JFK, LBJ,

and the

Democratic Party

SUNY series on the Presidency:

Contemporary Issues

John Kenneth White, editor

JFK, LBJ,

and the

Democratic Party

Sean J. Savage

STATE UNIVERSITY OF NEW YORK PRESS

Published by
STATE UNIVERSITY OF NEW YORK PRESS
ALBANY

© 2004 State University of New York

For information, address
the State University of New York Press
90 State Street, Suite 700, Albany, NY 12207

Production, Laurie Searl
Marketing, Fran Keneston

Library of Congress Cataloging-in-Publication Data

Savage, Sean J., 1964–
    JFK, LBJ, and the Democratic Party / Sean J. Savage.
        p. cm. — (SUNY series on the presidency)
    Includes bibliographical references and index.
    ISBN 0-7914-6169-6 (alk. paper)
        1. Kennedy, John F. (John Fitzgerald), 1917–1963. 2. Johnson, Lyndon B.
    (Lyndon Baines), 1908–1973. 3. Democratic Party (U.S.)—History—20th century.
    4. United States—Politics and government—1961–1963. 5. United States—Politics
    and government—1963–1969. 6. Political culture—United States—History—
    20th century. 7. Massachusetts—Politics and government—1951– 8. Texas—
    Politics and government—1951– 9. Political culture—Massachusetts—History—
    20th century. 10. Political culture—Texas—History—20th century.
    I. Title. II. SUNY series in the presidency.

E841.S28 2004
324.2736'09'046—dc22   2004045294

10 9 8 7 6 5 4 3 2 1

This book is dedicated to my father,

John J. Savage (1910–1968),

my grandfather, John Savage (1880–1973),

and my nieces, Olivia and Victoria Vendola.

Contents

Preface

Much has been written about the lives, presidencies, and policies of John F. Kennedy and Lyndon B. Johnson. Surprisingly little has been written about JFK's and LBJ's individual and collective influence on the Democratic Party as presidential party leaders. No previous study of these two presidents as party leaders has thoroughly explored the relationships between their experiences in and behavior toward their home states' political cultures and party systems and their later behavior toward and influence on the national Democratic Party. This book is an effort to fill that gap in the scholarly literature on Kennedy and Johnson. Its contribution is especially needed since the Democratic Party undertook the most extensive organizational, procedural, and participatory reforms in its history immediately after LBJ's presidency.

In addition to its use and analysis of the ideas and research of prominent political scientists, historians, and journalists, *JFK, LBJ, and the Democratic Party* extensively utilizes archival sources ranging from those of presidential libraries and the Library of Congress to rarely used special collections, such as those of Boston College, Bowdoin College, Bates College, the University of New Hampshire, the Rockefeller Archive Center, Providence College, and the University of Connecticut. The primary sources also include the author's telephone and personal interviews with former Democratic National Committee officials and state and local Democratic Party chairmen and recently released telephone recordings from the JFK and LBJ presidential libraries.

Many people and institutions have enabled me to research, write, and prepare *JFK, LBJ, and the Democratic Party* for publication. I am grateful to several sources of research grants, including Saint Mary's College, especially its SISTAR program, the American Political Science Association (APSA), the Earhart Foundation, the Rockefeller Archive Center, and the foundations of the John F. Kennedy and Lyndon B. Johnson presidential libraries. Professor John K. White of the Catholic University of America graciously and generously provided his time, expertise, and advice in reviewing this manuscript. Jessica White and Ann Hoover, two of my students, provided diligent assistance in preparing this manuscript for submission.

CHAPTER ONE

JFK and His Party

According to political scientist and Kennedy biographer James MacGregor Burns, JFK's first electoral success "left him with a disdain for routine politics and 'party hacks' that he would not lose for many years, if ever. He had found that the Democratic Party hardly existed as an organization in the Eleventh District; after he won office and consolidated his position, he would say, 'I am the Democratic Party in my district.' Thus he learned the key to winning politics . . . was a personal organization, not the party committees."[1] Burns wrote these words in 1959 concerning John F. Kennedy's 1946 congressional campaign. As Kennedy's pre-presidential political career revealed, his highly personalized and occasionally suprapartisan approach to campaign organization, tactics, and intraparty decisions both reflected and contributed to his meteoric rise in statewide, regional, and then national party politics.

The well-known story of Kennedy's entry into Democratic politics as a congressional candidate in 1946 includes paternal pressure, a young veteran's decision to begin a career path, and the various campaign advantages that Kennedy enjoyed due to his family's wealth, politically famous middle and last names, and John Hersey's previously published account of Kennedy's war record in *Reader's Digest*.[2] The various accounts of Kennedy's 1946 congressional campaign, however, have not adequately analyzed the extent to which Kennedy's assets as a candidate and the nature of his Democratic Party affiliation were well served by the organizational conditions of the Massachusetts Democratic Party and, more broadly, by the characteristics of his state's political culture in the immediate post–World War II era.[3] The significance of the nature of Kennedy's political environment in Massachusetts became more evident in his upset victory in the 1952 Senate campaign.

In 1949, journalist William Shannon calculated that only about ten of the 351 cities and towns of Massachusetts had functioning Democratic local committees and dismissed them as "the private preserves of dead beats and stuffed shirts."[4] Despite this organizational fragmentation, the New Deal realignment, the steady numerical and proportional growth of this state's Catholic population, and the greater attraction of Democratic candidates to non–Irish Catholic voters made the Democratic Party of Massachusetts this state's majority party by 1946 in terms of voter registration and at least potential dominance in statewide elections.[5] Nonetheless, the better-organized, more cohesive Republican Party of Massachusetts continued to demonstrate its ability to frequently control both houses of the state legislature and equally compete with the Democrats for major statewide offices. It partially accomplished this by nominating multi-ethnic Republican slates and adopting moderately liberal "good government" positions on certain issues.[6]

Also, Massachusetts, like other nonsouthern states, experienced what political scientist David G. Lawrence described as a "mini-realignment" in voting behavior and party identification from 1946 to 1950.[7] During this period, a significant increase in split-ticket voting and weaker party identification occurred among normally Democratic voters primarily because of postwar affluence and an "increasingly Republican coloration to American foreign policy regarding Communism."[8] This first mini-realignment was especially evident in the federal election results of 1952 when the Republicans won the presidency and control of both houses of Congress, despite the fact that 51 percent of Americans polled in 1952 identified themselves as Democrats and 29 percent as Republicans.[9] These percentages were virtually the same in 1948 when the Republicans lost the presidential election and control of Congress.[10]

In addition to the impact of this mini-realignment on Massachusetts's politics, the political culture of this state was becoming more varied and complex. Since the middle of the nineteenth century, Massachusetts' political culture developed two distinct value systems. According to political scientist Daniel Elazar, moralism, the first subculture, originated in the WASP, or Yankee, Puritan reformist values. By the late 1940s, this ethos was most clearly represented by the two liberal, patrician Republican senators from Massachusetts, Leverett Saltonstall and Henry Cabot Lodge, Jr.[11] Political scientists James Q. Wilson and Edward Banfield more specifically identified moralism as the ethos of "good government," which contributed to anti-machine, party-weakening reforms in Massachusetts during the Progressive era, such as nonpartisan local elections and office-column ballots.[12]

Political scientist Edgar Litt formulated a typology of this state's political culture. He identified four types of political cultures in Massachusetts based more on socioeconomic differences than ethnic and religious ones. They are: patricians, managers, workers, and yeomen. Even though he found that in the immediate postwar era, there were more Catholic managers and fewer Yankee yeomen, the Democratic Party still generally expressed Elazar's immigrant-based individualism while the Republican Party still embodied the good government ethos, or Yankee moralism.[13] Duane Lockard and Neal Peirce likewise noted that despite the fact that more Catholics in this state became college-educated, suburban, middle-class, and white collar in the postwar era, many of them remained Democrats.[14]

These various characteristics of the immediate postwar political climate of Massachusetts provided the ideal environment for a political entrepreneur with John F. Kennedy's qualities. In particular, JFK's ideology, rhetoric, socioeconomic and educational background, and campaign tactics ideally positioned him to become the first Irish or "Green" Brahmin, that is, a Harvard-educated Catholic Democrat of inherited wealth who could personify and express the Yankee, patrician, good government ethos.[15] More broadly and theoretically, Banfield and Wilson noted that "the nationality-minded voter prefers candidates who represent the ethnic groups but at the same time display the attributes of the generally admired Anglo-Saxon model."[16]

This was a contrast to the image of David Walsh. Walsh was a conservative, isolationist Democrat who was the first Irish Catholic to be elected to the U.S. Senate from Massachusetts. Walsh was defeated for reelection in 1946 by Henry Cabot Lodge, Jr., a liberal, Brahmin Republican, partially because many younger, suburban Catholics voted for Lodge.[17]

Kennedy's voter appeal as an Irish Brahmin was not limited to younger, upwardly mobile, less partisan middle-class Catholics. It was, to the surprise and dismay of his Democratic opponents in his 1946 primary campaign, equally powerful among older, lower-income, urban "turf-bound" Catholics. The Democrats held a special primary in the Eleventh Congressional District because its most recent congressman, James M. Curley, was elected mayor of Boston in 1945. In sharp contrast to JFK, Curley was the prototype of the provincial Irish machine politician who clearly personified the immigrant ethos of individualism and blatantly appealed to ethnic, religious, class, and partisan differences throughout his colorful, controversial political career.[18]

Likewise, Mike Neville, former mayor of Cambridge, and John Cotter, an administrative assistant to Curley and his predecessor, challenged JFK in the primary by stressing their homegrown roots in and long service to the various working-class neighborhoods of the district. Neville and Cotter, JFK's most formidable opponents, and the other candidates portrayed Kennedy as a callow, silver-spooned carpetbagger with no demonstrated ability to represent and serve the district effectively.[19]

Although JFK's official residence in the district was a recently acquired, usually vacant apartment, his family had already established a well-known, lasting presence in the district. John F. "Honey Fitz" Fitzgerald, Kennedy's maternal grandfather, was a former mayor of Boston and had previously held this congressional seat. Fitzgerald and Curley had engaged in a bitter political rivalry. Less significantly, Patrick J. Kennedy, the future president's paternal grandfather, had been a state senator and ward boss whose constituency included several neighborhoods in the Eleventh District.[20]

Kennedy also benefited from the advice and campaign management of aides and allies who understood this district and its unusually parochial, often family-centered ward politics well. Joe Kane, a Kennedy cousin and professional political consultant familiar with this district's politics, Mark Dalton, a speechwriter for JFK, and David F. Powers, a young veteran experienced in the politics of Charlestown, a major, rather xenophobic community in the Eleventh District, were Kennedy's three top campaign aides. They were careful to ensure that Kennedy quickly familiarized himself with the leading religious, ethnic, labor, and veterans' organizations of the district and with its numerous economic problems and needs, especially those pertaining to public housing and its large number of longshoremen.

In a 1964 interview, however, Mark Dalton claimed that the real campaign manager was Joseph P. Kennedy.[21] The candidate's father was both famous and infamous among Massachusetts' Democrats for his abrasive personality and efforts to buy political influence through his fortune.[22] Richard J. Whalen, a biographer of Joseph P. Kennedy, noted that by promoting his son as a war hero, the elder Kennedy used free newspaper and magazine publicity to supplement "the most elaborate professional advertising effort ever seen in a Massachusetts Congressional election."[23] Joe Kennedy was aware, though, that he still attracted controversy due to allegations that as ambassador to Great Britain he was an isolationist and an appeaser. He was careful to avoid attracting publicity to himself.

Thus, there were actually two dimensions in JFK's 1946 primary campaign. The first was the lavishly financed, behind-the-scenes campaign supervised by Joe Kennedy. He fully exploited his political, Hollywood, business, and media connections to promote his son's candidacy through newspaper and magazine articles, billboards, radio commercials, and motion picture ads at movie theaters. Thomas P. "Tip" O'Neill, Jr., then a state representative who succeeded Kennedy as the congressman in this district in 1952, estimated "that Joe Kennedy spent $300,000 on that race, which was six times what I spent in a very tough congressional campaign in the same district six years later."[24] The former ambassador even contacted the publisher of the *New York Daily News* to have public opinion polls conducted, a campaign tool previously unheard of in this district's political campaigns.[25]

The second dimension was the exhaustive, door-to-door campaign conducted by JFK and his army of volunteers, many of them young veterans, friends from Harvard, and young women. Combined with a well-organized schedule of coffee and tea parties where voters could meet the candidate, this dimension gave the Kennedy campaign an image of youthful, idealistic amateurism. But, in organizing the coffee and tea parties, the two dimensions of the campaign converged. Women in the district were provided with the refreshments, china, and other necessary items for hosting parties for Kennedy. They were also paid $100 each for "cleaning" expenses.

Although *Look* magazine referred to John F. Kennedy as a "fighting conservative," he did not elaborate on his ideology during his primary and general election campaigns in 1946.[26] Like his opponents in the Democratic primary, he emphasized bread-and-butter liberalism, especially support for public housing, a higher minimum wage, and improved veterans' benefits.[27] Kennedy, however, was careful not to identify himself as a liberal. This lack of a clear, self-defined ideology characterized Kennedy during his congressional and Senate career. His campaign image was that of an ideologically undefined war hero and celebrity from a family widely perceived as the "aristocracy" of the Irish in Massachusetts. This served Kennedy well in an economically liberal yet socially conservative and militantly anti-Communist district.[28]

Kennedy's intellectual interest in politics was much greater in foreign policy than in domestic policy.[29] Thus, his few profound campaign speeches focused on foreign policy, especially the rebuilding of Western Europe and the containment of Communism. But except for the specific issue of loan legislation to aid Great Britain, Kennedy still spoke in terms of generalities on foreign policy. In an interview with the Harvard *Crimson*, Kennedy stated that the major issue facing the United States was "the struggle between capitalism and collectivism, internally and externally."[30] The ominous, martial tone of this excerpt echoed a concluding statement in Kennedy's first book, *Why England Slept*. "We can't escape the fact that democracy in America, like democracy in England, has been asleep at the switch. If we had not been surrounded by oceans three and five thousand miles wide, we ourselves might be caving in at some Munich of the Western World."[31] As a congressman, JFK would occasionally express strident criticism of the Truman administration's foreign policy in his roll-call votes and Churchillian "Munich lesson" rhetoric.

But the real "issue" in this 1946 primary campaign was John F. Kennedy. His opponents repeatedly, and sometimes imaginatively, portrayed him as an inexperienced, spoiled playboy whose actual residence was in Florida or Manhattan, not the Eleventh District. Mike Neville, one of JFK's most prominent opponents, wore a ten-dollar bill attached to his shirt pocket and referred to it as a Kennedy campaign button.[32] Joseph Russo, a Boston city councilor and another congressional candidate, bought newspaper advertising accusing Kennedy of carpetbagging.[33]

The focus, though, of Kennedy's opponents on his privileged background and family fortune seemed to enhance, rather than diminish, his celebrity appeal to many voters, especially women. Often accompanied by his sisters and mother in a reception line, Kennedy greeted thousands of well-dressed women eager to meet him and his family. Patsy Mulkern, a precinct worker for Joe Kane, noted that the sharp increase in business for hair stylists and dressmakers in the Eleventh District indicated how heavily attended Kennedy's coffee and tea parties were.[34] Journalist Francis Russell later wrote, "After a half a century of oafishness . . . this attractive, well-spoken, graceful, witty, Celtic, Harvard-bred and very rich young man was what every suburban matron would like her son to be. In fact, many of them came to see Jack as their son."[35]

Primary day, June 18, 1946, was rainy. The Kennedy campaign was careful to provide enough cabs and other hired automobiles to drive many of its targeted voters to the polls. Nonetheless, turnout was light. About 30 percent of the registered voters cast ballots.[36] In a ten-candidate field, Kennedy won the Democratic nomination with 40.5 percent of the votes. He received nearly twice as many votes as his closest rival, Michael Neville.[37]

Since victory in the Democratic primary was tantamount to election in this district, Kennedy's general election campaign was more relaxed and subdued, despite the anticipated Republican sweep of the 1946 midterm elections. The most common Republican campaign slogan, "Had Enough? Vote Republican," originated in Massachusetts. Confident of victory by a wide margin in November, Kennedy devoted several speeches to the nature of his party affiliation. In an August 21, 1946, address to the Young Democrats of Pennsylvania, he stated, "The philosophies of political parties are hammered out over long periods—in good times and in war and in peace. . . . From the days of Andrew Jackson the Democratic Party has always fought the people's fight, (sic) has always been the party that supported progressive legislation."[38]

Two months later, Kennedy gave a similar speech to the Junior League in Boston. He began his speech by blandly stating that, for him, as for "some 95 percent of this group here tonight," party affiliation was simply a matter of family inheritance.[39] JFK proceeded to speak in historical generalities about the policy and doctrinal contributions of such prominent Democratic presidents as Thomas Jefferson, Andrew Jackson, and Franklin D. Roosevelt. He concluded his speech by quoting John W. Davis, the conservative Democratic presidential nominee of 1924. " 'And do not expect to find a party that has always been right, or wise or even consistent; that would be scarcer still. Independent judgment and opinion is a glodious (sic) thing on no account to be surrendered by any man; but when one seeks companionship on a large scale, he must be content to join with those who agree with him in most things and not hope to find a company that will agree with him in all things.' "[40]

While this speech and his other previous and future speeches on party affiliation disclosed little or nothing about JFK's ideological identity, it is rather revealing that Kennedy included this particular quote from Davis. Kennedy implied a certain independence from the Democratic "party line" in Congress, which became especially pronounced during his early Senate years. The Democratic congressional nominee told an interviewer, "If you must tag me, let's make it 'Massachusetts Democrat.' I'm not doctrinaire. I'll vote 'em the way I see 'em."[41]

JFK's doctrinal vacuum and issue eclecticism worked well in 1946. He received 72 percent of the votes in the November election. Meanwhile, the Republicans of Massachusetts won nine of that state's fourteen U.S. House seats. They also now controlled both U.S. Senate seats since Republican Henry Cabot Lodge, Jr., defeated veteran Democratic Senator David I. Walsh by a margin of

20 percent. Likewise, incumbent Democratic Governor Maurice Tobin was defeated for reelection.[42] Throughout all of JFK's campaigns for the House and Senate, he performed distinctly better as a vote getter than most other Democratic nominees for major offices in Massachusetts. Kennedy's successful electoral performance was especially accentuated by the fact that he entered the House of Representatives in 1947 and the Senate in 1953 as a member of the minority party in each chamber.

JFK's six-year tenure in the House of Representatives was characterized by an often lackluster, unreliable attention to his legislative duties, especially his committee service. Kennedy's lackadaisical job performance especially irked John W. McCormack, the leading Democratic congressman from Massachusetts who served as House majority leader after the Democrats regained control of Congress in 1948. McCormack later clashed with Kennedy in 1956 over control of their state's Democratic committee and delegation to the 1956 Democratic national convention.[43]

JFK was careful to develop and maintain a high-quality staff in Massachusetts and Washington, DC, in order to provide responsive, effective constituency service during his House and Senate years. He was also careful to support most social welfare measures needed by his mostly working-class constituents, such as public housing and the Truman administration's proposal for national health insurance.[44] Kennedy's safe seat provided him with the political security to distinguish himself as the only Democratic congressman from Massachusetts to refuse to sign a petition written by John W. McCormack urging President Harry Truman to pardon James M. Curley, the former congressman and mayor of Boston imprisoned for federal crimes.[45] JFK supported the McCarran Internal Security Act of 1950, which required the registration of Communist groups and increased the power of the federal government to deport subversives. It became law over Truman's veto.[46] Kennedy also opposed direct, comprehensive federal financial aid to parochial schools.[47]

Kennedy's independence from the typical voting patterns of other northern, urban Democratic congressmen was also evident in the reluctance and ambivalence of his opposition to the Taft-Hartley Act of 1947. As a member of the House Education and Labor Committee, JFK believed that some union leaders had used their power to call strikes excessively and irresponsibly in the immediate postwar years and was concerned about the infiltration of Communists in some unions. Kennedy submitted a one-man report to this committee accusing both management and labor of selfishness. Ultimately, though, he opposed the Taft-Hartley Act for being too restrictive toward labor unions.[48]

JFK's seat on this committee was an asset for developing and publicizing his most prominent and consistent intellectual and programmatic interest as a congressman—the development of staunch yet sophisticated policies to effectively oppose the spread of both domestic and foreign Communism. On this issue,

JFK formed a cordial, constructive relationship with a fellow committee member, Republican Congressman Richard M. Nixon. While Nixon rose to national fame during his investigation of Alger Hiss, JFK had a similar yet more obscure experience investigating Harold Christoffel. Christoffel was a United Auto Workers (UAW) official suspected of instigating labor strife in 1941 as part of a plot by American Communists.

Although Christoffel was later tried, convicted, and imprisoned, civil libertarians were disturbed by Kennedy's aggressive questioning of the labor official and his hasty call for Christoffel's indictment.[49] Regarding the Christoffel case, a journalist referred to Kennedy as "an effective anti-Communist liberal" who "is more hated by Commies than if he were a reactionary."[50] During JFK's 1952 Senate campaign, the candidate issued a press release praising a Supreme Court decision upholding Christoffel's conviction for perjury. JFK concluded this press release by stating, "The Communists, when I demanded that Christoffel be indicted, called (sic) 'Witch Hunter' but I knew I was right. Now everybody should know."[51]

With his hawkish anti-Communism and occasional efforts to reduce federal spending as the basis for his identification in his 1946 campaign as a "fighting conservative," Kennedy elaborated on his occasionally conservative rhetoric and policy behavior as he prepared for his Senate campaign.[52] He was especially outspoken in his criticism of Truman's foreign policy toward the anti-Communist Chinese nationalists. In a January 30, 1949, speech in Salem, Massachusetts, Kennedy denounced Truman and the State Department for contributing to the "tragic story of China whose freedom we once fought to preserve. What our young men had saved, our diplomats and our President have frittered away."[53]

JFK's eclectic conservatism on foreign policy and some economic issues, ambivalent liberalism on most social welfare and labor issues, and aloofness toward Democratic leaders in Congress and in Massachusetts, the Democratic National Committee (DNC), and Harry Truman's presidential party leadership were especially evident shortly before and during his 1952 Senate campaign.[54] Democratic Senator Edmund S. Muskie of Maine stated in 1966 that liberals and veterans' rights activists in Massachusetts "were disturbed" by Kennedy's "apparent determination to be independent of the 'regular' party organization."[55] But, as political scientist James MacGregor Burns indicated, there was no meaningful "regular" Democratic party in Massachusetts. "The Democratic Party had become, more than ever before, less a unified organization than a holding company for personal organizations that often warred with one another more fiercely than with the Republicans."[56]

JFK recognized the need to develop a suprapartisan, personal organization on a statewide basis in order to successfully run for a statewide office. He began to speak regularly throughout Massachusetts in 1948 and more frequently after his 1950 reelection. The opportunistic nature of Kennedy's ideological, partisan, and policy identity during this period was most succinctly yet clearly revealed in an address given at Harvard University on November 10, 1950. Among other opinions that he expressed, the congressman criticized the Truman administration's conduct of the Korean War and spoke favorably about Senator Joseph R. McCarthy's anti-Communist crusade and Republican Congressman Richard M. Nixon's defeat of Democratic Congresswoman Helen Gahagan Douglas.[57] According to several sources, including the memoirs of Thomas P. "Tip" O'Neill, Jr., and Nixon, JFK personally delivered a $1,000 contribution to Nixon, and his father gave a total of $150,000 to Nixon's Senate campaign.[58]

In another appearance at Harvard in late 1951, Kennedy disclosed that he definitely intended to run for the Senate in 1952 against the Republican incumbent, Henry Cabot Lodge, Jr.[59] The titular leader of the Massachusetts Democratic Party, Governor Paul Dever, posed a possible obstacle to JFK's ambition to become a senator. It was widely assumed among Massachusetts Democrats and in the media that Dever would run for the Senate in 1952 instead of reelection as governor.[60] Congressman Kennedy maintained the façade of being equally available for either of the two statewide offices. He confided, though, to historian and later White House aide Arthur M. Schlesinger, Jr., his preference for the Senate. "I hate to think of myself up in that corner office deciding on sewer contracts."[61] Likewise, in 1946, Kennedy was relieved that he could begin his political career by running for a congressional seat instead of for lieutenant governor.[62] Developing his political career in Washington, DC, instead of in state government enabled JFK to separate himself from the intraparty conflicts and spoils of state government and exercise his intellectual interest in foreign policy.[63]

Shortly after a meeting between JFK and Dever, a Kennedy-Dever campaign organization was established in Boston.[64] This committee was chaired by John E. Powers, a well-known state senator from South Boston popular among party regulars, and its expenses were mostly covered by the Kennedy campaign. JFK avoided campaigning much with Dever. From JFK's perspective, the purpose of this committee was to nominally identify him with Dever's supporters, especially among party regulars who had long resented the fact that the Kennedys had rarely contributed much to the Democratic state and local committees.[65] The Kennedy campaign became aware that, except for Dever's most loyal allies in Boston, the governor was increasingly unpopular throughout Massachusetts. JFK was also aware of how popular Republican presidential nominee Dwight Eisenhower and, to a lesser extent, Senator Joseph McCarthy of Wisconsin were among Massachusetts voters later in his campaign. Kennedy was careful to limit rhetorically and visually identifying himself with President Truman, Democratic presidential nominee Adlai Stevenson, and Dever.[66]

The Kennedy-Dever campaign committee was one of the least important of the many committees that constituted JFK's campaign organization. The Kennedy campaign exploited state and federal campaign finance laws so that Joseph

Kennedy could spend heavily on it. Also, in order to conduct a truly independent, suprapartisan Senate campaign, a large, diverse network of Kennedy campaign organizations was created throughout Massachusetts.

As early as 1947, Congressman Kennedy had considered running for either governor or senator in 1948. JFK regularly spoke throughout Massachusetts during his House career in order to develop statewide name recognition, but he lacked a statewide organization.[67] While Joseph Kennedy privately developed the overall campaign strategy and provided seemingly unlimited funding, Robert F. Kennedy directly implemented this strategy and micromanaged its details. RFK created a statewide organization headed by 286 local campaign chairs known as "Kennedy secretaries."[68]

"Secretaries" signified that these local Kennedy campaign leaders were not necessarily part of regular Democratic committees. This distinction was especially important for local Kennedy committees in heavily Republican rural and suburban communities. Also, some of Kennedy's "secretaries" were independents and Republicans.

This terminology seemed to be more likely to attract a large number of previously apolitical women and less likely to antagonize local Democratic chairmen.[69] This connotation was compatible with the Kennedy campaign's effort to sharply increase voter registration in small and medium-sized cities outside the Boston area, especially among women and young adults. On election day, the percentages of registered voters casting ballots in these cities averaged 91 percent.[70]

The most dramatic, suprapartisan, and possibly bipartisan element of Kennedy's campaign organization was a committee entitled Independents for Kennedy. It was chaired by T. Walter Taylor. Taylor was a Republican businessman who helped to lead the effort of conservative Republicans in Massachusetts to nominate Senator Robert A. Taft of Ohio for president in 1952. In a letter to other pro-Taft Republicans, Taylor explicitly linked Taft to Joseph Kennedy. He also stated that he and other "Independents and Taft people" were "very happy at the privilege of bringing the Kennedy message to the people."[71] Ironically, Joseph Kennedy had financially contributed to Henry Cabot Lodge, Jr.'s 1942 reelection campaign in order to spite Franklin D. Roosevelt by implicitly opposing Lodge's opponent, Democratic Congressman Joseph Casey. Casey was previously opposed in a Democratic senatorial primary by John "Honey Fitz" Fitzgerald.[72]

In addition to Taylor's committee, the Kennedys also generated the support— or at least the nonvoting neutrality—of more anti-Lodge, pro-Taft Republicans in Massachusetts through the editorial endorsements of two pro-McCarthy, anti-Lodge publishers. Basil Brewer, a staunch Republican, was outraged by Lodge's aggressive support for Eisenhower against Taft at the 1952 Republican national convention. Moreover, in June 1951, General Douglas MacArthur told Joseph Kennedy that Lodge "was strictly a pro-Trumanite on foreign policy" and was increasingly alienating conservative Republicans.[73]

Brewer owned newspapers on Cape Cod and in New Bedford in southeastern Massachusetts. Like the rural areas of western Massachusetts, this region's mostly WASP small towns usually provided huge margins of electoral support for Lodge or any Republican nominee. Brewer praised JFK as a more effective anti-Communist than Lodge. Endorsed by Brewer, JFK carried New Bedford by approximately 21,000 votes and greatly reduced Lodge's support in heavily Republican small towns.[74]

As Congressman Kennedy attacked Lodge for being too soft and ineffective against Communism, his campaign still feared the prospect of Senator McCarthy suddenly traveling to Massachusetts to personally endorse Lodge.[75] Such an appearance might generate the winning margin of votes for Lodge from previously undecided, pro-McCarthy Democrats and Republicans. While a joint McCarthy-Lodge appearance was never held in Massachusetts, Kennedy received the endorsement of the *Boston Post*.[76] John Fox, its publisher, was not a Republican activist like Brewer. But he was even more stridently pro-McCarthy than Brewer. He purchased this newspaper in 1952 primarily to advocate his militant anti-Communism and criticism of Truman's foreign policy.

Fox had intended to endorse Lodge, but Brewer's intervention, and, possibly, the loan that he later received from Joseph Kennedy, persuaded Fox to endorse JFK.[77] With the *Boston Post*'s readership concentrated among pro-McCarthy, split-ticket Catholic Democrats, Fox's endorsement helped to further solidify and unite Catholic electoral support for Kennedy. Unfortunately for Lodge, the more cerebral, influential, widely circulated, Brahmin-owned *Boston Globe* remained neutral in the Senate race.

While Kennedy and his media backers relentlessly attacked Lodge from the right, JFK also lambasted Lodge from the left on domestic policy, especially the Taft-Hartley Act.[78] On such social welfare issues as public housing, minimum wages, Social Security coverage, and federal aid to education, JFK's and Lodge's legislative records were similarly liberal. But Lodge had voted for the Taft-Hartley Act. JFK, however grudgingly, had voted against it and had cordially yet eloquently debated it with Congressman Richard M. Nixon in Pennsylvania in 1947.[79]

Before labor audiences throughout Massachusetts, JFK repeatedly used the Taft-Hartley Act to exaggerate and dramatize his policy differences with Lodge and to excoriate Lodge for not doing enough to prevent the increasing migration of manufacturing jobs, especially in the textile and shoe industries, from Massachusetts to the South.[80] In particular, JFK blamed the right-to-work provision of this law for giving the South an unfair advantage over Massachusetts in labor costs. Kennedy then used this as the basis for other votes on economic issues in which Lodge allegedly failed to serve his constituents.[81] Despite JFK's chronic absenteeism from his own congressional district and poor attendance record in Washington, his most widely used campaign slogan was that he would more faithfully and diligently serve the policy interests of Massachusetts in the Senate than Lodge had.[82]

Another dimension of the Kennedy campaign was social, virtually apolitical, and issueless. Rose Kennedy, Joseph Kennedy's wife, her daughters, and daughter-in-law Ethel, RFK's wife, conducted heavily attended, well-advertised coffee and tea parties for women throughout the state. In particular, the Kennedys concentrated these parties in small to medium-sized cities outside the immediate Boston area where their campaign targeted voter registration and turnout drives. These parties highlighted the celebrity and aristocratic status of the Kennedy family, especially among Catholic women of all age cohorts and socioeconomic strata.[83] But the formality and dignity of the invitations and reception lines were especially attractive to working-class Catholic women. These often issueless, seemingly nonpartisan parties developed a large receptive audience of viewers for "Coffee with the Kennedys."[84]

"Coffee with the Kennedys" was one of several paid television programs financed by the Kennedy campaign. Consultants had previously coached JFK on the use of television, both in the use of free media, such as interviews on news programs, like *Meet the Press,* and paid media, such as call-in question-and-answer programs. Lodge, by contrast, spent far less on television advertising and often appeared stiff and uncomfortable when televised.[85] Two television stations in Boston reported that Kennedy spent about $15,000 and Lodge about $5,000 on television advertising.[86] Instead, Lodge emphasized the use of newspaper advertising which compared his voting and absentee records to JFK's.[87]

This advertisement, printed in every daily newspaper in Massachusetts, and Lodge's oratory criticizing the details of Kennedy's legislative record seemed to have little impact on the voters. In general, Lodge conducted a belated, hastily organized, lackluster reelection campaign with no clear, consistent strategy for counterattacks against Kennedy. He refused to indulge in the type of jeering accusations and ridicule about Joseph Kennedy's wealth and power used by Congressman Kennedy's Democratic primary opponents in 1946. The gentlemanly, dignified Republican tried to unite his Republican base, retain the support of Democrats and independents who had previously voted for him, and benefit from the coattails of Dwight Eisenhower. Eisenhower enjoyed a widening lead over Adlai Stevenson in the polls of likely voters in Massachusetts.[88] Lodge's rhetorical emphasis on the liberal, bipartisan nature of his foreign and domestic policy positions attracted few Democratic voters and further angered and alienated pro-Taft Republicans.[89]

Lodge refused to publicly request a campaign visit by Senator Joseph McCarthy, who had required that Lodge make such a request public. Lodge hoped that a televised, election rally with Dwight Eisenhower in Boston Garden would enable him to prevail. The enthusiasm of the crowds and strict television scheduling, however, prevented Lodge from introducing Eisenhower.

The 1952 election results in Massachusetts yielded a Republican sweep of the governorship, most of the state's U.S. House seats, most seats in both houses of the state legislature, and the popular and electoral votes for president for the first time since 1924.

They also included a 91 percent voter turnout and an upset victory for John F. Kennedy. JFK received 51.4 percent of the votes in the Senate race and a winning margin of 70,737 votes.[90] Analysts of and participants in JFK's first Senate campaign have not agreed on one common factor for his victory. Was it the popularity of the tea parties with female voters, sophisticated use of free television coverage and television advertising, the opposition to Lodge from pro-Taft Republicans, possibly influenced by Brewer's and Fox's newspapers, JFK's issue portrayal of Lodge as both anti-labor and soft on Communism, or the absence of a personal endorsement of Lodge by Joe McCarthy?[91] What is more evident and less disputable is that JFK's family-based, suprapartisan network of campaign committees enabled him to attract votes through all of these factors. The Kennedy campaign located offices in remote, staunchly Republican small towns that had rarely, if ever, experienced the presence of active Democratic campaign offices. The Independents for Kennedy committee cultivated the electoral support, or at least the neutrality, of anti-Lodge, pro-Taft Republicans in the Senate race.

The sharing and financing of one committee in Boston with Governor Paul Dever appeased party regulars suspicious of the Kennedys, but this committee had no significant influence on Kennedy's campaign strategy. JFK carefully distanced himself from Dever's floundering campaign. Lawrence F. O'Brien, a Kennedy campaign aide from western Massachusetts, commented that "we would let the regulars do or die for Dever; our only hope was to build our own independent Kennedy organization, city by city, town by town, and, if possible, to build it without offending the party regulars."[92] Kenneth P. O'Donnell and David F. Powers, two other Kennedy campaign aides, stated, "This was the first campaign for the U.S. Senate, incidentally, in which the candidate had a statewide organization with headquarters of his own in the various cities and towns."[93]

While this sprawling, decentralized network of campaign committees helped the Kennedy organization to actively campaign throughout the state, the actual strategy and tactics were privately orchestrated by Joseph P. Kennedy as de facto campaign chairman and publicly implemented by RFK as the official campaign manager.[94] In a 1967 interview, RFK bluntly stated, "We couldn't win relying on the Democratic political machine, so we had to build up our own machine."[95] The large number and diversity of campaign committees with such innocuous, misleading, apolitical names as "Improvement of the Textile Industry Committee" and "Build Massachusetts Committee," were also used to receive and expend vast sums of money from the Kennedy fortune and from Joseph P. Kennedy's political allies and business connections. All of these Kennedy committees officially reported $349,646 in expenditures to the Lodge campaign's official report of $58,266.[96]

But estimates of the actual amount spent by the Kennedy campaigns range from a half-million to several million dollars.[97] The officially reported figure does not include the funds spent on the extensive "pre-campaign" from 1947 until April 1952.[98] During this period, money was spent on polling and campaign operatives as Congressman Kennedy traveled and spoke throughout Massachusetts in order to strengthen his name recognition and help decide whether he would run for governor or senator in 1952 or further delay a statewide race. It also does not include the well-publicized contributions that the Joseph P. Kennedy, Jr. Foundation made to various religious and charitable institutions in Massachusetts.[99] Finally, it is impossible to accurately calculate the invaluable labor and expertise for the Senate campaign provided by employees and associates of the nationwide Kennedy business interests.

The Kennedy campaign organization was so impressive and successful in 1952 that it was the basis for JFK's reelection campaign in 1958, in which he received a record-breaking 73 percent of the votes and, to a lesser extent, his 1960 presidential campaign.[100] Within the politics of Massachusetts, JFK's victory in his 1952 Senate created, in effect, a new, enduring state party—the Kennedy party. Tip O'Neill, who was elected to JFK's congressional seat in 1952, later ruefully observed that the Kennedy organization "quickly developed into an entire political party, with its own people, its own approach, and its own strategies."[101] Almost fifty years after JFK's 1952 Senate campaign, political scientist Lawrence Becker concluded that, in Massachusetts, "the state's royal family, the Kennedys, essentially constitute a separate political party of their own."[102]

The Kennedy party developed into more than a personal following during the 1950s and 1960s. It became a highly effective, suprapartisan political entity that included a polyglot of voting blocs ranging from socially conservative, lower-income, Catholic, straight-ticket Democrats to socially liberal, "good government," ticket-splitting, upper-income WASP Republicans.[103] Its seemingly unlimited finances, prestige, and "winner" status enabled it to attract the best pollsters, media experts, and other campaign professionals and academic advisors, as well as thousands of enthusiastic volunteers. The Kennedy party often either co-opted rival Democratic politicians through campaign contributions, endorsements, or patronage, or decisively defeated opponents in bitter intraparty conflicts. These tactics made even the most determined anti-Kennedy Democrats reluctant to challenge the Kennedy party.

With the Republican-owned *Chicago Tribune* proudly echoing *Look*'s 1946 labeling of JFK as a "fighting conservative," one of the first phone calls of congratulations that the Massachusetts Democrat received on the election night of 1952 was from Senator Lyndon B. Johnson of Texas.[104] LBJ was currently serving as the Democratic majority whip of the Senate and soon became Senate minority leader because of the GOP's capture of the Senate. The thirty-five-year-old Democrat's unexpected triumph over a presumably secure liberal Republican incumbent closely associated with Eisenhower's candidacy was one of the few electoral successes for the Democratic Party in 1952.[105]

JFK's status as a freshman member of the minority party and one of a reduced number of nonsouthern Democrats actually benefited his already budding national ambitions. It made his frequent absences from the Senate floor and committee meetings seem less egregious, and his family's connection to Senator Joseph McCarthy less onerous as the increasingly controversial, beleaguered Wisconsin senator became primarily a burden and an embarrassment for the Republican majority of the Senate and the Eisenhower White House.[106] In his role as Senate minority leader, LBJ's style and strategy sought to position himself as a pragmatic, nonideological, less partisan, national (rather than regional) legislative leader who compromised and cooperated with Eisenhower and the Republicans to develop and pass moderate, consensual legislation in both foreign and domestic policy.[107]

LBJ's legislative behavior increased JFK's freedom to stake out independent positions on certain policy issues. For example, Kennedy initially compiled a Senate record as a fiscal conservative who supported Eisenhower's budget cuts, especially for agricultural subsidies and federal water and power programs, favored by most Republicans and opposed by most Democrats in Congress.[108] Johnson's policy of increasing the number of less senior, nonsouthern Democrats assigned to major committees also helped JFK. Kennedy now attracted favorable national publicity, especially for his image as an enlightened centrist regarding the threat of Communist expansion in the Third World and labor relations reform later in the 1950s.[109]

Besides benefiting JFK's status in the Senate, LBJ's friendly, often preferential treatment of JFK until the late 1950s freed the Massachusetts Democrat to devote more time and effort to solidifying his domination of the Democratic Party of Massachusetts and developing a national reputation as a popular speaker at party functions and guest in televised news programs.[110] These intraparty activities further enhanced JFK's position and reputation at the national level. Kennedy was determined to lead and deliver a united Massachusetts delegation to Adlai Stevenson at the 1956 Democratic national convention in Chicago.

JFK waged a successful yet contentious effort to oust the current Democratic state chairman, William "Onions" Burke, and replace him with John M. "Pat" Lynch. Burke was a party regular from western Massachusetts and a close ally of John W. McCormack, a Democratic congressman from Boston and House majority leader.[111] Earlier in 1956, Lawrence F. O'Brien provided JFK with a memo analyzing the importance of controlling the Democratic state committee "for the far more practical reason of self-preservation."[112] In addition to McCormack, JFK had also developed a mutually suspicious rivalry for control of the state party apparatus with Democratic Governor Foster Furcolo.[113]

Before JFK could effectively project a televised appeal to fellow Democrats at the 1956 convention in Chicago and campaign throughout the nation for

Stevenson, he needed to ensure that his own state's delegates were united under his party leadership. In his conclusion, O'Brien ominously warned the Democratic senator, "It is not necessary to cite other examples of specific adverse affect (sic) of failure to accept leadership. . . . Certainly this alone could be disastrous to any person seeking national recognition within the Party."[114] As the new Democratic state committee chairman, Pat Lynch was JFK's rubber stamp at the national convention. Lynch was also grudgingly acceptable to McCormack and Furcolo.[115]

From JFK's perspective, Chicago was an excellent site for the 1956 Democratic national convention. Joseph P. Kennedy owned the Merchandise Mart in Chicago. It was managed by one of his sons-in-law, R. Sargent Shriver, and they had cultivated a friendly political and business relationship with Mayor Richard J. Daley.[116] With Daley's control of the largest bloc of Democratic delegates from Illinois and his machine's ability to "pack the galleries" and deter demonstrations by an opponent's delegates, JFK was later disappointed to learn that the Democratic National Committee chose Los Angeles, not Chicago, to host the 1960 Democratic national convention. Also, Chicago's location and time zone were conducive to coast-to-coast television broadcasts of the proceedings.

Having so far remained aloof from the Americans for Democratic Action (ADA), whose liberal activism was unpopular with party regulars and southern conservatives, JFK had been chosen by the DNC to narrate its campaign film, *The Pursuit of Happiness,* and by Stevenson supporters to nominate Adlai Stevenson for president. Kennedy was selected for both speaking roles partially because of his popular reputation as a guest speaker at party functions and his acceptability to a broad spectrum and variety of often conflicting Democrats.[117] Furthermore, the fame of JFK's best-selling book, *Profiles in Courage,* and Joseph P. Kennedy's influence with the film's producer, Hollywood mogul Dore Schary, also helped to secure the selection of JFK as its narrator.[118]

In dictating notes for his memoirs in 1963, JFK stated that in every political contest it was essential for him to begin campaigning earlier than his opponents.[119] It was uncharacteristic, then, for JFK to reject his father's advice and suddenly compete for the Democratic vice-presidential nomination after Adlai Stevenson announced that he would let the convention select his running mate.[120] Stevenson had been previously warned by party leaders that his most likely running mate, Senator Estes Kefauver of Tennessee, was unpopular with southern conservatives for his moderate position on civil rights. Kefauver was also opposed by urban machine bosses for his televised committee investigation of organized crime that had revealed collusion between gangsters and local Democratic politicians during the Truman administration.[121] Stevenson disliked his former competitor for the presidential nomination. Some advisors believed that the convention needed to seriously and publicly consider the selection of a Catholic vice-presidential nominee in order to improve Stevenson's image with Catholic voters.[122]

With this unexpected opportunity, JFK, his staff, and family began to ac-tively lobby delegates for the vice-presidential nomination. The results of the first ballot for vice-presidential nominee indicated that, except for JFK, the delegate support for the twelve candidates competing against Kefauver was mostly scattered among favorite-son candidates. What embarrassed Kefauver and fur-ther weakened his delegate strength was the fact that all thirty-two of his home state's delegates voted for his junior colleague from Tennessee, Senator Albert Gore, Sr.[123] With 687 votes needed for the Democratic vice-presidential nomi-nation, Kefauver received 483$\frac{1}{2}$ votes to JFK's 304 on the first ballot.[124]

On the second ballot, Senator Estes Kefauver was nominated for vice presi-dent by a close margin of 755$\frac{1}{2}$ votes to JFK's 589.[125] At one point in this process, Kennedy came within thirty-eight votes of being nominated for vice president. The greater significance of the second ballot's results was the broad, diverse regional, factional, and ideological distribution of delegate support for JFK.[126] The Massachusetts Democrat received votes from almost all of the north-eastern and Illinois delegates, all of the delegates from Georgia, Kentucky, Loui-siana, Mississippi, South Carolina, Texas, and Virginia, and most of the delegates from Alabama and North Carolina.[127]

Impressed by the solid backing that he received from conservative, segrega-tionist southern delegates, the New England Catholic senator told journalist Arthur Krock, "I'll be singing 'Dixie' the rest of my life."[128] Determined to leave the delegates at the convention and the television audience a gracious impres-sion, JFK told his fellow conventioneers that the spirited contest for the vice-presidential nomination "proves as nothing else can prove how strong and united the Democratic Party is."[129] After JFK asked that the convention make Kefauver's nomination unanimous by acclamation, the convention responded with thun-derous applause.

While JFK conducted a national speaking tour promoting the Stevenson-Kefauver ticket, RFK traveled with the Stevenson campaign as an observer in order to learn how to manage a presidential campaign.[130] RFK later admitted that he voted for Eisenhower in 1956 because of his disgust with the inefficiency and disorganization of Stevenson's campaign.[131] With polls confirming the conven-tional wisdom that Dwight Eisenhower would be easily reelected, the actual, self-serving purpose of JFK's speaking tour was to convince the major Democratic power brokers that he was loyal and diligent to their party's presidential ticket. He also wanted to solidify his proven bases of delegate strength in the Northeast and South while cultivating Democratic activists elsewhere in the nation.[132]

Kennedy delivered a speech to the Young Democrats of North Carolina at the Robert E. Lee Hotel in Winston-Salem on October 5, 1956. The senator from Massachusetts dismissed Eisenhower's contention that the Republican Party was "the party of the future" oriented toward young Americans.[133] Criticizing the dearth of young men in the Eisenhower administration and its policies, JFK asserted that "it is the Democratic Party that is the party of change, the party of tomorrow as well as today."[134] Praising his party's domestic and foreign policy ideas as more progressive and appealing to youth and the prominent number of younger Democrats who held high elective offices, JFK concluded, "Adlai Stevenson, and the young men and women who are supporting him and running for office with him, truly represent a new America."[135]

From the time of his speaking tour for Stevenson in 1956 until he officially announced his presidential candidacy on January 2, 1960, JFK's speeches throughout the nation sought to transform one of his liabilities as a prospective presidential candidate, his youth, into an asset. He accepted a disproportionate number of speaking invitations from organizations of Young Democrats, civic associations oriented toward young businessmen and professionals, and colleges and universities. These speeches often combined an idealistic tone, especially concerning a new direction for American foreign policy in the Third World, with a pragmatic, centrist content, especially regarding the reform of labor-management relations.[136] JFK's rhetoric associated youth with a receptivity to new, bold ideas in contrast with the presumably backward looking stagnation of the Republican Party.

JFK and his chief speechwriter, Theodore C. Sorensen, cultivated an image of the Massachusetts Democrat as a reform-minded intellectual through his speeches and magazine articles.[137] They were careful to avoid having the public perceive JFK as a liberal ideologue. During his first year as a senator, JFK firmly stated to the *Saturday Evening Post* that he was not a liberal and did not belong to the Americans for Democratic Action (ADA), the most prominent group of liberal activists. Nevertheless, DNC chairman Paul M. Butler did invite JFK to join the Democratic Advisory Council (DAC) that the DNC established shortly after the 1956 election.[138] Since the DAC sought to formulate and advocate more distinctly and consistently liberal policies for future national platforms, including civil rights, JFK declined this invitation.[139] He formally justified this decision by citing the need to base his legislative behavior on the needs and interests of his constituents, rather than on partisan or ideological lines, as he prepared for his 1958 reelection campaign.[140]

Eleanor Roosevelt, a member of the ADA and DAC, emerged as a harsh, outspoken critic of JFK, partially because of her conviction that JFK lacked sincere liberal principles. But JFK did not want to antagonize Speaker of the House Sam Rayburn and Senate Majority Leader Lyndon B. Johnson. Rayburn and LBJ criticized the DNC for interfering with their congressional party leadership.[141] JFK waited until November 1959 to join the DAC. He did this a few weeks after a memo from an aide warned JFK that in order to secure the Democratic presidential nomination he needed to be identified "as a 1960 liberal in clear and unmistakable terms."[142]

Kennedy's voting record on legislation and, to a lesser extent, his campaign rhetoric became more consistently and emphatically liberal after the 1958 Senate election results. With a sharp increase in the number of nonsouthern, liberal

Democrats elected to the Senate, LBJ's position and effectiveness as a power broker for bipartisan, multiregional, nonideological centrism and compromise were greatly diminished.[143] Liberal activists and voting blocs, like organized labor and civil rights advocates, were now more confident that they could insist on a liberal platform and a liberal presidential ticket in 1960.[144]

On the issue of civil rights, however, JFK was still questioned and challenged about his commitment to stronger civil rights laws and their effective enforcement. White liberals and NAACP leaders were especially chagrined at JFK's distinction as one of the few nonsouthern Democrats to join southern Democrats and conservative Republicans in voting to refer the civil rights bill of 1957 to the Senate Judiciary Committee, chaired by James O. Eastland of Mississippi, an unyielding segregationist. JFK also voted to adopt a jury trial amendment for this bill, in effect a guarantee of usually all-white juries in the South for persons prosecuted for violating this statute.[145] Originally enlisted to maximize black electoral support in Massachusetts for JFK's 1958 reelection campaign, Marjorie Lawson, a black civil rights leader and attorney, served as JFK's spokeswoman and liaison with NAACP members and other civil rights activists to assure them of JFK's mostly liberal views on civil rights issues.[146] Nevertheless, Kennedy found it necessary to periodically defend his two controversial votes on the 1957 civil rights bill as matters of procedures and principles, namely, respect for typical committee procedures on any bill and for the Common Law tradition of trial by jury. He also distributed a memo to northern liberal Democrats outlining his entire record on civil rights issues.[147]

But Kennedy's speeches on civil rights, especially before southern audiences, were balanced and courteous enough in tone and substance to minimally satisfy the more moderate southern opponents of the federal integration of public education and other civil rights objectives. Angry with Eisenhower for appointing Earl Warren to the Supreme Court and sending the U.S. Army to integrate Central High School in Little Rock, Arkansas in 1957, southern whites were less inclined to vote Republican for president in 1960, especially if the Republican and Democratic national platforms of 1960 were similarly liberal on civil rights.[148] In the late 1950s, JFK usually stated that all Americans should respect and obey the authority of the Supreme Court but were also free to disagree with its decisions.[149]

When JFK criticized how Eisenhower enforced school integration in Little Rock, some southern politicians had the impression that a Kennedy administration would be more accommodating and "reasonable" in implementing federal court orders and civil rights laws than another Republican administration.[150] Consequently, the earliest southern supporters of JFK's still unannounced presidential candidacy were the segregationist governors of Mississippi and Alabama. John Patterson, then the Democratic governor of Alabama, later stated that he and other pro-JFK southern Democratic politicians hoped that if they contributed to JFK's election to the presidency then "we would have a place where we could get an audience for the problems that we had and could be heard."[151]

In short, JFK, as an unannounced presidential candidate from 1956 to 1959, succeeded in solidifying the base of support that he received for his impressive yet unsuccessful vice-presidential candidacy at the 1956 Democratic national convention and extending his appeal to party leaders and factions that were previously neutral or hostile toward his presidential ambition. JFK's sophisticated media skills, eclectic, centrist policy record, and idealistic, cerebral speaking style enabled him to attract the pre-convention support of a variety of often conflicting factions and interests within the national Democratic Party. In his biography of JFK, first published in 1959, James MacGregor Burns observed that the weak, decentralized nature and structure of the national Democratic Party were well suited to JFK's political assets and pursuit of intraparty support prior to 1960. "He is no more willing to be thrust into the role of organizational 'Democrat' than into any other. Kennedy is independent not only of party, but of factions within the party."[152]

JFK's prior experiences, struggles, and victories in his home state's steadily growing yet bitterly factionalized Democratic Party and his family's development of a superimposed Kennedy party in Massachusetts as the vehicle for his ambitions prepared him well for seeking the Democratic presidential nomination within such a byzantine, fragmented organizational environment.[153] Before JFK formally announced his presidential candidacy in 1960, he was able to campaign unofficially for the presidency through public speaking and private negotiations and generate favorable publicity because of his Senate activities and reelection campaign in Massachusetts. Fortunately for JFK, few journalists critically emphasized his frequent absences from the Senate while he campaigned to cultivate a broad, consensual bandwagon effect behind him among Democratic power brokers and grassroots activists before 1960.

Ironically, the Democrat who was instrumental in enabling JFK to use his Senate seat as the foundation for developing his presidential campaign was the same Democrat who eventually posed the greatest threat to JFK's nomination at the 1960 convention—Senator Lyndon B. Johnson. First as minority leader and then as majority leader, LBJ led the Senate Democrats throughout JFK's Senate career. Despite Kennedy's lack of seniority and his reputation for inattentive behavior toward the drudgery of committee duties, LBJ ensured that JFK was appointed to the highly coveted Foreign Relations and Labor Committees in the Senate.[154] LBJ's indulgence toward JFK made it easier for the Massachusetts Democrat to use these two committee positions, especially the latter, to attract favorable publicity.

Meanwhile, JFK was often absent from committee meetings and Senate roll-call votes as he campaigned frequently during the late 1950s.[155] The most significant event during the second balloting for the vice-presidential nomination at the 1956 Democratic national convention was LBJ's decision to switch all fifty-six of Texas's delegate votes from Al Gore, Sr., to JFK.[156] At the time, JFK may not have realized that Johnson was boosting Kennedy's political career in order to eventually help the Texan fulfill his own presidential ambition.[157]

LBJ and His Party

When JFK first ran for a congressional seat in 1946, he already enjoyed celebrity status among his future constituents because of the well-entrenched political fame of his middle and last names and his own highly publicized combat heroism in World War II. By contrast, LBJ's gradual evolution from being a congressional secretary in 1931 to a controversially nominated Democratic senatorial candidate in 1948 was heavily based on his skills as an ombudsman with the growing federal government for his constituents, regardless of whether they were poverty-stricken hill country farmers or wealthy contractors. But, like JFK, Johnson was careful not to clearly and consistently identify himself with an ideology or party faction that might currently or eventually threaten his progressive ambition. Biographer Robert Caro noted, "Johnson's entire career, not just as a Congressman's secretary, would be characterized by an aversion to ideology or to issue, by an utter refusal to be backed into firm defense of any position or any principle."[1]

LBJ, though, did have some ideological underpinnings in his family's history with the Democratic Party. As a state representative, Sam Ealy Johnson, Jr., LBJ's father, was a populist Democrat from the chronically poor hill country of west Texas. He crusaded against conservative Democrats serving business interests in the Texas state legislature and throughout the state government. LBJ's father also took courageous positions against the Ku Klux Klan and against legislation that discriminated against his German-speaking constituents. Refusing to accept bribes or even modest favors, like restaurant meals from lobbyists, Sam Ealy Johnson, Jr., could not afford to continue his legislative career. Debt-ridden, he subsisted on minor patronage jobs during his last years.[2]

LBJ absorbed his father's desire to use the powers and resources of government to benefit the poor, but he avoided the anti-business, class conflict rhetoric of pre–New Deal populists like his father and many New Deal liberals.[3] For LBJ to ascend in state and then national Democratic politics, he needed to succeed in the mercurial environment of Texas's one-party politics. He served as the secretary and de facto chief of staff for Richard Kleberg, a wealthy, reactionary, yet lackadaisical Texas congressman. With this position, LBJ tried to develop a

base of political support both in Washington, DC, among other Texas congressmen and congressional aides and in Kleberg's district through assiduous constituency service. He also identified himself with New Deal programs that
benefited Kleberg's district through frequent press releases. Realizing that it was
unlikely that Kleberg would voluntarily retire from Congress soon, LBJ agreed
to serve as the director of the National Youth Administration (NYA) in Texas in
1935. This position provided Johnson with an office in Austin, the state capital,
a staff, the authority to distribute NYA funds, jobs, and public works contracts.
Unofficially, the NYA provided LBJ with a statewide political organization and
the opportunity to distinguish himself to Franklin D. Roosevelt as the most
diligent and effective NYA director in the nation.[4]

LBJ most intensely identified himself with FDR as a congressional candidate in a special election in 1937 held to replace a deceased Democratic congressman, James P. Buchanan. Buchanan's district included Austin and Johnson
City. Competing against seven other candidates, LBJ decided to campaign as the
most pro-FDR candidate. Besides reminding the voters how much the New
Deal had helped to combat the Depression and his role in implementing the
NYA in Texas, Johnson dramatized his unequivocally pro-FDR platform by
being the only candidate to clearly and emphatically express support for the
president's court-reform or "court-packing" bill.

After FDR's landslide reelection in 1936, the Democratic president submitted a court-reform bill to Congress. Its provisions included the authority to add
new seats to the Supreme Court. Republicans and conservative Democrats denounced this bill as an unscrupulous effort by FDR to pack the Supreme Court
with liberal, pro-New Deal justices. The growing public controversy around this
bill also attracted the opposition of some New Deal liberals in Congress, especially those from the South.

With such slogans as "Franklin D. and Lyndon B.," and "Roosevelt and
Progress," LBJ's campaign effectively used the "court-packing" bill to dramatize
and simplify the issues of the whirlwind campaign, especially among poor whites
in the hill country who were grateful for the New Deal and still held anti-
business, populist opinions.[5] LBJ's campaign was also well financed and used
radio more than all of the other candidates combined. He obtained substantial
campaign contributions from the Brown and Root construction firm. Alvin
Wirtz, an Austin attorney and state senator acquainted with LBJ, informed
Johnson that Herman Brown was his client and needed a congressman who
could secure authorization and funding for the Marshall Ford Dam project that
was in jeopardy.[6] Governor James Allred, who eagerly supported the flow of New
Deal funds into Texas, privately backed LBJ's candidacy by directing Ed Clark,
his top fundraiser, to help LBJ.[7]

After winning this special election to a congressional seat, LBJ focused on
obtaining the necessary Public Works Administration (PWA) funds for comple-

tion of the Marshall Ford Dam and bringing electricity to his rural constituents through the Rural Electrification Administration (REA). In accomplishing these two initial objectives, LBJ cultivated political relationships with key White House aides, namely Thomas Corcoran and James H. Rowe, Jr. Rowe later stated that FDR was impressed with LBJ's electoral victory in light of LBJ's support for the controversial court-reform bill.[8] The president directed his staff and other administrative officials to give LBJ favorable treatment in the implementation of federal programs in his district.[9]

Upon the advice of FDR, Johnson sought and received a seat on the House naval affairs committee.[10] Although LBJ's congressional district was landlocked, he was able to use this committee seat to steer defense contracts to his campaign contributors, especially the Brown and Root firm. Unlike his mentor-protégé relationships with FDR and Sam Rayburn, a fellow Texan who became Speaker of the House in 1940, LBJ was unable to develop such a relationship with Carl Vinson, a Georgia Democrat who chaired the naval affairs committee. Nevertheless, after World War II began in Europe in 1939, the steady increases in defense spending further enhanced LBJ's political influence among his House colleagues.

With this greater political influence among his fellow House Democrats, LBJ was better able to log roll (i.e., exchange votes in the legislative process), in order to gain greater favorable treatment for federal programs benefiting a variety of his constituents, such as agricultural subsidies for farmers and public housing for blacks and Hispanics in Austin.[11] With his proven success as a fundraiser in his own campaigns, LBJ raised campaign funds for nonsouthern House Democrats, especially those facing tough reelection campaigns, in 1938 and 1940. Although the Democrats lost seventy House seats in 1938 and gained only seven seats in 1940, FDR, Rayburn, and John W. McCormack, who became House majority leader in 1940, valued LBJ's diligence and dedication to fundraising.[12]

In order to formalize and publicize his fundraising role for Democratic congressional campaigns, LBJ wanted to elevate his role to the chairmanship of the Democratic Congressional Campaign Committee (DCCC). The DCCC's chairman, Patrick Drewry, had proven to be chronically lethargic and ineffective in this role, but Rayburn refused to replace him. Later, LBJ sought to be appointed as "liaison officer" between the DCCC and the DNC or as secretary of the DNC. Edward J. Flynn, the DNC chairman, rejected LBJ's request for both of these positions. Finally, under pressure from Sam Rayburn, FDR directed Flynn and Drewry in October 1940 to formally announce that LBJ would "assist the Congressional Committee."[13]

Even though Johnson felt slighted and unappreciated by the chairmen of the DCCC and DNC, he continued to raise funds for House Democrats throughout the 1940s. He often gained favorable name recognition and gratitude from nonsouthern Democrats in competitive districts. In particular, LBJ served as a conduit for campaign funds from oil and gas interests and defense contractors in Texas to Democratic candidates nationally.[14] Frustrated with the bureaucratic inertia and lack of innovation in fundraising by the DCCC and DNC, Johnson developed an enduring, negative perception of national party committees that influenced his presidential party leadership.[15]

Thus, LBJ, as a young congressman, already demonstrated an ambition and an ability to perform a national role in the Democratic Party. Already, his congressional district in Texas was the foundation, rather than the extent, of his political power. He was determined to become more than just another Texas or southern Democratic congressman.[16] After his first few years in the House, it was evident to LBJ that his impatient desire for a quick ascent to national power would not be satisfied by patiently waiting for a committee chairmanship or obtaining a leadership position in a DNC apparatus dominated by northern urban Democrats.[17]

The death of Senator Morris Sheppard of Texas in 1941 created an opportunity for LBJ's political advancement. LBJ entered the special election competing against Governor W. Lee "Pappy" O'Daniel, Attorney General Gerald Mann, and Congressman Martin Dies. The special election soon developed into a close race between O'Daniel and LBJ.

As he did in his competition with JFK for their party's presidential nomination in 1960, Johnson underestimated his major opponent for the Senate seat. Prior to being elected governor in 1938, O'Daniel had become popular throughout Texas, but especially among low-income rural whites, for his radio program. Sponsored by a flour company, O'Daniel's broadcasts combined religious fundamentalism, economic populism, and country-western music.[18] Although O'Daniel failed to fulfill his promise of state old-age pensions for all elderly Texans and was actually an economic conservative in his policy behavior, he remained popular and was easily renominated and reelected governor in 1940.

Gerald Mann was a loyal New Dealer who worked in LBJ's 1937 congressional campaign. Unlike LBJ, though, Mann used "good government," idealistic rhetoric that appealed to reform-minded middle-class voters. Martin Dies was an isolationist who chaired the House Un-American Activities Committee (HUAC) and opposed FDR's internationalistic, pro-British foreign and defense policies.

Dies was a protégé of John Nance Garner. As vice president, Garner opposed FDR for the presidential nomination at the 1940 Democratic national convention. Opposing Dies, Rayburn, and most other Texas Democratic congressmen, LBJ, serving as vice chairman of the Texas delegation, openly supported FDR for a third term.[19] LBJ's pro-FDR position in this situation earned him the growing hostility of conservative Democrats to his ambition for higher office.

Meanwhile, the White House was determined to do whatever it could to surreptitiously and unofficially help LBJ to win this special election. Besides FDR's fatherly, personal fondness for LBJ, the president wanted to ensure that an isolationist like Dies or O'Daniel would not be elected to this Senate seat. In a memo to the president, White House aide James H. Rowe, Jr., told FDR that the "alternatives" to LBJ's becoming a senator "are too frightful for contemplation."[20] Rowe also reminded FDR that the election of either Dies or O'Daniel would further strengthen the anti-administration obstructionism of Senator Tom Connally and Jesse Jones, Reconstruction Finance Corporation (RFC) administrator and later Secretary of Commerce, both Texas Democrats.[21]

Unable to pressure or persuade Jones to endorse LBJ, the White House failed to effectively assist LBJ's campaign, other than through the provision of additional pork barrel projects. Nonetheless, LBJ, as he did in his first congressional campaign, closely identified himself with FDR and emphasized his record as an ombudsman for federal domestic programs benefiting Texas as well as his unqualified support for FDR's defense policies. Using the slogan "Roosevelt and Unity," LBJ's campaign rallies were often jingoistic, patriotic rituals. Well funded by the Brown and Root firm, LBJ's campaign heavily invested in radio broadcasts, mailings, and newspaper publicity.[22]

One day after the June 28 election, Johnson led O'Daniel by more than 5,000 votes, and a Dallas newspaper's headline anticipated LBJ's victory as "FDR'S ANOINTED."[23] Liquor interests led by former governor Jim Ferguson were determined to remove O'Daniel, who was fanatically anti-alcohol, as governor. They wanted Coke Stevenson, the lieutenant governor, to succeed O'Daniel. These and other forces in O'Daniel's coalition of supporters were more effective than LBJ's allies in buying blocs of mostly Hispanic votes from machine-controlled counties, especially those along the Mexican border.[24] O'Daniel also received a surprisingly large and suspiciously belated number of votes in rural east Texas, the region most favorable to Dies.[25] The state canvassing board eventually declared O'Daniel the winner by a margin of 1,311 votes.[26]

LBJ declined to risk his congressional seat and challenge O'Daniel in 1942 in the Democratic senatorial primary. After a brief, failed effort to compile a heroic combat record as a naval officer, LBJ continued to ingratiate himself with the White House, financial contributors, and fellow House Democrats. He continued his fundraising efforts for the 1942 and 1944 congressional elections. Despite his diligence, most intraparty recognition and gratitude for obtaining campaign funds from oil and gas interests were directed at Edwin Pauley, a California oil executive who had become DNC treasurer in 1942.[27]

Still seeking a national leadership position, LBJ briefly considered trying to get an appointment in Roosevelt's cabinet as Secretary of the Navy or Postmaster General. He also considered running for governor in 1944 if Coke Stevenson chose not to run for another term.[28] But LBJ's progressive ambition could not be satisfied with an appointed national position or elective state office. Like Kennedy, Johnson perceived state government to be a dead end for upward political mobility and a chaotic environment of factional conflict.

Political scientists James R. Soukup, Clifton McCleskey, and Henry Holloway noted that by the early 1940s "ordered political competition along liberal-

conservative lines developed in Texas."[29] World War II stimulated greater industri-
alization and urbanization, the decline of the cotton economy, hostility toward labor
unions, and formidable economic and political power for oil and gas interests.[30] The
rising domination of Texas Democratic politics by anti-Roosevelt, oil-financed conservatives was illustrated in two dramatic events in 1944. First, Sam Rayburn was
almost defeated for renomination by a well-funded conservative opponent.[31] Second,
the Democratic state convention bitterly divided the Texas delegation to the 1944
Democratic national convention between pro-FDR and unpledged, anti-FDR
delegates, the latter referring to themselves as Texas Regulars.[32]

Unable to unite his own state's delegates behind FDR's renomination,
Rayburn realized that he would not fulfill his ambition to become FDR's running mate in 1944.[33] Running for the Democratic presidential nomination as an
anti-FDR conservative, Senator Harry F. Byrd of Virginia received eighty-nine
votes on the first ballot, twelve of them from Texas.[34] Meanwhile, the Texas
Regulars derided LBJ as FDR's "yes man" and "pin up boy." In its decision in
Smith v. Allwright in April 1944, the U.S. Supreme Court struck down the all-
white Democratic primary of Texas. This decision inflamed the use of race
baiting by conservative Democrats against Rayburn, LBJ, and other beleaguered
pro-FDR Democrats in Texas.

LBJ once told James H. Rowe, Jr., "There's nothing more useless than a
dead liberal."[35] LBJ noticed how Maury Maverick, once the most liberal congressman from Texas, was defeated by a conservative primary opponent in 1938
during his second term.[36] Despite his moderate legislative record and status as
Speaker of the House, Sam Rayburn struggled to retain his congressional seat as
conservatives perceived him to be a servant and captive of liberal White House
policies hostile to Texas.

LBJ spent his remaining years as a congressman developing a more conservative legislative record, especially regarding civil rights, labor unions, and oil
and gas interests. Although LBJ had generally benefited the oil and gas industries
in his previous record, he had distinguished himself as one of the two Texas
congressmen to oppose the oil industry and support the Roosevelt administration's
price control policy on crude oil in a 1943 floor vote.[37] In the name of states'
rights and free enterprise, LBJ opposed federal anti-lynching legislation and the
creation of a permanent Fair Employment Practices Commission (FEPC) to
prohibit racial discrimination in hiring.

Johnson was careful to rhetorically differentiate between his support for the
economic interests of the "working man" and his opposition to the "labor bosses."[38]
He often portrayed the latter as corrupt, dictatorial, and collaborating with
Communists and gangsters. In a Republican-controlled Congress in 1947, LBJ
voted for the Taft-Hartley Act limiting the powers of labor unions. With a
coalition of Republicans and most southern Democrats behind it, Congress
overrode Harry Truman's veto, thereby enacting this legislation.[39]

After Senator W. Lee O'Daniel announced that he would not run for re-election in 1948, LBJ delayed a decision and belatedly and ambivalently entered the primary for the vacant Senate seat. He waited to learn if Congressman Wright Patman would enter this Senate campaign. Patman and Sam Ealy Johnson, Jr., had served together in the state legislature, and both Sam and LBJ respected and admired Patman.[40] With Patman declining to run for the Senate, LBJ had to decide whether he wanted to run against his most formidable opponent, former governor Coke Stevenson. The Democratic state organization, "court-house gangs," and most conservative Democrats alienated from the Truman administration favored Stevenson. George Peddy, an obscure yet well-financed corporate attorney for oil and gas interests and endorsed by the *Houston Post*, was expected to attract votes away from any candidate who seriously challenged Stevenson.[41] Finally, unlike in the special Senate election of 1941, LBJ would have to vacate his safe congressional seat and risk a permanent end to his political career.[42]

LBJ announced his Senate candidacy less than one month before the filing deadline of June 11, 1948. He quickly developed an effective campaign strategy employing the most modern methods ever used in a statewide Texas campaign.[43] At a time when very few Americans had seen a helicopter, LBJ regularly flew from one campaign stop to another in order to attract attention with his helicopter and its loudspeakers. Flying throughout Texas also helped LBJ to save time and address more crowds. LBJ's campaign effectively utilized modern polling techniques, frequent radio advertising, monitoring of newspaper coverage, and public relations specialists.[44] Unlike his first congressional campaign and, to a lesser extent, his 1941 Senate race, LBJ informed his campaign staff not to associate him with FDR in his speeches and advertising because of the former president's decline in popularity among the more prosperous, conservative Texans.

Although LBJ distanced himself from the Roosevelt and Truman administrations, he frequently emphasized his proven ability to deliver federal largesse to his constituents. During and after World War II, Johnson had enthusiastically promoted federal spending and programs that benefited the growing aerospace industries and facilities of Texas, both civilian and military. Unlike Coke Stevenson, LBJ understood that even ideologically conservative, affluent Texans often favored federal programs and spending that promoted prosperity and modern economic development in their state, such as highways, hospital and school construction, water and power projects, and government contracts for defense and public infra-structure.[45] In short, LBJ ran for the Senate in 1948 as a big government conservative. He contended that his congressional experience, platform, and vision would enable him, as a senator, to establish a symbiotic relationship between Texas and the federal government. Texas would use federal resources to expand and modernize its economy, thereby enabling it to contribute more effectively to an aggressively anti-Communist, internationalist foreign and defense policy.

Coke Stevenson, by contrast, failed to understand and counteract LBJ's themes of modernity and progress. Instead, the taciturn former governor campaigned for senator emphasizing the same ideology and rhetoric that he had used in his gubernatorial campaigns. Identifying himself as a "Jeffersonian Democrat," Stevenson usually made brief, bland, vague statements about the need to apply his philosophy and gubernatorial record of states' rights, low taxes, less spending, and fewer regulations on business to the federal government.[46] It was difficult and awkward for him to explain why the American Federation of Labor endorsed him. Usually reticent about his foreign and defense policy views, Stevenson conveyed the impression that he was an isolationist.

LBJ was careful not to underestimate Stevenson, as he had O'Daniel in 1941. During the final weeks of the July campaign, most polls showed that Stevenson was ahead of LBJ. Although Stevenson received almost 72,000 more votes than LBJ in the July 28 primary, Stevenson's percentage of the total votes was small enough so that a runoff primary between the two top candidates was scheduled for August 28.[47] LBJ realized that the results of the runoff primary, like those of the 1941 Senate election, would probably be decided by machine-controlled ballot boxes. LBJ and his allies intensified their lobbying of machine bosses who were undecided or wavering in their support for Coke Stevenson.[48]

In particular, a friendly reporter informed LBJ that George Parr, the machine boss of Duval County with some political influence in nearby Jim Wells County, was disgruntled with Stevenson. Parr had backed Stevenson for governor, but he might be willing to endorse LBJ. Johnson asked Parr for his support, and Parr reputedly promised it to LBJ without asking for any favors.[49] Parr wanted to spite Stevenson for appointing a district attorney that he had opposed in 1943.[50]

On August 31, three days after the runoff primary was held, the Texas election bureau announced that Stevenson was ahead by 349 votes with forty votes left to count.[51] But the Johnson campaign contended that various ballots throughout Texas had still not been counted. In particular, the highly questionable, belated votes for LBJ from Duval and Jim Wells counties provided him with an eighty-seven-vote margin of victory against Stevenson.[52]

LBJ received vital assistance from Washington when he defeated Stevenson's legal challenges to his still disputed eighty-seven-vote victory. James H. Rowe, Jr., Abe Fortas, a former government attorney in the Roosevelt and Truman administrations, Thomas Corcoran, a former New Deal lawyer now associated with a lobbying and law firm in Washington, and Joseph L. Rauh, Jr., a lawyer and ADA leader, were among the thirty-five Washington lawyers who provided LBJ with legal advice and representation.[53] Supreme Court justice Hugo Black, who was the presiding judge of the federal circuit that included Texas, ruled in favor of LBJ on September 28, 1948.

Upon taking office as a senator in 1949, LBJ entered a now Democratic-controlled Senate. Since the Republicans had lost control of the Senate in the

1948 elections, Democrat Les Biffle became secretary to the Senate majority. Biffle's "chief telephone page" and de facto chief of staff was Bobby Baker, a South Carolinian.[54] Shortly before being sworn in as a senator, LBJ asked Baker to provide him with all the inside information about the Senate so that he could increase his power, status, and effectiveness as quickly as possible. Due to his razor-thin, controversial election, he bluntly told Baker that he needed to be independent of the liberal policy goals of the Truman administration and the national Democratic Party in order to strengthen his political base in Texas. "Frankly, Mr. Baker, I'm for nearly anything the big oil boys want because they hold the whip hand and I represent 'em."[55]

LBJ then devoted his first two years as a senator to this task. He allied himself with another freshman Democratic senator, Robert Kerr of Oklahoma, in protecting and promoting the policy interests of the oil and gas industries. They led the successful opposition to Leland Olds, Truman's nominee for another term on the Federal Power Commission (FPC) in 1949.[56] Olds was a New Deal liberal who favored stricter federal regulations on public utilities.

Six days before the Senate voted to reject Olds, Truman stated at a press conference that a Democratic senator's loyalty to the Democratic national platform and the president's party leadership required him to vote for Olds. Truman also directed William Boyle, the DNC chairman, to lobby Senate Democrats on behalf of Olds's renomination.[57] LBJ proudly stated on the Senate floor that he was willing to suffer the "lash of a party line" from the president in order to vote his conscience.[58]

As he had done in the House, LBJ quickly cultivated friendships and mentor-protégé relationships with the most powerful, veteran southern Democrats in the Senate.[59] LBJ especially gained the friendship and counsel of Richard Russell, a Georgia Democrat who later chaired the Senate Armed Services Committee and pursued the Democratic presidential nomination of 1952. With Russell's sponsorship, LBJ gained access to the "inner club" of southerners who dominated the Senate.

But LBJ realized, as he had in the House, that it would take him many years to accumulate enough seniority to chair a major committee in a Democratic-controlled Senate. He also did not want to isolate himself and limit his progressive ambition by being perceived and treated as just "another southern Democrat" by nonsouthern Democrats in the Senate. LBJ found his opportunity for rapid advancement in a seemingly unlikely place—party leadership.

Political scientist James Sundquist stated that party leaders "are, by definition, the beneficiaries of the party system as it is."[60] During the last two years of the Truman presidency, the national Democratic Party in general and the Senate Democrats in particular were experiencing an intensified degree of dissensus. Dissensus is a condition of intraparty political behavior in which party members increasingly lack a shared ideology and policy agenda and become alienated from each other multilaterally, rather than just bilaterally, as they are confronted by new types of issues.[61]

The Democrats were not simply divided between pro-civil rights, urban, northern, pro-union liberals and anti-civil rights, rural, southern, antiunion conservatives. The civil rights' positions of southern Democratic senators ranged from that of Estes Kefauver of Tennessee, who supported a federal repeal of poll taxes, to that of James Eastland of Mississippi, who stridently opposed any federal intervention on any race-related issue like voting rights for blacks. While supportive of civil rights and labor unions, western Democratic senators like Warren Magnuson of Washington and Joseph O'Mahoney of Wyoming often voted with southern conservatives and against northeastern liberals on expanding federal water and electrification projects. When the issue and political movement of McCarthyism emerged in 1950, Democrats in Congress, regardless of ideological and regional differences, disagreed over whether to emphasize the protection of civil liberties for suspected Communists or to demonstrate equally militant anti-Communism through new legislation and red-baiting rhetoric, and over how to facilitate Senator Joseph McCarthy's political demise. Finally, Harry Truman's declining public approval ratings and the growing public frustration with his conduct of the Korean War motivated most Senate Democrats to distance themselves from Truman's party leadership.[62]

Scott Lucas, a moderate Democrat from Illinois, served as Senate majority leader during the 1949–1950 session of Congress and unsuccessfully tried to be a liaison between the president and Senate Democrats, especially the conservative southern bloc. Lucas and five other nonsouthern Democratic senators were defeated for reelection in 1950. This made the southern bloc even more cohesive and powerful within the reduced Democratic majority. The Democrats elected Ernest McFarland, an aging moderate from Arizona, as their new majority leader.

LBJ's opportunity to enter the party leadership appeared when Lister Hill of Alabama resigned as Senate majority whip in protest of Truman's FEPC proposal and foreign policy in Korea. Although McFarland passively opposed LBJ's candidacy for whip, he had to accept the Texan as his assistant because of LBJ's staunch support from the southern bloc.[63] While the listless McFarland minimized his role and responsibilities as majority leader, the dynamic LBJ maximized his. The Texas Democrat especially used the whip's position to expand and strengthen his contacts and quid pro quo legislative relationships with nonsouthern Democrats, especially Hubert Humphrey, during the 1951–1952 session. In the 1952 elections, the Republicans won the presidency and majorities in both houses of Congress. McFarland was defeated for reelection by Barry Goldwater, a Republican city councilman from Phoenix.[64]

The Senate Republicans, however, only had a one-seat majority, 48–47. Senator Robert A. Taft of Ohio was elected majority leader, but he died of cancer on July 31, 1953.[65] The Republicans then elected Senator William F. Knowland of California as Taft's successor. Lacking Taft's intellectual and rhetorical skills and less willing than Taft to compromise with Democrats on major policy issues, Knowland was a staunch ally of Joseph McCarthy and openly criticized Eisenhower's foreign policy toward China and the United Nations. The California Republican threatened to resign his leadership position in 1954 if Communist China was admitted to the United Nations.

Knowland retained his title as Senate majority leader for the remainder of the eighty-third Congress. The Republicans actually lost their numerical majority in the Senate when Taft died because the Ohio Republican was replaced by a Democrat, Thomas Burke. Wayne Morse, an independent and former Republican from Oregon, mostly voted with the Democrats until he became one in 1955.[66] Following the Democratic gain of one Senate seat in the 1954 midterm elections, LBJ formally became Senate majority leader. Regardless of whether or not his party had a numerical majority in the Senate, LBJ had instructed Bobby Baker to have the title Senate Democratic Leader printed on his stationery.[67] At LBJ's request, Senator Earle Clements of Kentucky was elected majority whip. This was a shrewd, consensus-building decision by LBJ since Clements was a moderately liberal, culturally southern border state senator. Clements was generally acceptable to both northern Democrats and southern, conservative "inner club" senators led by Richard Russell of Georgia. The Texan privately assured Hubert H. Humphrey that the Minnesota Democrat would be his unofficial "ambassador" to northern liberals.[68]

Besides seeking cooperation on an incremental, issue-by-issue basis from a variety of Democrats, LBJ also developed constructive relationships with some moderate and liberal Republicans, such as Margaret Chase Smith of Maine and Irving Ives of New York, who were alienated by Knowland's party leadership and McCarthyism. Although the 1954 elections had yielded a twenty-nine-seat majority for the House Democrats, Speaker of the House Sam Rayburn still had to deal with major committees controlled by the bipartisan conservative coalition, especially the House Rules Committee.[69] Like LBJ, Rayburn wanted the Democratic policy agenda in Congress to consist of bipartisan cooperation on more consensual domestic programs, like the construction of the interstate highway system and the St. Lawrence Seaway and expansion of Social Security, deference to Eisenhower on major foreign policy issues, and the offer of centrist alternatives to the president's more conservative, partisan proposals, such as tax cuts.[70]

Even more important to LBJ's leadership style than Rayburn, though, was Dwight Eisenhower. The Republican president disliked partisan conflict and reluctantly agreed to run for president in order to preserve and continue a bipartisan foreign policy and prevent anti-UN isolationist Republicans from nominating and electing their own presidential candidate. Eisenhower demonstrated little interest or initiative in trying to transform the Republican Party into the new, enduring majority party with an ideology and policy agenda clearly distinguishing it from the Democratic Party.[71] Eisenhower's bipartisan centrism and, apparently, that of most American voters during the mid-1950s were revealed in the 1956 election results. The Republican president was reelected with 57 percent of the popular votes while the Democrats increased their congressional majorities by one seat in the Senate and two seats in the House. Also, the percentage of voters identifying themselves as Republicans steadily declined from 1956 to 1960.[72]

With this modest yet steady electoral progress by the Democrats during the mid-1950s, LBJ was careful to remain publicly respectful of Eisenhower and even deferential on most foreign policy issues, such as his support of the president against the anti-UN Bricker amendment sponsored by conservative Republicans in the Senate. Meanwhile, LBJ directed more partisan, aggressive rhetoric at the most controversial members of the Eisenhower administration, especially Secretary of Agriculture Ezra Taft Benson, and the most obstructionist, conservative Republican senators.[73] George Reedy, who served on LBJ's Senate staff during the 1950s and briefly as his White House press secretary, observed, "There were practically no circumstances under which Johnson would countenance a 'Democratic' bill. He insisted that the changes be made by striking the language of key portions of an *Eisenhower* bill and inserting Democratic language in its place."[74]

As Eisenhower began his second term, other Democrats increasingly and openly criticized and opposed what Texas newspapers had praised as LBJ's "constructive conservatism" and "cooperative and conciliatory attitude toward the President."[75] Liberal activists, especially the Americans for Democratic Action (ADA) and "amateur Democrats" inspired by Adlai Stevenson, were frustrated by and impatient with Johnson and Rayburn's party leadership in Congress.[76] They were especially insistent that LBJ and Rayburn articulate liberal policy positions, such as on civil rights and federal aid to elementary and secondary education. Liberals wanted to distinguish the two major parties ideologically and programmatically, thereby mobilizing Democratic majorities for winning presidential elections and making the Democratic congressional record more reflective of the Democratic national platform.[77]

Richard Bolling, a Missouri Democratic congressman and protégé of Rayburn, dismissively referred to these liberal critics as "the irresponsible liberals who didn't care about the deeds and only cared about words."[78] Shortly after the 1956 elections, the DNC created the Democratic Advisory Council (DAC) for formulating and announcing Democratic policy positions. DNC chairman Paul M. Butler invited Rayburn and Johnson to join the DAC, but both refused and asserted that they represented the national Democratic policy agenda.[79]

James H. Rowe, Jr., one of LBJ's closest, most respected political confidantes, warned the Senate majority leader that he must address this criticism. The liberals regarded LBJ as "a turncoat New Dealer" and will intensify their opposition to his party leadership "until Lyndon Johnson can find an issue on which he can lead his party."[80] During the 1957–1958 session, LBJ pursued the issue that he had avoided the most—civil rights.[81]

LBJ realized that he could attract the reluctant support of the most liberal southern Democrats, like Tennesseans Gore and Kefauver, and only passive opposition from the more conservative southerners if he limited the definition and policy focus of civil rights to a modest increase in the federal protection of voting rights. Black voter registration and turnout had gradually increased without acts of Congress in the peripheral South (e.g., Texas, Tennessee, and Florida), since the 1940s. Senators from these states were less likely to feel politically threatened by such legislation.[82] LBJ also understood that it would be difficult for the most doctrinaire liberal critics of his party leadership, such as Paul Douglas of Illinois and the recently elected William Proxmire of Wisconsin, to vote against such a bill for being too weak and limited.

Johnson had been careful not to antagonize southern conservatives by diluting the obstructionistic power of the filibuster through reform of the cloture rules. But he had gradually and subtly reduced the power of the southern bloc in the Senate. LBJ increased and diversified the membership of the Senate Democratic Policy Committee to include more nonsouthern Democrats. Greater regional and ideological diversity in the Senate Democratic power structure was also achieved through the Johnson Rule.[83] This procedural reform reduced the significance of seniority in committee assignments so that senators with less seniority, usually liberal and moderate nonsouthern Democrats, were more likely to receive assignments to more desirable, prestigious committees. Freshman Democrats John F. Kennedy of Massachusetts, John Pastore of Rhode Island, Mike Mansfield of Montana, and Henry M. "Scoop" Jackson of Washington especially benefited from the Johnson Rule. LBJ calculated that most nonsouthern Democrats who had benefited from his party leadership would be willing to amend a civil rights bill in order to assure its passage, despite lobbying pressure for a tougher bill from the NAACP, ADA, and their more liberal, anti-LBJ colleagues.

Using the influence of his mentor-protégé relationship with Richard Russell, LBJ persuaded the Georgia Democrat to abstain from organizing a filibuster if a jury trial amendment was added to the civil rights bill.[84] Russell and most other southern conservatives actually resented the solitary, marathon floor speech of J. Strom Thurmond of South Carolina against the compromised civil rights bill of 1957. Following Thurmond's twenty-four-hour speech, the Senate passed the civil rights bill by a margin of 60 to 15.[85]

The passage of the Civil Rights Act of 1957 was, according to Johnson aide George Reedy, "the production of a master legislative mind at the height of his powers" and that the "civil rights battle could now be fought out legislatively in an arena that previously had provided nothing but a sounding board for speeches."[86] Leading the Senate Democrats since 1953, LBJ had assumed that his emphasis on bipartisan, multiregional compromises, centrism, public respect for Eisenhower, and shrewd distribution of prestigious committee assignments and other favors to grateful nonsouthern Democrats would gradually improve his national status within the Democratic Party. LBJ's zealous determination to pass virtually any civil rights bill that would not arouse the implacable opposition of Richard Russell made him focus on the legislative tactics and policy compromises necessary to pass a bill rather than on the substantive value and impact of such legislation on the actual voting rights of southern blacks.[87] Eisenhower publicly criticized the shortcomings of the bill and only reluctantly signed it into law. Black civil rights and labor leader A. Philip Randolph and maverick liberal senator Wayne Morse denounced it as a sham.[88] Joseph L. Rauh, Jr. of the ADA actually asserted that LBJ's leadership in passing this bill "proved his unfitness for national leadership."[89]

Eisenhower's use of the U.S. Army to implement the court-ordered desegregation of Central High School in Little Rock, Arkansas, shortly after the enactment of the 1957 civil rights bill further exacerbated divisions among Democrats.[90] Liberals demanded tougher, additional civil rights legislation to compensate for the shortcomings of the 1957 law and prepare for the 1960 presidential election.[91] Feeling betrayed by Eisenhower, LBJ, and their nonsouthern Democratic colleagues, southern senators became more hostile to future civil rights legislation.[92]

Another event of 1957 that complicated Johnson's effort to develop a consensual national status as a Democrat was the special election of Ralph Yarborough to the Senate from Texas. Yarborough's predecessor, Price Daniel, was more conservative than LBJ, especially on racial and economic issues, and had openly endorsed Eisenhower's presidential candidacy in 1952. In 1952, Daniel was the senatorial nominee of both the Democratic and Republican parties of Texas. Daniel also served as a liaison for LBJ with an even more conservative, pro-Eisenhower Democrat, Governor Allen Shivers. Although LBJ wanted Daniel to run for reelection to the Senate in 1958, Daniel was elected governor in 1956. Reflecting on his usually friendly, cooperative relationship with LBJ, Daniel stated that LBJ wanted to "work as a team . . . on Democratic Party machinery, such as the State Democratic Executive Committee . . . and that I would work with him in seeing his enemies didn't get on that Committee and take over the party in Texas."[93]

Daniel, Rayburn, and LBJ formed a triumvirate in 1956 to control the state Democratic apparatus, especially its Democratic delegates to the party's 1956 national convention and the pledging of the state's Democratic electors to Adlai Stevenson. Ideologically, with Daniel to his right and Rayburn to his left, LBJ, according to political scientist O. Douglas Weeks, was "more in the exact center because he had not deserted the party or truckled too openly with either the right or the left."[94]

The shaky coalition that LBJ and Rayburn had cobbled together with conservatives and liberals was short-lived. Inspired by Adlai Stevenson and identifying themselves with the ADA and DAC, the small but vocal cadre of liberal Democrats in Texas distrusted LBJ. Encouraged by the special election of Ralph Yarborough to the Senate in 1957, Texas liberal Democrats established the Democrats of Texas (DOT), similar to the pro-Stevenson, "amateur" Democratic clubs that were being formed throughout the nation, and a Texas chapter of the Democratic Advisory Council (DAC).[95] Margaret Carter, a member of the Texas DAC, commented in 1969 that LBJ, like Rayburn, "simply did not want any organized activity to be going on, because if you sponsor an organization, then you do have to keep in touch with it."[96]

Yarborough's presence as the junior senator from Texas made LBJ appear to be even more conservative than he was. Unlike LBJ, Yarborough used anti–big business populist rhetoric and openly cultivated the support of blacks, Hispanics, the more liberal labor leaders, and liberal activists like ADA and DOT members. Frankie Randolph, a pro-Yarborough, anti-LBJ liberal, was elected Democratic national committeewoman from Texas. She defeated LBJ's candidate, Beryl Bentsen, the wife of former congressman and future senator Lloyd Bentsen.[97] With Yarborough and Randolph as their power base in the party apparatus of Texas, the most liberal Democratic activists were determined that Texas would not provide united delegate support for a possible LBJ presidential candidacy at the 1960 Democratic national convention.[98]

Unable to gain the trust of liberal activists in his home state, LBJ had a shaky political base that was also threatened by the growing number of Texas Republicans, who often allied themselves with the most conservative Democrats on an issue-by-issue, candidate-by-candidate basis. For example, although Ralph Yarborough won the 1957 Senate election in Texas, he received 38 percent of the votes while his two leading opponents, Martin Dies, a conservative Democrat, and Thad Hutcheson, a Republican, respectively received 30.4 percent and 22.9 percent.[99] As he faced renomination and reelection to the Senate in 1960, it was unlikely that LBJ would attract the overwhelming primary support and the token Republican opposition of his 1954 campaign. Johnson's pragmatic centrism was becoming a liability, rather than an asset, in his home state's politics.

While LBJ pondered a presidential candidacy as an escape from the internecine politics of Texas, he continued to try to further develop a national reputation as a consensus-building power broker who could lead the formulation and passage of legislation that benefited the nation as a whole. During the 1957–1958 legislative session, LBJ focused on bipartisan efforts to initiate a space program, increase federal aid for school construction, provide college loans and graduate fellowships, especially in science and mathematics, admit Alaska as a state, and end the unpopular farm policies of Secretary of Agriculture Ezra Taft

Benson.[100] Unfortunately for LBJ, the Senate was not a microcosm of national Democratic politics in the late 1950s.

In disseminating analyses of the election results of 1956, DNC chairman Paul M. Butler focused on the fact that Eisenhower had received a near landslide 57 percent of the popular vote and had performed unusually well among such typically Democratic voting blocs as blacks, Catholics, and union members. Even black Democratic representative Adam Clayton Powell, Jr., of New York endorsed Eisenhower's reelection.[101] In a 1957 speech at Howard University, political analyst Samuel Lubell stated, "One of the striking paradoxes of the whole election was that the Negro and the white Southerner could cast a protest vote against one another by voting for the same man, Dwight D. Eisenhower."[102]

Even before the 1957–1958 recession began and the 1958 midterm elections were held, the growing consensus of the DNC headquarters, the DAC, ADA, Democratic big city mayors, civil rights leaders, union leaders, and other major influences on the presidential nominating and platform drafting processes of the national Democratic party was that the Democratic presidential ticket and platform in 1960 needed to be distinctly more liberal in order to attract maximum electoral support from the major nonsouthern voting blocs of the New Deal coalition and win the election.[103] During the 1956 Democratic national convention, John M. Bailey, the Democratic state chairman of Connecticut, distributed a statistical analysis of the growing, decisive influence of Catholic voting power in presidential elections.[104] Later attributed to JFK's speechwriter Theodore C. Sorensen, the Bailey Memorandum suggested that the future nomination of a Catholic to a Democratic presidential ticket would be not only helpful but even necessary for Democratic victory. As early as the fall of 1955, LBJ had reportedly rejected Joseph P. Kennedy's offer to finance his presidential campaign if the Texan became the Democratic presidential nominee in 1956 and chose JFK as his running mate.[105]

Compared to Johnson, JFK better understood and could master the political forces that influenced the 1960 Democratic presidential nomination. Unlike Johnson, JFK realized that the power to influence the decision of the 1960 Democratic national convention resided primarily with Democratic state chairmen, governors, big city mayors, union leaders, and party activists rather than with Democratic senators. In a 1957 *Life* magazine article, JFK warned that if he and his fellow Democrats "simply stay in the middle with a policy of 'moderation,' we will not . . . distinguish our position sufficiently to arouse the much-needed enthusiasm of our more progressive supporters, particularly in the West, and the presidential race will be reduced to largely a personality contest."[106]

The midterm election results of 1958, especially those for the Senate races, accelerated and intensified these more partisan, ideologically divisive political forces that benefited JFK's presidential ambition and hampered LBJ's. With a secure political base in Massachusetts, ample campaign funds, high-profile committee seats that attracted favorable publicity and greater national name recognition, and expert advisers and staff, JFK was able to identify and successfully adapt to this changing political environment. JFK extensively yet unofficially campaigned for the presidential nomination by frequently speaking at Democratic events throughout the United States. LBJ, by contrast, was increasingly imprisoned and burdened by his duties as Senate majority leader.[107] For both Democrats, the impact of the 1958 election results affected their initial rivalry and eventual alliance in the 1960 presidential campaign.

CHAPTER THREE

The 1960 Election: Rivals and Allies

The key policy issues, political actors, and results of the 1958 midterm elections were major influences on the initial competition and eventual cooperation between JFK and LBJ during the 1960 presidential campaign. Unlike LBJ, Kennedy proved his ability to adapt to and manipulate the political climate and forces of the late 1950s in his successful strategy to win the Democratic presidential nomination. But JFK later realized how essential LBJ was as a running mate to energize and unite the Democratic party enough to win the 1960 presidential election by a razor-thin margin.

Labor reform, essentially amending the Taft-Hartley Act of 1947, dominated the 1958 campaign season. There had been a steady growth in the number and percentage of working Americans belonging to labor unions, the AFL-CIO merged in 1955, and journalists conducted sensationalized investigations of local labor union corruption, especially collusion with gangsters.[1] The impetus that Senator Estes Kefauver's 1952 presidential candidacy had received from his televised committee hearings on organized crime and the public attention aroused by the highly acclaimed movie *On the Waterfront* made it likely that the Senate would conduct similar committee hearings on labor racketeering.[2]

Consequently, in February 1957, a Senate select committee on labor racketeering chaired by John McClellan of Arkansas, a conservative Democrat who had voted for the Taft-Hartley Act, was convened. It initially appeared that an active, televised role on such a committee would be detrimental to the presidential ambition of a pro-union, nonsouthern Democrat. The McClellan committee's investigations would inevitably be embarrassing to labor unions and arouse the antagonism of the two most powerful labor leaders at Democratic national conventions, AFL-CIO president George Meany and UAW president Walter Reuther.[3]

JFK, however, recognized his membership on this select committee and chairmanship of a labor subcommittee as excellent opportunities for his presidential candidacy. Bolstered by a very favorable rating by the AFL-CIO's Committee on Political Education (COPE) and a deferential, admiring constituency in Massachusetts as he ran for reelection, Kennedy had the freedom to develop and maneuver a moderate, reformist policy direction.[4] In pursuing this objective,

JFK benefited from the fact that his policy position on the McClellan committee was midway between the tougher labor reforms proposed by Republicans Barry Goldwater and Karl Mundt and the blatantly pro-union criticism of this investigation by Democratic Senator Patrick McNamara of Michigan. McNamara was a former union official and staunch defender of the UAW who eventually resigned from the McClellan committee in protest.[5]

JFK's brother Robert was the chief counsel of the McClellan committee and conducted the most outspoken, relentless televised questioning of union officials, especially James R. Hoffa, president of the Teamster's Union. From the perspective of television viewers, JFK was calmer and more judicious than the crusading, impassioned RFK, but both projected the appealing image to suburban voters of independent-minded, reformist young Democrats who were not beholden to labor bosses. Actually, the Kennedys, unlike the committee's chairman, John McClellan, were able to dominate the direction of the investigation so that it primarily focused on the Teamsters and avoided an equally extensive investigation of the UAW, which earned RFK and JFK the gratitude and trust of Walter Reuther.[6] Considering JFK's presidential ambition, the Teamsters were a safe target for the McClellan committee since Reuther, Meany, and national labor leaders had already perceived it as a disreputable, renegade union and expelled it from the AFL-CIO in 1957.[7]

This investigation also provided JFK with an opportunity to achieve an asset lacking so far in his Senate career and conducive to a serious presidential candidacy. He could now demonstrate legislative leadership by authoring and guiding a bill on a prominent policy issue from its inception to its enactment. JFK needed a bill that would be warily acceptable to the blue-collar Democratic electoral base in a presidential election, especially the AFL-CIO's national leadership, and satisfying to middle-class, pro-Eisenhower split-ticket voters who wanted bipartisan centrism in labor reform. Consequently, JFK co-sponsored a labor reform bill with Senator Irving Ives of New York in 1958. Ives was a liberal Republican and vice chairman of the McClellan committee who chose not to run for reelection in 1958.[8]

The Kennedy-Ives bill's content contained strict financial disclosure requirements for unions, and stronger protection of the rank and file's voting rights in union elections. Its major concession to business interests was its prohibition of "shakedown" picketing and improper unloading fees.[9] In essence, the Kennedy-Ives bill was presented by its sponsors as an advancement of the legal and political rights of honest union members in their relationships with their union leaders.

Nonetheless, the Kennedy-Ives bill was opposed by the U.S. Chamber of Commerce and the National Association of Manufacturers (NAM) for being too weak and the United Mine Workers (UMW), Teamsters, and the United Steel Workers of America (USWA) for being too tough.[10] The AFL-CIO reluctantly endorsed it. But after the Senate, over JFK's opposition, added the requirement that union officers swear non-Communist affidavits, the Senate ratified the Kennedy-Ives bill by a vote of 88–1.[11]

JFK's legislative victory, though, was short-lived. The Kennedy-Ives bill stalled and died in the House committee system. It was resubmitted as the Kennedy-Ervin bill in 1959 and omitted provisions advocated by Eisenhower. The Senate rejected this bill by a 46–45 vote after a "bill of rights" hostile to labor leaders' interests was added to it. Vice President Nixon cast the deciding vote.[12]

With the influence of Eisenhower and Secretary of Labor James Mitchell, who was reputedly seeking to become Richard Nixon's running mate, the bipartisan conservative coalition in the House of Representatives designed a bill that included many of Eisenhower's recommendations with a pro-business, pro-states' rights emphasis. Cosponsored by Democratic Representative Phillip Landrum of Georgia and Republican Representative Robert P. Griffin of Michigan, the Landrum-Griffin bill was endorsed by Eisenhower in a televised speech in August 1959.[13] In September 1959, both houses of Congress passed it and the president signed it into law.

Kennedy ambivalently voted for the Landrum-Griffin Act. He did not attract the criticism and opposition from major labor leaders and liberal Democrats that LBJ had anticipated. In using his power and influence as Senate majority leader to facilitate JFK's prominence on the labor reform issue, Johnson had calculated that JFK's highly public legislative effort would be successful enough to boost the Catholic Democrat's name recognition so that he would be a valuable running mate for LBJ in 1960 but unsuccessful enough to prevent JFK from securing the presidential nomination.[14]

In this instance, however, as in other stages of his pre-convention strategy, LBJ miscalculated. JFK's efforts on behalf of the labor reform legislation proved to be more beneficial than detrimental to his evident, yet still unannounced presidential candidacy. Reuther and Meany understood that, due to the current political climate, labor reform legislation was inevitable and that the Landrum-Griffin Act was much more hostile to their interests than the original Kennedy-Ives bill had been.[15] Since LBJ was the Senate majority leader, they and other labor leaders were more likely to blame LBJ rather than JFK for the Senate's adoption of the bill of rights amendment vigorously opposed by union lobbyists.[16]

Walter Reuther recognized that JFK had diligently tried to defeat the bill of rights amendment and had carefully limited the McClellan committee's investigation of the UAW. He announced in early 1959 that the UAW would wait until after the 1960 Democratic national convention to announce its endorsement for president.[17] The official neutrality of the UAW during the pre-convention phase and primary campaigns of 1960 was a boon to JFK's candidacy against the more liberal, pro-union Hubert Humphrey. JFK's campaign staff perceived the Minnesotan as a stalking horse for LBJ.[18]

Emboldened by the more conservative, antiunion direction that labor reform legislation had taken in Congress, Republicans and business interest groups
introduced "right to work" ballot proposals prohibiting union shop contracts in
six states, most notably California, for the 1958 midterm elections.[19] Republican
party leaders and activists in these states rejected the advice of RNC chairman
Meade Alcorn. Alcorn opposed these "right to work" campaign activities for fear
that they would stimulate powerful voter registration and turnout efforts by
labor unions and divide the liberal and conservative wings of these states' Republican parties.[20] That is exactly what happened. Voters rejected the "right to work"
proposals in five of these six states and these antiunion measures contributed to
the defeats of the Republican nominees for governor and senator in California
and to the election of freshman Democratic senators in the Midwest.[21]

Even after the 1957–1958 recession dissipated, public opinion and voting
behavior indicated a more liberal policy direction in economics at a time when
Eisenhower and most Republicans in Congress emphasized the avoidance of
higher budget deficits and the adoption of balanced budgets.[22] Determined to
leave a surplus in his last budget, Eisenhower pursued a more adversarial relationship with LBJ and Rayburn and vetoed Democratic bills on urban renewal,
the economic development of depressed areas, public housing, and public works.[23]
The Republican president was equally adamant in rejecting Democratic defense
spending proposals introduced in the wake of the Soviet launching of Sputnik
in 1957 and Democratic allegations of a missile gap with the Soviet Union,
partially citing fiscal responsibility.[24]

The strongest partisan, ideological, and policy differences were most graphically demonstrated in the results of the 1958 Senate elections. The Democrats
gained fifteen seats in the Senate, increasing their majority from 49–47 to 64–34.
The Democrats also gained forty-eight House seats and eight governorships.[25]

A few days after the November 4, 1958, election, LBJ announced the
Democratic legislative agenda for the Eighty-Sixth Congress. He emphasized
"progress and growth" in his statement. The Senate majority leader outlined new
legislation for such policy goals as airport modernization, greater research on
space exploration, improved relations with Latin America, and greater federal
spending for agricultural subsidies, water and power projects in the western
states, housing, and urban renewal.[26]

LBJ hoped that such a broad, diverse policy agenda for greater domestic
spending would satisfy the newly elected freshmen Democrats and enabled him
to continue his leadership style as a moderate unifying leader among the regionally and ideologically diverse Democratic senators and an effective mediator with
Republican senators and Eisenhower. The Texas Democrat still assumed that his
chances of being nominated and elected president in 1960 depended on his
ability to continue to prove his mastery of the Senate. Publicly dismissing any
connection between the 1958 Senate election results and the 1960 presidential

election in a magazine interview, LBJ stated, "I think the people elected a Congress to represent them in '59 and '60, and the election in '60 will be determined on the basis of how we conduct ourselves in '59 and '60, and not on the basis of what the issues are in '58."[27]

LBJ, though, failed to understand that many of the Democrats elected in 1958 were not simply nonsouthern liberals and moderates who wanted more domestic spending and desirable committee assignments. Freshman Democrats like Edmund S. Muskie of Maine and Philip Hart of Michigan were less deferential toward LBJ's domineering leadership style, the tradition-bound folkways of the Senate, such as the seniority system, and the maintenance, however fragile, of intraparty harmony with southern conservatives.[28]

Only eight of the fifteen Democratic freshmen voted for LBJ's weak revision of Rule 22 on cloture. This revision was acceptable to anti-civil rights southern Democrats, and LBJ had advocated and used it to measure the loyalty of first-term Democrats to his leadership.[29] While LBJ's compromise on Rule 22 passed by a vote of 72 to 22, his aggressive lobbying of the Democratic freshmen irked and embittered UAW leaders toward LBJ, a sentiment that later threatened the Texan's vice-presidential nomination.[30]

The fact that almost half of the Democratic freshmen voted against LBJ's motion motivated the more senior, maverick liberals led by Paul Douglas, William Proxmire, and Joseph Clark to more frequently and blatantly criticize and challenge LBJ's leadership on procedural and organizational issues, rather than primarily on the substance and value of his legislative compromises. These Democrats wanted to develop a more open, democratic legislative environment and structure in the Senate with more time for debate and the formulation of more complex yet more valuable policy ideas.[31] On March 9, 1959, Paul Douglas of Illinois delivered a speech on the Senate floor to criticize the inadequate number and proportion of pro-civil rights northeastern and midwestern Democrats on the policy and steering committees. He woefully concluded, "I am perfectly frank to say I do not know how long the Democratic Party can continue with this situation."[32] Two weeks earlier, the more flamboyant William Proxmire of Wisconsin accused LBJ of "one-man rule" of the Senate.[33]

With Johnson facing a growing and more publicly embarrassing fragmentation of the significantly enlarged Democratic majority in the Senate, JFK busied himself with laying the foundation for his nomination campaign. Unlike LBJ, Kennedy used his seat and service in the Senate as one dimension, but not the totality, of his presidential campaign strategy. Since his election to the Senate in 1952, JFK developed the combination of his public image, political alliances, and issue positions as an ever-widening series of concentric circles. JFK initially secured his political base in Massachusetts by superimposing the Kennedy party above the factionalized, regular Democratic Party organization. He focused on the economic policy interests of Massachusetts in his legislative record, which included conservative positions on agricultural and public power issues, and attracted frequent press coverage from the major newspapers of Massachusetts.[34] JFK soon became known as the "The Senator from New England" because of his highly publicized leadership in organizing the senators from New England, both Democrats and Republicans, to protect and promote their region's shared policy interests. This regional leadership effort also helped JFK to cultivate more partisan, personally ambitious connections with fellow New England Democrats as a united regional bloc of delegates and campaigners for the 1960 Democratic national convention and presidential primaries.[35]

JFK's expansion from a regional base to a national political network was first vividly illustrated at the 1956 Democratic national convention. Receiving a surprisingly large number of delegates from southern states for his vice-presidential candidacy, the Catholic senator from Massachusetts was one of the few nonsouthern Democratic senators to vote with southerners on the jury trial amendment of the Civil Rights Act of 1957.[36] JFK continued to speak throughout the South and privately solicit future political support from southern politicians after the 1956 election. He spoke cautiously about civil rights, thereby contrasting himself with outspoken liberals. Despite his fame as "The Senator from New England," JFK further gained a national reputation for political independence by becoming one of the few senators from New England to vote for the St. Lawrence Seaway. [37] This vote implicitly identified JFK with the theme of his Pulitzer Prize–winning book, *Profiles in Courage.*

After the 1956 elections, JFK's legislative record and rhetoric subtly and selectively became more liberal, especially on agricultural, public power, and social welfare issues. In a 1958 speech in Des Moines, Iowa, JFK actually asked his listeners for "forgiveness" for his previously conservative voting record on agriculture.[38] But JFK also assumed that the state and local party leaders who controlled blocs of delegates to the 1960 Democratic national convention would endorse him for president if he could demonstrate popularity and effectiveness as a vote getter through poll rating and impressive primary victories. Despite JFK's urban, Catholic, New England characteristics and his initially conservative record on farm programs, Gallup polls conducted in 1959 revealed that JFK was the top choice for their party's presidential nomination among Democratic county chairmen polled.[39]

JFK also realized that state and local party leaders would be more likely to have their delegations support him at the national convention if he demonstrated overwhelming electoral strength in his home state. Throughout 1958, Kennedy was busy not only speaking at Democratic functions and campaigning for candidates in other states but also running for reelection in Massachusetts.[40] Since his Republican opponent, Vincent J. Celeste, and his major Democratic nemesis, Governor Foster Furcolo, both had Italian surnames, JFK directed his staff to emphasize items in his legislative record that benefited Italy and Italian immigrants.[41] In order to refute Celeste's criticism of the Kennedy family's wealth, JFK and his family emphasized personal contact with the voters, rather than extensive television advertising, and Jacqueline Kennedy spoke Italian to constituents of Italian ancestry.[42] With JFK expecting a record-breaking margin of victory, his campaign not only maximized voter turnout from his mostly Catholic Democratic electoral base. It also attracted significant Republican support for JFK by emphasizing his friendly, cooperative relationship with Republican Senator Leverett Saltonstall on legislation benefiting Massachusetts and generated nonpartisan state pride in JFK's potential as a presidential candidate. An Ohio newspaper reported, "The Kennedy headquarters has instructed its men in the field to sell the message that a vote for Kennedy for the Senate is a vote for Kennedy in 1960."[43]

JFK's landslide reelection in 1958 stimulated exactly the type of favorable national media coverage and commentary and more private yet equally significant attention of Democratic power brokers that the Kennedys wanted. With 73 percent of the votes and a winning margin of more than 873,000 votes, JFK received the largest margin of victory for any candidate in the history of Massachusetts.[44] Besides receiving the almost unanimous electoral support of Catholics, Jews, blacks, and union members, JFK also won narrow majorities in mostly Protestant, staunchly Republican small towns and affluent suburbs.[45] He carried every city and county in Massachusetts.[46]

JFK's plurality also exceeded the reelection margin of Senator Stuart Symington of Missouri. Symington was widely regarded as the most likely dark horse, compromise candidate for president if the 1960 Democratic national convention became deadlocked. JFK's advance men and allies began to promote the demographics of his landslide reelection to Democratic politicians and party activists throughout the nation as evidence that JFK had proven his voter appeal beyond his fellow Catholic Democrats.[47]

Unfortunately for the Kennedy campaign, the 1958 elections had intensified the "Catholic issue" in the nation's political community and, possibly, in its future voting behavior. Catholic Democratic candidates won major gubernatorial and senatorial contests in 1958. Edmund G. "Pat" Brown, David Lawrence, and Michael DiSalle were respectively elected to the governorships of California, Pennsylvania, and Ohio. Because California had thirty-two Electoral College votes and eighty-one delegate votes at the 1960 Democratic national convention, Brown was already being discussed as a running mate if the Democrats nominated a Protestant for president.[48] Even though the convention would be held in Los Angeles, it was unlikely that Brown could even control his state's delegation because of the historically weak party organization of the California Democrats and his competition for state party leadership with Senator-elect Clair Engle and Jesse Unruh, who became speaker of the state assembly in 1961.

Pennsylvania had the same number of Electoral College and Democratic delegate votes as California in 1960. Lawrence, however, was able to exert much stronger, more reliable control over his state's delegates, thereby making him a more formidable, influential power broker in the politics of presidential nominations.[49] Lawrence, the longtime mayor of Pittsburgh and Democratic national committeeman, led efforts within the DNC and at Democratic conventions during the 1950s to ensure the loyalty of anti-civil rights southern delegations to the Democratic presidential ticket and to create the DAC as a source of liberal policy ideas for Democratic national platforms and to challenge Eisenhower's policies.[50]

Until 1958, Lawrence had repeatedly rejected requests that he run for governor because of his concern that his Catholicism would lose votes for the entire state Democratic ticket.[51] He continued to be concerned that a Catholic presidential nominee in 1960 would lose the election because of religious controversy. Among nationally influential Catholic machine bosses, Lawrence remained the most skeptical of JFK's presidential candidacy. A great admirer of Adlai Stevenson, Lawrence could provide a substantial bloc of delegates to Stevenson if the Illinois Democrat chose to run for the presidential nomination at the national convention.

Like Brown, Governor-elect Michael DiSalle of Ohio was already being discussed as a vice-presidential candidate, especially if the Democrats nominated Stuart Symington for president. But, also like Brown, it was doubtful that DiSalle could control all or most of his state's sixty-four delegates at the national convention, even if he ran as a favorite-son presidential candidate. DiSalle lacked unified control of Ohio's delegates because he competed with Senator Frank Lausche, a maverick conservative Democrat, Senator-elect Stephen Young, and Ray Miller.[52] Miller was a Notre Dame graduate and the Democratic boss of Cleveland who actively opposed DiSalle for control of Ohio's Democratic party. Although Miller was an early, enthusiastic backer of JFK's presidential candidacy, the Kennedy campaign wanted to avoid the appearance of siding with Miller's faction in Ohio's intraparty conflict.[53]

The 1958 midterm elections also sent three Catholic Democrats to the Senate who influenced the presidential elections of the 1960s in varying degrees. Edmund S. Muskie was the first Democrat to be popularly elected to the Senate from Maine and the first Catholic to serve in that position.[54] Muskie soon distinguished himself as one of the first freshman Democrats to rebel against LBJ's leadership of the Senate and to endorse JFK's presidential candidacy. Like Muskie, Eugene McCarthy of Minnesota was the first Catholic to be elected to the Senate from his state and joined the Maine Democrat in opposing LBJ's proposal for weakly revising the cloture rule on filibusters.[55] Proving himself to be less compliant toward LBJ than Hubert H. Humphrey, his senior colleague from Minnesota, McCarthy remained aloof of JFK's presidential candidacy. He later delivered an impassioned nominating speech for Adlai Stevenson at the 1960 Democratic national convention.

The electoral results of the national Democratic landslide of 1958 were especially notable in Connecticut. All six of Connecticut's House seats switched from Republican to Democratic control. Its governor, Abraham Ribicoff, was reelected with nearly two-thirds of the votes, and Thomas J. Dodd, a former congressman who lost his 1956 Senate race, defeated Republican Senator William A. Purtell with almost 58 percent of the votes.[56] Dodd was a militantly anti-Communist Catholic who balanced his outspoken, hawkish foreign policy positions with a usually liberal record on civil rights, social welfare, and labor issues.[57] Ribicoff and Democratic state chairman John Bailey led the regional effort to organize all of New England's 114 Democratic delegates behind JFK's presidential candidacy. Dodd remained disaffected from this effort and was determined to support LBJ for the presidential nomination at the national convention. As one of the few Democratic freshmen who voted for LBJ's compromise on the cloture rule, Dodd assiduously ingratiated himself with the Senate majority leader and was rewarded with seats on the Foreign Relations and Judiciary Committees.[58]

Both JFK and LBJ were sensitive to the "Catholic issue" in their still unannounced candidacies. The Texan's desire to make himself more attractive to Catholic Democratic politicians partially motivated LBJ's favoritism toward Dodd and his elevation of Senator Mike Mansfield, a Catholic from Montana, to the position of majority whip shortly after the 1958 elections.[59] Determined to discourage any perception of his political base being limited by his Catholicism, JFK assigned Abraham Ribicoff, a Jew, with the more formal, public role of boosting his presidential candidacy among Ribicoff's fellow Democratic governors nationally and leading the coalition of New England Democrats behind JFK.[60] Meanwhile, Bailey, a Catholic, fulfilled the more discreet yet significant function of privately lobbying mostly Irish Catholic Democratic machine bosses in upstate New York, such as Daniel O'Connell in Albany and Peter Crotty in Buffalo, to commit their delegates early for JFK at the 1960 convention.

James H. Rowe, Jr., a Washington lawyer and Catholic Democrat who urged LBJ to announce his presidential candidacy soon, later characterized JFK's presidential campaign organization as a "quiet-moving machine" that pursued the party's presidential nomination as FDR did in 1932.[61] Kennedy, like FDR, realized that he was more likely to be nominated on the first ballot and sought to prevent a deadlocked convention that would then nominate a compromise candidate for president. This could be accomplished if he and his campaign aides accurately identified the party leaders in each state who favored JFK and could definitely deliver delegates at the national convention, thereby stimulating a cumulative bandwagon effect long before the convention.[62] Throughout 1959, Kennedy aide Theodore C. Sorensen stated that JFK "learned also to tell the difference between those who were party leaders in name and those who actually spoke for delegates."[63]

As in 1932, most delegates to the 1960 Democratic national convention were not selected and committed to presidential candidates through binding primaries. Unlike the 1932 nomination, however, a minimum of a two-thirds majority of delegates had not been required for the Democratic presidential nomination since the abolition of the two-thirds rule in 1936. With the power of southern delegates at national convention steadily declining since then, a candidate only needed a simple majority of 761 delegate votes to become the Democratic presidential nominee in 1960. Even if most southern delegates voted for LBJ or another southern Democrat, JFK could still win the presidential nomination on the first ballot.[64]

The process of presidential nomination campaigns had changed enough since 1932 that JFK was the only Democratic presidential candidate in 1960 who understood that a successful campaign for his party's presidential nomination required a multiyear, virtually full-time effort by a candidate. The successful candidate had to be equally proficient at the wholesale politics of polling, advertising, public speaking, and managing news coverage and commentary and the retail politics of private negotiations with Democratic politicians, party activists, and interest group leaders, along with an intricate knowledge of the delegate selection rules in each state.[65] The Kennedy campaign assumed that its symbiosis of wholesale and retail politics in 1959 and early 1960 would generate the appearance of a bandwagon effect, thereby stimulating the reality of a bandwagon effect among delegate-rich power brokers attracted to the apparently most popular presidential candidate and conclude with a first ballot victory, however narrow, at the Democratic national convention.[66] It was not surprising, therefore, that JFK was the first presidential candidate to hire his own pollster, Louis Harris, in 1959.[67]

The first two major organizational meetings of JFK's presidential campaign occurred in 1959 and included Harris. The first meeting was held on the first two days of April at Joseph P. Kennedy's estate in Florida. The second meeting was held on October 28 in RFK's home in Hyannis Port, Massachusetts.[68] During the time between these two meetings, members of the Kennedy campaign traveled, researched, and polled several of the sixteen states that would hold presidential primaries in 1960 in order to decide which primaries to enter and contest for votes and delegates.

JFK and his staff discerned that they needed to carefully decide which primaries to enter and which ones to forgo. In particular, JFK only wanted to enter contested primaries in states in which he was confident of decisive victories that would discourage his rivals from initiating or continuing their presidential candidacies and also encourage Democratic party leaders to commit their delegates to him. If JFK, as an urban, moderately liberal Catholic from New England, could win unexpected primary victories in overwhelmingly Protestant, socially conservative, rural midwestern states, then he could prove his national voter appeal.[69]

Shortly after the April 1959 meeting, Lawrence F. O'Brien traveled to Indiana to assess its potential as a primary state for JFK to enter and probably attract opposition from another presidential candidate.[70] At this time, the Kennedy campaign perceived Senator Stuart Symington to be JFK's most formidable opponent for the 1960 presidential nomination, both in the primaries and at the convention.[71] Symington was a Maryland-born Protestant from Missouri who combined administrative experience as a corporate executive and Harry Truman's Secretary of the Air Force with a liberal legislative record on civil rights and labor issues.[72] These characteristics seemed to make Symington both a leading vote getter in the Midwest and the ideal compromise candidate at a brokered, deadlocked national convention in 1960. In a taped message to his father, JFK expressed his suspicion that the Teamsters would support Symington in the primaries.[73]

Months before Symington's landslide reelection to the Senate in 1958, Frank McKinney, an Indiana Democrat, approached Symington about officially entering the presidential race and the Indiana primary. Symington politely declined McKinney's invitation.[74] O'Brien initially calculated, however, that if JFK could defeat Symington in the Indiana primary it would be a major symbolic victory in securing the presidential nomination at the 1960 convention.

The dramatic results of the 1958 elections indicated that even an urban, northeastern Catholic like JFK might win a contested Democratic presidential primary in Indiana. With Indiana suffering from high industrial unemployment and low farm prices aggravated by the recession, the Democrats gained six U.S. House seats. They now controlled eight of the state's eleven congressional seats and the lower house of the state legislature. R. Vance Hartke, the mayor of Evansville, became the first Democrat in Indiana to win a Senate seat since 1934.[75]

O'Brien, though, finally advised JFK not to attract Symington or any other major opponent for the presidential nomination into a high-profile, contested primary in Indiana. O'Brien concluded that campaigning in Indiana would be too risky and might destroy JFK's presidential candidacy if he suffered a humiliating defeat there. JFK's Catholicism could be a serious liability among historically Democratic yet culturally conservative Protestants in rural, southern Indiana.[76] The New England Democrat's previously conservative legislative record on farm programs and limited knowledge of agriculture might alienate Indiana farmers who had voted Democratic in 1958 because of discontent with Benson's farm policies.

Hartke had already become a loyal follower of LBJ's party leadership in the Senate and could not be expected to endorse JFK.[77] The only reliable electoral base for Kennedy in this state consisted of the urban-industrial tier of northwestern Indiana with its high concentration of Catholics, blacks, and union members.[78] Fortunately for JFK, Symington never entered the Indiana primary, so JFK won it with 81 percent of the votes.[79]

Other than avoiding major contests in primary states like Indiana, the Kennedy campaign wanted to actively discourage the favorite-son presidential candidacies of Democratic governors, especially those from states with large delegations. Using polling data and research about their states' divisive Democratic politics, JFK warned Pat Brown and Michael DiSalle that he would enter the California and Ohio presidential primaries and defeat them if they ran against him as favorite-son candidates.[80] JFK also asked Brown not to make himself available for the vice-presidential nomination. Kennedy feared that Brown's availability as a Catholic running mate from California would make the Democrats more likely to nominate a Protestant for president.[81] Both governors challenged JFK's bluff, so the Massachusetts Democrat decided not to enter the California and Ohio presidential primaries of 1960. DiSalle agreed, though, to pledge his delegation to JFK if the governor could run unopposed in his state's primary.[82]

By the end of 1959, the Kennedy campaign had meticulously selected seven presidential primaries for JFK to enter. In Pennsylvania and Illinois, two large states with mostly machine-controlled delegates, the Kennedy forces were careful not to file nomination papers or actively campaign there in order to avoid offending Governor David Lawrence of Pennsylvania and Mayor Richard J. Daley in their bailiwicks. Instead, the Kennedy campaign deferred to these machine bosses and patiently waited for JFK to win both uncontested primaries as a write-in candidate.[83]

In most of these seven primaries, JFK faced little or no opposition. As much as possible, the Kennedy campaign wanted to accurately calculate and influence the outcome of each contested primary and the media's interpretations of it. For example, DNC chairman Paul M. Butler had strengthened the Democratic Party of New Hampshire during the 1950s, and JFK won 85 percent of the votes in its Democratic presidential primary of March 8, 1960. The Kennedy operatives, nonetheless, had previously intervened to improve the intraparty harmony of squabbling Manchester Democrats so that JFK's plurality would not be less than that expected by the media.[84]

The Kennedy campaign's perception and anticipation of Stuart Symington as the most formidable opponent in the primaries, especially those in the Midwest, did not materialize. The Missouri senator did not campaign in any of the sixteen Democratic presidential primaries and was a write-in candidate in only five of them. He refrained from making negative public statements about JFK and rhetorically emphasized the need for the next president to close the alleged missile gap with the Soviet Union.[85] Symington apparently hoped for a brokered national convention in which he would be nominated as the presidential candidate most acceptable, or the least offensive, to the conflicting factions and voting blocs of the Democratic Party.

James H. Rowe, Jr., was LBJ's most astute advisor on national party politics and the author of the shrewd campaign strategy that Clark M. Clifford had persuaded Harry Truman to adopt in the 1948 presidential election.[86] Rowe understood how important even a few primaries could be in influencing the nomination of a presidential candidate and repeatedly urged LBJ to enter the primaries. After LBJ convinced Rowe that he would not run for president, Rowe offered his campaign services to Hubert H. Humphrey, who readily accepted.

Because of the close relationship in the Senate between Johnson and Humphrey and Rowe's prominence in Humphrey's presidential campaign, the Kennedy campaign suspected that Humphrey was merely a stalking horse for LBJ's devious strategy of weakening JFK in the primaries, polls, and media commentary, thereby leading to a deadlocked convention that would nominate LBJ for president.[87] But there has never been any convincing, irrefutable evidence that this was true. Humphrey's progressive ambition to become president was as evident as his loquacious, ebullient liberal idealism.[88] He was an enthusiastic, leading member of the ADA and DAC. His policy interests and expertise extended far beyond the immediate constituency interests of Minnesota to include civil rights, nuclear arms control, and a more enlightened American foreign policy toward the Third World.

Like JFK, but less impressively, Humphrey ran for the vice-presidential nomination at the 1956 Democratic national convention. Although he had developed a more cooperative legislative relationship with southern Democrats, the Minnesota senator was still resented and distrusted by southern conservatives for his rousing civil rights speech at the 1948 Democratic national convention. If Humphrey were merely a pawn in a "stop Kennedy" movement engineered by LBJ, the Minnesotan's campaign against JFK certainly would have been better financed, more professionally organized, and a greater threat to JFK's nomination.[89]

Instead, Humphrey's brief presidential campaign was poorly funded, hastily organized, and amateurishly conducted. The Minnesotan announced his candidacy three days before JFK did on December 30, 1959.[90] Humphrey's initial strategy was to weaken and slow Kennedy's momentum by defeating him in the Wisconsin presidential primary of April 5. Since Minnesota bordered on Wisconsin, Humphrey proudly identified himself as "Wisconsin's third senator" because of his advocacy of the policy interests of grain and dairy farmers in both states.[91] The proximity of Wisconsin also enabled the Humphrey forces, which consisted mostly of unpaid volunteers from Minnesota, to travel into Wisconsin on weekends to campaign for the senator. Humphrey's plan was to strengthen his already favorable name recognition in western, rural Wisconsin and then promote it in other agricultural areas of the state while attracting enough labor support in the industrial cities near Lake Michigan to reduce JFK's support in heavily Catholic cities like Milwaukee and Green Bay.[92] Wisconsin and Minnesota also shared the upper Midwest's political culture of "good government" reformism and agrarian populism that frowned on the high-priced celebrity status and gritty machine politics of the Kennedys.[93]

JFK's campaign organization in Wisconsin, however, was well established and familiar with the political environment of the state by the beginning of 1960. JFK had been impressed by the political skills of Jerry Bruno, who had helped to organize William Proxmire's successful Senate campaign in Wisconsin's special election of 1957. Having first met Bruno in 1957, JFK asked him in June 1959 to go to Wisconsin and open his campaign headquarters in Milwaukee.[94] In a biography of her father, Helen O'Donnell stated, "Hiring Bruno was an inspired move, not only because he knew the state well from organizing Proxmire's campaigns but because Proxmire was very close to presidential aspirant Hubert Humphrey, a Minnesotan who would have a natural advantage in neighboring Wisconsin."[95]

JFK made other shrewd decisions in his campaign appointments in Wisconsin months before the primary. His selection of Patrick Lucey, an Irish Catholic and Democratic state chairman, and Ivan Nestinger, a Lutheran Scandinavian and mayor of Madison, to serve as co-chairmen of Citizens for Kennedy provided JFK's campaign with greater regional, religious, and ethnic balance.[96] A less publicized yet significant Wisconsin ally of the Kennedys was Congressman Clement Zablocki. His heavily Polish, Catholic, Milwaukee-based Fourth Congressional District was already expected to deliver an overwhelming, enthusiastic majority of votes for JFK.[97] Approximately 32 percent of Wisconsin's adult population identified itself as Catholic in the Bailey Memorandum of 1956.[98] The Kennedy campaign wanted to discourage any political or media perception that JFK would easily coast to a statewide victory by relying on high Catholic voter turnout in a few urban areas.

The Kennedy campaign wanted to accomplish two objectives in Wisconsin after Humphrey entered the primary. First, it wanted to decisively defeat Humphrey in most parts of the state so that he would end his presidential candidacy. Second, it wanted to portray a Kennedy victory in Wisconsin as a microcosm of JFK's national vote-getting appeal to a variety of Americans, including Protestant farmers. To achieve these goals, the Kennedy campaign divided its organization according to the boundaries of Wisconsin's ten congressional districts. Besides having JFK carry most of these districts, the Kennedy campaign wanted to depict JFK as an underdog in heavily Protestant, rural, presumably pro-Humphrey districts who then exceeded the expectations of the media and pollsters in the actual voting results.[99] Consequently, JFK, his family, and Wisconsin allies spent a disproportionate amount of time and effort in the more rural, Protestant districts, often using social functions that emphasized JFK's personality and celebrity status. JFK refused to debate Humphrey, partially out of fear that the Minnesotan would castigate his record on agricultural issues.

Patrick Lucey admired JFK's campaign in Wisconsin as "an effective presentation of a celebrity."[100]

The Kennedy campaign's "politics of celebrity" was reinforced by the content and tone of JFK's rhetoric. Regardless of where or to whom JFK was speaking in Wisconsin and later in other primaries, he focused on one overall, national theme: the need for the next president to be a dynamic, active leader who could make bold, new domestic and foreign policies so that the United States could compete successfully against the Soviet Union.[101] While JFK campaigned as a national figure with this common theme, Humphrey campaigned as if he were a candidate for local office. The Minnesota senator appealed to individual voting blocs by specifying domestic issue positions tailored to attract votes from each of them. This originally appeared to be a shrewd strategy since most local union officials, members of the state Democratic committee, farm organization leaders, and educators favored Humphrey.[102] Isaac Coggs, a black state representative from Milwaukee, switched his support from JFK to Humphrey because of Humphrey's more consistently liberal record on civil rights.[103]

As the Wisconsin primary contest neared its end, it was evident that there were limits and liabilities to Humphrey's strategy. He was embarrassed and angered by the endorsement of his candidacy by controversial Teamsters president James R. Hoffa and by scurrilous, anti-Catholic literature mailed from Minnesota into Wisconsin.[104] Also, Wisconsin's Democratic and Republican presidential primaries were open primaries. Since Richard M. Nixon was running unopposed in the Republican primary, Republican and independent voters were more likely to participate in the Democratic primary. In a 1965 lecture at Boston College, Kenneth P. O'Donnell frankly admitted that the Kennedy campaign wanted to attract Republican and independent voters in the Wisconsin Democratic primary.[105]

In the heavily Protestant, agricultural areas that favored Humphrey, an important concentration of voters for JFK consisted of rural German Catholic Republicans and independents. Many of them had previously supported former Republican Senator Joseph McCarthy. Shortly before the April 5 primary, a Republican state representative informed Humphrey that there was an effort to mobilize Republican voters for JFK.[106]

Unfortunately for the Kennedy campaign, the media began to portray Humphrey as the underdog and increased expectations for an overwhelming victory for the Massachusetts senator.[107] Lawrence F. O'Brien later admitted that some of JFK's campaign workers contributed to higher expectations by boasting to journalists that JFK would carry eight or nine of the ten congressional districts.[108] On the Sunday before the primary was held, the *Milwaukee Journal* published the numbers of voters in each county according to three categories: Democratic, Republican, and Catholic.[109]

JFK received 56.5 percent of the votes in the Wisconsin Democratic presidential primary and carried six of the ten congressional districts.[110] In a televised interview, pollster Elmo Roper attributed Kennedy's victory to Catholic Republicans.[111]

As predicted, JFK performed best in heavily Catholic, urban counties in east-ern and southern Wisconsin and worst in the most Protestant, rural counties located along the Minnesota state line.[112] The most damaging district-level analysis of the Kennedy campaign arose from JFK's failure to carry the Second Congressional District based in Madison. The media expected JFK to carry this district partially because the mayor of Madison had actively campaigned for him.[113]

Humphrey interpreted the results as "a victory . . . in projecting myself into the national scene as a genuine contender."[114] Humphrey was emboldened to enter the May 10 Democratic presidential primary in West Virginia, even though almost all of his campaign staff urged him not to. The fact that the West Virginia contest was a closed primary that allowed only registered Democrats to vote was encouraging to Humphrey. Since the unfavorable media analysis of the Wisconsin primary had not generated a bandwagon effect for JFK among large, boss-controlled state delegations, the Kennedy campaign reluctantly entered the West Virginia primary.[115]

Compared to the Wisconsin primary, the Kennedy campaign had a larger number and variety of objectives in West Virginia. First, JFK's campaign wanted to firmly defeat Humphrey and financially weaken the Minnesotan's campaign so badly that Humphrey would be forced to end his active presidential can-didacy. Second, unlike his "high-road" restrained rhetoric in Wisconsin, JFK was now willing to use negative campaign tactics against Humphrey, especially through surrogates like Franklin D. Roosevelt, Jr.[116] Third, using FDR, Jr.'s status as one of the founding members of the ADA and namesake of the late president revered by many West Virginians, Kennedy emphasized the most liberal elements of his legislative record and campaign platform. The Massa-chusetts senator wanted to assure not only the voters in West Virginia but also the national media and Democratic power brokers that he was sincerely com-mitted to New Deal liberalism. Fourth, unlike his evasion in Wisconsin, JFK directly addressed the religious issue, hoping to permanently end his Catholi-cism as a recurring campaign issue.[117] Because West Virginia was an almost entirely Protestant, mostly rural, poverty-stricken, culturally southern border state, the Kennedy campaign shrewdly understood that a decisive victory by an urban, wealthy New England Catholic in the West Virginia primary would be a great symbolic victory nationally.[118]

The Kennedy campaign had been researching the political climate of West Virginia since 1958. JFK spoke at Democratic party functions in this state in 1958 and 1959.[119] In January 1959, JFK asked Robert P. McDonough, a Parkersburg businessman, to conduct meetings in several communities to assess the degree of actual or potential voter and volunteer support for JFK in West Virginia. Louis Harris conducted a private poll for JFK in December 1959 that revealed that Kennedy's lead over Humphrey was 70 percent to 30 percent. Publicly, JFK repeatedly told the media that at best he would receive 40 percent of the votes.[120] One month later, McDonough had developed the basis for a campaign organization for JFK in thirty of the state's fifty-five counties.

Upon the advice of JFK's staff, McDonough emphasized to his fellow West Virginians that JFK was an impressive vote getter who was the only Democrat who could defeat Nixon in November. This was a powerful appeal in an overwhelmingly Democratic, economically depressed state that was hostile to Eisenhower's economic policies, especially his rejection of Democratic-sponsored area redevelopment programs.[121] This theme also fit into JFK's contention that Humphrey was merely a stalking horse for a "stop Kennedy" movement that would defeat JFK at the convention and ultimately contribute to Nixon's victory in the general election.[122]

Although JFK accused Hubert Humphrey of "gutter campaign tactics" in late April, FDR, Jr., implied that Humphrey was a draft dodger during World War II while praising JFK's combat heroism in an April 27 speech.[123] The deceased president's son repeated this insinuation on May 6. Kennedy belatedly dissociated himself from these remarks, but he did not publicly criticize Roosevelt for this accusation.

Prior to FDR, Jr.'s suggestive remarks about Humphrey's deferment from the draft, the Kennedy campaign's publicity was already dramatizing JFK's combat heroism in the South Pacific. This theme was especially appealing in West Virginia, a small state whose population suffered a disproportionate number of casualties in World War II and was proud of its tradition of distinguished military service.[124] JFK's war record was also used to address the religious issue through his assertions that just as there is no religious requirement for military service there should be no religious test for the presidency. In one television program, JFK placed his hand on a Bible and solemnly asserted his commitment to the separation of church and state.[125] The resentful interpretation of the Humphrey campaign was that JFK was asking West Virginians to prove their religious tolerance by voting for him.[126]

The media's portrayal of the West Virginia primary as a national referendum on religious tolerance masked the fact that many West Virginia voters were indifferent to the religious issue in choosing between JFK and Humphrey and that JFK's campaign volunteers included Protestant ministers. The national media and the Humphrey campaign also failed to understand the byzantine slate-making processes—with long, complex ballots overseen by county party organizations often run by county sheriffs. As early as the spring of 1959, Lawrence F. O'Brien had joined Robert McDonough in lobbying Democratic county committees, especially those with reputations for effective voter mobilization, to slate JFK, that is, to recommend Kennedy's name in giving ballot instructions to primary voters. The Kennedy campaign was also careful to remain neutral in an intraparty conflict over the gubernatorial nomination.[127]

Researchers and participants of the Kennedy campaign in West Virginia continue to debate whether JFK "bought" his primary victory through bribes to

county sheriffs and other machine politicians in that state. Journalist Seymour
M. Hersh claimed that, because of the intervention of Joseph P. Kennedy and
Frank Sinatra, Sam Giancana and other gangsters contributed $50,000 for the
campaign expenses of pro-JFK Democrats in West Virginia.[128] Boston area
Congressman Thomas P. "Tip" O'Neill, Jr. suggested that Eddie Ford and other
admirers of JFK from Massachusetts traveled to West Virginia to distribute cash
to county sheriffs who helped the Kennedy campaign.[129] Kennedy campaign
strategist Lawrence F. O'Brien admitted that he distributed money for slating.
But O'Brien justified this as a legitimate tactic in West Virginia politics that the
Humphrey campaign, allegedly funded by pro-LBJ forces, also practiced.[130] After
the primary, the FBI and the *Charleston Gazette* investigated and dismissed the
charges of illegal vote buying by the Kennedy campaign.[131]

Regardless of the ethical questions raised by the national media and JFK's
critics about the transactional relationship between slating by party organizations
and candidates providing funds allegedly for legitimate campaigns expenses only,
most West Virginians were not offended by this practice.[132] In an objective case
study of this primary, political scientist Harry W. Ernst concluded that direct
vote buying was rare in West Virginia. Voters were often attracted to candidates
who paid them or their relatives for such minor campaign services as distributing
slate sheets and driving voters to the polls.[133]

Learning from their mistakes in Wisconsin, the Kennedy campaign was
careful to consistently minimize media and polling expectations of JFK's electoral performance. On the night before the primary, JFK stated that he would
be lucky to get 40 percent of the votes. JFK's public pessimism was underscored
by a comment from DNC chairman Paul M. Butler. Butler suggested that if JFK
lost in West Virginia, then he should consider becoming Adlai Stevenson's running mate.[134] Privately, JFK and his closest campaign advisors resolved to continue their presidential campaign if Humphrey won the West Virginia primary.[135]

Instead, JFK won a significant victory in West Virginia. He won 61 percent
of the votes and carried forty-eight of the state's fifty-five counties.[136] Kennedy
even carried counties that had slated Humphrey. JFK's candidacy also attracted
votes from West Virginians who were offended by the pro-Humphrey campaign
activities of local Teamsters officials and Senator Robert Byrd, a former Ku Klux
Klansman. Byrd bluntly urged his fellow West Virginians to vote for Humphrey
as a way to end JFK's candidacy and nominate LBJ for president at the national
convention.[137] Since this was not a binding primary, the twenty-five delegates
that West Virginia would send to the Democratic national convention were not
committed to any presidential candidate. Earle Clements, a former senator from
Kentucky, persisted in lobbying the West Virginia delegates for LBJ. The Texan
had still not announced whether he was a presidential candidate.

JFK's resounding victory in the West Virginia primary nonetheless achieved
the major objectives of his campaign strategy. The favorable publicity and com-

mentary about the power of his voter appeal motivated more boss-controlled delegations, especially that of Illinois dominated by the Chicago machine, to commit themselves to Kennedy on the first ballot. If Adlai Stevenson was not backed by all or most of his home state's delegates, it was less likely that he would receive his third presidential nomination in 1960.[138]

Also, the stronger national name recognition that JFK gained from his West Virginia victory helped him to win the remaining two contested primaries that he had entered, those of Maryland and Oregon. In both primaries, Senator Wayne Morse of Oregon was JFK's leading opponent. Morse, a former Republican, was an outspoken critic of LBJ's leadership of the Senate and JFK's legislative record on labor reform.[139] JFK defeated Morse by margins of more than 50 percent in Maryland and almost 20 percent in Morse's home state.[140] In Oregon, JFK benefited from the fact that Representative Edith Green, an intraparty nemesis of Morse, actively supported his presidential candidacy.[141]

By the end of May, however, Kennedy was engulfed in an unexpected issue that threatened his credibility as a serious presidential candidate. Since the Soviet launching of Sputnik in 1957 and Fidel Castro's takeover of Cuba in 1959, the Democrats had increased the frequency and intensity of their attacks on the Eisenhower administration's foreign and defense policies. After the Soviet Union shot down a U-2 spy plane flown by Francis G. Powers, an air force pilot working for the CIA, on May 1, 1960, the Eisenhower administration initially claimed that the Soviets had shot down a U.S. weather plane. By the end of May, the Eisenhower administration admitted that the U-2 plane was on a regular, justified surveillance mission and refused to issue the apology demanded by Soviet premier Nikita S. Khrushchev.[142] The increased friction and distrust between Eisenhower and Khrushchev led to the collapse of a previously scheduled summit between the United States and the Soviet Union in Paris.

To many Democrats, the U-2 incident was an excellent opportunity to challenge the judgment and leadership ability of Eisenhower and, by insinuation, Nixon and the Republican party in a Cold War crisis. In an uncharacteristically impetuous statement, JFK asserted in Oregon that Eisenhower should have expressed "regret that the flight did take place."[143] Republican criticism of JFK's comment ranged from accusations of naïveté to appeasement.

During the six-week period between the end of the primaries and the opening of the Democratic national convention in Los Angeles, JFK's statement jeopardized his candidacy as his Democratic critics and opponents exploited his gaffe. Kennedy's comment about the U-2 incident solidified their contention that he was too young and inexperienced to be president. In particular, Senator Mike Monroney of Oklahoma and Washington attorney John Sharon accelerated their campaign to organize enough delegates to prevent a first ballot victory for JFK at the convention and eventually draft Adlai Stevenson as the Democratic presidential nominee.[144] Throughout the 1950s, Stevenson had articulated and advocated a more enlightened, farsighted, conciliatory foreign policy toward the Soviet Union. The U-2 incident and Stevenson's high-minded disdain for aggressively competing for the presidential nomination increased his appeal to liberal activists who were disturbed by or ambivalent about JFK's candidacy.[145]

As part of JFK's damage control over the U-2 incident and to quell any competition at the convention from Stevenson, the senator from Massachusetts visited Stevenson at his home in Libertyville, Illinois. Before their meeting, Newton Minow, one of Stevenson's closest advisors, discouraged JFK from offering Stevenson the position of Secretary of State in a Kennedy administration in exchange for Stevenson's endorsement.[146] This offer would only offend and alienate Stevenson. The former Illinois governor remained publicly neutral about the Democratic presidential race and inscrutable about his own intentions as the convention neared and his supporters promoted a draft Stevenson movement.[147]

The most prominent member of the draft Stevenson movement was Eleanor Roosevelt. With his permission, the former first lady issued a press release on June 13 that quoted Stevenson as stating, "I will serve my country and my party whenever called upon."[148] Stevenson then persuaded her to attend the convention in Los Angeles, which she had previously declined to do.

These developments, combined with Eleanor Roosevelt's well-established hostility to JFK's presidential ambition and Stevenson's earlier meeting with LBJ, convinced the Kennedy campaign that Stevenson was either disingenuously angling for the presidential nomination at the convention or was an active participant in a "stop Kennedy" movement that could eventually lead to the presidential nomination of LBJ or Symington.[149] Also, Governors Robert Meyner of New Jersey and Pat Brown of California continued to control their delegates through favorite-son candidacies. Likewise, Hubert Humphrey did not release his delegates, and Stuart Symington maintained his dormant yet revivable dark horse candidacy.[150] At a time in the post-primaries, pre-convention period when the Kennedy campaign had expected to unite liberals behind JFK, the growth of Kennedy's liberal support had stalled. Even JFK's most confident strategists doubted that he had enough delegate strength to win a first ballot victory by the narrowest margin.[151]

The development of a larger, shrewder pro-Stevenson campaign and a more precarious front runner status for JFK stimulated a bolder, more active, yet still unannounced, presidential campaign for LBJ. The Senate majority leader remained uncertain and ambivalent about officially announcing his presidential candidacy But he encouraged his aides and advisors, such as George Reedy, Clifton Carter, and John Connally, to travel and lobby uncommitted delegates, especially those from the South and West.[152]

A definitive explanation about why Johnson waited so long to enter the presidential campaign of 1960 has not yet been established. George Reedy suggests that LBJ's prolonged indecision was psychological, rather than political.

Reedy deduced that LBJ was in a midlife crisis and was uncertain what to do about his future. Should he run for president, run for the Senate again, or leave politics entirely and enrich himself in the private sector?[153] Senate aide Bobby Baker concluded "that Senator Johnson had convinced himself that his and Sam Rayburn's cronies in Congress would deliver their state delegations to him, out of a combination of affection and fear."[154] LBJ experienced prolonged denial that JFK's pre-convention campaign could win the presidential nomination and delusions that he would eventually be nominated as a compromise candidate. Tip O'Neill was amazed and amused that LBJ asked the Massachusetts congressman to vote for him after the first ballot.[155]

Regardless of whether LBJ's relative inertia prior to the 1960 Democratic national convention was a product of a miscalculated political strategy or psychological uncertainty about his future, a more sympathetic analysis indicates that Johnson lacked a more feasible alternative for pursuing the presidential nomination. If LBJ had announced his presidential candidacy at the beginning of 1960 and actively campaigned against Kennedy and Humphrey in major, contested primaries, he would have suffered one or more humiliating defeats that would have threatened his increasingly beleaguered position as Senate majority leader and perhaps even his reelection to the Senate.[156] Frequent absences from the Senate for nationwide travel, primary campaigning, and networking in nonprimary states would have undermined the credibility of LBJ's contention that it was necessary for him to remain in Washington in order to attend to the nation's legislative needs. Despite the more liberal, nonsouthern composition of the Democratic majority in the Senate since the 1958 elections, the Senate remained a more moderate, less ideological milieu than the Democratic presidential nominating process dominated by liberal interest groups and voting blocs. If LBJ moved his rhetoric and policy positions further to the left in order to placate labor unions, civil rights organizations, and liberal activists, he risked alienating the southern bloc in the Senate and his political base in Texas.[157]

In short, LBJ's long delayed, formal announcement of his presidential candidacy on July 5, 1960, was more a product of his frustrated fatalism about his political future than of any profound ignorance or naïveté about the politics of presidential nominations.[158] LBJ had tried to portray himself as a westerner rather than a southerner. But it was evident from the failed lobbying efforts of his campaign staff and surrogates that few delegates from the western states would commit themselves to his candidacy.[159] In a desperate attempt to use his Senate leadership position to win his party's nomination for president, LBJ and Sam Rayburn announced in late June that Congress's legislative session would resume shortly after the Democratic and Republican national conventions ended.[160] Edmund S. Muskie and Henry M. "Scoop" Jackson were the only Democratic senators to publicly endorse JFK before their party's national convention began on July 11.[161] LBJ's apparent effort to pressure his Senate colleagues to support his still unannounced presidential candidacy at the Los Angeles convention through a post-convention session aroused resentment rather than quiescent deference to the majority leader.

Fortunately for LBJ, the attention of the public and the media about the issues of duplicity and abuse of power pertaining to the nomination politics of the Democratic national convention was soon directed at Kennedy, not Johnson. On July 2, 1960, the same day that Congress began its pre-convention recess, former president Harry S. Truman held an unexpected press conference.[162] Truman announced his decision to resign as a delegate from Missouri, but he devoted most of his speech to an explicit criticism of the Kennedy campaign and an implicit criticism of DNC chairman Paul M. Butler for pressuring delegates and manipulating the arrangements for the convention to assure JFK's nomination for president.[163] As a product of machine politics and a veteran of "smoke-filled rooms" and brokered conventions, Truman was concerned that even before the Democratic national convention began it was "taking on the aspects of a prearranged affair."[164] Truman once dismissed presidential primaries as "eye wash." For him, a party's national convention that is held while that party is the "out party" should be a truly deliberative process in which there is a strong possibility that mostly uncommitted delegates could nominate a dark horse candidate for president.[165]

Truman elaborated that JFK's youth and inexperience were serious liabilities for his electability as a presidential candidate and his competence as a possible, future president. Although Truman stated that fellow Missourian Stuart Symington remained his first choice for president, he spoke approvingly about several other men who should be "properly sized up on the convention floor before a final choice."[166] Truman, however, spoke most specifically and favorably about LBJ as a presidential candidate. In particular, the Missourian expressed his confidence in Johnson's proven ability to be a national leader who was not limited or biased by his characteristics as a southerner and a Texan. "No sections of the nation need have any concern or doubt as for where he would stand when the interests of everyone in the country were involved."[167]

Truman's press conference emboldened the Johnson campaign to more aggressively attack JFK's presidential candidacy. At his July 5 press conference, echoing Truman's criticism of JFK's youth and inexperience and accusation that the convention was unethically and undemocratically rigged in favor of JFK's nomination. While formally announcing his presidential candidacy at this event, LBJ underscored a recurring theme: his devotion to his duties as Senate majority leader proved his ability to be president while JFK's frequent absenteeism from the Senate disqualified the Massachusetts Democrat.[168] In contrast to JFK's firm, unequivocal assertion that he would not accept the vice presidential nomination, LBJ inscrutably, and perhaps prophetically, left open the possibility of becoming the Democratic vice-presidential nominee at his press conference. "I have been prepared throughout my adult life to serve my country in any capacity where my country thought my services were essential."[169]

Before the first day of the Los Angeles convention on July 12, however, the anti-JFK rhetoric of Johnson and, even more so, his surrogates was so strident and occasionally scurrilous that RFK developed a lasting distrust of and animosity toward LBJ.[170] The tone and content of the Johnson campaign's charges against JFK's candidacy made it appear unlikely that LBJ was maneuvering for the vice-presidential nomination. It seemed even less likely that the Kennedy campaign would offer it to him. In particular, India Edwards, co-chair of the Citizens for Johnson committee and former director of the DNC's Women's Division, announced to the media on July 4 that JFK had Addison's disease and may be medically unfit for the presidency.[171] Oscar Chapman, the other co-chair, later told Edwards that LBJ was angry about her unexpected announcement. In her defense, Edwards stated in her memoirs that she mentioned JFK's chronic illness only after a reporter had asked about LBJ's fitness for the presidency because of his 1955 heart attack.[172] John Connally, LBJ's campaign director, verified her statement at the press conference.[173]

With these charges having no discernible impact on the widespread perception of JFK as a youthful, energetic campaigner, LBJ refuted Edwards's statement on July 5. While the Johnson campaign's operatives and allies engaged in increasingly shrill smear tactics against JFK's policy record, qualifications for the presidency, family fortune, and controversial father, LBJ tried to maintain a public veneer of dignity and modesty. He sought to portray himself as a westerner, rather than a southerner, who was better qualified for the presidency and who could unite the disparate elements of the national Democratic Party for victory in November and provide competent, seasoned statesmanship in the White House. This already shaky façade of a dignified presidential candidacy was shattered by LBJ's July 14 statement. In it, he implied that Joseph P. Kennedy was an appeaser toward Nazi Germany during the elder Kennedy's ambassadorship. "I wasn't any Chamberlain-umbrella policy man. I never thought Hitler was right."[174]

Nonsouthern delegates and liberal interest groups, already distrusting LBJ on civil rights and labor issues, became even more hostile to the Texan. Johnson contended that he was a westerner or even a national political figure despite the fact that almost all of his committed delegates came from the South. This disparity further confirmed the liberals' suspicion of LBJ as a duplicitous, ruthlessly ambitious southern conservative.[175]

Kennedy hesitated but eventually accepted LBJ's invitation to debate him before a televised audience of delegates from Massachusetts and Texas. LBJ emphasized his proven national leadership in the Senate, especially in the passage of civil rights legislation. He also stated that no American should be discriminated against because of his race, religion, or region. The third classification was a subtle reminder to LBJ's fellow southerners that there was a national bias against southern presidential candidates for the Democratic presidential nomination since the Civil War.[176]

After indirectly and sardonically criticizing JFK for missing key roll-call votes, LBJ warmly expressed his "affection" for Kennedy, admiration for his combat heroism, and pride in supporting the Massachusetts Democratic for vice president in 1956. In JFK's brief "rebuttal," he complimented LBJ's reliability in answering quorum calls and expressed his continued, unmitigated support for LBJ as Senate majority leader.[177] From the perspective of television coverage of the "debate," the most striking difference between LBJ and JFK was in their speaking styles. LBJ's seemed to be, at best, unctuous, and, at worst, overbearing to television audiences. His tone was bombastic and animated with exaggerated facial expressions and arm movements.[178]

JFK, by contrast, was calm, witty, and urbane with a personality that projected an engaging combination of a self-confident presence and self-deprecating humor. He exuded telegenic skills well suited for a television talk show.[179] LBJ's grandstanding speech seemed more appropriate for a Texas county fair.[180] During the first two days of the Democratic national convention, it was apparent to the Kennedy forces that no matter how energetically and ubiquitously LBJ lobbied nonsouthern delegations his strength on the first ballot would be limited to most southern and a few border state delegates. Fortunately for JFK, Senator George Smathers of Florida, a close friend and usher at his wedding, controlled all twenty-nine delegates from his state as a favorite-son candidate, thus depriving LBJ of any Florida delegates. Governor Ross Barnett of Mississippi, a militant segregationist, controlled all twenty-three of his state's delegates as a favorite son.[181]

Political scientist Fred Burke stated that "the Los Angeles operation of the Kennedy organization, seen primarily as a defensive mechanism, was in essence a communications system and can be most usefully studied from this angle."[182] Indeed, the Kennedy organization's use of sophisticated walkie-talkies, phone banks, cautious, underestimated calculations of the number of delegates committed to JFK, and RFK's tenacious lobbying of wavering delegates and implied promises of the vice-presidential nomination to several midwestern and western Democratic politicians highlighted the defensive nature of JFK's convention strategy.[183] RFK and other leading members of the Kennedy organization fumed at the denigrating remarks of Johnson and his surrogates directed at JFK's candidacy.

But JFK abstained from making similarly negative public statements about LBJ's candidacy. The content and tone of the Massachusetts Democrat's public rhetoric were cautiously confident of a first ballot victory and courteous toward Johnson, Stevenson, and the other more obscure presidential candidates.[184] JFK needed to limit LBJ's existing base of support to most southern delegates and a few, scattered western delegates. It was necessary for Kennedy to avoid antagonizing southern conservatives ambivalent about LBJ because of the Texan's leadership on civil rights and nonsouthern Democrats equivocal in their support of JFK. Otherwise, they might coalesce in a "stop Kennedy" bandwagon movement before and during the first ballot.[185]

The growing possibility, though, of a stop Kennedy movement consisting of an ideologically and regionally diverse and incompatible collection of anti-JFK Democrats developing at the convention emerged from liberal activists who favored Adlai Stevenson as a compromise candidate rather than from LBJ's forces.[186] Hubert H. Humphrey told Joseph L. Rauh, Jr., the vice chairman of the ADA who helped Humphrey win the District of Columbia's Democratic presidential primary, in a May 30 letter that JFK's presidential nomination was "all set, stacked and planned." He expressed his "constant admiration of the thoroughness of the Kennedy program. It is incredible, if at times not terrifying."[187]

Humphrey's statement to Rauh was uncannily prophetic. Before the balloting began, the Kennedy organization had predicted that JFK would receive $8^1/_2$ of Wyoming's 15 votes, thereby giving JFK a total of $758^1/_2$ votes, two and a half votes fewer than the 761 needed for the presidential nomination. Instead, Edward M. Kennedy vigorously lobbied the Wyoming delegates and persuaded them to give all of their votes to JFK on the first ballot, thus giving JFK a total of 765 votes.[188]

There probably never will be a definitive, widely accepted explanation of why JFK offered the vice-presidential nomination to LBJ and why Johnson accepted it. The current consensus, however, of the most persuasive scholarly perspectives and primary sources is that Kennedy concluded that he needed LBJ as his running mate in order to win the presidential election. LBJ readily, and even eagerly, accepted the offer of the vice-presidential nomination.[189]

Before the first balloting for the presidential nomination had concluded, RFK deceptively nurtured the vice-presidential hopes of several midwestern and western Protestant Democrats. In particular, the Kennedy forces wanted to attract at least some of Minnesota's delegates on the first ballot by asking Governor Orville Freeman to make the nominating speech for JFK and suggesting to Freeman that he was JFK's top choice for vice president.[190] Instead, all thirty-one of Minnesota's delegates voted for Hubert Humphrey.[191] The Kennedy campaign had encouraged the vice-presidential ambitions of Governors Herschel C. Loveless of Iowa and George Docking of Kansas. But Docking failed to deliver his state to Kennedy until all of the other states and territories had voted and JFK had secured enough votes for the presidential nomination.

A more seriously considered candidate for vice president was Senator Henry M. "Scoop" Jackson of Washington. John Salter, Jackson's top aide, participated in the first major strategy session of the Kennedy campaign in RFK's Hyannis Port home in 1959, regularly promoted the advantages of Jackson as a running mate to the Kennedys, and encouraged Jackson to endorse JFK before the Democratic national convention.[192] But Senator Warren Magnuson and Governor Albert Rosselini, the other leading Democrats of Washington, were staunch advocates of LBJ's presidential candidacy. Jackson managed to deliver only fourteen and a half of his state's twenty-seven delegates on the first ballot.[193] Like the other midwestern and western Democrats who were rumored to be possible running mates, Jackson failed to deliver all of his state's delegates to JFK, a key litmus test of the Kennedys.

Despite the conventional wisdom of the media and a later comment of RFK in his 1964 oral history interview, Stuart Symington was evidently not a top choice for JFK.[194] In a 1959 audiotaped message to his father, JFK expressed his suspicion that the Teamsters were boosting Symington's dark horse presidential candidacy to spite the Kennedys.[195] Joseph Alsop, perhaps the most influential columnist of this era regarding Cold War foreign policy and a confidante of the Kennedys, later revealed that JFK was dismissive toward Symington's intellectual depth and competence to serve as president or vice president.[196] RFK apparently encouraged Symington to consider himself the preferred running mate for JFK so that the Missouri senator would intentionally restrain his effort to deadlock the convention and emerge as a compromise candidate for president.[197]

Although disappointed at Henry M. "Scoop" Jackson's failure to deliver a united Washington delegation to JFK, RFK still admired the fact that Jackson was the first senator to publicly endorse JFK. The younger Kennedy also admired Jackson's stamina for hard work, courage in challenging Senator Joseph McCarthy during the Army-McCarthy hearings in 1954, and the western Democrat's mixture of domestic policy liberalism, especially on civil rights and labor issues, and Cold War hawkishness on foreign and defense policies. But Theodore C. Sorensen and other campaign advisors rejected further consideration of Jackson for being too similar to JFK and adding no significant, additional vote-getting strength and balance to the ticket.[198] RFK's guilt at misleading Jackson about the vice-presidential nomination later motivated him to secure Jackson's selection as DNC chairman for the remainder of the 1960 campaign.[199]

Kennedy's selection of Johnson as his running mate, therefore, was partially a consequence of the abrupt transition in strategic and electoral calculations from JFK's pre-convention campaign for the nomination to his post-convention campaign for the general election. In order to be nominated for president on the first ballot, JFK had to maximize his support from nonsouthern delegations. He needed to alleviate the fears and suspicions of liberal activists, especially pro-Stevenson ADA members, civil rights advocates, and labor leaders that he was insincerely and insufficiently liberal toward their policy interests in order to appease southern Democrats. Besides the addition of previously pro-Stevenson, prominent liberal intellectuals like Arthur M. Schlesinger, Jr., and John Kenneth Galbraith to his campaign, JFK also promoted the DNC's choice of Chester Bowles, a Connecticut congressman and an ADA leader, as chairman of the convention's platform committee.[200]

These symbolic appointments combined with JFK's more unequivocally liberal policy positions and rhetoric on the more divisive domestic policy issues since his 1958 Senate campaign helped to limit the influence of the pro-Stevenson demonstration and the divided California delegates on wavering liberal delegates. JFK allowed the ADA and DAC to heavily influence the content of the 1960 Democratic national platform. He eventually gained the endorsement of the ADA's national leadership, despite lingering apathy and ambivalence toward JFK among some local ADA members.[201] Shortly before and during the first ballot, RFK assured liberals, labor leaders, and civil rights activists that JFK, if nominated, would not choose LBJ as his running mate.

While the Kennedys managed to appease and court most nonsouthern delegates through the above promises, concessions, and tactics, they inevitably alienated most southern Democrats at the convention. As JFK's rhetoric and policy positions moved further to the left, especially on civil rights, he lost much of the good will that he had attracted from southern Democrats during and shortly after the 1956 Democratic national convention. By the time that the convention in Los Angeles began, many southern delegates perceived JFK as a northern liberal indistinguishable from Humphrey and Stevenson in his apparent willingness to impose unreasonable civil rights demands on the South.[202]

In addition to his now more rigorous civil rights liberalism, JFK's Catholicism was perceived by southern Democratic politicians in particular as a serious liability to their state Democratic tickets if he were nominated for president. For example, Terry Sanford, the Democratic nominee for governor of North Carolina in 1960, was the only major Democrat from his state to endorse JFK before the convention in Los Angeles was held. He was aware, though, that JFK was controversial among many of his state's voters and that Republican electoral strength had steadily grown in his state during the 1950s. Sanford avoided closely identifying himself with JFK during his gubernatorial campaign.[203]

Despite the misgivings that the more conservative, stridently anti-civil rights southerners had about LBJ and the Texan's long-delayed, erratic, fumbling presidential candidacy, Johnson received the overwhelming majority of the South's delegate votes for president on the first ballot. LBJ received 409 votes on the first ballot, more than half of JFK's 806 votes.[204] By contrast, most of Symington's and Stevenson's modest delegate support was scattered throughout the nonsouthern states. Although LBJ's delegate support came almost entirely from the South, his nomination for president was seconded by Senator Thomas J. Dodd of Connecticut, a New England Irish Catholic and nemesis of John M. Bailey, and Senator Daniel Inouye of Hawaii, a distinguished, disabled World War II veteran of Japanese ancestry.[205]

Polls used by the media and the private polls conducted by the Kennedy campaign indicated that JFK persistently lagged behind Nixon among voters in farm belt areas of the Midwest and West.[206] With a midwestern or western running mate well versed on agricultural issues, it was still unlikely that JFK could carry most of these states in November. The Democratic leaders in California were divided and squabbling among themselves, and Los Angeles had proven to be a major source of pro-Stevenson, anti-JFK liberal activism. It was increasingly doubtful that JFK could carry Nixon's home state with its thirty-two electoral votes.[207]

No sooner had JFK secured the Democratic presidential nomination, than it became evident that he needed to carry several southern states to win the general election. In particular, the Catholic Democrat from Massachusetts needed the twenty-four electoral votes of Texas. JFK also needed a southern running mate who could discourage the proliferation of state-level, favorite-son presidential candidacies and the slating of independent electors in the South that could deprive him of electoral votes needed to win. JFK's running mate had to have enough status and influence as a fellow southerner and a nationally renowned Democrat so that he could persuade more moderate yet reluctant southern Democrats to actively campaign for the Democratic presidential ticket in their home states.[208] But a southern vice-presidential nominee's recent domestic policy record and rhetoric, especially on civil rights, labor reform, and social welfare, could not be egregiously incompatible with JFK's record and the 1960 Democratic national platform.[209]

In short, JFK needed LBJ as his running mate. The Massachusetts Democrat was also being pressured by his father, columnist Joseph Alsop, and newspaper publisher Philip Graham to choose the Texan.[210] Senator George Smathers of Florida also strongly recommended Johnson as the Democratic vice-presidential nominee. Smathers received all twenty-nine of Florida's delegate votes on the first ballot as his state's favorite son. This prevented any of them from voting for LBJ. But now Smathers was determined for JFK to win the election and regarded LBJ as essential for victory.[211] Following the convention, Kennedy appointed Smathers as the regional coordinator of his campaign in the South.[212]

From the participants in JFK's decision to choose LBJ as his running mate and various scholars and observers of that decision, much has been written about how JFK allegedly offered the vice-presidential nomination to LBJ as a courtesy and under the assumption that the Texan would reject it. This perspective was advanced by RFK in his 1964 oral history interview and by aides and scholars closest to RFK, such as Kenneth P. O'Donnell and Arthur M. Schlesinger, Jr., especially after JFK's presidency.[213] According to RFK's version of the events, after JFK's announcement that Johnson was his choice, civil rights and labor leaders and liberal delegations, especially those from Michigan and the District of Columbia, were outraged and felt betrayed. JFK then had second thoughts and sent RFK to Johnson in order to ask the Texan to withdraw from the ticket and become DNC chairman.[214]

Jeff Shesol made a more recent, exhaustive study of a wide range of primary sources pertaining to RFK's version of JFK's selection of LBJ. Shesol concluded that RFK, "who despised LBJ even in 1960, remembered events as he saw them."[215] In her book about her father's close relationship with RFK, Helen O'Donnell claims that her father and RFK had originally gone to LBJ's hotel suite in order to tell the Texas senator that his vice-presidential candidacy was fiercely opposed by Walter Reuther of the UAW and George Meany of the AFL-CIO. Combined with RFK's offer of the DNC chairmanship as a consolation prize, LBJ interpreted RFK's visit to mean that JFK's offer was being withdrawn. But JFK then personally told LBJ, "Bobby was out of the loop," and assured LBJ that he wanted the Texan as his running mate.[216]

The analyses of Jeff Shesol and Helen O'Donnell are also substantiated by the eyewitness observations of James H. Rowe, Jr. and Philip Graham and the conclusion of journalist Theodore H. White.[217] JFK may have briefly experienced ambivalence about his offer to LBJ. But he was shrewd and calculating enough to realize that it would be detrimental, and perhaps fatal, to his presidential candidacy if he abruptly withdrew his offer for several reasons. First, such a decision would offend not only LBJ but most southerners at the convention and make it unlikely that he would carry any southern state, let alone Texas. Second, Johnson and Rayburn would dominate the August rump session of Congress and could use it to embarrass Kennedy and weaken his presidential campaign.[218] Third, JFK was still struggling to convince a skeptical public that, despite his youth and relatively brief service in the Senate, he had the maturity and judgment to make sound decisions and be an effective leader of the nation.[219] If he abruptly and impulsively reversed his decision about LBJ, his actions would have substantiated this criticism.

Also, JFK had previously and repeatedly stated that, after himself, he regarded LBJ as the most qualified man to be elected president in 1960 and that he would endorse Johnson for their party's presidential nomination if he was not running for it. Later, JFK repeatedly told reporters that his running mate would be the most qualified Democrat who, if necessary, could competently serve as president.[220] LBJ's harshest critics and opponents among Democrats, Republicans, and journalists could not convincingly contend that LBJ lacked the necessary experience and demonstrated leadership skills, no matter how much they distrusted him or disagreed with his policy record.[221]

Several accounts of LBJ's reaction to JFK's offer emphasize the Texan's morose fatalism in reluctantly accepting an unexpected bid to become the vice-presidential nominee.[222] The basis of their perception was LBJ's grim recognition that, regardless of who was elected president, his power and status as Senate majority leader would further decline. Furthermore, if LBJ rejected the vice-presidential candidacy and JFK lost the election, especially in Texas and the rest of the South, he would be blamed for JFK's defeat and forfeit any chance of being nominated for president in 1964 or 1968.[223] According to this theory, LBJ was pressured by his inner circle of advisors and allies at the convention, namely, John Connally, Sam Rayburn, and Bobby Baker, to accept the vice-presidential candidacy as a responsibility to the Democratic Party, the nation, and his own political future. LBJ finally relented.[224]

A more persuasive explanation of Johnson's acceptance of Kennedy's offer, consistent with Joseph Schlesinger's theory of progressive ambition, is the following. LBJ immediately and positively recognized the Democratic vice-presidential nomination as an asset in his long-term quest to emancipate himself from Texas politics, finally establish himself as an entirely national political figure, and maximize his chances of being nominated for president in 1968, assuming a two-term Kennedy presidency.[225] Political scientist and biographer Doris Kearns indicated in her assessment of LBJ's willingness to run with JFK that throughout LBJ's career he had advanced his career by serving an apprenticeship with a more powerful person. Regardless of whether LBJ's patron was Cecil Evans, the president of Southwest Texas State Teachers' College, Representative Richard Kleberg, Sam Rayburn, FDR, or Richard Russell, LBJ shrewdly nurtured and manipulated each mentor-protégé relationship in order to gain greater power and influence.[226] Kearns stated, "In the past, Johnson's willingness to accept a subordinate position had come from the conviction that initial deference was but a means to eventual replacement of the figure in the authority."[227]

LBJ had also demonstrated the ability to recognize the potential for power and status in an apparently modest position and then transform it into an office with powers and responsibilities that no one else had imagined.[228] He had done this with the Senate minority and majority leadership posts and was already considering how he could make his vice presidency the most powerful in history, tantamount to a co-presidency.[229] Musing about how he could run the Senate as vice president and exert an unusual degree of influence on the younger, less seasoned president as JFK's senior counsel, LBJ remarked to a convention ally, "Power is where power goes."[230]

After LBJ assured JFK that he was willing to risk a floor fight for the vice-presidential nomination, the JFK–LBJ alliance for the 1960 presidential campaign was established.[231] Immediately after the speeches nominating LBJ for the vice presidency, John W. McCormack, chairman of the Massachusetts delegation and a mutual ally of JFK and LBJ, asked convention chairman LeRoy Collins to suspend the rules and allow a voice vote on the vice-presidential nomination. After listening to the oral response of the convention, Collins ruled that LBJ had been "nominated by acclamation as the Democratic nominee for Vice President of the United States."[232] On the following day at the convention, Johnson met with groups of disgruntled, anti-LBJ delegates and pledged his loyalty to the Democratic national platform of 1960, the most liberal in the party's history, especially on civil rights and labor issues.[233]

In the introductory remarks that he made before his acceptance speech at the Los Angeles Coliseum, JFK praised LBJ as "a distinguished running-mate who brings unity to our ticket and strength to our Platform."[234] With the Democratic national platform promising more federal programs, regulations, and spending in a large number and variety of domestic policy areas, JFK wanted to convince anti-LBJ liberals and labor leaders of the greater electability of his presidential candidacy with LBJ balancing the ticket. He also wanted to assure southerners that LBJ's vice-presidential candidacy represented their inclusion in his presidential campaign and policy agenda.[235]

The Democratic presidential nominee then balanced and broadened his rhetorical appeal by emphasizing suprapartisan individual and collective self-sacrifice for the national good in foreign policy with a tone of Adlai Stevenson's idealism. The vision of America's future that JFK identified as the New Frontier was actually an amalgam of ideas primarily influenced by Payson Wild, a Harvard political scientist who had been one of Kennedy's teachers, FDR's Commonwealth Club address of 1932, and the concept of political courage articulated in JFK's *Profiles in Courage*.[236] Kennedy concluded that in deciding whether to choose the New Frontier in the November election Americans must choose "between the public interest and private comfort—between national greatness and national decline—between the fresh air of progress and the stale, dank atmosphere of 'normalcy'—between determined dedication and creeping mediocrity."[237]

Critics of JFK's acceptance speech focused on his delivery of it. To them, he seemed fatigued and spoke too quickly with a grating, erratic staccato voice.[238] The ideals of sacrifice, courage, civic duty, and national greatness in the New Frontier speech seemed to cynically contradict and camouflage the promises of greater federal largesse made to Democratic interest groups and voting blocs in the platform.[239] This criticism, though, underestimated the significance of the New Frontier speech's uplifting style and content as a shrewd appeal to undecided voters watching his televised speech, especially middle-class suburbanites who voted for Eisenhower.[240] Many of these voters might be oblivious of or even hostile to the intraparty machinations at the convention that produced the Democratic national platform and the Kennedy–Johnson ticket. They were more likely to be attracted to an apparently nonideological, suprapartisan campaign theme of energizing and inspiring split-ticket middle-class voters behind an activist, heroic, Lincolnian view of the presidency, in contrast to the backward, listless stagnation of the Eisenhower presidency.[241]

While many Democratic delegates and journalists were surprised at JFK's choice of LBJ as his running mate, Richard M. Nixon, the presumptive Republican nominee for president, had expected to run against the two men.[242] Nixon had anticipated, however, that LBJ would be the Democratic presidential nominee and JFK his running mate.[243] Nixon and Republican national chairman Thruston Morton planned to exploit the policy differences in the congressional records of JFK and LBJ and the negative comments of the supporters of JFK and LBJ about the two Democrats that were made shortly before Kennedy was nominated for president and Johnson became his running mate for the general election campaign.

Before Nixon could entirely concentrate on developing an aggressive, effective campaign strategy against the Democrats, he needed to unite the Republican

Party behind his candidacy and a broadly accepted platform. The vice president's major obstacle in achieving both intraparty objectives was Republican Governor Nelson A. Rockefeller of New York. Rockefeller encouraged several of his aides and allies within the Republican Party to conduct a quiet, tentative exploratory campaign for the party's presidential nomination. Studies of the missile gap in particular and American foreign and defense policies in general from the Rockefeller Brothers Fund's Special Studies Project influenced Rockefeller's decision. He considered running in the New Hampshire and Indiana primaries.

But, regardless of whether or not Rockefeller could run there or in other primaries, most of the delegates at the Republican national convention would be moderate and conservative party regulars loyal to Nixon. The New York governor's tax increase during his first year in office confirmed their earlier suspicion that Rockefeller was a fiscally irresponsible big spender. Rockefeller's foreign policy positions under FDR and Truman and his appointment of several Democrats to his administration made the party regulars who dominated Republican national conventions further doubt the New Yorker's loyalty to the Republican Party.[244]

Rockefeller announced on December 26, 1959, "I am not, and shall not be, a candidate for nomination for the Presidency."[245] He added, "I should not at any time entertain any thought of accepting nomination to the Vice Presidency, even if the honor were offered, for this would clearly run counter to all the considerations inspiring my present decision."[246]

Rockefeller's Republican critics mistakenly assumed that the New York governor's progressive ambition to eventually be elected president superseded any concern for their party's ideological character and policy direction. But Rockefeller's rhetoric and behavior in the spring and summer of 1960 revealed that influencing the content of the Republican national platform was his top priority. In early May, Rockefeller reaffirmed his earlier statement that he would not accept the vice-presidential nomination and rejected the RNC's offer of his becoming its 1960 national convention's keynote speaker.[247] He further stated that he might not attend the Republican national convention in Chicago.

After the emergence of the U-2 spy plane issue and the cancellation of the summit between Eisenhower and Khrushchev, Rockefeller acknowledged that he would be available to be drafted for his party's presidential nomination, primarily for the purpose of influencing his party's ideology and policy agenda on foreign and defense policy planks. The emphasis of his May 30 press release, however, was his criticism of the Eisenhower administration's record in foreign and defense policies and Nixon's failure to specify his policy proposals. Rockefeller concluded with a nine-point program that he wanted to be adopted in the Republican national platform of 1960. These proposals ranged from a sharp increase in defense spending and an ambitious civil defense program against nuclear attacks to a more liberal civil rights plank and substantial federal aid to education. The essence of Rockefeller's message was that in domestic and foreign policies the Republican Party and its presidential nominee must provide bold leadership with new ideas in the struggle against the Soviet Union.[248]

During the remaining six weeks before the Republican national convention opened in Chicago, Rockefeller continued to promote his nine-point program throughout the nation. The governor's speaking tour stimulated a "draft Rockefeller" movement in several states in the Northeast and on the West Coast, mostly notably in San Francisco where William N. Brinton was the de facto national leader of Citizens for Rockefeller.[249] For an increasing number of pro-Rockefeller activists, the primary appeal of the New York governor was the fact that he appeared to be more electable than Nixon in November. In a letter to Rockefeller, Alvin Diamond, a Philadelphia Republican, stated his confidence that the Republican delegates "will arrive at the inevitable conclusion that the Vice President cannot win. At this writing it is hard to determine what states, if any, Mr. Nixon could carry, whomever (sic) the Democratic nominee may be."[250]

Gallup polls conducted in the late spring and early summer of 1960, however, refuted the contention of Rockefeller's supporters that the New Yorker would be a more attractive, electable presidential nominee than Nixon, especially among independents and disaffected Democrats. A poll published on May 25 indicated that JFK would defeat Rockefeller by 14 percent, 79 percent of the Democrats polled would vote for JFK, and, most significantly, 62 percent of the independents in the sample would vote for JFK.[251] A poll released on June 24 indicated that only 8 percent of the Republican county chairmen preferred Rockefeller over Nixon and that 95 percent assumed that Nixon would receive their party's presidential nomination.[252] Other Gallup polls published in May and June indicated that the public preferred Nixon over JFK on foreign and defense policy issues by decisive margins.[253]

In his statements to the media, Dwight Eisenhower politely and calmly expressed confidence in American military strength relative to the Soviet Union and graciously stated that the "mere expression" of Rockefeller's dissenting position would not "wreck any party."[254] Privately, though, the president fumed about how a fellow Republican was echoing and inflaming Democratic charges of an alleged missile gap and questioning Eisenhower's legacy on foreign and defense policy.[255] Like Nixon, Eisenhower was determined to ensure at least a superficially united Republican Party behind Nixon's nomination and a national platform. The president understood and agreed with Nixon's need to compromise with Rockefeller on the platform, especially on defense spending, and to again offer the governor the vice-presidential nomination. As much as Eisenhower disliked the grandstanding New York patrician, he was determined to defeat the Democrats in November. He perceived a Nixon–Rockefeller ticket with a compromised, moderate platform as the most likely GOP combination to be victorious.[256]

Nixon was in the precarious position of having to appease Rockefeller without alienating the party regulars and conservative ideologues who dominated the

Republican national convention. But even before he met Rockefeller at the governor's apartment in New York City on July 22, 1960, the vice president still needed to periodically assure Republican activists of his conservative convictions. In a May 10 letter to an Arizona Republican, Nixon defensively stated "that throughout my public life I have consistently and outspokenly classified myself as an economic conservative."[257]

Before discussing changes in their party's platform, Nixon again offered Rockefeller the vice-presidential nomination. In his memoirs, Nixon expressed his ambivalent reaction to Rockefeller's expected rejection of the offer. "I was not altogether sorry, because Rockefeller's independent temperament would have made him a much more difficult running mate for me to deal with than Johnson would be for Kennedy. But this left me without the option of the kind of finely balanced ticket the Democrats had achieved."[258] In order to placate Rockefeller and prevent an embarrassing challenge to his presumptive presidential nomination, Nixon made several concessions in the Republican national platform. To maintain the distinction of the Republican Party as more fiscally responsible than the Democratic Party on domestic spending, Nixon rejected Rockefeller's proposal for compulsory national health insurance.

The vice president also did not want the Republican defense spending plank to specify Rockefeller's proposed increase of $3.5 billion or any other dollar amount.[259] But he did agree to the plank's wording of "no price ceiling on America's security."[260] On domestic policy, the vice president agreed with the governor's suggestions of more liberal policy positions and specific wording for the policy planks on civil rights and federal aid to education. In particular, the Nixon–Rockefeller agreement expressed "support for the objectives of the sit-in demonstrators" in the civil rights protests of the South and a proposed "equalization formula" in providing federal funds for school construction.[261]

Dubbed by the media as the "compact" or "treaty" of Fifth Avenue, the Nixon–Rockefeller compromise was bitterly denounced by conservative Republican Senator Barry Goldwater of Arizona as the "Munich" of the Republican Party.[262] Even before the Republican national convention opened in Chicago on July 25, Nixon wanted to concentrate his rhetoric and strategy in attracting undecided independent and disaffected Democratic voters to his candidacy. The vice president had to compensate for the significant Democratic advantage in voter identification and registration. Nixon readily appeased Rockefeller on the platform and offered him the vice-presidential nomination in order to prevent Rockefeller from challenging his candidacy. Nixon also wanted Rockefeller on his ticket to develop a more liberal image for attracting northeastern suburban voters who might otherwise support Kennedy.

Nixon was stunned by the hostile, cacophonous reaction of Republican delegates, especially members of the platform committee, to the "Compact of Fifth Avenue."[263] In particular, southern delegates, like John Tower of Texas and

Thomas E. Stagg, Jr., of Louisiana, feared that the more liberal Rockefeller–Nixon plank on civil rights would hamper the "southern strategy" of persuading more southern whites to vote Republican.[264] Other disgruntled delegates were conservative ideologues who resented the centrist "modern Republicanism" advocated and personified by Eisenhower and Nixon. They believed that the Republican national platform should consist of conservative principles, not campaign tactics or concessions to liberal mavericks like Rockefeller.

In general, though, indignant delegates were angrier with the way in which the Nixon–Rockefeller compact was made than in its content. Even moderate, pro-Nixon delegates were chagrined that key platform planks were privately compromised and rewritten by two rival candidates before the convention, despite the extensive, deliberative, democratic processes of the platform committee. Equally solicitous of his party's right wing, Nixon readily agreed to submit the compact to the platform committee. Fortunately for Nixon, Charles H. Percy chaired the platform committee. Percy was a young, amiable Illinois Republican and corporate executive whom Eisenhower had appointed to chair the Committee on Program and Progress. This was a party organization created in 1959 to specify and promote the centrist ideas and policy agenda of "modern Republicanism." Heavily influenced by Eisenhower and his staff, this committee's statements were sent to every delegate before the convention began.[265]

Shrewd and diplomatic, Percy helped Nixon to discourage the appearance of a bitterly divided convention to the public and the media. Eisenhower's staff intervened in order to delete any wording in the defense plank that was implicitly critical of Eisenhower's most recent defense policies. Nixon, though, was least willing to compromise on the wording of the more liberal civil rights planks that he and Rockefeller developed. In a private meeting with members of the civil rights subcommittee, Nixon firmly told these Republicans, especially the southern conservatives, that his position on civil rights was a personal, moral commitment that he refused to weaken.[266]

On civil rights, defense, education, and other contentious issues, the platform that was eventually adopted by the Republican national convention consisted of planks that were slightly more moderate, vaguely worded versions of the Nixon–Rockefeller compact. Political scientist Karl A. Lamb concluded, "The final document represented a viewpoint more acceptable to Republicans in the urban states of New England and the mid-Atlantic than to Republicans in rural areas of the Midwest and South."[267]

Nonetheless, Nixon, unlike JFK, was almost unanimously nominated for president on the first ballot with 1,321 of the 1,331 delegates voting for the vice president.[268] In an acceptance speech initially regarded as more eloquent and smoothly delivered than JFK's, Nixon emphasized the future of American foreign policy in the Cold War.[269] In order to sustain the public image, however fragile and superficial, of an internally harmonious, united Republican Party,

Nixon revealed that his top three choices for a running mate were, respectively, a conservative, Representative Walter Judd of Minnesota, a moderate, Senator and RNC chairman Thruston Morton of Kentucky, and a liberal, Henry Cabot Lodge, Jr., the U.S. ambassador to the United Nations.[270]

As he did with Rockefeller concerning the platform, Nixon made another effort to woo the East Coast, liberal wing of his party by choosing Lodge as his running mate. Besides hoping that Lodge's candidacy would force JFK to campaign more in the Northeast than he had expected, Nixon admired Lodge's public speaking and debating skills in his televised denunciations of Soviet foreign policy.[271] The vice president also hoped that the Nixon–Lodge ticket would strongly underscore his campaign's emphasis on experience and continuity in American foreign policy.[272] A Gallup poll conducted immediately after the Republican national convention indicated that Nixon was ahead of Kennedy, 51 to 49 percent.[273]

Nixon soon regretted his choice of Lodge and envied JFK for selecting a vice-presidential nominee with immense physical energy, political savvy, and a regional electoral base.[274] Lodge proved to be a lackluster, independent-minded campaigner. He committed perhaps the most damaging rhetorical gaffe of the Republican presidential campaign. Without consulting Nixon beforehand, Lodge announced on October 12 in Harlem that as president Nixon would appoint the first black cabinet secretary. He also promised more aggressive federal policies to end segregation, guarantee voting rights, and appoint more blacks to higher positions in the State Department.[275]

Nixon attempted damage control. Herb Klein, his press secretary, issued a press release blandly and awkwardly stating that a Nixon administration would not discriminate in its appointments. Nixon began to steadily lose southern white support in the polls. Meanwhile, blacks and white liberals perceived the Republicans' conflicting statements on civil rights to be insincere pandering.[276]

Although the Democratic and Republican national platforms of 1960 were similar in content and specificity in their civil rights planks, the Kennedy–Johnson campaign more shrewdly and consistently coordinated the rhetoric of JFK and LBJ in order to maximize the civil rights issue as an asset in the North and minimize it as a liability in the South. In an October 1 speech in Minneapolis, JFK closely identified himself and his party with the more outspoken civil rights liberalism of Hubert Humphrey. He also expressed hope that the next president "stands for equal rights, that he stands for a fair chance for all Americans to have a decent education, to get a job and to hold it."[277] Earlier, in a September 21 speech in Memphis, JFK concluded a speech that was mostly devoted to foreign policy and economic growth by stating, "I want to see an America which is free for everyone, which develops the constitutional rights of all Americans, which will serve as our symbol, our own identification with the cause of freedom."[278]

By using the words "constitutional rights" instead of "civil rights" in the South, JFK was following LBJ's example. Johnson realized that most southern whites outside of Mississippi and Alabama had gradually accepted voting rights for blacks in their states by 1960. Any reference to "civil rights" in the South could be limited to the modest voting rights provisions of the 1957 and 1960 civil rights acts. By consistently using the term "constitutional rights" during his vice-presidential campaign in southern and border states, LBJ allowed his mostly receptive audiences to interpret the meaning of "constitutional rights" for themselves. LBJ knew, of course, that most southern whites did not perceive constitutional rights to include the federally enforced racial integration of schools, housing, jobs, and public accommodations that the ADA, NAACP, and other liberal activists sought. LBJ also used the term "region" equally with the terms "race" and "religion." Although Johnson used the same wording in his civil rights statements wherever he campaigned, his implicit message to southern white audiences was that a Kennedy–Johnson administration, unlike a Nixon presidency, would be equally sensitive to southern white and southern black interests on civil rights issues.[279]

JFK and LBJ, however, were careful to publicly express loyalty to their party's liberal platform on civil rights and to ensure that their separate statements on civil rights did not contradict each other.[280] At his party's national convention, Nixon had assured his fellow Republicans that he would frequently remind the voters of stark differences and conflicts between JFK's and LBJ's voting records in the Senate. With the ADA and NAACP still wary about JFK's selection of LBJ, the Kennedy–Johnson campaign could not risk alienating liberals.[281]

Careful coordination and frequent communication between the two Democrats' campaigns were even more important because of the lead that Nixon gained in the public opinion polls and in campaign travel in August during the special session of Congress. Both the Nixon campaign and the media were impressed at the large, enthusiastic crowds that greeted his campaign in the South, especially in Atlanta and Birmingham.[282] During most of August, JFK and LBJ were confined to the Senate because of its special session. No major bills reflecting the Democratic national platform were passed. Roll call votes further embarrassed JFK and LBJ by highlighting the intraparty differences between northern liberals and southern conservatives.[283]

A Gallup poll released on August 17 revealed that Nixon was ahead of Kennedy 50 percent to 44 percent. In analyzing this poll, polling expert George Belknap suggested to JFK and RFK that the Democratic presidential campaign emphasize its party affiliation, as Harry Truman did in 1948.[284] Since JFK, unlike Nixon, was suffering from "image diffusion," Belknap concluded that the JFK–LBJ ticket needed to generate "a high turnout of people who prefer the Democratic to the Republican Party."[285]

Shortly before the special session of Congress began, JFK, LBJ, and their campaign staffs met in JFK's house in Hyannis Port, Massachusetts, to discuss campaign strategy. Although JFK eventually campaigned in almost all the states, he concentrated his efforts on the major metropolitan areas of the Northeast, Midwest, and West Coast while LBJ focused on southern and border states. LBJ, though, was eager to project himself as a national, rather than a merely regional, political figure by campaigning extensively outside of the South.[286] JFK agreed that LBJ could have more nonsouthern appearances than originally planned, but the main thrust of the Johnson campaign would still be in the South. George Reedy, a Johnson aide, later stated that LBJ's campaign speeches and meetings in the North, especially in New York City, helped JFK attract the votes and fundraising efforts of Jewish Democrats like Edwin Weisl who were close to LBJ and distrusted the Kennedys.[287] In a report on the politics of the JFK–LBJ campaign in his state, Minnesota governor Orville Freeman told RFK that Minnesota farmers were more attracted to the Democratic ticket because of LBJ.[288]

The organization of the JFK–LBJ campaign continued the nucleus of JFK's pre-convention structure. It added such new units as Citizens for Kennedy–Johnson, headed by Colorado attorney Byron White; a voter registration project administered by Representative Frank Thompson of New Jersey; and a southern regional organization coordinated by Senator George Smathers of Florida. Lawrence F. O'Brien was the director of organization, and Kenneth P. O'Donnell was in charge of JFK's scheduling.[289]

RFK, of course, continued to manage the overall presidential campaign. Senator Henry M. "Scoop" Jackson was the DNC chairman, but he primarily fulfilled a symbolic role as the first Protestant DNC chairman since the 1920s.[290] O'Brien, rather than Jackson, stayed at DNC headquarters to ensure that the various appendages of the Democratic presidential campaign, both within and outside the DNC's apparatus, implemented RFK's overall strategy and supplemented the traveling, separate campaigns of JFK and LBJ.[291] Unlike Adlai Stevenson's 1952 and 1956 presidential campaigns with their "dual headquarters," JFK was careful to centralize his personal campaign staff within the DNC headquarters in Washington, DC.[292]

Although O'Brien tried to maintain harmonious relationships between the presidential campaign organization and Democratic state and local committees, RFK's single-minded determination to elect his brother president occasionally disrupted the intraparty fence mending efforts of O'Brien. For example, Katie Louchheim, the long-time director of the DNC's women's activities and DNC vice chairman, was abruptly removed as vice chairman by RFK. He replaced her with Margaret Price, Democratic national committeewoman from Michigan.[293] In a more well-known incident, RFK offended both Tammany Hall regulars and anti-Tammany reform Democrats from New York by telling them, "I don't give a damn if the state and county organizations survive after November, and I don't care if you survive. I want to elect John F. Kennedy."[294]

RFK's abrasive retort to New York Democrats and similar statements and actions during the general election campaign clearly contradicted a memo to the campaign staff that he circulated in late July. RFK reminded campaign workers that "our main aim and effort should be to supplement the work of the regular Democratic organization. Any other direction for our efforts would be disastrous."[295] RFK further elaborated that such coordination was especially necessary for registering the large number of unregistered voting-age adults, especially young adults.[296] RFK estimated that approximately 70 percent of eligible, nonvoting adults would vote Democratic in the 1960 election if they were registered.[297]

JFK was determined to avoid the issue of his Catholicism in order to focus on issues that could unite and energize the Democratic base, which outnumbered the Republican base of registered voters by three to two. RFK agreed with speechwriter Theodore C. Sorensen to have the presidential campaign headquarters at the DNC establish an Office of Community Relations. At Sorensen's suggestion, RFK also appointed James Wine, an official from the staff of the National Council of Churches, to answer mail, circulate publicity, and coordinate similar pro-JFK state and local organizations regarding questions, discussions, and challenges about JFK's record on church-state issues.[298] In assessing this office's success in the campaign, Sorensen stated, "No office in the Kennedy-Democratic National Committee headquarters worked harder or made a more important contribution to the campaign."[299]

This DNC effort enabled JFK to concentrate his rhetoric on issue positions tailored to appeal to traditionally Democratic voting blocs, ethnic groups, and interest groups in the major metropolitan areas of such key states in his strategy as Michigan, Ohio, Pennsylvania, and California. JFK's speeches either specified or broadly included a range of policy issues such as unemployment, job training, defense spending, medical care for the elderly, economic redevelopment of depressed areas, a higher minimum wage, American foreign policy in the Cold War, and education.

Regardless of the issue, focus, location, or audience of a speech, JFK's overall theme was clear and consistent with his acceptance speech introducing the New Frontier. In order for the United States to prevail in the Cold War during the 1960s, it needed to end divided government, improve the quality and justice of American society through new domestic policies, and meet the unknown challenges of the future through space exploration and new, better ways of understanding and assisting the Third World, such as the Peace Corps. A unified government with a Democratic president and Congress would be more likely to make and implement those policies because of this party's legacy of progress and innovation under the New Freedom, New Deal, and Fair Deal and the respective, vigorous leadership of Woodrow Wilson, Franklin D. Roosevelt, and Harry Truman.[300]

In a September 5 speech in Flint, Michigan, JFK encapsulated economic issues into this theme of a future-oriented Democratic Party. He stated to this labor union audience, "Economic growth, automation, full employment—those are the issues of the 1960's, a decent life for all Americans. And what Franklin Roosevelt attempted to do in the 1930's, in a different scale, facing different problems, we are going to do in the 1960's."[301] JFK again reinforced this theme in his September 14 speech in St. Louis. "My campaign for the Presidency is founded on a single assumption, the assumption that the American people are tired of the drift in out national course, that they are weary of the continual decline in our national prestige, a decline which has led to economic injustice at home and peril abroad, and that they are ready to move again."[302]

During the first six weeks of the JFK–LBJ campaign, LBJ generally followed the advice of James H. Rowe, Jr. to faithfully adhere to and effectively implement the scheduling and strategy of RFK and the rest of JFK's campaign staff. Rowe recommended John Connally as LBJ's campaign manager because Connally "can, when he wishes, be fully as 'hard-nosed' as Bobby Kennedy."[303] LBJ wanted more joint appearances with JFK to illustrate the "Boston–Austin Axis" and more nonsouthern trips to prove his national voter appeal.

But he complied with JFK's decision of using the Texan to complement, rather than duplicate, Kennedy's rhetoric. For example, LBJ, unlike JFK, repeatedly and directly confronted the religious issue throughout the nation. LBJ was a southern Protestant whose ancestors had founded Baylor University and been prominent Baptist ministers. He stated in Hartford, Connecticut, on September 9 that if "people do apply a religious test as a qualification for office, then we tear up the Bill of Rights and throw our Constitution into the waste basket."[304] While addressing the religious issue in the South and especially in Texas, LBJ appealed to this region's strong tradition of military heroism. He often asserted that JFK's distinguished combat record in World War II proved why it is necessary and just not to have religious requirements for either military service or the presidency.[305]

A Gallup poll conducted at the end of August and released on September 14 indicated that the JFK–LBJ campaign's strategy, theme, and rhetoric had narrowed the gap with Nixon. JFK was now ahead of Nixon 48 percent to 47 percent.[306] But the Democratic campaign was still frustrated by polling figures suggesting that Nixon had a stronger name recognition and a more attractive image among Americans polled, especially undecided voters and independents. George Belknap, after analyzing similar polls at the DNC, informed JFK, "Nixon has had a reasonably good reputation with the people. When he is evaluated as a Vice President, he comes off well."[307] Belknap suggested that the Democrats avoid criticizing Nixon's "personal character" and emphasize Nixon as the personification of the Republican Party as an unpopular, backward minority party of failed policies.[308]

Democratic strategists were convinced that an effective projection of JFK's engaging personality, intelligence, and eloquence in a significant televised event would attract more independents and undecided voters to JFK. In an August 15, 1960, letter to JFK, Blair Clark, a CBS executive, stated that CBS president Frank Stanton was receptive to the idea of Kennedy–Nixon debates on live, national television. Stanton, however, "seemed to think that there were traps in it for either of you, or both."[309]

Before the first debate was held on September 26, JFK readily accepted an invitation to address the Greater Houston Ministerial Association on September 12. Johnson and Sam Rayburn had advised Kennedy against speaking before this televised audience of presumably hostile ministers. The Reverend Norman Vincent Peale, one of the most nationally prominent Protestant ministers, had recently contended that a Catholic president would inevitably face conflicts between his religious faith and his constitutional duties. LBJ and Rayburn worried that JFK's speech or questions from the clergy would further inflame, rather than mitigate, the religious issue, especially in Texas.[310]

JFK's Houston speech and answers to the ministers' questions were broadcast live by nineteen television stations in Texas.[311] The Catholic Democrat's gracious yet self-confident style and rhetoric expressed fidelity to the separation of church and state and the presidential oath of office.[312] The initial reaction of the public and media was so favorable to JFK that even Norman Vincent Peale praised Kennedy's performance and distanced himself from his earlier statement.[313] Richard and Jack Denove, JFK's filmmakers, taped this event and used half-hour, five-minute, and one-minute excerpts as campaign commercials. Media expert Kathleen Hall Jamieson calculated that most of the paid broadcasts of the half-hour tape were used outside the South. In particular, the Democratic presidential campaign concentrated the broadcasts of this commercial in heavily Catholic metropolitan areas of states that were closely contested by JFK and Nixon.[314]

Nixon may have made a tactical error in declining an invitation from the Greater Houston Ministerial Association. The vice president made a more serious mistake by agreeing to debate JFK in four nationally televised debates beginning on September 26, 1960, in Chicago.[315] Eisenhower tried but failed to discourage Nixon from debating Kennedy. Like JFK, Eisenhower realized that Nixon continued to hold the advantage of greater familiarity with voters.[316]

In particular, this stronger name recognition especially helped Nixon when he emphasized his foreign policy experience. Soviet premier Nikita Khrushchev's September visit to the United States, embrace of Fidel Castro, and speech to the United Nations had, in the words of journalist Theodore H. White, "succeeded in distracting a disproportionate amount of American attention from the serious business of choosing a President to his own meaningless but threatening presence."[317] With Khrushchev's visit dominating news coverage and commentary, JFK could not effectively counteract the repeated assertions of Nixon, Lodge, and Eisenhower that the next president must have the maturity, experience, and sound judgment to protect the United States and its vital security interests against Khrushchev.[318]

Furthermore, the Democratic campaign was frustrated by Gallup polls throughout September that repeatedly showed Nixon and Kennedy to be in a statistical dead heat among prospective voters surveyed.[319] Gallup polls that were released prior to the first debate revealed that anywhere from 5 to 8 percent of the Americans polled were undecided.[320] A Gallup poll released on September 25 indicated that 24 percent of its respondents held a highly favorable opinion of Nixon compared to 20 percent for JFK.[321]

A campaign memo advised JFK that he needed to be able to project confident, competent leadership for the next decade while simultaneously exposing Nixon to the public as "a highly contrived and calculating figure."[322] In another memo, political scientist George Belknap warned RFK, "The 1960 election will certainly have many areas of ambivalent feelings and a great number of uncommitted voters, many of whom will likely remain so until the very day of the election."[323] Belknap referred to a study by the Market Psychology, Inc. that indicated "a shift of 1 to 2 % of the voting population away from Nixon and away from uncommittedness toward Kennedy."[324]

JFK and LBJ had spent nearly two months before the first debate rallying the Democratic coalition, but they had made little progress among independents and undecided voters. The Democrats feared that a vigorous, well-funded, Republican blitz of frequent television commercials and broadcasts by Eisenhower during the two weeks of the campaign could deliver most of these voters to Nixon for a Republican victory. Besides being confident that he was a better debater than JFK, Nixon assumed that the television audiences would steadily increase during the debates. Nixon was also optimistic because the content of the fourth debate, which he expected to have the largest audience, was foreign policy, his forte.[325] Nixon assumed that he would provide his best performance during the last debate on October 21. He planned to then solidify his expected, wider lead in the polls.[326]

Unfortunately for Nixon, the first debate was viewed by the largest audience, approximately 75 million people. Television audiences for the three remaining debates steadily declined so that only 48 million people watched the fourth debate.[327] Also, television viewers were most likely to watch the entire one-hour debate on September 26 compared to the other three debates. Another lucky break for JFK is that J. Leonard Reinsch, the DNC's director of radio and television, won the coin toss for the first debate. Reinsch chose to have JFK make the opening and closing statements in the first debate.[328]

According to conventional wisdom, JFK won the first debate and probably or definitely the election because of his healthy, telegenic appearance and confident, articulate speaking style in sharp contrast to Nixon's gaunt, uneasy demeanor and occasionally hesitant, muddled rhetoric.[329] In his memoirs, Nixon complained, "It is a devastating commentary on the nature of television as a political medium that what hurt me most in the first debate was not the substance of the encounter, but the disadvantageous contrast in our physical appearances."[330] Historian Thomas C. Reeves concluded that for many Americans "Kennedy became the hero, Nixon the villain" because of the televised, visual differences in the two candidates' faces.[331]

These opinions underestimated the superiority of the content, structure, and coherence of JFK's rhetoric in the first debate. Although the first debate was intended to concentrate on domestic policy, JFK shrewdly explained his domestic policy positions, party affiliation, and concern for economic and social issues within the broader framework of foreign policy and national defense. The first debate began and ended with JFK providing viewers and listeners with a memorable, cogent understanding of the necessity of the United States making progress in social and economic issues at home in order to meet the challenges and dangers of Communism abroad. For JFK, the achievement of these goals and fulfillment of these responsibilities were necessary during the 1960s not only for national self-interest but also for preserving the greatest American ideals. He compared the American slavery of 1860 to the Soviet and Chinese Communism of 1960 in the first sentence of his opening statement. JFK ended the debate by concluding that the "great issue" of the 1960 election was the question: "Can freedom in the next generation conquer or are the Communists going to be successful?"[332]

JFK encapsulated the essence of his campaign theme and dramatized the entire election as a unique moment in world history. It is not surprising that Americans were far less interested in watching the fourth debate with its exclusive focus on foreign policy. A Gallup poll found that 43 percent of its respondents stated that JFK "won" the first debate and only 23 percent chose Nixon as the winner.[333] JFK now led Nixon in a voter preference poll 49 percent to 46 percent.[334] More significantly for JFK's pre-debate strategy, viewing the debates made previously undecided voters in one poll more likely to prefer JFK over Nixon by a ratio of three to one.[335]

JFK's success in the first debate also helped LBJ's campaign in the South. All but one of the Democratic governors from the Southern Governors Conference signed a telegram congratulating JFK on his "superb handling of Mr. Nixon and the great issues facing the country. It is the consensus of the Governors present that the masterful way in which you controlled this debate further accelerates the movement to the Kennedy–Johnson and Democratic ticket."[336] Most Democratic governors in the South were previously aloof toward Kennedy. Now, they became more active in campaigning for the JFK–LBJ ticket as their constituents' concerns about JFK's religion, maturity, and leadership ability dissipated.[337]

JFK's more attractive image as a nationally televised celebrity facilitated LBJ's reverse coattails strategy. LBJ used this partisan theme most emphatically and consistently during his whistlestop campaign of eight southern states that began on October 10 in Virginia.[338] Dubbed the "Cornpone Special" by reporters, LBJ's train tour encouraged straight-ticket voting by southern Democrats. Most of them had split their tickets and voted for Eisenhower in 1956. This was especially true in states of the peripheral South, such as Virginia, North Carolina, Florida, and Texas.[339] In an exaggerated southern drawl, LBJ constantly reminded audiences of still skeptical, undecided voters about how Democratic programs had benefited the South and how their continuation and future progress were threatened by the prospect of a more partisan Republican president opposing a Democratic Congress.[340]

Journalist David S. Broder noted that during JFK's more frequent campaign appearances in the South after the first debate the Massachusetts Democrat urged southerners to vote a straight ticket, so that their Democratic members of Congress would be better able to protect their states' policy interests with a Democratic president.[341] In a November 4 speech in Norfolk, Virginia, JFK told his listeners, "You cannot possibly put your confidence in Democratic Senators and Democratic Congressmen and suddenly put in reverse and elect a Republican President. What sense does that make in the sixties?"[342]

LBJ made some progress in cajoling more southern voters publicly and, more important, persuading more southern politicians privately to actively support the JFK–LBJ ticket.[343] But he confronted the growing possibility that Nixon could carry Texas even if JFK won the election. LBJ was disliked and distrusted by conservatives and liberals in the Texas Democratic Party. He was further embarrassed by the conservative-dominated Texas Democratic convention's rejection of the Democratic national platform, especially its liberal positions on civil rights and "right to work" laws.[344] Research conducted by LBJ aide Bill D. Moyers and others showed that older, rural, lower-income, white Protestants in Texas were still inclined to vote against JFK for religious reasons.[345] The affluent suburbanites of Houston, Dallas, and Fort Worth were expected to further realign with the Republican party.[346]

The DNC headquarters announced on October 22 that nineteen Democratic senators would campaign for the JFK–LBJ ticket in Texas. But it was unlikely that this additional effort within the strategy of reverse coattails would deliver the twenty-four Electoral College votes of Texas for the Democrats. Hispanics in general and younger, lower-income, urban blacks in particular were the Texans most favorable to JFK, but they were less likely than whites to be registered to vote. This was especially true among lower-income, less educated, rural Hispanics, despite the efforts of the Viva Kennedy Clubs and Hispanic leaders like Albert Pena, a Texas delegate at the Democratic national convention, and state senator Henry B. Gonzalez of San Antonio.[347]

The benefit that JFK later gained in receiving 91 percent of the Hispanic votes in Texas was minimized by the results of a recent, obscure change in the already confusing ballot laws of Texas.[348] Earlier in 1960, the secretary of state and attorney general of Texas ruled that county election boards no longer had to follow the custom of printing the Democratic column as the first column on their ballots. Many counties changed the order of the party columns on their ballots and required voters to cross out the columns of the parties that they did not choose. These new, complex requirements proved to be most confusing to the most pro-JFK Texans, namely, Hispanics, blacks, low-income whites, and first-time voters.[349] A disproportionate number of ballots cast for the Democratic presidential ticket in Texas was invalidated.[350]

Most analysts of the Democratic presidential campaign in Texas contend that the most decisive factor that enabled LBJ to end this stalemate and deliver his state to JFK was his shrewd manipulation of a media event provided by the Republicans in Dallas.[351] On November 4, four days before the election, Johnson and his wife were confronted and surrounded by a well-dressed crowd of right-wing protesters in the lobby of the Adolphus Hotel in Dallas. Led by Bruce Alger, the only Republican congressman from Texas, this crowd jeered and jostled LBJ and Lady Bird Johnson. They carried picket signs that denounced the Texas senator as a socialist traitor to his home state and region. Noticing that this scene was being televised, LBJ calmly accompanied his wife in slowly walking through the lobby in order to attract prolonged television coverage and later commentary.[352]

LBJ biographer Merle Miller found that this highly publicized incident generated a sympathy vote for Johnson among Texans and other southerners "when they saw their sacred concepts of courtesy and hospitality so violated."[353] This incident also convinced Senator Richard Russell of Georgia, Johnson's former patron and mentor in the Senate, to finally accept LBJ's request to campaign for the JFK–LBJ ticket in Texas for two days before the election.[354] It was the first time that Russell had campaigned for the Democratic presidential ticket since 1944.

Another unexpected, well-publicized event in the final days of the 1960 presidential campaign helped to swing a crucial bloc of electoral votes to JFK in several states that were toss-ups in the Electoral College. The organizational and operational challenge for the Democrats was to increase voter registration and turnout among blacks enough to swing such states as Ohio, Illinois, and California to JFK.[355] In reports to RFK, the DNC's campaign coordinators in these states expressed concern about apathy among blacks toward JFK's candidacy and slow progress in voter registration and the distribution of campaign literature among blacks in these states. Tom Quimby, the DNC's coordinator in Ohio, found "a lack of enthusiasm in the Negro community for the Democratic cause" in Cleveland and suspected that Republicans were paying black ministers to discourage their congregations from voting for JFK.[356] Pollster Louis Harris warned RFK that polling figures in Illinois "should be read as a challenge rather than a cause for exultation" and those in California revealed that a higher black voter turnout for JFK was needed to compensate for a slight decline in expected Hispanic support.[357]

On October 19, Martin Luther King, Jr., the most nationally prominent civil rights leader, was arrested along with other blacks for a sit-in at an Atlanta department store. Since King's arrest violated his probation on a previous traffic offense, Judge Oscar Mitchell sentenced King to four months of hard labor at Reidsville state prison. Hearing rumors that Nixon might ask the Eisenhower administration to intervene on King's behalf, Harris Wofford, JFK's civil rights co-director at the DNC, contacted R. Sargent Shriver, his fellow co-director. Shriver persuaded JFK to call King's wife. Fearing the loss of more southern white votes, RFK initially criticized his brother's phone call to Mrs. King. George Stewart, the Democratic state chairman of Georgia, persuaded RFK to call Mitchell and ask for King's release from jail. At the urging of Stewart, Mitchell told the media that JFK had helped King while Nixon did not.[358]

Wofford, Shriver, and Louis Martin, the DNC's liaison with the black press, then arranged to have labor unions finance the printing of two million copies of a leaflet contrasting JFK and Nixon regarding this incident. Nicknamed the "blue bomb," this leaflet was widely distributed among blacks, especially through black churches in the South. Martin Luther King, Sr.'s comment that he was switching his endorsement from Nixon to Kennedy was widely publicized.[359] Previously opposed to JFK because of the religious issue, "Daddy" King used his network of southern black ministers to generate a high turnout for JFK on election day. Most southern blacks had voted for Eisenhower in 1956 and tended to be more uncertain about or hostile to JFK's candidacy because of his Catholicism than nonsouthern blacks.[360] JFK carried South Carolina by less than 10,000 votes and approximately 40,000 South Carolina blacks voted for him.[361]

With the positive impact of these media events on the JFK–LBJ ticket, the final Gallup poll showed JFK ahead of Nixon 51 to 49 percent.[362] The Democrats were concerned, though, that Kennedy could still lose the election. Polls conducted by Louis Harris for JFK showed that states that were crucial to JFK's campaign strategy in the Electoral College, such as Ohio, California, Illinois, and New Jersey, were statistical dead heats less than a week before the election. In some of these states, intraparty conflicts among Democratic politicians, especially between Governor Edmund "Pat" Brown and future assembly speaker Jesse Unruh in California and between Governor Michael DiSalle and Senator Frank Lausche of Ohio, complicated and hampered the efforts of the DNC's campaign operations.[363]

Kennedy, unlike Nixon, had not promised the public that he would campaign in all fifty states. But Kenneth P. O'Donnell was determined that JFK adhere to his schedule. Deferring to O'Donnell, JFK reluctantly campaigned in New York on November 5. He was confident that two more days of campaigning in California would secure that state for him in the Electoral College.[364] With Governor Nelson Rockefeller zealously campaigning throughout New York for Nixon, even that heavily Catholic, northeastern state was becoming less certain for JFK.[365]

The Democratic presidential campaign tried to remain consistent with its theme of promoting progress in the 1960s by electing a unified Democratic national government. The Nixon campaign became more aggressive and explicit in refuting JFK's charge of American stagnation both at home and in the Cold War struggle. On November 2, 1960, RNC chairman Thruston Morton issued a press release that provided quotes from Soviet and Chinese newspapers and broadcasts agreeing with JFK's charges. Morton concluded that Kennedy gave "the Communist propaganda apparatus more ammunition than the Communists themselves ever dreamed possible."[366] On that same day, Nixon stated in Brooklyn, New York, that some of JFK's statements on foreign policy during their debates indicated that, if JFK were currently president, his decisions "might have led to war or surrender of territory, or both."[367] Also on November 2, Eisenhower stated at a campaign rally in New York City that a Nixon–Lodge administration will not "succumb to the threats of communism."[368]

In addition to Eisenhower's speeches on behalf of Nixon during the last week of the campaign, the Democrats struggled to counteract the Republicans' more pervasive and better coordinated advertising efforts on television and radio. With only 16 percent of the nation's newspapers endorsing Kennedy, the Democrats realized throughout the campaign that they needed to use the electronic media more skillfully than Nixon. But the Democratic efforts in television advertising during the last week of the campaign paled in comparison to those of the Republicans.

Ironically, the Democrats outspent the Republicans in direct payments to advertising firms for radio and television commercials. The Democrats directed their advertising campaign from Washington while their film had to be sent to New York City for processing. The mobile unit that JFK used to tape locally oriented television commercials on his campaign trail was mysteriously burned in Paris, Kentucky. There were also conflicts between the advertising firm hired by DNC chairman Paul M. Butler before the convention and that retained by the Kennedy family until the end of the campaign.[369] Samuel C. Brightman, the DNC's publicity director, later complained that the Kennedys failed "to utilize the party machinery, the Democratic National Committee contacts for maximum value not only for them but for other candidates."[370]

By contrast, Eisenhower, Nixon, and Lodge devoted a larger proportion and amount of their campaign efforts to nationally televised paid broadcasts than the Democrats did. They included Nixon's telethon, Lodge's fifteen-minute "Meet Mr. Lodge" ads and half-hour telecast, and Eisenhower's election eve broadcast.[371] Strictly following his schedule, Kennedy spent the last two days of the campaign mostly in southern New England, his three safest states, while LBJ frantically worked to carry his home state for JFK.[372] Kennedy formally ended his presidential campaign in Boston with a nationally televised speech on the night before the election.[373] Relaxing in his hotel room after this event, JFK's first words to scheduling aide Kenneth P. O'Donnell were: "Well, it's all over. I wish I had spent forty-eight hours more in California."[374]

The regrets and uneasiness expressed by JFK were well founded and evident in the results of the 1960 presidential election. With a voter turnout of nearly 63 percent, the highest in more than fifty years, JFK received 34,221,344 popular votes to Nixon's 34,106,671 and 303 electoral votes to Nixon's 219. JFK received 49.72 percent of the popular votes to Nixon's 49.55 percent. This gave JFK a winning margin of 114,873 votes.[375]

This plurality was almost half that of the total number of popular votes received by Governor Orval Faubus of Arkansas. Running in several states as the presidential nominee of the National States Rights party, Faubus received 214,541 votes. Faubus became nationally known in 1957 after he dramatically opposed the court-ordered integration of Central High School in Little Rock.

Other characteristics of the Democratic victory in the presidential election of 1960 raised questions about its legitimacy and made it more difficult for the future Kennedy administration to pursue its policy agenda with a Democratic Congress and the public. Despite spending a disproportionate amount of time and effort campaigning in Ohio, JFK lost this state by the unexpectedly wide margin of 162,928 votes. Always rueful about not campaigning more in California, JFK lost this state by only 35,623 votes out of approximately 6.5 million votes cast.[376] The Massachusetts Democrat carried New Jersey and Minnesota by approximately 22,000 votes each, despite New Jersey's large Catholic population and Senator Hubert H. Humphrey's use of his reelection campaign to benefit JFK in Minnesota.[377] Former president Harry Truman campaigned for the JFK–LBJ ticket in his home state and there was an unusually high voter turnout in St. Louis. But Kennedy carried Missouri by only 6,950 votes and attracted charges of Democratic ballot fraud, especially in St. Louis.[378]

Of course, JFK's transition to the presidency was plagued more by accusations and investigations concerning alleged ballot fraud in Texas and Illinois, especially votes from Chicago. Kennedy's respective yet disputed pluralities in these two states were 46,242 and 8,858 votes.[379] Combined, they provided the Democratic presidential ticket with a total of 51 electoral votes.[380] If Nixon had definitely carried Illinois and Texas, he would have won the election.

With LBJ on the Texas ballot for both vice president and senator, JFK was confronted with the embarrassing contrast of his running mate receiving 58 percent of the votes and a plurality of 379,952 votes in the Senate race as the JFK–LBJ ticket carried the state by a 2 percent margin with 46,242 votes.[381] Anti-Johnson Texans, both Democrats and Republicans, suspected widespread ballot fraud and voting irregularities by the Democrats, especially in heavily Hispanic urban wards and boss-controlled counties along the Mexican border.[382]

Despite the heavy concentration of blacks in Houston and Dallas and the fact that Texas had the largest number of black voters in the South, Nixon carried these cities and their counties. The Texas Election Board, dominated by pro-LBJ Democrats, tactfully dismissed a Republican lawsuit alleging that approximately 100,000 mostly Republican votes were illegally invalidated and demanding a recount. Fortunately for JFK and LBJ, this controversy gradually abated.[383]

The dispute over the Illinois results, however, was more contentious and persistent. With a voter turnout of 89.3 percent, Chicago provided Kennedy with a plurality of 456,312 votes. Other than Chicago's Cook County, JFK carried only eight of the other 101 counties in Illinois, yielding a statewide plurality of 8,858 votes. Within Chicago, JFK received his most overwhelming victory margins in the wards that were the most strictly controlled by the Daley machine, black Democratic Congressman William Dawson, and, more disputably, by gangster Sam Giancana.[384]

Nixon later regretted not having the Justice Department impound the ballots of Cook County on the day after the election.[385] He also did not reveal that, after Illinois Republicans challenged these votes, the Illinois state electoral board, with a four to one Republican membership, unanimously certified JFK as the winner of the electoral votes. The Republican-controlled board may have been concerned with the equally graphic accounts of voting irregularities and ballot fraud by Republicans in counties west of Chicago, such as Bureau and DeKalb.[386] In a letter to RFK, Harold Leventhal, an attorney representing the DNC in the Illinois recount case, told RFK that the Nixon Recount Committee was making "wild claims" that "are primarily assertions that certain ballots should *not* be counted."[387] Leventhal assured RFK that JFK's electors would probably be certified.[388]

Some journalists and other analysts were surprised that JFK, regardless of having LBJ as his running mate, performed as well as he did in the South.[389] Despite his status as a pro-civil rights, New England Catholic, Kennedy received 52 percent of the southern white vote, 3 percent more than Stevenson did in 1956.[390] Journalists Rowland Evans and Robert Novak concluded that JFK's Catholicism hurt his candidacy more among Protestant voters in the Midwest than those in the South.[391] A study by political scientist David Lawrence showed that most southern whites polled preferred the Democratic Party over the Republican Party on racial issues in the 1960 election.[392] His statistics suggest that JFK's liberal position on civil rights was less of a liability in attracting southern white votes than was previously assumed.

JFK received almost 67 percent of the southern black vote. The number of registered black voters in the eleven states of the former Confederacy increased from approximately 595,000 in 1947 to 1,363,345 at the beginning of 1960.[393] JFK carried seven of the eleven southern states in the Electoral College, giving him 63 percent of the South's electoral votes compared to Eisenhower's 52 percent in 1956.[394] Mississippi, the most militant southern state in disfranchising blacks, gave more popular votes to JFK than to Nixon. But its unpledged slate of electors cast Mississippi's eight electoral votes for Democratic Senator Harry Byrd of Virginia.[395] These initial, impressive figures masked how fragile and ephemeral JFK's electoral support in the South was. If, compared to the 1956 presidential election, southern blacks had not increased their voter registration and turnout and substantially shifted from Eisenhower to Kennedy, then JFK would have lost most of the seven southern states that he carried, including Texas.[396]

As electors throughout the nation prepared to formally cast their states' Electoral College votes in December, there was a growing possibility that several electors from Alabama, Louisiana, and Georgia would not vote for JFK. Even though the JFK–LBJ ticket won 57 percent of the popular votes in Alabama, Alabama's electors cast six votes for JFK and five for Byrd.[397] In Georgia, where JFK's 62.5 percent of the popular votes exceeded his percentage in Massachusetts, strict party discipline imposed by Senators Richard Russell and Herman Talmadge delivered all of that state's twelve electoral votes to JFK.[398] In Louisiana, despite its large Catholic minority and high black voter turnout for JFK in New Orleans, the state Democratic committee pledged its ten electoral votes to JFK by a vote of 52 to 51.[399]

The pyrrhic nature of JFK's victory for the entire Democratic Party was evident in the congressional election results of 1960. The Democrats lost twenty House seats, all of them outside the South, and two Senate seats. Most of the defeated House Democrats were freshmen who were elected in 1958 from midwestern agricultural districts as a protest against the recession and Ezra Taft Benson's farm policies. Political analyst Michael Barone found that JFK carried only 206 of the 437 congressional districts.[400]

In the nonsouthern states that JFK carried in the Electoral College, he experienced a reverse coattails effect more extensively than Harry Truman did in 1948. For example, Truman carried Illinois by 33,612 votes while that state's respective Democratic nominees for senator and governor, Paul Douglas and Adlai Stevenson, received pluralities of 407,728 votes and 572,067 votes.[401] Like Truman, JFK received between 49 and 50 percent of the popular votes and similarly high percentages from Catholics, Jews, blacks, and labor union members.[402] The national voter turnout of 63 percent in 1960 was much higher than the 52 percent of 1948, especially among nonsouthern Democrats.[403] JFK's success in both the popular votes and electoral votes was more concentrated in major northeastern and midwestern cities than Truman's was.[404]

Political scientists more formally compared the similarities between the 1948 and 1960 presidential and congressional election results. They defined 1948 as a maintaining election and 1960 as a reinstating election.[405] In both elections, the Democratic Party's majority party status in terms of voter registration and voting behavior was reflected in both the presidential election and partisan control of Congress. Truman and Kennedy won their victories mostly by energizing and mobilizing the key voting blocs of the New Deal coalition through a liberal platform in domestic policy while promising a tough yet innovative foreign policy in the Cold War.[406]

But the Democrats had ended Republican control of Congress in 1948 by gaining seventy-five seats in the House and nine in the Senate. This sharp increase in the number of nonsouthern Democrats in the House and election of outspoken liberals like Hubert H. Humphrey and Paul Douglas to the Senate made the Truman administration confident that it had a public mandate to pursue the Fair Deal's liberal policy agenda.[407] The Eighty-first Congress rejected most of the Fair Deal. It became apparent that most voters who supported Truman and the return to a Democratic Congress wanted to protect the benefits of New Deal–era programs and laws rather than extend liberalism into new, more controversial policies, such as civil rights and national health insurance.[408]

Compared to Truman, Kennedy was confronted with a more challenging, complex task as a party leader and legislative leader. He and Johnson had campaigned on the Democratic Party's most ambitiously liberal platform in its history. The loss of nonsouthern Democratic seats in Congress, however, portended a strengthening of the bipartisan conservative coalition in the House and greater difficulty in enacting these platform proposals.[409] The most liberal voting blocs and interest groups, especially civil rights leaders, the ADA, and organized labor, had high expectations for the New Frontier and JFK's legislative leadership. They were unlikely to tolerate the new president heavily compromising or diluting their policy priorities with Congress and the more conservative yet powerful elements of the Democratic Party.[410]

CHAPTER FOUR

The Party Politics of Public Policy

I n his 1942 book, *Party Government*, E. E. Schattschneider stated, "The vote in Congress on critical issues is the acid test of the locus of power in the parties."[1] Political scientist and Kennedy biographer James MacGregor Burns perceived the American party system to consist, in effect, of four "parties." Within each of the two major parties, a conservative wing dominated Congress, especially its major committees, while a more liberal, activist wing dominated presidential nominating conventions.[2] Publishing his theory of four-party politics during JFK's last year as president, Burns stated that "it was clear in Kennedy's third year that the Administration faced a widening gap between the slow progress of its program in Congress and its public hopes and commitments."[3] In his detailed, quantitative study comparing periods of unified government and divided government from 1947 to 1988, David R. Mayhew, however, found that approximately the same amount of major legislation was passed during each session of Congress, regardless of whether the same party controlled the presidency and Congress.[4]

Throughout his presidential campaign and especially during its final days, JFK had emphasized the preferability and even necessity of a unified Democratic government in order to assure progress in both domestic and foreign policies during the 1960s. Many Republicans and some Democrats in Congress asserted that JFK lacked the experience, skills, and legislative accomplishments to effectively lead Congress as his inauguration approached.[5] Theodore C. Sorensen later conceded that his boss "felt somewhat uncomfortable and perhaps too deferential with these men who the previous year had outranked him."[6]

The president-elect understood that he needed to develop credibility with Congress, the media, and public opinion as an effective leader of the New Frontier's policy agenda. At a December 20, 1960, meeting in Florida, JFK, LBJ, their staff, and several Democratic congressional leaders agreed that during the next session of Congress their legislative priorities were: a higher minimum wage, federal aid to education, economic development of depressed areas, more housing, and hospital insurance for the elderly.[7] With his initial focus on the enactment of legislation for a higher minimum wage and economic aid to depressed areas, JFK wanted to accumulate a series of quick, feasible legislative victories, however modest in content and scope. This success was necessary to develop the political capital and policymaking momentum needed to eventually pass more divisive domestic legislation, such as the racially and religiously controversial dimensions of federal aid to education.[8]

This cautious yet cumulative strategy also wanted to avoid the Truman administration's tactical error of submitting the most controversial Fair Deal legislation, especially repeal of the Taft-Hartley Act and a civil rights bill, as its top priorities with the Eighty-first Congress. These liberal proposals quickly mobilized the bipartisan conservative coalition in Congress and its allies among interest groups and lobbyists to not only defeat these bills early in 1949, but also to defeat or severely weaken more modest, subsequent Fair Deal legislation.[9]

In addition to gradually developing a productive relationship with Democratic congressional leaders, JFK needed to sign legislation to ameliorate the economic suffering of the recent recession. Robert Finch, one of Nixon's campaign aides, contended that JFK won the election entirely because 400,000 Americans lost their jobs in October 1960.[10] Although JFK's inaugural address concentrated on Cold War foreign policy, his first few months as "chief lawmaker" were mostly devoted to anti-recession policies. The new president signed legislation and issued executive orders that extended unemployment benefits, expanded the federal government's distribution of surplus food to the poor, and provided more funds for public works on highways, hospitals, and other federally subsidized public infrastructure.[11]

JFK was irked by liberal commentators and activists comparing his first hundred days in office to FDR's. Despite the recession, the national mood was certainly more conservative and less willing to support revolutionary domestic policies. The president was also concerned that comparisons to FDR's early presidency would lead to the frustration of high expectations among liberals and a renewal of their criticism and suspicion of him as a calculating opportunist. In 1961, political scientists James T. Crown and George P. Penty stated, "Essentially a moderate, Kennedy feels that liberalism still has not lost its appeal for the country but he is at best impatient of old New Dealers, with their emphasis on what he often feels are old solutions to new problems."[12]

After approving the most feasible and conventional economic relief measures, JFK then concentrated on securing passage of the Area Redevelopment Act (ARA) of 1961. Determined to leave the presidency with a legacy of fiscal responsibility, Eisenhower had vetoed similar legislation as wasteful, ineffective boondoggles in 1958 and 1960.[13] Championed by Senator Paul Douglas of Illinois since 1954, aid to depressed areas legislation was intended to encourage new industries to move into often isolated communities of states whose local economies declined during the 1950s. This federal aid would target these selected areas with job training and placement programs for the chronically unemployed, especially those displaced by automation in factories or by decreased consumption of certain domestically produced raw materials, such as coal from West Virginia and timber from northern Michigan.[14] The federal government would also provide low-interest, long-term loans to businesses that opened in these areas and assistance in the design and construction of highways, water and sewer systems, parks, and other public infrastructure to facilitate economic development in depressed areas.

Despite Eisenhower's opposition, congressional support for this type of legislation grew during the late 1950s. The sharp increase in the number of Democrats in Congress, especially in the Senate, because of the 1958 elections, the impact of the 1957–1958 and 1960 recessions, and a heightened public awareness of the complex problem of structural unemployment worsening even during periods of economic growth and general prosperity motivated all but the most fiscally conservative Democrats, especially Senator Harry Byrd of Virginia, chairman of the Senate Finance Committee, to support aid to depressed areas by early 1961.[15] Several liberal Republicans, such as Senators Jacob Javits of New York and Clifford Case of New Jersey, also favored this legislation.[16]

It was not surprising that the ARA bill passed the Senate by a voice vote on April 20, 1961, and the House by a margin of thirty votes six days later.[17] Douglas and a few other liberal, northern Democrats were disappointed, though, that, as a legislative compromise, the ARA would be administered by the Secretary of Commerce, Luther Hodges.[18] Some liberals perceived Hodges, a former governor of North Carolina and business executive, as an antiunion conservative who would be biased toward business and against labor in implementing the ARA programs, especially in the South.[19]

There seemed to be a regional bias in the ARA's orientation toward southern and border states. JFK was grateful to West Virginians for his decisive primary victory in their state on May 10, 1960. It was more than coincidental that JFK signed the ARA bill on May 1 and a bill increasing the minimum wage on May 5, 1961. JFK repeatedly told aides and administration officials that he was determined to provide immediate economic relief to West Virginia as well as address the more long-term economic problems peculiar to that state.[20] Realizing that his eventual legislative and executive decisions on civil rights would alienate southern congressmen from Black Belt areas of the South, JFK hoped to gradually increase public and congressional support for his presidency in overwhelmingly white, economically depressed areas of the peripheral South and border states less concerned with racial issues.[21] For example, ARA funds were sent to help a non-union, low-wage shirt factory in Arkansas, the home state of Senator J. William Fulbright, chairman of the Senate Foreign Relations Committee.[22]

Since LBJ had left the Senate, Senator Robert Kerr of Oklahoma had become chairman of the space committee and a key member of the finance and public works committees. Needing Kerr's influence on a wide range of major legislation, JFK's administration approved loans and grants totaling $9.5 million, twelve times the amount given to any other ARA project, to build resort lodges in Lake Eufaula, Oklahoma. These ARA funds were allocated in conjunction with more than $66 million in other federal funds for water development in Oklahoma.[23]

JFK understood, however, that even the shrewd use of the ARA and other federal funds, such as subsidies to cotton, tobacco, and other southern agricultural commodities, were not enough to deliver southern Democratic votes in Congress for major legislation. Lawrence F. O'Brien, who headed the White House's congressional relations office, estimated that JFK needed the votes of a narrow majority of the nearly one hundred southern Democrats in the House of Representatives to secure passage of White House bills.[24] If fifty-five or more southern Democrats, virtually all nonsouthern Democrats, and at least twenty Republicans in the House backed an administration bill, it could still be stalled and eventually killed by the House Rules Committee, the bastion of the bipartisan conservative coalition in the House.[25]

The liberal Democratic effort to weaken the conservative obstructionism of this committee had been developing since the late 1950s. The Democratic Study Group (DSG), an organization of liberal House Democrats, approached Speaker Sam Rayburn with a proposal to restore the twenty-one-day rule. This rule forced the House Rules Committee to act on a bill within twenty-one days after receiving it or else the chairman of any standing committee could directly send that bill to the House floor. Rayburn barely prevented a liberal revolt in late 1958 by promising DSG members that he would do something to reform the House Rules Committee. The Democratic national platform of 1960 urged that House rules "should be so amended as to make sure that bills reported by legislative committees reach the floor for consideration without delay."[26]

JFK had made several campaign speeches criticizing the House Rules Committee for killing liberal legislation, but he initially deferred to Rayburn's leadership on this matter. Most of the strategy that developed was based on the friendship between Rayburn and Representative Richard Bolling of Missouri.[27] Bolling, a leader of the DSG and a member of the House Rules Committee, was a protégé of Rayburn.[28] Trusting the Speaker's integrity and judgment, Bolling agreed that there were not enough votes to restore the twenty-one-day rule. The Missouri Democrat also conceded that a Democratic caucus vote to remove William Colmer, a conservative Democrat from Mississippi, from his seat on the House Rules Committee for supporting his state's independent electors against the JFK-LBJ ticket could antagonize many southern Democrats and arouse more determined opposition to liberal legislation.[29] Rayburn had dissuaded Truman from seeking a similar "purge" of several southern House Democrats from their committee assignments because of their open endorsement of J. Strom Thurmond's Dixiecrat presidential candidacy in 1948.[30]

Rayburn also convinced Bolling of the need to ally themselves with at least some southern conservatives and some Republicans. In order to attract bipartisan support for changing the House Rules Committee, Rayburn and Bolling decided to increase the size of the House Rules Committee by adding three seats—two Democratic and one Republican. Despite the Democratic loss of House seats in the 1960 congressional elections, Rayburn was confident that this proposal would attract enough support from Republicans for two reasons. First, there were some liberal Republicans who resented the conservative-dominated committee's defeat of recent legislation that they favored and assumed that this additional Republican seat would be held by one of them. Second, Rayburn, more so than Bolling and the other DSG liberals, knew that several Republicans, regardless of ideology, such as conservative Missouri congressman Thomas Curtis, resented the abrupt ouster of Representative Joseph Martin of Massachusetts as House minority leader in 1959 and his replacement by Representative Charles Halleck of Indiana.

These anti-Martin Republicans partially blamed the heavy Republican losses in the 1958 House elections on Martin's passive, lackluster leadership style and his cordial relationship with Rayburn.[31] Halleck, more conservative than Martin and rigidly partisan, imposed stricter party discipline than his predecessor. He also publicly announced his support for Democratic Representative Howard Smith's chairmanship of the House Rules Committee and opposition to its expansion, even though the Republicans would gain a seat. Halleck's blatant backing of the bipartisan status quo on this committee offended some Republican party regulars like Curtis and Glen Cunningham of Nebraska.[32]

In addition to the twenty-one Republicans who pledged to vote for Rayburn's proposal, the Texas Democrat benefited from the intervention of Representative Carl Vinson of Georgia, chairman of the House Armed Services Committee. Although Vinson was an anti-civil rights conservative, he was a party regular who was proud of the fact that Georgia provided JFK with a higher percentage of popular votes than Massachusetts in the 1960 election and wanted the Democratic president to have a fair chance of having White House bills passed.[33]

Despite the fact that Rayburn's refusal to purge Colmer and his alliance with Vinson attracted some southern votes that would have otherwise gone to Howard Smith, the chairman of the House Rules Committee was confident that he could assemble enough southern Democrats combined with Halleck's Republicans to defeat the proposed expansion of his committee. Smith mobilized conservative interest groups, namely, the American Medical Association (AMA), the National Association of Manufacturers (NAM), the U.S. Chamber of Commerce, and the American Farm Bureau, to lobby undecided or wavering congressmen on his behalf.[34] Increasingly pessimistic of victory, the Speaker of the House began to seek the votes of undecided southern and border state Democrats simply on the basis of personal loyalty and friendship toward him. Rayburn then rescheduled the floor vote on his proposed reform from January 24, 1961, to January 31.

Rayburn now perceived the use of presidential party leadership on this vote as a necessity rather than a liability. In his January 25 press conference, JFK expressed hope "that a small group of men will not attempt to prevent the Members from finally letting their judgments be known" on important legislation through floor votes. But the president also stated that "the responsibility rests with the Members of the House, and I would not attempt in any way to infringe on that responsibility."[35] More privately and aggressively, JFK immediately responded to Rayburn's request for help by calling undecided Democrats and lobbying for their votes. Phone calls from O'Brien, Hodges, and Stewart Udall, the Secretary of the Interior, threatened the denial of future patronage and pork barrel spending for their districts.[36] Although his constitutional duty was to be president of the Senate, LBJ also lobbied southern House members, especially Texas Democrats, to vote for Rayburn's proposal.[37]

Rayburn's impassioned speech for his resolution was received with thunderous applause by both Democrats and Republicans on January 31.[38] Rayburn's proposal to add three seats to the House Rules Committee was subsequently adopted by a vote of 217 to 212.[39] JFK was disappointed that his administration's alliance with the Speaker of the House yielded a five-vote majority after such intense lobbying. Sorensen noted, "Without the votes of more than one-third of the Southern Democrats and one-eighth of the Republicans, he would not have won at all."[40]

By contrast, JFK refused to actively support an effort by Senator Joseph Clark of Pennsylvania to amend Rule 22 of the Senate. Rule 22 required at least a two-thirds majority in the Senate to end a filibuster. Clark and other liberals wanted to make it easier to invoke cloture for the purpose of preventing or ending filibusters, especially those used or threatened by southern Democrats and their Republican allies for defeating or weakening civil rights legislation.[41] JFK and LBJ were confident that there were enough pro-administration Democrats and liberal Republicans in the Senate to pass most of JFK's major legislation. They did not want to alienate Russell, Kerr, and other leading southern senators. JFK and LBJ supported the effort of Senator Mike Mansfield of Montana, the recently elected Senate majority leader, to refer Clark's proposal to amend Rule 22 and six other Senate rules to the Senate Rules Committee, effectively defeating it.

Mansfield's motion passed by a vote of 50 to 46 on January 11, 1961. Among the Democratic senators, 32 voted for it, and 31 voted against it.[42] With an even division among Senate Democrats on a procedural matter and Johnson still embarrassed by the vociferous hostility of Democratic senators to the proposal that he preside over the Senate Democratic caucus, Kennedy did not want to become embroiled in any Senate rules reform campaigns led by liberal dissidents. Moreover, rules reforms in the Senate appeared to be less crucial than those in the House because of the sharp increase in the number of nonsouthern Democrats in the Senate since 1958. These Democrats now had greater representation on major Senate committees due to the Johnson Rule that primarily benefited less senior, nonsouthern Democrats.[43]

Since southern conservative Democrats had relatively more power in the committee system of the House than in that of Senate, the expansion of the House Rules Committee proved crucial for the viability of New Frontier legislation in the House of Representatives. Two liberal Democrats, Carl Elliott of Alabama and Bernie F. Sisk of California, were added to this committee.[44] A narrow majority of its members usually ruled favorably on JFK's bills.

For much of Kennedy's initial domestic policy legislation, the two most powerful House committees influencing their content and chances of passage were Ways and Means and Education and Labor. Chaired by Representative Wilbur Mills of Arkansas, the Ways and Means Committee was still dominated by the membership and policy perspectives of the bipartisan conservative coalition. Mills was especially hostile to taxing and spending policies that resulted in higher budget deficits and opposed financing and administering medical insurance for the aged within the Social Security system.[45]

The House Education and Labor Committee was no longer chaired by a southern conservative. Its chairman, Representative Graham Barden of North Carolina, retired from Congress in 1961. In 1960, he had opposed JFK's bill to increase the minimum wage to $1.25 an hour and expand its coverage to include such employees as laundry workers, retail clerks, and intrastate bus and truck drivers. A major obstacle to Truman's Fair Deal legislation, Barden also wanted to ensure that any federal aid to elementary and secondary education not be used to benefit parochial schools or to enforce the racial integration of public schools.[46]

Due to House seniority rules, Barden was succeeded as chairman by a northern, urban liberal, Representative Adam Clayton Powell, Jr., of New York. With his Harlem-based district, Powell soon emerged as the most powerful and controversial black congressman of the 1960s. An outspoken, flamboyant maverick, Powell had endorsed LBJ's presidential candidacy as early as 1959.[47] Like Barden, though, Powell was also influenced by racial considerations in his legislative behavior on this committee. The New York Democrat was determined that any federal laws and federal aid that originated in the New Frontier not have the effect of subsidizing and continuing racial discrimination in education, labor, and social welfare.[48] George Meany, president of the AFL-CIO, suspected that Powell's chairmanship would be as much of a liability to labor's policy interests as Barden's was. He denounced Powell's assumption of this committee's chairmanship in one word, "Terrible!"[49]

Kennedy, like Truman, hoped that Congress in general and the House Education and Labor Committee in particular would consider his labor and education bills separately from civil rights, thereby attracting the support of both southern and nonsouthern Democrats. Throughout his presidential campaign and during the post-convention special session of Congress, JFK had repeatedly emphasized his proposal for a higher minimum wage with expanded coverage to be a major difference between the Democratic and Republican parties. He even devoted an entire television commercial to this issue during his campaign against Nixon.[50] Congress passed JFK's economic relief legislation and the ARA bill fairly easily. With organized labor and O'Brien's office actively lobbying for JFK's minimum wage bill, it seemed likely to pass with most of its original content, including coverage of approximately 4.3 million workers not protected by the current laws, intact.[51]

Because JFK had specifically and repeatedly identified himself and the New Frontier with an increase to $1.25 an hour by 1963, it was politically difficult for him to accept a smaller increase.[52] Kennedy was compelled to compromise and surrender more than he had expected in the expansion of coverage. Although Powell's committee had favorably ruled on and released JFK's bill for floor debate on March 13, it already attracted intense, effective opposition from the U.S. Chamber of Commerce and other business lobbyists. Organized labor, O'Brien's legislative office, and the legendary surname of Representative James Roosevelt of California, the House sponsor of JFK's bill, could not save substantial categories of workers included in the proposed, expanded coverage.

The bipartisan, conservative opposition to JFK's bill was represented by the Kitchin-Ayres bill. Cosponsored by Democratic Representative Paul Kitchin of North Carolina and Republican Representative William H. Ayres of Ohio, this bill raised the minimum wage to $1.15 for currently covered workers and expanded coverage to 1.3 million workers. But these newly covered workers would receive a minimum wage of $1 an hour. In sharp contrast to JFK's bill, the Kitchin-Ayres bill had an especially restrictive interpretation of interstate commerce so that most smaller businesses were considered to be engaged in "intrastate" commerce only and were not required to pay any federal minimum wages.[53]

The ailing, elderly Rayburn was exhausted by the House Rules Committee struggle, and Roosevelt was publicly pessimistic that JFK's bill would pass. Carl Vinson soon emerged as the administration's chief liaison with southern conservatives in the House. The Georgia Democrat recognized that service-oriented businesses in the South, particularly those with large numbers of black, female workers, did not want to be required to pay any federal minimum wage. Vinson insisted that the only way to pass a bill that increased the minimum wage to $1.25 an hour was to exclude large numbers of workers from coverage, such as the approximately 150,000 laundry workers, mostly black women in the South and major northern cities.[54]

In a 1960 campaign speech in Buffalo, JFK specifically and passionately stated the need for laundry women to receive an adequate minimum wage and dramatized that issue as a major difference between the Democratic and Republican parties.[55] JFK and O'Brien reluctantly agreed to exclude laundry workers and several other categories in order to retain the $1.25 an hour provision. Adopting some of Vinson's recommendations, Rayburn and House majority whip Carl Albert of Oklahoma cosponsored a modified version of JFK's original bill. It retained the $1.25 an hour minimum wage increase but expanded coverage to 3.6 million new workers, approximately 700,000 fewer workers than Kennedy had wanted to cover.[56]

Bolling helped Rayburn and Albert to organize Democrats for a roll-call vote on their bill. Bolling calculated that the exclusion of laundry workers from their bill would gain ten to twelve votes from Democrats being pressured by large laundry businesses. During the March 24 floor debate, Vinson sarcastically joked on the House floor that his amendment to the Rayburn-Albert bill "washed laundries clean out of the picture."[57]

Vinson's remark, widely quoted and publicized by the media, injected the divisive issue of race into an already factious legislative battle. It threatened to disrupt intraparty relations among Democrats in Congress and between the president and congressional Democrats enough so that the passage of future, more controversial New Frontier legislation was jeopardized. The most economically and racially conservative southerners were emboldened to add more weakening amendments to the Rayburn-Albert bill and to continue House consideration of the Kitchin-Ayers bill. The House members who were the most liberal on civil rights, Democrats like Powell and Republicans like Representative John Lindsay of New York, were angry about this exclusion and less motivated to fight for the compromised administration bill.[58]

In JFK's most humiliating legislative defeat so far, the House rejected the Rayburn-Albert bill by a teller vote of 186–185 and passed the Kitchin-Ayres bill by a roll-call vote of 216–203.[59] In the vote on the Rayburn-Albert bill, O'Brien's office and Albert had miscalculated the number of House Democrats presumably favorable to this bill who would be present for the teller vote since their rate of absenteeism was unusually and inscrutably high.[60] For the remainder of JFK's presidency, this defeat made O'Brien and the House Democratic leadership determined to conduct a more reliable count and tenacious "whipping" of Democrats behind White House bills. Theodore C. Sorensen traced its impact on party organization and discipline among House Democrats to "that day early in 1961 when the minimum wage bill had been defeated by one vote with sixty-four Democrats absent."[61]

Fortunately for Kennedy, the more liberal membership of the Senate and its weaker bipartisan conservative coalition enabled his surrogates to prevent further emasculation of his original bill. After the Senate readily passed a slightly modified version of JFK's original bill, pro-JFK Democrats dominated the House and Senate membership of the conference committee. Charging that the continued

exclusion of mostly black laundry workers was racist, Senator Wayne Morse of
Oregon refused to sign the conference report on the bill. But it expanded coverage to 4.1 million new workers, about one half of a million more than the
defeated Rayburn-Albert bill.

Although coverage in general was expanded, southern Democrats from the
House in the conference committee secured the exclusion of employees of auto
and farm equipment dealers, cotton processors, and other farm-related businesses from this House-Senate compromise bill. On May 3, 1961, it passed the
House 230 to 196 and the Senate 64 to 28.[62] On May 5, JFK signed this bill,
officially named the Fair Labor Standards Amendments of 1961.

After praising Congress for passing it and labor union leaders "for their
long interest" in it, JFK expressed his hope "that we can move from this improvement into greater gains in the months and years ahead."[63] On June 22, the
president issued a memo to all federal agencies stating that they should voluntarily comply with the minimum wage requirements of this law, even though it
exempt the federal government as an employer. He added, "I want to make clear
these minimum rates should apply to federal laundry workers, even though such
workers in private employment are specifically exempted by the law."[64]

JFK's decisions to accept exemption of laundry workers in the private sector
as a legislative compromise, despite his emphatic campaign promise, and then to
quietly include government laundry workers in minimum wage rates through
executive action typified his cautious yet shrewd leadership in advancing his
domestic policy agenda. In announcing his presidential candidacy in January
1960, JFK identified the presidency as the "vital center of action." He asserted
that a president can be an effective legislative leader only if he is also an effective
party leader. Kennedy further contended that only unified government with an
activist Democratic president leading a Democratic Congress "will help restore
purpose to both the Presidency and Congress."[65] In this speech and throughout his
campaign, JFK criticized Eisenhower for not fully using his presidential powers to
make progress in domestic policy and prepare the nation for the 1960s.

JFK's energetic use of executive orders and official memos to agency officials was
not enough to satisfy the policy demands of liberal activists, especially ADA members and civil rights leaders.[66] Although most of them did not expect JFK to submit
a comprehensive civil rights bill to Congress in early 1961, they were disappointed
that he did not use his executive powers more vigorously and extensively to prohibit
racial discrimination in federal programs.[67] Civil rights activists mailed pens to the
White House because of JFK's campaign statement that Eisenhower could end racial
discrimination in federally subsidized housing "with a stroke of his pen" through
executive orders.[68] As early as February 4, 1961, Martin Luther King, Jr., reminded
the nation of this promise in a magazine article.[69]

JFK was determined to keep controversial, divisive civil rights issues separate from the rest of his domestic policy agenda during the 1961–1962 session

of Congress. His first housing bill aroused little opposition from southern Democrats since it was mostly an updated expansion of the Housing Act of 1949, the
only major Fair Deal bill passed by Congress. Like the 1949 law, it included
funds for slum clearance, urban renewal, and public housing. Unlike the previous law, the Housing Act of 1961 funded the construction of housing for the
elderly and for colleges, long-term, low-interest loans for the construction of
middle-income, private housing, and the promotion of mass transit and open
spaces in cities. In addition to its broad appeal to members of Congress from
major metropolitan areas, the 1961 omnibus housing bill was attractive to both
business and labor. Its $6.1-billion dollar budget was perceived as a necessary
stimulus for the sluggish economy.[70] In answering questions at his March 1 and
March 23 press conferences, JFK replied that executive orders banning racial
discrimination in federally assisted housing were being considered. But he did
not mention this in his June 22 bill signing ceremony.[71]

The New Frontier's first housing act appeared to be simply an extension and
modernization of the Fair Deal's housing act, thereby minimizing intraparty
conflict among Democrats in Congress. The housing issue, however, was inevitably entwined with urban renewal and racial conflict. With more middle-class
whites leaving major cities of the Northeast and Midwest after World War II for
their rapidly growing suburbs and more southern blacks moving to these cities,
the black percentage of Chicago's population grew from 14 to 23 percent and
of Detroit's from 16 to 29 percent during the 1950s.[72] In raw numbers, the black
populations of New York City and Philadelphia doubled from 1940 to 1960 to
approximately 1.1 million and 529,000, respectively. Meanwhile, the black
populations of Chicago and Detroit tripled and that of Los Angeles quintupled
from 1940 to 1960. In particular, Chicago's black population increased from
approximately 278,000 in 1940 to 813,000 in 1960 and was expected to reach
nearly one million in 1964.[73]

A major factor in JFK's electoral success in 1960 was his ability to attract
the votes of the sharply increased number of urban blacks, the decreasing number of racially conservative, urban white ethnics, and the growing number of
white suburbanites, especially suburban Catholics.[74] This was especially true in
states like Illinois, Michigan, and New Jersey that JFK narrowly carried. With
their large, rapidly growing black constituencies, big city mayors like Richard J.
Daley of Chicago and labor leaders like Walter Reuther of the UAW expected
the New Frontier's domestic policies to focus more specifically and publicly on
the economic needs and social problems of major cities and their low-income
black residents.[75]

JFK hoped that the creation of a new cabinet department, tentatively named
the Department of Urban Affairs and Housing, would provide the political
symbolism and policy specialization to satisfy these political demands. The
president's strategy was to first propose the establishment of this department to

Congress and then nominate its secretary. He would wait until after the 1962 midterm elections to quietly issue an executive order prohibiting racial discrimination in federally assisted housing.[76]

Kennedy assumed that the creation of this new cabinet department would be the least divisive and most attainable race-related policy goal. In his April 18, 1961, letter to Congress, the president explained his proposal in moderate, nonracial bureaucratic terms that emphasized cooperation with state and local governments. He added, "Thus, the new Secretary of Urban Affairs and Housing will be in a position to present the nation's housing and metropolitan development needs to the cabinet and will by virtue of his position provide the necessary leadership in coordinating the many Federal programs in these fields."[77] Eisenhower consolidated several New Deal agencies into the Department of Health, Education, and Welfare (HEW) in 1953. JFK assumed that, likewise, the creation of a Department of Urban Affairs and Housing would face little opposition from Congress if he presented it simply as a matter of reorganization in the executive branch.

Controversy soon swirled around the widespread assumption of Congress and the media that JFK would nominate Robert C. Weaver as this department's secretary. Weaver was the director of the Housing and House Finance Agency and began working for the Department of the Interior during the New Deal.[78] If this new department was authorized by Congress and JFK and the Senate appointed him as its secretary, Weaver would become the first black cabinet secretary. Weaver also served on the board of directors of the NAACP and was a Harvard graduate.[79]

Suspecting that JFK's real motive was to appease civil rights advocates and black voters by making Weaver the first black cabinet secretary in history, southern Democratic opposition in Congress to JFK's bill became entrenched. The congressional subcommittees on housing that received this bill were chaired by anti-civil rights Democrats from Alabama, Senator John Sparkman and Representative Albert Rains. After Kennedy submitted this bill to Congress in October 1961, he ended speculation about Weaver by publicly confirming at a press conference that he would nominate Weaver as the secretary of the new department. JFK hoped that publicly acknowledging Weaver as his first choice for secretary of a Department of Urban Affairs and Housing would motivate enough pro-civil rights Republicans in Congress to coalesce with nonsouthern Democrats in order to ensure this bill's passage.[80]

JFK's tactic backfired since he underestimated the determination and skill of southern Democrats to kill his proposal. Despite its expanded, more liberal membership, the House Rules Committee voted against the urban affairs bill nine to six in January 1962. Meanwhile, pro-civil rights Republicans in Congress resented what they perceived as JFK's attempt to portray Republican opposition to a Department of Urban Affairs and Housing as implicitly racist.[81] Nonsouthern

Democrats in the House from rural districts perceived this proposed department to be biased toward urban and black policy interests and assumed that it would provide little or no benefit to their constituents.[82]

The urban affairs bill fared no better in the Senate. Senate majority leader Mike Mansfield tried to circumvent the Government Operations Committee through a discharge petition. This motion further intensified the opposition of its chairman, Senator John L. McClellan of Arkansas, to this bill. The Senate voted 58 to 42 against Manfield's discharge petition on February 20, 1962. On the next day, the House voted 264 to 150 against the bill.[83] Senator Joseph Clark of Pennsylvania, a liberal Democratic member of the ADA, especially criticized Lawrence F. O'Brien for mismanaging White House lobbying for this bill.[84]

Clark did not refrain from publicly criticizing what he regarded to be the excessive caution and occasional bumbling of the White House in pursuing liberal legislative objectives throughout JFK's presidency. The Pennsylvania senator, however, proved to be indispensable in guiding the New Frontier's most innovative labor legislation, the Manpower Development and Training Act of 1962, through the Senate. As a member of the Senate Labor and Public Welfare Committee, Clark had previously promoted passage of the ARA Act of 1961 and the Accelerated Public Works Act of 1962.[85]

While Clark was often uncompromising and combative in his liberal advocacy of civil rights, he readily made the concessions necessary to gain enough Republican and southern Democratic votes to ensure passage of the Manpower Development and Training bill in both houses of Congress. In particular, Clark accepted a one-third reduction in the proposed program's budget and a one-year reduction of its existence from four to three years in order to appease fiscal conservatives of both parties.[86] The lingering effects of the recession, the growing public concern about structural unemployment worsening after the recession because of automation, the desire of both business and organized labor to obtain federal assistance in improving the job skills of industrial workers, and the correlation between the purpose of this legislation and that of the ARA for depressed areas provided JFK with a broad, bipartisan, multiregional consensus.[87]

The Senate version of JFK's bill passed by a vote of 60 to 31 on August 23, 1961. Sixteen of the thirty-three Republican senators voted for it, and only fourteen Democrats opposed it.[88] During the remainder of the 1961 legislative session, however, the House deliberations on this issue stalled in the House Rules Committee, partially because of differences between bills of Democratic Representative Elmer Holland of Pennsylvania and Republican Representative Charles Goodell of New York. The White House and Secretary of Labor Arthur Goldberg pressured Holland to yield to Goodell's bill, which was more similar to the Senate bill than Holland's.[89] The House Rules Committee subsequently released the Goodell bill for a floor vote, and the House passed it by a vote of 354 to 62 on February 28, 1962.[90]

Political scientist Charles O. Jones, noting that over 80 percent of the House members of both parties voted for this bill, concluded, "Here was an unusual case of partisanship at the committee stage, copartisanship leading to cross-partisan support in floor maneuvering, and eventual bipartisan voting."[91] After signing this legislation into law on March 15, 1962, Kennedy praised it as "perhaps the most significant legislation in the area of employment since the historic Employment Act of 1946."[92] More so than any other labor and social welfare legislation passed during the Kennedy administration, the Manpower Development and Training Act (MDTA) exemplified the New Frontier's desire to prepare the nation's labor force for the economic challenges and changes of the 1960s and JFK's 1960 campaign theme of "getting this nation moving again." From August 1962, until December 1964, nearly 5,000 MDTA training projects and almost 300,000 trainees were approved by the Department of Labor.[93] Partially on the advice of LBJ, Kennedy directed the MDTA to focus more job training for unemployed blacks, especially poor, inner-city young black men and teenagers by June 1963. Unlike his failed proposal for a Department of Urban Affairs and Housing and the laundry workers' issue concerning his minimum wage bill, Congress overwhelmingly passed JFK's recommended amendments to the MDTA in 1963. There were no racial conflicts regarding their preferential focus on unemployed and unskilled black youths.[94]

JFK's legislative success with the MDTA and its amendments also taught him a valuable lesson about the relationship between his roles as party leader and chief lawmaker. At the beginning of his presidency, JFK had tried to develop a symbiotic relationship between these two roles in dealing with Democrats in Congress. Lawrence F. O'Brien had estimated that JFK needed the votes of a narrow majority of the ninety-nine southern Democrats in the House to pass major New Frontier bills.[95] O'Brien also expected the White House legislation to receive less Republican support in the 1962 session of Congress than in that of 1961 as the Republicans prepared for the 1962 congressional election.[96] JFK and O'Brien hoped that the early, assiduous cultivation of southern Democrats through the administration's generous treatment of southern agricultural interests, the concentration of ARA projects in the Appalachian regions of southern and border states, and regular breakfast meetings with the most powerful southern Democrats in Congress would gradually develop enough party unity and personal loyalty to JFK so that the administration would need few Republican votes to pass its later, more divisive legislation.[97] The long-term policy goals of the New Frontier generally reflected those of the Democratic national platform of 1960, organized labor, the ADA, and what Burns termed the liberal "presidential wing" of the Democratic Party. The Kennedy–O'Brien strategy assumed that the most liberal Democrats in Congress would feel compelled to faithfully support the administration, no matter how dismayed they may be with JFK's cautious rhetoric on civil rights and constant wooing of southern conservatives.[98]

Instead, the exasperated president through his chief liaison with Congress learned that effective party leadership did not necessarily correlate to effective legislative leadership and vice versa. Each major bill that the White House submitted to Congress often required a different coalition of supporters in each house to ensure its passage. Some bills could only be passed by an aggressively organized, party-line vote while others required a meticulous assemblage of idiosyncratic bipartisan support in both houses.[99]

In the summer of 1962, JFK lamented to Theodore C. Sorensen, "Party loyalty or responsibility means damn little. They've got to take care of themselves first."[100] Even if party loyalty or responsibility had been more valuable in gaining congressional support for his bills, JFK was reluctant to personally ask or pressure members of Congress for their votes. Also, Senate majority leader Mike Mansfield and Speaker of the House John W. McCormack, who succeeded Rayburn at the end of 1961, were less able to mobilize and discipline Democrats in Congress than their predecessors had been.[101]

Mansfield, in sharp contrast to LBJ, intentionally allowed the Senate to operate as a more open, participatory, and egalitarian institution under his leadership. Democratic senators like Edmund S. Muskie, Paul Douglas, Albert Gore, Sr., and William Proxmire had chafed under LBJ's aggressive leadership and rebelled against it by the end of his Senate career. By contrast, they respected and valued Mansfield's deference toward their individualism.[102] In particular, Mansfield allowed more floor debate and greater autonomy to Democratic senators in introducing bills than LBJ had.

Mansfield's leadership style slowed the legislative process in the Senate, provided more time and opportunities for debate and proposed amendments to bills, weakened party discipline, and gave more influence to liberal mavericks like Wayne Morse and Paul Douglas. Preferring the greater legislative productivity and consistent efficiency of the Senate under LBJ's majority leadership, Bobby Baker lamented that Mansfield "failed to develop a close rapport with the White House. Relations between the White House and Capitol Hill, consequently, ranged from the ineffectual to disastrous."[103] The irony, of course, is that Democrats outnumbered Republicans by a two to one ratio in the Eighty-Seventh Congress and gained four seats in the 1962 Senate elections.

Because of Mansfield's passive, reactive leadership style and the impossibility of the vice president serving as a powerful, de facto majority leader, a power vacuum developed for Democratic party leadership in the Senate.[104] JFK usually deferred to McCormack, Albert, and O'Brien on party leadership and legislative matters in the House. But the president felt impelled to more directly and regularly intervene in the Senate in order to gain the necessary number of votes on New Frontier bills.

In particular, JFK solicited the advice and cooperation of Democratic Senator Robert Kerr of Oklahoma, dubbed "the uncrowned King of the Senate" by the media.[105] Besides steering a disproportionate amount of ARA projects and other federal public works funds to Oklahoma, JFK reluctantly omitted any reduction in the oil depletion allowance from his tax reform and tax cut proposals in deference to Kerr's vigilant protection of oil and gas interests.[106] Chairing the Aeronautical and Space Sciences Committee, Kerr ensured that Oklahoma companies received a substantial number of NASA contracts and that James Webb, his oil company's business manager during the 1950s, became NASA's director.[107] However ambivalent JFK was about Kerr's pork barrel uses of the space program, the Oklahoma Democrat successfully promoted JFK's ambitious space program so that NASA's budget doubled from fiscal year 1961 to 1962.[108]

Except for his implacable disagreement with JFK on how to structure and finance medical insurance for the aged, Kerr gradually moderated his economic conservatism. His legislative behavior became more compatible with and occasionally indispensable to the New Frontier's policy agenda.[109] With his seat on the Senate Finance Committee, Kerr managed to counteract the opposition of this committee's chairman, Senator Harry Byrd of Virginia, to JFK's investment tax credit bill and request to raise the debt ceiling of the federal government. Kerr voted with the Kennedy administration 59 percent of the time in 1961 and 74 percent in 1962.[110]

The peak of Kerr's power in managing JFK's legislation in the Senate occurred in the intense controversy surrounding the creation of the Communications Satellite Corporation, commonly known as Comsat.[111] Part of JFK's effort in 1962 to refute charges that his policies were anti-business was his proposal to establish Comsat as a mixed public-private corporation. American Telephone and Telegraph Corporation, whose Telstar satellite recently demonstrated its ability to transmit television pictures across continents, would be a major partner in Comsat. Although Senator John Pastore of Rhode Island was the administration's floor manager for the Comsat bill, Kerr attracted most of the liberal opposition to this bill. Kerr chaired the space committee that conducted extensive hearings on this issue, and an earlier bill that he submitted proposed the entirely private ownership and operation of Comsat. Denouncing Comsat as a monopolisitic "giveaway" to the American Telephone and Telegraph Corporation, Senators Paul Douglas and Wayne Morse led eight other liberal mavericks in a filibuster to defeat this bill. They wanted Comsat to be entirely under government control, either under the authority of the Atomic Energy Commission (AEC) or through the creation of a new separate agency similar to the Tennessee Valley Authority (TVA).[112] Kerr and LBJ helped Mansfield organize enough senators to invoke cloture by a vote of 63 to 27 on August 14, 1962.[113]

It was the first time since 1927 that the Senate invoked cloture to end a filibuster. In the Comsat bill that JFK signed into law, Comsat was a primarily private business since the president could appoint only three of its fifteen directors. Nevertheless, JFK, upon signing the Communications Satellite Act on

August 31, 1962, stated that "world peace and understanding" would be "accomplished though the joint efforts of private individuals and concerns, and agencies of the Federal Government."[114] Douglas was not surprised by Kerr's Machiavellian maneuvering behind the Comsat bill, but he was dismayed and stunned that the normally placid Mansfield resorted to hardball tactics. Douglas wrote in his memoirs, "Mansfield then really applied the gag rule, moving to table without debate every amendment, no matter how sensible. It was like a legislative lynching bee."[115]

Kerr was instrumental in organizing southern Democratic support in Congress for the Trade Expansion Act of 1962. Although, historically, southern Democrats have been most enthusiastic about reducing tariffs and increasing American exports, some southerners feared that an increase in cheap imports would reduce the domestic consumption of some southern agricultural and manufactured goods, especially textiles. Kerr persuaded JFK to accept amendments that made concessions to the American textile industry and domestic oil production.[116] The most controversial element of the Trade Expansion Act was its delegation of discretionary power to the president to make trade agreements. In particular, the act authorized the president for five years to reduce tariff rates by 50 percent, end tariffs on some imports, and retaliate with higher tariffs against other nations if they engaged in unfair trade policies toward the United States.[117]

With Kerr organizing support for this legislation in the Senate Finance Committee, JFK shrewdly advocated this bill as vital to Cold War foreign policy, especially in relations with Common Market nations and Great Britain.[118] In public debate, Kennedy's argument overcame conservative concerns that this bill gave the president excessive lawmaking powers and would increase budget deficits because of anticipated losses in tariff revenue.[119] JFK specifically thanked Kerr for his help in this bill after stating during his October 11, 1962, signing ceremony, that the Trade Expansion Act of 1962 was the most significant international economic legislation since the Marshall Plan because it "marks a decisive point for the future of our economy, for our relations with our friends and allies, and for the prospects of free institutions and free societies everywhere."[120]

Kerr's sudden death on January 1, 1963, doomed any potential for Senate passage of JFK's Medicare and tax cut legislation for the remainder of his presidency.[121] The Oklahoma Democrat's death also had the effect of increasing the power of Senator Everett M. Dirksen of Illinois, the Republican minority leader. Dirksen intentionally modeled his relationship with JFK on LBJ's relationship with Eisenhower as the leader of the opposition party in the Senate.[122] With his mellifluous voice and theatrical oratory, Dirksen had a weakness for presidential flattery and media attention. Like Johnson during Eisenhower's presidency, the Illinois Republican wanted his party to compile a record of both constructive criticism and eclectic support of New Frontier legislation and presidential decisions that he deemed to be in the national interest.[123] Dirksen's centrist pragmatism in dealing with Mansfield and Kennedy contrasted sharply with the more consistently partisan, acerbic conservatism of Representative Charles Halleck of Indiana, a self-identified "gut fighter."[124] Dirksen's cordial rapport with the Democratic president elicited opposition from liberal Republican senators for accepting JFK's delay on civil rights legislation and from conservatives for his support of JFK's bond proposal for bailing out the United Nations.[125]

Nevertheless, Dirksen managed to retain the respect of and influence with both his Republican colleagues and JFK. With only thirty-five Republicans in the Senate during the Eighty-Seventh Congress, Dirksen could organize a cohesive bloc of Republican votes at a crucial point in the legislative process.[126] For example, the Senate majority leader persuaded all but two Republican senators to vote for cloture against the liberal filibuster of JFK's Comsat bill, thereby providing most of the votes for cloture. He also delivered thirteen Republican votes in the Senate for JFK's investment tax credit bill. Most business interest groups initially opposed this bill because they perceived it as an inadequate substitute for accelerated depreciation allowances.[127]

JFK appreciated Dirksen's assistance in assembling bipartisan support in the Senate. Both the president and LBJ refrained from actively campaigning for Sidney Yates, Dirksen's Democratic opponent in his 1962 campaign. Mayor Richard J. Daley of Chicago strongly backed Yates, and Dirksen was vulnerable to defeat in 1962. Kennedy did not want to antagonize Dirksen or contribute to his defeat and risk his replacement as minority leader by a more confrontational, less cooperative Republican. JFK even violated the partisan norms of senatorial courtesy. The president periodically deferred to Dirksen's preferred candidates for federal judgeships and other patronage, thereby exasperating and offending the Democratic senator from Illinois, Paul Douglas.[128]

Although the Democrats gained four seats in the Senate and only lost four seats in the House in the 1962 elections, Kennedy was concerned that the most hawkish southern Democrats and conservative Republicans would coalesce in the Senate to prevent ratification of the Limited Nuclear Test Ban Treaty in 1963.[129] Bipartisan opposition could succeed in denying JFK the necessary two-thirds majority for ratification if the conservatives attracted allies from militantly anti-Communist, nonsouthern liberal Democratic senators like Henry M. "Scoop" Jackson of Washington and Thomas J. Dodd of Connecticut.[130] Dodd decided to vote for ratification.

Jackson remained uncommitted yet implicitly critical of the treaty until he expressed qualified support for ratification of what he termed a "loose commitment" with the Soviet Union and Great Britain rather than an actual treaty. Jackson had previously strained his relations with JFK and Mansfield. The Washington Democrat joined Senate conservatives in almost preventing the creation of the Arms Control and Disarmament Agency in 1961. His widely publicized 1962 speech alleged that JFK's foreign policy was excessively deferential toward the United Nations.[131]

The prospect of a Democratic-Republican coalition in the Senate denying ratification of the treaty evaporated after JFK signed a letter that Dirksen wrote for the president. In the public letter, Kennedy promised to continue to develop nuclear weapons if the treaty were ratified. Dirksen read the letter to the Senate before he eloquently advocated ratification to his colleagues.[132] The Senate voted 81 to 19 to ratify the Limited Nuclear Test Ban Treaty on September 24, 1963. Only eight Republican senators voted against ratification.[133] Ironically, JFK's most notable legislative and foreign policy accomplishment in 1963, an otherwise disappointing and frustrating year for his legislative priorities, depended on the party leadership skills of the Republican Party's leader in the Senate.[134]

In his memoirs, Lawrence F. O'Brien, JFK's chief liaison with Congress on legislation, proudly stated, "Kennedy's legislative record in 1961–63 was the best of any President since Roosevelt's first term."[135] O'Brien further specified, "We had sent Congress fifty-three major bills and we had won passage of thirty-three of them. Those thirty-three bills were, by way of contrast, more than had been passed in the final six years of the Eisenhower administration."[136] Fellow New Frontiersmen Theodore C. Sorensen and Arthur M. Schlesinger, Jr., expressed similar pride in defending the legislative record of JFK's presidency, especially that of the Eighty-Seventh Congress.[137]

The general perception of JFK's contemporary critics and later scholars is that Kennedy's record as chief lawmaker was mediocre and disappointing.[138] In contrast to O'Brien's impressive statistics, the *Congressional Quarterly Almanac* calculated that Congress passed only 27 percent of JFK's legislative proposals in 1963.[139] LBJ usually expressed gratitude and respect for JFK's treatment of him as vice president, but even LBJ later contributed to this negative assessment of JFK's reputation as a legislative leader. By the end of 1965, he increasingly made such comments as, "Kennedy couldn't get the Ten Commandments past Congress" and that JFK had a good legislative program "even if he did not know how to pass it."[140]

The following is a more objective, balanced analysis of JFK's legislative record in domestic policy. Despite the loss of twenty nonsouthern Democratic House seats and JFK's controversial, razor-thin popular vote margin in 1960, JFK was generally successful in submitting and securing passage of economic and social welfare legislation that reflected the New Deal-Fair Deal policy legacy.[141] With these bills, JFK was willing to compromise on specific provisions, deferred to the judgment and advice of veteran congressional leaders, and intended to wait until 1964 to submit a comprehensive civil rights bill to avoid the defeat of this type of legislation because of racial conflicts. Kennedy was most successful in securing the passage of legislation that increased the minimum wage and enlarged its coverage, expanded coverage of Social Security benefits, increased and temporarily extended unemployment compensation, accelerated public works spending, and provided new funds for hospital construction, school construction, and public housing.[142] All of these legislative accomplishments were based on the familiar quantitative liberalism of Roosevelt and Truman. The "pump-priming," anti-recession, New Deal–based, quantitatively liberal policies of social welfare benefits, higher minimum wages, and public works spending were broadly distributed throughout the nation.

In his domestic policy proposals that were more distinctly and unique those of the New Frontier, JFK's record with Congress was mixed. Kennedy submitted and secured passage of the first major act of Congress seeking to improve research, services, treatment, and institutions for mentally ill and mentally retarded Americans.[143] This dimension of the New Frontier's qualitative liberalism wanted to improve the quality of life for specifically targeted population groups often ignored or neglected by previous federal policies. In addition to the Mental Retardation Planning Act of 1963 and the Mental Retardation Facilities and Community Mental Health Centers Act of 1963, the local implementation of the Juvenile Delinquency Act of 1961 was the role model for the development of the Community Action and Model Cities programs of the Great Society.[144]

The Area Redevelopment Act of 1961 concentrated economic resources in chronically poor, isolated areas, especially Appalachia. The Manpower Development and Training Act of 1962 was the first federal law to address the complex problem of structural unemployment as certain industries steadily declined in some states and as other, growing industries needed fewer workers because of automation. In 1963, JFK had this law amended to concentrate more specifically on the educational and job training needs of poor, urban black youths.[145]

Other New Frontier proposals that could be categorized as qualitatively liberal were rejected by Congress. Congress denied JFK's bill to create a Department of Urban Affairs and Housing. Congress also rejected most of the New Frontier's proposed reforms in agricultural programs, especially its plan to impose mandatory supply management controls on feed grains, wheat, and dairy products. The urban affairs bill aroused racial controversies over the presumed nomination of Robert Weaver and the suspicion of southerners that this new department would be used to prohibit racial discrimination in housing. The prospect of supply management controls stimulated vigorous opposition from wealthy commercial farmers, especially the American Farm Bureau.[146]

Much of the unfavorable appraisal of JFK's legislative record is based on the status of four major pieces of legislation at the time of his death in November 1963. Referred to by political scientist Irving Bernstein as the "Big Four," they are JFK's bills for civil rights, federal aid to education, a major cut in income taxes, and Medicare. Partially pressured by the public outcry over the violent reaction of local and state officials and white vigilantes in the South toward peaceful civil rights demonstrators in June 1963 and the anticipated March on Washington rally for civil rights in August 1963, JFK submitted a comprehensive civil rights bill to Congress on June 19, 1963, after his televised address on this issue.[147] JFK and RFK carefully negotiated with leading Democrats and Republicans in Congress, including House Judiciary Committee chairman Emanuel Celler and the ranking Republican on this committee, William McCulloch. The Kennedys wanted to ensure enough votes from both Democrats and Republicans so that the House would pass it by late 1963 or early 1964.[148] On November 20, 1962, two days before JFK's assassination, the House Judiciary Committee voted to send the White House–backed, substitute civil rights bill to the clerk of the House.[149] Most of the criticism of JFK on civil rights is based on the fact that he did not make the submission and passage of his civil rights bill an earlier, higher priority in his presidency and did not secure its enactment by the end of 1963.

Other than appropriations for school construction, JFK's failure to secure passage of his federal aid to education bill can be attributed to the complications of racial and religious divisions over this issue. Kennedy, as the first Catholic president, had repeatedly assured the nation that he was committed to the strict separation of church and state and opposed federal aid to parochial schools.[150] The House Rules Committee, however, included three Catholic Democrats who were determined to have some of the proposed federal aid go to parochial elementary and secondary schools: Thomas P. "Tip" O'Neill, Jr., of Massachusetts, Ray Madden of Indiana, and James Delaney of New York.[151] JFK's original $2.3 billion education bill of 1961 exclusively applied to public schools. It faced opposition from other powerful Catholic Democrats in the House, such as New York congressman John Rooney of the Appropriations Committee and House majority leader John W. McCormack. With the religious issue inflamed by the outspoken opposition of Francis Cardinal Spellman to his bill, JFK reluctantly compromised and agreed to submit supplemental legislation that provided special-purpose loans to parochial schools.[152]

JFK's concession did not satisfy Delaney, who joined Republicans and southern Democrats on the House Rules Committee in rejecting the bill by a vote of eight to seven. But JFK, O'Brien, and Secretary of HEW Abraham Ribicoff persisted in promoting this legislation. It was acceptable to the Senate Labor and Public Welfare Committee. JFK's campaign promises, the ADA, the now defunct DAC's proposals, and the Democratic national platform of 1960 made expanded federal aid to elementary and secondary education a high priority for a Democratic administration. The administration managed to secure a floor vote for its bill despite its rejection by the House Rules Committee. With McCormack still wanting more significant aid to parochial schools and Speaker of the House Sam Rayburn opposing the bill's provision on supplements to teachers' salaries, the House defeated JFK's bill by a vote of 242 to 170 on August 30, 1961.[153] JFK succeeded in achieving congressional approval of the Higher Education Facilities Act of 1963, which included aid to church-affiliated colleges and universities. But he was unable to secure passage of extensive federal aid to elementary and secondary education for the remainder of his presidency.

Unlike the first two proposals of JFK's "Big Four," his legislation to reduce income taxes did not involve any racial or religious conflicts as obstacles. Kennedy did not submit his income tax cut bill to Congress until January 24, 1963. It reduced the number of personal income tax rates from twenty to fourteen and the percentages from a top rate of 91 percent to 65 percent. It also reduced the corporate income tax rate from 52 to 47 percent and gave special tax breaks to small businesses, the elderly, and the disabled. In order to reduce the revenue loss and promote fairness in the tax code, JFK's tax cut bill included minor reforms by restricting itemized deductions and credit allowances. If enacted, his bill would reduce personal and corporate income taxes by more than $13 billion over three years. JFK estimated that during the first year of the tax cut the annual budget deficit would not exceed Eisenhower's $12.8 billion deficit in 1958.[154]

JFK intentionally delayed the submission of this tax cut bill until 1963 for several reasons. First, his economic advisors, namely Walter Heller, Paul Samuelson, C. Douglas Dillon, and John Kenneth Galbraith disagreed about the validity of Keynesian economics and the impact of a tax cut on economic growth and budget deficits.[155] JFK was skeptical about Heller's proposed tax cut and deferred to the more fiscally conservative advice of Dillon, the Secretary of the Treasury and a Republican.[156] The president also wanted to wait and assess the immediate impact of his early policies, such as the investment tax credit and higher public works spending, on economic conditions and the federal budget. Finally, JFK and Heller, the chairman of the Council of Economic Advisers (CEA) and the foremost proponent of an income tax cut, wanted enough time to gradually persuade Wilbur Mills, chairman of the House Ways and Means Committee, to support an income tax cut.

Mills, like other fiscal conservatives from both parties in Congress and in the business community, suspected that a major income tax cut would lead to severe revenue losses, excessive budget deficits, and, eventually, high inflation unless Kennedy first reduced government spending. Mills already opposed JFK's Medicare bill and increasingly perceived the president as a reckless spender. JFK, O'Brien, Heller, budget director Kermit Gordon, and other administration officials gradually and patiently co-opted Mills by convincing him of the long-term benefits of Keynesian economics with only modest deficits. They promised to increase revenue through the closing of some loopholes and other reforms in the tax code and to control future increases in government spending.[157]

Understanding the importance of timing and of his alliance with Mills, JFK deferred to Mills's judgment that there were not enough votes to assure passage in the House until 1963. Mills's management of the tax cut bill minimized southern conservative opposition, so that House members voted strictly along party lines. On September 24, 1963, the House rejected a Republican motion to return the bill to the Ways and Means Committee by a vote of 226 to 199. The Republican motion was supported by 173 of the 174 House Republicans, and only the most fiscally conservative, anti-administration southern Democrats joined them.[158] The House subsequently passed JFK's tax cut bill 271 to 155 with forty-eight Republicans voting for the bill.[159]

After Robert Kerr's death, Senator Russell Long of Louisiana became JFK's chief contact on the Senate Finance Committee for his tax cut legislation. Like Mills, Long also prepared for a future committee vote and then a floor vote on this bill by gradually reducing the opposition of fellow southern Democrats.[160] Long, though, was also faced with the challenge of circumventing and reducing the obstructionistic power of his committee's chairman, Senator Harry Byrd of Virginia. Byrd, unlike Mills, was determined to weaken or kill JFK's bill through lengthy hearings that began on October 15.[161]

Besides Long, Senate Minority Leader Everett M. Dirksen was also a member of the Senate Finance Committee. He was willing to accept an amended tax cut bill in exchange for the elimination of several federal excise taxes.[162] JFK wanted Byrd's committee to vote on his bill by December 1963. A few days before JFK's assassination, however, Mike Mansfield told the Senate that he expected the Senate Finance Committee to report it out after January 1, 1964, and Dirksen estimated the approximate date as March 15, 1964.[163]

More so than JFK's civil rights bill, it is probable that the Senate would have passed his tax cut bill in early 1964 if JFK had remained president. The bipartisan coalition in the Senate Finance Committee led by Long and Dirksen still would have overcome Byrd's opposition. Although Kennedy intended to use the enactment of his tax cut legislation as a major issue in his 1964 reelection campaign, Republican resistance to this bill for partisan, electoral motives withered. Nearly one-third of the House Republicans defied Halleck's party leadership in voting for it, and the Senate minority leader was instrumental in reducing opposition among his Republican colleagues. The Senate passed the tax cut bill on January 30, 1964, by a vote of 77 to 21, and LBJ signed it into law on February 26, 1964.[164]

Medicare, the last of the New Frontier's "Big Four" legislation, involved a strict division along both partisan and ideological lines, a complex variety of counter proposals, and the opposition of one especially powerful, sophisticated interest group, the American Medical Association (AMA). JFK, as a congressman with a mostly working-class, urban constituency, passively supported the Fair Deal's proposal for compulsory, universal national health insurance as part of the Social Security system. The AMA, the bipartisan conservative coalition in the Democratic-controlled Eighty-First Congress, and private insurance companies, especially Blue Cross and Blue Shield, combined to quickly and easily defeat Truman's legislation.[165]

Wilbur Cohen, an economist who specialized in social welfare benefits, had worked on this issue during the Roosevelt and Truman administrations as an official of the Social Security system. During the Eisenhower administration, he concluded that there was enough public support for medical insurance for retired Americans similar to the old-age pensions of the Social Security system. As FDR had assumed with Social Security, Cohen believed that a federal program of medical insurance for the aged would most likely be accepted by most Americans if it were perceived as a legitimate entitlement that covered all retirees who contributed to its financing during their working years through payroll taxes.[166] By contrast, if such a federal program only covered the poorest elderly Americans and was financed from the general treasury instead of a separate trust fund, most Americans would regard it as charity. Most retirees struggling to meet high medical expenses on fixed incomes would receive no benefits.[167]

Representative Aime Forand, a Democrat from Rhode Island, submitted a bill in 1958 that proposed limited hospital and surgical insurance for all of the aged receiving Social Security pensions, regardless of their incomes, and would be financed by increased Social Security payroll taxes. JFK cosponsored a similar bill with Senator Clinton Anderson of New Mexico during his presidential campaign and the post-convention special session of Congress.[168]

The AMA originally opposed but later supported the Kerr-Mills Act of 1960. This law provided funds to the states from the general treasury and served as a welfare program for the poorest elderly by covering most of their medical needs. Although Congress had rejected the Forand bill, Kerr, Mills, the AMA, private health insurance companies, and most business interest groups concluded that the Kerr-Mills Act would prevent the emergence of a more politically potent version of the Forand bill in the future.

With the AFL-CIO and the Democratic national platform committed to Medicare for all retirees covered by Social Security, JFK submitted a bill to Congress on February 9, 1961. Kennedy's bill was similar to the Forand bill, but it omitted coverage of surgical expenses and included nursing home care. Portraying his bill as a reasonable amendment to the Social Security system, JFK concluded, "This program is not a program of socialized medicine. It is a program of pre-payment of health costs with absolute freedom of choice guaranteed. Every person will choose his own doctor and hospital."[169]

JFK's Medicare bill was cosponsored by Representative Cecil King of California and Senator Clinton Anderson of New Mexico. King and Anderson were Democrats who respectively served on the House Ways and Means Committee and the Senate Finance Committee.[170] Kerr and Mills, however, were inflexibly opposed to the King-Anderson bill. Senate Finance Committee chairman Harry Byrd was even more militantly opposed to Medicare than Kerr and Mills. Having assiduously co-opted Kerr and Mills for his tax cut legislation, JFK did not want to exert too much pressure on their committees prematurely.[171]

Instead, the Kennedy administration and the AFL-CIO decided to generate favorable public opinion toward Medicare as a means to soften congressional opposition and as a prelude to the White House and organized labor lobbying Congress.[172] Among the administration's officials, Secretary of HEW Abraham Ribicoff, Wilbur Cohen, now an assistant secretary of HEW, and Secretary of Commerce Luther Hodges conducted public hearings, addressed pro-Medicare rallies organized by the AFL-CIO and local Democratic politicians, and debated Medicare opponents on television and radio programs.[173]

With his Medicare legislation stalled in Congress, JFK personally involved himself in this public relations campaign by addressing a televised pro-Medicare rally in Madison Square Garden on May 20, 1962.[174] AFL-CIO officials who helped to organize this rally were disappointed by JFK's rushed delivery of his speech. Unfortunately for JFK, Edward R. Annis, a leading AMA spokesman, delivered a well-received, rousing speech after the pro-Medicare rally that further underscored JFK's poor performance.[175]

In contrast to JFK, the AFL-CIO, and other advocates of the King-Anderson bill, the AMA and its allies, such as the U.S. Chamber of Commerce and the American Farm Bureau, conducted a well-financed campaign of advertising, mass mailings, public information meetings, lobbying, and campaign contributions for the 1962 and 1964 election to prevent the passage of Medicare.

JFK was determined to keep Medicare alive as a campaign issue for nonsouthern Democratic candidates in the 1962 congressional elections. Although Mills was becoming more compromising on the content of a Medicare bill, it still had little chance of being favorably reported out of his committee for a floor vote.[176] Instead, JFK decided to circumvent both the House Ways and Means Committee and the Senate Finance Committee. He had his Medicare proposal added as a rider to a public welfare bill that the House already passed and was being considered by the Senate in July 1962.

Senator Robert Kerr of Oklahoma, however, orchestrated the defeat of this amended bill by a vote of 52 to 48 on July 17, 1962.[177] Kerr had gained the previously undecided vote of Senator William Jennings Randolph of West Virginia, usually a pro-administration liberal. Kerr had promised Randolph extra funds for public works and welfare for Randolph's impoverished state in exchange for his vote against this amended bill.[178] Since Randolph had rejected JFK's personal appeal for his vote, the president retaliated by canceling a public works project for West Virginia.[179]

JFK subsequently dropped the Medicare issue in dealing with Congress until the end of his presidency. In October 1963, JFK traveled to Arkansas to dedicate a dam and deliver a speech at the Arkansas state fairgrounds.[180] While there, the president conferred with Mills about the status of the King-Anderson bill in the House Ways and Means Committee. JFK learned that Mills was willing to support the Medicare bill if it had a more flexible tax and revenue

formula. Henry Hall Wilson, O'Brien's top aide for lobbying the House, negotiated with Mills on an acceptable formula. Wilson and Mills agreed to a financing
method on November 22, 1963, the day that JFK was assassinated.[181]

Of the "Big Four," the tax cut and civil rights bills were enacted in 1964,
and the education and Medicare bills became law in 1965. Since all of the "Big
Four" were not enacted during JFK's presidency, his critics often cite this fact as
proof that he had, at best, a mediocre legislative record.[182] JFK's allegedly poor
performance in pursuing the New Frontier's domestic policy agenda in general
and the "Big Four" in particular has been variously attributed to his ineptitude,
insincerity, or indifference.[183]

It is impossible, of course, to ascertain that all of the "Big Four" definitely
would have been enacted if JFK had lived and been reelected in 1964. LBJ
certainly had more experience and proven skills as a legislative leader when he
assumed the presidency than JFK did at the beginning of his presidency. Johnson,
however, had several advantages in securing congressional passage of the "Big
Four" that JFK lacked. The Texas Democrat received greater deference from
Congress, the media, and the public during the period of shock and mourning
following Kennedy's assassination. LBJ's landslide election margin in 1964, disarray within the Republican Party because of the controversial presidential candidacy of Senator Barry Goldwater of Arizona, a more prosperous economy than
that of 1960, and a Democratic gain of thirty-eight seats in the House in 1964
facilitated the enactment of the "Big Four" and the transition from the New
Frontier to the more activist, challenging policy agenda of the Great Society.[184]

Overall, JFK's performance as chief lawmaker in domestic policy and as a
party leader in his relationship with Congress can be rated as modestly successful. Kennedy understood the need to establish his credibility as an effective
legislative leader by initially submitting social welfare, economic, and public
works legislation that were familiar and acceptable to virtually all Democrats in
Congress, especially the southern conservatives who dominated the House committees.[185] After JFK established this initial New Frontier legislation within the
policy and party legacy of the New Deal and Fair Deal, he then tried to use these
more cohesive Democratic majorities in Congress to pass the New Frontier's
more unique, innovative proposals, such as the Manpower Development and
Training Act (MDTA) and agricultural reforms, with mixed results.[186]

JFK steadily improved his ability to develop and lead bipartisan coalitions.
He cultivated a mutually beneficial relationship with Senator Everett M. Dirksen
in order to secure favorable Senate action on such legislation as the Comsat, civil
rights, and tax cut bills.[187] Neil MacNeil, chief congressional correspondent for
Time, concluded, "Kennedy so enhanced the role of the President in the legislative process that he had become within a year of taking office not merely the
Chief Legislator of the United States, as Wilson and Franklin Roosevelt had
been, but also, in effect, the Chief Lobbyist for his legislative program."[188]

Like Truman, JFK learned to his chagrin that high poll ratings and widespread, bipartisan congressional, public, and media support for his foreign policy decisions often had little or no influence on the progress of his domestic policy agenda in Congress. Gallup polls conducted in early February and early March of 1961 showed JFK's job approval rating at 72 percent.[189] A Gallup poll conducted shortly after JFK publicly accepted responsibility for the disastrous Bay of Pigs invasion showed that his job approval rating had increased to 83 percent.[190] Except in the South after he submitted his civil rights bill in 1963, JFK generally received fairly high, stable job approval ratings ranging from 70 to 75 percent throughout his presidency. A Gallup poll released on December 5, 1962, measured JFK's job approval rating at 74 percent. It was conducted shortly after Kennedy had resolved the Cuban missile crisis and the Democrats had lost only four House seats and gained four Senate seats in the midterm elections. Later studies indicated that the widespread public support for JFK's leadership and decisions during the Cuban missile crisis had little or no influence on Democratic electoral success in 1962.[191]

Likewise, JFK was pleasantly surprised by the wide margin in which the Senate ratified the Limited Nuclear Test Ban Treaty of 1963. The Senate ratified it in the autumn of 1963, a period that journalists Rowland Evans and Robert Novak characterized as "the worst congressional revolt since the days of Harry Truman, resulting in an atrophy of the New Frontier's legislative dreams."[192] This clear, consist contrast between the extent of public and congressional support for JFK's foreign and defense policies and that for his domestic policies was often true of Truman and other presidents. According to political scientist Aaron Wildavsky, this phenomenon occurs because there are, in effect, "two presidencies": one for domestic affairs and the other for foreign and defense policies.[193] With presidential power much more discretionary, exclusive, and immediate in foreign and defense matters, especially during international crises, "it takes a great deal to convince congressmen not to follow the President's lead."[194]

Shortly after becoming president, LBJ consulted Lawrence F. O'Brien, Theodore C. Sorensen, and other administration officials about the current status of JFK's pending legislation, especially the "Big Four."[195] On November 27, 1963, Johnson, in his first presidential address to Congress, urged Congress to pass JFK's civil rights bill in order to "eloquently honor President Kennedy's memory" as well as pass the tax cut bill since "no act of ours could more fittingly continue the work of President Kennedy than the early passage of the tax bill for which he fought this long year."[196] In his January 8, 1964, State of the Union address, LBJ again emphasized the passage of civil rights and tax cut legislation as the top legislative priorities of the transition from the Kennedy to Johnson presidencies. He relegated the Medicare and education bills, with their more complex, intractable provisions and issues, to more obscure places in his speech.[197]

More reflectively, LBJ stated in his memoirs, "Rightly or wrongly, I felt from the very first day in office that I had to carry on for President Kennedy,

I considered myself the caretaker of both his people and his policies . . . I never lost sight of the fact that I was the trustee and custodian of the Kennedy administration."[198] Some of JFK's top aides, namely, Theodore C. Sorensen, were already concerned about Johnson's sincerity in continuing and fulfilling the rest of JFK's domestic policy agenda. In particular, Sorensen and other New Frontiersmen wondered if LBJ's request for budget cuts portended a more conservative approach to domestic spending than what Kennedy intended.[199]

LBJ's determination to reduce JFK's last budget proposal so that it would be less than $100 billion was actually a tactical maneuver to assure favorable congressional action, especially in the Senate Finance Committee, on the tax cut bill. After the death of Robert Kerr, Harry Byrd, the chairman of this committee, had even greater potential to stall or kill JFK's tax cut bill. As vice president, LBJ had privately advised JFK to reduce his budget bill for the next fiscal year in order to weaken Byrd's opposition to the tax cut.[200] LBJ also believed that if the president first achieved enactment of his tax cut bill then it was more likely that Congress would pass his civil rights bill.[201]

Upon becoming president, LBJ's legislative strategy in domestic policy was not one of cautious centrism or a sabotage of New Frontier liberalism. Rather, LBJ recognized the need to establish the political legitimacy of his presidency with the nation in general and Congress in particular following JFK's assassination. The new president also understood that the development of his political legitimacy depended not only on the continuity of his policy agenda with JFK's but also on proving his effectiveness with Congress in achieving enactment of JFK's remaining bills, especially the "Big Four."[202]

One of LBJ's tactics in promoting his effectiveness in policymaking was to appeal to Congress's institutional interest in proving to the American public that it could unite and cooperate in enacting major legislation to benefit the nation and respect the memory of JFK.[203] In telephone conversations with Senate Minority Leader Everett M. Dirksen and Republican Congressman Gerald R. Ford of Michigan, LBJ referred to James MacGregor Burns's theory of "four-party politics" in which the liberal Democratic "presidential party" was often frustrated in its legislative efforts with the often obstructionistic, conservative Democratic "congressional party."[204] Unlike Burns, with his preference for strong, disciplined party leadership in which each of the two major parties is distinct and unified in its ideology and policy agenda, LBJ emphasized the need to develop a suprapartisan consensus. For LBJ, the two parties within Congress and the president and Congress as separate branches should agree on broad national policy goals and then productively negotiate and compromise their differences for accomplishing these objectives for the national interest.

In his November 29, 1963, conversation with Dirksen, who also served on the Senate Finance Committee, LBJ underscored the importance of proving Burns and other critics of Congress wrong by getting the tax bill out of Byrd's committee and passed. The president flattered Dirksen and appealed to his patriotism and partisan self-interest. If the tax cut bill is passed, LBJ assured Dirksen that the voters will reward Republicans, "And you'd probably pick up a bunch of Senate seats because you're running the Senate like I ran it, you being pretty patriotic."[205] Ironically, LBJ called Dirksen immediately after calling Speaker of the House John W. McCormack and Democratic Representative Otto Passman of Louisiana and appealed to their patriotism and partisan self-interest.[206] Two hours later, LBJ called Gerald R. Ford and commented, "I was getting ready to tell MacGregor Burns he's right about the Congress—they couldn't function."[207]

After LBJ conducted a highly publicized campaign to reduce government spending by rooting out budgetary waste and excessive staff in federal agencies, he submitted a $97.9 billion budget to Congress on January 21, 1964. LBJ's budget cuts dissuaded Byrd from actively organizing a majority vote on his committee against the tax cut bill. Although Byrd still voted against this bill, the Senate Finance Committee voted for it twelve to five on January 23, 1964. The Senate passed it on February 7 by a vote of 77 to 21, and LBJ signed the House-Senate conference bill on the $11.5 billion tax cut on February 26, 1964.[208] In his televised remarks at the bill signing ceremony, Johnson concluded, "With your help and the help of this legislation let us unite, let us close ranks, and let us continue to build a nation whose strength lies in our program for prosperity and our passion for peace."[209]

On the issue of JFK's civil rights bill, LBJ's strategic perspective had changed from that of cautious gradualism as vice president to that of bold leadership as president. JFK had appointed LBJ chairman of the Committee on Equal Employment Opportunity. Within this capacity, LBJ hoped to improve economic and educational opportunities for blacks by persuading and cooperating with business, education, and civil rights leaders. In leading Senate passage of the 1957 and 1960 civil rights acts, LBJ realized that if these laws exclusively focused on voting rights, however weak and inadequate their provisions, then only the most unyielding anti-civil rights southern Democrats and the most extreme conservative ideologues among the Republicans would oppose them.[210] The Civil Rights Act of 1957 was the first civil rights legislation to be enacted since 1875, so LBJ perceived it as an important legal and historical precedent for eventually enacting more comprehensive, effective civil rights laws that pertained to other facets of racial discrimination.[211]

During the last few months of the Kennedy presidency, LBJ was pessimistic about the prospect of JFK's civil rights bill being passed during the 1963 to 1964 legislative sessions. In particular, the bill's provisions on the prohibition of discrimination in public accommodations (e.g., restaurants, hotels, and movie theaters) and in both public and private employment threatened to arouse greater opposition from the more racially moderate southern Democrats and the most economically conservative Republicans in Congress. In a phone conversation with Theodore C. Sorensen, Johnson told Sorensen to "get the Republicans in on this thing."[212] LBJ was especially concerned that, without early, reliable support from Republican leaders like Dirksen and Halleck, the more partisan, conservative Republicans could exploit the failure of Kennedy's civil rights bill as a divisive, partisan issue in the 1964 elections.[213]

Actually, the hopeful omen that the civil rights bill would not die in the House occurred three weeks before the assassination when House Minority Leader Charles Halleck agreed to accept JFK's bill and work for its passage.[214] Shortly after returning to Washington from Dallas, LBJ reaffirmed Halleck's civil rights pledge over breakfast. LBJ's next break on the civil rights bill in the House occurred when Representative Clarence Brown of Ohio, the ranking Republican on the House Rules Committee, pressured Howard Smith, the committee's anti-civil rights chairman, to begin hearings on H.R. 7152, the White House civil rights bill, on January 9, 1964.[215] After conducting open hearings, the House Rules Committee voted eleven to four, with Smith in dissent, on January 30 to send H.R. 7152 to the House floor.

With a growing bipartisan momentum favoring this bill's passage, LBJ made it clear to civil rights leaders and to Democrats and Republicans in both houses of Congress that he would not agree to amendments that would weaken the civil rights bill, especially its provisions on public accommodations and job discrimination.[216] He gave a leading, prominent role to Attorney General RFK in lobbying Congress for the bill. Journalist Robert Mann later commented, "In many respects, Johnson had become the most unlikely proponent of a no-compromise strategy. After all, striking legislative bargains had been his stock in trade, the primary coin of his realm."[217]

The bipartisan cooperation of Emanuel Celler and William McCulloch, the respective chairman and ranking Republican of the House Judiciary Committee, guided the House floor debate and helped to defeat weakening amendments proposed by southern Democrats and the most conservative Republicans.[218] After less than two weeks of floor debate, the House voted 290 to 130 on February 10, 1064 to pass H.R. 7152, a civil rights bill even broader than JFK's original bill. The 130 opponents included 86 southern Democrats and 10 southern Republicans.[219]

During the evening of February 10, LBJ made phone calls praising John McCormack, Emanuel Celler, and other House members crucial to this victory.[220] He then called the attorney general. The president told RFK to consult Senate Majority Leader Mike Mansfield and White House Congressional liaison Lawrence F. O'Brien about the best legislative strategy for assuring quick passage in the Senate. In particular, LBJ told RFK, "I really think they ought to put it on the calendar and take it up the first day they can," before voting on the tax cut bill in order to attract interest group pressure from businesses in favor of the civil rights bill.[221] The president also wanted to avoid having the bill stalled or severely amended by the Senate Judiciary Committee. Its chairman, Senator James Eastland of Mississippi, was an implacable segregationist.[222]

Following the passage of the tax cut bill, Mansfield wanted to bypass Eastland's committee by bringing H.R. 7152 directly to the Senate floor. Not only southern Democrats but also several nonsouthern Democrats led by Wayne Morse of Oregon and several Republicans led by Everett M. Dirksen opposed Mansfield's motion for violating regular Senate committee procedures. The Senate passed Mansfield's motion 54 to 37, but there was still the danger of a successful southern filibuster.[223]

Mansfield and Senate Majority Whip Hubert H. Humphrey, the floor leader for H.R. 7152, needed the assurance of Dirksen that he could deliver enough Republican votes to invoke cloture against a southern filibuster. To obtain Dirksen's cooperation, Mansfield and Humphrey agreed to a few minor changes in the bill, namely, the inclusion of state and local authorities in reviewing civil rights grievances from Title II (Public Accommodations) and Title VII (Equal Employment Opportunity).[224] In response to a mandatory jury trial amendment proposed by Senator Herman Talmadge of Georgia, Mansfield and Dirksen proposed a substitute amendment that gave federal judges the discretion to decide if a person charged with criminal contempt should receive a jury trial.

On April 29, five days after the Senate adopted the Mansfield-Dirksen substitute, LBJ called Mansfield. Despite his long, mutually beneficial friendship with Dirksen, LBJ suspected that Dirksen might not be sincerely committed to the passage of a strong civil rights bill. Mansfield expressed his reluctance and ambivalence about making concessions to Dirksen. The Montana Democrat stated, "But we've got those twenty-three to twenty-five votes" from Republicans in order to ensure cloture.[225]

During the longest Senate debate in history, LBJ remained firm in his decision not to bargain with Dirksen or with Richard Russell and the other southern Democrats. He deferred these tactical decisions to Mansfield and Humphrey. The president and the two Democratic senators were confident that, if they appealed to Dirksen's patriotism, sense of history, and pride in his party's Lincolnian heritage, then he would provide enough votes for cloture.[226]

In a June 10, 1964, phone conversation, Humphrey informed LBJ that there were at least sixty-eight senators committed to cloture, one more than necessary. Of those sixty-eight, Humphrey estimated that twenty-six were Republican even though, "Dirksen tells me he's got twenty-eight votes, but I don't think he has. I think he's got twenty-six."[227]

Actually, Dirksen delivered twenty-seven Republican votes when the Senate voted 71 to 29 for cloture on June 10.[228] The most prominent Republican senator who voted against cloture was Barry Goldwater of Arizona, the presumptive Republican nominee for president. Mansfield and Humphrey intentionally waited until after the June 2 Republican presidential primary in California to seek a vote on cloture in order to persuade pro-Goldwater Republicans to vote for it.[229] On June 19, the Senate passed the civil rights bill as amended by Dirksen and Mansfield by a vote of 73 to 27. The Democratic and Republican party leaders of the House and Emanuel Celler and William McCulloch on the House Judiciary Committee readily agreed to accept the Senate-passed bill by foregoing conference committee deliberations.[230] On July 2, 1964, the House voted 289 to 126 to concur in the Senate amendments to H.R. 7152.[231] Of the ninety-one House Democrats who voted against the bill, eighty-eight were from the South. The only Democratic congressman from the Deep South who voted for the bill was Charles Weltner of Georgia. Representing an Atlanta-based district, Weltner stated, "We must not remain forever bound to another lost cause."[232]

With the civil rights bill ready to be signed by the afternoon of July 2, LBJ understood that the uniquely suprapartisan, historical, and moral significance of the civil rights bill required appropriate timing. Congress would soon recess for the Fourth of July and the Republican national convention would begin on July 13 in San Francisco. LBJ was not sure if he should hastily organize a bill-signing ceremony for the evening of Thursday, July 2, sign it on July 4 in order to highlight its historical importance, or wait until later in the summer.

The president called several people including RFK, Roy Wilkins of the NAACP, and White House press secretary George Reedy to consult them about the best day for signing the bill. The attorney general was concerned about the immediate problems of enforcing the civil rights law. RFK told LBJ that if the bill were enacted at the beginning of the Fourth of July weekend, "with Negroes running all over the South figuring that they got the day off, that they'll go into every hotel and motel, and every restaurant" and suggested that the president postpone the signing of the bill until Monday, July 6. LBJ listened patiently but reminded RFK that the signing ceremony needed to be scheduled soon enough so that Dirksen, Halleck, McCulloch, and other pro-civil rights Republicans could attend.

In his subsequent conversations with Reedy, LBJ told Reedy that the television and radio network executives were "selfish bastards" for being reluctant to provide live coverage of the ceremony during prime time.[233] Despite his evasiveness with RFK, Johnson told Reedy that he decided to sign the bill that evening after the White House got the bill from Congress. Reedy informed LBJ that Lawrence F. O'Brien "is fairly sanguine" about the bill being ready by 3 P.M. Reedy agreed that LBJ should sign the bill that evening or else signing it the following week would appear to be "a big public relations ploy. Actually, it will be, of course, but it won't look like it this way."[234]

Reedy was able to arrange for a live network broadcast of the signing ceremony for the civil rights bill at 6:45 P.M. eastern time on July 2, 1964, a little earlier than LBJ preferred. The White House managed to invite a wide range of civil rights supporters on short notice, including Dirksen, Halleck, AFL-CIO president George Meany, Martin Luther King, Jr., and Whitney Young of the National Urban League. Before signing the bill and distributing seventy-one pens to his invited guests, LBJ praised "our late and beloved President John F. Kennedy," "the bipartisan support" of Congress, and "the thoughtful support of tens of thousands of civil and religious leaders in all parts of this Nation." Appealing to the humanitarian, civic spirit of Americans, LBJ characterized the Civil Rights Act of 1964 as "a challenge to all of us to go work in our communities and our States, in our homes and in our hearts, to eliminate the last vestiges of injustice in our beloved country."[235]

The remaining two legislative goals of the "Big Four," federal aid to elementary and secondary education and Medicare, were not enacted until 1965. The fact that LBJ could not sign this legislation until 1965 reflected the change in the nation's political environment since the summer of 1964.[236] As a consequence of the 1964 presidential and congressional elections, LBJ was able to redefine the nation's political center to the left of where it had been during the first few months of his presidency. Besides receiving more than 60 percent of the popular votes, Johnson rarely mentioned partisanship in his campaign speeches. LBJ portrayed Republican presidential nominee Barry Goldwater as a dangerous extremist whose domestic policy positions, such as his opposition to the Civil Rights Act of 1964, made him oblivious and even hostile to the nation's policy needs.[237] Moderate and liberal Republicans in Congress, especially those from the Northeast, were either aloof from Goldwater's campaign or publicly denounced his candidacy. The House elections of 1964 included a Democratic gain of thirty-eight seats, the defeat of most of the northern Republicans who voted against the Civil Rights Act of 1964, and the replacement of seven conservative Democrats from Alabama, Mississippi, and Georgia with freshman Republicans, thereby reducing bipartisan conservative power in key committees.[238]

LBJ tried to publicly and gradually develop a suprapartisan, unifying consensus that favored liberal legislation as early as March 15, 1964. During a televised interview with several journalists, LBJ told Eric Sevareid that he had not thought of a slogan for his policy agenda, such as the New Deal or New Frontier, but he did suggest the "Better Deal."[239] In his State of the Union message of January 8, LBJ referred to his anti-poverty proposals as the "war on poverty," a more inspiring phrase whose words expressed the quality of life that his policies sought for all Americans, not only the poor. Eric Goldman, a Princeton University historian and special consultant to the president, suggested to Richard Goodwin, a speechwriter for LBJ, the words Great Society. Goldman recalled the title of columnist Walter Lippmann's book, *The Good Society*. In this 1937 book, Lippmann had referred to the influence of a book entitled *The Great Society*, written by Graham Wallas, a British socialist, and published in 1914. Despite its socialist origins, the "great society" was also an expression used by publishing magnate Henry R. Luce in a 1939 speech to the Economic Club of Detroit.[240]

Similar in tone and theme to FDR's Commonwealth Club address of 1932, Luce urged his fellow businessmen to assume greater social responsibilities and "take part in the creation of the Great Society."[241]

This concept of the Great Society appealed to LBJ's unusual combination of characteristics. He was a multimillionaire businessman, a Texas senator who effectively served the interests of oil and gas companies, and a New Dealer with family roots in hill-country populism. As a Democratic politician and party leader, he disliked the use of divisive, anti-business, class conflict rhetoric by labor leaders and some northern, urban Democrats.[242] He wanted to involve business leaders as active participants in the Great Society. The Democratic president wanted mostly Republican business executives to rise above partisan, ideological differences and join him in not only reducing poverty and unemployment among the poorest Americans in a mostly affluent nation but also in improving the quality of life for the entire nation in such areas as education, culture, environmental protection, and race relations.

He expressed these beliefs in an April 27, 1964, speech to the U.S. Chamber of Commerce. LBJ warned these business leaders that if they did not participate in building "a great society for tomorrow," then "what you have and what you own and what you hope to acquire is not secure when there are men that are idle in their homes and there are young people that are adrift in the streets, and when there are thousands that are out of school and millions that are out of work, and the aged are lying embittered in their beds."[243]

In a less ominous tone, LBJ made his most famous articulation of the Great Society at the University of Michigan on May 22, 1964. In particular, Johnson wanted to develop a consensus for the Great Society among college students and the suburban middle class. In this address, LBJ provided the most succinct yet revealing definition of the Great Society. "The Great Society is a place where every child can find knowledge to enrich his mind and to enlarge his talents. It is a place where leisure is a welcome chance to build and reflect, not a feared cause of boredom and restlessness. It is a place where the city of man serves not only the needs of the body and the demands of commerce but the desire for beauty and the hunger for community."[244]

It is not merely a coincidence that LBJ's most notable speech about the Great Society was made at a major university. For LBJ, expanding, improving, and redefining the federal government's role in education was a top priority. The Higher Education Facilities Act of 1963 was one of the first bills that LBJ signed as president on December 16, 1963.[245] JFK's bill that was enacted after his death concentrated on federal aid to colleges and universities, including church-affiliated institutions, for the construction of libraries, classroom buildings, and other academic facilities. Compromises over the bill's content and purpose made public community colleges and postsecondary technical institutes eligible for this aid and excluded college scholarships and any aid to elementary and secondary education.

Despite the demographic and financial demands on all levels of education because of the baby boom, LBJ wanted the federal role in education to extend beyond providing more funds for school construction. As an integral part of the Great Society's consensus-building philosophy and policy agenda, education represented more than universal literacy and job training.[246] For LBJ, improving the quality and variety of access to education at all levels, ranging from the Head Start programs for underprivileged preschool children to a sharp increase in graduate school enrollment and night school opportunities for adults in the full-time labor force, served as the primary means for developing a future American society that would not only have less poverty, illiteracy, and racial discrimination but also a more vibrant, participatory, and enlightened cultural and intellectual environment.[247] Although JFK had submitted proposals for college scholarships and federal funds to supplement public school teachers' salaries, Congress rejected these provisions.

LBJ had a political asset on this issue that JFK lacked. As a southern Protestant, LBJ could bargain with Catholic congressmen, clergy, and lobbyists from the National Catholic Welfare Council (NCWC). LBJ could gain their support in a way that JFK as the first Catholic president could not. Title IV of the Civil Rights Act of 1964 authorized the U.S. Office of Education, upon the request of local school boards, to assist in the planning or implementation of racial desegregation policies, and Title VI prohibited racial discrimination in the conduct of federally financed programs.[248] These provisions made Representative Adam Clayton Powell, Jr., chairman of the House Education and Labor Committee, less insistent on attaching uncompromisable desegregation amendments to an education bill and made southern Democrats more fatalistic about and less resistant to an education bill that might eventually be used to implement desegregation.[249] LBJ could confidently assume that all or most of the fifty-six nonsouthern freshmen Democrats in the House would vote for an elementary and secondary education bill if it survived the committee system and went to the floor for a vote.[250]

Ironically, the greatest challenges to LBJ's education bill, officially numbered H.R. 2362 and sponsored by Representative Carl Perkins of Kentucky in the House and by Senator Wayne Morse of Oregon in the Senate, came from nonsouthern, white liberal Democrats like Representative Edith Green of Oregon. Green was an especially influential member of the House Education and Labor Committee and reflected the policy interests of the National Education Association (NEA), an increasingly powerful union and lobby for public school teachers. Green wanted to ensure adequate local control of the use of these federal funds and that the mostly Catholic parochial schools would not financially and unconstitutionally benefit from this bill.[251] Green and other Democrats in Congress also wanted to ensure that the federal aid formula in this bill provide enough funds for nonsouthern urban and suburban public school districts with higher educational costs.[252]

Anticipating Green's criticism of these details, Wilbur Cohen, an assistant secretary of HEW and a member of LBJ's education task force, included the "child benefit" theory in H.R. 2362. In the *Cochran* decision of 1930 and *Everson* decision of 1947, the Supreme Court respectively upheld a Louisiana law that provided free textbooks to both public and parochial school students and a New Jersey law that subsidized the transportation of both public and parochial school students. Under the administration-backed bill cosponsored by Perkins and Morse, federal funds would not be directly given to nonpublic schools or used by parents to pay for tuition at nonpublic schools.

In preparing the bill, Lawrence F. O'Brien and LBJ's task force on education worked closely with Hugh Carey. Carey was a New York Democratic congressman who served on the House Education and Labor Committee. The White House, other members of this committee, and his fellow Catholic Democrats in the House generally deferred to him to ensure provisions that satisfied parochial school interests and were constitutionally and politically acceptable. Carey ensured that H.R. 2362 made parochial school students, especially those from poor families, eligible for the same special educational services, such as tutoring in reading, that public school students received under this bill. At Carey's suggestion, LBJ's bill was also amended so that any textbooks that public schools bought with these federal funds could be loaned, but not given, to parochial school students.[253] During the House Education and Labor Committee hearings, Carey and Perkins had to assure both Democratic and Republican critics that public school districts could only send public school teachers into parochial schools to provide federally aided special education and not general education. In an amendment proposed by Representative Frank Thompson of New Jersey, each public school district could define the distinction between special and general education.[254]

H.R. 2362 focused on providing compensatory education to children from low-income families in order to improve their academic performance. But the federal aid formula in this bill was partially designed for the purpose of satisfying the constituency interests of representatives and senators from states with higher living costs and higher levels of per pupil state and local spending on public education.[255] With these compromises, the House passed H.R. 2362 on March 26, 1965, by a vote of 263 to 153. Approximately 98 percent of the nonsouthern Democrats, 43 percent of the southern Democrats, and 27 percent of the Republicans in the House voted for H.R. 2362.[256]

Chairing the Senate Labor and Public Welfare Committee's subcommittee on labor, Wayne Morse had agreed not to add any amendments to H.R. 2362, named S. 600 in the Senate, to avoid weakening or killing the bill. Among the ten members of this subcommittee, the most critical questions and the only potentially divisive amendments during the hearings came from Democratic Senators Robert F. Kennedy (RFK) of New York and Edward M. Kennedy

(EMK) of Massachusetts. RFK aggressively questioned Francis Keppel, the U.S. Commissioner of Education, about the vague wording of the Perkins-Morse bill and expressed skepticism about the broad discretion given to local public school authorities.[257] EMK proposed an amendment to the bill that would create a Teacher Corps for recent college graduates. It was similar in purpose and philosophy to the Peace Corps.[258] The House had excluded a Teacher Corps from H.R. 2362 because of opposition from the NEA and others. Nevertheless, Morse's subcommittee unanimously approved the Perkins-Morse bill with no new amendments.[259]

The Senate Labor and Public Welfare Committee generally deferred to Morse's subcommittee and unanimously passed H.R. 2362. The full Senate passed H.R. 2362 on April 9, 1965, by a vote of 73 to 18. All but four Democrats and most Republicans voted for it.[260]

In one of LBJ's most picturesque bill signing ceremonies, LBJ traveled to Johnson City, Texas, in order to sign this bill, formally named the Elementary and Secondary Education Act (ESEA) of 1965, on Palm Sunday, April 11, 1965. Accompanied by Kate Deadrich Loney, the first teacher who taught him, Johnson signed the bill at the elementary school that he attended. The president stated that the ESEA "represents a major new commitment of the Federal Government to quality and equality in the schooling that we offer our young people. I predict that all of those of both parties of Congress who supported the enactment of this legislation will be remembered in history as men and women who began a new day of greatness in American society."[261]

Medicare, the last proposal of JFK's "Big Four" to be enacted, benefited the most from the momentum in the legislative process generated from the passage of earlier JFK-LBJ legislation, LBJ's landslide victory over Goldwater, the sharp increase in the number of liberal and nonsouthern Democrats in the House, and disarray within the weakened Republican opposition in Congress. Of course, two significant events during the last year of JFK's presidency facilitated the passage of Medicare in 1965, more formally known as the King-Anderson bill. First, there was the death of Senator Robert S. Kerr of Oklahoma at the beginning of 1963. As long as Harry Byrd and Kerr remained implacably opposed to the King-Anderson bill, it was unlikely that the Senate Finance Committee would favorably report this legislation to the full Senate. With Kerr's death, Senator Russell Long of Louisiana emerged as a more persuadable member of this committee for the purpose of organizing more moderate southern Democrats in the Senate and circumventing Byrd's obstructionism toward Medicare.[262]

Second, Henry Hall Wilson, representing JFK on the King-Anderson bill, and House Ways and Means Committee chairman Wilbur Mills agreed to a taxing and funding formula on the morning of JFK's assassination. Mills was more ideologically flexible and politically pragmatic than Kerr. Mills eventually recognized the inadequate, limited medical coverage of the aged under the Kerr-Mills Act of 1960. Mills decided to support the King-Anderson bill after the

White House convinced him that its taxing and financing formula under the Social Security system would not endanger future funding of retirement benefits or become excessively expensive.[263]

LBJ wanted to get the Medicare bill enacted or at least favorably reported out of the House Ways and Means Committee before the 1964 election. Mills was more cautious. The chairman calculated that there was only a one-vote majority among his committee's members in favor of Medicare. Mills wanted to wait until after the election to conduct a committee vote; he hoped that the election results would stimulate a larger majority within his committee and on the House floor in favor of Medicare. LBJ had already exploited Goldwater's controversial, unpopular proposal to make Social Security voluntary in television commercials and now wanted to link this position to Republican opposition to Medicare.

In a September 3, 1964, phone conversation with House Majority Leader Carl Albert, LBJ told Albert, "They got us screwed on Medicare. . . . We've been screwed good." "If Wilbur were for it, we could do something," Albert replied.[264] One hour later, LBJ called congressional liaison Lawrence F. O'Brien about the Medicare bill. O'Brien echoed Albert's frustration and pessimism about the inertia of the Medicare bill in the House for the remainder of 1964. "Mr. President, in substance, the House will be out of business this coming week," O'Brien told LBJ.[265]

LBJ still believed, though, that some legislative progress on Medicare could be made in the Senate before the election. On September 24, 1964, LBJ discussed the status of the Medicare bill in the Senate Finance Committee with Senator Russell Long of Louisiana. Long implied that Mills misled him and LBJ about the feasibility of Medicare passing in the House. "I'm in a hell of a spot because Harry Byrd wants to beat this thing . . . I think we're in trouble."[266] At Long's suggestion, LBJ then called Senator Clinton Anderson of New Mexico, co-sponsor of the Medicare bill. Anderson expressed his confidence that after the election there would be enough political pressure on Mills to send the King-Anderson bill to the House floor.[267]

On October 4, 1964, a House-Senate conference committee on the King-Anderson bill announced a deadlock. The House Ways and Means Committee opposed a Senate rider on a bill to increase Social Security retirement benefits that would have added Medicare as a collection of amendments to this routine bill. In exchange for their votes in opposition to this rider, Mills promised pro-Medicare Democrats that action on the Medicare bill would be his committee's top priority in January 1965.[268] The White House and leading supporters of the King-Anderson bill in the House and Senate increasingly suspected Mills of deceiving them and wanting to weaken or kill the bill through delaying tactics.[269]

Actually, Mills wanted to achieve enough of a broad, bipartisan consensus within his committee and throughout the House to pass an amended Medicare bill. By January 1965, the administration's Medicare, or King-Anderson, bill officially named H.R. 1 in the House and S.1 in the Senate, attracted two alternative bills within the House Ways and Means Committee. Influenced and promoted by the AMA, the Eldercare bill was cosponsored by Democratic Representative A. Sydney Herlong of Florida and Republican Representative Thomas Curtis of Missouri and officially designated as H.R. 3737. The Eldercare bill basically expanded the Kerr-Mills Act by covering almost all medical costs for the low-income elderly.[270] John Byrnes of Wisconsin, the ranking Republican on the House Ways and Means Committee, proposed a bill, H.R. 4351, that was similar to Eldercare. Like Eldercare, the Byrnes bill covered more medical expenses than Medicare so that doctors' services and prescription drugs were included. Membership and coverage were voluntary, however, under the Byrnes plan. Payments to finance this medical plan were scaled according to a participant's ability to pay, based on his or her Social Security cash benefits. Under the Byrnes plan, the poorest elderly who joined this insurance plan paid the least in Social Security taxes while receiving the same medical coverage as the more heavily taxed, higher-income participants.[271] While one-third of the costs of the Byrnes plan were financed by the higher Social Security taxes of its voluntary participants, the remaining two-thirds were financed by general revenues from the federal budget, initially increasing it by $2 billion.[272]

Despite the huge Democratic majority in the House in 1965 and the expanded membership of the House Ways and Means Committee with a two to one Democratic majority diluting Mills's power, the White House did not want to lose momentum on Medicare and the rest of its ambitious legislative agenda for the Eighty-eighth Congress. It reluctantly agreed to Mills's suggestion of a "three-layer cake" compromise bill, H.R. 6675.[273] The first layer or foundation of H.R. 6675 was Medicare Part A, generally based on the King-Anderson bill. Medicare Part A covered all Social Security retirees, regardless of income, paid for hospital and nursing home care, and was financed and administered by the Social Security system. The second layer, Medicare Part B, reflected the Byrnes bill. It was a supplemental, voluntary insurance plan for Social Security retirees that covered doctors' services and was financed by uniform premiums from its participants and from the general federal budget. The third layer, based on Eldercare and the Kerr-Mills Act, became known as Medicaid. It provided medical coverage for the poorest elderly and was expanded to include the eligible poor below the age of sixty-five. Medicaid would be administered by the states, financed by a federal-state matching fund formula, and allowed the use of private health insurance companies.[274]

Ironically, in the case of Medicare, it was Wilbur Mills, rather than LBJ, who contributed to the broad, suprapartisan consensus on major legislation that LBJ valued.[275] By waiting until 1965 and adopting the "three-layer cake" compromise in H.R. 6675, Mills's strategy significantly reduced the opposition of the bipartisan conservative coalition on the House floor when the full House voted on H.R. 6675 on April 8, 1965. The House passed this bill by a vote of

315 to 115 and sent it to the Senate.[276] Fifty-nine of the ninety-nine southern Democrats and all but two nonsouthern Democrats voted for H.R. 6675. The House Republicans were almost evenly divided with sixty-five of them voting for the bill and seventy-three voting against it.[277]

The amended Medicare bill faced fewer procedural obstacles in the more liberal Senate. But the AMA made a last ditch-effort to kill or amend the Medicare bill during the Senate Finance Committee hearings from April 29 until May 18, 1965. The AMA seized an opportunity to divide and weaken the now broad yet fragile consensus behind the Medicare bill in Congress by supporting the Long-Ribicoff amendment. Senators Russell Long of Louisiana and Abraham Ribicoff of Connecticut, Democratic members of the Senate Finance Committee, proposed that Part A of the Medicare bill eliminate time limits on hospitalization and nursing home coverage.[278] Wilbur Cohen, an assistant secretary of HEW and chief architect of Medicare, represented the White House's concern that the Long-Ribicoff amendment would greatly increase Medicare costs and contribute to loss of support in the House, especially from the cost-minded Mills, in the conference committee.[279]

In a June 26, 1965, phone conversation with LBJ, Senate Majority Leader Mike Mansfield told Johnson that Long had promised that if his amendment failed, he would refrain from proposing other amendments.[280] The Senate narrowly rejected the Long-Ribicoff amendment by a vote of 43 to 39. With the White House and most senators agreeing to extend time coverage for hospitalization, the Senate passed the Medicare bill by a vote of 68 to 21 on July 9, 1965.[281] During the two weeks of the House-Senate conference on the Medicare bill, the conferees generally deferred to Mills's domination of the proceedings regadring the compromise bill. It emerged from the conference containing almost none of the Senate's changes.[282] On July 27, 1965, the House passed the final Medicare bill 307 to 116, and the Senate passed it 70 to 24 on July 28.[283]

LBJ's bill-signing ceremony for Medicare was even more historically and politically poignant than that for the ESEA. Against the advice of Horace Busby, a White House speechwriter, LBJ arranged to sign the Medicare bill with Harry and Bess Truman as honored guests at the Truman presidential library in Independence, Missouri. He would then issue Harry and Bess Truman the first two Medicare cards.[284] Since Harry Truman had proposed compulsory national health insurance for all Americans, Busby was concerned that the prominent inclusion of the former president would revive the suspicions of the AMA and Republicans that LBJ's intention was to use Medicare as the precedent for eventually instituting socialized medicine.[285] LBJ had recently invited AMA leaders to the White House in order to gain their cooperation in the implementation of Medicare.[286]

LBJ was determined to symbolize the enactment of the Medicare-Medicaid legislation, formally known as the Social Security Amendments of 1965, as not only the greatest accomplishment in health care policy of his presidency, but also as the greatest legislative achievement of the social welfare agenda of Democratic liberalism since FDR's signing of the Social Security Act of 1935.[287] In connecting the Great Society with the New Frontier, Fair Deal, and New Deal, LBJ emphasized the programmatic and political debt that he and other liberal Democrats owed to the late Senator Robert F. Wagner of New York. Wagner proposed health insurance as part of the Social Security Act of 1935.[288] Despite the exclusion of this proposal, Wagner persisted in proposing federal grants to the states to provide health care in 1939 and cosponsored legislation in 1943 and 1945 to add compulsory medical and hospital insurance to the Social Security system.[289]

After paying tribute to FDR, Truman, JFK, and leading members of Congress and his administration for their contributions to the Medicare-Medicaid legislation, LBJ did not want to end his speech with this partisan emphasis. As he did with other major legislation of the Great Society, Johnson concluded with the underlying theme that the Medicare-Medicaid bill was a product of not only a suprapartisan, unifying consensus but also of the Social Gospel. "And this is not just our tradition—or the tradition of the Democratic Party—or even the tradition of the Nation. It is as old as the day it was first commanded: 'Thou shalt open thine hand wide unto thy brother, to thy poor, to thy needy, in thy land.' "[290]

With the enactment of all of the New Frontier's "Big Four" legislation, LBJ was able to concentrate his leadership and political capital more specifically and consistently on items of the Great Society's policy agenda that distinguished his presidency from Kennedy's. Journalists Rowland Evans and Robert Novak stated that the Great Society "was the badge of this particular President and this particular administration, of the uninhibited Johnsonian style, of the restless quest for new ways in which to use the presidential power, of the search for consensus, of government programs made by Johnson, as distinguished from those inherited from Kennedy."[291]

JFK developed ideas and tentative plans for an anti-poverty effort through task forces and as a major theme for his reelection campaign.[292] It is not clear that JFK definitely intended his future anti-poverty programs to be as expansive and ambitious as LBJ's War on Poverty. JFK lacked LBJ's visceral identification and personal experience with New Deal liberalism. JFK's rather diffident, deferential relationship with southern conservative Democrats in Congress on domestic legislation and his skeptical, detached nature in analyzing his policy options indicate that his future anti-poverty programs during a second term might have been more limited and experimental than LBJ's.[293] JFK also lacked his successor's mentor-protégé relationship with FDR and did not exhibit LBJ's almost obsessive, frenzied determination to equal or surpass FDR's legislative record as a champion of the underprivileged.[294]

Walter Heller, chairman of the Council of Economic Advisers, had struggled for years to persuade a skeptical, cautious JFK to intentionally engage in Keynesian deficit spending by cutting taxes as the best way to stimulate economic growth and more tax revenues for the New Frontier's domestic programs and higher defense spending. Until 1963, JFK leaned toward the more orthodox, budget-balancing fiscal policy advocated by his Republican Secretary of the Treasury, C. Douglas Dillon. Heller was pleasantly surprised when LBJ immediately and unequivocally embraced JFK's tax cut bill and the Keynesian theory behind it on the day after JFK's assassination.[295]

Two books that influenced the purposes, methods, and philosophy of the Great Society were John Kenneth Galbraith's *The Affluent Society*, published in 1958, and Michael Harrington's *The Other America* in 1962. Galbraith, a Harvard economist and JFK's ambassador to India, argued that the widespread prosperity of the 1950s had led to a growing contrast between more conspicuous consumption of private goods and services fueled by more consumer debt and an underfunded inadequate public infrastructure. Privately opposing JFK's tax cut bill, Galbraith advocated greater domestic spending, including budget deficits if necessary, in order to improve the quality of public life in such areas as environmental protection, public parks, culture, and education.[296] In an August 20, 1962, letter to JFK, Galbraith warned the president that "we could easily find ourselves with a remission of taxes for the rich, well-born and Republican and no other important change."[297]

Michael Harrington, a freelance writer, was influenced in his critique of the American economy by his participation in the Catholic Worker movement and the American Socialist Party. Harrington asserted that he wrote *The Other America* partially as a refutation of *The Affluent Society*'s "implicit assumption that the basic grinding economic problems had been solved in the United States."[298] Harrington elaborated on his personal experiences with and research of the poor and concluded that approximately fifty million Americans, more than one-fourth of the population and far more than what the American public and the federal government estimated, were poor. While urging more aggressive, innovative government intervention to reduce poverty among such population groups as the elderly, slum dwellers, migrant farm workers, and ghetto blacks, Harrington defined poverty broadly enough so that it "should be defined psychologically in terms of those whose place in the society is such that they are internal exiles" and "absolutely, in terms of what man and society could be."[299]

Toward the end of JFK's presidency, New Frontiersmen debated whether to emphasize Galbraith's qualitative liberalism or Harrington's quantitative liberalism in their proposals and in JFK's domestic priorities.[300] LBJ readily embraced both perspectives in the Great Society. LBJ was confident that if the tax cut stimulated enough economic growth with low inflation and low unemployment, then the economy would generate enough revenue to finance a variety of anti-poverty programs and policies developing a higher quality of life for all Americans in federal budgets that incurred modest deficits.[301]

The programmatic and theoretical foundation of LBJ's War on Poverty, the primary expansion of quantitative liberalism in the Great Society, was the Office of Economic Opportunity (OEO). The OEO was established by an act of Congress in 1964. Concerned about the political legitimacy of his presidency before the 1964 election, LBJ appointed R. Sargent Shriver, a Kennedy brother-in-law and Peace Corps director, as director of the OEO.[302] With the popularity of the Peace Corps and Shriver's reputation as a persuasive lobbyist before congressional committees, LBJ was confident that Congress would pass the OEO legislation.

In order to further improve chances of passage, the president had the bill sponsored by Georgia Democratic congressman Phillip Landrum, a southerner whose positions on labor issues were acceptable to the bipartisan conservative coalition. LBJ privately agreed to abandon his intention to appoint Adam Yarmolinsky, a Defense Department official who helped to draft the OEO bill, as Shriver's assistant. Shriver warned LBJ that the OEO bill might be defeated in the House because of rumors that Yarmolinsky's parents had been Communists and that he had held Communist sympathies in his youth. Landrum even felt compelled to publicly state on the House floor that Yarmolinsky would not be an official in the OEO.[303] After the House passed the OEO bill on August 8, 1964, LBJ firmly stated at two press conferences that neither he nor Shriver ever intended to appoint Yarmolinsky to be the deputy director of OEO.[304]

Before signing the Economic Opportunity Act of 1964 on August 22 1964, LBJ grandiosely announced, "Today for the time in all the history of the human race, a great nation is able to make and is willing to make a commitment to eradicate poverty among its people."[305] On a more modest, programmatic level, LBJ then appealed to middle-class values of economic self-sufficiency for the poor and long-term savings in social welfare spending. "In helping others, all of us will really be helping ourselves. . . . Every dollar spent will result in savings to the country and especially to the local taxpayers in the cost of crime, welfare, of health, and of police protection."[306] On behalf of all Americans, LBJ expressed gratitude to Shriver and others who developed and supported the OEO bill because "those who have an opportunity to participate in this program will vindicate your thinking and vindicate your action."[307] In order to discourage turf battles among the cabinet departments and enable LBJ to exert direct control over its programs, the OEO was placed within the Executive Office of the President (EOP). Like FDR with the WPA and other New Deal agencies, LBJ assumed that having a new, separate agency administer the anti-poverty programs would make them more innovative and flexible and less susceptible to the bureaucratic pathologies of existing cabinet departments.[308] Actually, much of the content and purpose of the various programs created by the Economic Opportunity Act of 1964 and administrated by the OEO were similar to those of the New Deal. Influenced by his experience as the NYA director of Texas during the Great Depression, LBJ was especially attentive toward underprivileged and often minority children, teenagers, and young adults.[309] These OEO programs were Head Start, Job Corps, and the Neighborhood Youth Corps (NYC). They emphasized an improvement of learning skills and job skills, job placement, and public service. Structured as a domestic version of the Peace Corps, Volunteers in Service to America (VISTA) hoped to tap into the idealism and altruism of recent college graduates. VISTA recruits often focused their efforts on remedial education, adult literacy, public health, and home building in urban slums, Appalachia, Indian reservations, and migrant farm worker communities.[310]

The Teacher Corps was not part of the OEO and was not created until its inclusion in the Higher Education Act of 1965. But it was often identified as an anti-poverty program similar to VISTA because it usually sent recent college graduates to the poorest urban and rural school districts [311] In his public statements on the War on Poverty, LBJ often emphasized these programs since they were usually the least controversial, most consensual elements of the OEO. They reflected the perspectives, assumptions, and values of the Social Gospel, the settlement house movement of Jane Addams, and the Progressive era.[312] Shriver's assiduous lobbying of IBM, RCA, General Electric, and other major corporations to participate in OEO's job training and placement policies evoked the "welfare capitalism" encouraged among socially responsible business executives during the 1920s.[313]

The most unique and, eventually, the most controversial and divisive OEO programs were the Community Action program and Legal Services.[314] Influenced by David Hackett's use of local residents in administering JFK's juvenile delinquency program, Title II of the Economic Opportunity Act of 1964 encouraged "maximum feasible participation" of the residents of a community receiving OEO programs. The authors of Title II assumed that if the poor were active participants, rather than passive recipients, in the OEO programs, then the War on Poverty would be more effective in adapting to socioeconomic problems and policy needs peculiar to these communities.[315] Besides authorizing the creation of new organizations for community action, Title II also allowed local communities to designate existing nonprofit organizations, such as the United Way or the National Urban League, as a Community Action Agency (CAA).[316]

More so than any other OEO program, Community Action addressed the psychological and sociological dimensions of the culture of poverty to which Michael Harrington and LBJ alluded. LBJ told Joseph Califano, the White House domestic policy advisor, that he especially wanted to help the hard-core poor who "were born to parents who gave up hoping long ago. They have no motivation to reach for something better because the sum total of their lives is losing."[317] In short, the culture of poverty, which was inextricably entwined with the intergenerational cycle of poverty, included a poverty of spirit in which the poor felt powerless to improve their lives.

Community Action's premise that the poor should be empowered to influence their environment was bolstered by the addition of the Legal Services program to OEO in 1965. Lawyers from this program represented the poor in legally redressing their grievances against landlords, public housing authorities, and urban renewal programs. They also organized and pursued class action suits against state and local governments that significantly broadened eligibility for welfare benefits and their number of recipients.[318] Increasingly, lawyers from Legal Services perceived themselves as activists for social change and legal reform who would not only represent the poor but also organize and motivate them to challenge public and private institutions.[319]

The Economic Opportunity Act of 1964 was worded broadly and inclusively enough so that members of Congress with many rural constituents, especially those from southern and border states, could reasonably assume that the rural poor would benefit from the OEO programs as much as the urban poor.[320] By the end of the summer of 1965, the OEO programs, however, were more specifically focused on the social and economic problems of poor blacks in major cities. From LBJ's perspective, this new focus was partially necessitated by the perplexing irony that a major race riot began in the mostly black Watts section of Los Angeles five days after he signed the Voting Rights Act of 1965 on August 6, 1965. Two months before he signed this legislation, LBJ stated at the historically black Howard University, "For Negro poverty is not white poverty. . . . One of these differences is the increased concentration of Negroes in our cities."[321]

LBJ decided to connect his anti-poverty programs with his civil rights efforts as a means of reducing racial unrest among urban blacks. This decision was most formally exemplified by the creation of the Department of Housing and Urban Development (HUD) on September 9, 1965. HUD's purposes and scope extended beyond the Department of Housing and Urban Affairs that JFK had proposed and Congress rejected. At the bill-signing ceremony for HUD, LBJ stated, "It is not enough for us to erect towers of stone and glass, or to lay out vast suburbs of order and conformity. We must seek and we must find the ways to preserve and to perpetuate in the city the individuality, the human dignity, the respect for individual rights, the devotion to individual rights, the devotion to individual responsibility that has been part of the American character and the strength of the American system."[322]

LBJ wanted HUD to do more than simply continue federal programs in slum clearance, urban renewal, and public housing. He wanted it to develop and implement new ways of improving the social health of cities, nurturing a sense of community and civic spirit, and helping them to become more accommodating to a greater diversity of residents in urban populations. With the urban crisis increasingly identified with racial unrest, LBJ hoped that the appointment of Robert Weaver as the Secretary of HUD, and the first black secretary of a cabinet department in American history, would symbolize the race-related significance of this new department and its purposes.[323]

HUD's most novel effort to ameliorate the often race-related social problems of cities was the Model Cities program, originally named the Demonstration Cities program. The Model Cities program was advocated by UAW president Walter Reuther and developed by a task force chaired by Robert C. Wood, a political scientist from the Massachusetts Institute of Technology.[324] The Model Cities' concept implicitly recognized the criticism of conventional urban renewal as "Negro removal" for destroying poor yet cohesive black neighborhoods to provide land for economic and highway development in major cities and often failing to provide enough new housing to replace the housing that was eliminated.[325]

One goal of Model Cities was to make urban renewal projects more sensitive and responsive to the needs and concerns of inner-city residents most affected by them. Consequently, the Model Cities Act of 1966 wanted to encourage citizen participation in its programs.[326] Although it was administered by HUD, new programs funded by Model Cities, such as the constriction and operation of new recreational and public health facilities, were to be implemented by existing local organizations. The primary function of HUD's Model Cities program was to coordinate, not control, existing and future federal, state, and local urban policy programs and to ensure that the recipients of Model Cities' funds satisfied the 1966 law's policy goals and methods.[327] In short, the Model Cities program wanted to analyze and address a particular city's social and economic problems and needs from a holistic, comprehensive perspective.[328]

In its December 1965 report to LBJ, Wood's task force proposed that the Model Cities program be applied to sixty-six cities ranging from the nation's largest to those with populations under 250,000. For five years, each of the selected Model Cities would concentrate its funds and coordinate all of the nation's public and private anti-poverty, urban redevelopment activities in a specific, blighted neighborhood. After an intense period of policy experimentation and programmatic coordination in a few cities, federal officials could assess the results and decide if more cities should receive Model Cities programs.[329]

The experimental, tentative intent of the task force's proposal was soon forgotten. LBJ's expansive, utopian rhetoric in announcing the Model Cities bill in 1966 and the pork barrel politics of congressional logrolling meant that the $12 million in planning funds for Model Cities were broadly and thinly distributed among many smaller cities, possibly as many as 400.[330] Determined to preserve the original Model Cities bill as much as possible, the White House managed to pressure and persuade the House Banking and Currency Committee to approve the mostly unamended bill for a floor vote on June 28, 1966.[331]

But LBJ, Califano, and O'Brien decided to delay the House floor vote until the Senate Banking and Currency Committee conducted hearings, amended, and voted on the Model Cities bill. They assumed that the more liberal, compliant Senate would more quickly and easily pass the Model Cities bill, thereby pressuring the House to pass it. To the surprise and dismay of the White House, the bill's prospect for Senate passage was soon endangered in a subcommittee of the Senate Banking and Currency Committee. Senator John Sparkman of Alabama was its chairman, and Senator Paul Douglas, the next leading Democrat on this committee, had introduced the Model Cities bill in the Senate. Both faced tough reelection campaigns and did not want to concentrate on Model Cities at this time.[332] Califano then lobbied the committee's next key Democrat, Senator Edmund S. Muskie of Maine. With Maine being a mostly rural, almost entirely white, sparsely populated state, LBJ told Califano to promise Muskie that the senator could choose any Maine city for inclusion in the first Model Cities budget.[333]

Muskie reluctantly agreed to negotiate with Califano on behalf of the other Democrats on his committee, but he convinced Califano to drastically reduce the appropriations that LBJ wanted. In addition to the $12 million in planning grants, LBJ wanted Congress to appropriate $2.3 billion in implementation funds over five years. Democratic Senator Thomas J. McIntyre of New Hampshire, a member of Muskie's subcommittee, was also concerned about the high cost of implementation and his own bid for reelection in 1966 in a fiscally conservative state. At Califano's suggestion, LBJ, Muskie, and McIntyre agreed that the Model Cities bill authorize $900 million in implementation funds for the first two years of the programs and let future legislation determine the implementation funds for the subsequent years. With that compromise, Muskie's subcommittee favorably voted on the Model Cities bill, and the Senate passed it on August 19, 1966.[334]

Despite LBJ's concession on the amount of requested implementation funds, the Model Cities bill was soon besieged by criticism from not only Republicans and southern Democrats but also from northern Democrats. Influenced by the growing criticism from their districts' local officials toward OEO programs, especially Community Action, for unjustified federal interference, these representatives denounced the Model Cities bill as another Great Society attempt to weaken federalism by centralizing power in Washington and usurping local authority. Republican congressman Paul Fino of New York emphasized the racial implications of this bill. He denounced Model Cities as a "tool of black power" and urged his colleagues to reject this bill in order "to draw the line and stand up to black power."[335] Although the House rejected all of Fino's proposed amendments, it emphasized greater local control in planning and using Model Cities' grants in amending the Model Cities bill. The House passed this bill on October 14, 1966, by a vote of 178 to 141, and both houses of Congress passed the conference committee's version of it by the end of October. On November 3, 1966, five days before the midterm elections, LBJ signed the Model Cities bill into law.[336]

In his memoirs, LBJ stated that the Model Cities Act of 1966 "provided a graphic test of the federal government's ability to work in harmony with other

levels of government."[337] Compared to the greater friction and controversy between local government officials and the community participation requirements
of most of the OEO programs, the Model Cities program did have a relatively
harmonious, or at least a less antagonistic, relationship with the selected cities.
Learning from the previous, contentious experiences that beleaguered OEO
officials suffered with irate local politicians and their members of Congress,
HUD officials tended to be more deferential to local governments and Congress
in implementing the Model Cities program.[338] In particular, HUD weakened
and obscured the citizen participation requirements in order to appease local
governments and members of Congress and facilitate the implementation of
Model Cities. These programs increasingly became merely additional sources of
federal funds for public schools, public health clinics, police departments, parks
departments, and other existing local government agencies.[339]

Congress subsequently nurtured "harmony" between the executive and legislative branches and between the federal and local levels of government by
sharply increasing the number, location, and diversity of cities selected to receive
Model Cities grants. The number of recipients increased from 63 cities in 1966
to 150 in 1967. The typical congressional politics of bipartisan logrolling and
widespread distribution of pork barrel projects contributed to the selection of
such cities as Smithfield, Tennessee, Pikesville, Kentucky, and Portland, Maine
for Model Cities grants to assure the continuation of this Great Society program.[340] Historian John Andrew III concluded, "The problem with Model Cities, in short, was not too much federal supervision but too little."[341]

Although funding for the Model Cities program did not end until 1973,
the legitimacy and efficacy of its efforts, like those of the OEO programs, to
improve the social health of poor, urban neighborhoods and empower their
residents through "maximum feasible participation" were aggressively challenged
and disputed by the late summer of 1967. During that summer, several cities,
especially Newark and Detroit, experienced their most destructive, prolonged
race riots of the 1960s. Ironically, Walter Reuther, in his early advocacy of a
Model Cities program, initially suggested that LBJ choose Detroit as the first
and only "demonstration city" for receiving a concentrated infusion of federal
funds, services, and planning for significantly improving its social, economic,
and civic health.[342] Nevertheless, after investigating the summer riots of 1967, a
presidential commission chaired by Governor Otto Kerner of Illinois optimistically stated, "The Model Cities program is potentially the most effective weapon
in the federal arsenal for a long-term, comprehensive attack on the problems of
American cities."[343]

LBJ, Reuther, the Kerner Commission, and other liberal policymakers were
confident that Model Cities, OEO programs, and other Great Society policies
concentrating on the urban poor needed more money, time, and minor correc-
tions in order to eventually succeed. But the white, suburban middle class, the

foundation of LBJ's consensus, was more skeptical. Less than one month before LBJ signed the Civil Rights Act of 1964, a Gallup poll showed that 57 percent of its respondents expected race relations to worsen during the next six months. In a May 12, 1965, poll, a plurality of nonsouthern whites claimed that LBJ was "pushing integration too fast." One year later, another Gallup poll showed that less than half of its sample expressed a favorable opinion of LBJ's anti-poverty programs. In a Gallup poll released on September 28, 1966, 52 percent of the nonsouthern whites stated that LBJ was "pushing integration too fast" while only 8 percent of them said that his promotion of racial integration was not fast enough.[344] As LBJ promoted legislation in 1967 that eventually became the Fair Housing Act of 1968, a Gallup poll released on March 29, 1967, showed that only 35 percent of its respondents supported the enactment of a fair, or "open," housing law.[345]

By contrast, two of the "Big Four" domestic policy goals of the New Frontier and Great Society, the income tax cut and Medicare, enjoyed consistent, widespread public support in the Gallup polls. For example, a poll released on September 28, 1963, showed that 60 percent favored and only 29 percent opposed JFK's tax cut bill. Even for the purposes of reducing inflation and a budget deficit, 76 percent opposed an income tax increase in a May 11, 1966, poll.[346] In general, except for the Civil Rights Act of 1964, a suprapartisan, centrist consensus among the white middle class favoring liberal programs for poor, powerless, neglected segments of the American population, such as blacks and Hispanics in urban slums, did not seem to exist.[347] Historians, political scientists, economists, and members of the Kennedy and Johnson administrations often agree that most of the New Frontier and Great Society programs focusing on these underprivileged groups were the products of liberal policymaking elites. They were not the result of the American public demanding and expecting these new programs.[348]

The New Frontier and Great Society programs and policies that were the most popular with suburban, middle-class Americans were those that clearly appealed to their economic self-interest, such as the income tax cut and Medicare, their cultural and intellectual aspirations, such as federal aid for public television and radio stations, the arts, and higher education, and their desire for a more aesthetic, accessible natural environment, such as the significant expansion of national parks, greater protection of the wilderness and wildlife, and Lady Bird Johnson's anti-billboard, highway beautification, tree planting, and anti-litter campaigns.[349] Also, the higher expectations that middle-class Americans developed for healthier and safer living conditions and consumer products were reflected in new federal regulations for automobile and highway safety, children's clothing and toys, air and water pollution, and pharmaceuticals that were enacted during the 1960s.[350] On a more selfless, altruistic level, the Peace Corps, VISTA, and the short-lived Teacher Corps appealed to and nurtured the idealistic desire of more middle-class Americans, especially college students, to help and uplift the less fortunate both domestically and internationally. After working in the fledgling Peace Corps, Richard Goodwin commented, "The Peace Corps volunteers and the men who organized them . . . were more closely attuned to this indefinable and still undefined spirit of the sixties than were the vast bureaucracies that surrounded them."[351]

LBJ occasionally expressed his distaste for the "politics of principle" and modeled his policymaking behavior on the premise that only compromise, negotiation, and pragmatism within Congress and between the executive and legislative branches and the two parties could generate steady progress in domestic policy.[352] For LBJ, according to political scientist Stephen Skowronek, "The Great Society was to alleviate conflicts between North and South, black and white, labor and capital, left and right—all the conflicts that had riddled liberal politics since its inception."[353] Instead of reflecting and then strengthening a centrist, suprapartisan consensus based on middle-class values, the Great Society contributed to the rise of ideological conflict and extremism in politics and society that LBJ had tried to prevent and discourage throughout his political career.[354]

JFK was also a pragmatist who had publicly expressed his discomfort with ADA members and other outspoken liberal ideologues during his Senate career. Like LBJ, Kennedy understood the necessity of gradually developing political legitimacy with the Democratic-controlled Congress and credibility as chief lawmaker on more conventional legislation before he could propose groundbreaking legislation.[355] In his study of the partisan dimensions of presidential policymaking with Congress, political scientist John H. Kessel noted, "John Kennedy and Lyndon Johnson prior to 1964, working with smaller Democratic majorities, had the greatest propensity to ask for large old programs."[356]

No matter how willing and able JFK and LBJ were to mute partisan or ideological oppsition and cultivate ad hoc bipartisan support in Congress for each piece of major legislation, both of these Democratic presidents based their power and performance in domestic policymaking on symbiotic, interactive relationships between their roles as party leader and chief lawmaker. Much of the Democratic national platform of 1960 was a product of policy proposals generated by Democrats in Congress, liberal interest groups like the AFL-CIO and the ADA, and the DNC's Democratic Advisory Council.[357] From the time of the post-convention 1960 special session of Congress to preparations for his 1964 reelection campaign, JFK's behavior as both party leader and chief lawmaker in dealing with Democrats in Congress indicated that he intended to achieve domestic policy goals that had mostly been established by the Democratic Party before he even announced his presidential candidacy.[358] LBJ referred to the New Deal and Fair Deal as the ideological and programmatic foundation of his domestic policy agenda more frequently and explicitly than JFK did.[359] Both, however, faithfully and effectively pursued domestic policy goals that reflected and fulfilled FDR's 1941 pledge "to insure the continuance of liberalism in our government. I believe, at the same time, that it is my duty as the head of the Democratic party to see to it that my party remains the truly liberal party in the political life of America."[360]

1   JFK speaking at Faneuil Hall in Boston, July 4, 1946.
Seated behind JFK is Mayor James M. Curley. Seated at
left is John "Honey Fitz" Fitzgerald.

2

2   JFK and his wife Jacqueline visit Assumption College in Worcester, Massachusetts on June 3, 1955.

3   LBJ with campaign helicopter in 1948.

4

4   DNC chairman Paul M. Butler.

5   Free speech demonstration at Berkeley on November 20, 1964.

6   Harry S. Truman, JFK, and LBJ at a Democratic dinner in Washington, DC on March 9, 1961.

5

7

7   JFK arrives in Quonset Point, Rhode Island on August 27, 1962.
    The photo was taken by George W. Locksie, Jr.

8   LBJ takes oath of office aboard Air Force One, November 22, 1963.

8

9

9   LBJ on the phone in the White House, January 10, 1964.

10

10   RFK at a cabinet meeting, January 28, 1964.

11

11   LBJ greets crowds in Providence, Rhode Island on September 28, 1964.

12   LBJ and RFK campaigning in Brooklyn, New York on October 14, 1964.

13

13   Hubert H. Humphrey at the White House on June 21, 1965.

14   LBJ and Harry S. Truman at the bill signing ceremony for Medicare, July 30, 1965. In the background are Lady Bird Johnson, Hubert H. Humphrey, and Bess Truman.

15   DNC chairman John M. Bailey in the Oval Office, January 7, 1966.

14

16

18

16   LBJ visiting American troops in South Vietnam on October 26, 1966.

17   LBJ visiting wounded soldiers in South Vietnam on October 26, 1966.

18   Cesar Chavez in 1966.

19

19   LBJ and John M. Bailey at DNC headquarters on July 20, 1967.

20   Senator Philip Hart and Mayor Jerome Cavanaugh survey riot destruction in Detroit in 1967.

21   Senator Eugene M. McCarthy campaigning in New Haven, Connecticut on April 3, 1968.

20

22

22   RFK campaigning in Mishawaka, Indiana, 1968.

23   RFK and Ethel Kennedy campaigning in South Bend, Indiana in 1968.
       With them are Democratic county chairman Ideal Baldoni, vice chairman
       Freda Noble, and Jeanne Baldoni.

23

24

25

26

27

29

27 Police preparing for riots in Chicago in August, 1968.

28 An antiwar demonstration in Chicago in August, 1968. Photo by Earl Seubert.

29 1968 campaign photo of Hubert H. Humphrey and Edmund S. Muskie.

30

30　JFK and LBJ in 1960 campaign photo.

JFK, LBJ, and the DNC

In studying the changes that occur in the roles of each of the two major parties' national committee chairmen, political scientists distinguish between the "out-party" chairman and the "in-party" chairman.[1] The "out-party" is the major party that does not control presidency while the "in-party" is the major party that does. Since the president is the titular national leader of his party, the "in-party" national chairman is relegated to a minor, subordinate role. The president will decide how active or inactive, extensive or limited, controlled or independent his party's national committee chairman will be in performing such roles as fundraiser, patronage dispenser, party spokesman, party publicist, manager of the president's reelection campaign, and administrator of any changes in party organization and procedures.[2] Since the growth of the modern presidency beginning with FDR, presidents have typically relied on their White House aides more and on the "in-party" chairmen less to perform these intraparty functions.

By contrast, the "out-party" chairman often has more discretion, opportunities, and power to define his various intraparty functions and make significant innovative changes in his party's national organization, fundraising methods and sources, procedures at national conventions, national platform, and cultivation of voting blocs outside of his party's electoral base.[3] The "out-party" chairman may be unusually influential in these facets if his party has also suffered devastating losses in the most recent presidential and congressional elections, has accumulated a large debt, and is the smaller of the two parties. For example, these were the circumstances under which John Raskob became DNC chairman in 1928. Raskob, a former Republican, a Catholic, and a General Motors executive, used his position as "out-party" chairman to change the location of the DNC's headquarters, influence the selection of Chicago as the site of the 1932 convention, and substantially reduce the DNC's debt.[4] He almost succeeded in making the Democratic national platform similar to the Republican national platform in advocating high tariff, pro-big business policies and making the repeal of prohibition the party's top policy goal despite the Great Depression.[5] Political scientists Cornelius P. Cotter and Bernard C. Hennessy concluded that "there is a tendency, or at least an opportunity, for the national chairman of the out-party to indulge more vigorously the chairman's roles as image-maker, hell-raiser, and administrator."[6]

Regardless of whether a DNC chairman has been an "in-party" or "out-party" chairman, the conduct of his duties has been influenced by the Democratic Party's need to provide adequate representation and opportunities for participation to its large, diverse coalition of interest groups and voting blocs since the New Deal realignment. The smaller, more homogeneous, and cohesive Republican Party has enabled RNC chairmen to concentrate more on party organization, fundraising, and campaign strategy.[7] DNC chairmen since the late 1930s have been confronted with the challenge of maintaining intraparty harmony and cooperation in the conduct of national convention proceedings and resolving the growing conflicts between the DNC and Democratic state parties and among the Democratic state parties, especially on such issues as civil rights, labor union policy interests, and whether or how to punish disloyal Democratic electors after presidential elections. For example, extensive hearings by an advisory committee of the DNC and deliberations at the 1952, 1956, and 1960 Democratic national conventions on the issue of loyalty to the Democratic presidential ticket failed to ensure the loyalty of Democratic electors in several southern states to the JFK-LBJ ticket.[8]

A DNC chairman's position by the 1950s was further complicated by the intensifying friction between the liberal-dominated presidential wing of the Democratic party and its conservative-dominated congressional wing.[9] After the Democratic national convention of 1936 abolished the two-thirds rule, the South could no longer exercise a regional veto over presidential and vice-presidential nominees and, to a lesser extent, platform planks objectionable to southern policy interests. Beginning with the 1940 Democratic national convention, nonsouthern, urban, pro-union liberals increasingly dominated the selection of the presidential ticket as well as the ideological character and programmatic direction of the national Democratic Party through its platform. Despite widespread opposition from southern delegates, FDR was nominated for a third term, Henry Wallace, a pro-civil rights former Republican with close ties to leftist CIO unions, was nominated for vice president, and the first civil rights plank specifying "equal protection of the laws" and "legislative safeguards against discrimination" for blacks was adopted.[10] The wording of Democratic platforms steadily became more distinctly, unequivocally, and militantly liberal, especially on such divisive issues as civil rights, federal aid to education, and "right to work" laws.[11]

The liberal forces that authored them and increasingly dominated the presidential nomination processes were less willing to compromise with or even consider dissident, conservative, and often southern policy positions.[12] By the mid-1950s, this widening ideological, regional, and policy gap between the mostly nonsouthern, liberal presidential wing and mostly southern, conservative congressional wing of the Democratic Party made the DNC chairman's position even more difficult. Furthermore, Cordell Hull of Tennessee was the last southerner to be DNC chairman, serving from 1921 to 1924. Every DNC chairman from John Raskob elected in 1928 until JFK's designation of Senator Henry M. "Scoop" Jackson of Washington as DNC chairman for the 1960 presidential campaign was a northern Catholic. Southern conservative Democrats in Congress who were the most alienated from the national Democratic Party often perceived the DNC chairman to be a representative of its liberal presidential wing rather than a neutral arbiter of intraparty differences.[13]

This was the political environment that Paul M. Butler entered on becoming DNC chairman. Butler was a Catholic Democrat from South Bend, Indiana, and had earned his law degree at the University of Notre Dame. He successively served as president of the local Young Democrats, the Democratic chairman of Indiana's third congressional district, and Democratic national committeeman from Indiana. After Stephen Mitchell decided not to seek reelection as DNC chairman after the 1954 midterm elections, Butler actively campaigned among his fellow DNC members to succeed Mitchell. Although Harry Truman and former DNC chairman Frank McKinney, a fellow Indiana Democrat, opposed Butler's candidacy, the South Bend Democrat was easily elected DNC chairman at a DNC meeting in New Orleans on December 4, 1954.[14] George C. Roberts, Butler's biographer, noted that "his selection was seen as the first undictated selection of a national chairman since 1912."[15]

As an "out party" DNC chairman, Butler's position was even more unique in that his party's congressional wing won control of Congress in the 1954 midterm elections while a Republican presidency continued. Butler was not the first "out-party" DNC chairman to be confronted by such an unusual partisan configuration. The two key questions were: Who would represent the Democratic Party during the remainder of a Republican administration, the DNC chairman or the Speaker of the House and the Senate Majority Leader? Regardless of who formally represented the Democratic Party's policy agenda as the "out party," how will that policy agenda be developed, by the DNC or by congressional Democratic caucuses?

Paul M. Butler did not formally and emphatically address these questions in his public rhetoric and organizational and procedural behavior until after the 1956 election. Since he was not DNC chairman during the 1952 Democratic national convention and presidential campaign, Butler did not believe that it was appropriate for him to publicly represent and interpret the 1952 platform during the 1955–1956 sessions of Congress. Instead, he spent the first year and a half of his chairmanship reducing the DNC's debt, raising funds for the 1956 campaign, preparing for the 1956 convention in Chicago, and improving the visibility of the DNC's headquarters and activities through his frequent, nationwide speaking tours and publication of the *Democratic Digest*.[16]

Following the 1956 election, Butler's status as "out-party" national chairman became even more unusual in that Eisenhower defeated Adlai Stevenson by a landslide margin even greater than his 1952 victory. The Democrats further increased their majorities in Congress, and most voters continued to identify themselves as Democrats. With Eisenhower constitutionally ineligible to run again in 1960, the Democratic Party seemed to have a good chance of winning the next presidential election.

But the liberal, presidential wing, with its high concentration of ADA members, academic elites, pro-Stevenson "amateur" Democrats from California, anti-Tammany Hall "reform" Democrats in New York, labor union leaders, and civil rights activists, was more pessimistic. In the 1956 presidential election, Eisenhower had received almost half of the Catholic vote, more than one-third of the black vote, and half of the votes of manual laborers.[17] Many nonsouthern liberal Democrats concluded that their party would lose the 1960 presidential election if it did not formulate and regularly advocate a comprehensive, liberal platform that distinguished the national Democratic Party from even the relative centrism of the Eisenhower Republicans.[18] If the DNC or a DNC-affiliated organization or process developed liberal policy positions for the next four years, then most delegates at the 1960 Democratic national convention would presumably adopt them and only nominate a liberal presidential ticket that would sincerely embrace such a platform and implement it if elected.

Before and during his 1956 presidential campaign, Adlai Stevenson received policy ideas and proposals from a group of liberal academics, lawyers, and former Truman administration officials led by Thomas Finletter. Finletter was a New York Democrat who had served as Secretary of the Air Force under Truman.[19] At the first DNC meeting after the 1956 elections, several DNC members, Paul Ziffren of California, Neil Staebler of Michigan, and Camille Gravel of Louisiana, suggested that the DNC create a party council similar to the "Finletter Group." It would research, discuss, and announce Democratic policy positions in contrast to those of the Eisenhower administration in particular and the Republican Party in general.[20] In the minutes of the DNC executive committee's November 27, 1956, meeting, Ziffren complained, "Lyndon Johnson, during the last four years, we feel, has arrogated to himself . . . the position of spokesman for the Party."[21] After the executive committee agreed to create the Democratic Advisory Council (DAC), Gravel warned the other executive committee members "that we may be getting in some trouble, not only with Johnson, but some of the other members of the Democratic Party of the South."[22]

As Gravel anticipated, southern Democrats in general and LBJ and Sam Rayburn in particular resented what they perceived as an encroachment on the prerogatives of congressional Democrats in the legislative process. Publicly rejecting Butler's offer of membership in the DAC, the Speaker of the House and Senate Majority Leader continued to insist that they would cooperate with

Eisenhower and Republicans on legislation that was best for the nation. Earlier in 1956, LBJ had defined partisanship as "sincere disagreement as to the course that is best for the nation."[23] For LBJ, the fact that under his party leadership the Democrats won control of the Senate in 1954 and gained more seats in 1956 despite Eisenhower's landslide reelection proved that his emphasis on a bipartisan, centrist consensus within Congress and between the two branches satisfied most voters, who increasingly engaged in split-ticket voting.[24] Furthermore, by cooperating with Eisenhower more than the most conservative Republicans did, LBJ believed that his practice of "responsible" partisanship would benefit the Democrats electorally in 1958 and 1960 by dividing the Republican Party.[25]

Except for Hubert Humphrey and Estes Kefauver, Democrats in Congress spurned Butler's initial offer to join the DAC. Representative Edith Green of Oregon withdrew her earlier acceptance of membership. JFK waited until the end of the 1959 to join the DAC and, unlike Humphrey, was a passive, silent member who rarely attended DAC meetings. Nonetheless, John Kenneth Galbraith and Chester Bowles were prominent members of the DAC and provided Kennedy with economic and foreign policy advice for his presidential campaign.[26]

Butler was careful, however, to ensure that there was broad regional membership in the twenty-member DAC so that southern and border state Democrats would not feel neglected.[27] In order to add prestige to the DAC and reduce intraparty criticism of it, Butler appointed Harry Truman, Eleanor Roosevelt, Adlai Stevenson, (W.) Averell Harriman, and former Secretary of State Dean Acheson.[28] Butler was personally committed to pro-civil rights New Deal liberalism and wanted the DAC's research, meetings, and policy statements to influence the adoption of a liberal national platform in 1960 and the nomination of a presidential ticket committed to it. But he was careful to maintain the traditional neutrality of "out-party" DNC chairmen in performing his duties.[29]

For example, Butler persuaded the DNC to choose Los Angeles as the location of the 1960 Democratic national convention partially because he perceived it as a politically neutral city.[30] JFK preferred Chicago. Philadelphia, the leading alternative to Los Angeles, was divided by intraparty squabbles between Representative William Green of Philadelphia and a faction led by Philadelphia mayor Richardson Dilworth and Senator Joseph Clark. Dilworth, Clark, and David Lawrence, a member of the DNC and DAC, favored Adlai Stevenson for the 1960 presidential nomination.[31] Philadelphia was also the home town of Matthew McCloskey, the DNC's treasurer. Butler found McCloskey to be lackadaisical in performing his duties and resistant to Butler's efforts to emphasize grassroots fundraising by appealing to a large number of small donors.[32]

Drexel A. Sprecher served as deputy chairman of the DNC from 1957 to 1960. In a 1972 interview, Sprecher stated that Butler "felt the party needed a national chairman that wasn't completely candidate oriented and who could build party apparatus which was more or less like a civil service group."[33] Benefiting from the donations of wealthy patrons of Eleanor Roosevelt and Adlai Stevenson, the DAC had a budget separate from the DNC. The DAC's financial independence strengthened its ability to hire staff to research and issue policy statements that party regulars and southern conservatives found objectionable.[34]

Most Democrats in Congress and among the DNC members generally appreciated the high quality of research and analysis that the DAC's staff provided in helping the DAC to issue policy statements, especially on foreign and defense policy after the Soviet launching of Sputnik and Castro's takeover of Cuba.[35] However, the DAC policy statements on domestic issues, especially education, social welfare, and civil rights, were often more liberal than those of the 1956 Democratic platform and generated opposition from southerners. Although Camille Gravel, Louisiana's Democratic national committeeman and a member of both the DNC's executive committee and the DAC, disagreed with the DAC's civil rights statements, the Louisiana Democratic state committee voted to remove him because of his association with the DAC.[36] The Louisiana Democrats took this action three weeks after the DAC issued a statement supporting the racial integration of Little Rock Central High School that enraged virtually all southern Democrats.[37]

Despite this growing intraparty conflict over race, Butler became bolder in his civil rights liberalism. He had the DNC sponsor its first national caucuses for black Democrats and did not want to entrust the DNC's activities for blacks to William Dawson, a black congressman from Chicago. Butler regarded Dawson as too passive and deferential to southern Democrats on civil rights.[38] The 1958 elections sharply increased the number of nonsouthern Democrats in Congress, and public opinion on domestic policy became more liberal during and after the 1957–1958 recession. Butler subsequently became more emphatic and assertive in his rhetoric about the need for the Democratic Party to adopt a liberal platform and nominate a liberal presidential ticket.[39]

Butler tried to avoid the appearance of any favoritism toward the presidential candidacy of JFK. But LBJ and other southerners became convinced that Butler was unethically using his powers as DNC chairman in order to benefit Kennedy at the convention and discriminate against southern Democrats in general and Johnson in particular.[40] The growing conflict over Butler's chairmanship from late 1958 until the conclusion of the 1960 Democratic national convention was not limited to LBJ, Rayburn, and other southerners. After Butler spoke at a Democratic women's conference in Hartford on June 6, 1959, Senator Thomas J. Dodd of Connecticut, a pro-civil rights Democrat who backed LBJ for the 1960 presidential nomination, sent the DNC chairman a letter denouncing Butler's alleged exclusion of southern Democrats from influencing the Democratic national platform and presidential ticket of 1960. Dodd stated, "You are, by your efforts to eliminate Southerners and Southwesterners from consideration for the Presidency, taking a position that is manifestly unjust and which belies the ancient Democratic claim that our party is America's only national party."[41] One month later, Harry Truman wrote to Sam Rayburn, "I noticed that Paul Butler is 'firing from the hip,' without any consultation with Democrats that count."[42] Six weeks after his letter to Rayburn, Truman rhetorically asked Dean Acheson, "Should we quit the Advisory Committee or should we not? If Butler has his way we'll nominate a loser and elect Nixon for President!"[43]

Butler also wanted to make the discussion and development of major planks of the 1960 platform as participatory and open as possible among Democrats at the grassroots level. In January 1960, Butler asked Richard Murphy, the DNC's director of the Young Democrats Clubs (YDC), and John M. Redding, the DNC's publicity director during the 1948 campaign, to organize platform hearings on major issues in ten cities. Each city's platform hearing concentrated on a different topic. For example, the first platform meeting, held in Philadelphia, focused on civil rights, and the last meeting was held in Miami Beach and concentrated on health insurance for the aged.[44] Butler wanted to ensure that the drafting of the 1960 national platform faithfully and accurately reflected the liberal policy content and ideological character of the results of these nationwide hearings and the DAC's policy statements. He chose Chester Bowles as chairman of the convention's platform committee and Philip Perlman as its vice chairman. Perlman had served as solicitor general under Truman and was primarily responsible for the wording of the civil rights plank of the 1960 Democratic national platform.[45]

Although party regulars like Harry Truman and David Lawrence and southern Democrats like LBJ and Rayburn chafed under Butler's dynamic, innovative chairmanship, Butler also gained the respect and admiration of other Democrats. These Democrats wanted a coherently and cohesively liberal Democratic national party whose policy agenda, organization, and procedures were consistent with and conducive toward the ideological and programmatic positions of the dominant voting blocs and interest groups of its presidential wing.[46] Most Young Democrats, Michigan Democrats led by Neil Staebler and Governor G. Mennen Williams, ADA members, labor and civil rights leaders, the anti-machine reform Democrats of New York, and pro-Stevenson "amateur" Democrats of California enthusiastically supported Butler's chairmanship in general and creation of the DAC in particular.[47]

Academics who were members of the DAC or its staff were impressed by the fact that Paul M. Butler was the first national chairman of either party who tried, whether intentionally or not, to implement the "responsible" party model delineated and promoted by the American Political Science Association (APSA) in a 1950 report.[48] In introducing its proposals, which included a "party council" similar to the DAC, the APSA stated, "The party system that is needed must be democratic, responsible and effective—a system that is accountable to the public, respects and expresses differences of opinion, and is able to cope with the great problems of modern government."[49] James L. Sundquist, a political scientist who worked as a DAC researcher, favorably analyzed the roles of Butler and the DAC in *Politics and Policy*, his thorough study of the relationship between party politics and policymaking during the Eisenhower, Kennedy, and Johnson administrations.[50] For Sundquist, the accomplishments of the DAC and Butler enabled the national Democratic Party to "fulfill its role—it succeeded in defining a concrete program that presented the voters with a true choice in reaching their public decision in November 1960."[51]

As presidential party leaders, JFK and LBJ did not share this enthusiasm and admiration for Butler's persistent, assertive promotion of the academic idea of party responsibility for the Democratic Party.[52] JFK maintained a cordial yet awkward relationship with Butler. Prior to the opening of the Democratic national convention in Los Angeles, JFK did not want to convey any impression that Butler was unethically manipulating the convention's proceedings in order to help a fellow Catholic become president. Also, JFK was well aware of the vehement criticism of Butler's chairmanship from southern conservatives and party regulars. Any association and apparent collaboration with Butler could weaken and damage JFK's chances of being nominated. Finally, throughout his political career, JFK always had his own well-financed, professional, highly effective political organization that was separate from the regular party organization of Massachusetts. From JFK's perspective, most of his experiences with the formal party committees in his home state, such as his conflict with William "Onions" Burke over the Democratic state committee in 1956, had been frustrating and burdensome.

Kennedy seemed to be ambivalent about Paul M. Butler's legacy as DNC chairman and the application of the APSA's "responsible" party model through the DAC and the 1960 Democratic platform. By contrast, Johnson was openly hostile and dismissive.[53] LBJ's political status in Texas during the 1950s had become more precarious as Texas Democrats divided into more ideologically incompatible, conflicting party organizations, like the liberal Democrats of Texas (DOT) clubs. Both the left and right wings of the Texas Democratic Party distrusted LBJ as an unprincipled, manipulative opportunist.[54] After learning that LBJ had rejected membership in the DAC, a pro-Butler Texas Democrat scolded LBJ for not helping Butler "to unite our Party—and decide what (if anything!) we are going to stand for."[55]

LBJ also found it impossible to believe that even an "out-party" national chairman could sincerely and impartially serve the best interests of the Democratic Party in general without favoring or secretly representing certain politicians or factions of the party while opposing rival politicians and factions. Shortly before the convention in Los Angeles began, LBJ publicly agreed with Truman that Butler rigged the arrangements to benefit JFK's candidacy for the presidential nomination. After the convention, LBJ resented the fact that, as Senate majority leader and JFK's running mate, he had to promote platform-based liberal legislation that had little or no chance of being passed during the special session of Congress.[56] The Texas Democrat was also embarrassed and burdened in his simultaneous reelection campaign to the Senate by the fact that the conservative platform of the Texas Democratic Party blatantly rejected most of the national platform, including its subtle threat to end the oil depletion allowance.[57] The impact of Butler's chairmanship, the DAC's influence, and the assertive liberalism of the 1960 Democratic national platform inextricably committed the presidencies of JFK and LBJ to the major domestic policy goals of 1950s' liberalism, especially on civil rights, education, and health care.[58]

More so than previous presidents, JFK and LBJ realized, perhaps somewhat ruefully, that their party's presidential wing would evaluate their presidencies according to their performance in securing enactment of this platform's most controversial priorities in domestic policy.[59] The irony is that the issue-oriented demands of the theory of party responsibility and of its practice in the application of the 1960 platform to the Kennedy and Johnson presidencies often required a diminution and an occasional rejection of strict party discipline by JFK and LBJ. These Democratic presidents, especially LBJ, often engaged in bipartisan or even suprapartisan rhetoric and policymaking behavior in order to gain congressional majorities for platform-based policy goals.[60] After examining the impact of the DAC on the DNC, Philip A. Klinkner concluded "that the DNC's policy orientation weakened the party in the long run. One possible implication of the DNC's emphasizing policy to the exclusion of organization and procedure was that it failed to develop the organizational strength and autonomy that they suffered in the 1960s."[61]

The supremacy of legislative leadership over party leadership was best illustrated by the contrast between Lawrence F. O'Brien and DNC chairman John M. Bailey. Historically, it has generally been true that "in-party" chairmen like Bailey have less influence and prominence than "out-party" chairmen like Butler.[62] Bailey's functions, power, and status as DNC chairman were further diminished by the power and significance that JFK and LBJ invested in O'Brien's White House office of congressional relations.

In JFK's first formal presidential address to the DNC on January 21, 1961, JFK frankly stated about the newly elected DNC chairman, "I will feel that he is doing a good job when you all say 'Well, Kennedy is all right, but Bailey is the one who is really making the mistakes.' "[63] The president was even more explicit in emphasizing the linkage and subordination of the party's organization to its legislative agenda. "The party is not an end in itself—it is a means to an end. . . . The party is the means by which programs can be put into action."[64]

The subordination of DNC considerations to legislative accomplishments was most evident in the different roles of Bailey and O'Brien on patronage decisions. In order to answer questions and requests about where to send inquiries and recommendations regarding patronage jobs, JFK made the following distinction for DNC members. Other than ambassadorships and vacancies in regulatory agencies, all politically appointed federal positions, including federal judgeships and Justice Department jobs, would initially be considered by Bailey.[65]

The reality, though, was that O'Brien determined which Democratic members of Congress would be rewarded or punished on patronage and pork barrel decisions according to their voting records on JFK's legislative priorities. With the loss of twenty Democratic House seats in the 1960 elections, O'Brien especially needed to use the manipulation of patronage and pork to pressure moderate southern and border state Democrats in the House who were undecided on such legislative issues as the expansion of the House Rules Committee and JFK's minimum wage bill. In his memoirs, O'Brien revealed that he and Bailey developed the following system. O'Brien informed Democrats in Congress about approval of their patronage requests while Bailey informed them of the denial of patronage. "In other words, John took the heat when we had to refuse someone and the White House took credit, for the President, when we made an appointment that pleased some member of Congress."[66]

Kenneth P. O'Donnell, the White House aide who managed the president's schedule, occasionally yet powerfully intervened on patronage. In fulfilling patronage requests, James Farley, FDR's first DNC chairman, gave preference to Democrats who were FRBC—For Roosevelt Before Chicago—that is, those Democrats who actively supported FDR's candidacy long before he was nominated at the 1932 convention.[67] O'Donnell, likewise, periodically used this criterion to decide which Democratic politicians were more likely to receive a patronage favor or an appointment with JFK in the Oval Office.[68]

This patronage system of the Kennedy administration, of course, did not always prevent announcements on federal jobs that were embarrassing to JFK. On March 6, 1963, JFK called Henry Fowler, Undersecretary of the Treasury, to express his anger and surprise at IRS commissioner Mortimer Caplin's announcement that he would close an IRS facility in Scranton, Pennsylvania and move its operations to Boston for the purpose of cost cutting and efficiency. JFK complained that Caplin "may be a genius but he doesn't have any God damn sense" since it looked as if the president "is screwing Pennsylvania in order to help Teddy" during his younger brother's first year in the Senate. JFK asked Fowler if Caplin had discussed this decision with O'Brien first. JFK emphatically told Fowler, "Tell him in the future to talk to O'Brien. Christ, I'm the one who gets all the hell on these things. Caplin doesn't."[69]

With Bailey having little actual influence over patronage and pork barrel decisions, he and JFK met in early 1961 to discuss the purpose of the DNC's apparatus. In a February 17, 1961, memo to Bailey, JFK asked the DNC chairman to discuss with him opposition research on Republican voting records, communicating with and strengthening local party organization, and "What plans are we now making to have a massive registration drive in 1962 and

1964."[70] A few months later, Bailey announced his reorganization plan for the DNC's apparatus. He explained his plan to divide the DNC into ten subcommittees for political action. These ten covered voting blocs such as nationalities, young voters, senior citizens, and women, and support groups, such as labor and farmers.[71]

Despite the impressive, specialized organizational chart that Bailey created, the DNC had little money for funding a full-time research division, and expanding its publicity operations.[72] After the 1960 elections, the DNC had a debt of $3.82 million while the RNC had a surplus of approximately $750,000.[73] Besides maximizing the use of the DNC's staff and publicity division to raise enough funds to liquidate this debt and prepare for the 1964 presidential campaign, JFK also expected Bailey to significantly improve voter registration and turnout for the next two national elections. Regardless of JFK's personal popularity among blacks, Hispanics, and young adults toward the end of his presidential campaign, these three mostly Democratic demographic groups had relatively low rates of voter registration and turnout in 1960. JFK had either carried or lost such crucial states in the Electoral College as California, Illinois, Ohio, and Texas by very close and controversial margins. Higher rates of pro-Democratic voter turnout among blacks and Hispanics would have enabled him to have carried all these states by wider margins in 1960. Assuming that he would carry fewer southern states in 1964 than in 1960 because of impending civil rights legislation, JFK wanted to ensure higher voter turnout among blacks and Hispanics in nonsouthern states that had significant numbers of either or both of these ethnic groups.[74]

Although the DNC headquarters did not provide substantial funding to black, Hispanic, and labor voter registration projects, it coordinated and advised their efforts and those of state and local party organizations. While Bailey was still careful not to antagonize southern Democratic politicians and state committees that discouraged voting by blacks, the Justice Department supported legal actions challenging poll taxes and literacy tests. JFK also encouraged foundations to subsidize the officially nonpartisan, civil rights-oriented Voter Education Project (VEP).[75]

Bailey realized that he had to be especially tactful and even stealthful about increasing voter registration in Texas. He carefully adhered to the understanding between JFK and LBJ that decisions on most federal appointments in Texas were to be cleared through the vice president. In general, Johnson was the conduit for the Kennedy administration's relationship with the Texas Democratic Party. The efforts of blacks, Hispanics, labor unions, and white liberals in Texas to reduce and eventually end that state's poll tax aggravated intraparty conflicts. Two weeks before JFK was assassinated in Dallas, Charles Roche, one of Bailey's assistants, told the DNC chairman that "it was decided to forward financial assistance to the State of Texas through confidential channels in order to assist in turning out the vote for the Anti-Poll Tax Amendment Saturday."[76]

Bailey and the DNC staff tried their best to avoid favoring one faction or candidate over another in intraparty disputes within the states, but this typical DNC neutrality was difficult to follow in Texas. John Connally, one of LBJ's closest political confidantes, resigned as Secretary of the Navy and was elected governor of Texas in 1962.[77] Connally represented the pro-business, conservative faction of the Texas Democratic Party. Most conservative Democrats in Texas opposed repeal of the poll tax and efforts to increase voter turnout among blacks, Hispanics, and poor whites, fearing that most of these voters would support the more liberal, pro-labor candidates in Democratic primaries.[78] After John Tower became the first Republican since the Reconstruction era to be elected to the Senate from Texas in 1961, Ralph Yarborough became the state's only Democratic senator. Yarborough resented the fact that LBJ superseded his authority on federal appointments in Texas and suspected that LBJ was encouraging Connally to oppose him in his 1964 senatorial primary.[79] As the most consistently liberal southern senator on both economic and civil rights issues, Yarborough was also frustrated and embittered by the fact that his staunch loyalty to the New Frontier was not being adequately rewarded. Meanwhile, Connally became increasingly outspoken in his criticism of certain policies of the Kennedy administration.[80]

In preparation for the 1964 presidential campaign in Texas, LBJ did not want to alienate either the pro-Connally conservatives or the pro-Yarborough liberals among Texas Democrats. Republican voting strength continued to inexorably increase in this state. During his career as chief of staff to Congressman Richard Kleberg and as the NYA administrator of Texas, LBJ had cultivated Hispanic political support by channeling public works jobs, public housing, and other New Deal programs to Hispanics, especially in Austin and San Antonio. During his first year as a senator, LBJ arranged to have Felix Longoria, a Hispanic Texan killed in World War II, buried at Arlington National Cemetery after his home town's cemetery refused to bury him because of discrimination.[81] The vice president regarded the conservative Connally and Henry B. Gonzalez, a pro-Yarborough congressman from San Antonio, as protégés. LBJ first allied himself with Gonzalez in the late 1950s when the Hispanic Democrat was a state senator. The vice president actively campaigned for Gonzalez in the 1961 special election that made him the first Hispanic congressman from Texas.[82] Partially on the advice of LBJ and Gonzalez, Bailey appointed Carlos McCormick, national chairman of the Viva Kennedy Clubs in 1960, as a DNC aide for Hispanic Democrats. McCormick used this position not only to lobby for more federal appointments for Hispanics but also to help mobilize Hispanic voters for the 1964 presidential election.[83]

For the politically pragmatic vice president, there was nothing inconsistent or duplicitous about attracting more votes for JFK in Texas from Hispanics, blacks, and other liberal elements of the Texas Democratic Party while also seeking campaign contributions for the DNC from oil and gas companies, defense and NASA contractors, and other business interests affiliated with the pro-Connally conservative Democrats. At JFK's request, Bailey, O'Donnell, LBJ, and Connally organized fundraising dinners in major Texas cities for the fall of 1963. JFK originally planned to arrive in September.[84]

Kennedy wanted to concentrate on Dallas and Fort Worth since he assumed that these two cities would be the most lucrative for fundraising. In order to placate Henry B. Gonzalez, JFK agreed to spend more time in San Antonio.[85] The eventual strategy for JFK's ill-fated trip to Texas in November 1963 was for JFK to alternate between improving his poll numbers and future voting strength in Texas by appealing to crowds of mostly pro-Yarborough liberals, blacks, and Hispanics through motorcades, handshaking, and his wife's brief speeches in Spanish, and raising DNC funds through dinners, speeches, and private receptions attended by mostly pro-Connally, wealthy conservatives.[86]

The DNC's solicitation of large sums of money from small numbers of party donors was a practice used throughout the Kennedy and Johnson presidencies. This elite method of fundraising was a rejection of and contrast to Paul M. Butler's preference for raising large amounts of small donations from large numbers of rank-and-file Democrats. In particular, the Dollars for Democrats Drive began in 1956 and distributed fundraising booklets to the state and local Democratic committee chairmen. The chairmen's responsibility was to mobilize volunteers who solicited donations door-to-door for $5 each. The donor was given a certificate of membership in the Democratic Party. Butler's perspective was that how the DNC raised its money was more important than how much money was raised. Although the Dollars for Democrats Drive raised less than $110,000 from 1959 to 1960, Butler believed that its grassroots, decentralized process stimulated more participation by state and local party committees and rank-and-file Democrats, thereby attracting more Democratic voters and campaign volunteers for the elections.[87]

Richard Maguire, a Massachusetts Democrat who served as DNC treasurer under JFK and LBJ, dissolved this program and emphasized the raising of large sums of money from fewer donors. In particular, Maguire created the President's Club in which Democratic contributors paid $1,000 each to attend dinners with JFK. The President's Club grossed approximately $400,000 on May 16, 1962, and over $500,000 on January 18, 1963.[88] The President's Club had about 4,000 members in 1964. Almost $2 million was raised by the President's Club from 1961 to 1963 and nearly $2.3 million in 1964. The DNC's nearly $4 million debt from the 1960 campaign was erased by 1963.[89] Maguire also promoted the sale of advertising in the program book of the 1964 Democratic national convention. Advertising cost $15,000 a page, and the DNC earned $1 million in profits from it.[90]

Wanting to protect the anonymity of President's Club members, the DNC refused to disclose their names to Congress when it filed its financial reports after the 1964 election.[91] *Congressional Quarterly Almanac* calculated that the percentage of DNC donors who were Fat Cats increased from 30.3 percent in 1960 to 57.4 percent in 1964. Fat Cats were donors who gave $10,000 or more.[92]

In addition to receiving large donations from lawyer-lobbyists and businessmen receiving federal contracts, the DNC also tapped into Hollywood for large contributions. Journalist Ronald Brownstein found a regular, formal connection between the President's Club and movie and television executives, namely, Lew Wasserman of MCA in California and Arthur Krim of United Artists in New York. Although Wasserman supported LBJ's brief, ill-fated presidential candidacy in 1960, he became active in organizing President's Club dinners among Hollywood executives and movie stars only after the Justice Department's 1962 anti-trust action against MCA. He simply wanted to develop political influence with JFK and later LBJ in order to prevent or at least mitigate future federal intervention that he perceived as detrimental to the movie industry in general and MCA in particular. Wasserman later declined LBJ's offer to be nominated Secretary of Commerce. But he developed a close rapport with LBJ aide Jack Valenti, who became president of the Motion Picture Association of America in 1966.[93]

Wasserman also raised funds for Governor Edmund "Pat" Brown's 1962 reelection campaign and for California Democrats in general, including former JFK press secretary Pierre Salinger in his unsuccessful Senate campaign in 1964. Eugene Wyman, a Beverly Hills lawyer and Democratic state chairman, developed a regular, symbiotic, bicoastal relationship between Wasserman and Krim. With his connections with leading Wall Street law and investment firms, Krim coordinated his fundraising activities with Wasserman, Maguire, and O'Donnell.[94] In particular, Krim organized the highly lucrative, televised birthday party for JFK in Madison Square Garden in 1962.[95] Krim and Wasserman also provided technical expertise and supervision for the media productions of the 1964 Democratic national convention.[96]

Unlike Wasserman, Krim was a liberal, issue-oriented intellectual who apparently had no desire to use his fundraising accomplishments to benefit his economic interests. He wanted to help JFK and LBJ fulfill their liberal policy agenda on civil rights, social welfare programs, education, and health care. Krim decided to regularly organize fundraising events for JFK and the DNC after O'Brien, O'Donnell, and Maguire explained the linkage between the president's fundraising success and his policy success. They told Krim that JFK needed his own separate, substantial source of campaign funds, although funneled through the DNC, for persuading and rewarding Democrats in Congress to support the New Frontier. These funds would also reduce and possibly end the president's and the DNC's traditional dependence on the often inadequate, unreliable contributions of state and local Democratic committees.[97] Brownstein observed that the President's Club money "was also raised on the basis of personal loyalty to the president, not necessarily to the party. As far as the club was concerned, the president stood independent of the party."[98]

In an oral history interview released to the public in 2002, Krim identified the primary reason why so many wealthy donors, especially in the entertainment business, gave so generously and continuously to the President's Club. Krim explained that membership in the President's Club "got you an awful lot of fun for yourself and a feeling of being close to the charisma of power . . . and it had started with Kennedy."[99] Investigative journalist G. William Domhoff less tactfully concluded that fundraising organizations, like the President's Club, that provide prestigious socializing with the president have "snob appeal" to nouveaux riche Jews who felt excluded by old money WASP Republicans in business and social circles.[100]

JFK seemed to anticipate this mutually beneficial relationship between popular entertainment figures like singer and actor Frank Sinatra and the president as a celebrity. In his address as president-elect to the pre-inaugural fundraising event in Washington organized by Sinatra, JFK stated that "the Democratic Party had been identified with excellence, and we saw excellence tonight. The happy relationship between the arts and politics which has characterized our long history I think reached culmination tonight."[101] Matthew McCloskey, DNC treasurer until 1962, announced that this event grossed $1.4 million for the DNC.[102]

LBJ was less personally appealing than JFK as a celebrity to politically active entertainers, but the Texan developed a close friendship with Arthur Krim. Krim frequently visited LBJ at his ranch in Texas and in the White House. The president had Krim closely monitor DNC treasurer John Criswell and reduce the DNC's debt from the 1964 campaign.[103] By the spring of 1966, the DNC's debt was more than $5 million. Krim's fundraising efforts, primarily through the President's Club, eliminated two-thirds of it by the end of 1966.[104] In addition to the activities of the President's Club, Krim planned sixty-five theater parties throughout the nation through the DNC's voter education committees during the fall of 1965. Krim would show unreleased, premiere movies to guests who bought tickets and $15,000-per-page advertising in program books. He expected to collect $2 million from the theater parties and advertising.[105]

Senator John J. Williams of Delaware, a Republican, revealed that corporations were able to deduct the cost of this advertising from their taxes. He used public outrage to pressure Congress to end this tax loophole.[106] Williams previously led the Senate investigation of corruption charges against Bobby Baker, former secretary of the Senate under LBJ.

Johnson had long perceived Williams as a relentless, vindictive publicity seeker determined to portray him as unethical and even criminal in campaign financing. During the 1964 presidential campaign, Williams conducted hearings that linked Baker's conflicts of interest with former DNC treasurer and ambassador to Ireland Matthew McCloskey. McCloskey's construction firm had gotten a contract for the construction of a new sports stadium for Washington, DC. He allegedly received a $35,000 contribution for the DNC's 1960 presidential campaign fund from an insurance executive who also paid Baker a fee in exchange for an insurance policy on the stadium.[107] LBJ failed to defeat Williams in his 1964 reelection campaign by funneling DNC money to the Republican senator's opponent, Elbert Carvel.[108] LBJ lamented to Attorney General Nicholas Katzenbach and congressional liaison Lawrence F. O'Brien about how the honest mistakes of DNC headquarters were embarrassing him and tainting his presidential campaign.[109] Ignoring any role for DNC chairman John M. Bailey in this problem, the president told O'Brien, "You make this McCloskey thing your personal business."[110]

By the summer of 1965, LBJ had developed an even lower opinion of DNC headquarters and its operations. Bypassing Bailey entirely, LBJ had Clifton Carter, a longtime political aide from Texas, serve as his liaison with the DNC and implement his 1965–1966 effort to substantially reduce the expenses, staff and activities of DNC headquarters.[111] Sam Brightman, the DNC's publicity director who had impressively served the DNC since 1947, was laid off. The DNC's voter registration project and radio and television facilities to assist congressional Democrats ended.[112]

The dismissal of John M. Bailey's chauffeur perhaps best symbolized the even lower status of the DNC chairman under LBJ's party leadership. Bailey had wanted to resign as early as January 1965, but LBJ persuaded him to remain DNC chairman.[113] LBJ wanted to maintain the appearance of leadership continuity at the DNC with JFK's party leadership. While Bailey was one of the few Kennedy political operatives whom LBJ trusted, the president also wanted to purge the DNC of staff whom he suspected of being loyal to RFK and disloyal to him. Shortly after becoming president, Johnson ordered Bailey to fire Paul Corbin, a DNC aide who was rumored to be promoting a write-in campaign for RFK for vice president.[114] On the previous day, February 10, 1964, LBJ told Clifton Carter to conduct an audit of the DNC's budget and submit a list of the names and salaries of everyone on the DNC payroll. LBJ implied that he wanted disloyal, pro-RFK employees of the DNC headquarters dismissed.[115]

The Democratic losses in the 1966 House elections were partially attributed to LBJ's diminution of the DNC's staff and operatives and his inadequate campaigning. Nevertheless, the president continued the DNC's apparatus as a hollow entity with Bailey as a figurehead. Bailey spent most of his time in Connecticut where he served as Democratic state chairman since 1946.[116] As his Vietnam War policies became more controversial and divisive within the Democratic Party and his public approval ratings declined, LBJ became more obsessed with the personal loyalty of his appointees. He increasingly equated Democratic criticism of his war policies with personal animosity toward him and support for future RFK opposition to his renomination in 1968. LBJ subsequently centralized and personalized his party leadership even further through (W.) Marvin Watson, the White House appointments secretary, the same position held by Kenneth P. O'Donnell during JFK's presidency.[117]

After Watson managed the details of the 1964 Democratic national convention in Atlantic City, he was elected, with the help of LBJ and John Connally, Democratic state chairman in Texas. Watson had a reputation as an antiunion conservative since his career as a steel company executive. His emergence as LBJ's most powerful, trusted liaison with the DNC and on all intraparty matters was the result of his unqualified loyalty to LBJ and his unquestioning implementation of LBJ's decisions.[118] Having worked with Watson on the write-in campaign for LBJ in the 1968 New Hampshire presidential primary, Bernard Boutin later said about Watson, "Whatever he said was pure Lyndon Johnson."[119] On behalf of LBJ, Watson closely monitored the use of government cars and the phone calls of White House aides. He wanted to determine if they were meeting or communicating with journalists or Democrats suspected of being hostile to the president.[120] LBJ publicly praised Watson with perhaps his highest compliment. "Marvin is as wise as my father and as gentle as my mother, and he is as loyal as another East Texan I know, Lady Bird."[121] Lady Bird Johnson later asked Watson to deliver the eulogy at LBJ's funeral in 1973.[122]

Arthur Krim rivaled Watson in LBJ's degree of trust on party affairs. Unlike Watson, though, Krim was more likely to provide advice that he knew LBJ would probably reject. For example, after the extent and methods of LBJ's fundraising became controversial, Krim urged LBJ to strengthen and improve the structure, staff, and activities of the DNC and its organizational relationship with state and local party organizations. Krim did not believe that a huge campaign treasury alone could ensure LBJ's renomination and reelection in 1968.[123] According to Krim, LBJ "told me that he didn't give a damn about the committee, he just wanted those debts paid."[124]

LBJ's dismissive attitude toward and denigration of the traditional grassroots activities of vibrant party organizations and thousands of party activists ultimately connected to the DNC chairman were also a product of his suprapartisan, non-ideological, unifying consensus politics.[125] His confidence in a suprapartisan consensus was bolstered by the crucial Republican support for the Civil Rights Act of 1964 and his landslide popular vote margin in 1964. In that election, he carried the most staunchly Republican states in the Electoral College. Many moderate Republicans either voted for LBJ or refused to vote at all as they rejected the ideological extremism of Barry Goldwater.[126] In his campaign speeches before Democratic audiences, LBJ repeatedly emphasized that he wanted to be the president of all Americans, regardless of their differences in party affiliation or wealth, and that the Great Society should be supported by both Democrats and Republicans in Congress.[127] Analyzing the large number of executive positions that LBJ gave to Republicans, political scientists Richard L. Schott and

Dagmar S. Hamilton noted that for LBJ "loyalty came to be perceived in terms of a candidate's commitment to the Great Society programs."[128] LBJ did not hesitate to appoint a liberal Republican, John Gardner, as his last Secretary of Health Education and Welfare (HEW).

LBJ perceived a strong, national party organization with regular publicity and activities emphasizing partisan differences to be a threat to the suprapartisan, centrist consensus that he wanted to develop for his presidency, the Great Society, and his policies in Vietnam, which he regarded as responsible, moderate, and restrained. LBJ concluded that his landslide victory, the Republican Party's bitter intraparty discord and devastating losses at all levels of government in 1964, and his success in fashioning bipartisan support in Congress for his impressive legislative accomplishments meant that he could transform the Democratic Party into a broad-based, consensual "big tent party."[129] It could then equally satisfy blacks and whites, northerners and southerners, business and labor, rich and poor. The Republican Party would marginalize itself further through right-wing extremism and would no longer be competitive in presidential elections and most congressional elections.[130]

LBJ also did not want a well-staffed, well-financed, active DNC apparatus that could become infiltrated and eventually captured by pro-RFK, anti-LBJ Democrats before the 1968 presidential primaries. The growth of large antiwar demonstrations, especially among college students, and opposition to the war and LBJ from younger, militant black and Hispanic political activists confirmed LBJ's perspective. Johnson recognized the potential for a pro-RFK, anti-LBJ coalition of these dissident elements and a DNC apparatus coopted by RFK's operatives.[131]

By 1967, LBJ's apparent desire to run for another term in 1968 was reflected in his party leadership strategy of minimizing the DNC's apparatus and chairman while maximizing personally controlled campaign funds under the trusted supervision of (W.) Marvin Watson and Arthur Krim. From December 1967 through January 1968, Krim and Watson held campaign preparation meetings with Supreme Court Justice Abe Fortas, Washington attorneys James H. Rowe, Jr. and Clark M. Clifford, and Postmaster General Lawrence F. O'Brien. DNC chairman John M. Bailey was conspicuously absent. Krim directed DNC treasurer John Criswell to coordinate his fundraising plans in California with assembly speaker Jesse Unruh. Krim estimated that fundraising activities for LBJ in California, Texas, and New York would yield approximately $15 million.[132]

Krim was also making arrangements to hire top advertising and polling firms for LBJ's reelection campaign. Despite Barry Goldwater's doomed presidential candidacy within a bitterly divided Republican Party, national-level Republican committees still spent approximately $3 million more than the total spending of the Democratic and labor committees in the 1964 election.[133] With the prospect of competing against the independently wealthy RFK for renomination and the immensely wealthy Nelson Rockefeller as the Republican presidential nominee in 1968, LBJ wanted to quickly and thoroughly gain overwhelming supremacy in campaign funds.[134] This advantage might deter RFK and more obscure dovish Democrats from opposing his renomination in the primaries.[135]

The Democratic president also needed the largest campaign treasury in order to effectively practice his consensus politics for renomination and reelection. LBJ still adhered to his belief in the politics of a suprapartisan centrist policy consensus.[136] He assumed that he could be reelected in 1968 by spending enough money on polling, advertising, changing his public image and style, and influencing the news media's coverage and analysis of his presidency and policies in Vietnam. Since poll ratings on public approval of his presidential performance in general and of his policies toward Vietnam, crime control, and inflation in particular were so volatile, they also seemed to be malleable and subject to improvement by the best experts.[137] The focus of a well-financed polling and publicity oriented campaign for LBJ's renomination and reelection in 1968 based on reshaping a new pro-LBJ consensus was the white, racially moderate, well-educated, suburban middle class.[138]

With its emphasis on issues and the personal qualities of candidates instead of their party affiliations, suburbia was expected to be the electoral battleground in 1968.[139] In an extensive analysis of LBJ's 1968 presidential campaign, Lawrence F. O'Brien wrote to LBJ, "There has been a mass movement to suburbia and the Democratic Party has not kept pace. A tremendous organizational effort is required in the suburbs. Nationally, Republicans are beating us to the punch in reaching new members of suburbia."[140]

O'Brien's September 29, 1967, report was the result of his extensive nationwide tour and consultation with Democratic state and local chairmen and major Democratic politicians. Most were loyal to LBJ and expected him to run in 1968. They emphasized, though, the need for Johnson or the DNC headquarters to more effectively and persuasively clarify and defend LBJ's policies, especially regarding Vietnam, crime, inflation, and race relations, to voters in their states. They also wanted LBJ to more effectively project an image as an experienced, responsible, moderate president best able to provide unifying leadership during a turbulent era.[141] O'Brien acknowledged the need for high-priced polling, public relations, and television advertising. He contended that the DNC's apparatus needed to become revitalized and better connected to state and local party committees in providing traditional party services and activities. "The Democratic National Committee is not staffed or equipped to conduct a successful Presidential election. The Democratic Party, to a greater or less extent, had lost contact with the voters."[142]

John P. Roche, a White House aide and former ADA chairman, was even blunter in his criticism. Roche observed that LBJ "was behaving in an absolutely absurd way in terms of any kind of organization of the Democratic Party. The DNC was just rotting on the vine."[143] In a 1987 interview, O'Brien admitted, "The DNC and its operation probably deserved all these negative comments. . . . We were at fault."[144]

Although O'Brien's campaign memo to LBJ, commonly nicknamed the "White Paper," recommended (W.) Marvin Watson as the director of organization for the 1968 campaign, O'Brien would presumably be LBJ's de facto campaign manager. More so than any of JFK's other political operatives, LBJ respected O'Brien's political judgment and trusted his loyalty throughout his presidency. Journalist Patrick Anderson observed, "Moreover, above and beyond the legislative program, O'Brien saw his loyalty as being to the Democratic Party, whether its leader was named Kennedy, Johnson, Humphrey, or whatever."[145]

The internal communications of White House aides and the advice of Krim, Fortas, Rowe, and Clifford recommended that LBJ run for renomination and reelection similar to Harry Truman's 1948 campaign strategy that was detailed in the Clifford-Rowe memorandum of 1947.[146] LBJ's campaign advisors assumed that former Alabama Governor George Wallace would fulfill the role of J. Strom Thurmond in his Dixiecrat presidential campaign of 1948. Unlike Thurmond, though, the LBJ campaign expected Wallace to attract much media attention and perform better in nonsouthern states, especially in industrial states. Many white blue-collar workers rejected the counterculture, regarded the antiwar movement as unpatriotic, and resented Great Society liberalism as soft on crime and indulgent toward unruly, ungrateful blacks.[147] LBJ was dismayed at how well Wallace performed in the 1964 Wisconsin and Indiana presidential primaries.[148]

As in 1948, the LBJ campaign expected that an antiwar presidential candidate on the left, similar to Henry Wallace in 1948, would oppose him in several primaries and possibly as a minor party candidate in November. If not RFK, then the antiwar presidential candidate might be J. William Fulbright or Wayne Morse, the two most frequent, outspoken Democratic critics of LBJ's Vietnam policies in the Senate. RFK's announcement at a Democratic dinner in 1967 that he supported LBJ for reelection in 1968 reassured LBJ's advisors and operatives that RFK would wait until 1972 to run for president.[149] White House aide John P. Roche told LBJ, "Forget (not *forgive*) the whole Kennedy caper— the point has been made to Bobby that if we go down, he goes with us. . . . He has nowhere else to go and your victory is imperative to his plans for 1972."[150]

The logic of LBJ's campaign strategists in late 1967 and early 1968 was that most voters, as in 1948, would vote against the extremism and irresponsibility of either or both the antiwar left and racist, right-wing populism. Just as most Democratic voters in 1948 were ambivalent or unenthusiastic about Truman, most of them would vote for LBJ as a way to vote against extremism. Bolstered by analysis from pollster Louis Harris, White House aide Fred Panzer told LBJ, "Therefore, your greatest strength is to overtly run against Wallace in the South and the peace party in the North. . . . It would also insure national coverage so that Negroes in the North would know of your attacks on George Wallace, and farmers, small towners and Southerners would know of your attacks on the peace wing."[151]

Harris's polling analysis also led LBJ's campaign strategists to conclude that the intraparty conflict over the Democratic presidential nomination would actually strengthen LBJ's candidacy and make it more difficult for the Republicans to defeat him in November. Regardless of whether the Republicans nominated Nixon, Rockefeller, or Governor George Romney of Michigan for president, LBJ's centrism "would force GOP criticism to join either extreme— the Wallace-ites or the peaceniks. Or if they avoid this, to conduct an empty campaign."[152]

In order to best protect the gradual improvement of LBJ's image, credibility, and approval ratings in the polls, O'Brien advised Johnson not to personally campaign in the primaries. Since most of the delegates to 1968 Democratic national convention were not chosen through binding primaries, O'Brien suggested that LBJ run as a write-in candidate in New Hampshire and other key primaries by having pro-LBJ Democratic politicians, like Governor John King of New Hampshire, represent the president for the purpose of winning and controlling blocs of delegates. Meanwhile, LBJ should not actually declare his candidacy. Instead, O'Brien's strategy wanted to generate the appearance of a publicly spontaneous, yet privately well-orchestrated, draft movement within the Democratic Party for LBJ's renomination. The theme of the pro-LBJ campaign literature and advertising, to be regularly tested through polls, was that LBJ was not campaigning in these states or making campaign statements from the White House because he was a dedicated, diligent, experienced president. As such, LBJ was so busy concentrating on making steady progress on the Vietnam War and other policy areas that he refused to be distracted by personal ambition and intraparty conflict.[153]

The expectation of LBJ's campaign strategists that a "peacenik" presidential candidate, similar to Henry Wallace in 1948, would soon emerge was fulfilled by Democratic Senator Eugene McCarthy of Minnesota. McCarthy had a reputation in the Senate for laziness, acerbic wit, and aloofness. More so than RFK and most other Democratic senators, however, McCarthy was an early, consistent, outspoken critic of LBJ's policies in Vietnam. As early as January 1966, the Minnesota senator denounced LBJ's bombing of North Vietnam and suggested that the Viet Cong be included in a coalition government in South Vietnam.[154]

In announcing his challenge to LBJ's renomination on November 30, 1967, McCarthy readily admitted that he probably could not defeat LBJ for their party's presidential nomination. McCarthy did not actually state that he was running for president. Instead, he intended to campaign in five or six primary states as a forum for critiquing LBJ's foreign policy in Vietnam and stimulating intraparty debate on this issue in order to pressure LBJ to change his policy direction in Vietnam. McCarthy stated, "I am concerned that the Administration seems to have set no limit to the price which it's willing to pay for a military victory."[155] McCarthy also told the media that he informed RFK beforehand of his announcement and that the New York senator did not indicate that he would later enter the primaries.

Neither LBJ nor John Bailey issued a public statement responding to McCarthy's announcement. RFK's repeated denial of any intention of running for president in 1968 combined with McCarthy's disclosure of his earlier consultation with RFK now made it more difficult for RFK to oppose LBJ for the presidential nomination without appearing to be duplicitous and egregiously ambitious. If RFK still decided to enter the primaries and McCarthy refused to withdraw, it seemed reasonable to conclude that McCarthy and RFK would divide the votes of the most antiwar, anti-LBJ, liberal Democrats and weaken each other's candidacy.

In his memoirs, Lawrence F. O'Brien observed, "McCarthy's candidacy was not taken seriously by anyone around the President. It was regarded as a joke, an annoyance."[156] McCarthy lacked a significant Democratic voting bloc, such as blacks or union members, in his national electoral base. The White House assumed that, like Henry Wallace in 1948, McCarthy's unconventional, quixotic "peacenik" candidacy would attract some of the most controversial, extreme antiwar activists. They would then prove to be more of a liability than an asset to McCarthy as the media and public opinion perceived him as the dupe of left-wing extremists.[157] A Gallup poll released on February 4, 1968, but conducted before the Tet Offensive, showed that Democrats preferred LBJ over McCarthy 71 percent to 18 percent and favored LBJ over RFK 52 percent to 40 percent for their party's presidential nomination in 1968.[158]

In addition to Gallup polls published by the media, O'Brien also used polls privately conducted and analyzed by pollsters Louis Harris, John Kraft, Oliver Quayle, and Richard Scammon.[159] O'Brien believed that a large number and variety of expertly conducted and analyzed polls on LBJ's prospects for reelection were necessary to persuade DNC members, Democratic state and local chairmen, and Democratic politicians in key states to openly and actively back LBJ for renomination. O'Brien hoped that this particular use of polling could solidify LBJ's base among wavering, ambivalent Democratic organizational leaders, especially in states with significant degrees of antiwar, anti-LBJ sentiment, such as Wisconsin, Massachusetts, New York, and California.[160] O'Brien also planned to use a revitalized DNC apparatus to stimulate and develop a unifying, pro-LBJ intraparty consensus as the foundation for a suprapartisan consensus behind LBJ in the general election.[161]

LBJ conducted highly publicized trips in December that included consultations with the pope in Rome and the president of South Vietnam in Australia and visits to American troops in Thailand and South Vietnam.[162] O'Brien assumed that LBJ's diplomatic missions, following optimistic explanations of American military progress by General William Westmoreland and U.S. Ambassador Ellsworth Bunker in November, might reduce LBJ's credibility gap with the public and make Americans more optimistic about and patient with LBJ's policies in Vietnam.[163] O'Brien and Bailey decided to hold more frequent meetings of the DNC and conduct DNC-organized regional meetings of Democratic state and local officials in such cities as Salt Lake City and Des Moines.[164]

At these regional meetings held from January to March of 1968, Hubert H. Humphrey and other prominent Democrats, including former DNC chairman James Farley, defended and explained LBJ's policies in Vietnam. At the DNC's regional conference in Salt Lake City on January 13, 1968, Farley harshly denounced Senator J. William Fulbright's critique of LBJ's policies. Farley declared, "I say that a man who attacks the morals of the armed forces, the integrity of the President and the motives of his country is as close to being their ally as even the Communists could wish."[165] More tactfully than Farley, Humphrey defended LBJ's Vietnam policies at the southern and New England regional conferences in February and March 1968.[166]

At the direction of Watson and O'Brien, Bailey had large quantities and a wide variety of DNC pamphlets explaining and defending LBJ's foreign policy produced and distributed to DNC members and state and local party leaders. Many of them would be delegates at the 1968 convention. In one pamphlet, entitled "The United States and Eastern Asia," Bailey stated, "Instead of a liability, the President's skillful and courageous handling of a difficult Southeast Asia situation is becoming an asset."[167] Another DNC pamphlet issued by Bailey explicitly rebuked Democratic opponents of LBJ's Vietnam policies. Comparing Johnson to Harry Truman in 1948, this pamphlet contended that "these same fair-weather fighters in the Democratic Party still have their guns trained on the President, Johnson this time. . . . Wolves from both parties and George Wallace for good measure are at his throat."[168] A DNC pamphlet issued on January 21, 1968, boasted that a poll of delegates from the 1964 Democratic national convention favored LBJ over RFK by a ratio of twenty-three to one and LBJ over McCarthy by a ratio of twenty-five to one. A DNC pamphlet issued on February 23, 1968, criticized the ADA for endorsing McCarthy and lamented, "The ADA is fast painting itself into a tiny corner."[169]

Since LBJ had not announced any intention to run for reelection and McCarthy was opposing his renomination, many anti-LBJ, antiwar Democrats regarded Bailey's rhetoric and the DNC's campaign literature to be a blatant violation of the DNC chairman's traditional neutrality in contested primaries. Even some pro-LBJ Democratic politicians were uncomfortable with the DNC publicity's scathing criticism of antiwar Democrats and implication that patriotism required support for LBJ's renomination. For example, Senator Edmund S.

Muskie of Maine, chairman of the Senate Democratic Campaign Committee, decided to establish a research and publicity operation for his campaign organization separate from the DNC. He also asserted his intraparty neutrality in distributing campaign funds to Senate candidates regardless of their positions on the Vietnam War and LBJ's renomination. Journalists Rowland Evans and Robert Novak concluded, "To Muskie, the Party structure must treat hawks and doves alike."[170]

Eugene McCarthy was disturbed by the fact that Bailey was using his chairmanship and DNC events to deny and suppress any discussion of intraparty differences on the Vietnam War. Bailey did not reply to McCarthy's telegram asking the DNC chairman if he could address a DNC meeting in January in Chicago that was planning their party's national convention for 1968.[171] In his January 8, 1968, speech to the DNC in Chicago, Bailey confidently stated, "Many who reviled President Johnson, both within and without our party, are now softening their criticism. Most of the undecided, after listening to all the heated Vietnam arguments, are now quietly lining up behind President Johnson."[172] Privately, Bailey bluntly told McCarthy that "the Democratic National Convention is as good as over. It will be Lyndon Johnson again, and that's that."[173]

In an article written for *Look* magazine, McCarthy stated that he was running against LBJ for other reasons in addition to the Vietnam War. He claimed that LBJ's insatiable appetite for power and control led the Texan to personalize and corrupt every institution that he influenced, including the Senate and the DNC. "What we have is a personalized presidency, somewhat independent of the government and somewhat independent of the political party from which the president has come. . . . We are getting a reflection of this in the administration's shocked and angry reaction to the challenge within the party in a presidential election year."[174]

Although Lawrence F. O'Brien was the primary architect of LBJ's overall campaign strategy, (W.) Marvin Watson generally managed the New Hampshire primary campaign from the White House. John M. Bailey conducted a tour of the northeastern states to assess LBJ's chances in their primaries. In a January 5, 1968, report, Bailey warned Watson about the difficulty of mobilizing a large write-in vote for LBJ in New Hampshire's March 12 primary.[175] The DNC chairman was also concerned that if too many pro-LBJ Democrats ran for delegate positions to the national convention then that surplus of candidates could further dilute the pro-LBJ vote. Bailey and DNC treasurer John Criswell discussed the possibility of meeting with pro-LBJ New Hampshire politicians in Boston "but I thought it might be looked upon as a sign of our worry over the situation," according to Bailey.[176]

Instead of Bailey, though, Watson's main operatives in New Hampshire were Governor John King, Senator Thomas J. McIntyre, and Bernard Boutin, a local businessman who previously served as director of the Small Business Administration (SBA) and deputy director of the OEO.[177] Watson did not want the appearance that LBJ or anyone from his administration was intervening in New Hampshire. Since McIntyre and King belonged to rival factions of the New Hampshire Democratic Party, Boutin served as a liaison between them and as Watson's chief contact in the state.[178] Bailey and O'Brien stayed out of New Hampshire.[179]

Like Bailey, Boutin expected problems with LBJ's refusal to declare himself as a candidate for the New Hampshire ballot and to have a well-known New Hampshire Democrat run as his "stand in." The New Hampshire Democratic state committee decided to issue pledge cards in order to assist it in targeting and mobilizing pro-LBJ voters on primary day. Boutin assured Watson that "the Citizens for Johnson Committee as a subsidiary of the State Committee" was the official vehicle for processing campaign funds, calling voters, and publishing pro-LBJ literature. Boutin told Watson that, for McCarthy, "I think a good walloping in New Hampshire might keep him out of other primaries where his efforts could be more harmful."[180] All but one of the fifteen members of the New Hampshire Democratic state committee voted to dismiss a motion by a pro-McCarthy Democrat to recall all of its pro-LBJ campaign literature in a February 20 meeting.[181]

Throughout the write-in campaign, the pro-LBJ politicians in New Hampshire were more confident than LBJ's campaign strategists in the White House and the DNC. On January 30, 1968, one day before the Tet Offensive in Vietnam, a poll reported that McCarthy would only receive 15 percent of the votes in the New Hampshire primary.[182] In a February 5, 1968, memo to LBJ, John Criswell expressed his concerns about the write-in campaign after a DNC aide, Spencer Oliver, visited New Hampshire. McCarthy's campaign in the state was well financed, heavily advertised, and seemed to showcase McCarthy's Catholicism in order to appeal to New Hampshire's mostly Catholic Democratic voters.[183] Oliver told Criswell that Boutin, King, and other pro-LBJ leaders "were very confident of their ability to pull off a stunning Johnson victory."[184] Oliver "found the secondary, rank-and-file Democrats, however, to be somewhat less than enthusiastic and not nearly as confident."[185] He estimated that McCarthy could get up to 35 percent of the votes, unlike the 5 to 15 percent projected by the top LBJ supporters.

The Watson-directed campaign from the White House continued to conduct its own polls through Oliver Quayle's firm in order to gain a more objective, scientific survey of New Hampshire voters. According to Fred Panzer's analysis of one of Quayle's polls, "Democrats are overwhelmingly hawkish and hence opposed to McCarthy's cut and run position."[186] LBJ's best issue, therefore, was "Vietnam—force it as a choice between backing down or remaining firm in our commitments."[187] In its conclusion, the Quayle poll stated, "It would hurt McCarthy if some of the more extreme young protesters started campaigning for him."[188] The firm's conclusion recommended "that President

Johnson will launch a program to improve his image with respect to the credibility gap."[189]

LBJ's credibility gap worsened significantly after the Tet Offensive. After
conducting and assessing another poll in New Hampshire in late February, the
Quayle firm still found LBJ with a wide lead over McCarthy, 57 percent to15
percent.[190] On the Saturday before the New Hampshire primary, John Criswell
reported to Watson that thousands of college students were canvassing the state for
McCarthy. The pro-LBJ leaders, though, were mobilizing labor union members,
and one of them "thinks they have the best set-up to get out the vote he had seen
in New Hampshire."[191] The White House received a less scientific, more pessimistic report from Gordon St. Angelo, the Democratic state chairman of Indiana, five
days before the New Hampshire primary. In his visit to New Hampshire, St.
Angelo noticed far more campaign activity in terms of volunteers, pamphlet distribution, and advertising for McCarthy than for LBJ. St. Angelo observed, "Not
a soul had contacted me to offer me literature, a button, or a pledge card."[192]

The McCarthy campaign increasingly used the pledge card as an issue. It
accused the pro-LBJ forces of violating the spirit of a secret ballot and of intimi-
dating voters through Orwellian authoritarianism. The most strident rhetoric of
King and McIntyre equated votes for McCarthy with the appeasement of Communist aggression in Vietnam and possibly treason. This offended many previously undecided or passively pro-LBJ voters.[193] Nevertheless, six days before the
primary, Boutin reported to Watson that LBJ would defeat McCarthy 37,000 to
15,000 votes, a ratio of more than two to one.[194]

Watson, Bailey, and other LBJ strategists in Washington generally gave the
New Hampshire Democrats broad discretion to choose and utilize their own
tactics. They also gave the pro-LBJ New Hampshire operatives little or no guidance about how to respond to McCarthy's attacks and those of the Republicans
in their New Hampshire primary. In February and early March, the broadcast
airwaves of New Hampshire were filled with anti-LBJ television advertising from
the McCarthy campaign and pessimistic news coverage and analysis of American
foreign policy in Vietnam, Secretary of Defense Robert S. McNamara's resigna-
tion, the Senate's hearings on the Gulf of Tonkin Resolution, and the military's
request for approximately 206,000 additional American troops in Vietnam.[195]
Despite all of these current events rapidly changing the political environment,
the pro-LBJ Democrats in New Hampshire persistently emphasized the theme
inspired earlier by O'Brien's "White Paper" and the DNC's pamphlets—"A Strong
Man in a Tough Job." This literature and LBJ's surrogate campaigners continued
to underscore the president's experience and proven, responsible leadership.

Although this persistent theme was now less effective among the increasingly skeptical New Hampshire voters, the pro-LBJ Democrats especially communicated it to lower-income, blue-collar, older voters, especially the elderly.
Polls indicated that they were the most loyal to LBJ.[196] Unfortunately for LBJ's

write-in campaign, the weather in New Hampshire on primary day, March 13, 1968, was cold, snowy, and icy. Older, pro-LBJ Democrats were less likely to vote; they were also more likely to be discouraged from voting and have their votes invalidated because of confusion about the write-in process.

The result was that LBJ received 49.6 percent of the votes and McCarthy 41.9 percent in the New Hampshire Democratic primary. Although LBJ defeated McCarthy by more than 4,200 votes in the Democratic primary, McCarthy received 5,511 write-in votes to LBJ's 1,778 write-in votes in that state's Republican presidential primary.[197] In a post-primary analysis to (W.) Marvin Watson, Boutin identified George Romney's withdrawal from the Republican presidential race as perhaps "the worse (sic) thing that happened" because "at least 6 or 7,000 votes for McCarthy can be attributable to the Romney withdrawal."[198]

The national pollsters who had been advising Watson, O'Brien, and Criswell mostly blamed Boutin and the other pro-LBJ Democratic leaders in New Hampshire. In particular, Louis Harris criticized the use of pledge cards and Governor King's red-baiting, "Hanoi is listening," mud-slinging rhetoric against McCarthy. Richard Scammon was blunter than Harris. He blamed a "lack of leadership" by pro-LBJ Democrats in New Hampshire. They conducted a much weaker campaign than McCarthy's and, by "fouling up on the delegates' slates," pro-McCarthy Democrats won twenty of New Hampshire's twenty-four delegate seats to the Democratic national convention.[199] Scammon informed White House aide Ben Wattenberg that he was very impressed by the thousands of college students who worked in McCarthy's campaign, enabling McCarthy to run "a European-style campaign: canvassing door-to-door throughout the state."[200] The typical media analysis of the voting statistics in New Hampshire compared the total votes for McCarthy and LBJ in both parties' primaries to calculate that LBJ had beaten McCarthy "by only 230 votes in what was supposedly one of the most patriotic and warlike states of the Union," according to journalist Theodore H. White.[201]

Because he had greatly exceeded expectations, Eugene McCarthy was widely declared to be the "winner" of the New Hampshire primary and publicly vowed to win the presidential nomination, rather than simply use his campaign to protest LBJ's Vietnam policies. The next contested primary was held in Wisconsin on April 2. O'Brien flew to Wisconsin on March 28 and found the McCarthy campaign to be vibrant and enthusiastic with thousands of student volunteers while LBJ's campaign was inert and demoralized. He told the stunned LBJ that the president might be defeated by a ratio of two to one.[202] RFK's announcement of his presidential candidacy on March 16 further complicated the intraparty conflict. However, on March 31, 1968, Johnson announced in a televised address to the nation, "I shall not seek and I will not accept the nomination of my party for another term as your President."[203]

Although LBJ told several people since 1967 that he might not run again in 1968, his staff, advisors, and DNC chairman John M. Bailey assumed that he would. The 1968 Democratic national convention in Chicago was intentionally scheduled so that LBJ would be renominated on his birthday, August 27.[204] It was later learned that LBJ chose March 31 to announce his withdrawal from the renomination process because it was almost the same day, March 29, in 1952 when Harry Truman announced that he would not run for another term.[205] Like LBJ, Truman suffered an embarrassing electoral performance in the New Hampshire primary after Senator Estes Kefauver of Tennessee defeated him 55 to 44 percent.[206]

During and after his presidency, LBJ often paralleled Truman's experiences with the Korean War and his experiences with the Vietnam War in terms of growing intraparty discord, his application of the limited war concept in both diplomacy and military strategy, his unpopularity as the American public and Congress became frustrated with the stalemate in an Asian war, and his fear of another period of McCarthyism.[207] Unlike Truman, though, LBJ had an unusually prominent, powerful rival within the Democratic party—RFK. LBJ told biographer Doris Kearns that if he withdrew from Vietnam, then "there would be Robert Kennedy out in front leading the fight against me, telling everyone that I had betrayed John Kennedy's commitment to South Vietnam."[208]

The antiwar presidential campaigns of Eugene McCarthy and RFK also confronted LBJ and the traditional "in-party" roles of the DNC's chairman and apparatus with a baffling turbulence that Truman did not face—the transition from Old Politics to New Politics. Five days before LBJ announced his withdrawal from the presidential race, columnist James Reston wrote, "Party loyalty and party machinery have never been weaker than they are now, and for this and many other reasons the President may be in much deeper trouble than most voters believe."[209] He continued, "For we are now in a wholly new era of political action in America where the television, the popularity polls and new personalities can and often do topple the old power structures."[210]

Since the early 1960s, journalists, cultural and academic elites, and student activists had either examined or promoted the transition from Old Politics to New Politics. They identified the major values and modes of behavior of the New Politics to include open, grassroots citizen participation, a rejection of strictly disciplined political organizations controlled by traditional party leaders like Mayor Richard J. Daley of Chicago as anti-democratic and corrupt, and a demand for vigorous debates over previously consensual ideas, policies, and institutions, such as corporate liberalism and the Cold War's containment policy. The origins of the New Politics were often traced to the New Left with the formation of the Students for a Democratic Society (SDS) in 1962 and the free speech protests at Berkeley in 1964. Other commentators, though, dismissed differences in ideology and partisanship and included the right-wing populism of Barry Goldwater, Ronald Reagan, and George Wallace as well as the maverick campaigning and governing style of liberal New York City Mayor John Lindsay as examples of the New Politics. [211] Journalist and historian Jeff Shesol specified that the LBJ-RFK conflict within the Democratic Party "personalized, embodied, and crystallized growing rifts among Democrats. Their feud was, in large part, an ideological and generational struggle for the soul of the Democratic Party and the future of American liberalism."[212]

It was ironic that by 1968 LBJ was widely perceived as the personification of old-fashioned machine politics with its emphasis on party discipline and a powerful role for party chairmen. Even with its "in party" status, the DNC's chairman, apparatus, and activities were relegated to unusually dormant, anemic conditions during most of LBJ's presidency. Indecisive and ambivalent about running for another term, Johnson passively deferred to O'Brien's suggestion in late 1967 to mobilize the DNC's publicity, voter registration project, regional conferences, coordination with state and local Democratic committees, and the public speaking role of John Bailey for the purpose of generating a unifying intraparty consensus behind LBJ's renomination.[213]

Except for Mayor Richard J. Daley of Chicago, LBJ generally disliked and distrusted northern Democratic machine bosses.[214] Unlike JFK, Johnson often could not understand or empathize with the perspectives, interests, and values peculiar to northern, urban party regulars. Widely recognized as the powerful boss of a tightly disciplined state party organization in Connecticut, John M. Bailey served primarily as LBJ's token window dressing for northern, urban Democratic politicians rather than as a crucial liaison between the president and these Democrats. Bailey admitted to his biographer and future senator Joseph I. Lieberman that his role as DNC chairman was a "housekeeping job." Lieberman observed that LBJ "soon demonstrated that the magnetism and leverage of the Presidency obviate the need for a middle-man between him and Democrats anywhere."[215]

It is not surprising that LBJ informed his family, Arthur Krim, and (W.) Marvin Watson, but not John Bailey, that he would withdraw from the presidential race before his televised address of March 31, 1968. Two nights before his speech, LBJ called Krim and asked him to have Oliver Quayle conduct polls to compare his candidacy with those of McCarthy and RFK in the primary states of California, Indiana, Nebraska, and Oregon.[216] On March 21, Krim sponsored a lunch for LBJ's top contributors in which they pledged over $2 million for his renomination campaign.[217] According to Krim, though, LBJ was more concerned about whether Lawrence F. O'Brien would manage his campaign or RFK's and about Mike Mansfield's suspected disloyalty to his Vietnam policy and his presidency in general.[218] Nevertheless, Krim was stunned when LBJ invited him to the White House on March 30 and informed the movie mogul that he would announce his decision not to seek reelection in his televised speech on the following evening. After detailing his reasons for withdrawing, LBJ told Krim that he "did not believe it possible for him to be both president and candidate."[219]

During his remaining five months as DNC chairman, the beleaguered John Bailey was in an awkward, unprecedented position as an "in-party" national chairman. The Democratic president was a lame duck who concentrated almost entirely on his policies in Vietnam. LBJ seemed to be apathetic and rueful about having Vice President Hubert H. Humphrey succeed him as president and party leader. Suspecting that Humphrey might try to appease antiwar delegates by softening the party's platform on Vietnam, LBJ seriously considered running for renomination in the late spring or early summer of 1968.[220] According to Texas governor John Connally, LBJ sent (W.) Marvin Watson to the Democratic national convention in Chicago and asked Connally to discuss with other southern governors the possibility of using their blocs of delegates to mobilize a "draft Johnson" movement.[221] Mayor Daley could also be recruited as a key actor.[222] Daley's role would be similar to that of Ed Kelly, the mayor of Chicago during FDR's presidency. Kelly controlled the galleries and orchestrated a "spontaneous," successful floor demonstration to nominate FDR for a third term at the 1940 Democratic national convention in Chicago.[223] Earlier, LBJ seemed to prefer Nelson Rockefeller as his successor because of the Republican governor's combination of hawkishness on Vietnam, proven leadership as a chief executive, and liberalism on domestic policy, especially civil rights.[224]

Although he soon dismissed any further consideration of reentering the campaign, LBJ was determined that the convention would write and adopt a pro-administration plank on Vietnam in its platform. Persistent rumors and media speculation that LBJ was secretly micromanaging the Chicago convention from Texas through (W.) Marvin Watson as his operative further diminished John M. Bailey's status as national chairman. They also made it more difficult for Hubert H. Humphrey to secure the still contested presidential nomination. The violence and disunity that plagued the Democratic national convention cruelly mocked remarks that Bailey had made to DNC members on January 8, 1968, when they met in Chicago to plan their party's national convention. Bailey confidently predicted that the Republicans "are due for a blood letting that soon will begin in earnest. . . . Before next summer they're apt to refer to us as the Unity Party. The Republican Party will resemble a patchwork quilt, with more bleeding factions than we have seen in many a year."[225]

Despite the death of RFK in June, competition for the Democratic presidential nomination of 1968 became even more fragmented shortly before and during the convention. Appealing to antiwar delegates, especially those previously committed to RFK, Senator George McGovern of South Dakota announced his presidential candidacy. Several southern Democratic governors, most notably Lester Maddox of Georgia and John McKeithen of Louisiana, initiated favorite-son presidential candidacies. They wanted to pressure the credentials committee to rule in their favor on race-related disputes over the seating of their delegates and the unit rule issue.[226] There was also speculation that a "stop

Humphrey" movement that included antiwar activists and party regulars led by Daley and Jesse Unruh wanted to nominate Senator Edward M. Kennedy for president. Kennedy, however, was absent from the convention and repeatedly stated his refusal to accept the party's presidential or vice-presidential nomination.[227]

Pro-McCarthy delegates, politicians, and demonstrators periodically charged that Bailey was unethically using his powers to benefit Humphrey's candidacy and the adoption of a pro-LBJ Vietnam plank at the convention.[228] As an "in party" national chairman dealing with circumstances and forces at a convention that were unprecedented, Bailey scrupulously tried to be neutral while rendering decisions during his remaining few days as DNC chairman. For example, Humphrey, McCarthy, and McGovern had publicly requested that there be no floor demonstrations at the convention. The convention's arrangements committee ruled accordingly, and John M. Bailey formally announced this suspension of floor demonstrations on August 16, ten days before the convention opened in Chicago.[229] In general, Bailey was merely the caretaker of DNC decisions and processes that had mostly been determined before LBJ's announced withdrawal from the presidential campaign. Lawrence F. O'Brien, Humphrey's de facto campaign manager, succeeded Bailey as DNC chairman on August 30. He later observed, "The fact is that the Democratic National Committee did make an effort to remain evenhanded." O'Brien admitted, however, that "it's Lyndon Johnson's national committee and the national committee probably was having considerable difficulty getting guidance and direction."[230]

At the DNC's August 24 meeting, John M. Bailey read his last report to DNC members and executive officers. Bailey devoted most of his speech to praising the Democratic legislative record since JFK became president and he became DNC chairman in January 1961. In particular, he proudly claimed that 94 percent of the policy proposals of the 1964 Democratic national platform had been enacted. He emphasized that this impressive legislative success occurred because Democrats practice "the politics of promises kept."[231]

Bailey was quoting, perhaps unwittingly, the second half of the title of the DNC's laudatory film on LBJ, *Promises Made, Promises Kept*. The DNC paid David Wolper Productions $125,000 to make the film. Like Bailey's last speech to the DNC, Wolper's film highlighted and praised domestic policy progress under LBJ. After Johnson decided not to attend the convention, however, Bailey and DNC treasurer John Criswell, who was also executive director of the convention, cancelled the showing of the film.[232]

Lawrence F. O'Brien served as the last DNC chairman of LBJ's presidency. He wanted to expedite and centralize the development and implementation of Humphrey's post-convention campaign activities. O'Brien, therefore, simultaneously served as both DNC chairman and Humphrey's campaign manager, a rare duplication of roles that Henry M. "Scoop" Jackson in 1960 and John M. Bailey in 1964 did not have. This integration and simplification of campaign operations also applied to the Citizens for Humphrey-Muskie staff and the regular DNC staff. "Our plan was to take over the national committee and, as needed, supplement the existing staff. This would be a coordinated effort, the national committee and the Humphrey campaign," O'Brien stated in a 1987 interview.[233]

O'Brien identified the two chief problems of the Democratic presidential campaign as the public's association of the Humphrey-Muskie ticket with the pro-LBJ Democratic platform on the Vietnam War and fundraising. Shortly after the Democratic national convention, Humphrey was far behind Nixon in the polls, and George Wallace's minor party candidacy significantly reduced potential support for Humphrey among southern whites and northern blue-collar Catholics. Wealthy, antiwar liberals who had contributed generously to McCarthy's and RFK's campaigns initially gave little to Humphrey. They perceived him as a certain loser against Nixon and as either duplicitous or too similar to LBJ on the Vietnam War. Arthur Krim and other pro-LBJ fund raisers from the President's Club gave little until the end of the campaign when LBJ belatedly asked them to help Humphrey.[234]

O'Brien realized that he had to improve Humphrey's status in the public opinion polls in order to attract substantial contributions from the more pragmatic, less ideological wealthier contributors. O'Brien needed to rehabilitate Humphrey's candidacy and make it competitive enough to attract enough money from big contributors so that the DNC and the various Humphrey campaign organizations could make an effective media blitz during the last few weeks of the campaign. The foundation of Humphrey's revitalization was the most financially, organizationally, and electorally powerful bastion of the Old Politics—organized labor. "In the end, the fact that there was any Democratic campaign at all was largely due to organized labor," O'Brien readily observed in his memoirs.[235]

During the AFL-CIO's September 17, 1968, executive council meeting, Al Barkan, director of labor's Committee on Political Education (COPE), warned AFL-CIO president George Meany that the DNC's apparatus was "disorganized and in financial chaos." Lane Kirkland, Meany's executive assistant, commented, "I reached the point where I'd never go into Democratic headquarters. I'd go in feeling good and come out feeling terrible."[236]

Despite his qualms about Humphrey's fitness for the presidency and his rancorous rivalry with the more liberal Walter Reuther, Meany and the UAW president cooperated in spending millions of dollars and mobilizing thousands of union members in a voter registration and publicity campaign. Labor's campaign was initially directed at reducing blue-collar support for Wallace but later attacked both Wallace and Nixon as anti-labor. COPE spent $300,000 on a voter registration drive in sixteen swing states.[237] Although Reuther was a dove and Meany a hawk on the Vietnam War, the literature that COPE and the UAW distributed to union members and their families avoided the Vietnam issue. Reuther and Meany knew that both the war and antiwar activists were equally unpopular among union members. Instead, labor pamphlets emphasized the economic gains that union members had made under the Democratic administrations of JFK and LBJ, Humphrey's instrumental role in lobbying for the passage of Medicare, and the Minnesotan's liberal, pro-labor record as a senator.[238]

Unlike the weak, scattered, belated grassroots campaign activities of the DNC's apparatus, labor launched the most impressive campaign effort in a presidential election since 1948. COPE operated telephone banks with nearly 25,000 volunteers in 638 cities. It registered approximately 690,000 voters in Michigan and 492,000 voters in Pennsylvania. COPE also printed more than 115 million pieces of campaign literature.[239]

A Gallup poll released on September 15 estimated that 19 percent of the voters surveyed preferred Wallace for president. But UAW polls of its members at several factories showed much higher levels of support for Wallace.[240] Its polls in the late summer and early fall of 1968 revealed that UAW members' preference for Wallace ranged from 23 percent in Flint, Michigan, to 92 percent in a local chapter in New Jersey.[241] By the end of October, support for Wallace in Michigan, Ohio, Pennsylvania, New Jersey, and other states targeted by the UAW and COPE was significantly reduced among white blue collar workers and generally reflected the national average of 15 percent estimated in a Gallup poll.[242] Shortly after the 1968 election, national-level labor campaign committees reported that they spent $7,241,259, which was almost 13 percent of all general election campaign spending. By contrast, labor committees spent $3,816,242 in 1964 and $2,450,944 in 1960. These sums respectively composed 9 percent and 10 percent of all general election campaign spending for these years.[243]

Organized labor's vigorous, effective campaign substantially reduced nonsouthern, white blue-collar support for Wallace and slightly reduced their support for Nixon. Humphrey's standing in the Gallup polls increased from a preference of 28 percent in a poll released on September 29 to 40 percent in a poll released on November 4.[244] Humphrey's improved standing in the polls enabled DNC chairman Lawrence F. O'Brien and Robert Short, DNC treasurer, to quickly and significantly raise more money from wealthy individual contributors.

Humphrey's nationally televised speech in Salt Lake City on September 30 was widely interpreted as a more dovish position on Vietnam with some independence from LBJ. This speech helped to attract more funds from previously pro-McCarthy, antiwar liberals. Journalist G. William Domhoff estimated that forty-three people loaned between $3.1 and $5.9 million to Humphrey for television advertising during the final weeks of his campaign.[245] Lew Wasserman, president of MCA, gave $54,000. John L. Loeb, a New York investment banker, gave $90,000 and loaned $100,000 to the Democratic presidential campaign.[246] Wasserman and businessman John Factor each loaned about $240,000 to the Democratic presidential campaign, and Humphrey's request for donations during his Salt Lake City speech generated about $200,000.[247]

Richard Maguire, a former DNC treasurer, joined the Humphrey campaign to assist O'Brien and Short in fundraising. In its preliminary campaign finance reports, submitted to the Clerk of the U.S. House of Representatives in December 1968, Democrats disclosed that a total of sixty-three national-level campaign committees received a total of $7,969,402.30 for the presidential and congressional elections.[248] Of this total, the DNC had obtained $973,917.96.[249] This amount was much lower than the $2,989,462.00 that the DNC received in 1964.[250]

Unofficially, J. Leonard Reinsch, the DNC's director of radio and television, estimated that a much larger number of committees, ninety-six, received campaign contributions for Humphrey.[251] From September 1 to October 31, 1968, the Humphrey campaign reported receiving $2,110,000 in loans.[252] Although Maguire reactivated the President's Club, it reportedly received only $44,452.[253] Jeno Paulucci, a Minnesota businessman and major contributor to Humphrey, told communications scholar Kathleen Hall Jamieson that he, DNC treasurer Robert Short, and Robert Strauss, a Texas Democrat and future DNC treasurer, met with Texas oil executives in mid-October to discuss campaign contributions. The oil men offered to contribute $700,000 if Humphrey as president promised not to threaten the oil depletion allowance. After Paulucci refused to make that promise, he called Joseph Napolitan and said, "We have to cancel next week's advertising. We don't have the money."[254]

Napolitan was a campaign media consultant and a former business partner of O'Brien from Springfield, Massachusetts. Like O'Brien, he worked without a salary for Humphrey. Although Short usually provided Napolitan with enough money to produce effective television commercials, there was not enough to pay for broadcast time on a regular basis in key media markets.[255] As much as possible, Short and O'Brien want to save their scarce campaign funds for the last two weeks of the campaign when they intended to spend as much as Nixon on television air time.[256]

Nevertheless, the Humphrey campaign spent a total $3,525,000 on television air time compared to Nixon's $6,270,000 during the general election.[257] At a campaign staff meeting, Napolitan reported that the Humphrey campaign would spend $200,000 to $250,000 a day on radio and television advertising during the last two weeks of the campaign.[258] It was primarily this high-priced media blitz that enabled Humphrey to reduce Nixon's lead to 1 percent in the last Gallup poll before election day. Almost twenty years after Humphrey lost the 1968 election by approximately 500,000 votes, O'Brien stated, "I am absolutely persuaded that if we had been able to implement fully our campaign program as we developed it, Hubert Humphrey would have been elected. And it wouldn't have taken the additional two or three weeks."[259]

Although a product and personification of the Old Politics, Lawrence F. O'Brien was able to understand and readily adapt to the dimension of New Politics that emphasized poll ratings, fundraising, and television advertising.

Compared to the 1960 and 1964 Democratic presidential campaigns, these aspects of the New Politics in 1968 placed little value on the traditional concerns of the Old Politics.[260] The Old Politics often stressed an appeal to the voters' party loyalty, careful coordination of the DNC's organization with those of state and local Democratic committees, and active use of DNC special divisions, such as those for young adults, blacks, and women, to distribute campaign literature and mobilize these voting blocs.

O'Brien's unusually burdensome, heightened financial responsibility as a DNC chairman in the New Politics era was further complicated and exacerbated by his status as an "in-party" national chairman with two titular party leaders—a lame duck president and the Democratic presidential nominee. The fact that O'Brien simultaneously served as Humphrey's campaign manager and DNC chairman did not enable him to act as a liaison between Johnson and Humphrey so as to clarify the president's and vice president's campaign relationship. Humphrey's advisors, and perhaps Humphrey privately and internally, remained divided about what role, if any, LBJ should have in Humphrey's presidential campaign.

Both the hawks (e.g., James H. Rowe, Jr. and William Connell), and doves (e.g., George Ball and Joseph Napolitan), advising Humphrey hoped that LBJ would at least clandestinely help them raise funds. In particular, Robert Short was denied access to the membership lists of LBJ's President's Club and the $600,000 remaining in its treasury. Acknowledging this "lack of cooperation" from LBJ's contributors in a 1987 interview, O'Brien tactfully observed that "there were clear indications that the 'Johnson people' were most reluctant to be cooperative and were not forthcoming."[261]

In his memoirs, Humphrey was blunter and more obvious in his criticism of LBJ's apathy and ambivalence toward his candidacy, especially regarding fundraising.[262] The vice president paralleled LBJ's shabby, negligent treatment of his presidential candidacy with the Texan's treatment of the DNC's chairman, activities, and role in presidential party leadership.[263] Humphrey concluded, "Unless the President tells party leaders the Vice President speaks for him, all the smiles and small friendships count for little."[264]

From LBJ's perspective, however, the key to an upset victory for Hubert Humphrey was not more campaign funds to broadcast a dovish position on Vietnam. After Humphrey's defeat, LBJ asserted that his vice president would have won the election if Humphrey's campaign rhetoric had been clearly and consistently loyal to LBJ's Vietnam policy. In his memoirs, LBJ stated that Humphrey's Salt Lake City speech had made the South Vietnamese government "extremely nervous and distrustful of the Johnson-Humphrey administration and of the entire Democratic party. . . . That, I am convinced, cost Hubert Humphrey the Presidency."[265]

For LBJ, this was a rare, uncharacteristic correlation of the doctrine of party responsibility to effective presidential leadership in foreign policy and electoral victory. Throughout his political career, LBJ's rhetoric and policy behavior expressed his conviction that American voters reward politicians who, regardless of their party affiliation, cooperate in a suprapartisan consensus to make laws that benefit the nation in both foreign and domestic policy. As party leader of the Senate Democrats during Eisenhower's presidency and in his 1960 and 1964 presidential campaigns, LBJ proudly told Democratic audiences that he supported Eisenhower's foreign policy more often than most Republican senators did.

Now, however, at the end of his presidency and party leadership, LBJ associated Humphrey's continuity with his policies in Vietnam as the foundation for the Democratic Party's future credibility in Cold War foreign policy. LBJ subtly inserted this theme in his few campaign speeches in the fall of 1968. In a September 10 speech to the American Legion, Johnson emphasized the fidelity and consistency of his foreign and defense policies with those of Kennedy, Eisenhower, and Truman in the Cold War. North Vietnam's aggression against South Vietnam and the recent Soviet-led invasion of Czechoslovakia affirmed LBJ's assumption "that we must meet our commitments and keep our promises to use our strength in the face of common danger to oppose aggression."[266] Likewise, in his last formal address to the DNC on October 27, LBJ denounced the Republicans' "ugly and unfair charges that have been made about our security gap and the charges that have been made about our attempts to win peace in the world."[267]

Hubert H. Humphrey had developed a different concept of party responsibility for foreign policy in general and the Democratic administration's policies toward Vietnam in particular. Humphrey eventually adopted a rhetorical and programmatic position on Vietnam that was to the left of LBJ's hawkishness and to the right of Eugene McCarthy's dovishness. Humphrey's centrist position within the Democratic Party on the Vietnam War was more than a self-interested campaign strategy in trying to win the election. Unlike LBJ, Humphrey was a product of the citizen politics of the upper Midwest and Minnesota's traditions of agrarian populism, grassroots participation, and issue-oriented reformism. Humphrey was one of the founders of his state's Democratic Farmer Labor (DFL) party.[268]

Humphrey was also an active, prominent member of the ADA, which had earlier endorsed McCarthy because of the Vietnam War, and the defunct DAC. As a former instructor of political science, Humphrey may have been familiar with the APSA's statement at the end of its 1950 report, *Toward a More Responsible Two-Party System*. The APSA report warned in its conclusion, "If the two parties do not develop alternative programs that can be executed, the voter's frustration and the mounting ambiguities of national policy might also set in motion more extreme tendencies to the political left and the political right."[269]

The keynote address of Senator Daniel Inouye of Hawaii and the acceptance speeches of Hubert Humphrey and Edmund S. Muskie at the 1968 Democratic national convention implicitly recognized this danger of extremism. Unlike many of the more hawkish Old Politics Democratic politicians, they perceived the need for the Democratic Party in general and the future DNC and its chairman in particular to significantly change the rules, structure, and processes of the Democratic Party for expressing dissenting policy positions and gaining adequate representation of these views in the party's platform-making, nomination, and delegate selection processes.

The first wave of baby boomers (i.e., Americans born in 1946), were eligible to vote in 1968. Also, the minimum voting age was nationally lowered to eighteen in 1972. Thus, the party's recognition and responsiveness to the antiwar, New Left–influenced youth movement of the New Politics were essential to its future legitimacy and electoral success. Inouye, who had endorsed LBJ over JFK for the 1960 presidential nomination, stated that he and his fellow Democrats should not "fear their voices. On the contrary, whether we know it or not, the marching feet of youth have led us into a new era of politics and we can never turn back."[270]

Hubert H. Humphrey's presidential nomination exemplified an undemocratic, boss-controlled "rigged" convention of the Old Politics to many young, antiwar Democrats. Nevertheless, Humphrey proclaimed, "In the space of but a week this convention has literally made the foundations of a new Democratic party structure in America. From precinct level to the floor of this convention, we have revolutionized our rules and procedures."[271] Likewise, Muskie noted that the turmoil and extremism of many young antiwar activists "may be the products of impatience with results, of lack of confidence in our intentions, of lack of experience with the democratic process. . . . We must learn to work with these people, to insure their continued and more meaningful participation in the democratic process."[272]

These sympathetic expressions of inclusion to young antiwar Democrats contrasted sharply with some of the arrangements made for the 1968 convention and earlier pro-Johnson DNC decisions against the Young Democrats division. Six weeks before the convention opened in Chicago, journalists Rowland Evans and Robert Novak revealed that DNC treasurer John Criswell and other convention managers did not schedule a speech or any other role for the Young Democrats or the DNC's Youth Division.[273] As early as 1966, Criswell wrote to (W.) Marvin Watson expressing his anger about an editorial in a newsletter from the College Young Democrats Clubs. "It condemns the DNC for its part in the campaign, lauds the 'Kennedy Generation,' and is generally anti-administration. We pay the salary of a CYD staff man and have supported them in many mailings. They have become such an irritant that I recommend we nip the situation while it is still little more than a bud."[274]

Lawrence F. O'Brien, a prototypical representative of the Old Politics, served two nonconsecutive terms as DNC chairman. He was an "in party" chairman during the final months of LBJ's presidency. He then succeeded Senator Fred Harris of Oklahoma as DNC chairman in 1970, serving as an "out-party" chairman until 1973. Like Humphrey and Muskie, O'Brien was sensitive and responsive to the demands and perspectives of the New Politics in general and the young, antiwar Democrats in particular. In his memoirs, O'Brien acknowledged that the "antiwar forces won one important victory at the 1968 Convention— the creation of two commissions in party reform: the Commission on Rules and the Commission on Party Structure and Delegate Selection."[275]

O'Brien, though, was also ambivalent about the rules and procedural changes that these DNC commissions made for the 1972 national convention. He praised rules changes that made "the National Convention less of a circus and more of an efficient meeting."[276] With Harris appointing the members of both commissions, O'Brien was concerned that these members were excessively biased in favor of liberal activists. He also doubted the wisdom and practicality of requiring that all state Democratic Parties ensure that all of their delegates were elected by 1972 and that "affirmative steps" be taken to sharply increase the number and proportion of young adults, women, and racial minorities elected as delegates without using quotas.[277]

Besides being in the uneasy position of a national chairman overseeing DNC-imposed reforms that Old Politics stalwarts like Richard J. Daley and George Meany found to be objectionable, O'Brien also had the responsibility of reducing the DNC's post-election debt of approximately $8 million.[278] In addition to the $6 million in debts incurred in the post-convention Humphrey campaign, this total included approximately $2 million in the nomination campaign costs of RFK, Eugene McCarthy, and Hubert Humphrey. When O'Brien returned as DNC chairman in 1970, the DNC's debt totaled $9.3 million.[279]

Political scientist Philip A. Klinkner persuasively concluded that the DNC responded to its defeat in the 1956 presidential election by adopting a policy reform, that is, the creation of the DAC with its advocacy of a liberal policy platform for the 1960 Democratic national convention. According to Klinkner, the DNC responded to its defeat in the 1968 election and the discord of its 1968 convention by adopting procedural reforms that significantly changed the party's rules for its presidential nominating process, selection of delegates, and national convention. The Democratic Party's culture, organization, and history have reflected its diversity of voting blocs and need to address intraparty conflicts. Thus, Klinkner found that by the 1960s "the Democrats began a series of reforms that sought to make the party more representative, but also more participatory and inclusive."[280]

For both the post-1956 DAC reform and the post-1968 rules reforms, the mostly nonsouthern, liberal "presidential wing" or "presidential party" of the Democratic Party was able to increase its influence over the next national convention's platform and selection of presidential and vice-presidential nominations.[281] JFK and LBJ devoted most of their presidential party leadership to achieving the enactment of the liberal domestic policy agenda formulated and advocated by the DAC and adopted by the 1960 Democratic national platform. Both presidents, but especially LBJ, assumed that liberal activists would be satisfied with legislative success on such major domestic issues as civil rights, poverty, Medicare, and education. Neither JFK nor LBJ granted the DNC, its chairman, or its apparatus significant roles in this process. The possible exception was the DNC's publicity effort to counteract the AMA's opposition to Medicare during JFK's presidency.[282]

In 1987, Lawrence F. O'Brien admitted that, before he became DNC chairman, he, like JFK and LBJ, paid little attention to the DNC while he focused on his duties as the White House liaison with Congress and later as Postmaster General. "Neither President I was associated with purposely wanted to diminish the role of the national committee or render it ineffective . . . I was sensitive to it, but I did nothing about it."[283]

CHAPTER SIX

The Politics of Consensus:
1962–1964

The suprapartisan, centrist policy consensus that contributed to the eventual passage of the "Big Four" New Frontier bills, the initial Great Society legislation, and the landslide Democratic presidential and congressional election results of 1964 actually originated in the middle of Kennedy's brief presidency. JFK was less likely than LBJ to explicitly and consistently dismiss ideological and partisan differences in order to promote bipartisan cooperation and compromise in Congress for the sake of legislative productivity. Influenced by his state's competitive, two-party system in statewide elections, JFK understood and valued the need for party cohesion in order to defeat strong Republican opponents. In a 1964 interview, DNC chairman John M. Bailey noted that, as a Democrat from Massachusetts, JFK understood that the Democratic party "stands for certain things, it is a liberal party, and for the most part, more than a majority party."[1]

The presidential and congressional elections of 1960 had yielded a razor-thin popular vote plurality for JFK despite an unusually high voter turnout. The Republicans gained twenty House seats, JFK carried eleven states by margins of less than 1 percent of their popular votes, and there was a prolonged controversy over credible Republican allegations of Democratic ballot fraud and irregularities in Illinois and Texas. Despite these political liabilities, most nonsouthern Democrats expected JFK as chief policymaker and party leader to achieve enactment of the 1960 Democratic national platform, the most liberal in the party's history.

Kennedy was faced with the task of co-opting enough votes from southern and border state Democrats in the House to gain passage of his minimum wage increase, extension of Social Security efforts, and other early domestic legislation that modernized or expanded the policy legacy of the New Deal and Fair Deal. Even in the Senate, where nonsouthern Democrats held a stronger position in the party's majority status and committee chairmanships than in the House, JFK had to regularly rely on the support of Senator Robert Kerr of Oklahoma because of his seat on the Senate Finance Committee. Consequently, during JFK's first year and a half as president, he needed to mend fences and develop a broad base of intraparty support in Congress for legislation that often created strict, nearly exclusive divisions between Democrats and Republicans. He needed to prevent or at least discourage a resurgence of the bipartisan conservative coalition in Congress that diluted or defeated almost all of Harry Truman's Fair Deal proposals.

JFK mostly concentrated on social welfare and economic stimulus legislation during the Eighty-seventh Congress of 1961 to 1962 and nurtured a cooperative relationship between his party leadership of Democrats in Congress and his legislative leadership of such bills as those for area redevelopment and accelerated public works. In a speech given in Trenton, New Jersey, on November 2, 1961, JFK stated that the president's "responsibilities as a legislative leader" are inextricably entwined with his responsibility as the "head of a political party."[2] Kennedy elaborated further that "a political party, as Woodrow Wilson so often pointed out, is the means by which the people are served, the means by which those programs of benefit to our country are written into the statutes."[3]

In his memoirs, Lawrence F. O'Brien proudly noted that Congress passed thirty-three of the fifty-three major bills submitted or endorsed by JFK and forty of JFK's fifty-one proposals in 1962.[4] O'Brien attributed much of this legislative success, especially in the House of Representatives, to JFK's diligent yet tactful cultivation of southern and border state Democrats in the House.[5] This presidential effort improved party unity enough among House Democrats so that their roll-call support for JFK's bills increased from 81 percent in 1961 to 85 percent in 1963. By contrast, only about 52 percent of House Democrats opposed Eisenhower on roll-call votes in 1960.[6] O'Brien observed that, in the House of Representatives, "by 1962 we were lucky to pick up four or five Republican votes on most bills and often we got none. Thus, we now needed half the Southerners to pass any given bill and more often than not we got them."[7]

JFK and O'Brien both understood that such party unity and intraparty consensus in Congress could only be sustained if most of the administration's bills focused on nonracial, social welfare, public works, and economic legislation that stemmed from the policy foundation of New Deal and Fair Deal liberalism. Economically liberal yet racially conservative southern Democrats, like Senator Olin Johnston of South Carolina and Representative Carl Vinson of Georgia, voted for this legislation. JFK wanted to wait until after the 1964 Democratic national convention to introduce a comprehensive civil rights bill in order to prevent a southern revolt while Congress was in session or during the convention.[8] The president had already been weakened early in his administration by southern opposition to the prospect that Robert Weaver would become the first black cabinet secretary. He also decided to wait until after the 1964 election to promote congressional passage of federal aid to elementary and secondary education because of this legislation's racially and religiously divisive issues.[9]

With even the most liberal, maverick Republicans in Congress, like Senator Clifford Case of New Jersey and Representative John Lindsay of New York, rarely voting for major New Frontier legislation, Kennedy wanted to maintain enough party unity in Congress to publicly distinguish the two parties and minimize anticipated Democratic losses in the 1962 congressional elections. In his July 23, 1962, press conference, JFK stated, "November 1962 presents the American people with a very clear choice between the Republican Party which is opposed to all of these measures, as it opposed the great measures of the 1930s, and the Democratic Party—the mass of the Democratic Party—the administration, two-thirds or three-fourths of the Democratic Party, which supports these measures."[10]

JFK understood that he needed an impressive legislative record to be reelected by a comfortable margin in 1964. He had to rely on indispensable Republican support in Congress in order to prevail on the Comsat bill of 1962 and the Limited Nuclear Test Ban Treaty of 1963. The intervention of Senate Republican Minority Leader Everett M. Dirksen and Republican Senator Leverett Saltonstall of Massachusetts ended a liberal Democratic filibuster of JFK's Comsat bill and assured its passage. Saltonstall, Dirksen, and other moderate and liberal Republican senators likewise provided the necessary votes to ratify the 1963 treaty and counteract the opposition of several southern Democrats led by Senator Richard Russell of Georgia, chairman of the Senate Armed Services Committee.[11]

This treaty, combined with JFK's effort to persuade Congress to approve the sale of wheat to the Soviet Union with the help of funds from the Import-Export in late 1963 and his establishment of a telephone "hot line" with Soviet premier Nikita Khrushchev, signaled JFK's more cooperative, less confrontational foreign policy toward the Soviet Union following the Cuban missile crisis.[12] This more conciliatory Cold War foreign policy provided JFK with the necessity and opportunity to develop a suprapartisan, centrist consensus behind his foreign policy, especially in the Senate. Needing at least a two-thirds majority in the Senate to ratify future, more dovish treaties with the Soviet Union, JFK had to be able to rely on enough Republican votes to dilute the opposition of most southern Democrats and the most hawkish, nonsouthern, liberal Democratic senators, namely, Henry M. "Scoop" Jackson and Thomas J. Dodd.[13]

JFK realized that he must influence public opinion in order to pressure and persuade Congress that a more peaceful, cooperative relationship with the Soviet Union (i.e., détente), was now a feasible, responsible moderate policy goal rather than the aspirations of a few naïve, impractical liberals who were soft on Communism. JFK's most significant speech in articulating and advocating détente as a mainstream, pragmatic foreign policy that should supersede the ideological and partisan conflicts of American politics was his commencement address at American University on June 10, 1963. JFK emphasized that he and his fellow Americans must "reexamine our attitude" toward peace, the Soviet Union, and the Cold War because "we can seek a relaxation of tensions without relaxing our guard. And, for our part, we do not need to use threats to prove that we are resolute."[14]

Gallup polls taken in 1963 pertaining to American-Soviet relations revealed that JFK was generally successful in nurturing a broad, suprapartisan consensus in public opinion that favored détente. A poll released on September 11, 1963, reported that 63 percent of the Americans polled stated that the Senate should ratify the Limited Nuclear Test Ban Treaty. There was little partisan difference since 67 percent of the Democrats and 58 percent of the Republicans polled supported ratification. More significantly, 52 percent of the Goldwater supporters polled endorsed ratification, despite the fact that Senator Barry Goldwater opposed the treaty.[15]

Likewise, in a Gallup poll released on October 2, 1963, only 25 percent of the Americans surveyed stated that the threat of war with the Soviet Union was the most serious problem facing the United States.[16] In a poll released on October 25, 1963, 55 percent of its respondents supported more trade between the United States and the Soviet Union while only 33 percent were opposed. In particular, 60 percent of its respondents approved the selling of surplus American wheat to the Soviet Union.[17]

By the spring of 1963, it was evident that the need for JFK to develop a centrist, suprapartisan consensus in public opinion and within Congress in favor of his civil rights legislation was more important yet more difficult to fulfill than in Cold War foreign policy. Prominent, dramatic, and tragic events in the civil rights movement in the South forced JFK to speak and act on civil rights sooner and more aggressively than he had intended and preferred.[18] Kennedy and O'Brien were stunned by congressional rejection of additional funds for the Area Redevelopment Administration (ARA). By a vote of 209 to 204, the House of Representatives defeated JFK's request for more ARA funding on June 12, 1963. The creation of the ARA received virtually unanimous support from House Democrats of all kinds, northern and southern, rural and urban, liberal and conservative, in 1961 and its purposes had no racial dimensions. Southern Democratic opposition to ARA funding on the June 12, 1963, vote was widely interpreted as the beginning of a southern Democratic revolt in Congress against more of the administration's bills because of JFK's recent, more assertive positions and actions on civil rights.[19] In particular, on June 11, 1963, he dramatically enforced the court-ordered racial integration of the University of Alabama and broadcast a televised address describing the civil rights crisis as "a moral issue. It is as old as the scriptures and is as clear as the American Constitution."[20]

JFK emphasized that his civil rights legislation addressed racial injustice as a national, and not entirely a southern, problem. But the president followed the advice of Speaker of the House John W. McCormack. McCormack had urged JFK not to submit any new, major legislation, such as the urban mass transit bill, to the House of Representatives during the summer of 1963. The speaker feared that more southern Democrats would coalesce with Republicans to defeat White House bills because of JFK's more divisive civil rights position. The speaker and the president also wanted to assure passage of the tax cut bill, which was expected to experience a mostly party-line vote in the House, before developing a bipartisan coalition behind JFK's civil rights bill.[21]

Fortunately for the president, leading southern Democrats like Representative Wilbur Mills of Arkansas, chairman of the House Ways and Means Committee, and Senator Russell Long of Louisiana, who succeeded Robert Kerr as JFK's closest contact on the Senate Finance Committee, separated their adamant opposition to the civil rights bill from their willingness to compromise and cooperate with JFK on his tax cut bill. Most House Democrats, both southern and nonsouthern, conservative and liberal, eventually decided to support the bill and the House passed it on September 25, 1963.[22] This vote was taken fifteen days after JFK federalized the Alabama National Guard and enforced federal court decisions that desegregated public schools in three Alabama cities, with the strident, grandstanding opposition of Governor George Wallace.[23] On that day, September 10, while JFK was concentrating on the civil rights crisis in Alabama, the House Ways and Means Committee approved the president's tax cut bill.[24]

The results of the 1962 midterm elections and the growth of ideological, programmatic, factional, and congressional leadership conflicts and rival presidential ambitions within the Republican Party also helped to stimulate the suprapartisan, centrist policy consensus in public opinion and congressional voting behavior that JFK and later LBJ needed to achieve their policy goals in civil rights, détente, tax cuts, and Medicare. RNC chairman William Miller and Republican congressional leaders targeted two issues for attacking the Democratic Party in general and JFK in particular during the 1962 campaign. First, they accused JFK and the Democrats in Congress of fiscal irresponsibility because of the growing budget deficit and increases in domestic spending. Second, Republicans denounced JFK's policies toward Cuba from the failure of the Bay of Pigs invasion to the beginning of the Cuban missile crisis in August 1962. Liberal northeastern Republicans, like Senator Kenneth Keating of New York, and conservative midwestern Republicans, like Senator Homer Capehart of Indiana, were equally strident in criticizing JFK's allegedly soft, indecisive treatment of Cuba and urged a quick American military invasion of Cuba to remove the missiles and overthrow Fidel Castro.[25]

The Republican exploitation of the Cuban missile crisis backfired on the GOP. The American public seemed to prefer JFK's moderate yet firm policy course of conducting a naval quarantine of Cuba while pressuring Khrushchev to remove the missiles. JFK's public approval rating increased from 62 percent in a September 20, 1962, Gallup poll to 73 percent in a November 16, 1962, poll.[26] Also, in another November 1962 Gallup poll, 49 percent of the poll's respondents, a plurality, stated that what they liked best about Kennedy was his leadership during and resolution of the Cuban missile crisis.[27]

Partially because of his vehement carping at JFK's decisions in the Cuban missile crisis and his neglect of domestic policy issues in his Senate campaign, Republican Senator Homer Capehart of Indiana was narrowly defeated for re-election by Democratic state representative Birch Bayh. With the help of public school teachers, Young Democrats, labor unions, and JFK's campaign appearance in Indiana, Bayh defeated Capehart by 10,944 votes.[28] Republican congressman Walter Judd of Minnesota, the McCarthyistic ranking Republican on the House Foreign Affairs Committee, was also defeated for reelection in 1962. Roger Hilsman, JFK's director of intelligence for the State Department, observed, "After the crisis was over, Keating apparently began to fear that he was vulnerable to charges that he had been peddling refugee rumors or that he had failed to give the government information vital to national security."[29] Despite Keating's zealous efforts to dissociate himself from Barry Goldwater's presidential campaign and reassert his liberal voting record on civil rights, social welfare programs, and American foreign policy toward Israel, Keating lost his reelection bid to RFK in 1964.

Richard M. Nixon was another Republican casualty of the Cuban missile crisis. After Nixon announced his candidacy for the governorship of California, both Democrats and right-wing Republicans in that state denounced Nixon for having little knowledge about or interest in such prominent California issues as water systems, highway construction, air pollution, taxes, crime, and public education. Positioning himself as a moderate Republican, Nixon ran against and defeated Joseph Shell, a conservative Republican who was the minority leader in the California assembly, for their party's gubernatorial nomination in the June primary by a two to one margin.[30]

Before the primary, Nixon denounced Robert Welch, founder of the John Birch Society, a right-wing extremist organization whose membership had grown rapidly in California.[31] Welch had accused Eisenhower and former Republican Secretary of State John Foster Dulles of being Communist agents. Although only two of California's Republican congressmen were members of the John Birch Society, Shell and other right-wing Republicans in California were careful not to antagonize and alienate the Birchites. The Birchites increasingly infiltrated local Republican Party organizations in southern California and became an important source of votes, campaign volunteers, and financial contributions to conservative Republican candidates.[32]

The association of the conservative wing of the California Republican Party with Birchites and other right-wing extremists further exacerbated intraparty conflicts with the moderate-liberal wing of the state's Republican Party led by Senator Thomas Kuchel. Kuchel was a protégé of Earl Warren during the Supreme Court chief justice's popular, liberal governorship. Kuchel had offended Birchites and right-wing Republicans in California with his 1961 speech calling for a congressional investigation of the John Birch Society and his liberal positions on civil rights, the United Nations, and nuclear arms control. Meanwhile, Birchites and right-wing Republicans persisted in antagonizing moderate and liberal Republicans with billboards and pamphlets urging the impeachment of Earl Warren.[33] With Kuchel running for reelection in 1962, Nixon managed to prevent an even wider rift between the two wings of the California Republican Party. The former vice president persuaded John Rousselot, a Republican congressman and leading Birchite, not to run against Kuchel in the senatorial primary for the sake of party unity.[34]

Since Nixon's announcement of his gubernatorial candidacy paralleled the publication of his book, *Six Crises*, the former vice president was frequently vocal about his opinions on JFK's foreign policy, especially toward Cuba near the end of the campaign. Nixon readily provided his foreign policy views and cited his experiences in fighting Communism at home and abroad. Even when Nixon tried to assure voters of his knowledge and concern about water systems, taxes, and other bread-and-butter gubernatorial issues, his most strident speeches criticized Democratic Governor Edmund "Pat" Brown for being lax and inept in combating Communist influence in California. Polls consistently showed that nearly two-thirds of the likely voters in the gubernatorial election assumed that Nixon only wanted to use the governorship as a political base for a presidential campaign in 1964 and that he was more interested in national and international issues than in addressing California's policy needs.[35]

Nixon blamed high taxes, growing unemployment, and rising crime rates in California on Brown and Democratic control of the state legislature. But most voters seemed satisfied with Brown's record on such key issues as water systems, public education, and highways. Kuchel remained aloof from Nixon during his reelection campaign. Both the right wing and the moderate to liberal wing of the California GOP remained unenthusiastic and wary of Nixon's candidacy. With Democratic voter registration exceeding that of the Republicans by approximately 1.3 million voters, Nixon needed to attract approximately 90 percent of the Republican votes and at least 20 percent of the Democratic votes to defeat Brown. Trying to reduce Republican apathy toward Nixon's campaign, the former vice president struggled to attract favorable news coverage and analysis of his campaign.

Instead, Californians focused on the Cuban missile crisis and a seven-game World Series between the New York Yankees and the San Francisco Giants.[36] The extent to which Californians engaged in split-ticket voting in the 1962 midterm elections was evident when Brown defeated Nixon by a margin of 296,758 votes. Kuchel was easily reelected by a margin of 727,644 votes.[37] Nixon's humiliating defeat, bitter diatribe at his "last" press conference, and return to New York to resume his law practice eliminated him as a viable candidate for the 1964 Republican presidential nomination. Apparently, at the time, they also ended his political career and any significant influence in future party affairs.[38]

In July 1962, former president Dwight Eisenhower hosted a "unity rally" for Republican Party leaders in Gettysburg, Pennsylvania. Eisenhower urged his fellow Republicans to avoid and dismiss using what he called the "shopworn and meaningless" labels of liberal and conservative.[39] Eisenhower's hospitality and bland platitudes advocating intraparty harmony, however, did little to mend the increasingly bitter, apparently irreparable conflicts between the conservative and moderate-liberal wings of the GOP. Most Republicans at the Gettysburg event decided to create and finance an All Republican Conference whose membership would include independents and disaffected Democrats. But conservative activists and party regulars suspected that this was a duplicitous effort of the moderate to liberal, Eastern Establishment wing of the GOP to expand its political base in order to control the Republican presidential nomination, national convention, and platform in 1964.[40]

In general, except for occasional speeches at Republican functions to promote an increasingly unlikely party unity, Eisenhower, unlike Truman, avoided taking an active, regular role in party affairs as an ex-president. Nixon was currently unable and Eisenhower unwilling to be a unifying, titular "out-party" leader for the GOP. In order to counteract JFK's attractive media image and growing personal popularity, Senate Minority Leader Everett M. Dirksen and House Minority Leader Charles Halleck conducted regular, televised press conferences to explain Republican policy positions and critique JFK's public statements and Democratic policies.

Both in their mid-sixties, Dirksen and Halleck did not provide serious visual and rhetorical competition for the young, urbane, eloquent president. Lampooned as the vaudeville-like "Ev and Charlie Show" by the Washington press corps, Dirksen and Halleck also proved to be incompatible spokesmen for the congressional Republicans. Reporters nicknamed Dirksen the "Wizard of Ooze" because of his long-winded, mellifluous speaking style and vain, unctuous personality. Halleck, by contrast, seemed uncomfortable in front of television cameras and often spoke in a harsh, combative partisan tone.[41]

Halleck proved to be especially unpopular among younger House Republicans, regardless of their ideological and policy differences, because they perceived his poor television appearance to be a liability for the GOP among voters. As the "in party" during the 1962 congressional elections, the Democratic Party performed unusually well by losing only four House seats. Led by Republican congressmen Robert Griffin of Michigan and Charles Goodell, the House GOP members voted 86 to 78 to remove Charles Hoeven, a Halleck ally, as chairman of the Republican Conference and replace him with Representative Gerald R. Ford of Michigan in January 1963.[42] Handsome, amiable, and popular with his colleagues, Ford was generally acceptable to both the conservative and moderate-liberal wings of the House GOP. Following the devastating Republican loss of thirty-eight House seats in the 1964 elections, House Republicans replaced Halleck with Ford as minority leader by a vote of 73 to 67 in January 1965.[43]

With this instability in House party leadership, Dirksen's cooperative relationship with JFK and LBJ, and no unifying, broad-based front runner for their party's 1964 presidential nomination, the Republicans were still uncertain about what strategic lessons to learn from Nixon's narrow defeat in 1960 and how to run a competitive presidential campaign in 1964. Moderate and liberal Republicans attributed Nixon's defeat to his failure to generate enough votes from ethnic and racial minorities and suburban independents in major metropolitan areas of the Northeast and Midwest. They especially criticized Nixon's halfhearted southern strategy for being a doomed, futile attempt to carry most of the South against the Kennedy-Johnson ticket and offensive to blacks and white liberals who might have otherwise voted for Nixon if they had perceived him as stronger on civil rights than JFK.[44] Emmet Hughes, a liberal Republican and former speechwriter for Eisenhower and later Rockefeller, told novelist James Michener, a Democrat, that Republicans would "rather lose with a regular they can control than win with a newcomer they can't. Yet victory with Rockefeller would have been so easy."[45]

The moderate to liberal wing's perception of the primary causes of Nixon's defeat and the electoral basis for a strong Republican performance in the 1964 presidential election were revealed in a report issued by the RNC's Committee on Big City Politics. Led by Ohio Republican state chairman Ray Bliss, this special committee recommended the invigoration and expansion of Republican Party organizations in major cities. It especially wanted to increase voter registration and subsequent Republican voting behavior among blacks and other urban ethnic groups, particularly eastern European nationalities with militantly anti-Communist beliefs.[46] Also, while conservative Republicans in particular were disappointed with the congressional election results on 1962, the moderate to liberal wing of the GOP was emboldened by the gubernatorial victories of Rockefeller in New York, William Scranton in Pennsylvania, and George Romney in Michigan.

Like Rockefeller, Scranton was a liberal patrician from a wealthy family active in his state's Republican party. For a Republican, Scranton proved to be unusually attractive to blacks and labor union members in Pennsylvania. He defeated his Democratic opponent, Philadelphia Mayor Richardson Dilworth, by a margin of 486,291 votes.[47] Romney, a devout Mormon and president of the American Motors Corporation, ended fourteen years of Democratic control of the governorship of Michigan. Romney's combination of civil rights liberalism, "good government" reformism, and maverick independence from the regular Republican Party organization made him especially attractive to independent voters, blacks, liberal Republicans, and disaffected Democrats in Michigan.[48]

While leading congressional Republicans were disappointed with the GOP's loss of Senate seats and gain of only a few House seats, both the conservative and moderate to liberal wings of the GOP's "presidential party" were pleased with the midterm elections of 1962. Frank S. Meyer, a conservative commentator, wrote in the *National Review:* "The elections of this year registered, I believe, a basic shift in the structure of American politics—a shift which has for the first time brought the conservative challenge to Liberalism into the center of the American political arena."[49] Meyer and other conservatives were pleased with the electoral performance of statewide Republican candidates in historically one-party Democratic southern and border states. Henry Bellmon became the first Republican to be elected governor of Oklahoma. Republican Senator Thruston Morton of Kentucky, a former RNC chairman, easily defeated Wilson Wyatt, a founder of the ADA for whom JFK actively campaigned. In Alabama, where no Republican had been a senator since 1871, James Martin, a previously unknown Republican, almost defeated veteran Democratic Senator Lister Hill. Since his election to the Senate in 1938, Hill had been careful to balance his economic liberalism with racial conservatism. Despite Hill's emphasis on the benefits of his seniority to the policy interests of Alabama and his vocal opposition to Kennedy's civil rights legislation, the Alabama Democrat defeated Martin by less than 7,000 votes.[50]

In Texas, Tennessee, and Florida, Republicans gained House seats. Conservative Republican Congressman Peter Dominick defeated the reelection bid of Democratic Senator John A. Carroll of Colorado, a liberal who had received a 100 percent approval rating from the ADA in 1961 and 1962.[51] While Nixon's unsuccessful gubernatorial campaign awkwardly tried to remain neutral between the feuding conservative and liberal factions of the California GOP, Max Rafferty, an outspoken, divisive, conservative Republican, was elected California's superintendent of public instruction by a margin of nearly 250,000 votes.[52]

Outside of the Northeast and the most industrialized, urbanized states of the Midwest, conservative Republicans optimistically concluded that there was a growing, grassroots conservative reaction against both the "creeping socialism" of liberal Democrats like JFK and LBJ and the "me too" complicity of the moderate to liberal wing of the GOP led by Rockefeller, Nixon, and Dirksen. From their perspective, a conservative-dominated Republican Party could motivate nonvoting "stay at home" conservative Americans who were disillusioned with and frustrated by "me too" moderate Republican presidential nominees and national platforms from 1940 to 1960. This invigorated, expanded GOP could then develop a conservative, electoral majority that would elect a conservative Republican as president in 1964 or 1968.[53]

Disappointed with Dwight Eisenhower's apparent apathy in transforming the GOP into a truly conservative party and left leaderless by the death of Senator Robert A. Taft of Ohio in 1953, the conservative wing of the GOP cooperated with non-Republican, conservative intellectuals and activists. They sought to develop a grassroots conservative ideology that appealed to middle-class Americans, especially suburbanites in the Southwest, West, and key metropolitan areas of the South. They also wanted to avoid alliances with the John Birch Society and other extreme right-wing organizations as well as with the White Citizens Councils of the Deep South and other blatantly racist organizations.[54]

For these conservatives, it was possible to develop and advocate a nonracist, uncompromising opposition to federal civil rights legislation and federally enforced school desegregation based on the appealing principles of states' rights, property rights, freedom of association, and free market capitalism.[55] In his best-selling book, *The Conscience of a Conservative*, Senator Barry Goldwater criticized the reasoning of the Supreme Court's school desegregation decision in *Brown*. The Arizona Republican stated that, while he personally opposed racial segregation and discrimination, "I am not prepared, however, to impose that judgment of mine on the people of Mississippi or South Carolina, or to tell them what methods should be adopted and what pace should be kept in striving toward that goal. That is their business, not mine."[56]

The conservative wing's principled, seemingly nonracist opposition to civil rights legislation and federal intervention on racial issues in general nonetheless led to the following realization of GOP leaders at the RNC's June 1963 meeting in Denver. According to journalist Robert Novak, "A good many, perhaps a majority of the party's leaders, envisioned substantial political gold to be mined in the racial crisis by becoming in fact, though not in name, the White Man's Party."[57] The emergence of a more militant civil rights movement and growing racial unrest in major northeastern and midwestern cities made it more likely that a significant segment of mostly Democratic, Catholic white voters in these areas might vote for a blatantly anti-civil rights Republican presidential candidate in 1964 as a protest against rising crime rates and declining property values.[58]

Conservative ideologues who sought to increase their influence in the 1964 Republican presidential campaign were also encouraged by the establishment of the Conservative Party of New York in 1962 and the Young Americans for Freedom (YAF) in 1960. Anti-Rockefeller Republicans gleefully noted that the obscure Conservative gubernatorial nominee attracted approximately 142,000 votes while the New York governor was reelected by a narrower margin in 1962 than in his upset victory of 1958.[59] Nurtured by *National Review* editor William F. Buckley, the YAF proved to be popular among conservative college students, increasingly infiltrated and even dominated local chapters of the Young Republicans, and provided the potential for a large number of enthusiastic campaign volunteers for a charismatic conservative Republican presidential candidate.[60]

Unlike previous, isolationist GOP conservatives, the conservative activists of the early 1960s combined their advocacy of minimal federal intervention on social and economic issues with more aggressive, interventionistic foreign and defense policies against international Communism. Among conservative intellectuals and political activists, both libertarians championing free market capitalism and individual liberty and traditionalists seeking to preserve moral, religious, and cultural values were dissatisfied with the American foreign policy of the early 1960s. For them, the bipartisan, cautious, defensive containment policy of Eisenhower, Dirksen, JFK, and LBJ seemed to be, at best, inept and unable to stop the expansion of Communism in the world. At worst, this foreign policy facilitated the growth of international Communism by appeasing the Soviet Union, subordinating American sovereignty to the "One World" United Nations, and providing substantial economic aid to socialist countries. John Stormer, chairman of the Young Republicans of Missouri, asserted in 1964 that "the Kennedy-Johnson Administration based nearly every foreign policy decision—in Laos, Cuba, Africa, Geneva, Berlin—on the assumption that communists have 'mellowed,' despite all the evidence to the contrary."[61] In promoting Barry Goldwater's presidential candidacy, Phyllis Schlafly rhetorically asked, "How long can we tolerate this Communist base in Cuba, with Castro insulting and harassing us, spreading his infection throughout the Western Hemisphere giving the Soviets the opportunity to zero in their missiles on American cities?"[62]

This type of zealous, pro-actively militant anti-Communism unified and energized the numerous and diverse factions and strands of the conservative intellectual movement and right-wing activism.[63] As much as they valued the ideological fervor, volunteer services, mass mail publicity, and fundraising efforts of right-wing activists, conservative Republican politicians were divided about whether to co-opt or dissociate themselves from these right wingers because of their controversial reputation with the media and American public. The more politically cautious and ambitious right-wing GOP politicians like Barry Goldwater and John Tower eventually and belatedly distanced themselves from the Birchites, Minute Men, and other prominent extremists.[64] Nonetheless, Birchite founder Robert Welch, who had denounced Eisenhower as a Communist agent, wrote the following about Goldwater as early as 1958. "I'd love to see him President of the United States, and maybe one day we shall."[65] Other Republican politicians, like congressmen John Rousselot and Edgar Hiestand of California, perceived their joint memberships in the GOP and the John Birch Society as political assets, not liabilities. For these conservative Republicans, cooperating with right-wing organizations outside the Republican Party would enable them to gradually gain control of the presidential nominating and platform-making processes of Republican national conventions and eventually achieve a conservative majority among American voters.[66]

The moderate to liberal wing of the Republican Party, however, was still confident that it would prevail at the 1964 Republican national convention. After all, with its financial base in Wall Street and major corporations, it still attracted most of the GOP's contributions, especially from wealthy individuals and well-funded economic interest groups like the AMA, NAM, and U.S. Chamber of Commerce. Despite the rapid growth of right-wing activism and conservative capture of local Republican organizations in the South, Southwest, and southern California, most delegates in 1964 would not be chosen through binding primaries. The moderate to liberal wing was confident that it could provide enough delegates from heavily populated northeastern and midwestern states to determine the selection of the Republican presidential nominee and dominate the writing of the party's platform in 1964.

Unlike the most outspoken, ideologically conservative Republican politicians, the moderate to liberal wing of the GOP was especially sensitive and responsive to the general public's perception of the Republican Party and its relationship to right-wing organizations. Moderate and liberal Republican candidates and their campaign strategists were still convinced that only a centrist, "good government" image of efficiency, honesty, and integrity expressed by the GOP's policy agenda, national conventions, and presidential tickets could attract enough independents, moderates, split-ticket Democrats, and middle-class racial minorities to run a competitive presidential campaign in 1964. The GOP could then win the presidency in 1968, when, presumably, JFK would be ending his two-term presidency. Since Wendell Willkie's 1940 presidential campaign, moderate and liberal Republicans had emphasized that, unlike Democratic presidents and nonsouthern Democrats in Congress, the GOP was not burdened and embarrassed by a need to make legislative concessions to an influential, racist, reactionary wing of its party.[67] Instead, a broad-based, centrist GOP that controlled the presidency and Congress could provide more innovative, efficient policy progress in social welfare programs, environmental protection, federal aid to education, civil rights, and bureaucratic reform, and a more rational, competent peacekeeping foreign policy than if the Democrats controlled the presidency and Congress.[68]

The moderate to liberal wing's concern about not having the GOP associated with the John Birch Society and other right-wing extremists was understandable. Gallup polls indicated that as the general public became more aware of the John Birch Society it was more likely to have an unfavorable opinion of it. Gallup polls released on April 21, 1961, February 16, 1962, and August 5, 1964, revealed that the proportion of Americans polled who had heard of the John Birch Society respectively increased from 37 percent to 53 percent and then to 68 percent.[69] The proportion of respondents who expressed a favorable opinion of the John Birch Society was only 8 percent in both the 1962 and 1964 polls.[70] Furthermore, only 11 percent of the Republicans polled in 1962 had a favorable opinion about this organization while 42 percent of Republicans had an unfavorable opinion and the remaining Republicans were undecided.[71] In an October 21, 1964, speech, liberal Republican Congressman Silvio Conte of Massachusetts publicly accused the John Birch Society of being "linked directly to the organized hate groups of the United States."[72]

The moderate to liberal wing of the GOP was pleased with the gubernatorial election results in the Northeast and Midwest in 1962. Republican victories in New York, Michigan, and Pennsylvania suggested that either Nelson Rockefeller or a candidate with a similarly centrist, "good government" appeal and attractive media image would be a formidable opponent to JFK in 1964. A Republican like this would compel the Democratic president to spend an unexpected and disproportionate amount of time, money, and other resources campaigning in the major metropolitan areas of the Northeast and Midwest, his strongest electoral base.[73] In assessing the election results of 1962, journalist David S. Broder noted the decline of the northern urban and southern rural voting blocs of the New Deal coalition and the rise of the non-ideological, pragmatic, less partisan, centrist middle-class suburbanites throughout the nation. He concluded, "The triad of issues that move these people is the same from coast to coast: Jobs, Schools, Taxes."[74]

In his statistical analysis of the 1962 elections, pollster Elmo Roper reached a similar conclusion. Roper declared 1962 to be "the year of the ticket splitter" and that "sectional and regional differences are gradually becoming more faint."[75] For example, Vermont elected its first Democratic governor since the Civil War. Alabama almost elected its first Republican senator since the Reconstruction Era, and Oklahoma elected its first Republican governor.

More ominously for the Democratic Party, Roper calculated that the percentage of the Democratic congressional vote had steadily declined from 56.5 percent in 1958 to 51.9 percent in 1962. Outside of the South, it was 50.3 percent in 1962.[76] Despite the nation's attention to the Cuban missile crisis in October, JFK's dramatic resolution of it, and the subsequent increase in his public approval rating, Roper found no evidence that this foreign policy issue benefited Democratic candidates or had any noticeable influence on voting behavior.[77] Roper concluded that the most significant races in 1962 were decided by the winning candidates' personalities and public images and local issues. Roper further surmised that JFK's party affiliation would be less significant in his electoral appeal in 1964 than in 1960 and the "public is in a mood to elect exceptional Republicans wherever it finds them."[78]

Private polls sponsored by the DNC and the White House reached similar conclusions. Earlier in 1962, political analysts E. John Bucci and J. V. Toscano informed JFK that his major advantages for his reelection campaign were incumbency and his consistently high public approval ratings. They warned him that "lurking menacingly in the shadows of national politics are Rockefeller and Romney ready to capitalize on any Kennedy mishap."[79] In his analysis of the midterm elections, pollster Louis Harris warned JFK that more of the most racially and economically conservative southern whites would vote Republican in 1964 and 1966, thereby further developing "an ultra right-wing GOP in the South, based in the heart of the Goldwater spectrum."[80] Harris, though, asserted that the increase in Republican voting behavior among Catholic ethnics in 1962 was more troubling for JFK's reelection campaign. "The Republicans can make strong appeals to ethnic minorities in the big cities, which show signs of rebellion, but at the same time can appease the conservative South to score gains there . . . they could make the 1964 election a close one, indeed."[81]

During the summer and fall of 1963, JFK conferred with Kenneth P. O'Donnell, RFK, Lawrence F. O'Brien, John M. Bailey, Louis Harris, Richard Maguire, and Richard Scammon, director of the U.S. Census Bureau, about preliminary plans for his reelection campaign. O'Donnell, JFK's appointments secretary, and Maguire, DNC treasurer and founder of the President's Club, were arranging his schedule for fundraising and public speaking purposes, especially in Texas. They originally wanted to plan a fundraising trip to Texas for September, 1963.[82] Through public appearances and statements as well as firm, clear instructions to his staff, JFK wanted to dispel any and all rumors and speculation that he intended to replace LBJ as his running mate in 1964.[83]

One rumor, advanced by Evelyn Lincoln, JFK's White House secretary, was that Kennedy wanted to replace Johnson with Terry Sanford, the young, racially moderate governor of North Carolina. Sanford, though, long after JFK's death, dismissed this. Howard E. Covington, Jr., and Marion A. Ellis, Sanford's biographers, stated, "To Sanford, replacing one Southerner for another would have made no political sense and only created more problems for a Kennedy reelection campaign, which was already in trouble in the South."[84]

O'Brien agreed with this analysis in his memoirs. "I saw no indication that Kennedy had considered dropping Johnson in 1964 as some have suggested. There was no reason for him to do so."[85] Indeed, Texas, with its twenty-five electoral votes in 1964, might prove to be even more important for JFK than in the 1960 election. Since JFK's televised speech on civil rights following the race-related violence in Birmingham, Alabama, in June 1963 and the subsequent submission of a comprehensive civil rights bill to Congress, the president's public approval ratings in the South were consistently and significantly lower than in other regions during the summer and fall of 1963. Although Nelson Rockefeller's reputation and policy position on civil rights were more consistently, clearly, and emphatically liberal than JFK's, a June 30, 1963, Gallup poll revealed that southerners preferred Rockefeller over Kennedy as a presidential nominee for 1964, 47 percent to 45 percent.[86] According to a July 7 poll, JFK received a 71 percent job approval rating outside of the South but only a 33 percent rating in the South.[87] By late September, Gallup polls also indicated that JFK's job approval rating in the South had improved only slightly to 44 percent and that in a presidential trial heat against Barry Goldwater only 44 percent of the southerners polled five days later would vote for JFK.[88]

Gallup polls of this period revealed that the public in general associated the Kennedy administration with the civil rights movement. Most whites, regardless of region, increasingly perceived both as too demanding and extreme on civil rights. Nearly half, 48 percent, of nonsouthern whites in an August 11, 1963, poll agreed that the Kennedy administration was "pushing integration too fast." Forty-four percent of Catholics agreed with this statement.[89] Of those respondents who had heard about the upcoming civil rights march on Washington, DC, led by Martin Luther King, Jr., 63 percent expressed an unfavorable opinion of it in an August 27, 1963, poll.[90] In a Gallup poll released on November 20, two days before JFK's assassination, 45 percent of nonsouthern whites agreed that "the Kennedy Administration is pushing integration too fast" and only 30 percent replied that the administration's promotion of racial integration was "about right."[91]

In their initial analysis of the 1962 election results, JFK's political advisors expressed their concern about the decline in Democratic voting behavior among white, non-Hispanic Catholics compared to 1960. They expected a decrease in electoral support for JFK among Catholics in 1964 for the following reasons. First, the absence of the excitement and novelty of electing the first Catholic president reduced religious solidarity among Catholic voters. Second, as Catholics continued to experience greater affluence, upward socioeconomic mobility, and migration from cities to suburbs, they were more likely to vote Republican, as they did in the 1950s compared to the 1930s and 1940s. Third, and perhaps most troubling, working-class and lower middle-class Catholic ethnics who lived in major cities experiencing growing racial tensions and rising crime rates associated with inner-city blacks were becoming more skeptical and even hostile to the civil rights movement, increasingly identified with JFK and RFK. Some of these Catholics might vote Republican or for a minor party presidential candidate as a protest vote in 1964.[92]

Besides being director of the U.S. Census Bureau, Richard Scammon also served as chairman of the President's Commission on Registration and Voting Participation. This commission suggested the abolition of poll taxes. Unofficially and more surreptitiously, it aided the DNC's effort to liberalize and eventually abolish Texas's poll tax law in order to increase black and Hispanic voter registration and turnout for 1964. John Connally and other conservative Democratic politicians in Texas were, at best, ambivalent about high voter turnout among these minorities. Scammon also helped White House special counsel Theodore C. Sorensen prepare voting statistics that the DNC needed to apportion delegates for the 1964 Democratic national convention in Atlantic City, New Jersey.[93]

In fulfilling his partisan, campaign role for JFK, Scammon met with the president ten days before Kennedy's assassination. JFK was especially interested in having Scammon explain to him how socioeconomic mobility affected the voting behavior and party affiliation of various Catholic ethnic groups. The president was impressed by and grateful for the partisan and personal loyalty of Polish Americans. JFK remarked that, as Catholics earned higher incomes, moved to suburbs, and voted Republican, "It's going to be a new kind of politics."[94]

Despite the statistical evidence of his current unpopularity among southern whites and the declining party loyalty of Catholic Democrats, JFK had already decided to run for reelection as a bold, pioneering liberal rather than as a cautious moderate. While linking the nation's economic growth and greater affluence to his administration's policies, the president planned to emphasize the contrast between prosperity and the persistence of poverty in his reelection campaign. In particular, JFK wanted to educate the voters and gain their support for his emerging anti-poverty programs by highlighting the similarities between the impoverished social and economic conditions of rural, Appalachian whites and those of urban blacks.[95]

With his more aggressively liberal positions on poverty and civil rights, JFK was confident that he could at least carry Texas and Florida among the southern states in the 1964 election. In addition to his family's longtime vacation residence in Palm Beach, the president enjoyed close friendships with Senator George Smathers of Florida and LeRoy Collins, a former governor of that state and chairman of the 1960 Democratic national convention. Although Smathers opposed JFK on civil rights, Collins was regarded as a New South politician because he urged his fellow southern governors to voluntarily obey the *Brown* decision on school integration. Except for its panhandle region, Florida was generally a more racially moderate state than others in the Deep South. Its voting behavior was increasingly influenced by the growing number of northern retirees in its population.[96]

JFK traveled and spoke in Florida a few days before arriving in Texas on November 21, 1963. In Tampa, Kennedy addressed the Florida Chamber of Commerce and the United Steelworkers' Union. In both speeches, the president emphasized that his administration's policies on trade, taxes, and economic growth benefited both business and labor. He replied to a question about his civil rights policies at the Chamber of Commerce event by acknowledging that his position was not popular in Florida. JFK pragmatically told his fellow whites that "if we are going to have domestic tranquility, if we are going to see that our citizens are treated as I would like to be treated, and as you would like to be treated, that they have to meet a standard of conduct and behavior, but they are not automatically excluded from the benefits which other citizens enjoy merely because of their race, their creed, or their color."[97]

On that same day, November 18, 1963, JFK addressed the Inter-American Press Association and the National Education Association (NEA) in Miami. JFK was aware that the failure of the Bay of Pigs invasion, his pledge to the Soviet Union that the United States would never again support an invasion of Cuba, and his embryonic détente with the Soviet Union were unpopular with Cuban exiles in Florida, right-wing activists, and the most conservative governments in Latin America. The president attributed the success of the Alliance for Progress and American economic aid to that region as major factors in reducing the appeal of Castro and Communism in Latin America. "Castroism, which a few years ago commanded the allegiance of thousands in almost every country, today has far fewer followers scattered across the continent," JFK asserted.[98] To the NEA, the president confidently stated, "This Congress must be judged, in my opinion, by what it is able to do in the important field of education certainly as much as in any other field before it goes home next July or next August."[99]

The president privately understood that it was unlikely that Congress would pass either his civil rights bill or the elementary and secondary education bill before the 1964 election.[100] Leading Republicans in both the moderate to liberal and conservative wings of the GOP attacked JFK's policy record and current legislative agenda as fiscally irresponsible and contradictory by combining tax cuts with increases in federal spending and a major new entitlement, Medicare, all of which threatened inflation. If the moderate to liberal wing controlled the 1964 Republican national convention and nominated Rockefeller for president, it could unfavorably contrast the New York governor's record on civil rights and education to the wide gap between JFK's liberal promises and the legislative stalemate exacerbated by the persistent conflict between southern and nonsouthern Democrats in Congress.

Moderate and liberal Republicans often agreed with the broad domestic and foreign policy goals of JFK. Thus, they often focused their criticism on the methods of and spending by the Kennedy administration and the Democrats in Congress as wasteful, inefficient, involving too much federal control, and providing pork barrel projects for Democratic politicians and interest groups.[101] As early as March 6, 1963, JFK complained to Undersecretary of the Treasury Henry Fowler, "Rockefeller is always yakking about efficiency."[102]

Despite Rockefeller's comfortable reelection margin in 1962, JFK was less concerned about running against Rockefeller in 1964 than he was in 1960. A major theme in Rockefeller's reelection campaign was that he had not broken his promise not to raise taxes. As 1963 began, however, his state's budget faced a $100 million deficit.[103] The New York legislature rejected his proposal to raise automobile license fees, but passed his bill to raise liquor taxes.

Rockefeller insisted that both revenue proposals were fees, not taxes. Nonetheless, the governor's fellow Republicans, especially more conservative GOP legislators from upstate, rural areas, were angry at what they perceived as the governor's duplicity and broken promise. Partially out of spite, these Republicans joined Democrats in the state legislature to cut $67 million from Rockefeller's spending proposals.[104] To conservative Republicans throughout the nation who opposed Rockefeller's budding presidential candidacy, this Republican tax revolt against Rockefeller proved that the New York governor was a liberal big spender like JFK.

Rockefeller's desired image of providing an honest, efficient administration for New York as a role model for the federal government was also tarnished by a political scandal in the New York liquor authority. With liquor licenses scarce, expensive, and difficult to obtain, Frank Hogan, the district attorney in New

York City, uncovered bribery, conspiracy, and influence-peddling activities. The scandal's participants included Martin Epstein, chairman of the state liquor authority and a Rockefeller appointee, and L. Judson Morhouse, the Republican state chairman and a close political confidante of the governor. Rockefeller had also appointed Morhouse chairman of the New York Thruway Authority. The most sensationalized case in this investigation included Hugh Hefner's Playboy Club in Manhattan. The prosecution charged that Morhouse demanded $100,000 and other financial benefits from the Playboy Club to secure its liquor license.[105] Morhouse was later convicted, briefly imprisoned, and pardoned by Rockefeller in 1970.[106]

Nonetheless, Rockefeller conducted an unannounced yet obvious exploratory campaign for the Republican presidential nomination during the spring of 1963. He hoped to position himself within the GOP as a centrist who was acceptable to both the moderate-liberal wing and the more pragmatic conservatives like Republican congressman Robert A. Taft, Jr., of Ohio. The New York governor awkwardly tried to co-opt conservative Republicans by hawkishly attacking JFK's new foreign policy toward the Soviet Union as appeasement concerning Cuba.[107] Rockefeller was cautiously calculating his chances for being elected president in 1964. He and his strategists firmly told Republican politicians favorable to his candidacy not to openly endorse him yet or organize pro-Rockefeller campaign committees in their states, including key primary states like California.[108]

Rockefeller's caution was justified. When he was running for reelection in 1962, his poll ratings dropped sharply after the public learned that the governor and his wife had divorced in March 1962. The governor's status in the New York polls soon rebounded, and his divorce apparently had little or no influence on voting behavior in the gubernatorial election. On May 4, 1963, shortly after conducting his political tour of several states, Rockefeller married Margaretta "Happy" Murphy. They were married one month after she divorced her first husband, a microbiologist for the Rockefeller Institute.[109]

Rockefeller's new wife was almost twenty years younger than he and had four young children. Before Rockefeller's divorce in 1962, there had been rumors among journalists who covered the governor and in New York circles that "Happy" Murphy was Rockefeller's mistress. Rockefeller and his advisors had anticipated a negative yet brief public reaction to his second marriage.

The fledgling campaign underestimated how severe and prolonged the intraparty controversy over the governor's sudden remarriage would be. A Gallup poll released on April 28, 1963, indicated that 43 percent of the Republicans surveyed favored Rockefeller for their party's 1964 presidential nomination and only 26 percent favored Goldwater. Two months later, a Gallup poll revealed that 38 percent of them favored Goldwater and only 28 percent preferred Rockefeller, a 15 percent decline for the New York governor.[110] Letters and telegrams to RNC members and Republicans in Congress showed that Rockefeller's controversial second marriage was especially repugnant to older Republican women and Protestant clergy.[111]

Rockefeller's speeches in Denver and San Francisco denouncing right-wing extremism during the summer of 1963 and his September trip to Europe to highlight his foreign policy credentials failed to rejuvenate his unannounced yet floundering presidential campaign. Rockefeller decided, therefore, to officially announce his presidential candidacy on November 7, 1963, and travel to New Hampshire to begin campaigning for that state's March 10 presidential primary.[112] The New York Republican was confident that if enough voters met him and his charming, vivacious wife, then the so-called "morality issue" would dissipate and he could win primaries, boost his poll ratings, and secure blocs of delegates from currently skeptical party leaders.[113]

Before leaving for Texas, JFK dismissed Rockefeller's recently announced presidential candidacy. The president told his campaign strategists that Rockefeller lacked the perseverance and courage to conduct a long, arduous, risky campaign.[114] The New York Republican demonstrated in his brief, tentative exploratory presidential campaign in late 1959 and his reconsidered presidential candidacy in the spring of 1960 that he was unwilling to boldly and vigorously run for president unless he was confident of victory.[115] JFK noticed that Rockefeller seemed as uncertain, indecisive, and ambivalent about his current presidential candidacy as he was about the 1960 presidential campaign.[116] Unlike Kennedy in 1960, Rockefeller was so afraid of losing a presidential campaign that he was ultimately unwilling and unable to do everything that he must do to win.

Conversely, JFK worried about running against George Romney if the Michigan governor became the Republican presidential nominee in 1964. Only a few months after Romney was inaugurated as governor, JFK told his close friend Paul "Red" Fay, "The one fellow I don't want to run against is Romney. That guy could be tough. . . . Imagine someone we know going off for twenty-four or forty-eight hours to fast and meditate, awaiting a message from the Lord whether to run or not to run."[117]

Indeed, Romney's sincere, zealous Mormon faith proved to be appealing not only in Michigan but nationally among Republicans from both the moderate to liberal and conservative wings of the GOP. Rockefeller's messy divorce and quick remarriage continued to distract the media and the public from his campaign message as his second wife accompanied him on his political appearances. For the politically pragmatic strategists of the GOP's "presidential party," who previously dominated their party's presidential nomination, Rockefeller's personal life was becoming an irreparable burden to his feasibility as a strong presidential candidate. Conservative party regulars and right-wing ideologues, however, had always detested and distrusted Rockefeller. Many of them blamed Rockefeller for Nixon's narrow defeat in 1960 because the New York governor pressured Nixon to make liberal concessions in the GOP's national platform. From their perspective, this "Munich of Fifth Avenue" branded Nixon as another "me too" candidate who disillusioned and alienated conservative voters and reduced Nixon's electoral potential in the South.

Conservative activists were planning to emphasize the issue of moral decline in 1964. They focused on the apparent failure of liberal domestic policies to successfully address rising rates of violent crime and juvenile delinquency and the highly publicized influence-peddling scandals of Bobby Baker and Billy Sol Estes that were linked to LBJ's Senate career.[118] For them, Rockefeller's marital controversy justified their perception of the New York governor as the personification of the moral decadence of wealthy, liberal eastern elites.

In addition to Romney's religious devotion and wholesome family life, he was a Horatio Alger success story who gradually worked his way up the corporate ladder of the American Motors Corporation (AMC) to become its president in 1954.[119] He was active in civic affairs, especially regarding race relations and the formation of a nonpartisan citizens' organization in 1959 that succeeded in persuading the voters of Michigan to adopt a new state constitution. As a corporate executive, Romney was popular with AMC's management and investors by improving the company's competitiveness and profitability and with employees for improving worker morale, participation in the workplace, and race relations.[120]

Romney's rhetorical and campaign style and content were suprapartisan, enthusiastic, and personable but also unpredictable, mercurial, and outspoken. He sharply criticized both the John Birch Society and UAW president Walter Reuther. In his primary and general election campaigns for governor in 1962, Romney criticized the state's Democratic Party for its domination by labor unions and the Republican Party for its domination by big business, especially Ford and General Motors. According to political scientist Peter Kobrak, Romney's "victory hardly terminated these party-interest group relationships, but it did cement in Michigan's political culture the good government expectation that candidates and parties must demonstrate a broader aspiration of the public interest."[121]

Having proven his ability to attract the votes of most Republicans, nearly all independents, and a substantial, multi-ethnic, biracial segment of typically Democratic, blue-collar voters, Romney was an equal match for Rockefeller regarding civil rights liberalism and a record, albeit in the private sector, of competent, reform-minded, innovative administration. Romney's reputation as a fiscal manager was soon tarnished by his failure to persuade the Michigan legislature to adopt the governor's proposed income tax on individuals and corporations in November 1963. This proposal was part of Romney's platform in 1962 to reform the state's tax base and to assure a fair distribution of the tax burden and provide adequate revenue for balanced budgets and improved state services.

This legislative defeat was mostly induced by a revolt of conservative, rural Republican legislators against Romney. In addition to their growing suspicion that the governor was becoming a liberal big spender, conservative Republicans in Michigan resented Romney's developing presidential "boomlet" in the spring of 1963. To them, this was apparent in his out-of-state political speeches, and his tendency toward controversial grandstanding. For example, Romney participated in a civil rights demonstration against housing discrimination in the wealthy Detroit suburb of Grosse Point.[122] Regardless of their ideological, regional, and factional differences, Michigan Republicans found their governor to be a party leader who eschewed the powers and responsibilities of state party leadership and appeared to be an erratic, eccentric loner. During his gubernatorial campaign, Romney refused to identify his party affiliation in his campaign literature, publicly endorse his fellow Republican candidates, or operate his campaign out of the state party headquarters.[123]

Journalist Robert Novak shrewdly observed that Romney's ideological, programmatic, and partisan identity were so unique and inexplicable that it was impossible to categorize Romney as a conservative, liberal, or even a moderate within the GOP. Instead, Novak explained, "He is a follower of something of his own creation called Romneyism more than any conventional ideology."[124] No matter how inscrutable and perplexing Romneyism may have been, it proved to be very appealing to rank-and-file Republicans polled during the spring and early summer of 1963. A March 31 Gallup poll revealed that 14 percent of its respondents preferred Romney for the 1964 Republican presidential nomination while 44 percent chose Rockefeller and 21 percent selected Goldwater. In an April 28 poll, Romney's support among Republicans surveyed was virtually unchanged with 13 percent preferring him as he remained in third place. In a May 26 poll, however, Goldwater was now in first place, at 35 percent, only 30 percent favored Rockefeller, and Romney's support jumped to 22 percent.[125]

In a November 3, 1963, poll, however, Romney's support among Republicans had declined and stabilized to 16 percent with a continuation of his third place position while Goldwater's first place preference had increased to 45 percent. On February 16, 1964, three weeks before the New Hampshire presidential primary, the Gallup firm released a poll revealing that Romney was in sixth place at 5 percent among Republicans asked to state their preferred presidential nominee.[126] Romney, of course, had knowingly diminished his potential for higher poll ratings by firmly repeating his intention to keep his promise to the people of Michigan to complete his four-year term and not run for president in 1964.

If Romney had insincerely yet effectively promoted a "spontaneous" grassroots citizens movement to promote his presidential candidacy in key primary states in late 1963 and early 1964, it was unlikely that the moderate-liberal wing of the GOP and at least some leading conservative Republicans would have coalesced around the Michigan governor. They briefly flirted with the prospect that Romney could prove to be a dynamic, unconventional presidential candidate who could unite both wings and energize a suprapartisan, inclusive electoral base that could either win the 1964 election or at least run a tough race against JFK and later LBJ in preparation for a more likely GOP victory in 1968. At various times, Nixon and Eisenhower had urged Romney to run in order to defeat Goldwater and spare the GOP the inevitable intraparty chaos spawned by the Arizonan's most extreme activists.[127]

They soon learned, to their dismay, bewilderment, and wary irritation, the same lesson that GOP regulars and politicians in Michigan had already learned. George Romney played by his own rules. He was too independent and unpredictable to readily cooperate and compromise with, and ultimately submit to, the machinations and plans of party elders in order to have the opportunity to run a professional, serious presidential campaign. Shortly before the Republican national convention of 1964 opened in San Francisco, Romney reconsidered running for his party's presidential nomination. But, characteristically, it was not a resurgence of presidential ambition but a quixotic crusade to save the GOP from Goldwater's extremism, especially on civil rights.[128]

Toward the end of JFK's presidency, it was clear that Barry Goldwater would probably become the Republican presidential nominee of 1964. It was now unlikely that the moderate to liberal wing of the GOP and the party's more pragmatic, compromising conservative politicians would unite behind a viable, alternative candidate who could defeat Goldwater for the nomination. Before leaving for Texas, Kennedy jokingly and confidently told his campaign strategists and advisors that he could defeat Goldwater so easily that, "I won't even have to leave the Oval Office."[129]

JFK and RFK personally liked the amiable, unassuming Arizona senator. But they were convinced that Goldwater would self-destruct as a candidate because of his lack of political savvy, tendency to publicly make outspoken, controversial remarks, and rigidly conservative voting record that isolated him from most Republican senators. For example, the Senate passed the heavily compromised Kennedy-Ervin labor reform bill on April 25, 1959, by a vote of ninety to one. Goldwater was the only senator to vote against it.[130]

Both humorously and seriously, JFK told his campaign strategists, "Don't waste any chance to praise Barry. Build him up a little. Don't mention the others."[131] JFK consistently practiced his own advice in his final public statements about Goldwater. In his replies at press conferences and in political speeches, Kennedy treated Goldwater, already known for his outspoken, controversial comments, with a mixture of patronizing courtesy and sardonic humor. On October 19, 1963, a reporter asked JFK to comment on Dwight Eisenhower's article expressing concern and uncertainty about Goldwater's policy positions. JFK replied, "I don't think Senator Goldwater has ever been particularly deceptive. I think he has made very clear what he is opposed to, what he is for. I have gotten the idea. I think that President Eisenhower will, as time goes on."[132]

At his October 31 press conference, JFK was less subtle in portraying Goldwater as alienating himself from not only the suprapartisan, centrist policy consensus that JFK was developing but also from Eisenhower and the rest of the moderate to liberal wing of the GOP. The Democratic president deflected a reporter's question about Goldwater's charge that Kennedy was manipulating the news to improve his chances for reelection. Instead, JFK replied, "I am confident that he will be making many charges even more serious than this one in the coming months. And, in addition, he himself has had a busy week selling TVA and giving permission to or suggesting that military commanders overseas be permitted to use nuclear weapons, and attacking the President of Bolivia while he was here in the United States, and involving himself in the Greek election. So I thought it really would not be fair for me this week to reply to him."[133]

JFK also understood that Goldwater's candidacy would enable him to further expand and solidify the suprapartisan, centrist policy consensus that the Democratic president was trying to develop. This consensus was needed to gain eventual passage of his Medicare, civil rights, anti-poverty, and education legislation and to further develop détente with the Soviet Union through trade and more extensive nuclear arms control treaties. JFK and later LBJ wanted to make this more liberal direction in domestic policy, and, to a lesser extent, in foreign policy appear to be moderate, responsible, and constructive, rather than divisively partisan and narrowly ideological.[134]

The phrase "Goldwater movement" was somewhat of a misnomer. Goldwater had not initiated a fledgling presidential candidacy which then stimulated a conservative, personal following. Instead, a conservative movement, within and, to a greater extent, outside the Republican Party had grown during the late 1950s and early 1960s. Conservative Republicans were disappointed by the staggering GOP losses in the 1958 midterm elections, especially in the Senate, embittered by Nixon's narrow defeat in 1960 allegedly because of his vacillating "me too" rhetoric and strategy, alienated by Eisenhower's "dime store New Deal" and "modern Republicanism," and chagrined by the triumph of moderate to liberal Republicans like Rockefeller, Romney, and Scranton in 1962. During this period, most conservative intellectuals and activists outside the GOP tried to slowly develop a conservative majority in public opinion through publications like *The National Review* and *Human Events* and radio programs like the *Manion Forum*.

They also created or expanded right-wing organizations like the John Birch Society, Young Americans for Freedom, and the Christian Anti-Communist Crusade. Many of these interest groups focused on criticizing and portraying current American foreign policy as the ineffective appeasement of Communism. The more popular, grassroots local conservative organizations, however, focused on single-issue causes in state and local governments, such as opposing the fluoridation of water, anti-discrimination laws concerning the sale and rental of housing, the expansion of labor union membership, and higher property taxes.[135]

Other conservative activists had not given up hope on the potential for the disparate individuals, organizations, and publicity activities to successfully influence presidential elections by either forming a conservative third party or eventually dominating Republican national conventions by infiltrating and then dominating local Republican Party organizations.[136] Clarence Manion, a Notre Dame law professor and founder of a popular, conservative radio program, had been a staunch defender of Senator Joseph McCarthy and previously supported Senator Robert A. Taft's 1952 presidential candidacy. After establishing a right-wing group, For America, Manion championed the obscure presidential candidacy of T. Coleman Andrews in 1956. Andrews advocated the abolition of the income tax and a rejection of the *Brown* decision on school desegregation as judicial tyranny over the states. Manion briefly considered the idea of promoting a conservative, minor party presidential candidacy for Orval Faubus, the Arkansas governor who had dramatically opposed school desegregation, in the 1960 election. Manion, though, began to publicly promote Barry Goldwater for the 1960 Republican presidential nomination as early as the spring of 1959.[137]

Manion and Brent Bozell, a *National Review* editor, were impressed by Goldwater's landslide reelection to the Senate in 1958. The GOP's moderate-liberal wing perceived Rockefeller's narrow, upset victory as the only bright spot in the 1958 elections. It was already boosting Rockefeller as a more attractive, electable presidential candidate than Nixon. Liberal Democrats and the DAC, meanwhile, were celebrating the results as a resurgence of New Deal liberalism and a harbinger for Democratic victory in the next presidential election.

Manion and Bozell noted that Goldwater ran against the same Democratic opponent in 1952 and 1958 and increased his winning margins from less than 7,000 votes to more than 35,000.[138] Goldwater was only the second Republican to be elected to the Senate from Arizona and had proven his ability to attract Democratic and independent votes in what had recently been a conservative yet virtually one-party Democratic state. Goldwater generously devoted his time and labor during the 1950s to developing a larger, stronger, more electorally successful Republican Party in Arizona. Leading this blossoming, dynamic, thoroughly conservative state Republican Party, Goldwater attracted dedicated allies and protégés. They included Phoenix congressman John Rhodes, Republican state chairman Richard Kleindeinst, Denison Kitchel, an antiunion corporate lawyer, and campaign manager Stephen Shadegg.[139]

Unlike conservative ideologues who had become alienated from the national GOP, Goldwater demonstrated his party loyalty by diligently and successfully chairing the Senate Republican Campaign Committee from 1955 to 1963. He proved to be a popular speaker at Republican fundraising events and wrote a syndicated newspaper column. With the help of Bozell, Goldwater wrote a book, *The Conscience of a Conservative*, and Manion arranged to have it published in 1960.

Manion assumed that the book would have a limited readership. He was pleasantly surprised that by September 1960 more than 100,000 copies were printed.[140] At the Republican national convention of 1960, Goldwater managed to retain the respect of both conservative ideologues outraged and embittered by Nixon's concessions to Rockefeller on the platform and moderate to conservative party regulars who emphasized the need for Republican unity behind the Nixon-Lodge ticket and the compromised platform. The Arizona senator was acerbic and unequivocal in denouncing the Nixon-Rockefeller agreement on the platform as the "Munich of the Republican Party" and "immoral politics" on July 23. Then, on July 27, Goldwater urged all conservatives throughout the nation to "grow up" and actively work for Nixon's election because the Democrats were "dedicated to the destruction of this country."[141]

During and after the 1960 presidential campaign, Goldwater continued to help the GOP raise funds. His rhetoric combined conservative principles and party unity. Goldwater's unselfish, admirable dedication to both the welfare of the Republican Party and his uncompromising, seemingly idealistic brand of conservatism gained the Arizona Republican more admirers and followers from a broader range of GOP politicians and party regulars. He also attracted a greater number and variety of right-wing activists and conservative intellectuals who had previously felt alienated from the "me too" centrist domination of the GOP.[142]

Unlike JFK, Rockefeller, and Nixon, Goldwater seemed to lack the insatiable progressive ambition necessary for a politician to secure his party's presidential nomination and run a competitive race in the general election. Goldwater would be up for reelection to the Senate in 1964. He was reluctant to give up his Senate seat if he were nominated for president in 1964. Unlike LBJ's dual position on the 1960 Texas ballot as a nominee for the Senate and the vice presidency, Goldwater flatly refused to run for both the Senate and the presidency in Arizona. Running for two offices on the same ballot seemed unethical to him. Goldwater appeared content to use his Senate seat and especially his seat on the Senate Labor and Public Welfare Committee to nationally promote his conservative belief in the libertarian symbiosis between economic freedom and political freedom.

As early as 1961, Arizona Republicans and Goldwater admirers throughout the nation, ranging from Ohio congressman John Ashbrook to *National Review* publisher William Rusher, met to discuss the formation of a mass movement to draft Goldwater for a presidential candidacy in 1964. In addition, Arizona campaign professional Stephen Shadegg and F. Clifton White, a former political science instructor and public relations consultant from New York, provided most of the organizational strategy that enabled pro-Goldwater activists to eventually gain control of the Republican national convention in 1964 and nominate Goldwater. They were confident that they could persuade and pressure Goldwater to accept the GOP's presidential nomination. They appealed to the Arizona senator's sense of duty and commitment toward ideologically moving the "presidential party" of the GOP from its persistent domination by the moderate to liberal wing since 1940 to making the GOP a truly conservative party in presidential elections.[143]

The organizational strategy of the Goldwaterites was to gradually win control of Republican Party committees at the local level. Many Republican state committees and RNC members and staff were hostile to the conservative movement in general and to the prospect of a Goldwater presidential candidacy in particular.[144] Besides recruiting pro-Goldwater Republicans to run for local party positions, the National Draft Goldwater Committee also began a direct mail, grassroots fundraising operation. Its purposes were to generate a large number of small donations that reduced the moderate to liberal wing's Wall Street-based advantage in fundraising from big business and to stimulate enthusiasm in the draft movement among masses of conservative voters by involving them in it through small contributions.[145]

Peter O'Donnell, Republican chairman of Texas, was another leading strategist in the movement to draft Goldwater. O'Donnell, White, and Kitchel focused their efforts to gain grassroots control of local and then state Republican committees and conventions in the South, Southwest, and Far West, especially in rural areas and small towns. They understood how solidly the moderate to liberal wing of the GOP dominated state and local party organizations in major metropolitan areas, especially in the Northeast, Midwest, northern California, and Pacific Northwest. The conservatives were confident that by the summer of 1963 they could persuade most Republicans that Goldwater could win their party's presidential nomination and defeat JFK in 1964. Privately, O'Donnell and Kitchel noticed that grassroots support for Goldwater and public perception of Kennedy as a liberal extremist on race relations grew significantly after JFK's June 1963 speech following the Birmingham demonstration and his subsequent submission of a civil rights bill to Congress.[146] They were also emboldened by the ubiquity and intensity of pro-Goldwater sentiment in sharp contrast to the paucity of enthusiasm for Rockefeller at the RNC's meeting in Denver in late June 1963.[147]

A few days later, Young Republicans held their national convention in San Francisco. The meeting was clearly dominated by conservative delegates. Many of them also belonged to the YAF and had been previously organized into a conservative caucus of the Young Republicans by F. Clifton White. Meanwhile, Nelson Rockefeller was shocked by the militant tactics of conservatives at the Young Republicans' convention and widespread talk at the RNC's Denver meeting about making the GOP a "white man's party."[148]

The New York governor chose Bastille Day, July 14, 1963, to issue a public statement denouncing the "tactics of totalitarianism" of the conservative activists at the San Francisco convention and found these Republicans similar to the John

Birch Society leaders and "others of the radical right and lunatic fringe."[149] Rockefeller also implicitly criticized the RNC's Denver meeting for its attendees' anti-civil rights remarks and the Goldwater movement's strategy of primarily wooing conservatives in the South and West. Rockefeller vowed, "I for one will do everything in my power, working with others to counter the influence of these forces and to defeat their purposes."[150] Rockefeller's cogent assertion of mainstream principles and pledge to combat the rising conservative domination of the GOP's organizational apparatus, however, did not unite and energize the moderate-liberal wing of the GOP behind his presumptive presidential candidacy. Instead, Rockefeller's Bastille Day declaration aroused greater determination by conservative activists to nominate Goldwater for president and write the GOP's 1964 platform.

The battle lines within the GOP soon formed around the party's ideological character and not merely around Rockefeller's ambition to become president. Goldwater became increasingly receptive to the idea of running for president as a way to solidify this conservative revolution within the GOP. By the late summer and early autumn of 1963, however, O'Donnell, Shadegg, Kitchel, and White were worried that the draft Goldwater movement was losing its momentum and irritating the *National Review* because of Goldwater's refusal to publicly announce his candidacy. The senator's public reticence about his intentions also made it more difficult for them to develop a well-financed, well-organized campaign for the New Hampshire presidential primary.[151] Shadegg thought that Goldwater might still decide to run for reelection to the Senate and definitely reject a presidential candidacy.[152]

Although Barry Goldwater did not formally and publicly announce his presidential candidacy until January 3, 1964, it was evident to Goldwater's inner circle by October 1963 that he would probably run for president. During that month, he received a memo from Raymond Moley, a conservative columnist and former New Dealer who had belonged to FDR's first Brain Trust. Moley subscribed to the assumption of many Goldwaterites that there was a latent conservative majority among the voters. They could be mobilized to win a presidential election by an attractive, articulate conservative nominee who rejected the cautious "me tooism" of Nixon and Rockefeller.

Moley recommended that Goldwater's campaign organization be divided into two parts. The first division would dedicate itself to ideas, policy proposals, and speechwriting. The second division would specialize in political organization, voter mobilization, campaign finance, and scheduling. Moley assumed that such a clear, exclusive division of labor would minimize conflict, confusion, and inefficiency within the campaign structure.[153]

For the most part, Goldwater followed Moley's advice. In late 1963, Denison Kitchel opened a campaign office for Goldwater in Washington, DC, ostensibly to prepare for either a Senate reelection campaign or a presidential one. With the help of William Baroody from the American Enterprise Institute and Washington attorney Edward McCabe, Kitchel soon eclipsed the influence of Shadegg, White, and O'Donnell in the Goldwater campaign.[154] This created friction with these leaders of the National Draft Goldwater Committee. Journalist Robert Novak perceived Kitchel as politically inept as both a theoretician and manager. He concluded that Goldwater chose Kitchel to lead his presidential campaign because Kitchel "was a close friend he could confide in and whose advice he could rely on."[155]

In order to protect the integrity of the Goldwater movement and the Arizona senator's reputation as an honorable, principled politician, Kitchel carefully purged Goldwaterites who were members of the John Birch Society and other controversial right-wing organizations. It was later revealed, however, that Kitchel had briefly belonged to the John Birch Society from 1960 to 1961. He feared that the media or the Democrats would discover this fact and publicize it to smear and discredit Goldwater.[156] But Goldwater's campaign staff and later the RNC headquarters found it impossible to prevent or even effectively react to the proliferation of extremist literature, canvassing, and other grassroots activities that were conducted on behalf of the Goldwater campaign. During Goldwater's California primary campaign against Rockefeller, one of his campaign organizers wearily stated, "We've got super patriots running through the woods like a collection of firebugs, and I keep running after them, like Smokey Bear, putting out fires. We just don't need any more enemies."[157]

Unfortunately for Goldwater and his campaign strategists, JFK's assassination made their task even more difficult. Before assassin Lee Harvey Oswald was identified as a pro-Castro Marxist, many Americans initially suspected that a conspiracy of right-wing extremists had killed the president.[158] Indeed, Birchites in Dallas had distributed pamphlets along JFK's motorcade route that accused the Democratic president of "treasonous activities against the United States."[159] Goldwater personally liked Kennedy and looked forward to an enlightening presidential campaign that emphasized the ideological and policy differences between the two parties. Depressed by JFK's tragic death, Goldwater considered not running for president, partially because of his personal animosity toward LBJ and his firm belief that the American people did not want to have three different presidents within such a brief period.[160] Kitchel, Baroody, and other Goldwater advisors finally convinced the Arizona senator that he must run for a president as a duty of principle to the many conservatives who had dedicated themselves to the draft Goldwater movement.

No matter how confident JFK and then LBJ were of easily defeating Goldwater, they were concerned about the threat of the growing conservative movement to the development of a suprapartisan centrist consensus behind their policy agenda. Both Democratic presidents used the DNC headquarters, campaign funds, the IRS, the FCC's Fairness Doctrine, ghostwriters, and the unwitting collaboration of leading moderate and liberal Republicans to disrupt and discredit the conservative movement, especially its radio broadcasting. In a lengthy memo to attorney general RFK, Victor Reuther, brother of the UAW president, suggested that the Justice Department publicly identify various right-wing organizations, including the John Birch Society, as subversive organizations that will be investigated.[161] JFK directed White House aide Myer Feldman to have IRS commissioner Mortimer Caplin investigate and then revoke the tax-exempt status of right-wing groups and left-wing groups critical of his Cold War foreign policy.[162]

The Kennedy and Johnson administrations' public threats to investigate several conservative, allegedly nonpolitical, nonprofit organizations and the sources of their tax-deductible contributions proved to be an effective form of legal harassment against groups such as the National Education Program and the Christian Anti-Communist Crusade.[163] Several Democratic campaign strategists, namely, John M. Bailey, James H. Rowe, Jr., Kenneth P. O'Donnell, and Richard Maguire, helped to establish the National Council for Civic Responsibility. They combined it with the preexisting Public Affairs Institute so that the former benefited from the latter's tax-exempt status. The National Council for Civic Responsibility was an officially nonpartisan organization led by Arthur Larson. Larson was an anti-Goldwater, liberal Republican who had served as Eisenhower's undersecretary of labor and director of the U.S. Information Agency.[164] With Larson's organization able to solicit and receive tax-deductible contributions, its largest donor was the DNC, which gave $50,000.[165]

The DNC also contracted with the public relations firm of Ruder and Finn to use the National Council for Civic Responsibility to funnel DNC funds to freelance writers like Fred Cook. Cook was paid to research and write the book, *Goldwater: Extremist of the Right*. In it, Cook refers to Goldwater as "a Phoenix Country Club McCarthy."[166] Wayne Phillips, a former *New York Times* reporter contacted by Kenneth P. O'Donnell, hired Wesley McCune to keep abreast of right-wing broadcasting for O'Donnell and other Democratic campaign strategists. At the request of Phillips and with research from McCune, Cook wrote an article for *The Nation* about right-wing radio programs, "Hate Groups of the Air."[167]

JFK and LBJ perceived the extreme right wing's greatest threat to their nurturing of a suprapartisan, centrist policy consensus, especially the beginning of détente with the Soviet Union, to be the influence of right-wing radio broadcasts on public opinion. Their concern even affected their policies in Vietnam. According to Kenneth P. O'Donnell, JFK planned to wait until after the 1964 election to begin withdrawing American troops from Vietnam.[168] JFK feared that if he announced or even implied the possibility of a complete withdrawal from Vietnam before 1965, then right-wing opposition to his foreign policy would become more extreme and widespread. Likewise, LBJ was concerned that if he did not conduct at least a defensive, limited war in Vietnam, similar to Truman's strategy in Korea, then the United States would experience another era of McCarthyistic hysteria that would destroy the Great Society.[169]

The White House was especially disturbed by right-wing radio broadcasts denouncing the Limited Nuclear Test Ban Treaty and urging listeners to pressure their senators to reject it.[170] The White House and DNC had quietly promoted the establishment of the Citizens Committee for a Nuclear Test Ban Treaty. It was an ostensibly nonpartisan, civic organization since James J. Wadsworth, a Republican and former U.S. ambassador to the United Nations, chaired it. Furthermore, it was mostly financed by the contributions of wealthy liberals like Norman Cousins, publisher of the *Saturday Review,* who contributed $400,000, and Lenore Marshall, a New York poet prominent in the arts community, who gave $50,000.[171]

The true partisan and ideological character and purpose of this "citizens" committee were evident in the fact that Ruder and Finn, the DNC's public relations firm, took care of research, publicity, and refutations of right-wing, anti-treaty propaganda. Although the Senate ratified the treaty by a vote of 80 to 19 on September 24, 1963, the White House and DNC wanted to continue and even expand this operation. They discerned that if they regularly investigated and monitored right-wing broadcasters' use of the FCC's Fairness Doctrine, then they could limit and diminish right-wing opposition to JFK's reelection and to his other policy goals, such as Medicare and the sale of wheat to the Soviet Union. Based on its 1963 decision in the case of WKUL's anti-treaty broadcast in Cullman, Alabama, the FCC broadened its definition of the Fairness Doctrine so that it applied to all issues and asserted that the public's right to hear opposing opinions on an issue superseded all other interests.[172]

Benefiting from substantial funding funneled by the DNC into various "civic organizations" and the legal expertise of Nicholas Zapple, counsel to the Senate Communications Subcommittee, the campaign strategists for JFK and LBJ directed surrogates like Fred Cook and Wayne Phillips to regularly demand equal time from radio and television stations to respond to right-wing broadcasts and threaten legal action through the FCC.[173] During and shortly after the 1964 presidential campaign, DNC chairman John M. Bailey became more aggressive and public about the DNC's criticism of right-wing broadcasts and the alleged laxity of the FCC in enforcing the Fairness Doctrine. Bailey specified ten radio stations with regularly violating the Fairness Doctrine, including *Manion Forum* broadcasts accusing the State Department of being controlled by Communists.[174]

Fred Cook's widely distributed article in *The Nation* generated personal attacks against right-wing broadcasts. Cook received the assistance of the DNC, the National Council of Civic Responsibility, Ruder and Finn, and Wesley McCune's Group Research, Inc. in demanding free air time from radio stations throughout the nation to make rebuttals. Martin F. Firestone provided the most effective, influential legal assistance to Cook and others invoking the Fairness Doctrine against right-wing broadcasts. Firestone was an attorney and former counsel for the FCC who volunteered for the DNC during the 1964 campaign.[175]

Of the two hundred radio stations contacted by Cook, fewer than fifty offered him free air time for rebuttals. One of those that refused was WGCB in Red Lion, Pennsylvania. Cook, Firestone, Phillips, and the DNC decided to make an example of WGCB's unyielding refusal. Even after LBJ's landslide victory in the 1964 election, the DNC wanted the FCC to rule against WGCB and use the precedent to weaken and intimidate right-wing broadcasters for future elections and protect LBJ's policy consensus from hostile broadcasts.[176] The FCC and eventually the Supreme Court ruled against WGCB. Gradually, more and more radio stations refused to carry the programs of right-wing commentators like the Reverend Billy James Hargis and Clarence Manion. They feared costly litigation, lost advertising revenue, and fines or license suspensions from the FCC.[177]

The FCC did not want to be accused of a pro-administration, anti-conservative, liberal bias in its rulings against right-wing broadcasters. In 1964, the FCC began to grant greater discretion to the National Association of Broadcasters (NAB) to regulate the content of their member stations' programs. The NAB's application of a code of ethics to its members included stricter regulations on broadcasting personal attacks that had the effect, whether intended or not, of further discouraging the most extreme, right-wing broadcasts.[178]

The efforts of the White House, FCC, DNC, moderate and liberal Republicans like Arthur Larson, and the NAB combined to contain and then significantly reduce the prevalence of right-wing broadcasts and their influence on public opinion. The increasingly irreconcilable ideological policy and factional differences between the moderate to liberal "presidential party" of the GOP and the sporadic yet evident interaction between the most conservative congressional Republicans and right-wing extremists also contributed to the potential growth of the Kennedy-Johnson administration's suprapartisan, centrist policy consensus. In a January 28, 1964 phone conversation with Hubert Humphrey, Johnson commended Humphrey for his optimistic, policy-oriented response to RNC chairman William Miller's denunciation of LBJ as a "wheeler dealer" and promise that the GOP would link LBJ to Bobby Baker's shady business deals during the presidential campaign.[179] LBJ suggested, "Just every day you ought to say the Democratic party is the one party left for America because the other fellows don't stand for anything. Just God pity them for they know not what they do."[180]

As confident as LBJ was that the voters would reward the Democrats for representing legislative productivity and progress in the 1964 elections, he was concerned about two intraparty threats to the further development and solidification of consensus. First, Governor George Wallace of Alabama, best known for his nationally televised defiance of court-ordered integration of the University of Alabama in 1963, ran surprisingly well among nonsouthern white voters in the

Wisconsin, Maryland, and Indiana Democratic presidential primaries of 1964. Two weeks before JFK's assassination, DNC chairman John M. Bailey publicly accused the Republicans of using "racist appeals" in their recent, unsuccessful campaigns for mayor of Philadelphia and governor of Kentucky.[181] While the House Judiciary Committee was deliberating on JFK's civil rights bill in early 1964, LBJ, White House staff, and Democratic pollsters were concerned about the increasingly evident "white backlash" in major metropolitan areas of the Northeast and Midwest, especially among mostly Democratic, white, blue-collar voters.[182]

Coincidentally, two days before Bailey's denunciation of the Republicans' "racist appeals" in the Philadelphia and Kentucky elections, George Wallace spoke at Harvard University, Kennedy's alma mater, on November 4, 1963. With his insatiable appetite for national media attention, Wallace readily accepted the suggestion that he conduct a national speaking tour of colleges and universities beginning with Harvard. Faced with hecklers and occasionally violent, militant civil rights protesters, the Alabama governor responded shrewdly and tactfully. After providing historical, sociological, and legal reasons why he opposed the growth of federal intervention in state and local governments, especially on race relations, Wallace disarmed hostile academic audiences with his self-deprecating humor. He also made provocative assertions about the hypocrisy of northern white liberals for denouncing segregation laws in the South while often ignoring de facto segregation and racial discrimination in northern cities.[183]

In essence, Wallace's rhetorical question that he repeatedly asked his collegiate listeners in particular and fellow Americans in general was the following. If the Kennedy administration and their liberal allies were sincere in their determination to end racial segregation and discrimination, why don't they initially concentrate on encouraging state, local, and private efforts in nonsouthern states to end racism outside of the South? Journalists who covered Wallace's visit to Massachusetts noted how friendly and receptive working-class whites, especially police officers and taxi drivers, were toward Wallace in JFK's home state.[184]

Wallace resumed his speaking tour after LBJ became president in December 1963. He eventually spoke at over twenty colleges and universities in the Northeast, Midwest, Far West, and West Coast. In addition to informing nonsouthern audiences of his pro-states' rights, southern, segregationist perspective, Wallace also learned about the racial fears of many nonsouthern whites. The Alabamian especially realized that not only racially conservative, urban working-class whites but also pro-civil rights, middle-class suburbanites were hostile toward, or at least apprehensive about, fair or "open" housing laws (i.e., laws prohibiting racial discrimination in the sale and rental of housing). State fair housing laws were increasingly controversial in several states, especially California and Wisconsin. Liberal Democrats in the White House and Congress decided not to add a fair housing provision to the Kennedy-Johnson administration's civil rights bill for fear that it would kill the rest of the civil rights legislation.[185]

As a matter of fact, shortly after Wallace began his speaking tour in November 1963, California realtors established the Americans to Outlaw Forced Housing Committee. This organization was committed to repealing California's Rumford Fair Housing Act, passed in June 1963 after vigorous lobbying by Governor Edmund "Pat" Brown.[186] One year later, as LBJ easily carried California in the presidential election, California voters repealed the Rumford Fair Housing Act by adopting Proposition 14.[187]

The more immediate impact of Wallace's calculated exploitation of the fair housing issue among nonsouthern whites appeared in the Democratic presidential primary of Wisconsin, held on April 7, 1964. Lloyd Herbstreith, a Wisconsin businessman active in right-wing causes, including Senator Joseph McCarthy's political career, convinced Wallace that he could stun the White House and the media with an unexpectedly strong showing in his state's Democratic primary. Advising Wallace and his staff on campaign strategy, Herbstreith assured the Alabama Democrat that he could benefit from Wisconsin's open primary law. This law allowed Republicans and independents to vote in the Democratic presidential primary. Ironically, JFK benefited from this feature when Catholic Republicans and independents voted for him in that state's 1960 Democratic presidential primary. Since the 1964 Republican presidential primary was uncontested, Wisconsin's Republican and independent voters were more likely than usual to participate in the Democratic presidential primary.

Wallace addressed especially enthusiastic crowds in working-class, mostly Democratic Polish and other white ethnic neighborhoods of Milwaukee and other industrial cities. Besides asserting his implacable opposition to both federal and state fair housing laws, the Alabama governor warned blue-collar audiences that the administration's civil rights legislation threatened to eliminate the seniority system in labor unions and impose racial quotas on union jobs. He also broadened his rhetoric to include his populist brand of nonracial cultural conservatism. For example, he praised the patriotism, family values, and piety of Polish Catholics while denouncing the Supreme Court's 1962 decision that rejected government-authorized prayer in public schools.[188]

The Wallace campaign in Wisconsin also benefited from blunders by LBJ and John Reynolds, the Democratic governor of Wisconsin. Johnson refused to officially announce his presidential candidacy until the Democratic national convention in Atlantic City, New Jersey, was held in August 1964. LBJ, therefore, was represented in state presidential primaries as either a write-in candidate or by favorite-son presidential candidates, often pro-LBJ Democratic governors like Reynolds in Wisconsin and Matthew Welsh in Indiana. Unfortunately for LBJ, Reynolds was currently unpopular among a wide range of white voters, Catholic and Protestant, WASP and Slavic, urban and rural, working class and middle class, because of his policy positions. In particular, his tax increases offended rural voters and his prominent yet unsuccessful advocacy of a state fair housing law alienated both urban and suburban whites.[189]

Reynolds made a serious tactical error in playing the "expectations game" with the media and pollsters. The Wisconsin governor publicly warned the voters of his state that Wallace could receive as many as 100,000 votes on April 7. Reynolds assumed that this apparent overestimation of potential Wallace support would motivate labor unions, the NAACP, churches, Democratic party organizations, and other anti-Wallace groups and their leaders to mobilize an unusually high voter turnout for the governor's stand-in candidacy.[190]

Nevertheless, campaign events for Reynolds were often sparsely and unenthusiastically attended. By contrast, Wallace often addressed cheering, overflowing crowds, both in heavily Democratic blue-collar ethnic neighborhoods in Milwaukee and other industrial areas and in heavily Republican, Protestant rural areas. The most numerous and aggressive anti-Wallace crowds usually consisted of urban blacks and white college students. The hostile and occasionally violent reaction of anti-Wallace demonstrators to the Alabama governor seemed to generate more sympathy and support for Wallace among other Wisconsinites.[191]

LBJ did not publicly identify Reynolds as his "stand-in" candidate for Wisconsin's Democratic delegates to the 1964 Democratic national convention. On April 4, three days before the Wisconsin primary, a reporter asked LBJ at a press conference to comment on Wallace's primary campaigns in Wisconsin, Indiana, and Maryland. The president curtly replied, "I think the people of those States will give their answer at the time designated. I don't care to speculate or anticipate it."[192] Throughout the spring and early summer of 1964, LBJ persisted in publicly stating that he was "the president of all the people," wanted to focus on leading the passage of major legislation with bipartisan cooperation in Congress, and would wait until the summer to discern if "the American people will be willing for us to serve next year in the Congress and in the executive department."[193]

As much as Johnson projected the apolitical, disinterested façade of a humble public servant, he privately and steadily increased his intervention toward the campaign behavior of his "stand-in" candidates in Wisconsin, Indiana, and Maryland. Although the president did not travel to Wisconsin, he wired a widely publicized telegram to John Reynolds praising the Wisconsin governor for his patriotism and devotion to public service. At the prompting of the White House, RFK and Postmaster General John Gronouski, the first Polish American cabinet member and a Wisconsinite, traveled to Wisconsin to actively campaign for Reynolds. The attorney general fervently denounced the Alabama governor's record and rhetoric on civil rights and urged Wisconsinites to provide a "substantial victory" for Reynolds in order to assure passage of the pending federal civil rights bill.[194]

The results of Wisconsin's Democratic presidential primary revealed that Reynolds received 522,405 votes to Wallace's 266,136 votes, providing Reynolds with 66 percent of the votes to Wallace's approximately 34 percent.[195] While barely 300,000 Wisconsinites voted in the Republican presidential primary, almost

800,000 Wisconsin voters participated in the Democratic presidential primary. Wallace's 266,136 votes greatly exceeded Reynolds's gloomiest, most alarming projection. Many journalists and pollsters grimly concluded that the Wallace vote in Wisconsin signified a growing white working-class "backlash" against blacks outside of the South that endangered not only passage of the JFK-LBJ civil rights bill but also anti-poverty legislation targeted at poor, urban blacks.[196]

Reynolds defensively and awkwardly stated that Wallace's relatively and surprisingly strong showing only indicated that Wisconsin had "a lot of people who are prejudiced."[197] Despite the massive, nationwide Democratic landslide in November, Reynolds was defeated for reelection. Actually, a more reflective analysis of the Wisconsin primary indicated that the Wallace vote was mostly a protest vote against Reynolds and several of his policies on state issues rather than the harbinger of a mostly Catholic, nonsouthern, blue-collar backlash against LBJ and federal civil rights legislation. Reynolds was especially unpopular among Democratic white ethnics in Milwaukee for his advocacy of a state fair housing bill, but this policy position also made him unpopular among more affluent, racially moderate Republicans in the suburbs who feared that this legislation threatened their property values.[198] Beyond any race-related issues, mostly Republican rural voters resented Reynolds' recent tax increases and voted for Wallace in the Democratic primary as a way to retaliate against the liberal governor.[199]

LBJ, however, immediately internalized the Wallace vote in Wisconsin as the precursor of a growing threat to his public identification with the civil rights bill and other liberal legislation as the programmatic foundation of a suprapartisan, centrist policy consensus and his own presidential nomination in Atlantic City. In an April 8, 1964, phone conversation with George Reedy, his press secretary, LBJ regretfully and defensively stated that if he, rather than the politically inept and unpopular Reynolds, had had his name on the ballot in Wisconsin then it would "have been mighty easy for me to let my name go on the ticket and roll up a heavy vote."[200] The president advised Reedy to tell that to the White House press corps, "And we find that a two-thirds vote is a pretty good vote. . . . The fact that we got more votes than Wallace is pretty satisfactory to us."[201]

LBJ hoped that a positive spin on the Wisconsin primary results might be enough to satisfy the press and end its growing speculation about a presumed, nonsouthern white backlash. Nonetheless, the president decided to more directly manage the primary campaigns of his "stand-in" candidates in the Indiana and Maryland Democratic presidential primaries. In Indiana, Democratic governor Matthew Welsh agreed to run as LBJ's stand-in candidate in that state's May 5 Democratic presidential primary. The president announced trips to several depressed areas, including South Bend, Indiana, in late April for the official purpose of assessing their economic conditions as he prepared his anti-poverty legislation. During this officially nonpolitical trip, LBJ met Welsh and Democratic Senators R. Vance Hartke and Birch Bayh of Indiana in South Bend on

April 24, 1964. In his speech, the president closely linked South Bend's economic needs with the national goals of his domestic policy agenda. He stated, "I am here to see that what the Federal Government can do to work with you to help us all improve the lot of our fellow Americans."[202] On the following day, Senator Edward M. Kennedy addressed a Democratic Jefferson-Jackson Day dinner in Indianapolis and emphasized the connection between support for Welsh's presidential primary campaign and LBJ's domestic policy agenda, including the civil rights bill.[203]

Welsh was alarmed by an April poll that projected Wallace winning 45 percent of the votes in the Indiana Democratic presidential primary. Like Milwaukee, Gary, Indiana, had experienced increasing racial tensions between working-class Catholic ethnics and blacks. Indiana hosted the national headquarters of the Ku Klux Klan during the 1920s, and the John Birch Society was founded in Indianapolis. Indiana state law did not prohibit de jure racial segregation in public schools until 1949.[204] While Welsh was elected governor by a margin of 23,177 votes in 1960, JFK lost Indiana by a margin of 222,762 votes.[205] Much of the wide disparity of votes between Welsh's narrow victory and JFK's landslide defeat in Indiana was attributed to anti-Catholic prejudice among rural, Protestant Democrats who voted for Welsh but not for JFK.[206]

Nonetheless, Welsh was confident that he could decisively defeat Wallace. Realizing that Hoosiers were more likely to vote for state Democratic officials than national Democratic figures like JFK and LBJ, Welsh did not seek help from the White House or the DNC. "Although we made contact with the Democratic National Committee and the White House, there was no practical service they could render, and we asked for none," Welsh later stated.[207]

Unlike Governor John Reynolds of Wisconsin, Welsh was not running for reelection in 1964 because the Indiana constitution prohibited a governor from succeeding himself. Since Welsh was a lame duck, it was unlikely that Indiana voters would vote for Wallace as a protest vote against the Democratic governor. Despite opposition from Republicans and some Democrats in the state legislature to his tax proposals in 1963, Welsh was generally popular and respected as an honest, competent administrator and a moderate reformer. Welsh was proud of his efforts to improve race relations in Indiana and was determined not to let Wallace's candidacy tarnish this legacy.[208]

In conducting his primary campaign against George Wallace, Welsh had certain advantages in Indiana that Reynolds lacked in Wisconsin. Unlike Wisconsin's open primary law, Indiana's presidential primaries were closed. Although an obscure provision of Indiana law allowed Republicans to vote in the Democratic primary if they completed a cumbersome affidavit process, it was unlikely that there would be a significant amount of crossover voting, as there was in Wisconsin. Furthermore, unlike the anti-party, good government reformism of Wisconsin, Indiana continued to operate strong, well-financed, highly disciplined party organizations.

The party that controlled the governorship of Indiana also controlled thousands of state patronage jobs. Party regulars administered auto license bureaus as franchises in which a percentage of their revenue was sent to the campaign treasury of the governor's party.[209] State patronage employees were also expected to contribute 2 percent of their salaries to the state committee of the governor's party. State party conventions still controlled nominations for U.S. senator and governor, and local party organizations often determined nominations for lesser state and local offices.[210] If Wallace did manage to carry a few counties, the Democratic state committee had the authority to impose a unit rule so that Welsh could still deliver all of Indiana's delegates to LBJ on the first ballot at the Democratic national convention.[211]

Welsh shrewdly portrayed the campaign against Wallace as a nonpartisan crusade to prove to the nation that Hoosiers were not receptive to Wallace's subtle racist appeal. The Indiana governor conducted a well-coordinated media strategy that included frequent television commercials and press conferences broadcast throughout the state. Welsh defused the Democratic presidential primary as a partisan matter by organizing a joint, televised press conference in which both the Republican and Democratic state chairmen denounced Wallace's candidacy. The Welsh campaign also appealed to the patriotism of Hoosiers by distributing literature that included a photograph of the Confederate flag flying above the American flag at the Alabama Capitol building.[212] Perhaps the best publicity tool of Welsh's campaign was a taped interview of Charles Morgan that was frequently broadcast on radio and television. Morgan, an Alabama lawyer and former supporter of Wallace, revealed to Indiana voters that Wallace became a racist and extreme segregationist because of his ruthless political ambition.[213]

The efforts of Birchites, the Christian Freedom Fighters, the American Nazi Party, and other extremists to help Wallace probably lost him potential support. The Alabama governor was put on the defensive and failed to convince many voters that his campaign was based on states' rights and property rights, rather than on racism. Wallace avoided criticizing Welsh or even defending himself against Welsh's aggressive rhetoric. In one speech, the Indiana governor referred to Wallace as "the man whose beliefs were responsible for the deaths of innocent children in a Montgomery (sic) Church."[214] Welsh also directed state employees to prevent Wallace from campaigning on state property, and pressured businesses and organizations receiving state contracts or funds not to help the Wallace campaign schedule appearances, post advertising, or distribute leaflets.[215]

In the 1964 Democratic presidential primary of Indiana, Welsh received approximately 65 percent of the votes to Wallace's 30 percent.[216] Wallace refused to specify an anticipated percentage of votes to the media. Barry Goldwater stated that if Wallace received more than 25 percent in the Indiana Democratic primary, then his electoral performance should be perceived as a victory and evidence of significant, nonsouthern opposition to the federal civil rights bill under consideration in the Senate.[217] The Arizona Republican accurately predicted Wallace's receipt of 30 percent of the votes in Indiana a few days before that state's Democratic primary was held.[218]

Goldwater also expected Wallace to perform even better in Maryland's May 19 Democratic presidential primary. In Indiana, Welsh had contained the Wallace movement effectively enough so that the Alabama governor carried only two counties, both located in the Gary-Hammond metropolitan area of northwestern Indiana. It was an area that was similar to Milwaukee in its recent racial tensions.[219] But racial conflicts in Baltimore had been even more severe than those in Milwaukee and Gary, and Wallace's candidacy could also be popular along Maryland's eastern shore and other culturally southern parts of the state. Daniel Brewster, Maryland's Democratic senator and LBJ's stand-in candidate, lacked Welsh's political savvy and a strong, disciplined party organization. Initially, Brewster could only rely on organized labor, blacks, and the more racially moderate white voters living in the Maryland suburbs of Washington, DC, as the electoral base of his primary campaign.

When asked at his May 6 press conference to comment on Wallace's performance in the Wisconsin and Indiana primaries, the president dismissed Wallace's percentages in those primaries for not being "any overwhelming endorsement of a man's record."[220] But LBJ included Maryland in his ostensibly nonpolitical tour of selected states promoting his anti-poverty programs, and told George Reedy, his press secretary, to persuade *Baltimore Sun* reporter Phil Potter to "expose Wallace. I think they ought to point out that Wallace is now under investigation for frauds, highway contracts in Alabama that are paying his expenses. . . . The FBI is now investigating it."[221]

Regardless of the sources of Wallace's campaign funds, he was able to spend more on broadcast advertising in Maryland than in Wisconsin and Indiana. He used his speeches and advertising to more explicitly exploit racial fears and prejudice among whites than he had in the previous two states. In particular, Wallace delivered an impassioned speech in Cambridge, Maryland, on May 11 denouncing the federal civil rights bill. Because of earlier racial disturbances in Cambridge, the Maryland national guard regularly patrolled that city. The state troops used tear gas to disperse an altercation between Wallace supporters and civil rights activists following Wallace's speech.[222]

Although church leaders, labor leaders, civil rights organizations, and several Democratic senators campaigned for Brewster, Wallace's crowds became larger and more enthusiastic and Brewster's remained small and lackluster as primary day neared. On May 19, Brewster received 53 percent of the votes to Wallace's approximately 43 percent in Maryland's Democratic presidential primary.[223] Despite his second-place finish, Wallace carried sixteen of Maryland's twenty-three counties and most of Baltimore's white ethnic neighborhoods.[224]

Fortunately for LBJ, the primary results of May 19 proved to be the peak of Wallace's 1964 presidential campaign. On that same day, Senate Minority Leader Everett M. Dirksen announced at a Republican Senate caucus and then to reporters that he planned to vote for the administration's civil rights bill. He urged his fellow Republican senators to support both the bill and cloture against filibusters.[225] Dirksen had again helped LBJ to protect the emerging suprapartisan centrist policy consensus behind civil rights legislation and squelched the hopes of southern senators that Wallace's performance in Maryland in particular would eventually lead to the defeat or dilution of the Kennedy-Johnson civil rights bill.[226]

Wallace did not campaign in any more Democratic presidential primaries in 1964. The Alabama governor announced on June 5 that he decided to run for president as an independent. His last major campaign appearance was held on July 4 in Atlanta. He devoted his speech to a diatribe against LBJ's signing of the Civil Rights Act of 1964 two days earlier.

But the national media paid little attention to Wallace's speech and the white crowds that cheered him in Atlanta. After Barry Goldwater announced his opposition to the Kennedy-Johnson civil rights bill on June 18, 1964, the most zealous opponents of federal civil rights legislation and greater federal intervention in general lost interest in Wallace. They intensified their efforts to assure Goldwater the Republican presidential nomination and to deliver southern electoral votes to him in November.[227] During the Republican national convention in San Francisco, the Goldwater campaign learned that Wallace was willing to become a Republican if he could be Goldwater's running mate. On July 19, 1964, three days after Goldwater accepted the Republican presidential nomination and one day after racial violence erupted in New York City, Wallace announced the withdrawal of his presidential candidacy on the television news program *Face the Nation*.[228] Any lingering influence that Wallace's defunct candidacy might have exerted on the 1964 presidential election outside of the Deep South was minimized by Johnson and Goldwater's agreement on July 24 "to avoid the incitement of racial tensions" in their campaign rhetoric and tactics.[229]

Unlike George Wallace's ephemeral, quixotic presidential candidacy of 1964, RFK's enduring presence in the Johnson administration and in the nation's political consciousness proved to be LBJ's greatest, and progressively more intractable, challenge as party leader. During LBJ's despondent, frustrating vice presidency, he sensed growing hostility from RFK and the attorney general's allies in the Kennedy administration, the DNC headquarters, and the media. In particular, he concluded that the highly publicized investigations of Billy Sol Estes and Bobby Baker were being orchestrated by RFK and pro-RFK Democrats in order to pressure JFK to replace LBJ as his running mate in 1964.[230] After he became president, LBJ's suspicion developed further as he assumed that RFK would challenge him for their party's presidential nomination in 1968 and possibly as early as 1964.[231]

LBJ, though, was determined to solidify the political legitimacy of his presidency with the public in general and liberal Democrats in particular. He did this by emphasizing a smooth transition from and continuity with JFK's presidency by shepherding major legislation identified with JFK, especially the civil rights bill, through Congress. He also justified his policies in Vietnam by claiming that he was faithfully fulfilling Kennedy's commitment to South Vietnam's security. LBJ initially suspected that if he appeared to soften his military intervention in Vietnam, RFK would then openly oppose him for abandoning his brother's commitment.[232]

RFK, of course, was equally hostile and suspicious toward LBJ. In a 1964 oral history interview for his brother's presidential library, RFK described JFK as "a gentleman and a human being" and LBJ as "mean, bitter, vicious—an animal in many ways."[233] In this interview, RFK did not explicitly reject an interest in becoming vice president. The attorney general did, however, express how futile and powerless his vice presidency under LBJ would be. RFK stated, "I think it's possible to be Vice President. . . . But who am I going to have influence with? He's not going to pay any attention."[234]

LBJ assumed that RFK was already determined to ruthlessly replace LBJ as president in order to continue an apparent Kennedy dynasty. The Texan did not understand that the withdrawn, grief-stricken attorney general was uncertain about his future during the post-assassination period of late 1963 and early 1964. RFK's comments and the observations of his closest associates indicate that he considered leaving politics entirely and moving back to Massachusetts to write. Rumors about RFK considering a gubernatorial candidacy in Massachusetts in 1964 also circulated. He found it difficult to concentrate on his duties as attorney general and spent much time consoling Jacqueline Kennedy and her children and overseeing the development of JFK's presidential library. Lawrence F. O'Brien later commented that if RFK had seriously considered becoming LBJ's running mate, then such a thought was "a measure of Bobby's deep confusion in the months following his brother's death."[235]

LBJ held an unyielding conviction that RFK, in the words of Jeff Shesol, "controlled a government-in-exile, a party-within-the-party" that was determined to eventually replace LBJ with RFK as president. LBJ's suspicion was confirmed by the machinations of Paul Corbin in New Hampshire.[236] Corbin was a shadowy political operative who joined JFK's Wisconsin primary campaign in 1960. Corbin had once been associated with Communists and was investigated by HUAC and the FBI.

But he had also been known as a rabid McCarthyite in Wisconsin. After meeting RFK in the role of JFK's campaign manager, Corbin entirely attached himself to RFK.[237] The Wisconsinite devoted himself to whatever he perceived as RFK's personal and political welfare. Corbin even converted to Catholicism because he wanted RFK and Ethel Kennedy to be his godparents.[238]

In January 1964, Corbin began to promote a write-in movement to draft RFK for vice president in the New Hampshire Democratic presidential primary. LBJ suspected that RFK had directed or at least encouraged Corbin to initiate this campaign in the Democratic primaries of New Hampshire and later Massachusetts. Corbin was also testing the waters for RFK in New York.[239]

Because Corbin worked as a staff aide at DNC headquarters, LBJ called DNC chairman John M. Bailey on February 11, 1964. Bailey attested to allegations of Corbin's "Communist leanings" and the fact that Corbin had a reputation for being unpopular and obnoxious among RFK's most trusted associates, like Kenneth P. O'Donnell, but Corbin had a job at the DNC headquarters as a favor to RFK. Still uncertain if Bailey was more loyal to the Kennedys than to the president, LBJ told Bailey to send all of Corbin's personnel records to the White House. In subsequent conversations with Bailey, LBJ was careful not to express any animosity and suspicion toward RFK. Instead, the president conveyed the modest, reasonable message that as party leader he had to ensure that employees and officials of the DNC must be neutral concerning the future nomination for vice president.

In order to ensure continuity and harmony with JFK's party leadership, LBJ had retained Bailey but did not seem to trust Bailey on intraparty affairs regarding RFK. The president was even less reliant on Kenneth P. O'Donnell. O'Donnell and RFK had been close ever since they played on the Harvard football team together.[240] LBJ was aware that O'Donnell had opposed JFK's selection of LBJ as his running mate as vociferously as RFK.[241]

Among JFK's appointees at the DNC, Johnson seemed to be the most trusting of Richard Maguire, the DNC treasurer. LBJ apparently hoped that Maguire would communicate to other Kennedy Democrats how gracious and generous he was "to show my friendship for all of President Kennedy's hierarchy, the top men."[242] In his February 11, 1964, telephone call to Maguire, the president added that he had politely yet firmly told RFK that the attorney general could employ Corbin in the Department of Justice, but Corbin must leave the DNC staff. LBJ ominously told Maguire, "It's going to be a problem and it's going to be serious."[243]

Clifton Carter, a fellow Texan and longtime LBJ confidante, had already become the president's chief liaison with Bailey and DNC headquarters. LBJ had previously ordered Carter to conduct an audit of all of the DNC's "liabilities and assets" and submit it on March 1.[244] Publicly, LBJ wanted to promote the idea that he was emphasizing frugality and efficiency in government expenditures and at the debt-ridden DNC headquarters. Privately, Johnson entrusted Carter, not Bailey or Maguire, with the task of identifying and removing all the allegedly pro-RFK, anti-LBJ employees from the DNC's payroll.

On February 13, 1964, LBJ ordered John M. Bailey to fire Corbin. By early March, LBJ was furious to learn that Corbin continued to boost RFK's write-in candidacy in New Hampshire. Even worse, Corbin was reportedly being paid by the Joseph P. Kennedy, Jr. Foundation.[245] William Dunfey, the Democratic national committeeman from New Hampshire, had warned Clifton Carter that RFK might outpoll LBJ in New Hampshire, thereby embarrassing the president. This electoral result might generate a bandwagon effect that could spread the pro-RFK write-in effort to other primary states, namely Wisconsin and Massachusetts, and eventually threaten LBJ's nomination.[246] Peter Crotty, the Democratic county chairman in Buffalo, had announced that his party organization endorsed RFK for vice president.

On March 6, 1964, four days before the New Hampshire primary, the Gallup polling firm released a poll indicating that RFK was the top choice for vice president among Democratic voters. Thirty-seven percent favored RFK, 25 percent named Adlai Stevenson, and only 13 percent chose Hubert Humphrey, placing the Minnesota senator in a distant and embarrassing third place.[247] Humphrey suspected earlier that Paul Corbin was responsible for the dirtiest campaign tactics that the Kennedys had used against him in the 1960 Wisconsin primary. Humphrey wrote to Bailey in 1961 that Corbin "has no place at the DNC unless we are trying to make enemies and lose friends. . . . To say the least, I am shocked and to be frank about it, I am damned good and mad."[248]

On the following day, March 7, 1964, Newsweek editor Benjamin Bradlee called White House aide Jack Valenti. He informed Valenti of Newsweek's upcoming article on Corbin's write-in effort for RFK. Bradlee, a friend and confidante of JFK, told Valenti that Corbin was a "terrible little guy." But Bradlee assumed that RFK wanted to be vice president because RFK could have ended Corbin's effort by merely making a few phone calls to New Hampshire. Bradlee repeatedly stated his assumption that RFK would publicly deny the validity of the Newsweek article.[249]

LBJ's concerns about the New Hampshire primary and its impact on subsequent presidential primaries intensified after his phone conversation with Speaker of the House John W. McCormack later on March 7. McCormack, who chafed under the rise and dominance of the Kennedys in Massachusetts politics, warned LBJ that the pro-Kennedy Democratic state chairman was requiring voters to vote for delegates to the Democratic national convention individually rather than by slates. McCormack grumbled to LBJ that this would be done for the April 28 primary, "so that they would roll up a big vote in Massachusetts for the Kennedys"— EMK for senator and RFK for vice president as a write-in candidate.[250]

Five days before the New Hampshire primary, RFK belatedly announced through Edwin Guthman, his public relations officer, that LBJ "should be free to select his own running mate. The Attorney General, therefore, wishes to discourage any efforts on his behalf in New Hampshire or elsewhere."[251] Skeptics noted that RFK's statement did not actually reject any interest in being nominated for vice president. On March 10, 1964, voters in the New Hampshire

Democratic primary gave LBJ 29,317 write-in votes for president and RFK 25,094 votes for vice president.[252]

Publicly, LBJ remained calm. Johnson was still a write-in candidate for president and refused to formally announce his availability for the Democratic presidential nomination until the Democratic national convention was held in August. He stated on television that Democrats should not be competing for the 1964 Democratic vice-presidential nomination.[253] He later remarked at his March 15 press conference, "I would be less than frank if I said that I thought that it was wise at this stage of the game for either the President or the Vice President to be carrying on a campaign for office."[254]

Privately, though, LBJ was furious and embarrassed by the close vote in New Hampshire. Paul Corbin appeared in Wisconsin to organize a "Draft Robert F. Kennedy for Vice President of the United States Groundswell Committee" in preparation for that state's April 7 primary.[255] This committee soon dissolved, but RFK made officially nonpolitical yet popular speeches in the primary states of Pennsylvania, Wisconsin, and West Virginia. He appeared on the widely viewed television talk show hosted by Jack Paar and told the nation that he was uncertain about his future.[256]

A Gallup poll released on April 12, 1964, indicated that RFK's popularity as a possible vice-presidential candidate had surged since February. Of the Democrats polled, 47 percent chose RFK, 18 percent chose Adlai Stevenson, and only 10 percent selected Hubert H. Humphrey.[257] Despite his instinctive, personal preference for Humphrey, LBJ wanted to keep the media, public, and Democratic power brokers guessing about his future choice until he secured the Democratic presidential nomination in Atlantic City. Johnson told Humphrey a few days after the New Hampshire primary, "If I just had my choice, I'd like to have you as the vice president."[258]

Humphrey, of course, was familiar with how inscrutable, unreliable, and devious LBJ was in making statements like this. After all, LBJ had qualified this apparent offer with the insinuation that he was not currently in a position to choose anyone whom he wanted as his running mate. Besides Humphrey's abysmally low ratings in the Gallup polls, LBJ knew that the Minnesota senator was especially unpopular and controversial among business executives and southern Democrats. The former perceived him as anti-business, and the latter perceived him as a radical on civil rights.[259]

From the middle of March until the opening of the Democratic national convention in late August, LBJ quietly and gradually groomed Humphrey for the vice-presidential nomination by improving Humphrey's status with business executives and southern Democrats. He also tested Humphrey's political skills and value to the White House. The president evaluated how well Humphrey functioned as Senate majority whip, especially concerning the tax cut and civil rights bills. LBJ's final test for Humphrey was to give him the responsibility for resolving the race-related dispute over the credentials of Mississippi's delegates at the Democratic national convention in August.[260]

While LBJ simultaneously built up and tested Humphrey's political assets as his presumptive running mate, he also distracted the media and tried to diminish RFK's standing in the polls. He did this by floating trial balloons about possible choices for vice president. Johnson especially flabbergasted the pundits and Democratic county chairmen when he suggested that Secretary of Defense Robert S. McNamara, a Republican and an Episcopalian, would make a good vice president. Realizing that RFK was especially popular among Catholics, LBJ dispersed and reduced the previously monolithic Catholic support for RFK's undeclared yet viable vice presidential candidacy. The president promoted media speculation that the Texan would balance the ticket by choosing a Catholic running mate. At various times in the spring and summer of 1964, LBJ encouraged speculation that he was considering such Catholic Democrats as Kennedy brother-in-law R. Sargent Shriver, Mayor Robert Wagner of New York City, Governor Edmund "Pat" Brown of California, and Senators Eugene McCarthy, John Pastore, and Thomas J. Dodd.[261] Nevertheless, a May 31 Gallup poll revealed that the preferences of Democratic voters surveyed had barely changed since the April 12 poll. Forty-one percent favored RFK, 26 percent chose Stevenson, and only 11 percent chose Humphrey.[262]

In his May 14, 1964, oral history interview, RFK spoke as if he were willing to serve as vice president but understood that LBJ would not select him. "Because the one thing Lyndon Johnson doesn't want is me as Vice President, and he's concerned about whether he's going to be forced into that . . . I think he's hysterical about how he's going to try to avoid having me or having to ask me."[263] During that same month, Clifton Carter tried and failed to persuade several Democratic state chairmen to adopt resolutions for their delegates stating that LBJ "shall have the free choice of selecting his running mate as Vice-President."[264]

LBJ, Washington lawyers James H. Rowe, Jr. and Clark M. Clifford, Governor John Connally of Texas, and other Johnson allies were steadily and quietly solidifying support for Hubert H. Humphrey among Democratic state and county chairmen. RFK was still popular enough with the public in general and future Democratic delegates in particular by late July so that an enthusiastic demonstration for RFK at the convention could force LBJ to offer him the vice-presidential nomination. LBJ directed the convention's arrangements committee to schedule the film commemorating JFK to be shown at the convention after the delegates nominated the vice president. LBJ suspected that RFK might exploit his introduction of this film to stimulate a bandwagon momentum among the delegates to nominate him.[265]

After the Republican national convention was over, LBJ decided to definitely end the prospect of RFK becoming vice president. He wanted to exclude RFK without providing credibility to the media's impression of animosity between the two. Shortly after 6 P.M. on July 30, Johnson read a brief statement to the White House press corps. "In reference to the selection of a candidate for Vice President, I have reached the conclusion that it would be inadvisable for me to recommend to the convention any member of the Cabinet or any of those who meet regularly with the Cabinet."[266] LBJ specifically included R. Sargent Shriver and Adlai Stevenson in the latter group. Earlier that day, Kenneth P. O'Donnell informed LBJ, "Whatever you want to do is all right with him"—that is, RFK.[267]

As the final move in privately selecting Humphrey as his running mate before the Democratic national convention began, Johnson used James H. Rowe, Jr. as his liaison with Humphrey. The president wanted Rowe to elicit a promise from Humphrey that the Minnesota senator would be unequivocally loyal to LBJ and would not challenge him for the Democratic presidential nomination in 1968.[268] The president also expected Humphrey to prevent or mollify any liberal opposition to LBJ at the convention, especially from UAW president Walter Reuther and ADA leader Joseph L. Rauh, Jr. Johnson bluntly and ungrammatically told Rowe, "If he don't want to be my wife, he oughtn't marry me."[269]

Later on July 30, Humphrey called LBJ and stated that Rowe was visiting him. The senator solemnly told the president, "If your judgment leads you to select me, I can assure you—unqualifiedly, personally, and with all the sincerity in my heart—complete loyalty. . . . Right to the end of the line."[270] He proudly told LBJ that an Associated Press poll of Democratic delegates showed that they preferred Humphrey over RFK for vice president by a vote of 341 to 230.[271] In abruptly ending his conversation with Humphrey, LBJ did not commit himself to the Minnesota senator.

Johnson wanted to wait and see if Humphrey would succeed in resolving a potentially disruptive intraparty conflict that was simmering before the Democratic national convention opened on August 24. Although George Wallace had announced the end of his presidential campaign on July 19, LBJ feared the resumption of a white backlash that could disrupt the nationally televised convention in Atlantic City and plague him in the general election campaign.[272] On June 21, three civil rights workers, two of whom were white, were murdered in Mississippi, apparently by Ku Klux Klansmen collaborating with local police. Eleven days later, LBJ signed the Civil Rights Act of 1964. The three murdered civil rights workers had been promoting voter registration in Mississippi, and the 1964 law had increased federal intervention on voter registration.

With the media focusing on the murder investigations in Mississippi and regularly highlighting that state's explosive racial climate, a mostly black, pro-civil rights group of Mississippi Democrats planned to go to Atlantic City and ask to be seated as that state's delegates. They called themselves the Mississippi Freedom Democratic Party (MFDP).[273] In its brief to the DNC's credentials committee, the MFDP asserted that if the national Democratic Party seated the delegates of the "regular," all-white, racist Mississippi Democratic Party, then "the National Democratic Party . . . shall walk backward with the bigoted power structure of Mississippi."[274]

The MFDP leaders and their allies in other civil rights organizations obtained promises from several Democratic delegations, such as those of Massachusetts, Michigan, New York, and Minnesota, to vote to seat MFDP members as Mississippi's delegates in Atlantic City.[275] The MFDP also retained Joseph L. Rauh, Jr., an ADA leader and close associate of Hubert Humphrey, as its attorney at the Democratic national convention. LBJ became concerned about the possibility of most southern white delegates leaving the convention in protest if the MFDP delegates were seated instead of those from the regular Mississippi Democratic Party. In a July 23 phone conversation with John Connally, Johnson told the Texas governor that he suspected that, regarding the MFDP controversy, "It may very well be that Bobby has started it." The president assured Connally, "Humphrey is trying his best to put an end to it."[276]

LBJ had imposed a daunting task on Humphrey. Before the Democrats convened in Atlantic City, the Minnesota Democrat had only a few weeks to formulate and gain acceptance to a compromise that would accomplish the following, seemingly incompatible objectives. Humphrey needed a solution to the controversy that would at least prevent floor demonstrations and other embarrassing protests at the televised convention from the MFDP and its sympathizers from organized labor, the NAACP, the ADA, and white liberal politicians influenced by black voters as well as from the white regular Mississippi delegates and southern Democrats in general whom Humphrey had been courting for his vice-presidential candidacy. If he did not successfully complete this delicate balancing act, Humphrey could not become LBJ's running mate and eventually fulfill his own presidential ambition.[277]

With Joseph L. Rauh, Jr. representing the MFDP, Walter Mondale, Minnesota's attorney general, Walter Reuther, the UAW president, and David Lawrence, chairman of the convention's credentials committee, assisted Humphrey.[278] Since Rauh also worked as the UAW's general counsel, Johnson calculated that Reuther could pressure Rauh to soften the MFDP's demands.[279] Behind the scenes, though, LBJ, not Humphrey, was the driving force in seeking a compromise before the Democratic national convention began its proceedings. On August 12, he assured Governor Paul Johnson of Mississippi that his state's all-white delegation would be seated at the convention.[280] The president also suggested to Senator James Eastland of Mississippi on August 22 that if the regular Mississippi delegates simply pledged loyalty to the presidential nominee, then the credentials committee would seat them. According to LBJ, the Mississippi delegation could word its statement of loyalty to the presidential ticket vaguely enough so that it could disagree with the Democratic national platform and the convention's selection of a vice-presidential nominee. With Johnson's appeasement of Eastland's anti-civil rights, anti-RFK positions, the Mississippi senator replied, "Just fine."[281]

LBJ's original position was that if Mississippi and other southern states with all-white delegations had complied with the current party regulations for elect-ing delegates, then they should be seated. The entire convention's delegates in Atlantic City would then adopt new rules to prohibit racial discrimination in the selection of delegates that would take effect at the 1968 convention. He assumed that this position would satisfy most southern whites and most northern, urban delegations that included black party regulars like Representatives William Dawson from Chicago and Charles Diggs from Detroit. At LBJ's behest, Humphrey and Reuther asked Rauh to refrain from seeking a pro-MFDP minority report from the credentials committee or a roll-call vote on the convention floor.[282]

Rauh refused to yield, and the MFDP's position was further strengthened by the nationally televised testimony of MFDP activists before the credentials committee. In particular, Fannie Lou Hamer, a black Mississippian, graphically and emotionally described how she was physically attacked and jailed in Missis-sippi for trying to register to vote. Hamer tearfully concluded, "All of this on account we want to register, to become first-class citizens, and if the Freedom Democratic Party is not seated now, I question America."[283]

The White House and the nonsouthern delegations in Atlantic City were soon inundated with telegrams sympathetic to Hamer. On August 23, LBJ, through Humphrey as his liaison, offered the MFDP members passes as "hon-ored guests" of the Democratic national convention, but Rauh refused to con-cede. Rauh's allies on the credentials committee were becoming more numerous and intransigent, especially Representative Edith Green of Oregon. In an August 25 phone conversation with LBJ, John M. Bailey referred to Green as "a bitch." Bailey could not dissuade her from leading the drafting of a pro-MFDP minor-ity report and demanding a roll call on it. "I'm distressed that they would treat me that way," LBJ morosely replied.[284] Bailey gloomily admitted that even in his dual capacity as DNC chairman and Connecticut Democratic chairman he could not prevent most of the Connecticut delegates from supporting the pro-MFDP minority report in a roll-call vote.[285]

The MFDP controversy spun out of control and Humphrey and Bailey seemed powerless to resolve it before the convention opened in Atlantic City on August 24. LBJ remained in Washington, DC, but began to more directly micromanage the situation. Walter Jenkins, LBJ's most trusted, longest-serving assistant, and Thomas Finney, an attorney in Clark M. Clifford's law firm, implemented the president's decisions on the MFDP issue in Atlantic City. The president decided that he needed to abide by his original decision of not letting the credentials committee and then the majority of delegates in a roll-call vote to refuse to seat the all-white, regular Mississippi delegation.[286] Otherwise, there could be a massive southern walkout at the convention, a white backlash that would help Goldwater and conservative Republican congressional candidates in November, and a legal precedent for unseating duly elected state delegations at future Democratic national conventions.[287]

Thus, unlike the vaguely worded loyalty oath that LBJ had mentioned to Senator James Eastland of Mississippi, Johnson now had the credentials committee require the pledged loyalty of delegates to Democratic presidential and vice-presidential nominees as well as to the national platform, including its most liberal planks, adopted in Atlantic City. LBJ understood that such a strict loyalty oath would motivate most or all of the regular, white Mississippi delegates to voluntarily refuse to take their seats and to leave the convention. He hoped that their voluntary exit would at least partially satisfy the MFDP, black Democrats in general, and white liberals. In order to discourage a general, voluntary walkout by most delegates from the Deep South, especially Alabama and Georgia, LBJ called Senator John Sparkman of Alabama and Senator Richard Russell and Governor Carl Sanders of Georgia urging them to prevent their states' delegates from joining the Mississippi regulars.[288]

Besides motivating the regular Mississippi delegates to leave the convention on their own volition, LBJ realized that he could not seat the MFDP as voting delegates from their state without violating existing party rules for delegate selection. The MFDP slate of delegates and alternates consisted of sixty-four blacks and four whites. LBJ rejected Rauh's proposed compromise that both the entire delegation of the MFDP and the Mississippi party regulars be seated.[289] With the Mississippi regulars bound to leave the convention over the stricter loyalty pledge, LBJ knew that the convention had to grant the MFDP at least some voting power as legitimate delegates, but not as Mississippi delegates.

After consulting with his advisors both in Washington and Atlantic City, LBJ had Walter Reuther communicate the following concession to Rauh. Two of the MFDP members would be delegates at large, but not representing Mississippi, and the others would be honored guests of the convention.[290] The DNC would also create a special committee to enforce anti-discrimination rules for selecting delegates from the states that would take effect at the 1968 Democratic national convention. Reuther adamantly impressed on Rauh that these were all of the concessions that LBJ would ever make to MFDP.[291] After Rauh reluctantly conveyed the White House proposal to MFDP members, most of them angrily rejected it.[292]

Humphrey, Reuther, and other White House emissaries, however, had already gained the endorsement of the NAACP and CORE leaders and Martin Luther King, Jr., for this compromise. Robert Moses and other MFDP members, especially those who also belonged to the leftist Student Non-Violent Coordinating Committee (SNCC), were outraged. They felt betrayed by the mainstream black civil rights leaders and white liberals like Rauh, Reuther, and Humphrey.[293] They were especially bitter that the White House chose the two

MFDP delegates at large, Aaron Henry and Edwin King. They regarded Henry, a middle-class black pharmacist, and King, a white minister, to be unrepresentative of the mostly poor, disenfranchised blacks of Mississippi and the more militant, leftist leadership of the MFDP.[294]

Finally, LBJ and his operatives had Representative Carl Albert of Oklahoma, the convention chairman, take a voice vote, rather than a roll-call vote, of the delegates to adopt the MFDP compromise.[295] LBJ wanted to ensure that there was no numerical record of the delegates passing this compromise by an embarrassingly narrow majority. He suspected that RFK had engineered the MFDP controversy in order to embarrass him or belatedly pressure LBJ to choose RFK as his running mate.[296] The Texan briefly yet seriously considered telling the convention that he would not accept the presidential nomination and that the delegates were free to nominate whomever they wanted for president. After suggesting his withdrawal from the presidential campaign to press secretary George Reedy, on August 25, the stunned Reedy gloomily replied, "This will throw the nation into quite an uproar, sir."[297]

LBJ's paranoia about RFK's political intentions was abated by the news earlier that day. RFK had formally announced his candidacy for a Senate seat from New York. According to journalist William Shannon, LBJ facilitated RFK's receipt of the Democratic senatorial nomination by pressuring Mayor Robert Wagner of New York City not to run for the Senate and assuring Wagner that the White House and DNC chairman would still defer to the mayor's preferences on federal patronage.[298]

The potential dangers of the MFDP dispute and the "Bobby problem" were now minimized for the remainder of the Democratic national convention in Atlantic City. On January 11, 1964, the DNC adopted a new apportionment formula for delegates. It increased the number of convention votes from 1,521 in 1960 to 2,316 in 1964, an increase of 52 percent.[299] In addition to providing delegates and alternates to the District of Columbia, Guam, Puerto Rico, and the Virgin Islands, the new formula rewarded large states that had voted for the JFK-LBJ ticket in the Electoral College and by large margins in their popular votes. This formula had the effect of significantly increasing the voting power and representation of large, urban, industrial states of the Northeast and Midwest at the 1964 and subsequent Democratic national conventions. Conversely, it furthered diminished the mostly conservative influence of southern and border state delegates at Democratic national conventions.[300]

Despite this greatly enhanced liberal presence in Atlantic City, LBJ was determined to fulfill his original plan to make the 1964 Democratic national convention, in the words of journalists Rowland Evans and Robert Novak, "a Great Society convention, and, in the summer of 1964, that meant a consensus convention. Controversy, dispute, and rancor were forbidden."[301] Regardless of how stiff and awkward LBJ's formal, televised addresses often were, he shrewdly understood the emotive, visceral power of television. At the raucous, bitterly divided Republican national convention, Goldwaterites jeered and heckled Nelson Rockefeller and other liberal Republicans. Barry Goldwater's most memorable words from his acceptance speech seemed to advocate extremism and reject moderation. Meanwhile, during the spring and summer of 1964, television news broadcasts included coverage of race-related violence and disorder in Harlem, Rochester, New York, Philadelphia, and other northern cities, the murders of civil rights activists in the Deep South, and noisy left-wing student demonstrations.[302]

LBJ was determined to ensure that the televised average and media analysis of the Democratic national convention convey a contrasting visual and emotional impression of placid unity, moderation, and responsible leadership. Its proceedings would symbolically signify the last phase of a smooth, respectful transition in the presidency and party leadership from the legacy of JFK to LBJ. Unlike the Republican national convention, the Democratic national convention planned and orchestrated by LBJ was intentionally bland, tightly controlled, predictable, and carefully scripted.[303] In his memoirs, LBJ fondly recalled, "Atlantic City in August 1964 was a place of happy, surging crowds and thundering cheers. To a man as troubled as I was by party and national divisions, this display of unity was welcome indeed."[304]

Johnson did not arrive in Atlantic City until the evening of August 26, the night before his fifty-sixth birthday, to deliver his acceptance speech and announce his recommendation of Hubert H. Humphrey as his running mate. Earlier in the day, the president directed Humphrey and Senator Thomas J. Dodd of Connecticut to share a highly publicized flight and limousine ride from Atlantic City to the White House in order to further confuse the media.[305] Before Humphrey and Dodd left Atlantic City, White House aide Bill Moyers assured LBJ, "Tomorrow needs to be the mark. It needs to become Lyndon Johnson's convention and Lyndon Johnson's party. And I think it will." [306]

Although Senator John Pastore of Rhode Island delivered a fiery, combative keynote address to the convention on August 24, most of the major addresses, especially the acceptance speeches of LBJ and Humphrey, communicated a moderate, restrained, and, paradoxically for a party convention, almost suprapartisan tone.[307] In his long-winded, ponderous acceptance speech on the evening of August 27, LBJ proclaimed the Democratic Party to be "a party for all Americans, an all-American party for all Americans."[308] The remainder of LBJ's acceptance speech emphasized national unity, policy progress, compassion, and idealism, while avoiding references to ideological, coalitional, and programmatic differences between the two parties.[309] In his slightly more partisan speech to the DNC on the next day, LBJ stated that the Great Society "is going to be a program that is fashioned for all the people of all parties, but it is not going to be one that is built on the past."[310]

While LBJ's acceptance speech was calm, grandiose, and did not mention Goldwater, Humphrey's acceptance speech systematically vilified Barry Goldwater as a dangerous reactionary and extremist who had alienated most Republicans in Congress. Humphrey specified Senate votes on such major issues as the Limited Nuclear Test Ban Treaty of 1963, the tax cut of 1964, the Civil Right Act of 1964, and the creation of the U.S. Arms Control and Disarmament Agency that most Republican senators supported "but not Senator Goldwater, the temporary Republican spokesman." Unusual for an acceptance speech at a Democratic national convention, Humphrey's impassioned yet highly statistical, fact-filled address openly welcomed "responsible, forward-looking Republicans" to follow "the banner of Lyndon B. Johnson," while omitting any mention of the Democratic Party.[311] Humphrey even spoke sympathetically of the Republican Party for being captured by Goldwaterites who transformed the party of Lincoln into a party "of stridency, of unrestrained passion, of extreme and radical language."[312] Both LBJ and Humphrey were nominated by acclamation with no roll-call votes.

Regardless of how liberal the content of the 1964 Democratic national platform was, its tone and wording were moderate, restrained, and harmonious. The platform conveyed the suprapartisan, centrist policy consensus that LBJ promoted, despite the unprecedented degree and variety of greater federal intervention that the Great Society represented. The Democratic national platform of 1964 began and ended with suprapartisan references. Its preamble invited "all to join us who believe that narrow partisanship takes too small account of the size of our task," and its last section concluded that "the achievements of the nation over this period outreached the contribution of any party: they are the work of the American people."[313]

Since the Republicans had previously written and adopted their platform in July, the Democrats were able to insert planks that explicitly rejected "Goldwaterism." They also adopted positions that moderate and liberal Republicans in San Francisco had tried but failed to include in the GOP platform. For example, Nelson Rockefeller was booed and rebuffed by the pro-Goldwater majority at the Republican national convention when he proposed a plank denouncing and refuting extremism.[314] The Democratic national platform of 1964, by contrast, condemned "extremism, whether from the right or the left, including the extreme tactics of such organizations as the Communist party, the Ku Klux Klan and the John Birch Society."[315]

During the first six weeks after the Democratic national convention ended, LBJ campaigned little. He wanted to project the image of an experienced, responsible president who was busy in Washington conferring with White House task forces and congressional committees that were developing legislation. This was consistent with his consensual theme of being "president of all the people," regardless of partisan, interest group, or ideological differences among Americans. In one of LBJ's rare campaign addresses outside of Washington, DC, in September, the Democratic president addressed the Pennsylvania Democratic state committee in Harrisburg on September 10. Johnson warned his fellow

Democrats about "extreme factionalism" and asserted "that our Nation can only be served by parties which serve all of America, and which serve all Americans in all segments in all sections of the country."[316]

During this period, though, LBJ assumed that his presidential decisions and policy statements from the White House on Cold War foreign policy would contrast his responsible, experienced, moderate leadership with Goldwater's reckless, controversial statements on foreign and defense policy issues, especially the use of nuclear weapons and Vietnam. In his memoirs, LBJ wrote, "I decided that the best answer to Goldwater's repeated suggestions that we consider using 'tactical' nuclear weapons on the battlefield was my relentless search for a détente with the Soviet Union and my insistence on restraint in Vietnam."[317]

Hubert H. Humphrey campaigned ubiquitously and garrulously after he left Atlantic City. The content and tone of Humphrey's speeches reflected the two purposes of his vice presidential campaign. First, the Minnesota senator continued to graphically portray Barry Goldwater as a dangerous, irresponsible extremist unfit for the presidency whose controversial policy positions and statements threatened the peace and prosperity of the nation.[318] Second, Humphrey wanted to assure certain voting blocs and interest groups, namely, southern whites, business leaders, and more conservative, affluent midwestern farmers, that he shared LBJ's suprapartisan, centrist policy consensus and was not a liberal extremist on racial and economic issues.[319] In an October 21 speech in Carbondale, Illinois, Humphrey stated that Goldwater "has made millions of Americans uneasy and apprehensive about placing his nervous finger on the nuclear trigger."[320] The Minnesota liberal also presented himself as an economic pragmatist who was helping LBJ protect agricultural subsidies, public power projects like the TVA and REA, and other New Deal–based programs from the threat of a Goldwater presidency. In a September 29 speech in Atlanta, Humphrey warned that a Goldwater administration would shut off electricity in rural areas and force impoverished farmers to move to the cities and "root, hog, or die."[321]

The most dramatic, controversial Democratic effort to frighten voters about the prospect of a Goldwater presidency was the infamous "Daisy Girl" television commercial that was broadcast only once because of the public outcry that it generated. The Johnson-Humphrey campaign retained the services of the advertising firm of Doyle, Dane, and Bernbach (DDB). The DDB firm hired Tony Schwartz to produce a commercial depicting Goldwater as reckless on the use of nuclear weapons and the health dangers of radiation in the atmosphere because of his vote against the Limited Nuclear Test Ban Treaty and his most controversial statements on nuclear arms. The "Daisy Girl"commercial did not mention Goldwater's name or use any quotes from him. Instead, it attracted and shocked a viewer's senses of sight and sound by pairing a little girl's plucking and counting of the petals of a daisy with the sound of a male voice finishing the count followed by a loud, visually expansive nuclear explosion. The commercial ended with LBJ's soothing, reassuring voice solemnly stating, "These are the stakes. To make a world in which all of God's children can live, or go into the dark. We must either love each other or we must die."[322]

The "Daisy Girl" ad aired once on the evening of September 7. The Johnson-Humphrey campaign withdrew it after the White House was inundated with phone calls and telegrams criticizing the alarmist, fear-mongering nature of the ad. The controversy over the "Daisy Girl" and the similar "Ice Cream Cone" ads soured the official beginning of LBJ's presidential campaign after he addressed an enthusiastic, UAW-organized crowd in Cadillac Square in Detroit earlier that day. Unlike the unsettling, divisive impact of the "Daisy Girl" ad, LBJ's speech in Detroit concluded with his benevolent reaffirmation of the suprapartisan, centrist policy consensus. "So today I say to these thousands assembled here, whose only concern is what is best for their country, let us bring the capitalist, the manager, the worker, and the Government to one table to share in the fruits of all of our dreams and all of our work."[323]

LBJ was careful not to let his name or voice be identified with any more negative, controversial television advertising like the "Daisy Girl" commercial. According to journalist Theodore H. White, the Johnson-Humphrey campaign was organized into five "teams": Team A, Team B, Team C, Team D, and Team E.[324] Team D, nicknamed the "Five O'Clock Club" or "Anti-Campaign" consisted of young White House aides and Washington attorneys active in Democratic politics. Led by former JFK aide Myer Feldman, Team D conducted a clandestine operation of negative research and publicity against the Goldwater campaign. Team D's activities were often not communicated and coordinated with the other teams so that its most scurrilous decisions and tactics could not be publicly identified with the other teams, especially Team A. Managed by future press secretary Bill Moyers, Team A included speechwriters Richard Goodwin, Horace Busby, and Douglass Cater, communicated with the DDB advertising firm, and received information on federal agencies and policies from Secretary of Labor Willard Wirtz.[325]

Since Team A was the closest team to LBJ organizationally and physically after he began his active, frequent traveling campaign in late September, Team D had much independence, discretion, and financing to smear Goldwater's policy positions, public statements, and personal character and alienate him from mainstream Republican politicians. According to conservative freelance writer Victor Lasky, Bill Moyers asked the FBI to find out if there were homosexuals on Goldwater's campaign and Senate staffs. Lee Edwards, the RNC's deputy director of publicity, found evidence of the FBI's illegal wiretapping of the phone calls of Goldwater's campaign officials and supporters in order to provide advance notice of Goldwater's campaign schedule, speeches, and tactical decisions to LBJ's campaign and any damaging information on Goldwater or his inner circle. White House use of the surveillance and investigative services of the

FBI and CIA disrupted Goldwater's campaign appearances and intimidated Goldwater supporters.[326]

Besides the efforts of Team D, the other teams and members of the Democratic presidential campaign sent anti-Goldwater information and rumors to friendly, receptive journalists, columnists, and editors. Group Research, Inc. and the National Council for Civic Responsibility, both subsidized by Democratic campaign funds, served a similar research and publicity function in the campaign against Goldwater.[327] Vic Gold, Goldwater's assistant press secretary, found Moira O'Connor, who claimed to be a freelance writer, surreptitiously distributing copies of an anti-Goldwater flier to reporters on Goldwater's campaign train. She admitted to Gold that she worked as a researcher for the DNC.[328]

Why did the Democratic presidential campaign and its various appendages and allies engage in duplicitous dirty tricks? After all, even before the divisive, contentious Republican convention was held, a Gallup poll released on July 22 showed that 62 percent of the voters surveyed preferred LBJ. Gallup polls released on August 9, August 23, September 16, October 18, and November 2 revealed that anywhere from 59 to 65 percent of the voters surveyed chose LBJ.[329] The alarmist warning of the Goldwaterites that LBJ's Great Society represented the further advancement of socialism and the greatest threat in American history to economic freedom and personal virtue was received apathetically or dismissively by most Americans. With *The Wall Street Journal*, automotive magnate Henry Ford II, and Robert Anderson, former Secretary of the Treasury under Eisenhower, endorsing LBJ, it was difficult for the Goldwater campaign to convince many voters that LBJ was an enemy of capitalism. Of the forty-five business executives who belonged to the National Independent Committee for President Johnson and Senator Humphrey, approximately 75 percent were Republicans.[330]

Although Barry Goldwater was an underdog and a challenger zealously supported by a small yet intense political base, he was often on the defensive. The efforts of the Democrats, media, and moderate and liberal Republicans to saturate the public with Goldwater's most controversial comments and policy positions forced the Arizona Republican to frequently qualify and rephrase his statements in order to defend himself and accuse his critics and opponents of distorting, exaggerating, or blatantly lying about his rhetoric, record, and platform.[331] He and his campaign spokesmen also had to publicly disavow and denounce campaign advertising and activities from the most extreme right-wing groups that were not formally affiliated with Goldwater's campaign organization.[332] F. Clifton White, the director of Citizens for Goldwater-Miller, later admitted, "The slogan dreamed up by an advertising agency and approved by his managers—'In your heart, you know he's right'—was transparently defensive. And so were his speeches."[333]

Since Goldwater's policy positions and statements on social welfare, economic, and civil rights issues were unpopular with most voters, the only two issues remaining for Goldwater to use offensively against LBJ were foreign policy and morality in government. In his acceptance speech at the Republican national convention, the Arizona senator castigated Democratic foreign and defense policies for failing to stop Communist aggression and expansion. "Failures proclaim lost leadership, obscure purpose, weakening wills and the risk of inciting our sworn enemies to new aggressions and to new excesses," Goldwater announced.[334]

But the public seemed to prefer LBJ's foreign policy experience and continuity with JFK's legacy of encouraging détente with the Soviet Union since the Cuban missile crisis and apparent restraint in Vietnam over Goldwater's dire predictions of more Communist aggression, wasted foreign aid, a debacle in Vietnam, and UN domination of American foreign policy if LBJ continued as president.[335] Congressman William E. Miller of New York, Goldwater's running mate, told a Republican audience in Austin, Texas, "This war in South Vietnam is never going to be concluded and it is never going to be won until Barry Goldwater is in the White House of this country."[336] Despite such grim statements from Goldwater and Miller, an August 26 Gallup poll revealed that 71 percent of the Americans interviewed stated that American foreign policy in Vietnam was "as well as could be expected" and 16 percent criticized it.[337] A Gallup poll taken shortly after the November election and released on December 4, 1964, showed that 58 percent agreed that "a peaceful settlement of our difficulties with Russia" was possible and only 24 percent disagreed.[338]

Since the beginning of LBJ's presidency, the incumbent was plagued by the public perception of him as ethically questionable or even corrupt. Prolonged congressional investigations of corruption allegations against two prominent, former associates of LBJ, Bobby Baker and Billy Sol Estes, fueled this public uneasiness about the president's moral character. An April 10, 1964, Gallup poll showed that Republican county chairmen cited the "Bobby Baker scandal and corruption in government" as one of the top three issues that they wanted to use in the upcoming presidential campaign.[339] As the campaign progressed and it appeared Johnson would win the election by a landslide, political analyst Samuel Lubell interviewed a lifelong Republican who stated, "I don't trust Lyndon Johnson at all, but I'm troubled by Senator Goldwater."[340] Some voters who decided to cast their ballots for LBJ used words like "corrupt" and "wheeler dealer" to describe the president. An informal, person-to-person survey conducted by a presidential aide in the Midwest concluded that most voters questioned who planned to vote for LBJ believed, "It's a choice between a crook and a kook."[341]

The Goldwater campaign decided to solidify and exploit these apparently widespread concerns about LBJ's ethics.[342] Its publicity increasingly communicated the message that LBJ personified and somehow accelerated the moral decline of American society evidenced by race riots, juvenile delinquency, sleazy entertainment, corruption in government, and less piety.[343]

F. Clifton White, director of Goldwater's major campaign committee, obtained Goldwater's permission to produce a campaign film connecting this moral decline with LBJ. White hired Rus Walton, a former publicist for the National Association of Manufacturers (NAM), to produce a 30-minute campaign film on this theme that he intended to broadcast entitled *Choice*. It was sponsored by Mothers for a Moral America (MOMA), an affiliate of the Citizens for Goldwater-Miller. This film's images included black rioters in Harlem, a buxom woman in a scanty bathing suit, strippers, and books entitled *Call Me Nympho, Men for Sale*, and *Sex and Hypnosis*.

These images of the "New America" under LBJ were symbolically linked to the image of a speeding Lincoln sedan. The driver of the Lincoln tossed out an empty can of Pearl beer. This was the brand of beer that LBJ drank at his ranch and the subject of a well-known news story about his drinking and driving with reporters in Texas.[344] With these garish images and sounds, the film's narrator grimly and ominously warned, "Demoralization, chaos, this is the changed other America that the people slowly wake up to."[345] The film contrasted the immorality and danger of LBJ's "New America" with Goldwater's America that was represented by clean-cut, wholesome youths, patriotism, piety, the Bible, and John Wayne.[346]

White and Walton let a cross section of RNC members preview the film. A former Eisenhower aide told White, "It has got to be shown."[347] Because of this enthusiastic, initial reception of the film, White and Walton made hundreds of prints and distributed them to local Goldwater and Republican campaign organizations and several reporters. Well-known, influential columnist Drew Pearson, who had previously written about the Goldwaterites as "fascists," obtained a print of the film and so did the DNC.[348]

White had planned to have *Choice* nationally broadcast, but Goldwater rejected that idea. Goldwater was concerned that the images of black rioters would motivate the media and the Democrats to accuse him of racism.[349] The news media quickly and broadly disseminated the story that the Goldwater campaign had produced, distributed, locally shown, and almost nationally broadcast a vulgar and possibly obscene campaign film.[350] This story's credibility with the public was solidified by NBC's announcement that it would not broadcast scenes from *Choice* that were "unduly suggestive" and a formal dissociation from *Choice* by the RNC's advertising firm. In his account of Goldwater's campaign, Stephen Shadegg, Goldwater's regional director of western states, ruefully concluded, "If *Choice* had been shown as scheduled, it would not have won the election for Goldwater, but the announcement of cancellation was accepted as a confession by the candidate that Rus Walton and his helpers had produced a vile, offensive, immoral, racist movie."[351]

The only remote possibility that the Goldwater campaign could effectively use the morality issue against LBJ appeared from an unexpected source—the

White House, namely, LBJ's closest, long-serving aide, Walter Jenkins. Jenkins had been LBJ's closest confidante and assistant since 1939 when he joined LBJ's congressional staff. Jenkins knew about LBJ's most confidential political and business affairs. He attended all cabinet meetings and was authorized to sign LBJ's name to letters. Republicans had wanted Jenkins to testify before the Senate Rules and Administration Committee about the Bobby Baker investigation, but the Democratic-controlled committee voted to end this investigation on May 25, 1964.[352]

On the evening of October 14, 1964, RNC chairman Dean Burch issued a press release stating that the White House was "desperately trying to suppress a major news story affecting the national security."[353] Earlier on that day, Abe Fortas, a member of Team B with Clark M. Clifford and James H. Rowe, Jr. called LBJ and informed the president that Walter Jenkins had been arrested on a morals charge on October 7 in the men's room of a YMCA in Washington, DC. Jenkins was actually arrested for homosexual behavior and was previously arrested for this in 1959. Because someone in the FBI had apparently leaked the fact of Jenkins's arrest to the RNC staff, Goldwater learned about this before LBJ. But the Arizona senator chose not to specifically exploit the Jenkins's scandal in his speeches on moral decline.[354]

Burch, however, believed that it was legitimate for him to publicly criticize the White House for trying to prevent newspapers from publishing news about Jenkins's arrest because Jenkins had access to highly classified national security intelligence. It was widely assumed that homosexuals should not hold any government positions with access to such information because they could be blackmailed and forced to compromise national security. The hoarse, exhausted president conducted a flurry of phone conversations for several days with Fortas, Clifford, acting Attorney General Nicholas Katzenbach, FBI director J. Edgar Hoover, and evangelist Billy Graham. LBJ initially suspected that the Republicans had framed Jenkins. He then wanted to ensure that he had the facts to prove, if necessary, that Jenkins had never compromised national security because of his homosexuality or the possible psychological reasons for his current hospitalization.[355]

Ironically, two unexpected news stories provided LBJ with the most effective damage control of the Jenkins scandal. On October 15, Soviet premier Nikita Khruschev was removed from power, and on October 16, Communist China exploded its first nuclear bomb. Front-page headlines, television broadcasts, articles, and commentaries explained and speculated on the impact of these events, and, to a lesser extent, the election of a Labour government in Great Britain on the future of American foreign policy.[356] The major daily newspapers and television networks were squeamishly reluctant to cover and further explore a homosexual scandal. They immediately marginalized or ignored the Jenkins incident in favor of these international events.

On Sunday, October 18, the three major networks gave LBJ free air time to inform the nation about the significance of the events in the Soviet Union, China, and Great Britain to American foreign policy. The Goldwater campaign spokesman demanded equal time for Goldwater to reply to LBJ's address. The networks refused, and the FCC and a federal court of appeals upheld their denial of equal time.[357] In his October 18 address, LBJ referred to himself in the third person as "your President" and calmly assured his fellow Americans that "the key to peace is to be found in the strength and the good sense of the United States of America. Tonight we are the strongest nation in all the world, and the world knows it."[358]

This televised address was a prominent and politically beneficial example of LBJ's ability to skillfully use his incumbency to dominate the news. This presidential advantage enabled Johnson to minimize any damage to his candidacy from unexpected incidents like the Jenkins scandal and lingering questions about his personal ethics, and to reduce and subordinate news coverage of Goldwater's campaign.[359] Using free media coverage and air time in this way combined LBJ's initial desire to conduct a dignified "front porch" campaign from the White House similar to that of William McKinley in the 1896 presidential election with Bill Moyers's strategy of steadily increasing the projection of LBJ's personal image to the public as both a reassuring, experienced statesman and a folksy, compassionate, amiable candidate.[360]

The smooth combination of these two publicity goals in Moyers's campaign strategy was evident in LBJ's press release of September 26 followed by his campaign tour of New England that began on September 28. On September 26, LBJ announced his decision to improve public safety after reviewing the FBI report of the race-related summer riots in several cities. The president prudently concluded that all Americans, regardless of race, were "entitled" to both "equal justice" and "security . . . in his person on our city streets or in the country-side."[361] During that weekend, public awareness of the need for its faith in the ability of political institutions to investigate, explain, and protect the nation from violence was heightened by widespread newspaper and television coverage and analysis of the Warren Commission's final report to LBJ.[362] Signed and sent to LBJ on September 24, 1964, the Warren Commission's extensive investigation, explanation, and analysis of JFK's assassination stated in its introduction, "This report endeavors to fulfill that right and to appraise this tragedy by the light of reason and the standard of fairness. It has been prepared with a deep awareness of the Commission's responsibility to present to the American people an objective report of the facts relating to the assassination."[363]

JFK had been especially popular among and was still deeply mourned by his fellow Catholic Democrats in New England. On September 25, 1964, the day after the Warren Commission sent its final report to the president, LBJ traveled to Texarkana to dedicate John F. Kennedy Square. Johnson praised Kennedy and recalled their joint appearance in Texarkana during the 1960 campaign. Adding JFK to a pantheon of great former presidents, LBJ concluded, "I also remember that the men who lived in this house before me kept one cause and one aim in their hearts. What is right and what is best for the American people."[364]

On September 28, LBJ arrived in Providence, Rhode Island, for the officially nonpolitical purpose of addressing Brown University in its commemoration of its 200th anniversary. Before this ceremony, LBJ's motorcade was tumultuously engulfed by the most enthusiastic crowd of spectators that greeted him during the fall campaign. Delighted and exhilarated by this reception in the heart of Kennedy country, LBJ stood from the rear seat of a convertible with diminutive Senator John Pastore of Rhode Island occasionally holding the president's legs to steady the tall Texan. Speaking to cheering crowds in Providence and then Hartford, Connecticut, through a bullhorn or microphone, LBJ simply greeted them and welcomed them to his inauguration in January. The virtually issueless theme that LBJ built on this extemporaneously budding cult of personality in southern New England was encapsulated by journalist Theodore H. White. "We're in favor of a lot of things, and we're against mighty few," LBJ frequently proclaimed.[365]

Later in the campaign, *Washington Star* correspondent David S. Broder wrote, "Some Democrats fretted before the campaign began that Johnson was so eager to woo Republicans and independents for himself that he would not plug hard for other Democratic candidates. Those fears were needless. In Johnson's world, one can be nonpartisan, bipartisan and super-partisan all in the same speech."[366]

For LBJ, it was certainly not paradoxical for his campaign to further nurture and broaden a suprapartisan, centrist policy consensus whose purposes included providing coattail effects for Democratic candidates running in traditionally Republican states and congressional districts. This purpose was especially evident in LBJ's campaign swing through the mostly Republican, Protestant, rural states of northern New England. Since the late 1950s, these three states were showing signs of greater Democratic electoral strength. This was especially evident when the Democrats nominated candidates with a suprapartisan appeal and the Republicans were internally divided.[367] Under these circumstances, Edmund S. Muskie became the first Democrat to be elected from Maine to the U.S. Senate in 1958. In 1962, New Hampshire elected Democrats as governor and senator for the first time, respectively, since 1922 and 1932, and Vermont elected its first Democratic governor since the Civil War.

Public opinion polls and more private, limited political surveys indicated that New England Republicans were particularly alienated from Goldwater's campaign.[368] Shortly after the Republican national convention ended in San Francisco, a Maine Republican asked Muskie for "some anti-Goldwater, pro-President Johnson literature." He then added, "As I said, I'm not whole-heartedly in accord with the Democratic Party philosophy, but if the choice is between it and Goldwater-ism, why I don't see how there can be any choice at all for any thinking American."[369]

LBJ certainly wanted to make it easier for disaffected Republicans like Muskie's constituents to not only vote for the president but also for Muskie and other Democratic candidates for major offices. In his memoirs, the president made it clear that he did not want to win the election with the votes of Republicans, independents, and even some Democrats merely on the basis of anti-Goldwater sentiment. He wanted most Americans, regardless of their partisan, ideological, regional, racial, and socioeconomic differences, to vote for him as the symbol and spokesman for shared national values like racial and economic justice, enlightened progress, peace, and the compassion of the Social Gospel. LBJ later wrote that his "frontlash" strategy was "an attempt to practice a politics of consensus that would make it as easy as possible for lifelong Republicans to switch their votes in November to the Democratic column."[370] The president assumed that if this frontlash, unifying, suprapartisan dimension of his campaign resulted in a landslide victory, then he would have "a rare opportunity to further the cause of social reform. Having inherited the entire political center, if only for the time being, I decided to seek a new mandate from the people."[371]

LBJ was confident that his frontlash strategy was developing a policy mandate as he spoke before historically Republican audiences. In Burlington, Vermont, LBJ effusively praised Democratic Governor Philip Hoff and Republican Senator George Aiken, and added, "No party has a monopoly on good judgment or good service, or on patriotism."[372] On that same day, September 28, the Democratic president praised the public service and virtues of Democratic Senator Edmund S. Muskie and Republican Senator Margaret Chase Smith. LBJ promised Mainers that he, Muskie, Smith, and Republican Governor John H. Reed "are going to unite and try to get this job done for all you people, whether you are Democrats or Republicans."[373]

Johnson continued this suprapartisan theme during his October campaign appearances in the Midwest. In a speech in Indiana, a state that had not voted Democratic for president since 1936, LBJ told a crowd in Indianapolis, "Let all the good people of Indiana, of all religions, of all colors, of all parties—let us all as good Americans do not what is good for the Democratic Party or what is good for ourselves, or what is good for the Republican party. Let us, on November 3rd, go and do what is best for our country."[374] On November 3, 1964, Indiana voted mostly Democratic for president, U.S. senator, and governor.[375]

In mostly Republican Iowa, LBJ was greeted by Democratic Governor Harold Hughes for a campaign speech in Des Moines. Hughes was narrowly elected governor in an upset victory in 1962.[376] LBJ emphasized the importance of a restrained, responsible bipartisan foreign policy, especially in Vietnam. He reminded his Iowa audience that as Democratic floor leader in the Senate he helped Dwight Eisenhower conduct a bipartisan foreign policy. LBJ then complimented Republican Senator Bourke Hickenlooper of Iowa "who sits on the Foreign Relations Committee and comes in and advises with us. In matters of foreign policy, it is not Democratic, it is not Republican. It is what is best for your country."[377]

Ironically, Hickenlooper was almost as conservative as Goldwater on domestic policy issues and received single digit or zero ratings from the ADA when it measured the liberalism of members of Congress.[378] The results of the 1964 elections, however, gave Iowa the most dramatic partisan change of any state in its congressional delegation. Iowans voted 62 percent for LBJ and 68 percent for Hughes as they changed the party affiliation of Iowa's congressional delegation from six Republicans and one Democrat to six Democrats and one Republican. The lone Iowa Republican to win a House seat in 1964 was incumbent H. R. Gross. He was barely reelected by a disputed margin of 419 votes.[379] The Democrats also won control of the lower house of the Iowa state legislature for the first time in thirty years as well as the state senate.[380]

In his November 4 phone conversation with Harold Hughes, LBJ awoke the exhausted Iowa governor at 3:15 in the morning Eastern Standard Time.[381] The president first asked, "Did you clean out that damn Republican, mean delegation that up there . . . is harassing me all the time?" "I think we got all seven seats, Mr. President," Hughes replied. "What happened to me in Iowa?" LBJ asked. "I think around 63 percent," the governor answered. "It's just tremendous, sir."[382]

In concluding his phone call, LBJ implied that he would not be satisfied unless Republican congressman H. R. Gross of Iowa was definitely defeated.[383] Although LBJ frequently stated that Hughes and John Connally were his two favorite governors, both eventually distanced themselves from him. Connally became more conservative and increasingly opposed LBJ's Great Society programs.[384] Before his election to the Senate in 1968, Harold Hughes was one of the earliest, most outspoken doves criticizing LBJ's policies in Vietnam. In his autobiography, Hughes claimed that by the beginning of 1966 LBJ became aloof toward him. "For I knew that in his eyes I had become an enemy," Hughes observed.[385]

LBJ had very high, unrealistic expectations of the results of the 1964 presidential and congressional elections. The president was not satisfied to merely defeat Barry Goldwater in a landslide and increase the number of liberal, nonsouthern Democrats in Congress. He also wanted to permanently destroy right-wing extremism within and outside the GOP. If the 1964 elections did not accomplish this, he feared the emergence of another wave of McCarthyism. McCarthyism during the remainder of the 1960s could destroy the centrist, suprapartisan consensus within Congress and public opinion for responsible, restrained American foreign and defense policies, especially in Vietnam. He also wanted to eradicate the remnants of the bipartisan conservative coalition of southern Democrats and conservative Republicans in Congress, especially in the

House, that had weakened or killed liberal domestic legislation since the 1938 congressional elections.[386]

LBJ had hoped that Congress would have passed and he could have signed the Medicare bill before the election. Johnson was angry with and felt betrayed by House Ways and Means Committee chairman Wilbur Mills for not reporting out the Medicare bill earlier.[387] The president understood the necessity of increasing the number of liberal Democrats in Congress to facilitate the passage of pending legislation on Medicare, education, and anti-poverty programs, especially those focusing on the needs of poor, urban blacks. Moreover, a substantial number of pro-LBJ, liberal Democrats in Congress were crucial for the passage of additional, more controversial civil rights and voting rights legislation.

LBJ wanted to not only defeat Goldwater by a wide margin. He also wanted Democratic and anti-Goldwater Republican surrogates and appendages of his campaign to thoroughly discredit the Arizona Republican and end Goldwater's political career. Goldwater, unlike Richard M. Nixon, would then become a pariah in the GOP. The moderate to liberal wing of the GOP could resume its dominance of its party in presidential elections and in Congress. With Goldwater defeated and delegitimized within the GOP, Johnson expected moderate leaders of the GOP in Congress, namely, Everett M. Dirksen in the Senate and Gerald R. Ford in the House, to be more likely to cooperate with the White House on major domestic legislation and in foreign policy.[388] Journalist David S. Broder concluded that LBJ perceived both political parties "as unwanted intruders on the process of consensus government."[389]

In addition to Arthur Larson, Republicans who held high positions in the Eisenhower administration led the National Citizens for Johnson and Humphrey organization. Oveta Culp Hobby and Maxwell Rabb, who respectively served as secretary of HEW and secretary of the cabinet under Eisenhower, co-chaired it.[390] A few weeks after the 1964 elections, LBJ told the press, "I want a stronger Republican party so that it can do more to help me and the country."[391] This statement was merely a broader, more public repetition of LBJ's private phone conversation with Senate Majority Leader Everett M. Dirksen on the morning after the 1964 election. With Dirksen hospitalized for back problems, the Democratic president courteously and generously stated to the Illinois Republican, "I want to work awfully close with you and I think that you got a wonderful chance now to make a great contribution to your party and the country, and I hope that you take the leadership on it." The president added, "We got to keep our underlings from going hog wild. . . . We got to unite the country and do like we did under Eisenhower."[392] Again, LBJ wanted to flatter and co-opt Dirksen by comparing their legislative relationship to that of LBJ as Senate Democratic floor leader during Eisenhower's presidency, especially concerning American foreign policy in Vietnam.[393]

In the immediate aftermath of the 1964 elections, the various electoral statistics indicated an impressive victory for LBJ's suprapartisan, centrist policy consensus in domestic and foreign affairs and for the Democratic Party outside the Deep South. Receiving 61.4 percent of the two-party popular vote, LBJ was disappointed that he did not exceed FDR's 1936 record of 62.45 percent of the two-party vote.[394] Nearly two million more Americans voted in 1964 compared to 1960, and the voter turnout of 61.9 percent in 1964 was only 1 percent lower than the 62.8 percent turnout of 1960.[395] Although the results of the presidential election had seemed dull and predictable since July, the DNC's voter registration and mobilization project significantly contributed to this unusually high voter turnout and to LBJ's plurality of more than fifteen million votes. In particular, the DNC's Voter Education Project concentrated on the registration and mobilization of black voters in the peripheral South and in major nonsouthern cities.[396] Blacks were more likely to vote for LBJ than for JFK in 1960 with 94 percent of them voting for LBJ in 1964. They also engaged in more straight-ticket Democratic voting in 1964 than in 1960.[397]

The Vote Profile Analysis of CBS found that the number of blacks voting in general and those voting a straight Democratic ticket increased substantially in Illinois and New York. LBJ easily carried these states while his coattails among blacks narrowly reelected Democratic Governor Otto Kerner of Illinois and helped RFK to narrowly defeat liberal, pro-civil rights Republican Senator Kenneth Keating of New York. In Tennessee and Florida, nearly twice as many blacks voted in 1964 compared to 1960. In Tennessee, 60 percent of the black voters cast ballots for JFK in 1960 compared to 99.5 percent for LBJ in 1964.[398] The more widespread straight-ticket voting among blacks in Tennessee especially helped the reelection of Democratic Senator Al Gore, Sr., who had voted against the Civil Rights Act of 1964, as LBJ carried Tennessee by a wider margin than Gore.[399]

The Democrats gained two Senate seats and reelected all of the liberal, nonsouthern Democratic senators from the "Class of 1958," such as R. Vance Hartke of Indiana and Edmund S. Muskie of Maine. But the Democrats made much more impressive gains in the U.S. House of Representatives and in state legislatures. The Democrats gained thirty-eight House seats so that they now held 295 House seats to the Republicans' 140 seats during the 1965–1966 sessions of Congress.[400] In particular, the most conservative nonsouthern House Republicans, namely those who opposed the Civil Rights Act of 1964, were the most likely to lose seats. By contrast, Representative John Lindsay of New York, the most liberal, maverick Republican in the House who publicly repudiated Goldwater, was reelected with nearly 72 percent of the votes while his district's voters backed LBJ by almost the same percentage.[401] In three states of the Deep South that Goldwater carried, Alabama, Mississippi, and Georgia, five conservative, anti-civil rights Republicans were elected to the U.S. House.

But even this pyrrhic victory for the GOP embarrassed and burdened the House GOP leadership while helping liberal Democrats to further weaken the obstructionistic power of southern conservatives within the House Democratic majority.[402] In state legislatures, Republicans lost more than five hundred seats, approximately one hundred in state senates and more than four hundred in the lower houses in the 1964 elections.[403] In a series of decisions from 1962 to 1964, the Supreme Court ruled that states must reapportion their state legislative and congressional districts. With Democratic control of nearly two-thirds of the nation's state legislatures and governorships, redistricting was most likely to benefit Democrats outside the South and the more racially moderate, economically liberal white Democratic candidates in major southern cities.[404]

The New Republic and the ADA were established after World War II to articulate and promote an anti-Communist liberal consensus in American politics, or what historian Arthur M. Schlesinger, Jr., termed "the vital center."[405] Like the ADA's public statements and other political activities, *The New Republic's* articles, editorials, and columns combined grudging, ambivalent admiration for LBJ's legislative and leadership skills with frequent criticism of his moral compromises and personal character. In a November 14, 1964, commentary, *The New Republic* observed, "Mr. Johnson is also, we think, one of the supreme masters of the terribly difficult art of parliamentary control and consensus achievement. And what is an American political party anyway, but a collection of coalition minorities hunting for a consensus? The president has a capacity for finding common ground that is almost hypnotic . . . Mr. Johnson, in short, seems to us after long and patient observation to have many qualities of greatness, and now it remains to be seen whether he has greatness itself."[406]

In the immediate aftermath of this great personal and party victory in the elections of 1964, LBJ understood its potential for presidential greatness, especially in legislative productivity. He also recognized the equal and perhaps greater potential for errors of judgment in exceeding the limits of what this suprapartisan, centrist policy consensus allowed him to do. Now that he was elected president in his own right, LBJ's reference point for his presidential performance was no longer JFK. It was FDR.

Johnson was disappointed to learn that he received a smaller percentage of the two-party proportion of the popular votes and fewer Electoral College votes than FDR in the 1936 election. He was elated when Eric Goldman, a Princeton University historian and special consultant in the White House, informed him that his percentage of all of the popular votes exceeded FDR's 1936 percentage, although by a margin of less than 0.3 percent.[407] LBJ was determined to avoid Harry Truman's mistakes in the Korean War in his conduct of the Vietnam War. LBJ also resolved not to waste his political capital with Congress, as FDR had done with the submission of his ill-fated court-packing bill in 1937.[408] Busy with White House task forces on policy proposals and with Lawrence F. O'Brien on congressional relations, LBJ ended 1964 determined to exceed FDR's First Hundred Days in the speed, volume, and long-term significance of domestic legislation passed during the Eighty-ninth Congress.[409] Eric Goldman estimated that during the 1965 session of Congress from January 4 to October 23, Congress approved 86 of the 89 major bills that LBJ sponsored or supported.[410]

LBJ perceived and prized a suprapartisan, centrist policy consensus as the foundation and stimulus for legislative productivity, greater social and economic progress, and less partisan and ideological conflict. He also understood how ephemeral and fragile this consensus was. Shortly after LBJ's inner circle celebrated the 1964 election results, the president made a rather mournful, ominous observation and political forecast to the staff of the White House congressional liaison office in January 1965. "I was just elected President by the biggest popular margin in the history of the country, fifteen million votes. Just by the natural way people think and because Barry Goldwater scared the hell out of them, I have already lost about two of these fifteen and am probably getting down to thirteen. If I get in any fight with Congress, I will lose another couple of million, and if I have to send any more of our boys into Vietnam, I may be down to eight million by the end of the summer."[411]

CHAPTER SEVEN

The Politics of Dissensus:
1966–1968

Like most conventional politicians, LBJ assumed that any public mandate that he received from the 1964 election to make major changes in domestic policy would steadily diminish after his inauguration in 1965. Earlier, during the summer and autumn of 1964, LBJ directed the various White House policy task forces to secretly develop the large volume and extensive variety of Great Society legislation with which he inundated Congress during its 1965–1966 sessions. Always shrewd, cautious, and obsessed with timing in the legislative process, LBJ wanted the Republicans and the media to know as few specifics as possible about his future policy intentions so that they would not be criticized and reduce his victory margin.[1]

In an editorial published one week before the 1964 election, *Time* magazine chastised LBJ for the superficial "pettifoggery" of his campaign rhetoric. "Confident of victory, he had a readymade opportunity to set forth national policies and win a mandate for them. But he put off any action that might possibly prove embarrassing until after November 3, and talked about urgent matters only in generalities. He failed to deliver on his own pre-campaign pledge to furnish a blueprint for 'the Great Society.' "[2]

Nonetheless, as the first session of the Eighty-ninth Congress began in 1965, it was difficult to argue that LBJ and liberal Democrats in Congress had not received a public mandate for the Great Society, no matter how vaguely and inadequately Johnson had explained it. In the Senate, Democrats enjoyed a more than two-to-one majority. In the House of Representatives, there were now 295 Democrats and 140 Republicans. Democrats controlled thrity-three governorships, and the Republicans controlled both houses of only six state legislatures.[3] Thus, one irony of LBJ's suprapartisan, centrist policy consensus was how much it benefited liberal Democratic candidates outside the South in the 1964 elections.

The sharp increase in the number of liberal Democrats in Congress, especially in the House, greatly reduced the power and ability of the bipartisan conservative coalition to weaken or kill liberal legislation. This coalition's obstructionism was formidable during JFK's presidency and, to a lesser extent, during the first year of LBJ's presidency. *Congressional Quarterly Weekly* estimated that in House roll-call votes, the bipartisan conservative coalition won 74 percent in 1961, 67 percent in 1963 and 1964, and only 25 percent in 1965.[4]

More so than most presidents, LBJ assumed that the quality of his presidency would be judged by his contemporaries and future scholars by the legislative productivity of Congress during his administration, especially during the Eighty-ninth Congress. Just as LBJ was determined to exceed FDR's 1936 popular vote percentage in his 1964 victory, the Texan wanted to surpass the legislative productivity of FDR's "First Hundred Days."[5] LBJ, though, also wanted to avoid or at least delay the obstacles that had hampered or destroyed progress in domestic policy for Democratic presidents from Woodrow Wilson to JFK.[6]

Secretary of HEW Wilbur Cohen recalled LBJ telling him and other administration officials at the end of January 1965 the following warning. "Every day that I'm in office and every day that I push my program, I'll be losing part of my ability to be influential, because that's in the nature of what the president does. He uses up his capital. Something is going to come up, either something like the Vietnam War or something else where I will begin to lose all that I have now."[7]

Understanding how vulnerable the policy mandate based on his landslide victory and broad yet fragile consensus was, LBJ immediately moved to increase the prospect of getting most of the Great Society legislation, including major landmark bills for Medicare, immigration reform, voting rights, elementary and secondary education, the creation of the Department of Housing and Urban Development (HUD), and a wide range of lesser known, specialized legislation on environmental protection, consumer protection, the expansion of national parks, and highway beautification enacted. He did this by prominently involving key members of Congress, especially Senate Democrats, in the formulation and shepherding of legislation that pertained to their policy specialties, such as Edmund S. Muskie on air and water pollution and RFK on public housing and urban renewal.[8] LBJ biographer and political scientist Doris Kearns noted, "Johnson would not approve the draft until the relevant Cabinet member had presented him with a statement that he had carried out the necessary consultations with Congress giving proof that he had done his homework."[9]

While LBJ sensitively sought cooperation and provided lavish recognition to leading Democrats as well as some Republicans like Everett M. Dirksen and Margaret Chase Smith for their roles in developing and passing Great Society bills, he wanted to minimize floor debates to maintain the momentum of legislative productivity. He reduced the opposition of business interest groups to his domestic legislation by lowering his original budget proposal for fiscal year 1966 to less than $100 billion. His cut in excise taxes was calculated to satisfy both business and consumers.[10] The president even considered combining the departments of labor and commerce into a single, new cabinet department for the

purposes of cost-cutting efficiency and symbolizing the greater cooperation between labor and business that LBJ's consensus sought.[11]

Organized labor, of course, was disappointed by the failure of LBJ and
liberal Democrats in Congress to secure repeal of section 14(b) of the Taft-
Hartley Act, which allowed states to enact "right to work laws." Likewise, civil
rights activists were startled that the Eighty-ninth Congress could pass the Voting Rights Act of 1965 but not home rule legislation for Washington, DC. In
his memoirs, Lawrence F. O'Brien, however, asserted that both the qualitative
and quantitative legislative successes of the Johnson administration and the Eighty-
ninth Congress were more impressive than those of FDR's "First Hundred Days."
O'Brien estimated that 84 of the administration's 87 major bills submitted to
Congress in 1965 and 97 of its 113 major bills in 1966 were passed.[12] O'Brien
concluded, "Yet I tend to think, granting my deep personal involvement that the
breakthroughs of the Eighty-ninth Congress—in education, in medical care, in
civil rights, in housing—exceeded the New Deal achievements in their impact
on American society... Lyndon Johnson made his mistakes and he paid for
them, but his record with the Eighty-ninth Congress will live on as a monument
to his energy, his vision, and his compassion."[13]

As LBJ grimly anticipated, his consensus in domestic policy was deteriorating
by the early spring of 1965 because of foreign policy, especially but not entirely
in Vietnam. The president sent the first large contingent of American ground
combat troops to South Vietnam for the official purpose of protecting American
air bases and other installations from Viet Cong attacks. Congress overwhelmingly
approved LBJ's request for additional defense spending. What was more controversial with Congress and the public, though, was LBJ's initiation of major American bombing raids in North Vietnam because of its support of the Viet Cong.[14]
LBJ's military intervention in the Dominican Republic in the spring of 1965 also
aroused controversy and briefly diverted the attention of the public, media, and
Congress away from Great Society legislation.

On March 25, 1965, LBJ reassured his fellow Americans, "The United
States still seeks no wider war. . . . The United States will never be second in
seeking a settlement in Viet-Nam that is based on an end of Communist aggression."[15] Johnson continued to repeat his previous assertions that he was not
expanding the war in Vietnam but was merely continuing the commitment to
South Vietnam's safety and independence that Eisenhower and JFK had made.[16]
A Gallup poll released on April 7, 1965, however, revealed that public opinion
was evenly divided on American foreign and defense policies in Vietnam. While
41 percent of the Americans polled agreed that the United States should negotiate a peace settlement with Communist leaders, 42 percent wanted to send
more American troops to Vietnam.[17]

A Gallup poll released on April 23 showed American public opinion to be
even more fragmented. A plurality of those surveyed, 28 percent, expressed no

opinion while the policy options suggested ranged from 17 percent advocating complete American withdrawal from Vietnam to 19 percent wanting to "go all out" with a declaration of war and a decisive military victory. Only 14 percent supported LBJ's current policy of combining incremental increases in military action with a willingness to negotiate on terms that would preserve South Vietnam as a non-Communist nation.[18]

Despite his frequent consultation with and interpretation of public opinion polls, LBJ's chief concern was the current state of congressional opinion, especially in the Senate, toward his policies in Vietnam. Because the Gulf of Tonkin Resolution passed almost unanimously in Congress, LBJ believed that he had avoided a mistake that Harry Truman had made in the Korean War by not obtaining a similar resolution from Congress. The Texan was careful to privately consult leading members of Congress on foreign policy, especially Democratic senators J. William Fulbright and Richard Russell and Republican Minority Leader Everett M. Dirksen, but could not tolerate public criticism from fellow Democrats, especially Fulbright, chairman of the Senate Foreign Relations Committee.[19]

Since Fulbright had previously been an outspoken critic of Truman's foreign policy in Korea, LBJ perceived another parallel between the Vietnam War and the Korean War.[20] LBJ also felt a sense of personal betrayal and perceived a lack of patriotism by Fulbright because the Arkansas senator had been one of LBJ's floor leaders in defending and advocating the Senate's adoption of the Gulf of Tonkin Resolution. In an April 17, 1965, phone conversation with journalist Philip Potter, LBJ complained that the Senate Foreign Relations Committee "really has no great strong leadership . . . Fulbright philosophizes. . . . He just doesn't want to take on anything that's real tough."[21]

From his perspective, Fulbright concluded that LBJ had deceived him about the alleged North Vietnamese attack in the Gulf of Tonkin and manipulated the Arkansas senator in order to gain overwhelming Senate support for this vaguely worded resolution granting the president broad, discretionary war-making powers in Southeast Asia.[22] Fulbright later stated, "The greatest mistake I made in my life was to accept Lyndon's account of what happened and those of his men."[23] Despite his distrust of LBJ, Fulbright continued to communicate his most serious concerns and criticisms of the administration's actions in Vietnam privately to LBJ, Robert McNamara, and Dean Rusk. Fulbright's April 5, 1965, memo warned LBJ that a large-scale American ground and air war in Vietnam would ultimately fail and threaten the potential for détente with the Soviet Union that had been developing since the Limited Nuclear Test Ban Treaty. Also, since it would be independent of China and the Soviet Union, a Communist regime that governed all of Vietnam would be similar to Tito's government in Yugoslavia. This would be more beneficial to American foreign policy than an unstable anti-Communist government in South Vietnam dependent on more and more American troops and funds to survive. Fulbright's memo also urged

LBJ to halt American bombing missions in order to persuade both the North and South Vietnamese governments to negotiate.[24]

Fulbright was initially optimistic that LBJ would adopt some of his memo's suggestions and perspectives. In his April 7, 1965, address at Johns Hopkins University, LBJ expressed his desire to help develop all of Vietnam economically through programs similar to the TVA and improve nutrition, education, and public health among all Vietnamese. But, despite Fulbright's recommendations, the president asserted that Communist China dominated North Vietnam's aggression toward South Vietnam and warned North Vietnam, "We will not withdraw, either openly or under the cloak of a meaningless agreement."[25]

LBJ's military intervention in the Dominican Republic in late April and early May of 1965 further alienated Fulbright and motivated him to be more strident, frequent, and open in his public criticism of LBJ's foreign policy. The president justified this intervention on his assumption that the government of the Dominican Republic was in danger of being overtaken by a Castro-supported Communist faction and that Americans living there needed to be protected. LBJ assured the American public on May 2, 1965, that he had conferred with several Latin American governments and the Organization of American States (OAS). "The American nations cannot, must not, and will not permit the establishment of another Communist government in the Western Hemisphere," the president vowed.[26]

Fulbright, though, again concluded that LBJ had deceived and misled him and other members of the Senate Foreign Relations Committee about exactly what happened in the Dominican Republic and whether American military intervention was definitely necessary.[27] Besides Fulbright, an increasing number of Democratic senators, including Eugene McCarthy, Frank Church, and R. Vance Hartke, became more openly critical of LBJ's foreign policy in general as it seemed to become more blatantly and consistently militaristic. Journalists Rowland Evans and Robert Novak assessed what they termed "the deeper significance of Johnson's split with the liberals in the Dominican intervention. It sheared off the liberal end of his consensus precisely at the moment he needed it most, when the torment of Vietnam already menaced the Johnson consensus and threatened wholesale erosion of his support."[28]

When the Senate Foreign Relations Committee televised hearings on the Vietnam War on February 4, 1966, LBJ's relationship as party leader and president with Senate Democrats on the Vietnam War had dissolved into dissensus. Dissensus is a condition of intraparty relations and mode of intraparty political and policy behavior in which the party fragments multilaterally, rather than bilaterally, on a growing number of new, complex issues and lacks a shared ideology or policy agenda. In terms of issue positions, ideological and regional differences, and interest group conflicts, the Democratic Party in Congress had often been divided bilaterally: northern and southern, rural and urban, liberal and conservative, labor and business, pro-civil rights and anti-civil rights. During his impressive career as Democratic floor leader in the Senate and as a Democratic president shepherding major, landmark domestic legislation through Congress, LBJ proved himself unequalled as a master of compromise, consensus, and centrism in formulating and passing legislation within the context of such bilateral differences among Democrats and even among some Republicans.[29]

LBJ again perceived the increasing volume, extent, and variety of criticism of his policies in Vietnam among Senate Democrats through the prism of Truman's experiences with Democrats in Congress, especially J. William Fulbright, during the Korean War.[30] Conservative Democrats in the Senate like Patrick McCarran of Nevada joined conservative Republicans like Joseph McCarthy and Robert A. Taft in criticizing Truman's military decisions in Korea for being too cautious, limited, and ineffective. Meanwhile, foreign policy liberals like Fulbright criticized Truman's conduct of the Korean War from the left.[31]

LBJ occasionally telephoned the frail, elderly former president in order to commiserate about Fulbright. They both perceived Fulbright, whom Truman derisively nicknamed "Halfbright," as an irresponsible, grandstanding intellectual dilettante. On April 19, 1965, LBJ complained to Truman about "this damn fool Fulbright who fights me on everything. He wants [to run] foreign relations, and he's in with Chou En-lai and the Russians this morning on wanting me to stop bombing out there. . . . Can you imagine putting handcuffs on Americans bombers and saying, 'We ought to let them shoot at you, but you can't shoot back.' "[32]

Unlike the Democratic congressional critics of Truman's policies in Korea, however, LBJ's critics and opponents in Congress could not be easily categorized in terms of ideology, region, or faction. They divided multilaterally on the Vietnam War, leading to dissensus on this issue. While some leading Democratic senators were publicly yet tepidly loyal to LBJ's policies in Vietnam, they were privately critical and skeptical, but for different reasons. For example, Senate Majority Leader Mike Mansfield of Montana was emerging as a dove who privately expressed reservations to LBJ that were similar to Fulbright's.[33] Like Mansfield, Richard Russell of Georgia, chairman of the Senate Armed Services Committee, usually maintained a public façade of loyalty to LBJ's decisions on Vietnam. Privately, though, the Georgia Democrat's advice to Johnson was to either fully mobilize the American people for a decisive military victory in Vietnam or withdraw.[34]

The earliest, most outspoken dovish critics of LBJ's Vietnam policies were often Democratic senators from the upper Midwest and Far West, such as Frank Church of Idaho, George McGovern of South Dakota, Gaylord Nelson of Wisconsin, and Wayne Morse of Oregon.[35] LBJ was accustomed to Morse's reputation, rhetoric, and policy behavior as a quirky, unpredictable maverick who was one of the two senators to vote against the Gulf of Tonkin Resolution. But he was especially angry and vindictive in his behavior as presidential party leader toward Church, McCarthy, and later Senator R. Vance Hartke of Indiana for their dovish opposition.[36] All of them had been members of the "Johnson Network" who had benefited from LBJ's distribution of pork barrel favors, campaign contributions, and desirable, prestigious committee assignments during his leadership of the Senate Democrats. He now regarded Fulbright and most other Democrats on the Senate Foreign Relations Committee as ungrateful and disloyal toward his party leadership and untrustworthy and irresponsible toward his foreign policy.[37] The president subsequently recognized Gale McGee of Wyoming, a hawkish Great Society liberal, as his chief contact on the Senate Foreign Relations Committee and de facto spokesman and defender of his policies in Vietnam. McGee also belonged to the Democratic, freshman "class of 1958" and was a member of the "Johnson Network" in the Senate.[38]

During the 1965–1966 period, LBJ's expansion of American military activities in Vietnam was generally supported by liberal, Catholic Democratic senators from the Northeast, especially Thomas J. Dodd of Connecticut and John Pastore of Rhode Island and, more ambivalently, by the Kennedy brothers and Edmund S. Muskie of Maine.[39] Although consistently liberal on domestic issues like civil rights, social welfare, anti-poverty programs, and labor, Dodd was one of the most stridently and outspokenly hawkish nonsouthern Democrats in the Senate and intensely loyal to LBJ.[40] Like McGee, Dodd was a fellow member of the Senate Foreign Relations Committee, the freshman "class of 1958," and the "Johnson Network."

As early as February 23, 1965, Dodd delivered a Senate floor speech in which he denounced "the new isolationism" that was influencing some senators, implicitly including Fulbright.[41] The Connecticut senator elaborated that the "propositions" of this isolationism "would strike at the heart of our national effort to preserve our freedom and our security; and collectively add up to a policy which I can describe by no other name than 'appeasement,' subtle appeasement, unintentional appeasement to be sure, but appeasement nonetheless."[42] Dodd then alluded to Cold War, domino theory assumptions and perspectives, such as the Munich Lesson, the need for American foreign policy to persist in a long-term, arduous war in Vietnam to protect the freedom of the United States and its allies from monolithic Communism, and the perception of Vietnam as "only one symptom of the disease, the epidemic, we are resisting."[43]

Almost one year later, Senator Russell Long of Louisiana, a hawkish southern moderate, echoed Dodd's 1965 speech. Long criticized the recent televised hearings of Fulbright's committee. He stated, "I want to say that these advocates of retreat, defeat, surrender, and national dishonor have not been doing the country any good when they went before a television network suggesting that this Nation was not committed to fighting aggression in this area. . . . We are committed to resisting Communist aggression. That is what this is all about."[44]

LBJ usually deferred to hawkish surrogates like McGee, Dodd, and Long to defend his policies in Vietnam and rebut his critics. The president was also quick to use the media to counteract and occasionally preempt both dovish and hawk-ish congressional opposition to his policies in Vietnam. Johnson made a major speech on Vietnam at Johns Hopkins University a few days after he received Fulbright's memo and significantly expanded the American military effort in Vietnam. This speech, like future speeches on LBJ's policies in Vietnam, com-bined an assertion of American resolve to resist Communist aggression and fulfill its collective security agreements like SEATO and NATO with an expressed desire for a responsible, peaceful settlement of the war and an offer of substantial humanitarian, economic, and technological aid to Southeast Asia.

On February 4, 1966, the first day of the Fulbright committee's televised hearings on the Vietnam War, LBJ held a televised press conference. The presi-dent announced American food relief to famine-plagued India and stated that he was traveling to Honolulu to confer with Henry Cabot Lodge, Jr., U.S. ambas-sador to South Vietnam, and General William Westmoreland, the commander of American forces in Vietnam, and South Vietnamese leaders.[45] In addition to the secretaries of state and defense, LBJ would be accompanied by the secretaries of agriculture and HEW. They would have "both military and non-military briefings," discuss American military and diplomatic strategy in Vietnam, and "explore and inaugurate certain pacification programs in the fields of health, education, and agriculture in Vietnam."[46]

During the rest of that week, as the Senate Foreign Relations Committee conducted its televised hearings, LBJ and his administration's officials dominated the news with the president's trip to Honolulu. At the Honolulu International Airport on February 6, the president declared that "it is vitally important to every American that we stop the communists in South Vietnam" and "we will leave here determined not only to achieve military victory over aggression, but to win victory over hunger, disease, and despair."[47] Two days later at the Los Angeles International Airport, LBJ announced the success of the Honolulu conference and his administration's plans to combine enlightened humanitarian aid, international cooperation, and effective yet limited military efforts. He pledged that "we shall fight the battle of aggression in Vietnam to a successful conclu-sion. We shall fight the battle for social construction and throughout the world we shall fight the battle for peace."[48]

Through such rhetoric and calculated media events, LBJ's purpose went beyond an effort to refute and delegitimize the criticism of his hawkish and dovish critics in Congress, the media, and the American public. He wanted to develop a compromised, centrist policy consensus on his Vietnam policies—first, on an intraparty basis among Senate Democrats; second, on a bipartisan basis in Congress; and, third, on a suprapartisan basis among Americans in general.[49] The president was also determined to prevent the growing commitment of American funds and troops to Vietnam that might end the Great Society. World War II halted any further progress of FDR's New Deal, and the Korean War destroyed any potential for Truman's major Fair Deal proposals to be enacted.[50] As LBJ glumly predicted, liberal doves in Congress expected him to reduce American military action in Vietnam in exchange for their support of the increasingly controversial, additional Great Society legislation, especially race-related policies like the fair housing bill and Community Action. Meanwhile, conservative hawks wanted him to reduce domestic spending and avoid tax increases in exchange for their support of LBJ's policies in Vietnam and higher defense spending.[51]

LBJ struggled on an issue-by-issue basis to forge shaky, temporary bipartisan coalitions to continue both the Great Society and the Vietnam War. He engaged in more duplicity. He intentionally underestimated and obscured the actual costs of the war in funds and troops. Johnson exaggerated or even fabricated the appearance of American diplomatic and military progress in Vietnam. LBJ's manipulative, misleading rhetoric and policy behavior added another ingredient of dissensus that plagued his presidency—the credibility gap. This gap first developed in Congress, especially the Senate, and soon extended to the general public.

British political scientist Michael Foley observed that the evaporation of LBJ's consensus with the Senate and emergence of his credibility gap by 1966 occurred at a time when the Senate realized "that the enhanced scope of Johnson's power was a reflection of the legislature's own emasculation and produced a growing renaissance in institutional consciousness and independence. Even among Johnson's most fervent congressional supporters, there developed a marked antipathy toward many of the president's secretive and manipulative tactics."[52] Mike Mansfield's passive leadership encouraged debate and participation in the Senate, further contributing to greater assertiveness by LBJ's critics. Gallup polls revealed that public approval of LBJ's handling of the Vietnam War declined from 50 percent on March 6, 1966, to 41 percent on June 8, 1966.[53] In his analysis of LBJ's presidency, journalist Hugh Sidey concluded that "credibility became the single biggest problem in Lyndon Johnson's four years of leadership."[54]

To some extent, LBJ's credibility gap was an unexpected product of his calculated, domestic political strategy toward the Vietnam War. LBJ wanted a maximum degree of discretion and flexibility in his diplomatic and military decisions in Vietnam so that he could eventually achieve a peace settlement similar to that of the Korean War while avoiding what he regarded as the two worst consequences of the Korean War: massive Chinese military intervention and the rise of McCarthyism in American politics.[55] Military historian H. R. McMaster condemned LBJ's apparent subordination of military strategy to domestic political concerns. He stated, "Because policy decisions were made based on domestic political expediency, and because the president was intent on forging a consensus position behind what he believed was a middle policy, the administration deliberately avoided clarifying its policy objectives and postponed discussing the level of force that the president was willing to commit to the effort. Indeed, because the president was seeking domestic political consensus, members of the administration believed that ambiguity for the objectives for fighting in Vietnam was a strength rather than a weakness."[56]

Actually, LBJ's campaign strategy in the 1964 election and his subsequent expansion of American military intervention in Vietnam shared a common, domestic, political purpose. LBJ intended both of them to crush and thoroughly discredit right-wing extremism. He wanted to prevent a resurgence of McCarthyism and ensure the continuation of the centrist, bipartisan containment policy that began under Truman and that LBJ helped Eisenhower to protect from the threat of McCarthyites, "the China lobby," and isolationists among right-wing Republicans in Congress during the 1950s.[57]

By late June 1965, LBJ was confronted with the question of whether to ask Congress to approve the politically controversial, unpopular possibility of calling up military reserve units because of the need for more American troops in Vietnam. He waited until Congress passed the Medicare and voting rights bills and appropriated $2 billion for his anti-poverty legislation.[58] Throughout July, he periodically consulted Eisenhower to gain the former president's cooperation in influencing the Republican leadership in Congress to support his possible, pending request for the mobilization of the reserves.[59] In a July 23, 1965, phone conversation, Eisenhower assured LBJ that he had spoken with leading Republicans in Congress. "I just wanted to calm these people down by telling them I talked to you," Eisenhower stated.[60] LBJ later decided not to call up the reserves.

In addition to Eisenhower's intervention on his behalf among Republicans in Congress, LBJ appreciated the generally supportive position of Senate Minority Leader Everett M. Dirksen. The Illinois senator increasingly demanded that LBJ cut domestic spending in order to compensate for higher defense spending. Like Eisenhower and LBJ, Dirksen also wanted to preserve a bipartisan, centrist foreign policy and protect it from right-wing extremism.[61] By the spring of 1966, dissensus on the Vietnam War seemed to be occurring among Republicans in Congress.

House Minority Leader Gerald R. Ford criticized LBJ's policies in Vietnam while Dirksen publicly rebuked Ford and defended LBJ. In April 1966, Ford referred to LBJ's "shocking mismanagement" of the Vietnam War and later dismissed the president's diplomatic trip to the Philippines in October 1966 as a "political gimmick." Dirksen publicly reprimanded Ford through such statements as, "You don't demean the chief magistrate of your country at a time when a war is on," and "You don't denounce the commander in chief before the whole, wide world."[62] RNC chairman Ray C. Bliss quietly negotiated an uneasy rapprochement between Ford and Dirksen in order to prepare the GOP for the 1966 congressional elections.

To maintain this increasingly fragile, vulnerable, bipartisan, centrist consensus in Congress, LBJ eventually decided to reject the request of the Joint Chiefs of

Staff to call up the reserves and the recommendation of McNamara and other top civilian officials that he raise taxes.[63] Instead, the president announced on July 28, 1965, that he was increasing the number of regular American troops in Vietnam "from 75,000 to 125,000 men almost immediately" and "we will use the authority contained in the present Defense appropriation bill under consideration to transfer funds in addition to the additional money that we will ask."[64] Toward the end of this press conference, he assured the reporters, "Up to now, we have had ample authority, excellent cooperation, a united Congress behind us, and—as near as I could tell you from my meetings last night with the leaders, and from my meetings today with the distinguished chairmen of the committees and the members of both parties—we all met as Americans, united and determined to stand as one."[65] As additional evidence of bipartisan unity, LBJ announced the return of Henry Cabot Lodge, Jr., a liberal Republican and Nixon's running mate in 1960, to South Vietnam for a second tour of duty as U.S. ambassador.[66]

LBJ chose not to call up the reserves and continued to provide incremental, rather than overwhelming, increases in the number of American troops in Vietnam, usually less than what the Joint Chiefs of Staff recommended. He feared that doing so might arouse hawkish extremism from Congress and the public demanding total victory.[67] Dean Rusk, McGeorge Bundy, and other top civilian officials and advisers shared LBJ's concern. In his memoirs, Rusk stated, "Since we wanted to limit the war, we deliberately refrained from creating a war psychology in the United States. We did not try to stir up the anger of the American people over Vietnam . . . we felt that in a nuclear world it was just too dangerous for an entire people to become too angry."[68] Two weeks before LBJ's July 28, 1965, announcement of another 50,000 troops being sent to Vietnam, Bundy warned the president that such a troop increase was necessary in order to restrain the domestic political appeal of the "Goldwater crowd" since right-wing hawks were "more numerous, more powerful and more dangerous than the fleabite professors," that is, left-wing doves.[69]

Nonetheless, LBJ was a president who constantly consulted public opinion polls for domestic policy, election campaigns, and his public approval ratings. It is somewhat perplexing that from the spring of 1965 until the end of 1967 LBJ's decisions on Vietnam, so closely attuned to the nuances of two-party congressional politics and the influence of the media, did not include public opinion as a significant factor.[70] Historian George Herring observed the following in his 1990 lecture at the U.S. Air Force Academy. "Vietnam makes abundantly clear that a—perhaps the—central problem of waging limited war is to maintain public support without arousing public emotion. . . . Vietnam was not fundamentally a public relations problem, and a more vigorous and effective public relations campaign would not have changed the outcome. Still, what stands out quite starkly from an examination of this topic is the small, indeed insignificant role played by public opinion in the decisions for war."[71]

Since LBJ and his administration carefully calculated their military and diplomatic decisions and their public rhetoric on Vietnam to limit hawkish criticism and opposition in Congress, they were sequentially oblivious, dismissive, and then clumsily reactive toward the various antiwar youth movements and antiwar leftist intellectuals.[72] George W. Ball, Undersecretary of State for Economic Affairs, was an early, persistent critic of a greater American military commitment to Vietnam and warned LBJ about the domestic political impact of antiwar sentiment on the left as early as 1965.[73] LBJ replied to Ball, "Don't worry about the hippies and the students and the Commies; they'll raise a lot of hell but can't do real damage. The terrible beast we have to fear is the right wing; if they ever get the idea that I'm selling out Vietnam, they'll do horrible things to the country, and we'll be forced to escalate the war beyond anything you've ever thought about."[74]

In particular, LBJ could not understand or effectively respond to the angry, sometimes violent, dissent and rebelliousness of the mostly white, affluent students at elite universities who often identified with the New Left. As the student-based, New Left antiwar protests became larger, more frequent, and more extreme in their policy demands and political tactics, a flabbergasted LBJ frequently asked his White House aides, "But what in the world do they want?"[75] White House speechwriter Harry McPherson observed that LBJ could not understand the alienated baby boom generation and the New Left because these youths "judged the society in the light of its professed ideals, or of their own, and invariably found it wanting." By contrast, Johnson "was a manipulator of men, when the young were calling for everyone to do his own thing; a believer in institutions such as government, universities, business, and trade unions, when these were under constant attack on the campuses; a paternalist, in a time of widespread submission to youthful values and desires."[76]

The New Left in general and the student-dominated, grassroots antiwar movement in particular added complex, novel, and seemingly intractable dimensions to the developing dissensus of the Democratic Party by the late 1960s. The New Left especially challenged the two ideological and programmatic foundations of the Democratic Party: a bipartisan, centrist containment policy in the Cold War and New Deal–based liberalism with its emphasis on regulations, social welfare entitlements, economic subsidies, policy experts, bureaucrats, and interest groups bargaining to address domestic policy needs.[77] By 1968, the antiwar New Left's influence within the Democratic Party was strong enough to influence the dovish, insurgent presidential candidacies of Eugene McCarthy and RFK. The New Left's ideological and programmatic criticism extended beyond LBJ's Vietnam policies to include the growth of a larger, more centralized federal government in domestic policy, especially in the Great Society's antipoverty programs. Presidential historian Jeff Shesol suggested that the New Left-New Politics influence on RFK furthered aggravated the antagonistic relationship between RFK and LBJ and personified the New Left's contributions to Democratic dissensus. Shesol rhetorically asked, "Would liberals, like LBJ, continue to represent unions, federal paternalism, and globalism? Or would they move with RFK toward a 'newer world'—a broader coalition, more decentralized decision-making, and 'empowerment' of the underprivileged?"[78]

At a less political and more cultural and sociological level, LBJ personified the 1950s-style, centrist, suprapartisan, pragmatic power broker. He emerged during the divided government of the Eisenhower era and filled the leadership vacuum created by the apparent "end of ideology" proclaimed by sociologist Daniel Bell. According to Bell's theory, centrist, bipartisan compromises reduced sharp ideological and partisan differences by the end of the 1950s as a mostly middle-class, relatively apolitical, increasingly homogeneous, bureaucratized, and mechanized "mass society" developed.[79] Bell prophetically warned, "Social tensions are an expression of unfulfilled expectations. It is only when expectations are aroused that radicalism can take hold."[80]

For LBJ, this type of "mass society" was the desirable and essential social and political foundation necessary for consensus-building progress in achieving long-delayed, stalled domestic policy goals, such as Medicare and civil rights for blacks, and the fulfillment of American foreign and defense policy responsibilities in the Cold War. LBJ carefully relied on the lessons of the Korean War and the Formosa Resolution of 1955 as the basis for his decisions in the Vietnam War. He depended on the social fabric, congressional environment, two-party politics, and institutional perspectives of the 1950s for the conduct of his presidency in the 1960s.[81]

LBJ's ideal political milieu was a macrocosm of the Senate cloakroom during the peak of his career as Senate majority leader. It maximized policymaking, compromise, and the preservation of a cooperative, suprapartisan centrist consensus about shared, broad policy goals for the nation. It also discouraged and minimized discussion, debate, grassroots participation, dissent, and individualism.[82] LBJ assumed that the average American wanted the president to be an effective, pragmatic problem-solver who led Congress to made steady progress in public policy and cared little about the methods, processes, and compromises that the president used to fulfill his responsibilities.[83]

The New Left, though, regarded LBJ's "consensus" to be repugnant, repressive conformity imposed by "the Establishment" that LBJ personified and protected. C. Wright Mills, a maverick sociologist whose iconoclastic ideas inspired many students in the New Left, explicitly rejected Bell's theory in his 1960 "Letter to the New Left." Mills wrote, "The end-of-ideology is a slogan of complacency, circulating among the prematurely middle-aged, centered in the present."[84] He concluded, "If there is to be a politics of a New Left, what needs to be analysed (sic) is the structure of institutions, the foundations of politics."[85] Earlier, in his definitive 1956 book, *The Power Elite*, Mills characterized the

United States as "a conservative country without any conservative ideology" and scornfully dismissed New Deal–based American liberalism as "a set of administrative routines" that was "readily made to sustain the conservative mood."[86]

By the time of his death in 1962, Mills had given up hope of a revitalized alliance of labor unions, or even non-unionized workers, and leftist intellectuals similar to that of the Old Left shortly before World War I and during the 1930s.[87] For Mills, the most powerful labor leaders, most notably AFL-CIO president George Meany and, to a lesser extent, UAW president Walter Reuther, had been co-opted by big business and government, especially through the higher wages and better benefits that the wealth of the "military-industrial complex" provided their union members.[88] The typical blue-collar worker was too socially conservative and concerned with his own economic security to be attracted to the New Left's revolutionary consciousness. Also, the aging, scattered remnants of the Old Left seemed obsessed with ideological and factional squabbles among Trotskyites, Maoists, pro-Soviet Communists, and anti-Communist Socialists.[89]

As far-fetched as it appeared to LBJ, perhaps the shrewdest political tactician of "the Establishment," the Students for a Democratic Society (SDS) believed that a politically influential New Left could be developed from the masses of undergraduate students inspired and organized by graduate students, professors, and leftist writers. The UAW invited the SDS to use its summer camp in Port Huron, Michigan, to host its 1962 conference. The SDS was actually founded in 1960 as a successor of the Student League for Industrial Democracy (SLID). SLID had its origins in several labor unions, most notably the International Ladies Garment Workers Union (ILGWU).[90] The UAW also financed the Educational Reform and Action Projects (ERAP) of the SDS. By 1964, the ERAPs concentrated their educational, community organizing, anti-poverty, and public health efforts in black, urban neighborhoods. In terms of its purpose, methods, and ideology of grassroots participation and individual empowerment, ERAP was a forerunner of Community Action, VISTA, and other Great Society programs.[91]

The Port Huron Statement of 1962 made it clear that the SDS was not merely a subordinate, subsidized student association for organized labor. This document's major theme is one of alienation rather than rebellion. It expressed its members' generational, intellectual, and sociological alienation from the power structures of major institutions in American society: big business, organized labor, universities, the military, government, and the two-party system. The SDS was especially dismayed at the enduring influence of the racist, reactionary Dixiecrats within the Democratic Party, especially in the committee system of Congress and in the platforms of national conventions.[92]

Meanwhile, the American voter had little meaningful influence over the content and direction of public policy, especially foreign policy. The SDS dismissed the campus Young Democrats since they were often dominated by ambitious, career-minded students who wanted to become co-opted into the anti-democratic, elitist system of two-party politics with no significant policy and ideological differences between the two major parties. "Rather than protesting the state of politics, most politicians are reinforcing and aggravating that state. While in practice they rig public opinion to suit their own interest, in words and ritual they enshrine 'the sovereign public' and call for more and more letters. Their speeches and campaign actions are banal, based on a degrading conception of what people want to hear. They respond not to dialogue, but to pressure: and knowing this, the ordinary citizen sees even greater inclination to shun the political sphere."[93]

Despite its bitter, cynical, and alienated critique of the American political system, the Port Huron Statement was optimistic about the potential of the SDS to gradually reform American politics in particular and American society in general. The SDS intended to eventually reform the American political system and achieve liberal policy objectives in domestic and foreign policies by first revolutionizing values. Like Mills and the "beat poets" of the 1950s, the SDS rejected the post–World War II values of social conformity, consumerism, hierarchical, bureaucratic power structures, ideologically vapid centrism and moral compromises in politics, and the suppression of emotions. The SDS embraced, articulated, and promoted among their fellow Americans the values of local-level, direct community participation in education, economics, and government, greater freedom of expression, respect for the uniqueness of each individual, and a rejection of elitism and inequality. "We would replace power rooted in possession, privilege, or circumstance by power and uniqueness rooted in love, reflectiveness, reason, and creativity."[94]

In this excerpt and other words of utopian idealism in the Port Huron Statement, there was no indication that the SDS would engage in civil disobedience on a regular basis against policies and institutions that they regarded as immoral, unjust, and illegitimate. Before the SDS wrote and issued the Port Huron Statement, several SDS members, most notably Tom Hayden, had already participated in civil rights demonstrations in the South that included violations of state and local segregation laws. Influenced by SNCC, a more militant, youthful civil rights organization than Martin Luther King, Jr.'s organization or the NAACP, the SDS was also inspired by the nonviolent civil disobedience of black students who conducted lunch counter sit-ins that began in the South in 1960.

Also, in 1960, the illegal yet peaceful sit-in demonstrations of Berkeley students against hearings by the House of Un-American Activities Committee (HUAC) at the San Francisco city hall were ended by police using fire hoses and billy clubs as they physically removed the demonstrators.[95] Many of these student demonstrators were also members of Berkeley's chapter of the Young People's Socialist League (YPSL). YPSL members were picketing Woolworth's because this company had not integrated the lunch counters of its stores in the South.

With its membership and leadership mostly derived from students and recent graduates of the University of Michigan, the SDS realized even before its convention in Port Huron that it had the potential to become a nationwide movement by co-opting or coalescing with similar New Left student organizations. New Left leaders at the Ann Arbor and Berkeley campuses recognized and exploited a grievance shared by many of even the most apolitical, seemingly conventional students. The rapid growth in the size, enrollments, and funding of major research-oriented state universities had contributed to the disillusionment and alienation of many students. Professors seemed more concerned with their research, obtaining grants, and gaining prestige in their disciplines than with the intellectual development of their students. The administration and staff seemed to be an impersonal, authoritarian bureaucracy that treated students like punch cards processed in computers.[96] As early as 1957, Berkeley students had established a student political party named SLATE, which was not an acronym for anything. SLATE's original purpose was to nominate and elect student government leaders who would challenge the administration and provide a greater student role in university policies, such as an end to compulsory participation in ROTC.[97]

Like SDS members, SLATE and other leftist students from Berkeley were radicalized further by their experiences in Mississippi during the summer of 1964. They joined other students throughout the nation, SNCC, and CORE to teach black children in Freedom Schools and register black voters. What appalled and embittered the New Left students in Mississippi more than the expected racism and violence of the Ku Klux Klan, white mobs, and state and local officials and police were the apparent hypocrisy and callous neglect of a liberal Democratic administration.

Although LBJ signed the Civil Rights Act of 1964 and sent federal officials to investigate the murders of three civil rights activists in Mississippi, the New Left focused on the fact that the president did not send federal officials or troops earlier to prevent racist violence and protect their summer projects. The New Left concluded that the incorrigible insincerity of LBJ and the Democratic Party toward civil rights, voting rights for southern blacks, and meaningful, inclusive participation in the Democratic Party was evident at the 1964 Democratic national convention. Johnson and his surrogates made token concessions to the MFDP delegates while seating the all-white, racist delegation of regular Democrats from Mississippi at their Atlantic City convention.[98]

The SDS was especially disillusioned by Walter Reuther's role in pressuring the MFDP and its lawyer, Joseph L. Rauh, Jr. into accepting LBJ's superficial offer. Despite promising and acting upon the most ambitious, liberal policy agenda of any Democratic president, LBJ was perceived by the New Left as a corrupt, scheming tool of "the Establishment" and mainstream middle-class conformity. To the SDS, Barry Goldwater's right-wing candidacy seemed more like quixotic eccentricity than a serious threat. The activities and publications of the SDS expressed little or no hope of ever transforming the Democratic Party into a truly liberal, idealistic, participatory organization that would finally purge itself of Dixiecrats, corrupt big-city machines, and labor leaders who had "sold out" to big business and government. At the end of 1964, Tom Hayden wrote and issued an SDS pamphlet, *Liberal Analysis and Federal Power.*[99] In it, he stated, "The southern segregationist Democrats are able to act in this spectacularly evil manner because they have learned that liberalism is defused, lacking a point of moral explosion. Liberal laxness and federal policies of laissez-faire in times of violence in the South, whether for decent or opportunistic or whatever reasons, help to breed conditions in which segregationist hordes have the incentive to go unchecked."[100]

In the fall of 1964, Berkeley's Free Speech Movement (FSM) dramatized what many New Left activists regarded as the hypocrisy and repression of another presumably liberal institution—the University of California. Its administration was proud of the fact that more Peace Corps volunteers were graduates of Berkeley than any other college or university, welcomed JFK as its speaker on Charter Day in 1962, and prided itself on its racial liberalism.[101] But in September 1964, the administration prohibited students from setting up tables for the purposes of soliciting donations and promoting their political views. Seasoned by his experiences in Mississippi, student activist Mario Savio organized a free speech sit-in demonstration. Part of Savio's appeal to students was his frequent use of profanity in denouncing the administration as oppressive. Consequently, critics of the Free Speech Movement (FSM) at Berkeley called it the "Filthy Speech Movement."[102] By January 1965, the administration and regents had acceded to most of the FSM's demands. Historian Irwin Unger noted that the success of FSM revealed "the ambiguous relationship between radical politics and cultural dissent that would characterize the New Left to its end."[103]

The FSM and other New Left activists in Berkeley were influenced by the "beats" and a desire for greater freedom of cultural expression. By contrast, the SDS more strongly and deeply focused on current, national policy issues, both domestic and foreign. The SDS consciously chose to formally grant visitor status to Communists. The SDS believed that everyone who accepted its values should be welcome in it and wanted to avoid the infighting between Communists and Socialists that plagued the Old Left.[104] Unlike other major New Left student movements before the spring of 1965, the SDS especially wanted to change American foreign policy. It perceived Fidel Castro as a grassroots, nationalist revolutionary rather than as a puppet of the Soviet Union who threatened American national security.[105]

In general, the SDS was sympathetic toward Third World nations and assumed that they simply wanted to be neutral in the Cold War struggle between the two superpowers and determine their own destinies. The SDS was repelled by American economic and military support of corrupt, brutal dictatorships, like that of South Vietnam.[106] More so than any other issue, the SDS fervently believed that American policies in the Cold War corrupted and co-opted universities, business, labor, and the political system and practiced elitist, anti-democratic decision-making under the guise of "corporate liberalism."[107] Regardless of whether JFK or LBJ was president and which party controlled the White House and Congress, Cold War, anti-Communist perspectives and policies perpetuated "corporate liberalism."

LBJ's significant expansion of the American military commitment to South Vietnam and military invention in the Dominican Republic in the spring of 1965 increased the number of members and chapters in SDS and motivated the New Left in general and the SDS in particular to more specifically and militantly concentrate on the issue of the Vietnam War for the remainder of LBJ's presidency. The New Left perceived these two decisions by LBJ to be the most egregious, blatant examples of corporate liberalism's Cold War imperialism. Since Johnson had campaigned only a few months earlier as the "peace candidate" in contrast to Goldwater's reckless jingoism, these major foreign policy actions in the early spring of 1965 proved to the New Left how meaningless and fraudulent elections and differences between the two parties were.

The SDS and other leftist groups organized demonstrations in Washington, DC, to protest the failed Bay of Pigs invasion in 1961 and JFK's nuclear showdown with the Soviet Union during the Cuban missile crisis.[108] But the April 1965 March on Washington organized by the SDS was much greater in size, with nearly 20,000 participants, and intensity than these previous protests. In his analysis of the SDS, Kirkpatrick Sale observed that the 1965 demonstration signified the movement of the SDS "away from its old roots, its liberal heritage, its period of reformism" and toward active, illegal resistance to the Vietnam War, especially the draft laws.[109] The New Left initially promoted legal methods of anti-draft behavior, such as application for conscientious objector status and continuation of higher education, but it later encouraged illegal methods, such as draft card burning and duplicitous efforts to fail military medical exams.

The New Left's promotion of draft resistance and its role in organizing the antiwar demonstrations of approximately 80,000 people in fifty cities in October 1965 led to Attorney General Nicholas Katzenbach's announcement that the Justice Department would investigate the SDS.[110] Privately, LBJ asked FBI director J. Edgar Hoover to investigate the SDS for evidence of Communist infiltration.[111] The suspicions of the White House and the FBI were further raised after Tom Hayden and several other SDS activists arrived in North Vietnam on a Chinese flight after changing planes in Prague, Moscow, and Beijing in December 1965. After this unauthorized fact-finding trip to Hanoi, Hayden concluded in his memoirs, "The Hanoi visit definitely deepened my sense of isolation from an America at war."[112]

Ironically, the SDS did not even endorse, let alone organize, the October 1967 March on the Pentagon. It attracted approximately 100,000 antiwar demonstrators to Washington, DC.[113] By that time, the SDS was increasingly divided into squabbling factions, eventually leading to its capture by Maoists and the formation of the Weathermen. The Weathermen explicitly committed themselves to terrorism as a means of forcing an immediate end to the Vietnam War.[114]

Even before the emergence of the Weathermen in 1969, it was evident by the fall of 1967 that the prominence of the SDS in the student-oriented antiwar movement and, more broadly, in the New Left was receding. In July 1967, *Time* magazine published a cover story on the so-called "hippies" who had dropped out of society, including politics, and focused on self-fulfillment and escapism through drugs, sexual promiscuity, bohemian-style communal living, and unconventional cultural expressions, especially in the Haight-Ashbury section of San Francisco.[115] Despite their apparent, self-chosen status as dropouts from society, "hippies" led by Abbie Hoffman and Jerry Rubin, who had been active in the FSM at Berkeley, attracted much media attention for their outlandish, prankish rhetoric and behavior in Washington, DC during the March on the Pentagon. Rubin and Hoffman subsequently founded the Youth International Party, nicknamed Yippies.

SDS activists often disdained the Yippies for undermining the efforts of the SDS to make the antiwar movement intellectually and morally provocative and politically influential.[116] The antics of the Yippies and the increasing militancy of more SDS activists also made it more difficult for the New Left youth movements to cross generational lines and coalesce with the growing number of older, middle-class liberals, such as ADA members, who openly opposed LBJ's policies in Vietnam. After all, the March on the Pentagon was sponsored by the National Mobilization Committee to End the War in Vietnam (Mobe), not the SDS. Mobe was led by David Dellinger, a fifty-two-year-old pacifist, in 1967, and its leading members mostly consisted of middle-aged and some elderly clergymen, professors, and writers and included the nationally renowned pediatrician Benjamin Spock and Nobel Prize–winning chemist Linus Pauling.[117] Journalist Jack Newfield, who belonged to the SDS from 1961 to 1964, lamented that "the effect of this grouping will be to harden the generational lines, and thereby diminish the chances for the forging of a broadly based opposition to the Johnson consensus."[118]

In addition to the failure or refusal of most SDS and other young antiwar activists to cross generational lines, the antiwar New Left was also a mostly white, middle- to upper-middle-class movement that did not successfully coalesce with the more militant, antiwar activists among blacks and Hispanics. Although Tom Hayden and other SDS members worked with SNCC and CORE in the early to mid-1960s, younger, more leftist black leaders wanted to exclude whites from any influential role in their organizations. With an emphasis on black power and black pride, SNCC formally announced in May 1966 that it was no longer a pacifistic organization and elected Stokely Carmichael as its new chairman.[119] Influenced by murdered black Muslim leader Malcolm X, Carmichael advocated racial separatism for blacks rather than integration.[120]

With an emphasis now on group identity, feminists formed the National Organization for Women (NOW) in 1966. NOW was primarily established to counteract the persistence of job discrimination and socioeconomic inequality of women and lacked a close association with the male-dominated New Left. Female activists in the New Left, like Casey Hayden, were increasingly disillusioned with and frustrated by the sexism and subordinate roles that they experienced with many male New Left leaders. In January 1968, the Jeanette Rankin Peace Brigade conducted the first all-female antiwar demonstration in Washington, DC and included a "Burial of Traditional Womanhood" to symbolize the independence of women.[121]

While the New Left fragmented into increasingly exclusive groups through the politics of identity, another movement appeared by the mid-1960s that was distinct from the student, black, feminist, counterculture, and antiwar movements. The political activism of Hispanics during the 1960s was initially concentrated in the efforts of middle-class Hispanic businessmen and professionals to increase Hispanic representation and influence in the 1960 and 1964 presidential elections, at Democratic national conventions, in Congress, in the executive branch, and in the state and local politics of southwestern states and California. They attempted to accomplish this through private lobbying and their influence with Hispanic voters through such organizations as the Political Association of Spanish-Speaking Organizations (PASO), the Viva Kennedy and Viva Johnson clubs, the League of United Latin American Citizens (LULAC), and the Mexican American Political Association (MAPA).

After the election of Henry B. Gonzalez as the first Hispanic congressman from Texas in 1961, these mainstream Hispanic leaders often relied on Gonzalez as their liaison with LBJ during his vice presidency and presidency. Carlos McCormick, a leader of the Viva Kennedy clubs in the 1960 election, served as an assistant to John M. Bailey at DNC headquarters.[122] Leaders of these organizations also pressured the White House, the DNC chairman, and federal agencies to appoint more Hispanics to high-level government positions, direct the services and programs of the Great Society more toward Hispanic needs, and focus more on reducing job discrimination suffered by Hispanics. Consequently, Johnson held separate White House civil rights conferences for blacks in 1966 and for Hispanics in 1967.[123] As the Vietnam War became more controversial and a disproportionate number of Hispanics served in Vietnam, most of these mainstream Hispanic leaders were careful not to openly challenge LBJ's policies in Vietnam.[124]

But the political methods and objectives of these older, middle-class Hispanics during the 1960s were similar to those of middle-class Irish Catholics and

Jews during the Roosevelt and Truman administrations. They simply used the greater voting power of their ethnic groups to gradually gain more and better federal jobs and more influence in policymaking, policy implementation, and the Democratic Party's processes and decisions. In his study of the leaders of the Viva Kennedy clubs, historian Ignacio M. Garcia concluded, "Their perspective represented a hybrid of southwestern nationalism, New Deal politics, and middle-class accomodationism."[125]

The year 1966 marked a turning point in Hispanic political activism. The White House and DNC headquarters were alarmed by the sharp drop in Hispanic voter turnout in the 1966 midterm elections. Meanwhile, conservative Republican Ronald Reagan attracted nearly half of the Hispanic votes in his victorious gubernatorial campaign in California.[126] LBJ became more cautious about appearing to favor Hispanic political interests in Texas in 1966 because John Connally was running for reelection as governor and was increasingly unpopular among Hispanics there. Also, by the end of 1966 and the beginning of 1967, more militant, younger Hispanics, especially college students, formed organizations like United Mexican American Students (UMAS), Mexican American Youth Organization (MAYO), and later La Raza Unida.[127] Often identifying themselves as Chicanos, they reflected the New Left emphasis on group consciousness and cultural expression by promoting bilingual education and greater respect for Mexican culture.[128]

Compared to the SDS and SNCC, however, the Hispanic New Left was much smaller in size and potential national political influence. Its presence was mostly limited to a few major universities and cities in Texas and California. Instead, from 1966 to 1968, a different type of Hispanic political movement attracted the most national attention and played a major factor in the rivalry between LBJ and RFK for leadership of the Democratic Party and competition for the 1968 Democratic presidential nomination—the United Farm Worker (UFW) movement of Cesar Chavez. Chavez and the UFW did not have any clear intellectual, ideological, or organizational origins in the New Left or the antiwar movement.

Chavez was the son of a small farmer and migrant laborer and began working as a migrant farm laborer during his childhood. The Wagner Act of 1935 and subsequent labor union laws as well as federal and state minimum wage laws denied coverage to migrant farm laborers. Many migrant farm workers and their families in California and the Southwest were Mexican immigrants or first-generation Mexican Americans who experienced low wages, long work hours, unsanitary living conditions, little or no formal education for their children, few or no medical services, and unscrupulous employers. After participating in several unsuccessful strikes, Chavez joined the Community Service Organization (CSO) of San Jose, California, in 1952.

Through the CSO, Chavez conducted voter registration drives among Hispanics in California and provided assistance in immigration laws and welfare services. During the 1960 presidential campaign, he briefly met RFK when RFK came to California to manage JFK's campaign there.[129] Chavez resigned from the CSO in 1962 after its board rejected his plan to organize the migrant farm workers into a labor union.[130]

Originally named the National Farm Workers Association (NFWA) at its founding in 1962, the UFW had difficulty attracting members, political legitimacy, and bargaining power with the growers. Chavez declined the offer of a well-paying job as a Peace Corps director in order to continue organizing farm workers. In September 1965, eight hundred Filipino grape pickers, who were members of the Agricultural Workers Organizing Committee (AWOC), an AFL-CIO affiliate, began a strike for higher wages.

Chavez led his union in a sympathy strike, but his efforts soon broadened to include demands for formal recognition of both unions from the grape growers and other agricultural employers in California.[131] To symbolize and demonstrate the economic suffering of migrant workers and their families and to pressure the growers to recognize and negotiate with both AWOC and the NFWA, Chavez led a peaceful, 300-mile protest march from Delano, California, to Sacramento. The march culminated in a crowd of over 10,000 people supporting the cause of the farm workers. Governor Edmund "Pat" Brown, facing a tough reelection bid in 1966 and criticized by conservative Democrats and Republicans as too liberal and soft on law and order, remained publicly aloof from the farm worker movement.[132]

Several months later, the Chavez-led movement gained greater political legitimacy and power after Chavez agreed to establish the United Farm Workers Organizing Committee (UFWOC) and affiliate it with the AFL-CIO in July 1966. UFWOC combined and absorbed the members of both the now defunct NFWA and the AWOC. By September 1966, several major growers of wine grapes capitulated to the UFWOC's demands because of its growing labor influence and the effects of boycotts, public sympathy, and unflattering Senate investigations spearheaded by RFK. They recognized the UFWOC, agreed to negotiate with it exclusively, and signed contracts providing higher wages and better working and living conditions.

From 1966 to 1968, the activities and demands of UFWOC attracted more sympathy and less criticism from the American public than any other nationally prominent protest movement of the mid- to late 1960s. Middle-class Americans were predisposed to be sympathetic to the plight of farm workers and their families because of the 1960 CBS news documentary, *Harvest of Shame*, and John Steinbeck's novel, *The Grapes of Wrath*. News coverage and the Senate investigation of this prolonged labor conflict conveyed images of the growers and local police as callous and oppressive and of Chavez and the UFWOC leaders as peaceful and reasonable in their tactics, rhetoric, and demands.[133]

Much of the political and eventual economic success of and widespread sympathy for the farm worker movement in California, though, can be attributed to how Chavez personified this movement for the media, the middle class, and liberal Democratic senators like RFK and Harrison Williams of New Jersey. In a 1968 speech on the Senate floor defending the UFWOC, Williams stated that the UFWOC's members "are solemnly dedicated to non-violent, direct action as a tactic to obtain human dignity, and to guarantee by contract improved living and working conditions" and "Cesar Chavez is proving to the world his dedication to the aspirations of his own people, and indeed to the needs of all men."[134] With no clear identification with the increasingly controversial, divisive, and radical elements of the New Left, Chavez refused to make the UFWOC an exclusively Hispanic organization. Meanwhile, the SDS, SNCC, and the Brown Berets, a Hispanic version of the Black Panthers, respectively engaged in generational, racial, and ethnic separatism. Chavez, for example, rejected the demands of younger, militant Hispanic activists that he exclude Filipinos and whites from UFWOC.[135]

Despite police brutality toward UFWOC picketers and the growing advocacy and use of violence by more New Left activists and the Brown Berets, Chavez persisted in promoting pacifism. He began a twenty-five-day fast on February 14, 1968, to protest the violence that more militant Hispanics advocated.[136] At a time of increasingly strident, harsh, confrontational rhetoric and behavior, Chavez represented a quiet, gentle, devoutly Catholic, self-sacrificing call for economic justice and human dignity for an exploited, long neglected, and previously powerless segment of workers and their families.

As RFK became more liberal in his political rhetoric and policy behavior after 1965, the New York senator generally resisted being identified with the New Left. By contrast, he readily and enthusiastically embraced Chavez and his movement in California.[137] RFK traveled to Delano, California, in early March 1968 to share communion with Chavez at an ecumenical mass that ended the Hispanic labor leader's hunger strike for nonviolence. Journalist Jack Newfield characterized RFK as the Chavez movement's "best publicist and fundraiser."[138] LBJ and his staff suspected that Chavez had long been RFK's political operative in California and was organizing Hispanic voters for that state's winner-take-all Democratic presidential primary on June 4.[139]

For LBJ and other critics of RFK, it seemed too coincidental that Bert Corona, president of MAPA, announced that over 700,000 additional Hispanic voters had been registered in California, more than 40,000 of them in Los Angeles, in January 1968. Corona subsequently endorsed RFK and began establishing Viva Kennedy clubs for the campaign.[140] Also, RFK arrived in Delano on the same day of the New Hampshire presidential primary and conferred with Jesse Unruh, the speaker of the California assembly, who had been urging RFK to run for president.[141]

The origins of RFK's eventual decision to run for president in 1968 partially stemmed from the results of the 1966 midterm elections. They indicated the growing dissatisfaction with LBJ's party leadership among functionaries and politicians from the Old Politics' and New Politics' factions of the Democratic Party. Democratic politicians of the Old Politics, like Representative Thomas P. "Tip" O'Neill of Massachusetts and Mayor Richard J. Daley of Chicago, were often urban, northern, middle-aged Catholics who were publicly linked to LBJ's presidency and party leadership. Privately, though, they were increasingly ambivalent toward and skeptical of LBJ's policies in Vietnam and were acutely aware of how unpopular Johnson and the war were among their constituents, both young, antiwar academics and socially conservative blue-collar whites. They were also frustrated that the Great Society programs, which they had enthusiastically embraced, did little to ameliorate the racial unrest and dismayed at how the draft laws adversely affected and disproportionately burdened blacks, Hispanics, and working-class whites.[142]

In 1966, O'Neill distinguished himself as the first Old Politics Democrat in the U.S. House of Representatives to publicly question and then disagree with LBJ's policies in Vietnam and become a dove. In a June 1966 newsletter to his constituents, O'Neill told them that "there is no easy solution to this problem." He reluctantly concluded that he and they had no other choice but to hope and assume that LBJ "is doing what is proper and in the best interests of the Vietnamese people, the United States, and the Free World."[143]

This newsletter was soon followed by another, entitled "Vietnam: Solution or Stalemate." In it, O'Neill grimly concluded, "As a citizen, congressman, and father, I cannot help but wonder whether this may not be too high a price to pay for an obscure and limited objective."[144] In his memoirs, O'Neill noted that LBJ was furious with the congressman's public statement and accused him of being influenced by antiwar, left-wing students and professors at Harvard University, which was located in O'Neill's district. O'Neill could not convince the president that he had arrived at his opinion on the war independently of the antiwar movement and that his announcement was actually unpopular with his mostly blue-collar constituents.[145] O'Neill stated that, even after he reluctantly voted for the Gulf of Tonkin Resolution in 1964, "I couldn't prove it, but I had the feeling that the White House was using the Gulf of Tonkin incident as an excuse to open up a full-scale war."[146]

Unlike O'Neill, Daley did not publicize any dissent about LBJ's policies in Vietnam. Like many big-city mayors of the Old Politics, the Chicago mayor believed that politics stopped at the water's edge and that all Americans should defer to the president on foreign policy, especially during a war to stop Communist aggression. Privately, however, Daley was concerned about how the growing divisiveness and political extremism over the Vietnam War affected the social fabric of his city, already racked by racial turmoil, and would affect the 1966 state, local, and congressional elections in Illinois. The rising number of casualties among Chicagoans in Vietnam also worried Daley.[147]

The uneasiness and ambivalence of Democrats of the Old Politics toward LBJ and the war in Vietnam were amplified in the direct correlation between the public's perception of the effectiveness of LBJ's Vietnam policies and LBJ's over-all public approval ratings throughout 1966. A Gallup poll released on January 3, 1966, indicated a 56 percent public approval of LBJ's handling of the Viet-nam War, and a Gallup poll released on February 2, 1966, showed a 59 percent public approval of LBJ's overall job performance.[148] A March 9, 1966, Gallup poll, however, showed a wider gap between these two indicators. This poll gave LBJ a 56 percent approval rating for his overall job performance as president while only 50 percent approved his policies in Vietnam.[149]

Gallup polls released on September 18 and September 21 revealed that LBJ's overall job approval rating had fallen to 48 percent while public approval of his Vietnam policies had declined to 43 percent.[150] In his analysis of LBJ's use of polls and their impact on his political and policy behavior, political scientist Bruce E. Altschuler stated that "polls provided Johnson with the illusion that short-term approaches could succeed in reversing the decline. Even worse, they were used to reinforce his own rationalizations that there was no real decline."[151]

Johnson was well aware of how midterm election results were often used to assess the current status of public opinion toward a president and his policies. He chafed under the characterization and personification of the Vietnam War as "Johnson's War" by hawks and doves who disagreed with his policies. LBJ was confident, though, that he could revitalize the middle-class, centrist base of his suprapartisan consensus, improve his poll ratings, and thus minimize Demo-cratic losses in the 1966 elections by a dramatic, highly publicized trip to Asia that included a visit with American troops.[152] LBJ carefully timed his signing of bills increasing and expanding coverage of the minimum wage, creating the Department of Transportation (DOT), and enacting omnibus urban aid and housing provisions that included the Demonstration (or Model) Cities program to occur immediately before the November 8, 1966 elections.

Despite the turbulent, fundamental changes in American politics and public opinion that had occurred since Johnson became president, the Texan persisted in his assumption that most voters would reward a president and his party in elections if they proved to the voters that they were productive, effective, and responsible in both foreign and domestic policies. Thus, LBJ wanted to keep Congress in session as long as possible in 1966. This reduced the time that House Democrats could spend in their districts campaigning for reelection.[153]

In preparing for the 1966 congressional elections, LBJ paid little or no attention to the importance of party organization, especially the relationship between the DNC's apparatus and local Democratic Party organizations. In early 1965, there was much fanfare about how the DNC headquarters planned to help House Democratic freshmen with direct mail operations, speechwriting, policy research and data, computer, radio, and television services and fundraising. Soon, though, in the name of cost cutting, debt reduction, and efficiency, (W.) Marvin Watson, apparently at the direction of LBJ, ordered substantial budget cuts, fewer services, and layoffs at the DNC headquarters.[154] One year later, *Wall*

Street Journal columnist Alan L. Otten wrote, "Lyndon B. Johnson's behavior, always unpredictable, is at its most unfathomable in his current treatment of the Democratic National Committee and the freshman Democrats in Congress."[155] Otten speculated that LBJ "also appears sincerely to feel that by November this Vietnam policy will be a big plus for those Democratic candidates who support it—and he doesn't much worry about those who don't."[156]

There had been speculation that LBJ might reduce domestic spending and end, or at least suspend, further Great Society policy initiatives in order to reduce inflation and budget deficits. He presumably wanted to strengthen bipartisan support for his Vietnam policies and defense spending among fiscal conservatives and moderates of both parties.[157] LBJ, however, unequivocally dismissed this impression in his January 12, 1966, State of the Union address. He stated that "we will not permit those who fire upon us in Vietnam to win a victory over the desires and the intentions of all the American people. This nation is mighty enough, its society is healthy enough, its people are strong enough, to pursue our goals in the rest of the world while still building a Great Society here at home."[158]

By vowing the continuation of higher levels of both domestic and defense spending, LBJ unwittingly added another facet to Democratic dissensus. His rhetoric and policy behavior gradually alienated both hawks and doves among Democrats in Congress as the former blamed the Great Society programs and the latter blamed the escalation of the Vietnam War for rising inflation, interest rates, and budget deficits and the prospect of higher taxes after the midterm elections.[159] As early as the fall of 1965, Harris polls indicated that public approval of LBJ's job performance regarding inflation had declined from 44 to 28 percent between March and October of 1965.[160]

Johnson neglected the typical party leadership activities of campaign appearances and fundraising for his party's most vulnerable incumbents seeking reelection in 1966. Instead, he calculated that the voters would favorably respond to the legislative productivity of the Eighty-ninth Congress and his highly publicized "peace offensive" of late October and early November of 1966. The president expressed his relatively few, harshly partisan attacks on the Republicans in his respective campaign appearances in Newark, New Jersey, and Staten Island, New York on October 7 and 12. Most of LBJ's October 7 speech in Newark detailed and praised Democratic progress in domestic policy in sharp contrast to Republican inertia and obstructionism. The president also criticized the Republicans for not knowing "how to end the war in Vietnam, except to denounce the Commander in Chief."[161] Likewise, in his October 12 speech on Staten Island, LBJ stated, "The Republicans remember that the only way they have ever elected people is by scaring people. They always go back to one word—fear."[162]

Despite such sporadic, partisan rhetoric, LBJ risked much of the outcome of the 1966 elections on the hope that a successful foreign policy summit in Asia and a highly publicized visit with American troops in Vietnam would restore a suprapartisan, centrist policy consensus on his Vietnam policies and minimize Democratic losses as an expression of public discontent. At the October 24–25 conference in Manila, the leaders of SEATO and ANZUS nations, especially President Ferdinand Marcos of the Philippines, pledged to send more troops to Vietnam as an expression of united, allied participation in a collective security effort in Southeast Asia against Communist aggression in Vietnam.

In Manila, LBJ issued a declaration that politically resembled FDR's Four Freedoms Speech of 1941 and Atlantic Charter Conference with Winston Churchill. Johnson and the six other heads of state announced Goals of Freedom for Vietnam and the rest of Southeast Asia. These seven leaders also agreed with a statement from the South Vietnamese government that they would withdraw their troops "as soon as peace was restored."[163] In his memoirs, LBJ elaborated that the Declaration of Peace and Progress in Asia and the Pacific announced at the Manila conference encapsulated the essence of his foreign policy. "If there was a Johnson Doctrine, these were its cornerstones: opposition to aggression; war against poverty, illiteracy, and disease; economic, social, and cultural cooperation on a regional basis; searching for reconciliation and peace."[164]

The enlightened and humanitarian values and objectives that LBJ attributed to the so-called Johnson Doctrine were less evident in some of his statements expressed to American troops in Vietnam or in the apparently self-serving political purpose of the final declaration from the Manila conference. LBJ's occasionally bellicose language among American troops urged them to "come home with the coonskin on the wall."[165] The final declaration from the Manila conference on October 25 stated that the United States and its allies in the Vietnam War would withdraw their troops "as soon as possible and not later than six months after the above conditions have been fulfilled."[166]

The specification of a timed yet conditional withdrawal of American troops was a blatant attempt to appeal to war-weary American voters.[167] During the Manila conference, LBJ was careful to prevent General William Westmoreland's request for more troops from being leaked to the media. The *Pentagon Papers* noted, "McNamara and Johnson were not politically and militarily enchanted with a costly major force increase at that time, nor with the cross-border and air operations which ran grave political risks."[168]

There was a sharp, disingenuous contrast between LBJ's publicly announced willingness to conduct a quick yet conditional American withdrawal from Vietnam and his private yet reluctant plans to increase American troops in Vietnam and raise taxes after the midterm elections. LBJ's credibility gap with the media and beleaguered Democratic candidates widened further as he returned to the United States. Press secretary Bill Moyers previously announced that LBJ would conduct a fifteen-state, four-day campaign swing that included California, Oregon, Missouri, and Illinois.[169]

Instead, LBJ told a perplexed, skeptical press corps on November 4, 1966, "First, we don't have any plans, so when you don't have plans, you don't cancel plans."[170] Speaking at his ranch, LBJ truculently added, "We have no plans for any political speeches between now and the election. We know no requirement that we forgo them. I just don't think they are necessary."[171]

Governor Edmund G. "Pat" Brown of California was an endangered Democratic incumbent who had been anticipating and depending on campaign appearances by LBJ to mobilize enough blacks, Hispanics, and labor union members to help him win reelection. Brown was first elected governor in 1958 as a New Deal liberal who promised to improve state services and the public infrastructure and as a reaction of voters against the 1957–1958 recession. He easily defeated Richard M. Nixon in 1962 because of his record as a competent administrator and Nixon's evident lack of interest and experience in state and local issues. In the June 1966 Democratic gubernatorial primary, Brown narrowly won renomination by defeating Sam Yorty, a maverick, conservative Democrat and the outspoken, law-and-order mayor of Los Angeles.

Brown moved toward the political center by trying to co-opt Yorty's voters in the primary and distancing himself from the farm worker movement of Cesar Chavez, black civil rights leaders, and liberal activists who were identified with the antiwar movement and campus unrest.[172] Until the end of the general election campaign, Brown did not regard Ronald Reagan as a serious threat to his reelection. Brown's campaign ridiculed the prospect of a failed, mediocre actor with no prior experience in elective public office being elected governor of California.[173] But the Republican gubernatorial nominee gradually narrowed the gap in the polls between himself and Brown.[174]

Realizing that they would get little or no help from LBJ or the DNC, Brown's campaign strategists targeted Reagan's right-wing affiliations and rhetoric and his prominent campaigning for Barry Goldwater in 1964. But they failed to convincingly portray and delegitimize Reagan as a dangerous, right-wing extremist unfit for the governorship. Reagan's friendly, open accessibility to reporters covering his campaign and his folky, populist conservative rhetoric blunted the Brown campaign's ideological attacks.[175] Although Democrats greatly outnumbered Republicans among California voters, this state's tradition and practice of weak party loyalty meant that Brown could not rely on this numerical advantage. After all, Brown was a former Republican, and Reagan was a Democrat until 1962.

Despite polls and media commentary predicting a close election result, Reagan overwhelmed Brown by receiving 58 percent of the votes. Blacks, Hispanics, union members, and liberal activists expressed little enthusiasm for Brown's candidacy through their low voter turnout and the governor's surprisingly narrow majorities in the most liberal, Democratic areas of northern California. Reagan performed especially well among traditionally Democratic, white, rural voters in central California and among middle-class Hispanics. He also benefited from a high voter turnout and landslide victory margins among conservative suburbanites in southern California.[176]

In gubernatorial races, the Republicans made a net gain of eight seats in 1966. It was difficult for the Democrats to persuasively dismiss these results as a typical, predictable decision of voters to seek change in party control of governorships in midterm elections. With controversial tax increases and scandals in his administration, Nelson Rockefeller was reelected governor of New York. He defeated his Democratic opponent, Frank O'Connor, by a 6 percent margin in a four-candidate race.[177] Rockefeller's brother Winthrop became the first Republican governor of Arkansas. George Romney and John Rhodes, the Republican governors of Michigan and Ohio, were reelected by landslide margins. Pennsylvania voters continued Republican control of their state's governorship by electing Raymond P. Shafer to succeed Governor William Scranton. The traditionally Democratic states of Florida and Maryland also elected Republican governors, and Howard Callaway, a Republican, was almost elected governor of Georgia.[178]

In the Senate, the Republicans achieved a net gain of three seats. In Massachusetts, Edward Brooke, that state's attorney general and a liberal Republican, became the first black to be elected to the Senate since the Reconstruction era. Charles H. Percy, an Illinois businessman who mediated conflicts between liberals and conservatives within the GOP over their party's 1960 platform, defeated three-term Democratic Senator Paul Douglas with 55 percent of the votes.[179] More so than any other issue, federal fair housing legislation that LBJ sought and Douglas supported damaged the Illinois Democrat's candidacy. Led by Martin Luther King, Jr., black demonstrations against housing discrimination in Chicago generated a white backlash vote against Douglas.[180]

Polls revealed that more Americans were discontented with inflation, crime, racial conflict, campus unrest, and the prospect of higher taxes and a stalemate in Vietnam. But there was no clear, consistent evidence that public opinion and voting behavior had sharply turned to the right ideologically in the 1966 gubernatorial and Senate elections. Victorious Republicans in these races included Goldwaterite conservatives like Reagan and Senator John Tower of Texas. Mark Hatfield, the liberal Republican governor of Oregon, was elected to the Senate in 1966. He defeated a Democratic congressman, Robert Duncan, who was a staunch supporter of LBJ's policies in Vietnam.[181] Hatfield had nationally distinguished himself as the only Republican governor to vote against a resolution supporting the war in Vietnam at the Governors Conference in Los Angeles in April 1966.[182]

It was also not clear that Republican victories for these statewide offices were, except in Illinois, products of the white backlash. There were several races in which voters chose racially moderate Republicans over racially conservative Democrats. In Maryland, George Mahoney, the Democratic nominee for governor, ran a George Wallace-type of race-baiting campaign. He dramatized his opposition to fair housing legislation and emphasized tough crime control to address racial conflict. Instead, voters in this mostly Democratic border state elected Spiro Agnew, an obscure, racially moderate Republican who favored fair housing legislation, as governor.[183]

It was uncertain if the Republican gains in Senate and gubernatorial elections of 1966 conveyed any consistent, national message to LBJ about the Vietnam War and racial issues. Journalist Thomas Powers concluded, "The election of 1966 registered an indisputable discontent with the leadership of President Johnson, but failed to say anything unarguable about the war."[184] In Maine, once a Republican bastion that was one of only two states to vote against FDR in 1936, the 1966 elections yielded Democratic control of all of Maine's congressional seats. George J. Mitchell, the Democratic state chairman, proudly wrote to Maine Democrats, "We must now proceed to build upon this strong foundation an effective party organization which will assure us of even greater victories in future elections."[185] In a more ambivalently worded letter reflecting the national election results, Senator Edward M. Kennedy of Massachusetts told Mitchell, "Although there were many disappointments this year, I hope you agree with me that the Democratic Party of your State and throughout the Nation will emerge a stronger and more vital organization."[186]

Kennedy's reference to "many disappointments" euphemistically referred to the devastating losses that Democrats suffered in the U.S. House elections of 1966. The Republicans made a net gain of forty-seven House seats in 1966, exceeding the Democratic net gain of thirty-eight House seats in 1964.[187] While the Democrats gained approximately 500 seats in state legislatures in 1964, the Republicans gained 557 state legislative seats in 1966.[188] The Supreme Court's reapportionment decisions from 1962 to 1964 affected the redistricting of congressional and state legislative districts. Democratic strategists, however, had miscalculated and erroneously concluded that reapportionment would benefit Democratic candidates by increasing the electoral power of voters in major cities and blacks in the Deep South. They expected a sharp increase in voter registration and turnout among blacks, especially in the South.

Instead, reapportionment influenced the results of the 1966 congressional and state legislative elections by increasing the electoral influence of white voters in suburbs, especially in suburbs that surrounded major cities in the South and West.[189] In the South, the number of Republican congressional seats doubled from fourteen to twenty-eight between 1962 and 1966.[190] In Iowa, reapportionment reduced the voting power of traditionally Republican, sparsely populated rural areas while increasing the voting power of the more Democratic cities and suburbs. Nevertheless, Democrats won six of Iowa's seven congressional seats in 1964, but only two of them in 1966.[191]

The Democratic net loss of forty-seven House seats in 1966 was virtually the same as the Republican net loss of forty-eight House seats in 1958. Almost the same percentages of House incumbents, 90 percent in 1958 and 88 percent in 1966, were reelected in these midterm elections.[192] The weakening of party loyalty and growth of split-ticket voting, though, were evident between 1958 and 1966.[193] The percentages of party-line voters (i.e., Democratic or Republican identifiers who voted for the nominees of their parties), in House elections were 84 percent in 1958 and 76 percent in 1966. More ominously for the Democrats, all of the Democratic nominees for U.S. House seats in 1966 received 50.9 percent of all votes nationally, the lowest Democratic percentage since the Eisenhower sweep of 1952.[194]

The key to the Republican success in the 1966 elections was organization. Since 88 percent of all House incumbents were reelected in 1966, most of the Republican gains resulted from winning open seats vacated by retiring Democrats.[195] Orchestrated by RNC chairman Ray C. Bliss and former vice president Richard M. Nixon, the Republican strategy was non-ideological and pragmatic. It recruited, financed, advised, and promoted attractive Republican candidates for the U.S. House, regardless of ideological, policy, and factional differences among them. Thus, the RNC headquarters and Nixon's "Congress '66" organization assisted conservative Goldwaterites in the South and Southwest as well as moderate and liberal Republicans in the Northeast and Midwest.[196]

While DNC chairman John M. Bailey was often ignored by LBJ and received no clear guidelines about his role in the 1966 elections, Bliss focused entirely on what he called the "basics" or "nuts and bolts" of national party chairmanship when he became RNC chairman in 1965.[197] He spurned the role of an "out-party" spokesman and avoided attracting media attention to himself. Instead, Bliss methodically strengthened and expanded Republican Party organization at the precinct level, especially in major cities, encouraged growth and activism among Young Republicans at colleges and universities and established training workshops and seminars for local party functionaries and campaign volunteers.[198] Bliss also raised an impressive campaign treasury whose funds were targeted at underfinanced yet promising Republican candidates. Bliss appointed Lucius D. Clay, a retired general and a hero of the 1948 Berlin airlift, as finance chairman of the RNC. The RNC raised $4 million in 1965 and $7.1 million in 1966.[199]

Bliss also succeeded in partially absorbing the Boosters Club. This $1,000-per-member fundraising organization was the Republican equivalent of JFK's and LBJ's President's Club. The Boosters Club began in 1965 as part of the Republican Congressional Campaign Committee (RCCC). Bliss persuaded the RCCC to move this club's office to RNC headquarters and serve under the direction of General Clay. Research fellow Stephen Hess and journalist David S.

Broder observed that "even though he did not control it, the Boosters operation fulfilled a major criterion of Bliss's finance program: big money was raised
early and given to politicians to dispense without regard to their liberalism or
conservatism but solely on the basis of where the investment might pay the
greatest return."[200]

In preparation for the 1966 and later the 1968 elections, Bliss prevented a
resumption of ideological factionalism over the Republican national platform
that could destroy the vote-getting potential of his party building efforts. After
learning that Republican governors wanted to hold a conference to rewrite the
controversial Goldwater-dominated platform of 1964, Bliss and Wisconsin congressman Melvin Laird established the Republican Coordinating Committee
(RCC). Its membership included Eisenhower, Nixon, and Goldwater. The wording and tone of this committee's policy statements reflected Bliss's desire to avoid
factional and ideological divisiveness within the GOP. Its bland, ideologically
inscrutable policy statements were intended to offend as few Republicans as
possible while trying to attract more independents, young voters, and disaffected
Democrats to the GOP. For example, the RCC stated that the GOP opposed
extremism on both the left and right and challenged the Democratic Party to
assume "the same position toward ALL extremists." On Vietnam, the RCC
expressed virtually the same position as LBJ. "Our purpose is and must be, once
again, to repel Communist aggression, to minimize American and Vietnamese
casualties, and to bring about a swift and secure peace."[201]

The Republicans succeeded in the 1966 elections, especially in House races,
through a "bottom up" campaign strategy. This strategy emphasized the
micromanagement of candidate recruitment, the raising and channeling of substantial campaign funds to key races, and the mechanics of grassroots party
organization. By contrast, Johnson persisted in employing a "top-down" campaign strategy in his party leadership.[202] He wanted to continue the appearance
of being a suprapartisan, centrist president who was dedicated to achieving an
honorable, responsible end to the war in Vietnam. He apparently hoped that his
October "peace offensive" in Asia would yield favorable media attention, high
public approval ratings in the polls, and only modest Democratic losses in the
midterm elections.[203]

In his first press conference after the November 8 elections, LBJ casually
and confidently deflected questions about the Republican gains. Instead of addressing the staggering Democratic losses in the House, he emphasized the fact
that the Democrats only lost three Senate seats, of which only one was that of
a defeated Democratic incumbent, Paul Douglas.[204] Johnson soon returned to
his 1964 theme of a suprapartisan, centrist policy consensus. He expressed
confidence that Republicans like Eisenhower and Dirksen would continue to
provide bipartisan cooperation in foreign and defense policies. Praising Republican support for his domestic policy legislation during the Eighty-ninth Congress,

the president optimistically concluded "that on most roll calls on passage of what you would call the Great Society bills, we had a good many members of the other party. I expect, if our recommendations are meritorious, that they will command the support from some of them in the days ahead."[205]

The content and tone of LBJ's 1967 State of the Union address were more defensive and accommodating toward the greater Republican presence in the House of Representatives and the revitalization of this chamber's bipartisan conservative coalition. In this January 10, 1967, message to Congress, the president balanced his defense of the progress made under the Great Society and his vow not to abandon it with a proposal for new crime control legislation and greater flexibility to state and local governments in federal anti-poverty and anti-crime programs.[206] In order to control inflation and "finance responsibly the needs of our men in Vietnam and the progress of our people at home," LBJ proposed a 6 percent surcharge on individual and corporate income "to last for two years or for so long as the unusual expenditures associated with our efforts in Vietnam continue."[207]

In foreign policy, LBJ's 1967 State of the Union address emphasized the need for the United States to continue to fulfill its commitments of more progress on nuclear arms control with the Soviet Union and of protecting South Vietnam "because the United States of America and our allies are committed by the SEATO Treaty to 'act to meet the common danger' of aggression in Southeast Asia."[208] In his conclusion, LBJ expressed confidence in his military and diplomatic strategy of restrained, responsible military action and a relentless search for an honorable peace in Vietnam.

As he did privately, LBJ responded more to his hawkish than dovish critics. Johnson observed that Americans were "being tested" in Vietnam according to whether "we can fight a war of limited objectives over a period of time, and keep alive the hope of independence and stability for people other than ourselves; whether we can continue to act with restraint when the temptation is to 'get it over with' is inviting but dangerous . . . whether we can do these without arousing the hatred and the passions that are ordinarily loosed in time of war—on all these questions so much turns."[209]

In his relationships with Congress, public opinion, and the Democratic Party, LBJ persisted in using the style, tone, and wording of a suprapartisan, centrist consensus to revitalize and strengthen his political base during the 1967–1968 sessions of the Ninetieth Congress. The president tried to achieve further liberal policy objectives, such as a federal fair housing law, gun control, and more federal programs directed at poor urban neighborhoods, through more moderate rhetoric and methods of implementation and cooperative relationships with leading moderate and liberal Republicans in Congress.

But the House Republicans were not only more numerous in this Congress, they were also more united and effective in defeating or diluting LBJ's domestic legislation, especially in committees.[210] On January 10, 1967, the same date as LBJ's State of the Union Address, the House voted to repeal the twenty-one-day rule, which had facilitated the passage of liberal legislation in the Eighty-ninth Congress. In addition to rejecting LBJ's proposals for a surcharge on income taxes, gun control, and a new civil rights bill that included a fair housing provision, Republicans and southern Democrats in the House greatly reduced LBJ's funding requests and the extent of federal regulations for highway beautification, model cities, rent supplements, and the Teacher Corps. Political scientist Norman J. Ornstein calculated that the bipartisan conservative coalition in the House of Representatives was victorious in 73 percent of the roll-call votes in 1967 compared to 32 percent in 1966. By contrast, the bipartisan conservative coalition's percentage of "victories" in the Senate remained virtually the same, 51 percent and 54 percent, respectively, in 1966 and 1967.[211]

Before the 1966 congressional elections were held and had such debilitating effects on LBJ's legislative leadership, journalist David S. Broder wrote in October 1966 that LBJ's consensus politics was an experiment that had failed. Broder cited LBJ's experience in the previously one-party politics of Texas and his failure to adapt to the competitive, two-party environment of national politics. LBJ's landslide victory in 1964 and his legislative success with the "Great Society Congress" made the Texan less likely to recognize the flaws of consensus politics in the long term and adapt accordingly.[212] Broder faulted LBJ's party leadership, like his legislative leadership and relationship with public opinion, for excessively relying on the top-down approach of the "Johnson treatment." Johnson tried to personally negotiate with and persuade interest group leaders, foreign leaders, and politicians of both parties toward a compromised solution to each conflict or issue. While a party organization functions vertically, LBJ's "consensus politics operates on horizontal lines" so that "it is almost inevitable that a consensus President from a one-party state would ignore the party organization."[213]

In concluding his critique of the "Johnsonian system" of consensus politics, Broder noted the growing intraparty discord and antipathy toward LBJ, especially among younger Democratic politicians and activists who "are forsaking his leadership. . . . The President barely speaks the language of this new generation. His methods are not likely to be carried over into their era of ascendancy."[214]

A few months after the 1966 elections, Doris Kearns, then a graduate student at Harvard, coauthored an article entitled "How to Remove LBJ in 1968" for the *New Republic*. This article reflected Broder's warning that LBJ's consensus politics alienated young liberal intellectuals and Democratic activists like Kearns. For her and coauthor Sanford Levinson, liberal activists and students were alienated not only by LBJ's policies in Vietnam but also by his leadership style that discouraged public debate and grassroots participation. Kearns and Levinson suggested a third party that represented students, blacks, and the poorest farmers and laborers in the 1968 presidential election. This was necessary to force both the Republicans and Democrats to make their decision-making and policymaking processes more inclusive and participatory.[215]

If LBJ is reelected, then "the likelihood is that the consensus will further fragment and be replaced by mass disorder and violence."[216] The authors assumed that the Republican Party would not nominate either Nixon or Reagan for president in 1968. Kearns and Levinson asserted that an antiwar, leftist third party that contributed to a Republican victory and a Democratic defeat in 1968 "would make it possible for an acceptable Republican to carry those states and thus win the presidency" and would ensure that "the first objective is achieved—the removal of Johnson, Rusk, and Rostow from power in the American government."[217]

The first formal, organized attempt to establish an antiwar, anti-LBJ third party was a fiasco. Its failure seemed to justify LBJ's dismissive trivialization of leftist, antiwar activists. In late August and early September of 1967, the National Conference for New Politics (NCNP) held a national convention in Chicago. The NCNP wanted to capitalize on Martin Luther King, Jr.'s outspoken opposition to the Vietnam War and on an April 18 antiwar rally at the United Nations. This demonstration attracted over 100,000 participants and featured King as a speaker.

Martin Peretz, a wealthy antiwar and pro-civil rights liberal, financed much of the establishment of the NCNP and hoped to create a third party that would nominate King for president and Benjamin Spock, the famous pediatrician, for vice president. Peretz wanted to develop a viable antiwar, leftist third party for the 1968 presidential election that would include the more mainstream antiwar liberals and civil rights leaders, such as anti-Johnson ADA members, King, the anti-nuclear bomb organization SANE, and the more militant, anti-establishment New Left groups, such as SNCC and the SDS.[218]

Peretz evidently sought to co-opt radicals into the conventional political system as a means of redressing their grievances and sharing the mutual disdain of the delegates at the NCNP convention, black and white, liberal and radical, for LBJ and the Vietnam War. To the dismay of Peretz, the NCNP convention was soon dominated by the most extreme, militant leaders of SNCC and young white radicals. Peretz and many of the other older, antiwar liberals were Jewish. But SNCC delegates and their white allies devoted an inordinate amount of time and effort to denouncing Israel's foreign and defense policies because of the Six Day War. The black caucus of delegates soon overwhelmed the NCNP convention and won adoption of its Thirteen Points, the equivalent of a platform for the NCNP. The thirteen-point program included a characterization of the Six Day War as "the imperialist Zionist War," the personification of the "savage and beast like character that runs rampant in America" by LBJ and American Nazi leader George Lincoln Rockwell, the creation of an all-black armed militia, and a denunciation of a "United States system that is committed to the practice of genocide, social degradation, and the denial of political and cultural self-determination of black people."[219]

The divisiveness and irresolution of the NCNP convention were enumerated by its vote to decide whether the NCNP would create a third party for the 1968 presidential election or support local organization efforts for a variety of leftist causes and candidates. The delegates voted 13,519 to 13,517 to support local organizing over a third party.[220] The NCNP quickly dissolved as a meaningful political organization and a serious threat to LBJ's renomination in 1968.[221]

The more persistent, white, antiwar liberals who participated in the NCNP convention left Chicago disillusioned with their failed effort to coalesce with the New Left and Black Power movements. But they were still determined to force LBJ to withdraw from the presidential race. They decided to work within the Democratic Party to legitimize and politically empower antiwar, anti-LBJ sentiment at the party's local and state levels through their grassroots activism in several Democratic congressional and presidential primaries. Peretz eventually joined Eugene McCarthy's presidential campaign in making this transition from the NCNP.[222]

Peretz and other white, antiwar liberals had abandoned any hope of forming a politically effective antiwar, anti-LBJ coalition with the New Left, Old Left, and Black Power movement. But they were still pessimistic about the feasibility of working within the Democratic Party to force LBJ to withdraw from the presidential race and hasten an end to the war in Vietnam. Allard Lowenstein, however, was convinced that a successful challenge to LBJ's renomination could be launched if he found an attractive, antiwar presidential candidate to run in two key primaries, California and Wisconsin.

Lowenstein was a student organizer who had previously served as president of the National Student Association (NSA). On February 13, 1967, the NSA confirmed published reports that it had received substantial funding from the CIA, primarily for the purposes of financing its various seminars on foreign policy, student exchange programs, and the foreign travel of NSA officials, in order to prevent Communist infiltration of the NSA. The NSA did not receive CIA funds while Lowenstein was its president, but the SDS, SNCC, and other youth-oriented New Left organizations distrusted and scorned Lowenstein because of the NSA-CIA connection.[223]

Ironically, the fact the NSA-CIA connection made Lowenstein repugnant to the New Left increased his credibility with antiwar, anti-Communist liberals, such as ADA members and reform Democrats in New York, California, and major university communities who identified more with Adlai Stevenson than the Kennedys. Lowenstein's legitimacy as an antiwar Democrat and reputation as an effective campaigner were further enhanced in a 1966 Democratic congressional primary in New York City.[224] Although he failed to defeat the incumbent Democratic congressman for the nomination, Lowenstein ran a competitive race for the reform Democrats as their candidate to oppose Representative Leonard Farbstein.[225] Historian William H. Chafe observed, "In the end, Lowenstein had run a superb race. . . . Once again, as in college, he waged the good fight on issues of principle, in the process mobilizing a band of devoted followers who would never forget their introduction to politics, not least because of the bittersweet taste of feeling morally victorious even though politically defeated."[226]

More politically pragmatic by 1967, Lowenstein helped to persuade the California Democratic Council (CDC) to vote in March 1967 to run a slate of antiwar delegates against LBJ in that state's 1968 Democratic presidential primary. Although Lowenstein was a vice chairman of the ADA, he failed to persuade ADA leaders to adopt a resolution opposing LBJ's renomination at its September 1967 board meeting. Joseph L. Rauh, Jr. convinced most other leading ADA members that opposing LBJ's renomination was futile and that the ADA should sponsor a peace plank for the 1968 Democratic national platform.[227]

In lobbying the ADA's executive board, Allard Lowenstein found a valuable ally, Curtis Gans, for his Dump Johnson movement. Gans was a staff aide to the ADA and a founder of the SDS. Lowenstein and Gans were able to recruit younger, more outspoken antiwar ADA members in local chapters, raise funds from wealthy antiwar liberals in California and New York, and network with antiwar organizations, especially those consisting of students and faculty in large, liberal academic communities, such as Berkeley, Ann Arbor, and Madison, Wisconsin. During the summer and fall of 1967, their embryonic Dump Johnson movement grew further in participants, finances, and local chapters as major antiwar demonstrations were held in New York, California, and Washington, DC. Lowenstein urged students at the NSA's August convention at the University of Maryland to end the war by opposing LBJ's renomination.[228]

Besides organizing a grassroots movement of thousands of students and faculty to volunteer in California, Lowenstein privately lobbied liberal Democratic politicians for their support of the Dump Johnson movement. He tried to convince them of the growing electoral appeal of this movement among white, middle-class voters. He realized that he could not gain the assistance of these dovish politicians in key primary states unless he recruited a well-known, viable, dovish Democratic presidential candidate to oppose LBJ for the nomination.[229]

Not surprisingly, RFK was Lowenstein's top choice. Although RFK was one of the less outspoken, more moderate doves among Democratic senators, his animosity toward Johnson and fierce ambition to become president were well known. Since his 1964 Senate campaign, RFK had tried to be equally appealing to both party regulars and reform Democrats in the faction-ridden, byzantine Democratic politics of New York.[230] Lowenstein was known to RFK as a leading reform Democrat in Manhattan and for being refuted by the New Left. He was confident that he could gain direct access to RFK and persuade the senator to run for president in 1968.

Fortunately for Lowenstein, most of RFK's Senate aides were currently urging RFK to run against LBJ for the 1968 presidential nomination. On the day after the 1966 midterm elections, Adam Walinsky, a staff member and speechwriter for RFK, submitted the senator a memo stating, "Lyndon Johnson is a lame duck."[231] Throughout 1967, Frank Mankiewicz, RFK's press secretary, Richard Goodwin, a former speechwriter for LBJ, Peter Edelman, an aide on domestic policy, and other members of RFK's inner circle emphasized the political feasibility and the moral imperative of an antiwar, anti-LBJ presidential candidacy in 1968. In response to this lobbying, RFK seemed, at best, indecisive, and, more often, pessimistic about the ability of anyone to deny LBJ renomination if the Texan sought another term.

RFK's Senate staff readily welcomed Allard Lowenstein's effort to persuade RFK to run for president. After Lowenstein learned that RFK was flying to Los Angeles to attend a Democratic fundraiser on August 4, 1967, he took the same flight as RFK. Frank Mankiewicz traded seats with Lowenstein so that the former NSA president could sit next to RFK to lobby the senator. RFK firmly told Lowenstein that he would not run for president in 1968. RFK also warned Lowenstein not to become involved with the California Democratic Council (CDC). The New York senator regarded the CDC as a collection of left-wing extremists.[232]

Disappointed by RFK's rebuff, Lowenstein persisted in trying to recruit a Democratic presidential candidate. He admired Don Edwards, a Democratic congressman from San Jose, for Edwards's early opposition to LBJ's policies in Vietnam. In May 1965, Edwards joined six other House members in opposing a supplementary defense spending bill requested by LBJ for the rising costs of the Vietnam War. Edwards was also a former national chairman of the ADA and repeatedly tried to end funding for HUAC.[233] Edwards, though, declined Lowenstein's offer of support for a presidential candidacy.

The most fortuitous event of Lowenstein's August trip to California was his meeting with Gerald Hill, a San Francisco attorney and chairman of the CDC. On August 5, the day after he spoke with RFK, Hill and Lowenstein agreed to open and raise funds for a national campaign office in Washington, DC, for an organization that they named the Conference of Concerned Democrats (CCD). Hill told Lowenstein that he had contacted several dovish Democratic senators about running an antiwar slate of delegates in the 1968 Democratic presidential primary in California. Of them, only Senator Eugene McCarthy of Minnesota seemed seriously interested in his reply to Hill. McCarthy wrote to Hill that he would like to meet him in Los Angeles in late October. Lowenstein joined Hill and McCarthy for breakfast at the Ambassador Hotel in Los Angeles on October 20, 1967. Although McCarthy did not definitely state that he would run in the California presidential primary, Hill and Lowenstein left the hotel confident that he would become their antiwar candidate.[234]

From August until McCarthy announced his antiwar presidential candidacy on November 30, 1967, Lowenstein, Hill, Gans, and other members of the

CCD were busy raising funds, establishing local chapters in key primary states and major university communities, and trying to obtain the endorsement of regular Democratic politicians, Young Democrats, and local party chairmen. They succeeded in recruiting the Democratic state chairman of Michigan, Young Democrats in several midwestern states, the local Democratic chairman of Eau Claire, Wisconsin, and a Minnesota state representative. Perhaps the greatest public relations victory for the CCD in gaining national credibility with antiwar liberals before McCarthy's November 30 announcement was a front-page endorsement of the CCD from the *New Republic*.[235]

McCarthy's November 30 announcement provided unexpected, yet ideal, timing for the CCD's national convention that began on December 2, 1967, in Chicago. This convention attracted almost five hundred participants from forty-two states. Although their ranks included Democratic congressmen, state legislators, and members of state and local Democratic committees, a disproportionate number of the conventioners were academics and Stevensonian reform Democrats from California, New York, and the upper Midwest. After Allard Lowenstein gave the CCD convention a rousing, vitriolic denunciation of LBJ and the Vietnam War, Eugene McCarthy's speech was anticlimactic in tone, style, and content. McCarthy did not explicitly denounce Johnson and carefully avoided any rhetorical effort to emotionally appeal to the conventioneers, especially the students. Instead, he calmly and blandly quoted historical references from the Punic Wars, the Dreyfus case, and Adlai Stevenson's acceptance speech at the 1952 Democratic national convention. He did not specifically critique LBJ's diplomatic and military decisions in Vietnam and propose a dovish alternative. Rather, he vaguely referred to the American conduct of the war in Vietnam as immoral, domestically divisive, and detrimental to its relationships with other democratic nations.[236]

Following his speech, the solitary, aloof senator refused to address the thousands of students who waited to meet him or mingle with the CCD delegates. He told his staff that he would never again make a speech after Lowenstein.[237] Lowenstein was soon marginalized in the McCarthy campaign. McCarthy generally relied on Blair Clark, a wealthy Democrat and former CBS executive, to raise campaign funds and schedule his appearances. He depended on Curtis Gans and Sam Brown to organize student and faculty volunteers for his upcoming primary campaigns. Lowenstein tried to indirectly improve McCarthy's campaign through consultations with Gans and Brown.[238]

Eugene McCarthy persisted in his pensive, plodding campaign style. He seemed oblivious and occasionally dismissive toward the antiwar, anti-LBJ fervor of his mostly young, academic supporters. Until McCarthy's unexpectedly strong, close, second-place finish to LBJ's write-in candidacy in New Hampshire's Democratic presidential primary, the rhetoric and purpose of McCarthy's campaign were consistent with the November 30 announcement of his presidential candidacy. For three and a half months, the Minnesota senator spoke and behaved as if he were not seriously trying to defeat LBJ for their party's nomination and become president. McCarthy's campaign was, in the words of journalist Thomas Powers, "a one-issue referendum" on the Vietnam War.[239]

In retrospect, Eugene McCarthy revealed his shrewdness and insight rather than his reputed laziness and apathy. He made the unpopularity of the war, rather than his own qualifications, the political feasibility of his becoming president, or personal attacks on LBJ, as the entire raison d'etre of his campaign. McCarthy thereby attracted a broader, more diverse spectrum of primary voters to his campaign.

The Tet Offensive of late January 1968 sharply increased the desire of voters in key primary states like New Hampshire and Wisconsin to electorally express their disapproval of LBJ's policies in Vietnam. Both hawks and doves were angry at what they perceived as confirmation of LBJ's duplicity and incompetence in ending the war. A vote for Eugene McCarthy, with his bland, middle-aged, midwestern presence, seemed moderate and reasonable, rather than radical or unpatriotic to a growing number of middle-aged, middle-class voters who distrusted and disliked LBJ and his policies in Vietnam.[240] McCarthy's dovish proposal for a political settlement of the war and a gradual withdrawal of American troops attracted the scorn and denunciation of the New Left. This leftist criticism of McCarthy's position further made his candidacy seem moderate and legitimate to mainstream voters.[241]

Despite Lowenstein's insistence that he remained loyal to McCarthy's campaign, his unflagging devotion to RFK, alienation from McCarthy, and confidence that the Tet Offensive and the New Hampshire primary results confirmed the political feasibility of an antiwar candidacy for president motivated him to privately encourage RFK to enter the race.[242] By this time, most of RFK's inner circle, including historian Arthur M. Schlesinger, Jr., and pragmatic campaign professionals like Fred Dutton and Kenneth P. O'Donnell, were urging RFK to announce his presidential candidacy. EMK and Theodore C. Sorensen persisted in cautioning RFK to wait until 1972 to run for president.[243]

RFK was well aware of his assets and liabilities as an antiwar candidate against LBJ. In addition to his family's vast wealth for campaign finance, the New York senator had immediate access to some of the best campaign professionals, pollsters, and speechwriters in the nation. His impassioned rhetoric, youthful looks, and unconventional domestic policy proposals, which now included some of the New Left's criticism of corporate liberalism, labor leaders, and big bureaucracies, and embodiment of his martyred brother's presidency held the potential for attracting not only young, antiwar college students but also blacks, Hispanics, blue-collar Catholics, and the more dovish yet politically calculating Democratic politicians like Jesse Unruh.[244]

But RFK's liabilities were equally formidable. In addition to Johnson, RFK's critics on both the left and right perceived the New York senator as amorally opportunistic, ruthless, and impatiently ambitious to become president by exploiting the memory of the slain JFK. Johnson had long assumed that, in order to gain political advantage over him, RFK was equally willing to criticize the president's policies in Vietnam from both the dovish left and hawkish right.[245] RFK also faced the challenge of restoring his credibility with the media. After all, he had repeatedly and publicly stated throughout 1967 and in early 1968 that he had no intention of running for president in 1968. During his 1964 Senate campaign, RFK assured the voters of New York that if he were elected to the Senate he wanted to do a good job representing them so that he could be reelected in 1970 and, at the earliest, would only consider a presidential candidacy in 1972.

Moreover, RFK had periodically praised LBJ and pledged his support for the president's renomination and reelection in 1968. On June 3, 1967, RFK introduced LBJ at a Democratic fundraising dinner in New York. Kennedy effusively praised Johnson for bearing "the burdens few other men have even borne in the history of the world. . . . He has sought consensus, but he has never shrunk from controversy. He has gained huge popularity, but he has never failed to spend it in pursuit of his beliefs. . . . In 1964 he won the greatest popular victory in modern times, and with our help he will do so again in 1968."[246]

On December 10, 1967, less than two weeks after Eugene McCarthy announced his presidential candidacy, LBJ asked White House aide Ben Wattenberg to have DNC treasurer John Criswell, rather than DNC chairman John M. Bailey, distribute copies of RFK's flattering remarks to every DNC member in every state.[247] At his December 19 press conference, LBJ slyly insinuated that McCarthy and RFK were collaborating in the same campaign. "I don't know what the effect of the Kennedy-McCarthy movement is having in the country . . . I am not privileged to all of the conversations that have taken place . . . I do know of the interest of both of them in the Presidency and the ambition of both of them. I see that reflected from time to time."[248]

LBJ perceived McCarthy to be a stalking horse for RFK's de facto yet unannounced presidential candidacy. His assumption overlooked the long-standing animosity between McCarthy and the Kennedys. Ironically, RFK still bitterly regarded McCarthy's rousing nominating speech for Adlai Stevenson at the 1960 Democratic national convention to be part of a well-orchestrated Johnson strategy to deadlock the convention and nominate LBJ for president.[249] Nevertheless, through EMK as his liaison, RFK offered to conduct a joint, antiwar, anti-LBJ primary campaign with McCarthy in Wisconsin.[250] McCarthy refused.

RFK's essential decision to formally announce his presidential candidacy was further complicated by a poorly timed statement to the media. On March 13, 1968, the day after the New Hampshire primary, RFK told reporters, "I am actively reconsidering the possibilities that are available to me, and I imagine that other people around the country are doing the same." He further added that he was "reassessing the possibility of whether I will run against President Johnson."[251]

These unprepared remarks further complicated the task of RFK's speechwriters. The wording and tone of RFK's declaration of his candidacy had to convey noble, unselfish reasons for his pursuit of the presidency. RFK also had to assure a skeptical public that he was not entering the presidential race because of animosity toward Johnson or resentment of McCarthy's unexpectedly strong performance in New Hampshire.[252] In particular, the younger members of RFK's inner circle feared that the masses of student volunteers in McCarthy's campaign would be so bitter and suspicious toward RFK for apparently trying to exploit the results of the New Hampshire primary that they would never join his campaign. Feeling obligated to remain with McCarthy, Richard Goodwin observed in his memoirs, "By making his announcement only days after the New Hampshire primary, denying the McCarthy workers time to savor their victory, to let their sense of invincibility fade in the light of political realities, Bobby had incurred a harsh, hostile resentment among McCarthy's legions."[253]

The compromised, revised text that RFK and his advisors produced for his March 16 declaration of candidacy included elements of damage control for his March 13 remarks. His declaration also sought to apply a broader, more comprehensive theme to his candidacy by synopsizing ideas from the senator's book, *To Seek a Newer World*. It also expressed his disappointment with LBJ's seemingly callous, dismissive response to the Kerner Commission's report and policy recommendations regarding race-related urban riots. RFK announced his presidential candidacy in the same Senate caucus room that was the location of JFK's 1960 declaration of candidacy for president.

In his speech, RFK assured the public that his presidential candidacy was not a personal rivalry with Johnson and McCarthy. Instead, he wanted to advocate new policies to address not only an end to the Vietnam War but also the persistent, worsening problems of racial conflict, poverty, and alienated, angry youths. He insisted that he had to wait to enter the presidential campaign until the New Hampshire primary was concluded or else "my presence in the race would have been seen as a clash of personalities rather than issues."[254] RFK was careful to praise Johnson for his "utmost loyalty" to JFK and kindness toward the Kennedys following JFK's assassination. Also, "I have often commended his efforts in health, in education, and in many other areas, and I have the deepest sympathy for the burden that he carries today."[255] Nonetheless, the senator felt compelled to oppose LBJ for the presidential nomination because of "our profound differences over where we are heading and what we want to accomplish."[256]

Despite its tactful, respectful references to Johnson, RFK's announcement was skeptically and even harshly received by the print media. Tom Wicker's article for the *New York Times* was headlined, "Kennedy to Make 3 Primary Races; Attacks Johnson." In the second sentence of his article, Wicker wrote,

"With this severe attack on President Johnson, the brother of President Kennedy opened what may become the most serious challenge to the renomination of an incumbent President since Theodore Roosevelt failed to oust William H. Taft in 1912."[257] In general, the reaction of columnists to RFK's announcement was hardly flattering. It reaffirmed their long-held suspicion that RFK had been scheming to restore Kennedy control of the White House since JFK's assassination. He merely waited for the best opportunity and was too cautious, calculating, and even cowardly to enter the race until he analyzed the results of the New Hampshire primary.[258] Rejecting EMK's invitation to a St. Patrick's Day cocktail party honoring RFK's presidential candidacy, columnist Murray Kempton telegrammed EMK, "Your brother's announcement makes clear that St. Patrick did not drive all the snakes from Ireland."[259]

With little hope of attracting favorable coverage and commentary from the print media, RFK focused most of his efforts during the first two weeks of his campaign on privately lobbying Democratic Party leaders, especially governors, machine bosses, state and local committee chairmen, and DNC members, for their endorsements. As his campaign progressed, RFK primarily relied on Stephen Smith, his brother-in-law and 1964 Senate campaign manager, and EMK to fulfill this networking role. But RFK knew that he needed to personally contact politicians to persuade them to provide delegate support at the Democratic national convention. It was too late for RFK to enter the Wisconsin, Pennsylvania, and Massachusetts primaries. Any votes that he received as a write-in candidate would probably provide him with a distant, embarrassing third-place position behind McCarthy and LBJ. Such "losses" in these three primaries that he had not entered, especially in Massachusetts, could further damage his credibility with the power brokers at the convention. These party leaders would eventually select the presidential nominee since most of the delegates' votes at the 1968 convention would not be determined by binding primary results.[260]

RFK's adopted home state of New York would not hold its primaries until June 18, but RFK realized that he might suffer an embarrassingly narrow victory or even an upset defeat there. In 1964, RFK managed to easily win the Democratic senatorial nomination by first gaining the endorsements of party regulars and machine bosses like Peter Crotty of Buffalo, John English of Nassau County, Stanley Steingut of Brooklyn, and Representatives Charles Buckley and Adam Clayton Powell, Jr. RFK eventually gained enough support, however reluctant and ambivalent, from anti-machine reform Democrats and liberal activists to avoid a divisive contest for the Democratic senatorial nomination.[261]

By the time of RFK's March 16, 1968 announcement, the long-simmering resentment and distrust that reform Democrats and liberal activists in New York harbored toward him erupted in fury since many were McCarthy supporters. As a matter of fact, many were McCarthy's major financial backers and most articulate, influential advocates.[262] Furthermore, New York's Democratic senatorial primary held the prospect of a bitter intraparty conflict among a hawkish, pro-LBJ candidate, Representative Joseph Resnick, a leftist, dovish McCarthy supporter, Paul O'Dwyer, and an RFK ally, Eugene Nickerson.[263]

New York's party regulars were at least formally and publicly committed to LBJ's renomination. Nationally, Mayor Richard J. Daley of Chicago and most Democratic senators, ranging from hawks like Robert Byrd of West Virginia and Henry M. "Scoop" Jackson of Washington to doves like Wayne Morse of Oregon and Ernest Gruening of Alaska, the only senators who voted against the Gulf of Tonkin Resolution of 1964, publicly refuted RFK's candidacy. The *New York Times* published a poll on March 24, 1968, estimating that 65 percent of the nation's Democratic delegates would vote for LBJ's renomination at the party's August convention in Chicago.[264] But on that same day, the Gallup firm released a poll indicating that the Democratic voters surveyed preferred RFK to LBJ as their party's presidential nominee 44 percent to 41 percent. By contrast, in a different question, this poll's respondents preferred Johnson over McCarthy, 59 percent to 29 percent.[265]

Three days later, *New York Times* columnist James Reston wrote that the commitment of major labor leaders and big city mayors to LBJ's renomination meant little because of the decline of party organizations and the tumultuous political environment. He concluded, "This is, thanks to television, a more representative democratic process. The idea is getting around that politics is too serious a business to be left to politicians, just as war is too serious to be left to soldiers, and if this spreads even the will of an incumbent president can be overcome."[266]

Regardless of how much the power of party bosses and labor leaders over Democratic presidential nominations may have atrophied by 1968, the fact remained that during the first two weeks of RFK's campaign the party's power brokers remained committed to LBJ, however tenuously and superficially. Meanwhile, the masses of antiwar campaign volunteers, mostly college and graduate students, were even more enthusiastic about and devoted to McCarthy's campaign. RFK's strategy was to attract enough nationwide television coverage of his campaign appearances before large, enthusiastic crowds so that he could improve his poll ratings and gradually convince the party leaders who controlled the delegates that he was more likely to win the general election than LBJ. Before RFK embarked on a sixteen-state campaign trip during the first two weeks of his campaign, he and his staff made sure that their campaign's advance men organized overflowing, cheering crowds for his campaign speeches and motorcades. Jerry Bruno, RFK's chief advance man, later stated, "What I am sure of is that advance work has an enormous impact on campaigns and their outcome . . . the press and the media judge candidates by the visceral, physical facts—how big was the crowd, how many people turned out, were they turned on, or of failure."[267] Bruno also claimed that it was essential for a successful campaign relying on televised coverage to attractively project the candidate's personality. "Most people do not think of politics in terms of issues. They vote for people who strike them as being more honest, more trustworthy, more exciting, maybe sexier."[268]

Hoping to attract large numbers of student campaign workers, RFK made his initial campaign appearances at large universities in the Midwest and South. The Kennedy campaign's selection of Kansas State University, Vanderbilt University, and the University of Alabama reflected its strategy of symbolically using regionally and politically diverse locations. Televised coverage of RFK's appearances there could project the image of broad, national appeal for the Massachusetts-born, liberal, wealthy Catholic senator from New York. The mostly friendly reception that RFK attracted at the University of Alabama could also convey RFK's political courage in visiting the campus that he and JFK had integrated in 1963.[269] In staunchly Republican, agricultural, presumably hawkish Kansas, RFK was given a friendly reception by Kansas State University students and Governor James Pearson, a Republican.[270]

RFK's pollsters and staff assured RFK that the New York senator's visceral, long-held contempt for LBJ was now widespread among Americans. Regardless of differences in age, income, education, region, race, ideology, or positions on the Vietnam War, most Americans disliked and distrusted Johnson. RFK now felt free to caustically criticize not only LBJ's policies in Vietnam but also LBJ in general. Consequently, Kennedy's rhetoric at Kansas State University and other campuses during the first two weeks of campaign had an emotionally charged, dramatic tone that McCarthy's lacked. He was not constrained by charges of demagoguery and self-indulgent, ad hominem attacks on LBJ from his critics in the print media.[271]

In his March 18, 1968, speech at Kansas State University, RFK stated, "We are in a time of unprecedented turbulence, of danger and questioning. It is at its root a question of the national soul."[272] At Vanderbilt University, RFK expressed the value of dissent for Americans to correct their policy errors and injustices "and thus restore our place at the point of moral leadership, in our country, in our own hearts, and all around the world."[273] RFK's March 24 speech at the Greek Theatre in Los Angeles was perhaps his most scathing attack yet on LBJ's credibility and integrity. For RFK, the American moral and political crisis "is not simply the result of bad policies and lack of skill. It flows from the fact that for almost the first time the national leadership is calling upon the darker impulses of the American spirit—not, perhaps, deliberately but through its action and the example it sets—an example where integrity, truth, honor, and all the rest seem like words to fill out speeches rather than guiding beliefs."[274]

At his press conferences and in his speeches during the last two weeks of March, LBJ refused to publicly comment on RFK's campaign, other than to say that he was not surprised that the senator had entered the race. In his March 18 speech to the National Farmers Union and his March 25 speech to the AFL-CIO, the president criticized both hawkish and dovish opposition to his policies in Vietnam and made it clear that he would continue them. In his March 18 speech, LBJ compared the dovish position to the British appeasement of Hitler at the Munich conference. "But wanting peace, praying for peace, and desiring peace, as Chamberlain found out, doesn't always give you peace," he asserted.[275] On March 25, LBJ told the AFL-CIO, "Now, the America that we are building would be a threatened nation, if we let freedom and liberty die in Vietnam. We will do what must be done—we will do it both at home and we will do it wherever our brave men are called upon to stand."[276]

But the more unyielding LBJ sounded on his policies in Vietnam, the more unpopular he became. From February 18 to March 31, the president's public approval rating declined from 41 percent to 36 percent in the Gallup polls.[277] Gallup polls released on March 24 and March 27 revealed that Democratic voters surveyed preferred RFK over LBJ as their party's nominee and that Nixon defeated Johnson 41 percent to 39 percent in a trial heat.[278]

With Wisconsin's April 2 Democratic presidential primary approaching, Oliver Quayle reported to White House appointments secretary (W.) Marvin Watson that Eugene McCarthy was ahead of LBJ 43 to 34 percent in a poll that Quayle conducted in Wisconsin from March 23 to March 25. Since Republicans could vote in this open primary, Wisconsin Republicans preferred McCarthy to Johnson 58 to 19 percent.[279] Before leaving for Wisconsin to manage the president's dormant, dispirited write-in campaign in that primary, Lawrence F. O'Brien wrote to LBJ that "our problems in Vietnam transcend political consid-erations and our search for solutions must not be politically motivated. Never-theless, the widespread political anxieties I have found among out political friends and associates convince me that their fears reflect an ever deepening disenchant-ment among many segments of the population which have heretofore supported our actions in Vietnam."[280]

On March 31, 1968, two days before the Wisconsin primary, LBJ informed the nation that he would not seek or accept his party's presidential nomination. In the Wisconsin Democratic presidential primary, despite the voters' awareness of LBJ's withdrawal, the president received 34 percent of the votes to McCarthy's 56 percent. As write-in candidates, RFK received 6 percent while Hubert H. Humphrey and George Wallace each received approximately 0.5 percent of the votes.[281]

When RFK returned to New York from campaign appearances in New Mexico and Arizona, John Burns, New York's Democratic state chairman, in-formed RFK of LBJ's statement of withdrawal. At the beginning of his April 1 speech to the New York Overseas Press Club, RFK quoted the telegram that he sent to the president commending "new efforts for peace in Vietnam" and asked LBJ for "an opportunity to visit with you as soon as possible to discuss how we might work together in the interest of national unity during the coming months."[282] The remainder of this address was much more subdued than his recent speeches and was more respectful and deferential toward Johnson regarding the Vietnam War.

LBJ's March 31 speech provided RFK's campaign with both a dilemma and an opportunity. During the first two weeks of RFK's campaign, the New York senator's position on the Vietnam War had been more dovish than LBJ's but less dovish than McCarthy's. But LBJ had announced an end of American aerial bombings and of offensive military actions against North Vietnam and the beginning of peace negotiations with North Vietnam for a political settlement to end the war.[283]

Now, there were few meaningful differences between LBJ and RFK on the Vietnam War. Combined with LBJ's new, self-chosen status as a lame duck, it was less politically advantageous for RFK to continue his rhetorical theme of how the brutality, immorality, and failure of LBJ's policies in Vietnam and the prospect of his reelection threatened to worsen domestic policy conditions, world opinion of the United States, and the American public's distrust of its government. As journalist David Halberstam observed, LBJ's March 31 speech "destroyed Kennedy's most important issue, the war, and more important, removed his favorite opponent, for it was Johnson who made him look good, made him a necessity. . . . In the spring of this crucial year he had managed, because of his delayed entrance, to be at once too ruthless and too gutless for the liberals and the students, too radical for the middle class, too much the party man for some of the intellectuals, and too little the party man for some of the machines."[284]

LBJ's withdrawal from the presidential race and announcement of a bombing halt and the beginning of negotiations for an end to the Vietnam War freed RFK to devote most of his speeches' content to domestic issues, especially poverty and race relations, and to emphasize the need for Americans to reconcile their differences, resolve conflicts among themselves, and unite to develop a better, more just nation at home. RFK's speeches and motorcades continued to attract boisterous crowds, especially among blacks, Hispanics, and youths. The senator's rhetoric, though, seemed less rabble rousing and demagogic and more restrained and moderate to journalists and commentators.[285]

While the content and tone of Kennedy's campaign speeches changed after March 31, his objective remained the same. He formally entered his name as a candidate in six primaries. He energetically crisscrossed the nation to generate a bandwagon effect through televised news coverage and steadily improving poll ratings that the party bosses and their delegates at the Democratic national convention in Chicago would find irresistible. As April progressed, Martin Luther King, Jr., was assassinated on April 4, and Hubert H. Humphrey did not declare his presidential candidacy until April 27. Shortly after RFK learned of King's assassination, he urged blacks in Indianapolis not to resort to the mob violence that now engulfed other cities, including Washington, DC, and Chicago. In this speech, RFK concluded that "the vast majority of white people and the vast majority of black people in this country want to live together, want to improve the quality of our life, and want justice for all human beings who abide in our land."[286]

After attending King's funeral, RFK persisted in addressing the need for all Americans to work together to reduce not only race-related violence but also violent crime and the ubiquity of violence in American culture, such as the use of violent television shows to advertise toys for children.[287] The political impact of King's assassination on RFK's campaign meant that he was assured of overwhelming support from black voters in his six contested primaries. Monolithic support from black voters made it more likely that Democratic power brokers with large black constituencies, such as Mayor Richard J. Daley of Chicago and UAW president Walter Reuther, would back RFK at the Democratic national convention in August. His recent oratorical emphasis on national unity, healing, and cooperation in developing a more peaceful American society made him appear to be less of a divisive radical to white, middle-aged, middle-class Americans.[288]

Hubert H. Humphrey waited until the end of April to declare his presidential candidacy, so it was too late for him to formally enter any of the remaining primaries. By limiting the contested primaries to Kennedy and McCarthy, Humphrey evidently hoped to use the Old Politics strategy of presenting himself as the safest choice among the three Democratic presidential candidates to boss-controlled delegates, interest group leaders, big-city mayors, Democratic members of Congress, DNC members, and Democratic state and local chairmen.[289] The prospect of Humphrey's behind-the-scenes, smoke-filled room strategy to succeed was confirmed by his early success with the Maryland and Pennsylvania delegations. On April 29, two days after Humphrey announced his candidacy, the Maryland Democratic state convention voted to commit all of its forty-nine delegates to Humphrey through a unit rule. Although McCarthy won almost 72 percent of the votes in Pennsylvania's April 23 primary, that state's Democratic convention voted to commit two-thirds of its 130 delegate votes to Humphrey at its May 27 meeting.[290]

McCarthy was bitter at Humphrey for benefiting from the tactics of the Old Politics to deny him delegates and at RFK for using the campaign style and emotionally charged, personalized rhetoric of the New Politics to cut into McCarthy's following among antiwar activists and students. Nonetheless, McCarthy did not noticeably adapt to these rapidly changing political circumstances. He persisted in his phlegmatic, banal campaign style, self-righteously insisted that he had the most dovish position on the Vietnam War, recited his poetry, and generally spurned opportunities to lobby party regulars and interest group leaders for delegate support at the national convention.[291]

With LBJ out of the race, RFK decided to decisively defeat and end McCarthy's campaign by criticizing his domestic policy record in the Senate, only slightly less liberal than RFK's, because of the Minnesota senator's reputation for lethargy and apathy in the legislative process. Kennedy wanted to make the aloof, pedantic McCarthy appear to be callous and indifferent to the national crisis in race relations, domestic violence, and poverty. RFK also wanted to avoid harshly criticizing Hubert H. Humphrey in his primary campaign. He had confided to his inner circle that he definitely preferred Humphrey over McCarthy as the possible Democratic nominee for president. If Humphrey received their party's nomination for president, RFK did not want his campaign rhetoric to fatally damage Humphrey's campaign in the general election.[292]

Despite the conventional wisdom that Indiana was a hawkish, mostly rural, conservative state that would be hostile to RFK and McCarthy, Kennedy was confident that he could win that state's May 7 Democratic presidential primary by defeating both McCarthy and Governor Roger Branigin. Branigin was a favorite-son presidential candidate perceived as a stand-in for LBJ and later for Humphrey. In announcing his presidential candidacy in this primary on March 28, 1968, Branigin repeatedly emphasized his unqualified support of LBJ's policies in Vietnam as the purpose of his candidacy. In his press release, Branigin stated, "Half a million American boys and girls are involved in this struggle in the Far East. To desert them in these critical days—to give comfort and aid to the enemy—to show division and discord at home while our fighting forces press our effort to halt the Communist aggression in the Pacific is, as former Presidents Truman and Eisenhower have said recently, bordering upon treason."[293]

At a time of relative decline in the strength of party organizations and party loyalty among voters, Indiana had the most cohesive, disciplined statewide Democratic organization in the nation in 1968. As a Democratic governor, Branigin controlled thousands of patronage jobs and state contracts.[294] Both of Indiana's Democratic senators depended on Democratic state conventions for their nominations. Senator R. Vance Hartke was an early, outspoken dove, and Senator Birch Bayh was a close friend of EMK and RFK. They at least nominally supported Branigin.[295]

Originally, Gordon St. Angelo, the Democratic state chairman, had organized Democratic county, congressional, and precinct committee chairmen in Indiana behind an effort to promote Branigin as a favorite-son candidate for vice president. His purpose was to increase the bargaining power of the Indiana delegation at the Democratic national convention.[296] A few days after Branigin announced that he was now a favorite-son candidate for president, Indiana Democrats understood that the real purpose continued to be Branigin's effort to maintain a united Indiana delegation.

In an April 4, 1968, letter to Branigin, a newspaper publisher from Bloomfield, Indiana, wrote, "It is imperative that the State of Indiana have control of its delegates and deliver them for the Democratic Party's best interests at the National Convention. I regard Kennedy and McCarthy as intruders in our great state and it is our duty to show them that we Hoosiers will decide our own destiny."[297] A handwritten letter to Branigin dated April 18, 1968, denounced RFK as "the Black Man (sic) friend" and warned of "civil war" if RFK became president. Anonymously signed "Democrat," the letter's author urged the governor to "knock the little jerk out."[298]

All ninety-two of Indiana's Democratic county chairmen endorsed Branigin as did the AFL-CIO unions and the Teamsters' local chapters in Indiana. Since Indiana had closed primaries, the more numerous Republican voters of that state could not vote in the Democratic presidential primary for Branigin, despite the abundance of mail that the governor received from friendly Hoosier Republicans wishing him well against RFK and McCarthy.[299] If the May 7 primary yielded a first-place finish for Branigin, as most journalists expected, it would be perceived as a victory for the Old Politics of a strong party organization, and, indirectly, for Hubert Humphrey and an embarrassing defeat for the New Politics of RFK.[300]

Lawrence F. O'Brien, who resigned as Postmaster General to become RFK's director of organization, was pessimistic about RFK's chances in Indiana for the same reasons that he had persuaded JFK not to contest Indiana's Democratic presidential primary in 1960. With Branigin monopolizing Indiana's Democratic Party organization down to the precinct levels, Indiana's population seemed too white, rural, Protestant, conservative, and xenophobic for a Kennedy victory. By 1968, racial tensions between blue-collar Catholic ethnics and blacks in Gary and Hammond, industrial cities on the eastern outskirts of Chicago, were tenser than they were in 1964. In that year, George Wallace won nearly 30 percent of the votes and carried two counties that included Gary and Hammond in Indiana's Democratic presidential primary. Rural, southern Indiana still had a reputation for anti-Catholic, anti-black sentiment.[301]

RFK immediately recognized that Indiana, more than any other state in his agenda of contested primaries, held the potential for his greatest symbolic victory. An upset Kennedy victory could prove to the media, pollsters, and Democratic power brokers at the national convention in August RFK's ability to attract the votes of people who shared few, if any, of his regional, religious, socioeconomic, and ideological characteristics. In short, Indiana in 1968 would be for RFK what West Virginia was for JFK in 1960. Instead of cautiously concentrating his campaign in black and Catholic neighborhoods in Indiana's few industrial cities, RFK crisscrossed the entire state frequently stopping in staunchly Republican, virtually all-white small towns.

Especially among small-town Hoosiers and blue-collar whites in northwestern Indiana, RFK's rhetoric revived his image as a tough, relentless Irish cop who wanted to restore law and order as much as he wanted racial harmony and economic justice. He also attacked the "overcentralization" of federal programs and the democratic, participatory need for Americans to exert more local control over government services. This theme of decentralization and citizen participation appealed not only to urban blacks in Indianapolis and Gary who sought economic self-determination but also to Indiana's conservative political culture that valued minimal government, local control, and low taxes.[302]

The fact that local Teamsters' officials actively opposed his candidacy provided RFK with the opportunity to remind Hoosiers of his vigorous investigation of corruption in the Teamsters' union and the eventual conviction of Jimmy Hoffa. Ideal Baldoni, then the Democratic chairman of St. Joseph County, which includes South Bend, later surmised that the opposition of the Teamsters to RFK actually attracted antiunion, conservative, rural voters to RFK.[303] Despite heckling from some college students, RFK persisted in expressing his opposition to draft deferments for students, which McCarthy supported. RFK found that his position on the draft was especially popular among blacks and blue-collar whites who resented draft deferments as unfair privileges for affluent whites.[304]

As the May 7 primary date neared, it was evident that RFK's greatest task was to gain the confidence and affection of a solid plurality of Indiana's Democratic voters. The *Indianapolis Star* actively promoted Branigin's campaign while attacking RFK's and often ignoring McCarthy's. The folksy, easygoing governor leisurely ambled throughout the state shaking hands with small groups of Hoosiers in courthouses and town squares. Other than pledging his patriotic loyalty to LBJ's policies in Vietnam, Branigin rarely attacked the issue positions of RFK and McCarthy and conducted a low-key campaign. The Democratic county chairmen of Indiana unanimously endorsed Branigin, but many of them had constituents who enthusiastically supported RFK.[305] Their organizational activities for Branigin's campaign ranged from lackluster to inert in quality and energy.[306]

Meanwhile, Eugene McCarthy vainly tried to remind Indiana voters that their Democratic presidential primary was a competitive, three-candidate race. He focused his attacks on RFK, accusing the New York senator of distorting and even lying about his Senate record. He also publicly invited RFK to a televised debate, which Kennedy declined. Internally, McCarthy's campaign suffered from inept scheduling, wasteful, inefficient spending, bitter factionalism, and inadequate coordination among its staff and managers. It mistakenly adopted Curtis Gans's strategy of concentrating McCarthy's appearances in rural areas rather than in affluent suburbs and major university communities where McCarthy might have more appeal.[307]

Publicly, RFK and his staff portrayed Kennedy's candidacy in Indiana to reporters as an uphill battle. They privately hoped that the results of the Indiana primary would provide RFK with at least 50 percent of the votes and a first-place finish forcing McCarthy to end his presidential campaign.[308] Instead, RFK received 42.3 percent of the votes to Branigin's 30.7 percent and McCarthy's 27 percent.[309] Although his third-place finish in Indiana was far less impressive than his second-place finish in New Hampshire, McCarthy could claim that he had exceeded expectations in the Indiana primary. The last polls that the Harris and Quayle firms conducted before primary day projected McCarthy receiving 24 percent of the votes.[310] As the Kennedy campaign, its rivals, the media, and pollsters expected, RFK's greatest electoral strength in Indiana was derived from blacks, Hispanics, and east European Catholic ethnics, especially in the industrial corridor of northwestern Indiana stretching from South Bend to the outskirts of Chicago. One report calculated that RFK received 85 percent of the black votes in the Indiana primary.[311] The District of Columbia also held its Democratic presidential primary on May 7, and RFK won with 62.5 percent of the votes, mostly because of overwhelming black support. But McCarthy did not run in this primary.[312]

RFK's staff diligently tried to influence the media's analysis of the Indiana primary results by depicting it as the equivalent of JFK's victory in the 1960 West Virginia primary. They used the statistics of the voting patterns in Indiana to demonstrate that RFK carried nine of that state's eleven congressional districts, all of its largest cities except Evansville and Bloomington, seventeen of the twenty-five rural counties in southern Indiana, and 57 percent of Indiana's ninety-two counties. In short, they contended, RFK's electoral support was broadly and diversely distributed throughout Indiana, a microcosm of Middle America.[313] Furthermore, according to the rules of the Indiana Democratic Party, all of Indiana's sixty-three delegate votes at the Democratic national convention were committed to RFK on the first ballot.[314]

Most columnists, pollsters, and the McCarthy campaign refused to accept the Kennedy campaign's impressive depiction of the Indiana primary results. RFK's next challenge was to soundly defeat Eugene McCarthy in Nebraska's May 14 primary. By doing so, Kennedy hoped to finally force McCarthy to end his candidacy, absorb McCarthy's student volunteers and voters into his campaign, and energize a consensus-building bandwagon among Democratic power brokers by proving his vote-getting appeal among white, Protestant, middle-class farmers and businessmen.[315]

Demographically, Nebraska seemed even more hostile to a Kennedy candidacy than Indiana. Compared to Indiana, Nebraska was more rural, agricultural, and Republican with smaller percentages of blacks, Catholics, and labor union members in its population. There was also a much smaller Democratic electorate in Nebraska. While 776,513 voters participated in the Indiana Democratic presidential primary, only 162,611 Nebraskans voted in their state's Democratic presidential primary on May 14.[316]

Unlike Indiana, though, there already was a regular Democratic organization committed to RFK. Theodore C. Sorensen, one of RFK's speechwriters and campaign advisors, was a native of Nebraska. His father had once served as attorney general and his brother Philip as lieutenant governor. Philip Sorensen unsuccessfully ran for governor of Nebraska in 1966.[317] With the Sorensens well known and influential in the Nebraska Democratic Party, the Sorensen brothers and their operatives carefully and repeatedly contacted Democratic voters and mobilized them on primary day.

RFK campaigned by car and train throughout Nebraska and addressed agricultural issues more than he had in Indiana. He ended his Nebraska campaign with a speech in a black neighborhood in Omaha.[318] In the Nebraska primary, RFK received 52.5 percent of the votes compared to 31 percent for McCarthy and 8.4 percent for Hubert Humphrey as a write-in candidate.[319] RFK carried eighty-eight of Nebraska's ninety-three counties, including twenty-four of the twenty-five Nebraska counties in which he campaigned.[320]

McCarthy left Nebraska a few days before the primary was held and sent most of his staff to Oregon and California to prepare for their primaries. With McCarthy remaining in the race, Kennedy was now far less likely to attract McCarthy's dovish voters to his campaign in these two West Coast primaries. Beginning with his victory speech in Nebraska, RFK bluntly urged McCarthy's supporters in future primaries to join his campaign in order to prevent Humphrey from being nominated for president at the Democratic national convention. RFK publicly interpreted the combined percentages of his votes and McCarthy's votes in the Nebraska primary—nearly 83 percent—to represent an overwhelming repudiation of the Johnson-Humphrey administration in a conservative, rural state.[321]

As Kennedy and his staff prepared for the Oregon and California primaries, they were frustrated and perplexed by their failure to force McCarthy out of the race and persuade party bosses to commit their delegates to RFK as the only prospective Democratic presidential nominee who could win in November. After the staggering Democratic losses in the 1966 midterm elections, would not the most cynical, pragmatic, calculating Democratic politicians want RFK, rather than McCarthy or Humphrey, at the top of Democratic tickets in 1968 for coattail effects? With the unpopularity of Johnson and the Vietnam War now transferred to Humphrey as the embodiment of both, why were the party bosses and interest group leaders so quick to commit themselves and their delegates to the untested Hubert Humphrey, who did not enter and campaign in any of the contested presidential primaries?

The Kennedy campaign was also exasperated and puzzled by the fact that the positions of RFK, McCarthy, and Humphrey in the Gallup polls remained virtually the same from the day that Humphrey declared his presidential candidacy until the completion of the Nebraska primary. A Gallup poll released on April 28, 1968, reported that, of the Democratic voters surveyed, their preferences for their party's presidential nominee were RFK at 28 percent, McCarthy at 33 percent, and Humphrey at 25 percent. Gallup's May 15 poll revealed that these percentages remained virtually the same for McCarthy and Humphrey with their respective voter preferences at 33 percent and 22 percent. In this poll, the voter preference for RFK had improved to 34 percent, but this occurred mostly because of the movement of previously undecided voters to RFK.[322]

But, in 1968, this peak year of dissensus for the nation in general and the Democratic party in particular, small-town Hoosiers and Nebraska farmers had embraced the urban, liberal New York senator as a champion of law and order and reforms in agricultural economics. It was not surprising that southern, anti-civil rights conservative Democratic politicians and northern party bosses were tenaciously clinging to Hubert H. Humphrey as the only viable, "conservative," pro-establishment Democratic presidential candidate. Four years earlier, LBJ struggled to gradually persuade both of these factions that Humphrey was not an anti-business, race-mixing radical and a naïve idealist captured by the UAW and ADA so that the Minnesota senator could become his running mate. Other southern Democratic politicians who controlled most or all of their states' delegates, such as governors Lester Maddox of Georgia, John Connally of Texas, and John McKeithen of Louisiana and Senator George Smathers of Florida, were developing favorite-son presidential candidacies in order to bargain with Humphrey over the choice of his running mate and the content of the Democratic national platform.[323]

RFK had no other choice but to doggedly enter and win contested primaries against McCarthy. He had to gradually end McCarthy's presidential candidacy through a war of attrition and then attract McCarthy's antiwar voters and activists as the only politically feasible agent of change against Humphrey, the Republicans, and the status quo. When RFK began campaigning in the Oregon Democratic presidential primary, his prospect for victory initially seemed better than it had been in Indiana or Nebraska. Congresswoman Edith Green of Oregon offered the Kennedy campaign the use of her party organization in the primary.

Green was a powerful member of the House Education and Labor Committee and was one of the first House Democrats to endorse JFK's presidential candidacy. As an early dove, Green was one of seven House members to vote against a supplemental defense spending bill for the Vietnam War in 1965. LBJ also resented her interference with his efforts to settle the MFDP controversy at the 1964 Democratic national convention and her advocacy of amendments to LBJ's education bills that threatened to kill them in the House Education and Labor Committee.[324]

Green was also a divisive, controversial figure within the Oregon Democratic Party. Senator Wayne Morse of Oregon had clashed with Green over federal education bills and intraparty matters, such as the Democratic nomination of Robert Duncan, a hawk on Vietnam, for the Senate in 1966. Morse openly supported Robert Hatfield, Duncan's Republican opponent, because of Hatfield's dovish position on Vietnam. Hatfield won the election, and labor leaders resented Morse's involvement in labor-management disputes. Morse faced a tough reelection bid in 1968 and resented RFK's entry into the Oregon primary.[325]

Fortunately for Eugene McCarthy, his campaign in the Oregon primary was organized by Howard Morgan, the former chairman of the Democratic state committee. Unlike Green and Morse, Morgan was a popular, consensus-building Democratic Party leader, an excellent campaign manager, and an arbiter of intraparty conflicts. Morgan was often credited with transforming Oregon from a one-party Republican state into a more liberal, competitive, two-party state during the 1950s and 1960s.[326]

The crowds that greeted RFK's motorcades, train trips, and speaking engagements in Oregon were usually friendly. But they lacked the exhilaration, intensity, and overflowing size of his crowds in Indiana and Nebraska. Oregon was a generally liberal, dovish state, with Morse immortalized as one of the two Senate opponents of the Gulf of Tonkin Resolution. But its voters lacked the sense of urgency and alarm about ending the war compared to voters in other primary states. Oregon's major cities, Portland, Eugene, and Salem, did not have the large, white ethnic and black neighborhoods of Gary, Indianapolis, and Omaha. More so than in his other primary campaigns, RFK insisted to his listeners that he opposed Humphrey and the continuation of the status quo, not McCarthy.[327]

During the last week of his Oregon campaign, it appeared that RFK might eke out a narrow victory in the Oregon primary. An NBC poll released on May 22, 1968, revealed that RFK was ahead of McCarthy, 29 to 27 percent. The other respondents polled divided their intended votes among LBJ, Humphrey as a write-it candidate, and others. Twelve percent of those surveyed were undecided.[328]

Under the meticulous management of Howard Morgan and Blaine Whipple, a realtor, the McCarthy campaign in Oregon quietly and expertly identified and mobilized well-educated, dovish, middle class white voters. RFK increasingly divided his campaign appearances between Oregon and California. During the final days of the Oregon campaign, RFK's staff was pessimistic of victory. McCarthy defeated RFK in the Oregon primary, 44 percent to 38 percent.[329] A Kennedy campaign aide ruefully told journalist Theodore H. White, "Oregon is all one great white middle-class suburb. It's a good state. It had no problems. We frightened them."[330]

RFK's defeat in the Oregon primary was the first time a Kennedy had lost a contested primary or election. Although more confident of victory in California than he was in Oregon, RFK decided to join McCarthy in a televised debate, a forum that he had declined in previous primaries.[331] RFK had been following the conventional wisdom that the front runner should not debate his underdog opponent.

There was also the unpredictable, uncontrollable, potentially embarrassing nature of a live, televised debate. Reporters and McCarthy could ask Kennedy tough, unexpected questions about his own responsibilities for the Vietnam War and the shortcomings of New Frontier and Great Society programs. RFK accepted this risk in order to revitalize his stalled presidential campaign and magnify his domestic policy differences with McCarthy, especially on race-related housing and economic issues. The New York senator now perceived his competition with McCarthy as more of a personal rivalry. He was convinced that McCarthy persisted in running for the presidential nomination entirely because of personal antagonism toward him.[332] Kennedy also needed to successfully refute charges made by columnist Drew Pearson, published a few days before the Oregon primary, that as attorney general he approved the wiretapping of Martin Luther King, Jr.'s telephones.[333]

With Pearson's article, RFK feared the loss of black votes and the votes of civil liberties–minded white liberals in California. Kennedy could not risk the revived, negative image of "Ruthless Bobby" who had worked for Joe McCarthy, was callous toward the early civil rights movement, and had been a vindictive prosecutor indifferent to civil liberties. More so than in any other primary state, California politics was media and image politics.

Party organizations, including that of Jesse Unruh, the powerful pro-Kennedy speaker of the California assembly, meant little in influencing the outcome of major, statewide elections. Weak party loyalty and split ticket voting were common and well entrenched in California. In 1964, California voters gave 59 percent of their votes to LBJ while electing and giving nearly 52 percent to Senate candidate George Murphy. Murphy was a right-wing Republican and obscure tap-dancing actor with no prior experience in public office. Murphy defeated Pierre Salinger, the incumbent, appointed Democratic senator who had served as JFK's press secretary and was relying on LBJ's coattail efforts.[334]

Furthermore, like the Oregon primary, the California Democratic presidential primary was an open one. Republicans and independents could vote for McCarthy as a way to embarrass and defeat RFK. The winner of the California Democratic presidential primary would have all of that state's 174 delegate votes pledged to him at the Democratic national convention.[335]

Besides preparing for his June 1 televised debate with McCarthy, RFK actively campaigned throughout the state. In addition to touring and speaking in California's major cities, he visited the Central Valley, home of many Hispanic farm workers and rural whites descended from the "Okies" and "Arkies" who moved there during the Great Depression. Black politicians like California assemblyman Willie Brown assured the Kennedy campaign that Drew Pearson's column about wiretapping and a pro-McCarthy radio commercial that exploited it had little impact on black voters. Mobilized by UFWA leader Cesar Chavez, Hispanics were even more enthusiastic about RFK's candidacy than blacks were. While AFL-CIO unions in California remained staunchly pro-Humphrey, more UAW locals in California and other states began to endorse RFK individually.[336]

When his top advisors and Jesse Unruh coached and quizzed RFK for his debate with McCarthy, Unruh suggested that Kennedy emphasize his criticism of McCarthy's "ghetto dispersal" program. RFK favored targeting federal aid, public works programs, and business investment in black and Hispanic urban ghettos. He wanted to promote grassroots participation, economic self-determination, and home ownership in minority communities. By contrast, Unruh and RFK's staff interpreted McCarthy's race-related public housing proposals to include the federally subsidized migration of ghetto blacks to white suburbs.[337]

The first part of the June 1 debate mostly consisted of Kennedy and McCarthy accusing each of distorting the other's record and using misleading, negative advertising. The crucial event of the debate, though, was RFK's use of Unruh's suggestion. In referring to his policy differences with McCarthy on a wide range of anti-poverty programs, including Head Start, RFK added, "You say you are going to take 10,000 black people and move them into Orange County. . . . The property taxes, for instance, here in the state of California . . . are astronomically high."[338] McCarthy's campaign aides were startled and disappointed by McCarthy's rambling, dismissive rebuttal to RFK's charges. Thomas Finney, a member of Clark M. Clifford's law firm and a McCarthy advisor, lamented, "He flubbed it! Blew it! Threw it away. How can you get him elected?"[339]

Most columnists, the Californians who were polled, and even LBJ, in his comments to auto magnate Henry Ford II and actor Gregory Peck, perceived Kennedy as the "winner" of the debate.[340] On the evening of June 4, primary day in California and South Dakota, a CBS poll projected RFK ahead of McCarthy by 14 percent in California. With higher than usual turnout among blacks and Hispanics, RFK won about 90 percent of the black vote and 95 percent, and in some precincts 100 percent, of the Hispanic vote.[341]

As expected, most of the most dovish, affluent white liberals and New Left–influenced academics, especially in northern California, voted for McCarthy. But the Kennedy campaign managed to attract virtually half of the older Jewish middle-class voters and cut into previously and presumably pro-McCarthy support among antiwar, church-oriented voters and young white liberals. This was partially accomplished by the activities of the ecumenical Clergy for Kennedy Committee and the effort of Frank Mankiewicz, RFK's press secretary and a former Peace Corps official, to organize former Peace Corps and VISTA volunteers as Kennedy campaign activists.[342] The Hollywood for Kennedy Committee also reduced the significance of actor Paul Newman's prominent campaigning for McCarthy. It enlisted the endorsements of entertainment celebrities ranging from comedian Milton Berle and singer Trini Lopez to actor Sidney Poitier and director Otto Preminger.[343]

On June 2, 1968, two days before the California primary, the Gallup firm released a poll reporting that, when adjusted regionally, 67 percent of the Democratic county chairmen in the nation preferred Hubert H. Humphrey as the Democratic presidential nominee. Only 19 percent chose RFK and 6 percent chose McCarthy. If they had to choose between RFK and McCarthy, the Democratic county chairmen preferred RFK to McCarthy by only 3 percent, with 41 percent for RFK, 38 percent for McCarthy, and 21 percent undecided.[344]

Covering the Kennedy campaign during these primaries, journalist David Halberstam observed, "It was becoming clearer and clearer that Robert Kennedy's problem with the machines was very deep and serious, and that the apparatus was almost as hostile to him as it was to McCarthy. For the first time in many years, the party machinery, which had traditionally been reasonably sympathetic to the pressures and whims of the party eggheads and liberals, was unresponsive to two candidates representing the intellectual element."[345] Halberstam added, "If the existing officials of the Democratic party lack a powerful sense of social change, they do have a sense of survival. Robert Kennedy, like Gene McCarthy, threatened their survival. Hubert Humphrey did not."[346]

The results of the California Democratic presidential primary provided RFK with a comfortable, but not overwhelming, margin of victory over McCarthy. Kennedy received 46.3 percent, McCarthy 41.8 percent, and California attorney general Thomas Lynch, a pro-Humphrey stand-in candidate, approximately 12 percent.[347] RFK defeated McCarthy by a statewide margin of 135,303 votes. In Los Angeles County, RFK's winning margin over McCarthy was over 120,000 votes so that his statewide victory was almost entirely dependent on his electoral success in this county, especially among blacks, Hispanics, and lower-income whites. Furthermore, McCarthy carried thirty-eight of California's fifty-six counties.[348]

But even before RFK made his victory speech at the Ambassador Hotel in Los Angeles, both campaigns engaged in spin control to influence the media analysis and future political significance of these results. McCarthy dismissed the California primary results as another example of RFK's exploitation of "bloc voting" among minority groups that was unrepresentative of the American population in general. The Minnesota senator gave no indication that his defeat in California ended his presidential campaign.[349]

RFK's staff quickly circulated early returns from South Dakota's June 4 primary. In South Dakota, a state quite different from California and even more rural, WASP, and agricultural than Nebraska, RFK was defeating McCarthy by a more than two-to-one margin. The final, official results in South Dakota were: RFK at 49.5 percent, LBJ, officially listed as a candidate by state law, at 30 percent, and McCarthy a distant third at 20.4 percent.[350]

The Kennedy campaign's spin on the returns from these two primaries was that RFK's securement of all of California's 174 delegate votes now enabled him to impress and unite the warring factions of New York Democrats enough so that RFK's delegate slates would carry most of New York's forty-one congressional districts against pro-McCarthy and pro-Humphrey slates.[351] Kennedy aides estimated that RFK could now secure 132 of New York's 190 delegate votes as a consequence of its June 18 primary.

They distributed a chart to RFK and reporters. It illustrated that, with a minimum of 1,312 delegate votes needed for Democratic presidential nomination, RFK was projected to receive 1,432 delegate votes at the Democratic national convention.[352] Privately skeptical of such bandwagon optimism, RFK nonetheless told his aides to contact Allard Lowenstein, then a Democratic congressional primary candidate in New York's fifth district. RFK wanted to enlist Lowenstein's help in attracting pro-McCarthy Democrats in New York to his slates of delegates for the June 18 primary.[353]

Before RFK's victory speech in Los Angeles and subsequent assassination, his campaign staff was already planning his post-California strategy. Led by Theodore C. Sorensen, Stephen Smith, and David Hackett, RFK's advisors and managers intended to combine the most effective tactics of the Old Politics and the New Politics.[354] For the Old Politics, Smith, Hackett, O'Brien, EMK, and O'Donnell would lobby pro-Humphrey or uncommitted delegates from nonprimary states in the Northeast and Midwest to support RFK at the convention.[355] Meanwhile, representing the New Politics, Adam Walinsky, Jeff Greenfield, and Peter Edelman planned to arrange more Kennedy motorcades in minority neighborhoods in major northern cities of nonprimary states to further weaken the loyalty of big-city mayors and other party bosses to Humphrey's candidacy. Recognizing how older, more affluent Stevensonian liberals still preferred McCarthy to RFK, the Kennedy campaign wanted to produce and nationally broadcast a series of "fireside chats" in which RFK appeared calm, mature, and statesmanlike in contrast to their perception of RFK's televised image as an immature, emotionally volatile rabble rouser unfit for the dignity and responsibilities of the presidency.

RFK's advisors wanted to bolster Kennedy's gravitas by having the New York senator visit Europe. In addition to scenes of cheering crowds of Europeans greeting RFK, the New York senator would be shown having somber consultations with European officials. RFK also expected to publish his book on the Cuban missile crisis during the summer of 1968.[356]

If the northern bosses and labor leaders persisted in supporting Humphrey, then RFK would confer with them at the Kennedy compound in Hyannis Port before the Democratic national convention was held in Chicago. RFK's inner circle assumed that he would not accept the vice-presidential nomination as a consolation prize and that he would use his influence over the platform to insist that Humphrey adopt a more dovish position and become independent of LBJ on the Vietnam War.[357] Recognizing that the pro-Humphrey power brokers might still be intransigent and indifferent to RFK's media blitz and frenzied motorcades, Kennedy and his staff planned to play hard ball. They would influence the selection of members and chairmen to key committees at the convention, especially those for credentials, arrangements, and the platform.

In particular, RFK intended to challenge the credentials of mostly or entirely white delegations from the South.[358] The Kennedy campaign was already communicating with black Democrats in Mississippi to dispute the credentials of the regular Mississippi delegation.[359] It also wanted to challenge the unit rule that was being used to establish favorite-son presidential candidacies or entirely pro-Humphrey delegations from nonprimary states.[360]

RFK's aides and allies, as well as journalists favorable to his presidential candidacy, optimistically speculated, and sometimes confidently concluded, that RFK was on his way toward securing the Democratic presidential nomination and winning the election in November. This political forecast is mostly based on the following perceptions and assumptions. Kennedy had proven that, unlike Humphrey, McCarthy, and Nixon, he was a transitional figure between the Old Politics and New Politics. He showed that he could understand and develop a broader, winning coalition that included blacks, Hispanics, antiwar activists, UAW local officials, and socially conservative, lower-income whites, from Nebraska farmers to Slavic factory workers in Gary, Indiana.[361] It was only a matter of time before the more pragmatic, pro-McCarthy Democrats, party bosses, and labor leaders switched their allegiance to RFK after it became evident that the despised, feared, presumably hawkish Richard M. Nixon would become the Republican presidential nominee.[362] Since Kennedy would have a better chance of defeating Nixon than Humphrey or McCarthy, it seemed illogical to Kennedy supporters that the Humphrey and McCarthy forces were willing to forfeit the election to Nixon because of an unyielding animosity toward RFK.[363]

There is no conclusive evidence that RFK's campaign was on its way toward gradually co-opting boss-controlled, pro-Humphrey delegates at the time of RFK's death. RFK met Mayor Richard J. Daley of Chicago on February 8, 1968, to discuss the feasibility of RFK challenging LBJ for the Democratic presidential nomination.[364] Daley reaffirmed his commitment to LBJ, but RFK repeatedly told his advisors and journalists, "Dick Daley is the ball game."[365] RFK assumed that if he could eventually convince Daley, through higher poll ratings, impressive motorcades in Chicago, a media blitz, and primary victories, then the Chicago mayor would not only deliver the Illinois delegation to RFK, he would also use his rigid control of the Democratic national convention and influence with other boss-controlled delegations to assure RFK the presidential nomination.[366]

Daley privately confided to his aides that Hubert H. Humphrey could not carry Illinois in the Electoral College and had suggested to LBJ in 1964 that the Texan choose RFK as his running mate. Nonetheless, Daley perceived RFK differently than he did JFK and EMK.[367] For Daley, JFK and EMK were rational, predictable, calculating politicians whose presidencies would not threaten the Chicago machine legally or politically. Daley and other party bosses bitterly and vengefully remembered how RFK's Justice Department had vigorously prosecuted Democratic machine politicians in Gary, Indiana, and J. Vincent Keogh, the brother of New York congressman Eugene Keogh and a state judge.[368]

Also, in the spring of 1968, Daley suspiciously and angrily associated the New Politics of RFK with boisterous crowds in black neighborhoods that eventually rioted and pillaged in Chicago, as they did following Martin Luther King,

Jr.'s assassination. The mayor did not look forward to future Kennedy motor-cades and rallies in Chicago. They would further burden and complicate his efforts to avoid a "long, hot summer" of race riots and worsening tensions between blacks and white ethnics.

RFK's repeated, public efforts to welcome McCarthy's youthful, antiwar activists into his campaign also did not endear Kennedy to Daley. Daley and other machine Democrats made little distinction between antiwar activists like Abbie Hoffman, who promised disorder in Chicago, and Allard Lowenstein. The mayor expected thousands of antiwar demonstrators to arrive in Chicago and disrupt the convention.[369] Furthermore, RFK had encouraged the late Martin Luther King, Jr.'s decision to organize a mostly black, anti-poverty march on Washington. This movement established its "Resurrection City" in the nation's capital shortly before the California primary.[370]

Daley's persistent coolness toward RFK's candidacy and ambivalence toward Humphrey, whom he regarded as "safe" for the machine's interests but unelectable in November, were evident by June 1968. Weeks after RFK's assassination, he tried to persuade EMK to let the Chicago mayor begin a "draft Kennedy" movement among the boss-controlled delegations and those committed to the slain RFK. Grief-stricken and distraught, EMK insisted that he was not inter-ested in the Democratic presidential or vice-presidential nomination in 1968 and would not even attend the national convention in Chicago.[371] With Daley's sharply contrasting perceptions of and behavior toward RFK and EMK, it is not merely a coincidence that, within RFK's inner circle, EMK was the most out-spoken, implacable opponent of RFK's decision to run for president in 1968. Although EMK worked diligently yet reluctantly on his brother's behalf, he frequently cautioned RFK to moderate the style and tone of his New Politics' campaign, recognizing how repugnant it was to party bosses like Daley.[372]

Less than two weeks after RFK's assassination, a *New York Times* poll esti-mated that Hubert H. Humphrey had secured approximately 1,600 delegate votes, almost 300 more than the 1,312 needed for the presidential nomination. Eugene McCarthy later admitted that he agreed with the conventional wisdom assuring Humphrey the presidential nomination.[373] Nevertheless, McCarthy re-fused to end his presidential campaign. One week after RFK's assassination, he stated, implying a more leftist position on Vietnam, that the American public "is ready to accept even withdrawal" from Vietnam, rather than a gradual deescalation of the American military presence there.[374]

New York's June 18 primaries selected 123 of its 190 delegates for the Democratic national convention. Pro-McCarthy Democrats won a plurality of these delegate seats, and Paul O'Dwyer, an obscure, eccentric, pro-McCarthy, underdog candidate, won an upset victory in the Democratic senatorial pri-mary.[375] Two days before the New York primaries, McCarthy publicly stated that he was willing to support, but not lead, an antiwar minor party.

Despite, or perhaps because of, his willingness to bolt the Democratic Party with Hubert H. Humphrey as its presumptive presidential nominee, statements like this and the results of the New York primaries revitalized McCarthy's campaign in June and early July. His crowds were larger and more enthusiastic, and he received more campaign contributions. He further dramatized his more dovish position by announcing on June 23, 1968, that he wanted to confer with North Vietnam's diplomats during his visit to Paris in late July or early August.[376] At another time, McCarthy suggested that he might conditionally support Nelson Rockefeller for president.[377]

In addition to these erratic, unexpected statements from the enigmatic Minnesota senator, the McCarthy campaign was characterized by bitter factionalism among McCarthy's top campaign aides and advisors. One faction, led by Curtis Gans and Sam Brown, wanted to emphasize the student-oriented, New Politics, grassroots populism of McCarthy's primary campaign in New Hampshire and Wisconsin. Brown and Gans assumed that if McCarthy spoke to large, cheering, peaceful, antiwar audiences organized by student volunteers then this publicity and its impact on public opinion would pressure more delegates, especially those previously committed to RFK, to support McCarthy's candidacy at the Democratic national convention. A second faction of McCarthy's inner circle advocated different tactics. Led by Thomas Finney, these advisors suggested that McCarthy use dignified television commercials and favorable poll ratings to make McCarthy appear to be a more statesmanlike, viable presidential candidate to the party bosses and use this image to bargain for delegates before and during the convention. In short, the Finney faction represented the perspectives and tactics of the Old Politics.[378]

The third faction, led by former DNC chairman Stephen Mitchell, combined elements of the Old Politics and the New Politics. Like the Finney faction, the Mitchell faction wanted to avoid using student-organized, antiwar demonstrations since the radical statements and possible violence of their participants could taint and damage McCarthy's candidacy. Unlike the Finney faction and in the spirit of the anti-establishment New Politics, Mitchell wanted McCarthy to aggressively and comprehensively challenge the rules, committee members, and procedures of the Democratic national convention and the delegate selection methods of several states as undemocratic, racially discriminatory, and biased in favor of Humphrey. The Mitchell faction eventually persuaded McCarthy that their legalistic approach, referred to as "confrontation politics," offered the best chance of accomplishing Eugene McCarthy's two goals at the Democratic national convention—an anti-LBJ, dovish plank on the Vietnam War and party reform.[379] The victory of the Finney and Mitchell factions over the Brown-Gans faction was also evident in McCarthy's public statements urging his supporters not to come to Chicago and conduct antiwar demonstrations.[380]

Although Richard Goodwin returned to McCarthy's campaign and Lawrence F. O'Brien joined Humphrey's, most of the late RFK's staff and allies did not want to actively support either McCarthy or Humphrey before the Democratic national convention was held. On June 23, five days after he won the Democratic congressional primary in New York's fifth congressional district, Allard Lowenstein announced that a recently founded organization, the National Coalition for an Open Convention (NCOC), would hold a meeting on July 1 in Chicago. Similar to the CCD's Dump Johnson national convention in 1967, the NCOC attracted more than 1,000 participants, seventy-five of whom would be delegates at the Democratic national convention in August, from thirty-seven states.[381] The NCOC's decisions and purposes were explicitly anti-Humphrey but not necessarily pro-McCarthy since many of its attendees were RFK supporters. Although he was publicly identified as a McCarthy supporter, Lowenstein's public position was that the NCOC insisted on a more democratic, participatory Democratic national convention. The NCOC wanted the Democratic national convention to reflect the antiwar, liberal sentiment of most rank-and-file Democrats in its proceedings, rules reforms, platform, and selection of presidential and vice presidential nominees.[382]

Privately, though, Lowenstein had already given up hope in McCarthy's candidacy and wanted EMK to be the NCOC's candidate. With EMK's firm, public rejection of a presidential or vice-presidential candidacy by late July, Lowenstein had no alternative, viable antiwar presidential candidate, so the NCOC movement collapsed. Senator George McGovern's July 23 announcement of his availability as a stand-in presidential candidate for pro-RFK delegates did not arouse much enthusiasm from the NCOC.[383]

With the liberal, antiwar movement in disarray, leading anti-Humphrey Democrats gloomily and fatalistically accepted the inevitability of Humphrey's nomination for president at the convention. They decided to focus their efforts on writing and advocating a peace plank on the Vietnam War that most Democratic delegates would accept. Shortly after the Republican national convention ended its proceedings on August 8, 1968, Richard M. Nixon and Spiro Agnew, the respective Republican nominees for president and vice president, visited LBJ. Despite Nixon's earlier, hawkish criticism of LBJ's military strategy in Vietnam, he publicly adopted a more moderate yet inscrutable position on the war that differed little from Johnson's.[384]

From the perspective of the average, undecided voter, there were no meaningful policy differences between Nixon and Humphrey on the Vietnam War. Some of the Old Politics' doves from the RFK campaign, like Fred Dutton and Kenneth P. O'Donnell, wanted to convince Humphrey that a moderately dovish plank could be worded in such a way that the vice president could clearly distinguish himself as more dovish than Nixon on the Vietnam War without appearing to be disloyal to LBJ. Humphrey could thereby improve his chances of beating Nixon in November.[385]

The DNC's platform committee was chaired by Hale Boggs, the House majority leader and a staunch ally of LBJ. Most of its members were also loyal to Johnson's policies in Vietnam and Humphrey's candidacy. Nevertheless, shortly before the platform committee held its hearings, O'Donnell and other dovish party regulars, like former Ohio Congressman John Gilligan, were optimistic that most committee members could be persuaded to approve a moderately dovish plank in order to make Humphrey electable in November. Of course, the person who would ultimately decide the content and wording of the Vietnam plank was Johnson, not Humphrey.

O'Donnell, Gilligan, Galbraith, Sorensen, and other advocates of a compromised, dovish plank seemed to be making progress during the platform committee's hearings on August 19, 1968, the first day of platform hearings. Promoting a responsible, dovish plank, Roger Hilsman, former Assistant Secretary of State for the Far East under JFK and LBJ, told the platform committee, "There are no longer any dominoes in Southeast Asia. Vietnam, in fact, is turning out to be unique—unique in the sense that it will probably be the last Asian nation in which Communism captures the leadership of nationalism."[386]

Any potential for Hilsman's expert testimony and similarly reasonable statements supporting the minority plank was diminished by the following two events. On August 19, the same day that the Democratic platform committee began its hearings in Chicago, LBJ addressed the annual convention of the Veterans of Foreign Wars (VFW) in Detroit.[387] In a stirring, bombastic speech, LBJ asserted that his administration, including Hubert H. Humphrey, would not let South Vietnam and the rest of Southeast Asia fall to Communism. In sharp contrast to Hilsman's statement, Johnson asserted that, in the future, "the prosperity and the security of your United States will, with the passage of time, be more bound up with the fate of Asia—and not less."[388] Emphasizing the relevance of the Vietnam War to the domino theory and national defense, LBJ ominously added, "Laos, South Vietnam, Thailand, Malaysia, Singapore, Indonesia—pretty soon we could be back to the Philippines—and even back to Honolulu."[389]

On the following day, August 20, 1968, Soviet and other Warsaw Pact military forces entered Czechoslovakia to overthrow the reformist, democratizing government of Alexander Dubcek. On August 21, LBJ publicly denounced this Soviet-led intervention. "The Soviet Union and its allies have invaded a defenseless country to stamp out a resurgence of ordinary human freedom. It is a sad commentary on the Communist mind that a sign of liberty in Czechoslovakia is deemed a fundamental threat to the security of the Soviet system."[390]

Any remaining, remote possibility that Humphrey, LBJ, and a majority of the platform committee would adopt a moderately dovish plank on Vietnam ended with the intervention of Charles Murphy. David Ginsburg, a Washington, DC, attorney appointed by Humphrey to be his negotiator with the doves over the Vietnam plank, had written a proposed plank that was generally agreeable to McCarthy and the dovish negotiators. Ginsburg's plank draft stated, "Stop the bombing of North Vietnam. This action and its timing shall take into account the security of our troops and the likelihood of a response from Hanoi." Murphy, a former White House aide to Harry Truman, represented LBJ in these negotiations and asserted that Ginsburg's proposal was unacceptable to the president, who had read it. At most, Johnson would accept a Vietnam plank that stated "Stop all bombing of North Vietnam when this action would not endanger the lives of our troops in the field; this action should take into account the response from Hanoi."[391] Before the platform committee's hearings resumed on Monday, August 26, LBJ called Hale Boggs to the White House and secured the bombing plank that he wanted.[392]

Humphrey felt baffled and betrayed with this turn of events since he had cleared the wording of Ginsburg's draft with National Security Adviser Walt Rostow. Humphrey telephoned LBJ at his ranch, and the president insisted that his exact wording for the bombing plank must be adopted by the convention and embraced by Humphrey. In his memoirs, Hubert Humphrey grimly and regretfully observed, "Our choice was to stand and fight the President's emissaries or to give in to the inevitable. Now I know, in retrospect, that I should have stood my ground. I told our people I was still for the plank, but I didn't put up a real fight. That was a mistake. I am not sure it would have made any difference in the election, but once we had arrived at that point, at some consensus with the Kennedy people, I should not have yielded."[393]

On Monday, August 26, 1968, the first day of the Democratic national convention in Chicago, Hale Boggs led the platform committee in endorsing LBJ's bombing plank and other planks on the Vietnam War by a vote of 65 to 35.[394] This committee vote set the stage for a divisive, rancorous televised floor debate on the bombing plank in particular and LBJ's Vietnam policies in general that Humphrey had feared and struggled to avoid. More so than previously, antiwar demonstrators outside the convention hall and many of the McCarthy and Kennedy delegates at the convention were convinced that the convention's proceedings and decisions were rigged beforehand to benefit Humphrey.

Privately, Humphrey often felt powerless to influence the convention's decisions. Johnson and DNC chairman John M. Bailey rejected the vice president's request that the Democratic national convention be relocated to Miami Beach. This city had recently hosted the Republican national convention, and Humphrey wanted to reduce and confuse the number of antiwar protesters flocking to Chicago. Likewise, Mayor Daley ignored Humphrey's request that a separate hall in Chicago be reserved for peaceful, antiwar activists to meet.[395]

In his welcoming address to the delegates, Daley sternly promised, "As long as I am mayor of this town, there will be law and order in Chicago."[396] Daley and Postmaster General (W.) Marvin Watson rigidly micromanaged the convention on behalf of the absent LBJ. The beleaguered Humphrey was haunted by the possibility of LBJ accepting renomination in order to protect and continue his policies in Vietnam. This possibility became more credible after John Connally, governor of Texas and a Johnson confidante, explored the feasibility of joining other southern Democrats and some northern party regulars in initiating a "draft LBJ" movement at the convention. Connally was especially angry at Humphrey's August 21 statement advocating the abolition of the unit rule. Connally and other pro-Humphrey southern Democrats and some nonsouthern machine Democrats wanted to retain the unit rule. They suspected that William Connell, one of Humphrey's aides, had misled and betrayed them in promising that Humphrey would preserve the unit rule in exchange for their support of his presidential nomination.[397]

Briefly considering a campaign for vice president at the convention in order to increase his bargaining power, Connally finally decided to release the delegates of Texas to Humphrey after the convention decided to abolish the unit rule by a roll call vote of 1,350 to 1,206 on Tuesday, August 27.[398] After the convention's decision to end the unit rule, the McCarthy and Kennedy forces, combined with the more liberal Humphrey delegates, experienced some success in influencing the convention to adopt their positions on party reforms and in resolving race-related disputes over the credentials of delegates from several southern states, namely Georgia, Alabama, Texas, and Mississippi.[399] Chaired by Governor Richard Hughes of New Jersey, the credentials committee, after conferring with the equal rights committee, recommended and the convention ratified the seating of the mostly black Loyal Democrats of Mississippi as delegates instead of the all-white, regular delegation of Mississippi.[400]

Led by Senator Ralph Yarborough, a pro-McCarthy Democrat from Texas, other delegates challenged the credentials of Connally's Texas delegation for allegedly discriminating against full participation by blacks and Hispanics in Texas in the selection of delegates. The convention, though, rejected the minority report favoring this challenge by a vote of 1,368 to 955.[401] Through a voice vote, the convention adopted the credentials committee's recommendation that Georgia's delegate votes be equally divided between the all-white regular delegation led by segregationist Governor Lester Maddox and the mostly black Loyal National Democrats led by Julian Bond, a state representative and former SNCC leader. The convention rejected the liberal, pro-Bond minority report. This report favored the expulsion of all of the pro-Maddox regular delegates and the seating all of the Loyal National Democrats from Georgia as voting delegates.

Likewise, the convention adopted the credentials committee's recommended compromise that Alabama's all-white regular delegation would be seated if it signed a loyalty pledge to the Democratic national ticket. By a vote of 1,525 to 801½, the convention rejected a minority report promoted by pro-McCarthy Democrats. This minority report proposed that Alabama's entire delegation be replaced by members of the mostly black National Democratic Party of Alabama (NDPA).

The credentials committee and then the convention in general also rejected similar race-related challenges to the credentials of the North Carolina, Tennessee, and Louisiana delegations.[402] Despite these initial defeats by liberal delegates advocating party reforms, the credentials committee recommended and the convention adopted a proposal for a comprehensive study of all the states' delegate selection processes and formulation of any necessary reforms for the 1972 convention. This proposal wanted to ensure that all Democrats "will have meaningful and timely opportunities to participate fully in the election or selection of such delegates and alternates."[403]

Of course, most of the drama and disorder within the Democratic national convention of 1968 emanated from the floor debate on the platform committee's recommended, pro-LBJ majority report on the Vietnam War and the minority report cosponsored by dovish presidential candidates Eugene McCarthy and George McGovern.[404] The three most distinct and disputed features of the proposed McCarthy-McGovern planks on Vietnam were its unconditional end to the American bombing of North Vietnam, the phased withdrawal of all American and North Vietnamese troops from South Vietnam, and "a political reconciliation" between the National Liberation Front, which included the Viet Cong, and the current government of South Vietnam. The McCarthy-McGovern proposal solemnly concluded, "We are also resolved to have no more Vietnams. . . . We shall neither assume the role of the world's policemen, nor lend our support to corrupt oppressive regimes unwilling to work for essential reforms and lacking the consent of the governed."[405]

In making speeches to the convention endorsing the McCarthy-McGovern minority report, former Kennedy aides Pierre Salinger and Kenneth P. O'Donnell emphasized the need for the Democratic Party to clearly distinguish itself from the Republican Party on the Vietnam War. O'Donnell, a delegate from Massachusetts, stated that he and his fellow Democrats must "not delude the American people that we can adopt this platform in its domestic sense, meet our responsibility for vast expenditures of money to meet the problems of the United States of America and continue a foreign adventure, a foreign engagement, that is costing us $30 billion a year. This is the height of irresponsibility, and let us not leave this convention as the Republicans left Miami, promising all things to all people."[406] With a similar theme, Salinger, a California delegate, stated that the minority report "is offered because it offers the Democratic party a real chance for victory in November. I believe that to give the people of the United States a plank on Vietnam which is indistinguishable from what was offered by the Republicans in Miami is sheer suicide for our party."[407]

Of the several speeches urging the convention to adopt the pro-LBJ majority report on Vietnam, Senator Edmund S. Muskie of Maine gave the most persuasive, conciliatory address. Muskie emphasized the similarities between the majority and minority reports. In his conclusion, Muskie added, "I wish a spirit of compromise had moved to resolve the differences. Each of these planks commits us to an early negotiated settlement. Each supports the idea of calculated risk to move us toward that settlement."[408]

After the election, Muskie told journalist David Nevin, "I felt that Hubert would act to wind down the war faster than Nixon would, and that he could do so under either policy, the majority plank or the minority plank . . . I wanted to see the Democratic Party win and I wanted it to win through a war policy that would permit us to end the war."[409] Partially because of Muskie's speech and televised interviews on behalf of the majority report, it passed by the surprisingly wide margin of 1,567³/₄ votes to 1,041¹/₄ votes on August 28.[410]

Like Senate Majority Leader Mike Mansfield, Muskie had been publicly loyal to LBJ's policies in Vietnam while privately questioning and occasionally criticizing them in letters to the president, including JFK, as early as 1963. In a confidential memo to LBJ in January 1968, Muskie asked the president to stop the bombing of North Vietnam unilaterally.[411] Humphrey understood and respected the fact that, like himself and Mansfield, Muskie had tried to privately influence LBJ's decisions in Vietnam instead of publicly opposing them or LBJ's renomination as McCarthy and RFK did. In his memoirs, Humphrey revealed that Muskie had been his top choice for a running mate as early as April.[412] The vice president immediately recognized Muskie's advantage to his presidential campaign in not being "identified with the Johnson administration or with the Vietnam War."[413]

After Hubert Humphrey received the presidential nomination on the first ballot with 1,761³/₄ votes to McCarthy's 601 votes, he quickly moved to secure Muskie's agreement to be his running mate.[414] On August 29, Muskie was overwhelmingly nominated for vice president, receiving 1,941 votes. Of the 75¹/₄ votes cast for other candidates for vice president, Julian Bond received 48¹/₂ votes, even though he was constitutionally too young to run for vice president.[415]

More so than any other decision that Humphrey made at this convention, his selection of Muskie distanced him from LBJ. Johnson had disliked and distrusted Muskie ever since the senator from Maine, a member of the freshman class of 1958, refused to submit to LBJ's domination of the Senate in a key vote in 1959. Humphrey, nonetheless, informed LBJ by telephone of his choice of Muskie, knowing that it would displease and disappoint the president.[416] Lawrence F. O'Brien, who was named DNC chairman on August 30, later commented, "As it turned out, the nomination of Muskie was the best decision made in Chicago."[417]

Humphrey desperately needed whatever assets Muskie could provide to the Democratic ticket, especially in improving his strained relationship with dovish Democratic senators. Senator George S. McGovern, a now defeated presidential candidate running for reelection in South Dakota, urged his supporters to "get behind Humphrey" and later congratulated Humphrey at the podium following the vice president's televised acceptance speech.[418] Eugene McCarthy, however, left the convention less than twenty minutes after Humphrey was nominated for president.

McCarthy stated that he had not decided if he would endorse Humphrey. He might support, but would not lead, a new, antiwar minor party in the presidential election. Less than one hour later, Marcus Raskin, co-director of the Institute for Policy Studies, led other McCarthy supporters in a meeting to discuss the formation of such a party for the presidential election. Raskin told the other participants that this new party could have its slates of electors in at least five states.[419]

After an extended vacation on the French Riviera, McCarthy covered the 1968 World Series for *Life* magazine. He did not make another major campaign appearance until October 9, 1968, when he campaigned for Democratic senatorial nominee Paul O'Dwyer in New York. McCarthy declined to publicly endorse Humphrey until October 29, one week before the election.[420] Besides being tepid and tardy, McCarthy's endorsement was qualified according to whether Humphrey's future statements on the Vietnam War strictly adhered to the measures proposed by the McCarthy-McGovern minority report at the convention. On October 30, McCarthy publicly stated to an audience in California, "I'm voting for Humphrey, and I think you should suffer with me."[421]

While Hubert Humphrey did not need McCarthy's apathetic, contemptuous endorsement to win the election, the vice president needed the votes of supporters of McCarthy and RFK as well as the campaign contributions of wealthy, antiwar liberals who financed much of McCarthy's presidential campaign.[422] McCarthy made no effort to influence the ADA to switch its endorsement from him to Humphrey. The ADA had endorsed McCarthy before the New Hampshire primary.[423] The ADA's national board did not endorse Humphrey until the middle of October. It only did this because UAW attorney and ADA vice chairman Joseph L. Rauh, Jr. vigorously lobbied ADA leaders.[424] Many local ADA chapters remained indifferent or hostile to Humphrey's candidacy as election day neared.[425]

With the financial, organizational, and electoral support from antiwar liberals absent or unreliable, the Humphrey campaign closely followed a revised version of O'Brien's campaign plan known as the "O'Brien White Paper" and given to LBJ on September 29, 1967.[426] O'Brien patterned his 1967 campaign strategy for LBJ on the Clifford-Rowe memorandum submitted to Truman in 1947. O'Brien expected that the 1968 presidential election would be similar to that of 1948, regardless of whether LBJ or Hubert Humphrey was the Democratic presidential nominee in 1968.

In addition to the Democratic and Republican presidential nominees, O'Brien expected that a significant portion of the popular votes and perhaps some electoral college votes would be absorbed by a leftist, antiwar candidate, similar to Henry Wallace in 1948, and a right-wing, anti-civil rights southern candidate, similar to J. Strom Thurmond in 1948. From O'Brien's perspective, the Democratic presidential campaign of 1968 must initially unite and energize the centrist base of the party, namely, labor unions, big-city mayors, and racially moderate southern whites, and then try to minimize the voter appeal of the left-wing and right-wing minor party presidential nominees toward the end of the campaign. In this way, the Democratic presidential nominee of 1968 could win an upset victory similar to that of Harry Truman in 1948.[427]

With the profound, turbulent changes in the political environment that had occurred since the fall of 1967, the Vietnam War was even more of a liability for Humphrey than it had been for LBJ. O'Brien's recommended focus on domestic policy issues while avoiding detailed policy statements on the Vietnam War seemed to be the best rhetorical strategy for Humphrey. Most of the Humphrey campaign's literature, speeches, and television commercials emphasized his domestic policy positions. In 1948, Truman concentrated his campaign on defending New Deal economic, labor, and social welfare policies from the threat of Republican control of both Congress and the presidency. Similarly, the Humphrey campaign warned socially conservative, blue-collar whites that their improved economic conditions during the JFK and LBJ administrations would vanish if Richard Nixon were elected president or if they wasted their votes on George Wallace's minor party candidacy. Humphrey's publicity also tried to appeal to the more moderate, antiwar youth by promising liberal changes in domestic policy.[428]

On September 4, 1968, Richard M. Nixon officially began his general election campaign in Chicago. On that same day, Bill Claire, a Humphrey campaign aide, wrote the following assessment to Lawrence F. O'Brien. "Generally, I think the two areas most in need of work are in the two areas traditionally Democratic. Assuming a Truman-type campaign of '48, and the JFK turning points in 1960, we must, I think, give top priority to capturing the traditional Democratic and independent votes in '48 and '60, bearing in mind that several of the '48 votes are now—at this moment—in the suburbs, and nominally Republican. These are the most disillusioned people in the country, even though their present economic status is largely due to Democratic accomplishments."[429] Claire also suggested that the Humphrey-Muskie campaign avoid trying to absorb the pro-McCarthy antiwar activists. "Little or nothing can be done with this group, which will nonetheless have some ballot strength in the (sic) six or seven states."[430]

Democratic members of Congress who backed Humphrey, both hawks and doves, also tried to avoid discussing Humphrey's position on the war and emphasized their agreement with him on domestic policies as the reason for endorsing him, however passively and equivocally.[431] Democratic senators facing tough reelection battles, such as Birch Bayh of Indiana, Wayne Morse of Oregon, and Joseph Clark of Pennsylvania, avoided sharing platforms with Humphrey or even mentioning his name in their speeches, let alone mobilizing their campaign organizations behind Humphrey.[432] Despite the fact that Democratic senatorial nominee Alan Cranston of California was far ahead of his Republican opponent in the polls, he rebuffed Humphrey's plea to at least casually endorse the vice president in his speeches until the end of the campaign.[433]

In major campaign appearances in Philadelphia, Boston, San Francisco, and Seattle, Humphrey was often distracted and irritated by heckling, occasionally violent, antiwar protesters. Televised news coverage of Humphrey's appearances at these events often focused on the hecklers and police actions against them, rather than on the content of Humphrey's speeches and the occasionally warm, enthusiastic receptions that most listeners provided him. The print media often described the low turnout of Humphrey supporters and conveyed the impression of a dismal, hopeless campaign for the vice president. Pessimistic media coverage and analysis made it more difficult for Humphrey to improve his status in the polls and mobilize the Democratic base. On September 29, less than six weeks before the election, the Gallup firm released a voter preference poll that ranked Nixon at 43 percent, Humphrey at 28 percent, and Wallace at 21 percent.[434]

The AFL-CIO and UAW labor leaders, however, began to make steady progress in dissuading their union members from voting for Wallace and, to a lesser extent, for Nixon. Organized labor, of course, had even less optimism in the prospect of victory for Humphrey in 1968 than it had for Truman in 1948. As in 1948, its primary concern was the election or reelection of pro-union Democrats to Congress. It also did not want Wallace's racially divisive candidacy to inflict lasting damage on its efforts to improve race relations among its union members, especially in the UAW, and consolidate their votes behind union-endorsed candidates.[435] Labor's efforts in publicity, voter registration, and voter mobilization reminded union members and their families of Hubert H. Humphrey's and Edmund S. Muskie's consistently pro-labor legislative records, Richard Nixon's servitude to big business, and the antiunion, low-wage work environment of George Wallace's Alabama.[436] In its last voter preference poll, released on November 4, the Gallup firm reported that support for Wallace had declined to 14 percent.[437] Gallup exit polls on election day later revealed that, among voters who belonged to union families, 56 percent voted for Humphrey, 15 percent for Wallace, and 29 percent for Nixon.[438]

In addition to organized labor's vigorous anti-Wallace efforts, the Humphrey campaign benefited from the sharply contrasting public perceptions of the three vice-presidential nominees. Nixon and Wallace chose politically inept, outspoken, controversial running mates.[439] Among the most antiwar, previously anti-Humphrey liberals, Muskie gained some respect and sympathy for the Humphrey-Muskie ticket. He politely and patiently shared his campaign appearances with antiwar students and encouraged rational, calm debates with them on the Vietnam War.[440] Agnew sometimes equaled Wallace's strident, callous disregard and repression toward antiwar activists. Curtis LeMay, a retired air force general and Wallace's running mate on the American Independent Party (AIP) ticket, shocked the media and the American public with casual, blunt statements about his willingness to use nuclear weapons in Vietnam. Nixon's cautious, centrist campaign strategy wanted to attract votes from both southern conservative whites and moderate, suburban whites on racial issues. But he had to counteract Agnew's widely quoted references to "a Polack" and a Japanese journalist as the "fat Jap."[441] A Harris poll showed that voters preferred Muskie over Agnew by a margin of 17 percent.[442]

The Humphrey campaign eagerly promoted the taciturn, lanky Muskie's image as "Lincolnesque," not only in physical appearance but also in integrity and independence because of his political success in historically Republican Maine. The fact that Muskie was the son of a Polish immigrant tailor was also emphasized in internal campaign memos and some publicity as an asset in attracting Catholic ethnic voters, especially Polish Americans, who were tempted to vote for Wallace or Nixon because of racial unrest.[443] Other Muskie publicity underscored the Maine senator's policy specialization on air and water pollution in order to attract votes from environmentally conscious, Republican-leaning, or undecided suburban voters.[444]

The Democratic presidential campaign shrewdly used its promotion of Muskie's vice-presidential candidacy to highlight a broader theme: the character issue. It hoped that it could use the favorable public perception of Muskie to convince voters that Humphrey was not a lackey of LBJ and the product of an undemocratic, brutal, boss-controlled convention. Instead, the Democratic campaign wanted to persuade voters that Humphrey's choice of Muskie was an indication of the vice president's good judgment, experience, and integrity. Campaign aides and advisors concluded that effectively communicating these attributes of Humphrey to the public was especially important for appealing to undecided or Nixon-leaning suburban voters.[445]

The character issue was also used to emphasize each voter's responsibility in choosing a presidential candidate who was best for the nation. A Humphrey campaign flier solemnly stated, "On November 5, this country will elect a new President. And in a single day, a man will be chosen to change America. He must do more than talk about change. He must cause it. He must know what's right. He must know what's wrong. . . . And he must know how to make it happen. Hubert Humphrey is that kind of man."[446]

The Humphrey campaign further used the character issue as a way to encourage the voters and the news media to critically question Nixon's character, judgment, and qualifications to be president. This tactic paralleled the efforts of the 1960 Democratic presidential campaign to frighten and motivate a wide spectrum of Democrats, ranging from Joseph L. Rauh, Jr. to Sam Rayburn, to unite behind the JFK-LBJ ticket because of their shared revulsion at the possibility of a Nixon presidency. More uniquely and contemporaneously, the 1968 Democratic presidential campaign wanted to not only mobilize the Democratic base but also persuade undecided swing voters to reject the so-called "New Nixon" being touted by the Republicans. Humphrey's speeches, Democratic television commercials, and campaign literature portrayed the "New Nixon" as nothing more than the high-priced, Madison Avenue-created façade for the "Old

Nixon," that is, the "real Nixon." The real Nixon was still deceitful, unscrupulous, quick-tempered, ruthlessly power-hungry, and callous to the domestic policy needs of average Americans, and proved his poor judgment with his selection of Spiro Agnew.[447] When Nixon rejected Humphrey's repeated invitations to debate him on television, Humphrey used Nixon's rebuff as further evidence of Nixon's insincerity and duplicity.[448]

The Humphrey campaign understood that voters, especially Democrats, had weaker party loyalty in 1968 than in 1960. The Democratic criticism of Nixon in 1960 portrayed him as a rigidly partisan Republican who, if elected president, would be unwilling or unable, in contrast to Eisenhower, to cooperate with a Democratic Congress in making progress in domestic policy and in continuing a responsible, bipartisan foreign policy in the Cold War. In 1968, the Democratic presidential campaign attacked Nixon's personal character, instead of his partisanship, in order to revive the public's fears and suspicions about the Old Nixon.[449]

Nixon's repeated refusal to specify his "peace with honor" and "secret plan" because of his concerns about the progress of the Paris peace negotiations was a political asset against Humphrey until the final weeks of the campaign. After Humphrey publicly adopted a more dovish position on Vietnam with his September 30 speech in Salt Lake City, Democratic campaign commercials boldly challenged Nixon to explain his positions on Vietnam to the American voters.[450] The Democratic presidential campaign was now trying to use the Vietnam War issue to actually benefit Humphrey's candidacy and damage Nixon's by subordinating it to the character issue. In short, Humphrey had the honesty and courage to publicly detail his positions on Vietnam, and Nixon did not.[451]

By late October, Nixon's campaign had stalled while Humphrey's was improving in the polls, media commentary, and the vice president's more self-confident appearances before larger, friendlier crowds.[452] O'Brien's assumption that the 1968 presidential election would be similar to that of 1948 appeared to be coming true. Even from a Republican perspective, Nixon's well-financed, poll-driven, strictly scripted campaign with cautious, vapid issue positions seemed eerily reminiscent of Thomas Dewey's ultimately unsuccessful presidential campaign.[453] Later, Leonard Garment, a Nixon campaign advisor, recalled how he felt helpless and powerless to reverse Nixon's decline, or "slide," in the polls during the final weeks of the campaign. Garment stated, "The slide was a strange sensation; there was nothing you could do about it. We threw in everything. . . . Then, he squeaked through."[454]

Journalists critical of the apparently cynical vacuousness of Nixon's campaign were less charitable in their observations of it. Jack Newfield characterized Nixon as "the Howdy Doody of the new politics."[455] After the election, David Halberstam concluded, "In part because of his silence and his failure to come to terms with such an awesome issue, Nixon had helped turn a potential landslide into a cliffhanger."[456] Likewise, David Broder observed, "This outcome was hardly surprising, considering the 'no-risk' holding-operation kind of campaign Nixon chose to run."[457]

Of course, the Nixon campaign's greatest concern about losing the election stemmed from its inability to control or predict LBJ's military decisions in Vietnam or news from the Paris peace negotiations. The Republicans suspected that Johnson would manipulate his bombing decisions to help Humphrey win the election.[458] For his part, LBJ believed that Anna Chennault, the Chinese-born, pro-Nixon widow of an American general, was a liaison between the Nixon campaign and the South Vietnamese government, which refused to send a delegation to Paris.[459] The South Vietnamese government now perceived a Nixon presidency to be more protective of its interests in the peace talks than a Humphrey presidency.

During the last week of the 1968 presidential campaign, the Johnson administration and the Nixon campaign raised each one's suspicions of the other's motives. With Humphrey steadily gaining on Nixon in the polls throughout October, LBJ announced on October 31 that he ordered a halt to all bombing in North Vietnam to facilitate the peace talks. In this nationally televised, prime-time speech, the president confidently stated "that the action I announce tonight will be a major step toward a firm and honorable peace in Southeast Asia."[460]

On November 2, Nguyen Van Thieu, president of South Vietnam, issued a public statement criticizing LBJ's decision and announcing that his government would not send a delegation to Paris for the renewed peace talks scheduled to begin on November 6, the day after the presidential election. Secretary of Defense Clark M. Clifford, who helped to draft LBJ's October 31 speech, urged the president to halt the bombing. He also concluded that Anna Chennault, John Mitchell, Nixon's campaign manager, and Bui Diem, South Vietnam's ambassador to the United States, had persuaded the South Vietnamese president to make his announcement to help Nixon win the election. It seemed more than coincidental that President Thieu made his announcement on the same day that most polls showed Humphrey and Nixon in a statistical dead heat.[461] In his memoirs, Clifford mostly attributed Humphrey's defeat to "Thieu's treachery," "Nixon's clever deviousness," and "Chennault's interference."[462]

Nonetheless, in the closing days of their campaigns, the Humphrey and Nixon campaigns could not anticipate and did know exactly how to adapt to sudden, new developments from the Paris peace talks and the war in Vietnam and their effects on the polls, voter turnout, and voting behavior. With its rigid planning, the Nixon campaign had already prepared and paid for air time to broadcast election eve telethons for the East and West coasts, similar to Nixon's 1960 election eve telethon. By contrast, JFK did not conduct an election eve telethon in 1960.

Lawrence F. O'Brien decided that Humphrey and Muskie should conduct similar telethons. He believed that JFK's omission of a nationally broadcast telethon on the eve of the 1960 election was a mistake. He concluded that JFK's razor-thin popular vote margin over Nixon was partially a result of this mistake. O'Brien rejected the opposition of Joseph Napolitan and Robert Squier, Humphrey's media consultants, to the idea of a telethon. With inadequate campaign funds and even less time remaining before the election, Napolitan and Squier wanted to spend these scarce funds on well-timed television commercials. The Nixon campaign had saturated the air waves with advertising during the Olympics.

O'Brien wanted to make the most of Humphrey's recent surge in the polls and provide a televised visual contrast between the partnership of Humphrey and Muskie in the Democratic telethons and the absence of Agnew in Nixon's telethon.[463] O'Brien was also confident that the screening of questioners' phone calls could prevent the embarrassing calls that plagued Humphrey's telethon in the 1960 West Virginia primary.[464] From the polling and voter mobilization data that the Humphrey campaign received, O'Brien discerned that undecided voters were more likely to vote for Humphrey than Nixon if the Democrats also conducted election eve telethons.

In his memoirs, O'Brien commented that, of all of the Democratic presidential campaigns in which he participated from 1960 to 1972, he found Humphrey's 1968 campaign to be the most personally satisfying, despite Humphrey's narrow, heartbreaking defeat. O'Brien especially valued the fact that he was able to equally and simultaneously combine and fulfill the roles of campaign manager and DNC chairman. Humphrey generally deferred to O'Brien's judgment and gave O'Brien broad discretion to determine the strategy and tactics of the Democratic presidential campaign. O'Brien observed that "in 1968, Humphrey understood his needs, and he wanted me to have full authority over all aspects of the campaign—the media program, organization, issues, the whole thing. I savored the challenge, the day by day uphill struggle that took us so close to victory."[465]

Where was LBJ's presidential party leadership? After all, the suprapartisan, centrist policy consensus that he nurtured and promoted disintegrated shortly after he made a major commitment of American ground forces to South Vietnam in the spring of 1965. Congress, public opinion, and the voters rejected his determination to continue Great Society liberalism in domestic policy. Some of LBJ's political contemporaries, journalists, and recent scholarly interpretations concluded that LBJ's lack of political support for Humphrey in the general election campaign contributed to, or even caused, Humphrey's defeat.[466] In his book, *Flawed Giant*, historian Robert Dallek unequivocally stated, "Johnson's choice as his successor was New York's Republican Governor Nelson Rockefeller."[467] Dallek later added that "Johnson was reluctant to do anything that might help Humphrey win."[468]

Dallek and other critics of LBJ's treatment of Humphrey's general election campaign underestimate the extent to which Johnson was a liability to Humphrey after the vice president secured the presidential nomination in Chicago. Since late 1967, LBJ, on the advice of the Secret Service and FBI, greatly limited his public speaking appearances outside of Washington, DC, and military bases. If LBJ had barnstormed the nation on Humphrey's behalf in the fall campaign, televised news coverage and Nixon's campaign commercials would have highlighted the inevitable anti-Johnson demonstrations, hecklers, and imposing security precautions associated with LBJ's campaign appearances.

Moreover, after the convention and especially after Humphrey's Salt Lake City speech, the Humphrey campaign devoted much of its scarce and precious time and money portraying the vice president as a man of independence whom the voters could trust. Johnson told the nation on March 31 that he would not spend time on partisan matters in order to fully devote himself to achieving an honorable, responsible end to the Vietnam War during the remainder of his presidency. If LBJ had actively campaigned for Humphrey, the president would have exacerbated his serious credibility problem with public opinion, the media, and Congress. A wider credibility gap would have weakened the effectiveness and legitimacy of his military and diplomatic decisions and Humphrey's candidacy through their association with each other. In particular, Republicans could have more convincingly charged that LBJ's October 31 announcement of a bombing halt callously and cynically disregarded the safety of American troops in order to swing the election to Humphrey.[469]

Robert E. Short, the DNC's treasurer and Humphrey's chief fundraiser, complained after the election that LBJ did not do enough to raise campaign funds for Humphrey, particularly among oil executives.[470] In his memoirs, published three years after LBJ's death, Hubert Humphrey revealed that he had opportunities to receive substantial contributions from oil and gas interests. He knew that they wanted him to promise to protect the oil depletion allowance. He firmly told them that he wanted to substantially reduce this tax break in order to reform the tax code. Humphrey proudly concluded, "I kept my honor. They kept their money."[471]

If Johnson had been more assiduous in privately raising funds for Humphrey, it is unlikely that the president could have significantly narrowed the overwhelming financial advantage that Nixon's campaign had over Humphrey's. As Humphrey, O'Brien, and others have indicated, business interests and wealthy individuals who donated substantial or equal sums of money to both Democratic and Republican presidential nominees in the past gave little or nothing to Humphrey. These contributors pragmatically concluded that Humphrey would definitely lose the election because of the chaotic legacy of the Chicago convention, Nixon's wide lead in the polls until late October, and LBJ's status as an unpopular lame duck.[472] They perceived Nixon as a centrist, winning Republican candidate like Eisenhower in 1952 instead of a controversial, doomed extremist like Goldwater in 1964. There was nothing that LBJ could do to change that perception.

In addition to his announcement of a bombing halt on October 31 and his organization of a joint appearance with Humphrey at the Houston Astrodome on November 3, one of the most significant, unwitting, yet overlooked contributions that LBJ made to Humphrey's campaign was his persistence in trying to elevate Abe Fortas from associate justice to chief justice. If LBJ succeeded, Fortas would become the first Jewish chief justice of the U.S. Supreme Court. Republicans and southern Democrats on the Senate Judiciary Committee aggressively questioned Fortas about his financial interests, the impropriety and possible unconstitutionality of his role as an advisor to LBJ during his tenure as an associate justice, and his liberal jurisprudence.[473] Although this committee recommended Fortas's nomination, the Senate became embroiled in a mostly Republican filibuster opposing the appointment of Fortas as chief justice. After a Senate vote failed to invoke cloture on October 1, 1968, Fortas asked LBJ to withdraw his nomination.[474]

Throughout this ordeal, LBJ remained steadfast in his support of Fortas.[475] Paul O'Dwyer, the Democratic nominee for senator in New York, publicly and repeatedly accused some of Fortas's opponents in the Senate of being motivated by anti-Semitism. The American Jewish Committee provided evidence of the anti-Semitic basis for opposition to Fortas from extremist, right-wing groups.[476] In his study of campaign contributions from mostly Jewish investment firms in New York, journalist G. William Domhoff asserted that Abe Fortas was the most influential lawyer of the "Jewish-Cowboy" faction of the Democratic Party. Shortly after Fortas's nomination for chief justice became embroiled in a contentious filibuster that Johnson and his allies in the Senate tried to end, there was a sharp increase in contributions and long-term, high-risk loans to the Humphrey campaign from mostly Jewish financiers and attorneys from Wall Street and producers in Hollywood.[477]

Determined to achieve a responsible end to the Vietnam War and to appoint Abe Fortas as chief justice, LBJ persisted in his belief that the voters on November 5 would reward policy behavior that benefited the national interest with the election of Hubert Humphrey. The subordination of immediate partisan and campaign interests to productivity in public policy had always been the foundation of LBJ's suprapartisan, centrist policy consensus. In short, good government is good politics.

LBJ publicly reaffirmed his faith in the suprapartisan, national desire for good government in his endorsement of Hubert Humphrey in an address sponsored by the Democratic Victory Committee and broadcast on the evening of November 3. The president quoted several Republican presidents on the importance of the presidency as a nationally unifying, nonpartisan public trust. LBJ asserted that Americans "must never elect a man of narrow partisanship" and that the presidency "is supremely the place where political honor and public trust must coincide to guard the Nation's interest as well as to grant the people's will."[478] Toward the end of his speech, LBJ concluded that American voters could entrust Humphrey and Muskie with the presidency because "each had shown, throughout all of public life, the essential qualities of character that so many of our Presidents have singled out as the vital qualities of leadership: honor and conscience, reason and truth. A commitment to represent all of the people—and the ability to do so because they have earned the faith of all of the people."[479]

The words of LBJ's November 3 endorsement were consistent with his desire to rebuild and resume a unifying suprapartisan centrist policy consensus under Humphrey and Muskie and the theme of his 1964 presidential campaign. This theme was his determination for his candidacy, administration, policy agenda, and, somehow, the Democratic Party to broadly, inclusively, and consensually represent all reasonable interests and perspectives under a big tent. No matter how misguided, impractical, or oblivious to the dissensus of 1968 Johnson's tenacious faith in a suprapartisan, centrist policy consensus was, it influenced his behavior as president and party leader to the end of his presidency.[480]

It is still difficult to discern exactly what the 1968 election results revealed regarding LBJ's presidency and party leadership. A Gallup poll conducted immediately after the election and published on November 27 indicated that LBJ's job approval rating was 43 percent, a significant improvement on his September 4 rating of 35 percent.[481] A Gallup poll released on October 30, however, indicated that a plurality of its sample preferred the Republican Party over the Democratic Party as being "more likely to keep the United States out of World War III" and for controlling inflation. In this poll, the respondents slightly favored the Democratic Party over the Republican Party, 37 to 34 percent, for "keeping the country prosperous."[482]

Another Gallup poll, released on December 4, 1968, indicated that 25 percent of the voters surveyed were undecided about how to vote for president two weeks before the election. Also, 54 percent of the voters surveyed stated that they had voted a split ticket. The voting statistics of the 1968 election indicated ambiguity, indecision, and dissatisfaction among many voters. Voter turnout decreased only slightly from 61.7 percent in 1964 to 60.6 percent in 1968.[483] The number of southern blacks registered to vote increased from 2,164,000 in 1964 to approximately 3,124,000 in 1968.[484] George Wallace's American Independent Party (AIP) succeeded in being placed on the ballots of all fifty states. Wallace received 13.5 percent of the popular votes and forty-six electoral votes from five states in the Deep South and one "faithless elector" from North Carolina.[485] Political analysts Richard M. Scammon and Ben J. Wattenberg estimated that 70 percent of the Wallace vote would have gone to Nixon in a two-candidate election between Nixon and Humphrey.[486]

George Wallace fell far short of the bargaining position that he sought in the Electoral College. By winning enough Electoral College votes to deny either Nixon or Humphrey a majority, Wallace had hoped to extract policy promises on such issues as civil rights, crime, and Supreme Court nominees from one of them in exchange for his bloc of electoral votes or influence among southern congressmen in the House of the Representatives. Instead, Nixon's share of the Electoral College votes, 301, compared to Humphrey's, 191, was large enough so that this possibility was quite remote.[487]

Nixon's popular vote margin over Humphrey was surprisingly narrow. Nixon received 43.42 percent of the popular votes compared to Humphrey's 42.72 percent. This resulted in Nixon receiving 510,645 more votes than Humphrey of the 73,203,370 popular votes cast in the presidential election of 1968.[488] This was far less than the landslide, similar to Dwight Eisenhower's in 1952, that the polls suggested in the late summer and early fall. Despite the turbulence and dissensus afflicting the Democratic Party in 1968, Nixon's victory had no noticeable coattail effects on Republican congressional candidates. The national Democratic percentage of votes in House elections declined from 50.9 percent in 1966 to 50.2 percent in 1968.[489]

The Republicans made a net gain of four House seats and five Senate seats in 1968. Of the 401 House members who ran for reelection, 98.8 percent were reelected.[490] With 83 percent of the incumbent senators reelected, Republicans defeated two prominent, antiwar liberals, Wayne Morse of Oregon and Joseph Clark of Pennsylvania. The voters of Iowa replaced retiring Senator Bourke Hickenlooper, a hawkish conservative Republican, with Democratic governor Harold Hughes, a dove who nominated Eugene McCarthy for president at the Democratic national convention. This lack of a national ideological pattern or an issue position preference on the Vietnam War in Senate elections was also evident in the elections of Barry Goldwater to an open seat in Arizona and Alan Cranston, a dovish Democrat who avoided any association with Hubert H. Humphrey, in California.[491]

While Humphrey performed almost as well as LBJ did in 1964 among black and Jewish voters, he received 59 percent of the Catholic votes compared to LBJ's 76 percent.[492] Similarly, Humphrey received 56 percent of the votes of labor union members and their families compared to LBJ's 73 percent. Despite Democratic campaign strategists' earlier fears that Wallace would perform well among Catholic union members in major metropolitan areas, Wallace received only 8 percent of the Catholic votes and 15 percent of the votes of labor union members and their families.[493]

The most significant difference in voting behavior between the 1964 and 1968 presidential elections occurred among southern whites, even when the Wallace factor is discounted. Michael Barone estimated that Humphrey received less than 10 percent of the white votes in the Deep South.[494] In *The Emerging*

Republican Majority, Kevin P. Phillips likewise concluded, "All across the Deep South and even through much of the Outer South, Negroes were the only group to rally behind Hubert Humphrey."[495] In comparing southern white voting behavior in the 1964 and 1968 presidential elections, the statistical studies of Phillips and other scholars observed that southern whites in general were more likely to vote Republican in 1968 than in 1964, regardless of the differences among them in terms of location, income, and opinions on racial issues. For example, poor whites in the Deep South were much more likely to vote for Goldwater in 1964 than were affluent whites living in the suburbs of Richmond and Nashville.[496] But in 1968, Nixon's popular vote percentages in several states of the Deep South (e.g., 38 percent in South Carolina and 31 percent in Arkansas), were almost as high as those in the peripheral South (e.g., 40 percent in Texas and 38 percent in Tennessee).[497]

Another disturbing trend for the Democratic Party in future presidential elections was the weakening of party identification and loyalty among Democratic voters in particular. Among voters who identified themselves, LBJ respectively received 82 percent, 90 percent, and 77 percent of the votes of weak Democrats, independent Democrats, and independents in 1964. By contrast, Humphrey respectively received 68 percent, 64 percent, and 20 percent of the votes of weak Democrats, independent Democrats, and independents in 1968.[498] One study found that the national percentage of voters identifying themselves as Democrats decreased from 52 percent in 1964 to 46 percent in 1968. The percentage of Republicans remained virtually the same, 25 percent in 1964 and 24 percent in 1968, yet the percentage of independents increased sharply from 23 percent in 1964 to 29 percent in 1968.[499] Political scientists Everett C. Ladd, Jr., and Charles D. Hadley noted that the growth of independents was especially pronounced among southern white Protestants. While Republican identification among them increased slightly from 17 percent in 1964 to 22 percent in 1968, the proportion of independents increased from 30 to 39 percent. In 1964, 53 percent of southern white Protestants identified themselves as Democrats, but only 38 percent did in 1968.[500]

Kevin Phillips calculated that statistics like these indicated the beginning of a realignment that was developing a Republican majority in the nation. He concluded, "The emerging Republican majority spoke clearly in 1968 for a shift away from the sociological jurisprudence, moral permissiveness, experimental, residential, welfare and educational programming and massive federal spending by which the Liberal (mostly Democratic) Establishment sought to propagate liberal institutions and ideology—and all the while reap growing economic benefits."[501] Political scientist Walter Dean Burnham was far less confident of a Republican realignment. To him, Nixon's narrow victory was an "abortive landslide" in which the Republicans barely dented the large Democratic majorities in Congress and only slightly increased the percentage of voters identifying with the GOP.[502] It seemed likely that the dissensus that arose in the mid- to late 1960s and resulted in the dealignment of 1968 would persist well into the future with no clear majority party in voter identification.[503] For Scammon and Wattenberg, the party that was better able to satisfy the opinions and policy demands of most voters on social issues such as crime, racial conflict, campus unrest, and drug abuse would dominate future elections and domestic policymaking.[504]

When JFK and LBJ were developing their national political ambitions during the 1950s, their rhetoric and behavior within the Democratic Party, Congress, and the intraparty politics of their home states reflected that decade's emphasis on the apparent "end of ideology" and bipartisan, centrist pragmatism. JFK avoided being labeled a Catholic liberal as much as LBJ spurned being known as a southern conservative. Both of them were privately contemptuous of the ADA, the "amateur" Democratic clubs, and other mostly pro-Stevenson liberal activists. As Senate majority leader, LBJ openly opposed the DAC's efforts to formulate and advocate distinctly liberal policy positions to counteract the Eisenhower administration and Republicans in Congress. JFK declined the DAC's initial offer to join it and briefly became a silent, inactive member of it from 1959 to 1960. JFK and LBJ's shared pragmatism, centrism, and progressive ambition resulted in Kennedy becoming the only northern Democratic senator to join segregationist southern Democrats in voting for the jury trial amendment of the Civil Rights Act of 1957, and LBJ refusing to sign the 1956 Southern Manifesto opposing the *Brown* decision on school desegregation and subsequently shepherding compromised civil rights bills to their enactment in 1957 and 1960.[505]

Ironically, and to the occasional consternation of JFK and LBJ, the DAC's liberal ideas dominated the development and adoption of the 1960 Democratic national platform, especially in the policy areas of civil rights, poverty, health care, education, and urban renewal. As presidents and party leaders, they faced and eventually fulfilled their obligations to transform most of this liberal platform into laws.[506] JFK and LBJ assumed that the voters would evaluate their presidencies and the Democratic Party in general on their ability to fulfill their party's major domestic policy goals and to continue an effective, bipartisan containment policy in the Cold War. Thus, the activities of the DNC's apparatus were mostly limited to fundraising and voter registration among blacks, Hispanics, and young adults. The power and role of Lawrence F. O'Brien as the White House liaison with Congress greatly overshadowed the figurehead role of DNC chairman John M. Bailey. Most decisions on patronage and pork barrel spending that affected Democrats in Congress were made by O'Brien, not Bailey, for the purposes of facilitating passage of the president's policy agenda.[507]

The appearance of right-wing extremism and the presidential candidacy of Barry Goldwater in the early 1960s provided JFK and LBJ with the opportunity to portray the Democratic Party to the voters as a broad, inclusive, centrist engine of problem-solving pragmatism in public policy, rather than a bulwark of divisive, partisan, New Deal–based liberalism. After the far right damaged, divided, and disoriented the previously dominant moderate to liberal, pro-civil rights wing of the GOP, the Democratic Party outside of the South became modestly successful in co-opting socially and culturally liberal, middle- to upper-middle-class, white, Protestant, and Jewish Republicans.[508]

JFK's and LBJ's efforts to develop a suprapartisan, centrist policy consensus in the early to mid 1960s could not foresee, absorb, or counteract the dissensus that evolved from ideological, intellectual, and generational challenges of the New Left and the stylistic, participatory, and cultural demands of the New Politics.[509] Toward the end of his presidency, LBJ still believed that right-wing extremism posed a greater threat to the domestic policies of the New Frontier and Great Society and to moderate, restrained military and diplomatic policies in Vietnam and elsewhere in American foreign policy than the New Left and New Politics. The immediate, unfortunate legacy of JFK's and LBJ's presidential leadership of the Democratic Party is that it left the organization, rules, and processes of participation in their party unprepared and unable to resolve the disintegrating effects of dissensus and develop a new intraparty consensus in the Democratic Party's coalition, policy agenda, and ideology that would make it competitive in future presidential elections as Richard Nixon assumed the presidency.[510] JFK's and LBJ's legacy in party leadership seemed to fulfill the following, ominous warning of the APSA's 1950 study, *Toward a More Responsible Two-Party System*. "When the President's program actually is the sole program in this sense, either the party becomes a flock of sheep or the party falls apart. In effect this concept of the presidency disposes of the party system by making the President reach directly for the support of a majority of the voters."[511]

Epilogue

The 1960s was a tumultuous decade for the Democratic Party. The midterm elections of 1958 indicated greater public support for more federal intervention in economics, agriculture, education, and health care. In addition to these policy areas, liberal Democrats, represented by such organizations as the DAC, UAW, and ADA, advocated and formulated a Democratic platform for the 1960 presidential election that included the party's most liberal civil rights plank and more innovative Cold War foreign and defense policies, especially regarding the Third World and space technology.

It is not surprising that the mostly pro-Stevenson, liberal Democratic activists were initially dismayed and alarmed that their party's 1960 presidential ticket consisted of JFK and LBJ. After all, both appeared to be centrist, calculating politicians always willing to compromise or abandon liberal principles, especially on civil rights, for the sake of their ambition. Their administrations, however, proved to be dedicated and effective in fulfilling the policy priorities of the liberal-dominated Democratic national platforms of 1960 and 1964. In such policy areas as civil rights, federal aid to education, Medicare, Medicaid, and job training, the New Frontier and Great Society completed much of the unfinished policy agendas of the New Deal and Fair Deal.

As policymakers and party leaders, JFK and LBJ hoped to redefine the center of the American two-party system and public policy. They wanted the liberalism of the New Frontier and Great Society to eventually represent a suprapartisan, centrist policy consensus, instead of a divisive, partisan ideology and policy agenda limited to the most liberal, nonsouthern elements of the Democratic Party. Consequently, their presidential party leadership did little to organizationally prepare the Democratic Party, especially the regular activities of the DNC headquarters and its various appendages, such as the Young Democrats Clubs (YDC), for the political forces and events that buffeted and fragmented the party during the mid- to late 1960s. Both JFK and LBJ neglected the grassroots levels of the Democratic Party. Instead, they concentrated on raising large campaign contributions at elite levels and relied excessively on pollsters and media consultants to prepare for the 1964 and 1968 presidential elections. LBJ assumed that the best methods of polling, public relations, and media manipulation combined with steady policy progress in the Great Society and the Vietnam War could mold and move public opinion and then voting behavior in a desired direction.

The growth of right-wing extremism in the early 1960s, culminating in Barry Goldwater's presidential nomination and staggering losses for the Republican Party in 1964, led JFK and LBJ to overlook and underestimate the potential of the New Left and black militancy to challenge the Democratic Party and weaken its ability to win elections, especially presidential elections. Even after his presidency ended, Johnson still asserted that his administration and party leadership became unpopular mostly because of the public's uninformed, unreasonable impatience with his competent, responsible conduct of the Vietnam War. LBJ failed to realize that on a deeper, more complex level many politically active Democratic doves were frustrated and alienated by his refusal to provide them with adequate opportunities and processes for participation and consultation regarding American policies in the Vietnam War, especially at the 1968 Democratic national convention.

Robert F. Kennedy, Hubert H. Humphrey, Lawrence F. O'Brien, and Edmund S. Muskie, however, understood by the late 1960s that the Democratic Party needed to become more genuinely democratic, inclusive, open, and participatory in its presidential nomination, platform making, and delegate selection processes. They hoped to combine Old Politics and New Politics so that the Democratic Party could co-opt the more moderate, politically pragmatic elements of the New Left, antiwar movement, and black and Hispanic power movements while retaining enough of the shrinking New Deal coalition to win presidential elections and govern responsibly. With an "out-party" status after the 1968 election, the national Democratic Party began to undertake the most extensive, significant changes in its rules for delegate selection, platform making, primaries, and oversight over state Democratic parties in its history.

It was uncertain what the electoral, coalitional, ideological, and policy consequences of these procedural and participatory reforms would be. In their efforts to develop a suprapartisan, centrist policy consensus, JFK and LBJ wanted to diminish sharp ideological and partisan differences for the sake of greater, presidency-centered progress in policymaking. JFK and LBJ did not anticipate that their policies and party leadership would contribute to a fundamental, internal transformation of the Democratic Party's procedures and processes with such an inscrutable impact on its future.

Abbreviations

ADA	Americans for Democratic Action
APSA	American Political Science Association
APSR	*American Political Science Review*
BC	Boston College
BTC	Bates College
BU	Boston University
BWC	Bowdoin College
CHC	College of the Holy Cross
CQ	*Congressional Quarterly*
CR	*Congressional Record*
DAC	Democratic Advisory Council
DNC	Democratic National Committee
DSG	Democratic Study Group
EMK	Edward M. Kennedy
FC	Franklin College
FDR	Franklin D. Roosevelt
GPO	Government Printing Office
HHH	Hubert H. Humphrey
HST	Harry S. Truman
HUAC	House Un-American Activities Committee
ISA	Indiana State Archives
IU	Indiana University—Bloomington
JFK	John F. Kennedy
JFKL	John F. Kennedy Library
LBJ	Lyndon B. Johnson
LBJL	Lyndon B. Johnson Library
LOC	Library of Congress

MHS	Minnesota Historical Society
MTSU	Middle Tennessee State University
NAR	Nelson A. Rockefeller
ND	University of Notre Dame
NHSA	New Hampshire State Archives
NY	New York
NYT	*New York Times*
OF	Official File
OH	Oral History transcript
PC	Providence College
PCP	Presidential Campaign Papers
PF	Political File
POF	Political Office File
PPP	*Public Papers of the Presidents* (Washington, DC: GPO, 1958–1969) These volumes are cited by year and volume number.
PRPP	Pre-Presidential Papers
RCCC	Republican Congressional Campaign Committee
RFK	Robert F. Kennedy
RNC	Republican National Committee
SDS	Students for a Democratic Society
TTU	Texas Tech University
UCT	University of Connecticut—Storrs
UNH	University of New Hampshire
USNWR	*U.S. News and World Report*
UTA	University of Texas—Austin
UTN	University of Tennessee—Knoxville
VP	Lyndon B. Johnson, *The Vantage Point: Perspectives on the Presidency, 1963–1969* (New York: Popular Library, 1971)
WH	White House
WHCF	White House Central Library

Notes

CHAPTER ONE
JFK AND HIS PARTY

1. James MacGregor Burns, *John Kennedy: A Political Profile* (New York: Harcourt Brace Jovanovich, 1960): 69.

2. John Hersey, "Survival," *New Yorker* 20 (June 17, 1944): 31–43; Kenneth P. O'Donnell and David F. Powers, *"Johnny We Hardly Knew Ye"* (New York: Pocket Books, 1973): 73–74; Christopher Matthews, *Kennedy and Nixon* (New York: Simon and Schuster, 1996): 28–33; Ronald Kessler, *The Sins of the Father* (New York: Warner Books, 1996): 282–283; and Victor Lasky, *J.F.K.: The Man and the Myth* (New York: Macmillan, 1963): 320.

3. Herbert S. Parmet, *Jack: The Struggles of John F. Kennedy* (New York: Dial Press, 1980): 27–45; Matthews, 47–113; Nigel Hamilton, *JFK: Reckless Youth* (New York: Random House, 1992): 737–760.

4. William V. Shannon, "Massachusetts: Prisoner of the Past," in *Our Sovereign State*, ed. by Robert S. Allen (New York: Vanguard Press, 1949): 53.

5. Kristi Andersen, *The Creation of a Democratic Majority: 1928–1936* (Chicago: Univ. of Chicago Press, 1979): 4–16, 97–117; Earl Latham, *Massachusetts Politics* (New York: Citizenship Clearing House, 1957): 3–28; and Gerald H. Gamm, *The Making of New Deal Democrats* (Chicago: Univ. of Chicago Press, 1989): 183–202.

6. Latham, 33–56; Alec Barbrook, *God Save the Commonwealth* (Amherst: Univ. of Massachusetts Press, 1973): 22–23; and Duane Lockard, *New England State Politics* (Princeton: Princeton Univ. Press, 1959): 119–171.

7. David G. Lawrence, *The Collapse of the Democratic Presidential Majority* (Boulder: Westview Press, 1996): 6–7, 28–29.

8. Ibid., 7.

9. John K. White, *Still Seeing Red* (Boulder: Westview Press, 1997): 148.

10. Ibid.

11. Daniel J. Elazar, *American Federalism: A View from the States* (New York: Crowell, 1966): 96–122; Lockard, 119–120; and Neal R. Peirce, *The New England States* (New York: Norton, 1976): 93.

12. Edgar Litt, *The Political Cultures of Massachusetts* (Cambridge: MIT Press, 1965): 162–166; Edward Banfield and James Q. Wilson, *City Politics* (New York: Vintage, 1963): 138–186.

13. Litt, 7–25.

14. Lockard, 120–121; and Peirce, 62–63.

15. Burns, *John Kennedy: A Political Profile*, 102–103.

16. Banfield and Wilson, 43.

17. Jack Beatty, *The Rascal King* (New York: Addison-Wesley, 1992): 37–63, 508–523.

18. O'Donnell and Powers, 47–80; and Thomas P. O'Neill, Jr., *Man of the House* (New York: Random House, 1987): 75–76.

19. Peter Collier and David Horowitz, *The Kennedys: An American Drama* (New York: Summit Books, 1984): 26–41.

20. OH, Mark Dalton, Aug. 4, 1964, 11, JFKL.

21. Richard J. Whalen, *The Founding Father* (New York: New American Library, 1964): 381–408.

22. Ibid., 398.

23. Richard J. Whalen, 399.

24. O'Neill, 77.

25. Matthews, 32.

26. "A Kennedy Runs for Congress: The Boston-Bred Scion of a Former Ambassador Is a Fighting Conservative," *Look* 10 (June 11, 1946): 32–36.

27. Fletcher Knebel, "Pulitzer Prize Entry—John F. Kennedy," in *Candidates 1960*, ed. by Eric Sevareid (New York: Basic Books, 1959): 195; and JFK Papers, PRPP, Issues and Speeches folder, copy of JFK's 1946 platform, 5, JFKL.

28. Thomas Sugrue, "Crabgrass Roots Politics," *Journal of American History* 82 (Sept. 1995): 551–578; and Lasky, *J.F.K.: The Man and the Myth*: 95–96.

29. John F. Kennedy, *Why England Slept* (New York: Doubleday, 1961): 176–196; and Deirdre Henderson (ed.), *Prelude to Leadership: The European Diary of John F. Kennedy, Summer 1945* (New York: Regnery, 1995): ix–xlv.

30. Lasky, *J.F.K.: The Man and the Myth*, 95.

31. JFK, *Why England Slept*, 185.

32. Lasky, *J.F.K.: The Man and the Myth*, 95.

33. Matthews, 30.

34. O'Donnell and Powers, 72.

35. Ibid., 66.

36. Ralph G. Martin and Ed Plaut, *Front Runner, Dark Horse* (New York: Doubleday, 1960): 146.

37. Parmet, Jack, 162.

38. JFK Papers, PRPP, Speech Files 1946–52, speech to Young Democrats of Pennsylvania, Aug. 21, 1946, 3–4, JFKL.

39. Ibid., Boston Office Files, speech, "Why I am a Democrat," Oct. 23, 1946, 1, JFKL.

40. Ibid., page A.

41. Nigel Hamilton, 42.

42. CQ, *Guide to U.S. Elections* (Washington, DC: CQ Press, 1985): 508, 619, 963.

43. Parmet, *Jack*, 347–348.

44. Lasky, 108–109; and JFK Papers, PRPP, DNC booklet on health care, 1950, JFKL.

45. James M. Curley Collection, public letter, from Archbishop Richard Cushing, June 12, 1947, and, letter, John McCormack to Edward McCormack, undated, CHC.

46. Burns, *John Kennedy*, 87–92.

47. Ibid, 87–88.

48. Ibid., 76–78; and CR, v. 93, April 16, 1947, 3512–3513.

49. *Hearings Before the Committee on Education and Labor*, U.S. House of Representatives, 1st session (Washington, DC: GPO, 1947), v. 5, March 8–15, 1947, 3616.

50. Paul Healy, "Galahad in the House," *The Sign* 29 (July 1950): 10–11.

51. JFK Papers, PRPP, 1952 Senate Campaign, Box 105, undated 1952 press release, 2, JFKL.

52. Nigel Hamilton, 773.

53. JFK Papers, PRPP, Box 95, speech files, 1946–52 folder, Jan. 30, 1949, speech in Salem, MA, JFKL.

54. Parmet, *Jack*, 209–210.

55. OH, Edmund S. Muskie, Jan. 4, 1966, 3, JFKL.

56. Burns, *John Kennedy: A Political Profile*, 59.

57. John P. Mallan, "Massachusetts: Liberal and Corrupt," *New Republic* 127 (Oct. 13, 1952): 10.

58. O'Neill, 81; Richard M. Nixon, *RN: The Memoirs of Richard Nixon* (New York: Grosset and Dunlap, 1978): 75; Stephen E. Ambrose, *Nixon: The Education of a Politician* (New York: Simon and Schuster, 1987): 210–211; Matthews, 70; and Greg Mitchell, *Tricky Dick and the Pink Lady* (New York: Random House, 1998): 99–100.

59. Mallan, 11.

60. Thomas J. Whalen, *Kennedy Versus Lodge* (Boston: Northeastern Univ. Press, 2000): 59; and Burns, *John Kennedy*, 107.

61. Arthur M. Schlesinger, Jr., *A Thousand Days: John F. Kennedy in the White House* (Boston: Houghton Mifflin, 1965): 91.

62. Hamilton, 740–743; and Amanda Smith (ed.), *Hostages to Fortune: The Letters of Joseph P. Kennedy* (New York: Viking, 2001): 625 626.

63. Amanda Smith, 654–655.

64. JFK Papers, Box 106, Campaign Effort folder, letter, JFK to Stephen A. Mitchell, Aug. 19, 1952, JFKL.

65. Lawrence F. O'Brien, *No Final Victories* (New York: Ballantine, 1974): 28–29; and O'Neill, 76.

66. O'Brien, 36–37.

67. John A. Farrell, *Tip O'Neill and the Democratic Century* (Boston: Little, Brown, 2001): 119–120.

68. Thomas J. Whalen, 65.

69. O'Brien, 30–31.

70. Thomas J. Whalen, 183.

71. Lasky, *J.F.K.: The Man and the Myth*, 145.

72. Thomas J. Whalen, 364–365.

73. Amanda Smith, 653.

74. Thomas J. Whalen, 161.

75. JFK Papers, PRPP, Box 103, letter, Edward J. Dunn to RFK, Sept. 30, 1952, JFKL.

76. Thomas C. Reeves, *A Question of Character: A Life of John F. Kennedy* (New York: Free Press, 1991): 100–101.

77. Thomas J. Whalen, 129–130; and Kessler, 337–340.

78. JFK Speech Files, 1947–52, Box 93, undated 1952 speeches, "Civil Rights and the International Situation," "How Massachusetts Has Benefited from Two Decades of Federal Democratic Administration," and DNC files, Box 187, Henry Cabot Lodge folder, undated 1952 memo, JFKL.

79. Matthews, 49–50.

80. *Worcester Telegram and Gazette*, Oct. 24, 1952, 16.

81. JFK Papers, PRPP, Box 105, press release, Sept. 7, 1952, JFKL.

82. *Worcester Telegram and Gazette*, Oct. 22, 1952, 5, and Oct. 24, 1952, 16; and O'Brien, 30.

83. O'Donnell and Powers, 100–101; and Burns, *John Kennedy: Political Profile* 119.

84. Thomas J. Whalen, 149.

85. Vito N. Silvestri, *Becoming JFK: A Profile in Communication* (Westport, CT: Praeger, 2000): 35–37.

86. *Worcester Telegram and Gazette*, Oct. 30, 1952, 11.

87. William J. Miller, *Henry Cabot Lodge* (New York: James H. Heineman, 1967): 254.

88. Thomas J. Whalen, 152–153; Lasky, *J.F.K.: The Man and the Myth*, 148–149; Barbrook, 180; and Lawrence H. Fuchs, "Presidential Politics in Boston: The Irish Response to Stevenson," *New England Quarterly* (Dec. 1957): 435–437.

89. OH, Torbert MacDonald, Aug. 1, 1965, 50, JFKL.

90. Barbrook, 169, 174, 184; and CQ, *Guide to U.S. Elections*, 619.

91. O'Donnell and Powers, 101–106; Lasky, *J.F.K.: The Man and the Myth*, 144; Burns, *John Kennedy*, 118–119; Helen O'Donnell, *A Common Good* (New York: Morrow, 1998): 88–92; and Thomas J. Whalen, 157–162.

92. O'Brien, 29–30.

93. O'Donnell and Powers, 99.

94. OH, David F. Powers, April 3, 1969, 6, JFKL; OH, Dalton, 29; Matthews, 86–87; and Richard J. Whalen, 422–432.

95. Edwin O. Guthman and Jeffrey Shulman (ed.), *Robert Kennedy: In His Own Words* (New York: Bantam, 1988): 442.

96. Burns, *John Kennedy*, 118; Martin and Plaut, 183; and Hugh D. Price, "Campaign Finance in Massachusetts in 1952," *Public Policy* 6 (1955): 25–46.

97. Kessler, 342; and Lasky, *J.F.K.: The Man and the Myth*, 149.

98. Martin and Plaut, 155–162; and O'Donnell and Powers, 87–88.

99. Richard J. Whalen, 374; Martin and Plaut, 182–186; and Parmet, *Jack*, 255.

100. Barbrook, 116–117; *CQ, Guide to U.S. Elections*, 619; and JFK Papers, PRPP, Box 527, memo, O'Brien to JFK, May 16, 1957, JFKL; and Farrell, 149.

101. O'Neill, 76.

102. Lawrence Becker, "New England as a Region," in *Parties and Politics in the New England States*, ed. by Jerome M. Mileur (Amherst: Univ. of Massachusetts Press, 1997): 14.

103. Peirce, 67; Banfield and Wilson, 42–43; and Nicol C. Rae, *The Decline and Fall of the Liberal Republicans: From 1952 to the Present* (New York: Oxford Univ. Press, 1989): 146–147.

104. Thomas J. Whalen, 154–155.

105. Rae, 37; Ambrose, *Nixon*, 285–286; and Herbert S. Parmet, *The Democrats: The Years After FDR* (New York: Oxford Univ. Press, 1976): 95–102.

106. Arlene Lazarowitz, *Years in Exile: The Liberal Democrats, 1950–1959* (New York: Garland, 1988): 93.

107. Rowland Evans and Robert Novak, *Lyndon B. Johnson: The Exercise of Power* (New York: New American Library, 1966): 54–87; Duane Tananbaum, *The Bricker Amendment Controversy* (Ithaca, NY: Cornell Univ. Press, 1988): 145–146; and Howard E. Shuman, "Lyndon B. Johnson: The Senate's Powerful Persuader," in *First Among Equals*, ed. by Richard A. Baker and Roger H. Davidson (Washington, DC: CQ Press, 1989): 216–220.

108. Hubert H. Humphrey, *The Education of a Public Man: My Life and Politics* (New York: Doubleday, 1976): 180–182; and Lasky, *J.F.K.: The Man and the Myth*, 170.

109. LBJA Congressional Files, letters, Edwin C. Johnson to Jesse Jones, May 1, 1954, LBJ to Estes Kefauver, Jan. 10, 1957, LBJL; POF, copy, *Vital Speeches of the Day*, Aug. 1, 1956, 617–619, JFKL; Gary W. Reichard, "Division and Dissent: Democrats and Foreign Policy, 1952–1956," *Political Science Quarterly* 93 (1978): 51–72; and R. Alton Lee, *Eisenhower and Landrum-Griffin* (Lexington: Univ. Press of Kentucky, 1990):72–73.

110. JFK Papers, PPRP, Box 546, letters, JFK to Harry J. Blanchette, May 11, 1956, press release of John W. McCormack, May 17, 1956; POF, Box 31, undated 1956 statement from JFK on Democratic State Committee, JFKL; POF, Box 136, letters from H. Clinton Leef, Hallie Merrill, and Louise H. Pickering, all from Oct. 29, 1956 to JFK; and from Russell E. Taylor to JFK, Oct. 30, 1956, JFKL.

111. O'Donnell and Powers, 129–133.

112. JFK Papers, PRPP, Box 106, memo, Larry O'Brien to JFK, undated, 1956, 9, JFKL.

113. Ibid., 13; and Parmet, *Jack*, 291–295.

114. O'Brien memo, 12, JFKL.

115. John W. McCormack Papers, letters, John E. Powers to McCormack, Jan. 5, 1956, BU; OH, Joseph L. Rauh, Dec. 23, 1965, 17–18, JFKL; and OH, Kenneth P. O'Donnell, July 23, 1969, 2, JFKL.

116. Adam Cohen and Elizabeth Taylor, *American Pharaoh: Mayor Richard J. Daley* (Boston: Little, Brown, 2000): 249–250.

117. Joseph L. Rauh, Jr. Papers, Box 29, letter, Robert Nathan to Rauh, Aug. 16, Robert Nathan to Rauh, Aug. 16, 1956, LOC.

118. Parmet, *Jack*, 356–357; Thomas C. Reeves, 134; and Lawrence J. Quirk, *The Kennedys in Hollywood* (Dallas, TX: Taylor, 1996): 168.

119. Presidential Recordings, cassette K, item 39, undated 1963 memo, dictated by JFK, JFKL.

120. DNC, *Official Proceedings of the 1956 Democratic National Convention* (Chicago: DNC, 1956): 420–421.

121. Author's interview with William Woolsey, former reporter for the *Nashville Tennesseean*, in Louisville, KY, on June 24, 1993; author's interview with Wilson Wyatt, 1952 campaign manager for Adlai Stevenson, in Louisville, KY, on June 24, 1993; and Jeff Broadwater, *Adlai Stevenson* (New York: Twayne, 1994): 162–163.

122. John Bartlow Martin, *Adlai Stevenson and the World* (New York: Doubleday, 1977): 354.

123. Albert Gore, Sr. Papers, Democratic convention 1956 folder, letters, J. P. Coleman to Gore, Aug. 28, 1956, Gore to Sam Rayburn, Aug. 22, 1956, LBJ to Gore, Aug. 30, 1956, Sam Ervin, Jr. to Gore, Sept. 10, 1956, MTSU.

124. DNC, *Official Proceedings . . . 1956*, 464.

125. Ibid., 480.

126. OH, Camille Gravel, May 23, 1967, 5–12, JFKL; OH, John M. Bailey, April 27, 1966, 10–15, JFKL; and Richard D. Mahoney, *Sons and Brothers* (New York: Arcade, 1999): 20.

127. DNC, *Official Proceedings . . . 1956*, 480.

128. Arthur Krock, *Memoirs: Sixty Years on the Firing Line* (New York: Funk and Wagnalls, 1968): 359.

129. DNC, *Official Proceedings . . . 1956*, 482.

130. O'Donnell and Powers, 144–145.

131. C. David Heymann, *RFK* (New York: Dutton, 1998): 114–116.

132. LBJA Cong. Files, Box 55, letter, Stuart Symington to LBJ, May 25, 1956, Box 3, Thomas G. Corcoran folder, Corcoran folder, Corcoran to HHH, Aug. 31, 1956, LBJL; George H. Gallup, *The Gallup Poll: Public Opinion, 1935–1971* (New York: Random House, 1973), v. 3, 1430–1431; Parmet, *Jack*, 384–386; and Estes Kefauver to JFK, Oct. 1, 1956, UTN.

133. JFK Papers, PRPP, Box 815, speech, JFK to Young Democrats, Oct. 5, 1956, 2, JFKL.

134. Ibid., 3.

135. Ibid., 6.

136. Parmet, *Jack*, 399–416; Silvestri, 91–94; and JFK Papers, PRPP, Box 902, speech, JFK to Chamber of Commerce, Charlotte, NC, Jan. 15, 1959, JFKL.

137. Theodore C. Sorensen Papers, Box 10, letter, JFK to William Loeb, April 3, 1957, JFKL.

138. Philip A. Klinkner, *The Losing Parties: Out-Party National Committees, 1956–1993* (New Haven, CT: Yale Univ. Press, 1994): 22–24.

139. Theodore C. Sorensen Papers, letter, JFK to Paul M. Butler, Feb. 7, 1957, JFKL.

140. Parmet, *The Democrats*, 172.

141. Irving Bernstein, *Promises Kept* (New York: Oxford Univ. Press, 1990): 24–25; and author's interview with Sam Brightman, former DNC publicity director, on July 12, 1991, in Bethesda, MD.

142. Parmet, *The Democrats*, 174.

143. Evans and Novak, 196–212; and Nicol C. Rae, *Southern Democrats* (New York: Oxford Univ. Press, 1994): 99.

144. Bernstein, *Promises Kept*, 25–26; *Time*, v. 72 (Nov. 3, 1958): 16–19; and Joseph L. Rauh, Jr. Papers, Box 37, letter, Theodore C. Sorensen and Rauh, Nov. 18, 1958, LOC.

145. Mark Stern, *Calculating Visions: Kennedy, Johnson, and Civil Rights* (New Brunswick, NJ: Rutgers Univ. Press, 1990): 15–16.

146. OH, Herbert Tucker, March 9, 1967, 15–25, JFKL.

147. Stern, 21; and Abraham Ribicoff Papers, Box 11, unsigned, undated memo from JFK staff to Ribicoff, "IV. Civil Rights and Race Relations," LOC.

148. Earl Black and Merle Black, *The Vital South: How Presidents Are Elected* (Cambridge: Harvard University, 1992): 190.

149. Knebel in Sevareid, 207–208.

150. Stern, 72; and Lasky, *J.F.K.: The Man and the Myth*, 202.

151. OH, John Patterson, May 26, 1967, 15, JFKL.

152. Burns, *John Kennedy*, 221

153. Klinkner, 12–40; Lazarowitz, 132–157; and Stephen M. Gillon, *Politics and Vision: The ADA and American Society* (New York: Oxford Univ. Press, 1987): 75–128; and John K. White, *The Fractured Electorate* (Hanover, NH: Univ. Press of New England, 1983): 47.

154. Evans and Novak, 112–113.

155. Joseph C. Goulden, *Meany* (New York: Atheneum, 1972): 293; and OH, Joseph S. Clark, Dec. 16, 1965, 15–19, JFKL

156. DNC, *Official Proceedings, 1956*, 464–465, 480–481.

157. Merle Miller, *Lyndon: An Oral Biography* (New York: Ballantine, 1980): 243–244; and Robert A. Caro, *Master of the Senate* (New York: Knopf, 2002): 859.

CHAPTER TWO
LBJ AND HIS PARTY

1. Robert A. Caro, *The Path to Power* (New York: Vintage: 1982): 200.

2. Ibid., 93–94; Doris Kearns, *Lyndon Johnson and the American Dream* (New York: Harper and Row, 1976): 230; and Robert Dallek, *Lone Star Rising: Lyndon Johnson and His Times, 1908–1960* (New York: Oxford Univ. Press, 1991): 23–24.

3. Alonzo Hamby, *Liberalism and Its Challengers* (New York: Oxford Univ. Press, 1985), 240–241; Kearns, 92; and Paul K Conkin, *Big Daddy from the Perdernales River: Lyndon Baines Johnson* (Boston: Twayne, 1986): 214.

4. Ronnie Dugger, *The Politician* (New York: Norton, 1982): 185–190; and Dallek, *Lone Star Rising*, 126–138.

5. Ibid., 148–149.

6. Caro, *The Path to Power*, 394–396.

7. Ibid., 408.

8. OH, James H. Rowe, Jr., Sept. 9, 1969, 7–11, LBJL.

9. James H. Rowe, Jr. Papers, folder AC, 87–6, letter, Rowe to Missy LeHand, Aug. 10, 1939, LBJL.

10. William E. Leuchtenburg, *In The Shadow of FDR: From Harry Truman to Ronald Reagan* (Ithaca: Cornell Univ. Press, 1983):150.

11. Dugger, 197; and Conkin, 95

12. *CQ, Guide to U.S. Elections*, 1116; and OH, John M. McCormack, Sept. 23, 1968, 4–5, LBJL.

13. Caro, *The Path to Power*, 625–626.

14. Miller, *Lyndon*, 92–93.

15. Lewis L. Gould, "Never a Deep Partisan: Lyndon Johnson and the Democratic Party, 1963–1969," in Robert A. Divine (ed.), *The Johnson Years*, v. 3 (Lawrence: Univ. Press of Kansas, 1994): 21–52.

16. Conkin, 63; and Evans and Novak, 9–11.

17. Schlesinger, *A Thousand Days*, 33–40; and Dallek, *Lone Star Rising*, 204–206.

18. V. O. Key, Jr., *Southern Politics in State and Nation* (Knoxville: Univ. of Tennessee Press, 1985): 265–268; and James R. Soukup et al., *Party and Factional Division in Texas* (Austin: Univ. of Texas Press, 1964): 92, 113–114.

19. Charles R. Ashman, *Connally* (New York: Morrow, 1974): 54–55.

20. James H. Rowe Jr. Papers, folder AC, 87–6, memo for Rowe to FDR, April 10, 1941, LBJL.

21. Ibid., memo, Rowe to FDR, May 5, 1941, LBJL.

22. Dallek, *Lone Star Rising*, 214–218; Dugger, 228–230; and Ashman, 59.

23. John B. Connally, *In History's Shadow* (New York: Hyperion, 1993): 109.

24. Caro, *The Path to Power*, 718–723; and Connally, 107–110.

25. Conkin, 105.

26. Miller, *Lyndon*, 106.

27. Robert A. Caro, *Means of Ascent* (New York: Knopf, 1990): 74–75.

28. Dugger, 261.

29. Soukup et al., xiv.

30. Hart Stillman, "Texas: Owned by Oil and Interlocking Directorates," in *Our Sovereign State*, 314–320; and John Gunther, *Inside USA* (New York: Harper, 1947): 814–848.

31. D. B. Hardeman and Donald C. Bacon, *Sam Rayburn: A Biography* (Lanham: Madison Books, 1987): 296–300.

32. Richard C. Bain and Judith H. Parris, *Convention Decisions and Voting Records* (Washington, DC: Brookings Institution, 1973): 265; and Key, *Southern Politics*, 256.

33. Hardeman and Bacon, 301.

34. CQ, *Guide to U.S. Elections*, 202.

35. OH, Rowe, 15, LBJL.

36. Caro, *Means of Ascent*, 15; and James MacGregor Burns, *Roosevelt: The Lion and the Fox* (New York: Harcourt Brace Jovanovich, 1956): 364.

37. Bruce J. Schulman, *Lyndon B. Johnson and American Liberalism* (Boston: St. Martin's Press, 1994): 28.

38. Joe Phipps, *Summer Stock: Behind the Scenes with LBJ in '48* (Fort Worth: Texas Christian Univ. Press, 1992): 156.

39. Caro, *Means of Ascent*, 125–126; and Donald R. McCoy, *The Presidency of Harry S. Truman* (Lawrence: Univ. Press of Kansas, 1984): 98–99.

40. Phipps, 57–58.

41. Ibid., 151–153.

42. Connally, 114.

43. Ashman, 64–65.

44. Caro, *Means of Ascent*, xxxiii.

45. OH, John E. Babcock, Nov. 22, 1983, 40–41, LBJL.

46. Connally, 112–113; and Gunther, 840–841.

47. Ashman, 65.

48. Oh, Cecil E. Burney, Nov. 26, 1968,18, UTA.

49. Phipps, 306–307; Dugger, 320–321; and Caro, *Means of Ascent*, 184–191.

50. Dallek. 330; and Miller, *Lyndon*, 152–153.

51. Dugger 328

52. Ibid., 328–329; Phipps, 319; and Seth S. McKay, "The Mystery of Ballot Box 13," *Human Events*, 24 (June 6, 1964): 8.

53. OH, Joseph L. Rauh, Jr., July 30, 1969, LBJL; and Miller, *Lyndon*, 162.

54. Bobby Baker, *Wheeling and Dealing: Confessions of a Capitol Hill Operator* (New York: Norton, 1978): 34.

55. Ibid., 41.

56. Robert H. Ferrell (ed.), *Truman in the White House: The Diary of Eben Ayers* (Columbia: University of Missouri Press, 1991): 330–331.

57. Sean J. Savage, *Truman and the Democratic Party* (Lexington: Univ. Press of Kentucky, 1997): 68–69; Joseph P. Harris, "The Senatorial Rejection of Leland Olds," *APSR* 45 (1951): 674–692.

58. Evans and Novak, 37.

59. Rae, *Southern Democrats*, 98–99.

60. James L. Sundquist, *The Dynamics of the Party System* (Washington, DC: Brookings Institution, 1983): 283.

61. Savage, *Truman and the Democratic Party*, 166.

62. Ibid, 146–151.

63. Bobby Baker, 59–60.

64. Lee Edwards, *Goldwater* (Lanham: Regnery, 1995): 39–50.

65. James T. Patterson, *Mr. Republican: A Biography of Robert A. Taft* (Boston: Houghton Mifflin, 1972): 597–617.

66. Goodwin, 109–110.

67. Bobby Baker, 63.

68. HHH, *The Education of a Public Man*, 164–165.

69. Hardeman and Bacon, 389–394.

70. Stephen E. Ambrose, *Eisenhower* (New York: Simon and Schuster, 1990): 346–347; Arthur Larson, *A Republican Looks at His Party* (New York: Harper, 1956): 16–17; Robert L. Branyan and R. Alton Lee, "Lyndon Johnson and the Art of the Possible," *Southwestern Social Science Quarterly*, 44 (1963): 214–225.

71. David Reinhard, *The Republican Right Since 1945* (Lexington: Univ. Press of Kentucky, 1983): 156–158; Kent Beck, "What Was Liberalism in the 1950s?," *Political Science Quarterly*, 52 (Summer, 1987): 233–258; Gary W. Reichard, *Reaffirmation of Republicanism: Eisenhower and the Eighty-third Congress* (Knoxville: Univ. of Tennessee Press, 1975): 236–237.

72. CQ, *Guide to U.S. Elections*, 359, 1124; Rae, *The Decline and Fall of the Liberal Republicans*, 160–161; Angus Campbell and Warren E. Miller, "The Motivating Basis of Straight and Split Ticket Voting," *APSR* 51 (1957): 293–312; and Everett C. Ladd, Jr., and Charles D. Hadley, *The Transformations of the American Party System* (New York: Norton, 1975): 125.

73. Duane Tananbaum, *The Bricker Amendment Controversy* (Ithaca: Cornell Univ. Press, 1988): 145–146; and Herbert Parmet, *The Democrats: The Years After FDR* (New York: Oxford Univ. Press, 1976): 126.

74. George Reedy, *Lyndon B. Johnson: A Memoir* (New York: Andrews and McMeel, 1982): 92.

75. Senate Political Files, Box 19, Clippings, *San Antonio Express*, May 30, April 15, 1954, LBJL.

76. Gillon, 155–156; Klinkner, 14–25; and James MacGregor Burns, *The Deadlock of Democracy* (New York: Prentice-Hall, 1963): 179–195.

77. APSA, *Toward a More Responsible Two Party System* (New York: Rinehart, 1950): 3–4.

78. OH, Richard Bolling, February 27, 1969, 10, LBJL.

79. Parmet, *Jack*, 152–155; Burns, *Deadlock*, 253–254; and Brightman interview.

80. Thomas G. Corcoran, Papers, Box 66, undated 1956 memo, Rowe to LBJ, 1–2, LOC.

81. Stern, *Calculating Visions*, 132–134.

82. Black and Black, 145–151.

83. Robert G. Kaufman, *Henry M. Jackson: A Life in Politics* (Seattle: Univ. of Washington Press, 2000): 111–114.

84. John Goldsmith, *Colleagues: Richard B. Russell and His Apprentice, Lyndon B. Johnson* (Washington, DC: Seven Locks Press, 1993): 62–66.

85. Robert Mann, *The Walls of Jericho* (New York: Harcourt Brace and Company, 1996): 220–221.

86. Reedy, 130.

87. Richard A. Baker and Roger H. Davidson (ed.), *First Among Equals* (Washington, DC: CQ Press, 1991): 229.

88. Stern,14.

89. Dallek, *Lone Star Rising*, 526.

90. James C. Duram, *A Moderate Among Extremists: Dwight D. Eisenhower and the School Desegregation Crisis* (Chicago: Nelson-Hall, 1981): 143–144.

91. John F. Martin, *Civil Rights and the Crisis of Liberalism* (Boulder: Westview Press, 1976): 164–167.

92. Mann, *The Walls of Jericho*, 225–228.

93. OH, Price Daniel, June 5, 1970, 48, LBJL.

94. O. Douglas Weeks, *Texas in the 1960 Presidential Election* (Austin: Univ. of Texas, 1961):1.

95. OH, Edgar Ball, Jan. 29, 1983,1–4, LBJL; and James Q. Wilson, *The Amateur Democrat* (Chicago: Univ. of Chicago Press, 1962): 370.

96. OH, Margaret Carter, August 19, 1969, 13, LBJL.

97. OH, Burney, 31–34.

98. Weeks, 21–22; and Soukup et al., 4–5.

99. CQ, *Guide to U.S. Elections*, 632.

100. Dallek, *Lone Star Rising*, 535.

101. Clinton Anderson Papers, Box 125, DNC Analysis of 1956 election, February 1, 1957, LOC; and Charles V. Hamilton, *Adam Clayton Powell, Jr.* (New York: Macmillan, 1992): 273–281.

102. LBJA Subject Files, Box 65, Samuel Lubell's lectures, Howard University, February 25–March 1, 1957, 8, LBJL.

103. Author's telephone interview with Richard Murphy, former DNC official, Nov. 10, 2001.

104. *USNWR*, v. 41, Aug. 10, 1956, 41–46.

105. Dallek, *Lone Star Rising*, 490–491; and Paul R. Henggeler, *In His Steps: Lyndon Johnson and the Kennedy Mystique* (Chicago: Ivan R. Dee, 1991): 26.

106. W. Averell Harriman Papers, Box 390, clipping, *Life* (March 11, 1956): 166, LOC.

107. Kearns, 160–161.

CHAPTER THREE
THE 1960 ELECTION: RIVALS AND ALLIES

1. Lee, *Eisenhower and Landrum-Griffin*, 1–17; Arthur A. Sloane, *Hoffa* (Cambridge: MIT Press, 1991): 160–184; and Kevin Boyle, *The UAW and the Heyday of American Liberalism, 1945–1968* (Ithaca, NY; Cornell Univ. Press, 1995): 125–154.

2. William H. Moore, *The Kefauver Committee and the Politics of Crime: 1950–1952* (Columbia: Univ. of Missouri Press, 1974): 200–204.

3. Goulden, 296–303; and Boyle, 146–147.

4. OH, Clark, 19–30, JFKL.

5. Boyle, 140–141.

6. John Barnard, *Walter Reuther and the Rise of the Auto Workers* (Boston: Little, Brown, 1983): 97–121.

7. Sloane, 99–104; and Lee, *Eisenhower and Landrum-Griffin*, 56–57.

8. RFK, *The Enemy Within* (New York: Popular Library, 1960): 274–286.

9. Lee, *Eisenhower and Landrum-Griffin*, 81–82.

10. RFK, *The Enemy Within*, 304–307.

11. Parmet, *Jack*, 430.

12. Lee, *Eisenhower and Landrum-Griffin*, 102–111; and Parmet, *Jack*, 493–494.

13. Lee, *Eisenhower and Landrum-Griffin*, 156–159.

14. Miller, *Lyndon*, 272–273.

15. Boyle, 139–143.

16. Goulden, 296–297; and Miller, *Lyndon*, 274.

17. Boyle, 140.

18. OH, O'Donnell, 7, JFKL.

19. Frank H. Jonas, "Western Politics and the 1958 Elections," *Western Political Quarterly* 14(1959): 241–156; and Glenn W. Miller and Stephen B. Ware, "Organized Labor in the Political Process: A Case Study of the Right-to-Work Campaign in Ohio," *Labor History* 4(1963): 51–67.

20. Philip S. Wilder, Jr., *Meade Alcorn and the 1958 Election* (New York: McGraw-Hill, 1960): 27–28.

21. *CQ, Politics in America: The Politics and Issues of the Postwar Years* (Washington, DC: CQ Press, 1969): 29–31.

22. Gallup, 1523; and Ambrose, 494.

23. *PPP*, 1958, 690–691, 1959, 503–506, 647.

24. Dallek, *Lone Star Rising*, 537–538.

25. *CQ, Politics in America*, 30–31.

26. *USNWR*, 45 (Nov. 14, 1958): 35.

27. Ibid., 46.

28. Donald B. Matthews,"The Folkways of the United States Senate: Conformity to Group Norms and Legislative Effectiveness," *APSR* 53 (1959):1064–1089; George Goodwin, Jr., "The Seniority System in Congress," *APSR* 53 (1959): 412–436; and Ralph K. Huitt, "Democratic Party Leadership in the Senate," *APSR* 55 (1961): 333–344.

29. Dallek, *Lone Star Rising,* 547.

30. Evans and Novak, 202.

31. Michael Foley, *The New Senate: Liberal Influence in a Conservative Institution 1959–1972* (New Haven: Yale Univ. Press, 1980): 28–33.

32. Paul Douglas, "Party Responsibility in Congress," in *Politics 1960*, ed. by Francis M. Carney and H. Frank Way, Jr. (San Francisco: Wadsworth, 1960): 33.

33. Evans and Novak, 200; and OH, William Proxmire, Feb. 4, 1986, 1–3, LBJL.

34. Tristram Coffin, "John Kennedy: Young Man in a Hurry," *Progressive* 23 (December 1959): 10–18; and JFK, "New England and the South," *Atlantic Monthly* 193 (January 1954): 32–36.

35. OH, John M. Bailey, April 10, 1964, 2–16, JFKL; OH, Muskie, 8–22, JFKL; and Abraham Ribicoff Papers, Box 11, letter, Theodore C. Sorensen to Ribicoff, July 28, 1959, LOC.

36. Stern, 15–17.

37. Theodore C. Sorensen, *Kennedy* (New York: Harper & Row, 1965): 58–59.

38. Victor Lasky, *John F. Kennedy: What's Behind the Image?* (Washington, DC, Free World Press, 1960): 33.

39. Gallup, 1633–1634.

40. JFK Papers, PRPP, Box 527, letter, JFK to O'Brien, June 4, 1957, JFKL; and Sorensen, *Kennedy*, 74–77.

41. Burns, *John Kennedy: A Profile*, 54–57; and Theodore C. Sorensen Papers, memo, JFK to Sorensen, December 1957, undated, memo, Sorensen to Charles Patione, JFKL.

42. O'Brien, 54–57.

43. Theodore C. Sorensen Papers, clipping, *Youngstown Vindicator*, August 21, 1958, JFKL.

44. *CQ, Guide to U.S. Elections*, 619; and Sorensen, *Kennedy*, 77.

45. Knebel in Sevareid, 210.

46. Sorensen, *Kennedy*, 78.

47. O'Brien, 52–58.

48. OH, Frederick G. Dutton, May 3, 1965, 8–29, JFKL.

49. Theodore H. White, *The Making of the President 1960* (New York: Atheneum, 1961) 62.

50. Klinkner, 12–40; and OH, Camille Gravel, May 23, 1967, 20–22, JFKL.

51. Michael P. Weber, *Don't Call Me Boss: David L. Lawrence, Pittsburgh's Renaissance Mayor* (Pittsburgh: Univ. of Pittsburgh Press, 1988): 303–351.

52. White, *The Making of the President 1960*, 32.

53. O'Donnell and Powers, 170–174.

54. David Nevin, *Muskie of Maine* (New York: Random House, 1972): 33.

55. Miller, *Lyndon*, 265.

56. Joseph I. Lieberman, *The Power Broker: A Biography of John M. Bailey, Modern Political Boss* (Boston: Houghton Mifflin, 1966) 205; and James Boyd, *Above the Law* (New York: New American Library, 1968): 23.

57. White, *Still Seeing Red*, 172; Boyd, 24–27; and Thomas J. Dodd Papers, Box 1, folder 9, letter, Dodd to John M. Bailey, March 9, 1959, UCT.

58. Boyd, 28–33.

59. Francis Valeo, *Mike Mansfield: Majority Leader* (New York: M.E. Sharpe, 1999): 33–34.

60. Abraham Ribicoff Papers, Box 11, undated memo, Ribicoff and John Bailey to Theodore C. Sorensen, LOC; O'Brien, 76; Dennis Roberts Papers, Box 6, copy of memo, EMK to RFK, Dec. 23, 1959, PC; and John O. Pastore Papers, General Files, letter, JFK to Pastore, Jan. 13, 1959, PC.

61. OH, James H. Rowe, Jr., May 10, 1964, 12, JFKL.

62. OH, O'Donnell, 7–12, JFKL.

63. Sorensen, *Kennedy*, 115.

64. Fred G. Burke, "Senator Kennedy's Convention Organization.," in Paul Tillet, (ed.), *Inside Politics: The National Conventions, 1960* (New York: Oceana, 1962): 25–38; and Paul T. David, "The Presidential Nominations," in Paul T. David (ed.), *The Presidential Election and Transition: 1960–1961* (Washington, DC: Brookings Institution, 1961): 4–10.

65. Burke, 27–35.

66. White, *The Making of the President 1960*, 194–195.

67. O'Brien, 59, 68.

68. White, *The Making of the President 1960*, 63–64.

69. OH, Bailey, 14–50, JFKL.

70. O'Brien, 60–63.

71. Edward P. Morgan, "The Missouri Compromise—Stuart Symington," in Sevareid, 245–279.

72. OH, O'Donnell, 7, JFKL.

73. Telephone Conversation, cassette L, item 421, dictated 1959 memo, JFK to Joseph P. Kennedy, JFKL.

74. JFK Papers, POF, letter, JFK to Newton Minow, Jan. 13, 1960, JFKL.

75. (R.) Vance Hartke and Jack Redding, *Inside the New Frontier* (New York: MacFadden Books, 1962): 11–19.

76. Matthew E. Welsh, *View from the State House: Recollections and Reflections, 1961–1965* (Indianapolis: Indiana Historical Bureau, 1981): 30–31; and O'Brien, 60–61.

77. Evans and Novak, 264–265.

78. Author's interview with Ideal Baldoni: former Democratic chairman of St. Joseph County, Indiana, Sept. 28, 2001, in Mishawaka, Indiana.

79. CQ, *Guide to U.S. Elections*, 412.

80. Lasky, *J.F.K.: The Man and the Myth*, 325–326; OH, Bailey, 8–9, LBJL; and Sorensen, *Kennedy*, 130–131.

81. OH, Bailey, 18–19, JFKL.

82. O'Brien, 79.

83. OH, Bernard L. Boutin, June 3, 1964, 3–10, JFKL; Sorensen, *Kennedy*, 121; and author's telephone interview with Boutin, January 10, 1998.

84. Robert W. Merry, *Taking on the World* (New York: Viking Press, 1996): 342–350.

85. Author's personal interview with Richard Neustadt, political scientist and former adviser to JFK, July 24, 1991, Wellfleet, Massachusetts.

86. OH, O'Donnell, 7–10, JFKL.

87. HHH, 204–212.

88. OH, O'Donnell, 7–8, JFKL.

89. HHH, 205–206.

90. *NYT*, Dec. 31, 1959.

91. Austin Ranney, "The 1960 Democratic Convention: Los Angeles and Before," in Tillett, 9.

92. White, *The Making of the President 1960*, 100–109.

93. Elazar, 108–110; and James H. Fenton, *Midwest Politics* (New York: Holt, Rinehart, and Winston, 1966): 44–74.

94. Jerry Bruno and Jeff Greenfield, *The Advance Man* (New York: Morrow, 1971): 38–42.

95. Helen O'Donnell, 167.

96. OH, Patrick Lucey, Jan. 6, 1972, 26–39, JFKL.

97. OH, Clement J. Zablocki, Oct. 29, 1965, 11–31, JFKL.

98. Theodore C. Sorensen Papers, unsigned memo, "The Catholic Vote in 1952 and 1956," spring, 1956, JFKL; and "Can 'Catholic Vote' Swing An Election?" *USNWR*, v. 14 (Aug. 10, 1956): 41–46.

99. O'Brien, 66–67.

100. OH, Lucey, 26.

101. Silvestri, *Becoming JFK*, 95–96; and Theodore C. Sorensen (ed.), *"Let the World Go Forth": The Speeches, Statements, and Writings of John F. Kennedy* (New York: Delacorte Press, 1988): 89–90.

102. OH, Lucey, 24–31; OH, James E. Doyle, Jan. 15, 1966, 5–9, JFKL; and HHH, 204–208.

103. OH, Isaac Coggs, December 8, 1965, 2–5, JFKL; and OH, James Brennan, Dec. 9, 1965, 14–15, JFKL.

104. Sorensen, *Kennedy*, 135; and HHH, 208–209.

105. Vito N. Silvestri, "John F. Kennedy: His Speaking in the Wisconsin and West Virginia Primaries 1960," Ph.D. diss., Indiana University, 1966, 17–18.

106. HHH, 210–211.

107. OH, Brennan, 14–17, JFKL.

108. O'Brien, 66.

109. O'Donnell and Powers, 182.

110. O'Brien, 66; and *CQ Guide to U.S. Elections*, 410.

111. Sorensen, *Kennedy*, 137.

112. Silvestri, diss., 26–27.

113. Helen O'Donnell, 185.

114. HHH, 211.

115. Harry W. Ernst, *The Primary That Made A President: West Virginia 1960* (New York: McGraw–Hill, 1962): 1–8.

116. Lasky, *J.F.K.: The Man and the Myth*, 342–350.

117. White, *The Making of the President 1960*, 121–127.

118. Ernst, 3.

119. Ibid., 2.

120. OH, John E. Amos, Aug., 6, 1965, 4–5, JFKL.

121. Silvestri, diss., 134–135; and OH, Sidney L. Christie, July 16, 1964, 15–16, JFKL.

122. Lasky, *J.F.K.: The Man and the Myth*, 344.

123. White, *The Making of the President 1960*, 119–120.

124. Ernst, 8.

125. HHH, 214.

126. Ernst, 5–7; OH, Bailey, 2–6, JFKL; OH, Amos, 16–17, JFKL.

127. Ernst, 18–21; and Richard Bradford, "John F. Kennedy and the 1960 Presidential Primary in West Virginia," *South Atlantic Quarterly* 75 (Spring 1976): 161–172.

128. Seymour M. Hersh, *The Dark Side of Camelot* (Boston: Little, Brown, 1997): 100–101; and Sam Giancana and Chuck Giancana, *Double Cross* (New York: Warner Books, 1992): 284.

129. O'Neill, 91–92.

130. O'Brien, 69–71.

131. Silvestri, *Becoming JFK*, 111–112.

132. David R. Mayhew, *Placing Parties in American Politics* (Princeton: Princeton Univ. Press, 1986): 80–84.

133. Ernst, 16.

134. Silvestri, diss., 109.

135. O'Brien, 76.

136. Ibid., 77.

137. Ernst, 23–31; Sorensen, *Kennedy*, 141; and Evans and Novak, 259.

138. Porter McKeever, *Adlai Stevenson: His Life and Legacy* (New York: Quill, 1989): 446–455.

139. Parmet, *Jack*, 496; and Mason Drukman, *Wayne Morse: A Political Biography* (Portland: Oregon Historical Society Press, 1997): 325–327.

140. O'Brien, 78–80; and *CQ, Guide to U.S. Elections*, 413.

141. Drukman, 325–330.

142. Edwin M. Yoder, Jr., *Joe Alsop's Cold War* (Chapel Hill: University of North Carolina Press, 1995): 172–173.

143. Sorensen, *Kennedy*, 149.

144. White, *The Making of the President 1960*, 145–146.

145. Broadwater, 184–185.

146. McKeever, 448.

147. Martin, *Adlai Stevenson and the World*, 506–512.

148. Broadwater, 186.

149. Schlesinger, *A Thousand Days*, 25; and O'Donnell and Powers, 205.

150. Martin and Plaut, 436–437; and Morgan in Sevareid, 278–279.

151. O'Brien, 83–84.

152. Connally, 170–171; and Reedy, 140–142.

153. Reedy, 141.

154. Bobby Baker, 121.

155. O'Neill, 181–182.

156. Foley, 27–33; and Conkin, 146–147.

157. Dallek, *Lone Star Rising*, 518–519; Soukup et al., 6–9; and Caro, *Master of the Senate*, 956–957.

158. Bobby Baker, 121–122.

159. Evans and Novak, 276–278.

160. Ibid., 265.

161. OH, Muskie, 32–33, JFKL; and Kaufman, 118.

162. *NYT*, July 30, 1960.

163. Robert H. Ferrell (ed.), *Off the Record: The Private Papers of Harry S. Truman* (New York: Penguin Books, 1980): 386–387; and author's telephone interview with John Doran, DNC aide under Paul Butler, Oct. 20, 2001.

164. *NYT*, July 31, 1960.

165. Savage, *Truman and the Democratic Party*, 194–195.

166. *NYT*, July 3, 1960.

167. Ibid.

168. Dallek, *Lone Star Rising*, 570–573.

169. Evans and Novak, 266.

170. Jeff Shesol, *Mutual Contempt*, (New York: Norton, 1997): 30–38; and India Edwards, *Pulling No Punches* (New York: Putnam, 1977): 227–229.

171. India Edwards, 226–227; and India Edwards Papers, unsigned memo, June 29, 1960, LBJL.

172. India Edwards, 228–229.

173. Ashman, 74.

174. Evans and Novak, 272.

175. OH, Rauh, 18–24, LBJL.

176. DNC Files (1st Series), clipping, *Wall Street Journal*, March 22, 1960, LBJL.

177. Sorensen, *Kennedy*, 156.

178. Henggeler, *In His Steps*, 41–42.

179. William C. Spragens, "Kennedy Era Speechwriting, Public Relations and Public Opinion," *Presidential Studies Quarterly* 14 (Winter 1984): 78–86.

180. OH, John P. Roche, July 16, 1970, 2–3, LBJL.

181. DNC, *Official Report of Proceedings of the Democratic National Convention and Committee 1960* (Washington, DC: National Document Publishers, Inc., 1964): 168.

182. Burke in Tillett, 26.

183. RFK Papers, Political Files, letter, James Landis to RFK, June 24, 1960, JFKL.

184. Joseph Hajda, "Choosing the 1960 Democratic Candidate: The Case of the Unbossed Delegations," *Kansas Quarterly* 8 (1976): 71–87.

185. Paul G. Land, "John F. Kennedy's Southern Strategy, 1956–1960," *North Carolina Historical Review* 56 (1979): 41–63.

186. Martin, *Adlai Stevenson and the World*, 512–521.

187. Joseph L. Rauh, Jr. Papers, Box 20, letter, HHH to Rauh, May 30, 1960, LOC.

188. Burke in Tillett, 38–39; and Clymer, 30.

189. Evans and Novak, 292–306; Guthman and Schulman, 19–26; Miller, *Lyndon*, 311–320.

190. Abraham Ribicoff Papers, Box 11, letter, Robert A. Wallace to Ribicoff, June 9, 1960, 4, LOC.

191. DNC, *Official Report of the Proceedings of the Democratic National Convention and Committee: 1960*, 168.

192. Kaufman, 118–121.

193. DNC, *Official Report . . . 1960*, 168.

194. Guthman and Shulman, 23–24.

195. Telephone Recordings, cassette L, item 421, dictated memo, JFK to Joseph P. Kennedy, undated 1959, JFKL.

196. Merry, 350–351.

197. Shesol, 43.

198. Ibid., and Sorensen, *Kennedy*, 165–166.

199. Kaufman, 121–123; and Ralph M. Goldman, *The National Party Chairmen and Committees: Factionalism at the Top* (New York: M.E. Sharpe, 1990): 470.

200. Lieberman, 144, 249–254.

201. Joseph L. Rauh, Jr. Papers, Box 37, letter, Rauh to JFK, Aug. 30, 1960, and ADA press release, Aug. 27, 1960, LOC.

202. Black and Black, 104–108.

203. Howard E. Covington, Jr. and Marion A. Ellis, *Terry Sanford* (Durham, NC: Duke Univ. Press, 1999): 233–234.

204. *CQ, Guide to U.S. Elections*, 208.

205. DNC, *Official Proceedings . . . 1960*, 110–111.

206. Gallup, 1675, 1681.

207. RFK Papers, Political File, memo, "The Issues of Concern in California," by Louis Harris, Oct. 31, 1960, 6–8, JFKL.

208. Bernstein, *Promises Kept*, 54–55.

209. Schlesinger, *A Thousand Days*, 45–55.

210. Miller, *Lyndon*, 317–320; Theodore H. White, *The Making of the President 1964* (New York: Atheneum, 1965): 407–415; and Kessler, 383–384.

211. Evans and Novak, 28.

212. O'Brien, 91.

213. Guthman and Shulman, 19–26; Arthur M. Schlesinger, Jr., *Robert Kennedy and His Times* (New York: Ballantine, 1978): 222–227; and OH, O'Donnell, 11, JFKL.

214. Dallek, *Lone Star Rising*, 580.

215. Shesol, 50.

216. Helen O'Donnell, 217–218.

217. Dallek, *Lone Star Rising*, 580–582.

218. Bobby Baker, 121.

219. OH, Clifton C. Carter, Oct. 9, 1968, 19–20, LBJL.

220. Chester Bowles, *Promises to Keep: My Years in Public Life, 1941–1969* (New York: Harper and Row, 1971):297; Victor Lasky, *It Didn't Start With Watergate* (New York: Dial Press, 1977): 30; and David Burner and Thomas R. West, *The Torch Is Passed: The Kennedy Brothers and American Liberalism* (New York: Atheneum, 1984): 87.

221. Sorensen, *Kennedy*, 162–166; and Pierre Salinger, *With Kennedy* (New York: Avon Books, 1966): 71.

222. Miller, *Lyndon*, 302–320.

223. Connally, 162–166.

224. Hardeman and Bacon, 443–444; and Bobby Baker, 124–130.

225. Dallek, *Lone Star Rising*, 580–585.

226. Kearns, 159–163.

227. Ibid., 162.

228. Conkin, 154–155.

229. Gerald S. Strober and Deborah H. Strober (ed.), *"Let Us Begin Anew:" An Oral History of the Kennedy Presidency* (New York: Harper Collins, 1993): 21–26.

230. Evans and Novak, 280–281.

231. Jules Witcover, *Crapshoot: Rolling the Dice on the Vice Presidency* (New York: Crown, 1992): 158–159.

232. DNC, *Official Proceedings . . . 1960*, 219.

233. Dallek, *Lone Star Rising*, 582–583.

234. DNC, *Official Proceedings . . . 1960*, 540.

235. Joseph L. Rauh, Jr. Papers, Box 37, memo, Rauh to JFK, Aug. 30, 1960, LOC; and Black and Black, 104–107.

236. Parmet, Jack, 49–50; J. B. S. Hardman (ed.), *Rendez-vous with Destiny* (New York: Kraus, 1969): 32; and JFK, *Profiles in Courage* (New York: Harper & Row, 1956): 1–18.

237. DNC, *Official Proceedings . . . 1960*, 244.

238. White, *The Making of the President 1960*, 205; and Matthews, 134–135.

239. Lasky, *J.F.K.: The Man and the Myth*, 408–409.

240. Ladd and Hadley, 127–128.

241. Sorensen (ed.), *"Let the Word Go Forth,"* 19–23; Bernstein, *Promises Kept*, 23–26; Daniel Bell, *The End of Ideology* (New York: Free Press, 1962):25–31; and Samuel Lubell, *Revolt of the Moderates* (New York: Harper, 1956): 235.

242. Fawn M. Brodie, *Richard M. Nixon: The Shaping of His Character* (Cambridge: Harvard Univ. Press, 1983): 423.

243. Matthews, 126–128; and Anthony Summers, *The Arrogance of Power: The Secret World of Richard Nixon* (New York: Penguin Books, 2000): 203.

244. Rockefeller Family Collection, Record Group III 2 D, Box 25, memo, Thruston Morton to Republicans, July 20, 1959, RAC.

245. NAR Papers, Series 22, Subseries 4, Box 19, press release from NAR, Dec. 26, 1959, 1, RAC.

246. Ibid., 2.

247. White, *The Making of the President 1960*, 247.

248. Stewart Alsop, *Nixon and Rockefeller* (New York: Doubleday, 1960): 77–79.

249. NAR Papers, Series 22, Subseries 4, Box 18, NAR press release, July 6, 1960, RAC.

250. NAR Papers, Series 22, Subseries 4, Box 17, letter, Alvin Diamond to NAR, June 10, 1960, RAC.

251. Gallup, 1669.

252. Ibid., 1674.

253. Ibid., 1669–1675.

254. *PPP*, 1960–61, 555.

255. Ambrose, *Eisenhower*, 519–521.

256. Tom Wicker, *One of Us: Richard Nixon and the American Dream* (New York: Randon House, 1991): 221–223; and Rae, *The Decline and Fall of the Liberal Republicans*, 41–43.

257. Graham Molitor Papers, Box 5, letter, Nixon to Clarence B. Kelland, May 10, 1960, RAC.

258. Nixon, *RN*, 215.

259. Ambrose, *Nixon*, 551.

260. Earl Mazo and Stephen Hess, *Nixon: A Political Portrait* (New York: Harper & Row, 1967): 225.

261. White, *The Making of the President 1960*, 435.

262. Mazo and Hess, 226.

263. White, *The Making of the President 1960*, 227–228.

264. Karl A. Lamb, "Civil Rights and the Republican Platform: Nixon Achieves Control," in Tillett, 62–70.

265. Bain and Parris, 306–307.

266. Ibid., 307.

267. Lamb in Tillett, 83.

268. *CQ, Guide to U.S. Elections*, 208.

269. "Acceptance Speech by Vice-President Richard M. Nixon, Chicago, July 28, 1960," in Arthur M. Schlesinger, Jr. and Fred L. Israel (ed.), *History of American Presidential Elections: 1940–1968* (New York: McGraw-Hill, 1971): 3557.

270. Nixon, *RN*, 270.

271. William J. Miller, 307–308.

272. Nixon, *RN*, 216; and Wicker, *One of Us*, 224.

273. Mazo and Hess, 229.

274. Wicker, *One of Us*, 238.

275. Ambrose, *Nixon*, 580.

276. Black and Black, 194–195.

277. U.S. Senate Committee on Commerce (ed.), *The Speeches, Remarks, Press Conferences, and Statements of Senator John F. Kennedy*, Aug. 1 through Nov. 7, 1960, pt. 1 (Washington, DC: GPO, 1961–60): 432.

278. Ibid., 307.

279. Stern, 152–153; Dallek, *Lone Star Rising*, 582–583; Black and Black, 196–197; and OH, John Patterson, May 26, 1967, 14–16, JFKL.

280. Stern, 148–153.

281. Joseph L. Rauh, Jr. Papers, Box 37, letter, Rauh to Abram J. Chayes, July 25, 1960, Chayes to Rauh, Aug. 5, 1960 and Rauh to JFK, Aug. 30, 1960, LOC.

282. White, *The Making of the President 1960*, 304–308.

283. Stanley Kelley, Jr., "The Presidential Campaign," in David, 73–74.

284. RFK Papers, PF, memo, George Belknap to department head, Aug. 17, 1960, JFKL.

285. Ibid., 2.

286. White, *The Making of the President 1960*, 202–203.

287. Reedy, 141; and Michael R. Beschloss (ed.), *Taking Charge: The Johnson White House Tapes, 1963–1964* (New York: Simon and Schuster, 1997): 107–108.

288. POF, memo, Orville Freeman to RFK, Aug. 4, 1960, JFKL.

289. RFK Papers, PF, letter, George Smathers to RFK, Sept. 13, 1960, and report, Elizabeth A. Gernethy to DNC, "Strategy for Peace Campaign," undated, JFKL, and O'Brien, 89–95.

290. Kaufman, 123; and James W. Davis, *The President as Party Leader* (New York: Praeger, 1992): 910.

291. Daniel M. Ogden, Jr., "The Democratic National Committee in the Campaign of 1960," *Western Political Quarterly* 14 (Sept. 1961), Supplement, 27.

292. Goldman, 469.

293. Katie Louchheim, *By the Political Sea* (New York: Doubleday, 1970): 31–35; and Kathleen S. Louchheim Papers, Box 16, letter, Beatrice Schurman to Louchheim, July 31, 1960, LOC.

294. Quoted in Ralph de Toledano, *RFK: The Man Who Would Be President* (New York: Putnam, 1967): 169.

295. RFK Paper, PF, undated 1960, RFK memo, 3, JFKL.

296. Ibid., 3–4.

297. Toledano, 170.

298. Sorensen, *Kennedy*, 175–176.

299. Ibid., 176.

300. Hamby, *Liberalism and Its Challengers*, 201–202; Silvestri, *Becoming JFK*, 115–118; LBJA-Famous Names Collection, Box 8, letter, Arthur M. Schlesinger, Jr. to LBJ, June 15, 1957, LBJL.

301. *The Speeches . . . Senator John F. Kennedy*, pt. 1, 117.

302. Ibid., 228.

303. John Connally Papers, Series R-Z, Box 1, memo, James Rowe to LBJ, July 25, 1960, LBJL.

304. Quoted in Evans and Novak, 317.

305. Black and Black, 190–194; Dallek, *Lone Star Rising*, 585; and Henggeler, *In His Steps*, 51.

306. Gallup, 1683.

307. POF, memo, "The Nixon Imagery," George Belknap to JFK, August 22, 1962, JFKL.

308. Ibid., memo, "Public Opinion and the 1960 Campaign," 3, JFKL.

309. POF, letter, Blair Clark to JFK, August 15, 1960, JFKL.

310. Paul R. Henggeler, *The Kennedy Persuasion* (Chicago: Ivan R. Dee, 1995): 90; Miller, *Lyndon*, 324–325; Hardeman and Bacon, 444–445; and Sam Rayburn Papers, SRH—3U47 folder, letter, Ethel Hook to Rayburn, July 25, 1960, UTA.

311. Kathleen Hall Jamieson, *Packaging the Presidency* (New York: Oxford Univ. Press, 1984): 125.

312. *The Speeches . . . Senator John F. Kennedy*, pt. 1, 206–218.

313. Ibid., 124; and DNC Papers, Box 128, press release from Senator Sam Ervin, Sept., 27, 1960, JFKL.

314. Jamieson, 133–135.

315. John Connally Papers, Series P-B, Box 2, unsigned, undated 1960 memo, "Nixon's Visit to Texas," LBJL; and Donald C. Lord, *John F. Kennedy: The Politics of Confrontation and Conciliation* (New York: Barron's, 1977): 82–83.

316. Ambrose, *Eisenhower*, 526.

317. White, *The Making of the President 1960*, 334.

318. U.S. Senate Committee on Commerce (ed.), *The Speeches, Remarks, Press Conferences, and Study Papers of Vice President Richard M. Nixon, Aug. 1 through Nov. 7, 1960* (Washington, DC: GPO, 1961–62), pt. 2, 207, 239; and White, *Still Seeing Red*, 160.

319. Matthews, 144.

320. Gallup, 1683–1686.

321. Ibid., 1686.

322. POF, unsigned, undated 1960 campaign memo, 6, JFKL.

323. POF, memo, George Belknap to RFK, August 29, 1960, 2, JFKL.

324. Ibid., 4.

325. Nixon, *RN*, 217.

326. Mazo and Hess, 235.

327. Ibid., 236.

328. J. Leonard Reinsch, *Getting Elected: From Radio and Roosevelt to Television and Reagan* (New York: Hippocrene Books, 1991): 137.

329. Henggeler, *The Kennedy Persuasion*, 75–76; and Richard M. Nixon, *Six Crises* (New York: Doubleday 1962): 336–343.

330. Nixon, *RN*, 219.

331. Thomas C. Reeves, 196.

332. U.S. Senate Committee on Commerce (ed.), *The Joint Appearances of Senator John F. Kennedy and Vice President Richard M. Nixon and other 1960 Campaign Presentations* (Washington, DC: GPO, 1961–62): pt. 3, 92.

333. Matthews, 155.

334. Harold W. Stanley and Richard G. Niemi, *Vital Statistics on American Politics* (Washington, DC: CQ Press, 1994): 104.

335. Lord, 83; and Elihu Katz and Jacob Feldman, "The Kennedy-Nixon Debate: A Survey of Surveys," *Studies in Public Communications* 4 (Autumn 1962): 21–25.

336. *NYT*, Sept., 28, 1960.

337. RFK Papers, PF, reports from Matthew Reese and John Doran to RFK, Sept. 24, 1960, JFKL.

338. Dallek, *Lone Star Rising*, 586.

339. Sundquist, *Dynamics of the Party System*, 352–363; and Ladd and Hadley, 151–162.

340. Allan P. Sindler, "The Unsolid South: A Challenge to the Democratic Party," in Alan F. Westin (ed.), *The Uses of Power* (New York: Harcourt, Brace, and World, 1962): 280.

341. David S. Broder, *The Party's Over* (New York: Harper and Row, 1972): 29.

342. *The Speeches . . . of Senator John F. Kennedy*, 887.

343. Sorensen, *Kennedy*, 187–188; and James A. Farley Papers, Box 25, Farley to John N. Garner, Oct. 31, 1960, LOC.

344. Weeks, 49–50; and J. Evetts Haley, *A Texan Looks at Lyndon: A Study in Illegitimate Power* (Canyon, TX: Palo Daro Press, 1964): 202.

345. Evans and Novak, 318; and Sam Rayburn Papers, SRH-3U45, letter, Wright Patman to Henry Jackson, Oct. 15, 1960, UTA.

346. RFK Papers, PF, undated memo, Jim Wright to RFK, 1960, JFKL; and Soukup et al., 25–64.

347. Ignacio M. Garcia, *Viva Kennedy* (College Station: Texas A and M Univ. Press, 2000): 91–105; Julie L. Pycior, *LBJ and Mexican Americans* (Austin: Univ. of Texas Press, 1997): 116–120; and Clinton Anderson Papers, Box 977, speech by Anderson to Viva Kennedy Club, San Antonio, Nov. 4, 1960, LOC.

348. Garcia, 105–106.

349. Weeks, 60–62.

350. OH, Clifton Carter, Oct. 9, 1968, 25, LBJL.

351. Evans and Novak, 320–321.

352. Miller, *Lyndon*, 330–332.

353. Ibid., 332.

354. Gilbert C. Fite, *Richard B. Russell, Jr.: Senator from Georgia* (Chapel Hill: Univ. of North Carolina Press, 1991): 378–379, and Goldsmith, 81.

355. RFK Papers, PF, polls and memos on Illinois and Ohio, Louis Harris to RFK, Nov. 2–4, 1960, JFKL.

356. Ibid., memo, Tom Quimby to RFK, Sept. 24, 1960, JFKL.

357. Ibid., polls and memos on Illinois and California, Louis Harris to RFK, Oct. 31 and Nov. 2, 1960; and DNC—140 folder, memo, G. Mennen Williams to Marjorie Lawson, Oct. 3, 1960, JFKL.

358. Victor Lasky, *Robert Kennedy: The Myth and the Man* (New York: Trident Press, 1968): 159–160; and Taylor Branch, *Parting the Waters: America in the King Years, 1954–1963* (New York: Simon and Schuster, 1988): 351–366.

359. Stern, 36.

360. OH, Simon Booker, April 24, 1967, 16, JFKL; Black and Black, 198; Donald R. Matthews and James W. Prothro, "Southern Images of Political Parties: An Analysis of White and Negro Attitudes," in Avery Leiserson (ed.), *The American South in the 1960's* (New York: Praeger, 1964): 107–108; and Norman H. Nie, Sidney Verba, and John R. Petrocik, *The Changing American Voter* (Cambridge: Harvard Univ. Press, 1980): 226–229.

361. *NYT*, Nov. 27, 1960.

362. Stanley and Niemi, 104.

363. RFK Papers, POF, memo, Tom Quimby to RFK and O'Brien, Sept. 10, 1960, JFKL.

364. O'Donnell and Powers, 254–255.

365. NAR Papers, Box 16, letter, Oren Root to M. Mooney, Oct. 31, 1960, RAC.

366. NAR Papers, Box 19, RNC press release, Nov. 2, 1960, 1, RAC.

367. *The Speeches . . . of Vice President Richard M. Nixon*, pt. 2, 944.

368. *PPP*, 1960, 831.

369. Reinsch, 156–158; and Jamieson, 165–166.

370. OH, Samuel C. Brightman, Dec. 29, 1964, 13, JFKL.

371. *The Speeches . . . of Vice President Richard M. Nixon*, pt. 2, 1082–1119; Gene Wycoff, *The Image Candidates* (New York: Macmillan, 1968) 49; and *PPP*, 1960, 852–856.

372. U.S. Senate Committee on Commerce (ed.), *The Joint Appearances of Senator John F. Kennedy and Vice President Richard M. Nixon and other 1960 Campaign Presentations* (Washington, DC: GPO, 1961–62), pt. 3, 385; Miller, *Lyndon*, 332–333; Claiborne Pell Papers, Box 6, letter, John Lewis to local Democratic chairmen, Oct., 27, 1960, Box 4, Ray Nelson to Pell, Nov. 2, 1960, URI; and RFK Papers, PF, confidential memo, "Last 9 Days of Campaigning," unsigned, undated, JFKL.

373. *The Speeches . . . of Senator John F. Kennedy*, 953–958.

374. O'Donnell and Powers, 254.

375. Stanley and Niemi, 85; and *CQ, Guide to U.S. Elections*, 307, 360.

376. Sorensen, *Kennedy*, 221.

377. *CQ, Guide to U.S. Elections*, 360.

378. Ibid

379. Ibid.

380. Ibid.

381. Ibid.

382. Ibid., 632, 360; and "Johnson: His Candidacy Goes to Court," *Human Events* 17 (Aug. 11, 1960): 338.

383. Soukup et al., 126–130; and Robert Sherrill, *The Accidental President* (New York: Pyramid Books, 1968): 99.

384. Cohen and Taylor, 264–268; Len O'Connor, *Clout: Mayor Daley and His City* (Chicago: Regnery, 1975): 158; and Giancana and Giancana, 289–290.

385. Nixon, *Six Crises*, 413; and Brodie, 433.

386. Edmund F. Kallina, Jr., "The State's Attorney and the President: The Inside Story of the 1960 Presidential Election in Illinois," *Journal of American Studies* 11 (1978): 147–160.

387. RFK Papers, PF, letter, Harold Leventhal to RFK, December 10, 1960, JFKL.

388. Ibid.

389. *NYT*, Nov. 11, 1960; and Richard L. Strout, *TRB: Views and Perspectives on the Presidency* (New York: Macmillan, 1979): 211.

390. Black and Black, 199.

391. Evans and Novak, 316.

392. Lawrence, 64–65.

393. DNC Records, Box 150, clipping, *USNWR*, March 28, 1960, JFKL

394. Black and Black, 199.

395. Hersh, 152.

396. Sam Rayburn Papers, folder SRH-3U45, letter, Horace Merideth to Rayburn, Dec. 1, 1960, UTA.

397. OH, Patterson, 12, JFKL.

398. Fite, 377–381.

399. OH, Gravel, 69–70, JFKL.

400. Michael Barone, *Our Country* (New York: Free Press, 1990): 334.

401. *CQ, Guide to U.S. Elections*, 357, 499, and 615.

402. Stanley and Niemi, 105–106; and V. O. Key, Jr., *The Responsible Electorate* (New York: Vintage Books, 1966): 115–123.

403. Stanley and Niemi, 85–86.

404. Sorensen, *Kennedy*, 222; and Ladd and Hadley, 111–128.

405. Angus Campbell et al., *The American Voter* (New York: Werbel and Peck, 1964): 274–275.

406. White, *Still Seeing Red*, 155–163.

407. *CQ, Politics in America*, 39–41; and Savage, *Truman and the Democratic Party*, 138–143.

408. Ibid., 163–164.

409. Barone, 223–228.

410. RFK Papers, PF, DNC report, Adelaide Eisenmann to RFK, Nov. 7, 1960, JFKL.

CHAPTER FOUR
THE PARTY POLITICS OF PUBLIC POLICY

1. E. E. Schattschneider, *Party Government* (New York: Rinehart, 1942): 129.

2. Burns, *The Deadlock of Democracy*, 204–301.

3. Ibid., 317.

4. David R. Mayhew, *Divided We Govern* (New Haven: Yale Univ. Press, 1991): 1–7, 175–199.

5. Bernstein, *Promises Kept*, 6; and "Kennedy's Next Job: Congress," *Business Week* (Jan. 7, 1961): 17–19.

6. Sorensen, *Kennedy*, 345.

7. Allen J. Matusow, *The Unraveling of America: A History of Liberalism in the 1960s* (New York: Harper and Row, 1984): 97.

8. Parmet, *The Democrats*, 201–205; and Bernstein, *Promises Kept*, 228–234.

9. Savage, *Truman and the Democratic Party*, 144–164.

10. Mazo and Hess, 243.

11. *PPP*, 1961, 19–20, 100; Sorensen, *Kennedy*, 403; and James L. Sundquist, *Politics and Policy: The Eisenhower, Kennedy, and Johnson Years* (Washington, DC: Brookings Institution, 1968): 34–35.

12. James T. Crown and George P. Penty, *Kennedy in Power* (New York: Ballantine, 1961): 19.

13. Dwight D. Eishenhower, *Waging Peace: The White House Years, 1956–1961* (New York: Doubleday, 1965): 459–462; and Bernstein, *Promises Kept*, 168–169.

14. Ibid., 167–168.

15. Boyle, 148–149; Sar Levitan, *Federal Aid to Depressed Areas: An Evaluation of the Area Redevelopment Administration* (Baltimore: Johns Hopkins Univ. Press, 1964): 2–27; Mayhew, *Divided We Govern*, 96; and Sundquist, *Politics and Policy*, 98–107.

16. OH, Clark, 70, JFKL; and OH, Lawrence F. O'Brien, Oct. 30, 1985, III, 24, LBJL.

17. Bernstein, *Promises Kept*, 171.

18. OH, Luther H. Hodges, March 19, 1964, 6, JFKL.

19. Levitan, 246–254; and Paul H. Douglas, *In the Fullness of Time* (New York: Harcourt Brace Jovanovich, 1972): 521.

20. O'Brien, 128; and Bernstein, *Promises Kept*, 175.

21. Herbert S. Parmet, *JFK: The Presidency of John F. Kennedy* (New York: Dial Press, 1983): 275; and Schlesinger, *A Thousand Days*, 1008–1009.

22. Sundquist, *Politics and Policy*, 85.

23. Anne Hodges Morgan, *Robert S. Kerr: The Senate Years* (Norman: Univ. of Oklahoma Press, 1977): 221–223.

24. O'Brien, 138.

25. Tom Wicker, *JFK and LBJ: The Influence of Personality upon Politics* (Chicago: Ivan R. Dee, 1968): 87–88.

26. Kirk H. Porter and Donald B. Johnson (ed.), *National Party Platforms:1840–1960* (Urbana: Univ. of Illinois Press, 1961): 596.

27. Carl Elliott, Sr. and Michael D'Orso, *The Cost of Courage* (New York: Doubleday, 1992):199–203.

28. OH, Richard Bolling, Feb. 27, 1969, 1–3, LBJL; and Hardeman and Bacon, 418–420.

29. William R. MacKaye, *A New Coalition Takes Control: The House Rules Committee Fight of 1961* (New York: McGraw-Hill, 1963): 9–11.

30. Sean J. Savage, "To Purge or Not to Purge: Hamlet Harry and the Dixiecrats," *Presidential Studies Quarterly*, v. 27, n. 4 (Fall 1997): 773–791.

31. Reinhard, 149–150; and Rae, *The Decline and Fall of the Liberal Republicans*, 160–164.

32. Wicker, *JFK and LBJ*, 77; and Hardeman and Bacon, 440.

33. MacKaye, 15–16; and OH, O'Brien, III, 5–6, LBJL.

34. MacKaye, 18–22.

35. *PPP*, 1961, 11.

36. Wicker, *JFK and LBJ*, 74–77; and MacKaye, 23–26.

37. Hardeman and Bacon, 457–459.

38. *CR*, Jan. 31, 1961, 1504–1508; and *NYT*, Feb. 1, 1961.

39. Hardeman and Bacon, 464.

40. Sorensen, *Kennedy*, 464.

41. Alan Rosenthal, *Toward Majority Rule in the U.S. Senate* (New York: McGraw-Hill, 1963): 1–3.

42. Ibid., 24–25; and Valeo, 13–14.

43. Baker and Davidson, 212–213; and Foley, 121–122.

44. Elliott and D'Orso, 201.

45. Charles B. Seib, "Steering Wheel of the House," *New York Times Magazine* (March 18, 1962): 30, 140–141, 146; and Theodore R. Marmor, *The Politics of Medicare* (Chicago: Aldine, 2000): 28–29.

46. Sundquist, *Politics and Policy*, 163–164.

47. Charles V. Hamilton, 329–332; David Hapgood, *The Purge That Failed: Tammany v. Powell* (New York: McGraw-Hill, 1960): 9–22; and Michael Beschloss (ed.), *Reaching for Glory: Lyndon Johnson's Secret White House Tapes, 1964–1965* (New York: Simon and Schuster, 2001): 197–199.

48. Martin, *Civil Rights and the Crisis of Liberalism*, 221–223.

49. Charles V. Hamilton, 330.

50. Jamieson, 164–166.

51. O'Brien, 126–128; Goulden, 304; and Bernstein, *Promises Kept*, 196–197.

52. *PPP*, 1961, 49, 186, and 216.

53. Wicker, *JFK and LBJ*, 93–94; and *Amendments to the Fair Labor Standards Act*, Hearings before the Subcommittee on Labor, Senate, 87th Cong., 1st session, 1961, 35–38.

54. Wicker, *JFK and LBJ*, 96–97.

55. Giglio, 100.

56. Alfred Steinberg, *Sam Rayburn: A Biography* (New York: Hawthorne, 1975): 174–183.

57. Wicker, *JFK and LBJ*, 105.

58. Charles V. Hamilton, 349–356; and Wicker, *JFK and LBJ*, 116.

59. Bernstein, *Promises Kept*, 197.

60. Giglio, 100.

61. Sorensen, *Kennedy*, 356.

62. Bernstein, *Promises Kept*, 197–198.

63. *PPP*, 1961, 353.

64. Ibid., 470.

65. Sorensen (ed.), *"Let the World Go Forth,"* 20–21.

66. OH, Robert R. Nathan, June 9, 1967, 24, JFKL; OH, Clark, 61, JFKL; OH, Rauh, 105, JFKL; and Sam Rayburn Papers, folder SRH3U72, letter, Roy Wilkins to Rayburn, Aug. 16, 1961, UTA.

67. Gillon, 142–143; and Stern, 42–45.

68. Lasky, *J.F.K.: The Man and the Myth*, 561.

69. Martin L. King, Jr., "Equality Now," *Nation* 192 (Feb. 14, 1961): 91–95.

70. Giglio, 104; "Home Sweet Home: Kennedy's $6.1 Billion Housing Bill," *Time* 77 (June 30, 1961): 12; Robert C. Weaver, "What the Housing Bill Means for the Nation's Cities," *American City* 76 (August, 1961): 5; and Sundquist, *Politics and Policy*, 356.

71. *PPP*, 1961, 137, 218, 488, 489.

72. Ben J. Wattenberg and Richard Scammon, *This U.S.A.* (New York: Doubleday, 1965): 271–273.

73. White, *The Making of the President 1964*, 224.

74. OH, Thruston B. Morton, Aug. 4, 1964, 10–14 JFKL; Sugrue, 551–578; and John C. Donovan, *The Politics of Poverty* (New York: Pegasus, 1967): 106.

75. Dennis R. Judd, *The Politics of American Cities: Private Power and Public Policy* (Boston: Little, Brown, 1984): 303–305; Mark Gelfand, *A Nation of Cities: The Federal Government and Urban America, 1933–1965* (New York: Oxford Univ. Press, 1975): 321–325; Boyle, 147–151; Cohen and Taylor, 487; and Kenneth Fox, *Metropolitan America: Urban Life and Urban Policy in the United States, 1940–1980* (Jackson: Univ. Press of Mississippi, 1986): 196.

76. Sorensen, *Kennedy*, 476–482; and Stern, 52.

77. *PPP*, 1961, 285.

78. OH, Robert C. Weaver, Nov. 19, 1968, 4–7, LBJL.

79. Parmet, *JFK*, 77–78.

80. Sorensen, *Kennedy*, 481; and Harry Golden, *Mr. Kennedy and the Negroes* (New York: World Publishing, 1964): 119–120.

81. *CQ, Politics in America*, 45.

82. Neil MacNeil, *The Forge of Democracy: The House of Representatives* (New York: McKay, 1963): 448, and Giglio, 104–105.

83. Schlesinger, *A Thousand Days*, 711; and OH, Mike Mansfield, June 23, 1964, 37, JFKL.

84. OH, Clark, 72, JFKL.

85. Ibid., 70–86.

86. Foley, 139.

87. Sundquist, *Politics and Policy*, 85–86; and *CR*, v. 107 (July 7, 1961): 12053.

88. Sundquist, *Politics and Policy*, 89.

89. Ibid., 90–91.

90. Ibid., 91.

91. Charles O. Jones, *The Presidency in a Separated System* (Washington, DC: Brookings Institution, 1994): 259.

92. *PPP*, 1962, 233; Bernstein, *Promises Kept*, 188.

93. Bernstein, *Promises Kept*, 188.

94. Ibid., 189.

95. O'Brien, 108–109.

96. Ibid., 138.

97. Patrick Anderson, *The President's Men* (New York: Doubleday, 1968): 253–254.

98. Schlesinger, *A Thousand Days*, 711–712; and Gillon, 141–143.

99. Paul C. Light, "Domestic Policy Making," *Presidential Studies Quarterly*, v. 30, n. 1 (March, 2000): 123–124.

100. Sorensen, *Kennedy*, 346.

101. Davis, 53–56; Stephen J. Wayne, *The Legislative Presidency* (New York: Harper and Row, 1978): 174; and Barbara Kellerman, *The Political Presidency* (New York: Oxford Univ. Press, 1984): 82.

102. Valeo, 39–43; Nelson Polsby, *Congressional Behavior* (New York: Random House, 1971): 71; and Ross K. Baker, "Mike Mansfield and the Birth of the Modern Senate," in Baker and Davidson, 293.

103. Bobby Baker, 140.

104. Miller, *Lyndon*, 337.

105. Evans and Novak, 350.

106. Jack Anderson, *Washington Expose* (Washington, DC: Public Affairs Press, 1967): 212.

107. Barone, 340.

108. Michael E. Kinsley, *Outer Space and Inner Sanctums: Government, Business, and Satellite Communications* (New York: John Wiley, 1976): 11–54; and "Where the Space Billions Will Go," *USNWR* 53 (Oct. 1, 1962): 78–80.

109. Morgan, 198–227.

110. *Wall Street Journal*, Jan. 21, 1963.

111. Jonathan F. Galloway, *The Politics and Technology of Satellite Communications* (Lexington, MA: D.C. Heath, 1972): 18–42.

112. Roger A. Kvam, "Comsat: The Inevitable Anomaly," in *Knowledge and Power: Essays on Science and Government*, ed. by Sanford A. Lakoff (New York: Free Press, 1966): 271–292.

113. *CQ, Politics in America*, 45; and OH, Lawrence F. O'Brien, Dec. 4, 1985, IV, 19.

114. *PPP*, 1962, 657.

115. Douglas, 220.

116. Matusow, 35–36; Jim F. Heath, *John F. Kennedy and the Business Community* (Chicago: Univ. of Chicago Press, 1969): 92–93; and "Historic Victory for Free Trade," *Newsweek* 60 (Oct. 1, 1962): 17–18.

117. Giglio, 106.

118. OH, Mansfield, 6–13, JFKL.

119. *CQ, Federal Economic Policy* (Washington, DC: CQ Press, 1971): 66–67; O'Brien, 133–134; and "Byrd v. Kennedy," *New Republic* 47 (July 9, 1962): 2.

120. *PPP*, 1962, 759.

121. Jeffrey E. Cohen, *Presidential Responsiveness and Public Policy-Making* (Ann Arbor: Univ. of Michigan Press, 1997): 200–204.

122. Neil MacNeil, *Dirksen* (New York: World Publishing, 1970): 186–187.

123. Charles O. Jones, *The Minority Party in Congress* (Boston: Little, Brown, 1970): 168.

124. Henry Z. Scheele, *Charlie Halleck: A Political Biography* (New York: Exposition Press, 1966): 226; and Edward L. Schapsmeier and Frederick H. Schapsmeier, *Dirksen of Illinois: Senatorial Statesman* (Urbana: Univ. of Illinois Press, 1985): 132–133.

125. Byron C. Hulsey, *Everett Dirksen and His Presidents* (Lawrence: Univ. Press of Kansas, 2000): 163, 174; and Theodore C. Sorensen Papers, Box 30, letter, Mike Mansfield to JFK, June 18, 1963, JFKL.

126. Burdett Loomis, "Everett McKinley Dirksen: The Consummate Minority Leader," in Baker and Davidson, 255.

127. MacNeil, *Dirksen*, 197; Giglio, 134; Theodore C. Sorensen Papers, Box 31, memo, Walter Heller to JFK, Oct. 21, 1963, JFKL; and Donald Gibson, *Battling Wall Street: The Kennedy Presidency* (New York: Sheridan Square Press, 1994): 21–22.

128. Douglas, 573–574; Cohen and Taylor, 287–291; Schapsmeier and Schapsmeier, 143–144; and White House Staff Files, Larry O'Brien papers, Box 17, Claude Desautels to O'Brien, Feb. 20, 1962, JFKL.

129. Sorensen, *Kennedy*, 734–738; Philip J. Briggs, "Kennedy and the Congress: The Nuclear Test Ban Treaty," in *John F. Kennedy: The Promise Revisited*, ed. by Paul Harper and Joan P. Krieg (Westport, CT: Greenwood Press, 1988): 35–55; and Ronald J. Terchek, *The Making of the Test Ban Treaty* (The Hague: Martinus Nijhoff, 1970): 7–43.

130. Peter J. Ognibene, *Scoop: The Life and Politics of Henry M. Jackson* (New York: Stein and Day, 1975): 118–119; and Thomas J. Dodd Papers, letter, Dodd to Jean Farrel, Dec. 14, 1962, UCT.

131. Kaufman, 148–153, 257–258.

132. MacNeil, *Dirksen*, 219–220.

133. Sorensen, *Kennedy*, 739.

134. OH, Mansfield, 6–8, JFKL; and Hulsey, 178–180.

135. O'Brien, 106.

136. Ibid., 130.

137. Sorensen, *Kennedy*, 756–760; and Schlesinger, *A Thousand Days*, 1030.

138. Thomas C. Reeves, 416; Henry Fairlie, *The Kennedy Promise* (New York: Doubleday, 1973); "Criticism of Kennedy," *New Republic* 144 (May 18, 1963): 2; and John R. Alden, "Overrated and Underrated Americans," *American Heritage* 39 (July/Aug. 1988): 48–54, 56, 58–59, 62–63.

139. Paul Light, *The President's Agenda* (Baltimore: The Johns Hopkins Univ. Press, 1991): 26.

140. Quoted in Henggeler, *In His Steps*, 122; and in Eric F. Goldman, *The Tragedy of Lyndon Johnson: A Historian's Interpretation* (New York: Knopf, 1969): 24.

141. Hamby, 202–212; and Leuchtenburg, 94–106.

142. Sorensen, *Kennedy*, 759–760.

143. Edward D. Berkowitz, "The Politics of Mental Retardation during the Kennedy Administration," *Social Science Quarterly* 61 (June 1980): 128–143; and *PPP*, 1963, 14, 679–680.

144. Matusow, 108–115.

145. Ibid., 4–8.

146. Giglio, 108–111; "Abundance Abated," *Nation* 196 (June 15, 1963): 497–498; and "Controls Rejected," *Commonwealth* 78 (June 7, 1963): 293.

147. Stern, 88–93.

148. Charles Whalen and Barbara Whalen, *The Longest Debate: A Legislative History of the Civil Rights Act of 1964* (Cabin John, MD: Seven Locks Press, 1985): 29–70.

149. Stern, 109–110.

150. "Catholics vs. Kennedy," *Newsweek* 57 (March 20, 1961): 24–25; and Edward T. Folliard, "Kennedy's Dilemma: Federal Aid to Parochial Schools," *Saturday Review* 441 (April 15, 1961): 56–57.

151. Hugh D. Price, "Race, Religion, and the Rules Committee: The Kennedy Aid to Education Bills," in Westin, 19.

152. Giglio, 101–102; and *USNWR* 50 (Jan. 30, 1961): 54–55.

153. Price in Westin, 64–67.

154. Neil H. Jacoby, "The Fiscal Policy of the Kennedy-Johnson Administration," *Journal of Finance* 19 (May 1964): 353–369.

155. Matusow, 42–59.

156. Edward B. Claflin (ed.), *JFK Wants to Know, Memos from the President's Office, 1961–1963* (New York: Morrow, 1991): 180–181; and Bernard D. Nossiter, "The Day Taxes Weren't Cut," *Reporter* 21 (Sept. 13, 1962): 25–28.

157. Bernstein, *Promises Kept*, 149–159.

158. *CR*, v. 108 (Sept. 24, 1963): 17905–17913; and Randall Ripley, *Party Leadership in the House of Representatives* (Washington, DC: Brookings Institution, 1967): 178.

159. Sundquist, *Politics and Policy*, 51.

160. *CR*, v. 110 (Jan. 30, 1964): 1501.

161. Robert Mann, *Legacy to Power: Senator Russell Long of Louisiana* (New York: Paragon House, 1992): 210–211.

162. MacNeil, *Dirksen*, 214–215; and Evans and Novak, 394–395.

163. *NYT*, Nov. 19, 1963; and *CR*, v. 109 (Nov. 18, 1963): 22508.

164. Evans and Novak, 389–395.

165. Marmor, 6–8; Frank D. Campion, *The AMA and U.S. Health Policy Since 1940* (Chicago: Chicago Review Press, 1984): 138–142; and Savage, *Truman and the Democratic Party*, 152–157.

166. Irwin Unger, *The Best of Intentions: The Triumph and Failure of the Great Society under Kennedy, Johnson, and Nixon* (New York: Doubleday, 1996): 34–35; and Frank D. Campion, 37–42.

167. Marmor, 27–30.

168. Clinton Anderson Papers, Box 977, speech, Anderson to Viva Kennedy Club in San Antonio, Nov. 4, 1960, 14015, LOC.

169. *PPP*, 1961, 79.

170. Donald R. Campion, "Primer in Medicare" *America* 107 (June 9, 1962): 383–385.

171. Marmor, 35.

172. OH, O'Brien, III, 31–33, LBJL.

173. Frank D. Campion, 253–261.

174. *PPP*, 1962, 416–420.

175. Frank D. Campion, 262–263.

176. Sorensen, *Kennedy*, 343.

177. Frank D. Campion, 267.

178. Sundquist, *Politics and Policy*, 313–314.

179. Sorensen, *Kennedy*, 344.

180. *PPP*, 1963, 760–765.

181. Bernstein, *Promises Kept*, 258; and O'Brien, 145.

182. OH, Clark, 61–63.

183. Ted Lewis, "Congress versus Kennedy," *Nation* 195 (July 14, 1962): 4–6.

184. Sundquist, *Politics and Policy*, 476–481.

185. MacNeil, *The Forge of Democracy*, 265–266; Light, *The President's Agenda*, 49–50; and Kenneth Dameron, Jr., "President Kennedy and Congress: Process and Politics," Ph.D. diss., Harvard University, 1975: 11–37.

186. Hamby, 202–209.

187. MacNeil, *Dirksen*, 219–227.

188. MacNeil, *The Forge of Democracy*, 239.

189. Gallup, 1707, 1712.

190. Ibid., 717.

191. James E. Campbell, "Explaining Presidential Losses in Midterm Congressional Elections," *Journal of Politics* 47 (1985): 1140–1157; and Philip Grant, Jr., "Kennedy and the Congressional Elections of 1962," in *John F. Kennedy: Person, Policy, and Presidency*, ed. by J. Richard Snyder (Wilmington, DE: Scholarly Resources, 1988): 85–95.

192. Evans and Novak, 381.

193. Aaron Wildavsky, "The Two Presidencies," in *Perspectives on the Presidency*, ed. by Aaron Wildavsky (Boston: Little, Brown, 1975): 448–461.

194. Ibid., 454.

195. Irving Bernstein, *Guns or Butter* (New York: Oxford Univ. Press, 1996): 27–42; Beschloss, *Taking Charge*, 48–49; and Evans and Novak, 359–360.

196. *PPP*, 1963–1964, I, 9.

197. Ibid., 112–118.

198. LBJ, *VP*, 19.

199. Beschloss, *Taking Charge*, 38–39; Eric Goldman, 49–51; and Robert Dallek, *Fallen Giant: Lyndon Johnson and His Times, 1961–1973* (New York: Oxford Univ. Press, 1998): 60–63.

200. Telephone Conversations, cassette H, side 2, items 26 A.2, Aug. 16, 1963, JFK and LBJ; and item 26 B.2, Aug. ? 1963, JFK and John McCormack, JFKL.

201. Matusow, 94; and RFK Papers, Civil Rights Legislative File, letters, Norbert Schlei to RFK, June 4, 1963, JFKL; and Whalen and Whalen, 75–77.

202. Vaughn Davis Bornet, *The Presidency of Lyndon B. Johnson* (Lawrence: Univ. Press of Kansas, 1983): 47–48.

203. Jones, *The Presidency in a Separated System*, 36–37.

204. Beschloss, *Taking Charge*, 48 and 64; and Burns, *The Deadlock of Democracy*, 301–322.

205. Tape K6311.05, PN014, LBJ and Dirksen, Nov. 29, 1963, LBJL.

206. Ibid., PNO 12, LBJ and John McCormack, Nov. 29, 1963, LBJL.

207. Tape K6311.06, PNO 1, Side A, LBJ to Gerald Ford, Nov. 29, 1963, LBJL.

208. Miller, *Lyndon*, 437.

209. *PPP*, 1963–64, I, 314.

210. OH, James O. Eastland, Feb. 19, 1971, 7–9, LBJL; and OH, Hale Boggs, March 13, 1969, 12, LBJL.

211. Reedy, 130–131; Alex Poinsett, *Walking with Presidents: Louis Martin and the Rise of Black Political Power* (Lanham, MD: Rowman and Littlefield, 1997): 141–143; OH, Roy Wilkins, April 1, 1969, 9–13, LBJL; and OH, Whitney Young, Jr., June 18, 1969, 14–15, LBJL.

212. Quoted in Whalen and Whalen, 77.

213. Miller, *Lyndon*, 447.

214. Scheele, 223.

215. Beschloss, *Taking Charge*, 83.

216. Evans and Novak, 399.

217. Mann, *The Walls of Jericho*, 391.

218. OH, Emanuel Celler, March 19, 1969, 9–13, LBJL.

219. Whalen and Whalen, 109–111, 121.

220. Tape WH6402.14, LBJ's phone conversations with John McCormack, Peter Rodino, Emanuel Celler, and Eugene Keogh, Feb. 10, 1964, LBJL.

221. Ibid., LBJ and RFK, Feb. 10, 1964, LBJL.

222. OH, Eastland, 9–12, LBJL.

223. MacNeil, *Dirksen*, 234–238.

224. Hulsey, 188–190.

225. Beschloss, *Taking Charge*, 333.

226. LBJ, *VP*, 158–159.

227. Quoted in *Taking Charge*, 400.

228. LBJ, *VP*, 160.

229. Stern, 182.

230. Whalen and Whalen, 218–222.

231. *CR*, July 2, 1964, pt. 12:15869–15897.

232. *CQ, CQ Weekly Report* (July 3, 1964): 1331.

233. WH 6407.01, item 4101, LBJ and Reedy, July 1, 1964, and item 4117, LBJ and RFK, July 2, 1964, LBJL.

234. Ibid., item 4122, LBJ and Reedy, July 2, 1964, LBJL.

235. *PPP*, 1963–64, II, 446.

236. John A. Andrew III, *Lyndon Johnson and the Great Society* (Chicago: Ivan R. Dee, 1998): 6–9.

237. Bernstein, *Guns or Butter*, 147–151.

238. *CQ, Politics in America*, 60–61.

239. *PPP*, 1963–64, I, 367–368.

240. Eric Goldman, 154–165.

241. Hardman (ed.), *Rendezvous with Destiny*, 27–38; and Eric Goldman, 165.

242. Unger, 72.

243. *PPP*, 1963–64, I, 560–561.

244. Ibid., 704.

245. Bernstein, *Promises Kept*, 243.

246. Franklin Parker, "Federal Influence on the Future of American Education," *School and Society* (Oct. 28, 1967): 383–387.

247. Andrew, 10–22, 163–182; and Diane Ravitch, *The Troubled Crusade: American Education, 1945–1980* (New York: Basic Books, 1983): 159–161.

248. Whalen and Whalen, 240–241.

249. James W. Guthrie, "The 1965 ESEA: The National Politics of Educational Reform," Ph.D. diss., Stanford University, 1965, 8–71.

250. Sundquist, *Politics and Policy*, 214.

251. Ravitch, 144–145.

252. LBJ, *VP*, 208.

253. Ibid., 20; WHCF, LBJA2 File, letters, O'Brien to LBJ, March 8, 1965; and Jack Valenti to LBJ, March 23–24, 1965, LBJL; and OH, Douglass Cater, August 29, 1969, I, 1–16, LBJL.

254. *CR*, v. III (March 24, 1965): 5747–5748.

255. WH6503.13, items 7151–7152, LBJ and John McCormack, March 25, 1965, LBJL.

256. Bernstein, *Guns or Butter*, 196–198.

257. OH, Cater, I, 13–17, LBJL.

258. Andrew, 119–120.

259. Bernstein, *Guns or Butter*, 198–199.

260. *CR*, v. III (April 8, 1965): 7531–7532 (April 9, 1965):7710.

261. *PPP*, 1965, I, 413.

262. Morgan, 195–199, 227; and Marmor, 53–54.

263. Bernstein, *Guns or Butter*, 159–161.

264. WH6409.05, items 5469 and 5470, LBJ and Carl Albert, Sept. 3, 1964, LBJL.

265. Ibid., item 5473, LBJ and O'Brien, LBJL.

266. WH6409.05, item 5677, LBJL and Russell Long, Sept. 24, 1964, LBJL.

267. Ibid., item 5688, LBJ and Clinton Anderson, LBJL.

268. Marmor, 43.

269. WH6503.8, items 7078–7080, 7084–7085, 7088–7089, LBJ and Harry Byrd, HHH, Wilbur Mills, John Byrnes, and Mike Mansfield, all on March 18, 1965; and WH503.11, item 7142, LBJ and Wilbur Cohen, March 23, 1965, LBJL.

270. Marmor, 46–47; and John F. Manley, "The House Committee on Ways and Means: Conflict Management in a Congressional Committee," *APSR* 59 (Dec. 1965): 927–939.

271. Frank D. Campion, 274–275; and Robert J. Myers, *Medicare* (Bryn Mawr, PA; McLahan Foundation, 1970): 54–63.

272. *CR*, III (April 7, 1965): 7220; and Sundquist, *Politics and Policy*, 318.

273. Marmor, 50–55.

274. Frank D. Campion, 275.

275. Manley, 930–933.

276. Marmor, 52.

277. Bernstein, *Guns or Butter*, 173; and Unger, 112–113.

278. *Guns or Butter*, 176.

279. WHCF, Box 75, memo, Wilbur Cohen to LBJ, June 17, 1965, LBJL; and Eugene Feingold, *Medicare: Policy and Politics* (San Francisco: Chandler, 1966): 15–28.

280. WH6506.08, items 8196–8197, LBJ and Mike Mansfield, June 26, 1965, LBJL.

281. Sundquist, *Politics and Policy*, 320; and Unger, 115.

282. Richard Harris, "Medicare: We Do Not Compromise," *New Yorker* (July 16, 1966): 35–38; and OH, Lawrence F. O'Brien, July 24, 1986, XI, 543, LBJL.

283. Frank D. Campion, 277.

284. WH6507.08, item 8404, LBJ and Harry Truman, July 27, 1965, LBJL.

285. WHCF, Box 75, memo, Horace Busby to LBJ, July 2, 1965, LBJL.

286. OH, Kermit Gordon, Aug. 4, 1981, IV, 16–17, LBJL.

287. Hamby, 36–64; Leuchtenburg, 141; and Herbert E. Klarman, "Major Public Initiatives in Health Care," in *The Great Society*, ed. by Eli Ginzberg and Robert M. Solow (New York: Basic Books, 1974): 108–109.

288. Marmor, 7; and *PPP*, 1965, II, 814.

289. Frank D. Campion, 8–10, 128–142.

290. *PPP*, 1965, III, 814.

291. Evans and Novak, 449–450.

292. Richard Reeves, *President Kennedy: Profile of Power* (New York: Simon and Schuster, 1993): 656.

293. Burner and West, 188–192.

294. Leuchtenburg, 115–120; and Hamby, 208–209, 230.

295. Matusow, 56–57.

296. John K. Galbraith, *The Affluent Society* (New York: Mentor, 1958)

297. James Goodman (ed.), *Letters to Kennedy: John Kenneth Galbraith* (Cambridge: Harvard Univ. Press, 1998): 56.

298. Michael Harrington, *The Other America* (New York: Macmillan, 1962): 9.

299. Ibid., 175.

300. Matusow, 50–53.

301. Joseph A. Califano, Jr., *The Triumph and Tragedy of Lyndon Johnson* (New York: Simon and Schuster, 1991): 75.

302. Beschloss, *Taking Charge*, 202–203.

303. Califano, 75–76.

304. *PPP*, 1963–64, II, 941, 968–969.

305. Ibid., 1963–64, II, 989.

306. Ibid.

307. Ibid., 990.

308. Richard N. Goodwin, *Remembering America* (Boston: Little, Brown, 1988): 286–287.

309. Kearns, 521; LBJ, VP, 74–75; and WH6408.43, item 5279, LBJL and Dick West, Aug. 31, 1964, LBJL.

310. Bernstein, *Guns or Butter*, 105.

311. Andrew, 126–127; and Gareth Davies, *From Opportunity to Entitlement: The Transformation and Decline of Great Society Liberalism* (Lawrence: Univ. Press of Kansas, 1996): 108.

312. Richard A. Hofstadter, *The Age of Reform* (New York: Knopf, 1966).

313. Paul Carter, *The Twenties in America* (Arlington Heights, IL: Harlan Davidson, 1968): 107–108; and Matusow, 237.

314. Donovan, *The Politics of Poverty*, 30–33, 70–71.

315. Bernstein, *Guns or Butter*, 104–105.

316. Matusow, 244.

317. Califano, 75.

318. Richard M. Pious, "Policy and Public Administration: The Legal Services Programs in the War on Poverty," *Politics and Society*, 2 (May 1971): 365–391.

319. Edgar S. Cahn and Jean C. Cahn, "The War on Poverty: A Civilian Perspective," *The Yale Law Journal* (July 1964): 1317–1352.

320. Donovan, *The Politics of Poverty*, 29–38.

321. *PPP*, 1965. II, 638.

322. Ibid., 985.

323. Beschloss, *Reaching for Glory*, 160–161.

324. Califano, 130.

325. Judd, 274–276.

326. LBJ Papers, Box 124, memo, Califano to LBJ, Aug. 19, 1966, LBJL.

327. Fox, 191.

328. Charles M. Haar, *Between the Idea and the Reality* (Boston: Little, Brown, 1975): 80–82, 289–290; and U.S. Senate, 88th Cong., 2nd session, part 1, 25–26, 187–190.

329. Andrew, 136–137.

330. Bernstein, *Guns or Butter*, 464–465.

331. *NYT*, June 29, 1966; and Haar, 58–60.

332. Douglas, 543.

333. Califano, 132.

334. Ibid., 132–133.

335. Andrew, 143.

336. Dallek, *Fallen Giant*, 321–322.

337. LBJ, *VP*, 330.

338. Daniel P. Moynihan, "What Is Community Action?" *Public Interest* 5 (Fall 1966): 3–8.

339. Judd, 318–319; and Donovan, *The Politics of Poverty*, 137.

340. John J. Harrigan, *Political Change in the Metropolis* (New York: Harper Collins, 1993): 424.

341. Andrew, 146.

342. Boyle, 202–203.

343. National Advisory Commission on Civil Disorders, *Report to the President* (New York: Bantam, 1968): 479.

344. Gallup, 1884, 1939, 2004, 2031.

345. Ibid., 2057.

346. Ibid., 1842, 2005.

347. Earl Raab, "What War and Which Poverty?" *Public Interest* 3 (Spring 1965): 45–56; and Steven Lawson and Mark Gelfand, "Consensus and Civil Rights," *Prologue* 8 (Summer 1976): 65–76.

348. Daniel P. Moynihan, "The Professors and the Poor," in *On Understanding Poverty*, ed. by Moynihan (New York: Basic Books, 1969): 5–7; Theda Skocpol, *Protecting Soldiers and Mothers* (Cambridge: Harvard Univ. Press, 1992): 40–42; Carl M. Brauer, "Kennedy, Johnson, and the War on Poverty," *Journal of American History* 69 (June 1982): 98–119; and Richard M. Pious, "The Phony War on Poverty in the Great Society," *Current History* 61 (1971): 266–272.

349. *PPP*, 1961, 719–720, 1963–64, I, 621–627; Craig W. Allin, *The Politics of Wilderness Preservation* (Westport, CT: Greenwood Press, 1982): 267–272; Ravitch, 182–227; Carnegie Commission, *Public Television* (New York: Bantam, 1967): 105–112; and Douglass Cater Papers, memo, Cater to LBJ, Oct. 31, 1967, LBJL.

350. Dallek, *Fallen Giant*, 341–315; Clarence Davies III and Barbara S. Davies, *The Politics of Pollution* (Indianapolis: Pegasus, 1975): 173–220; and R. W. Barsness, "The Department of Transportation," *Western Political Quarterly* 23 (Sept. 1970): 500–515.

351. Goodwin, 220.

352. OH, Rauh, 7, LBJL; OH, Richard Bolling, Feb. 27, 1969, 10, LBJL; and Krock, 6.

353. Stephen Skowronek, *The Politics Presidents Make* (Cambridge: Harvard Univ. Press, 1993): 347.

354. Erwin C. Hargrove, *The President as Leader* (Lawrence: Univ. Press of Kansas, 1998): 116–122; Kellerman, 124; Jeffrey E. Cohen, 110–112, 110–112; and John H. Aldrich, *Why Parties?* (Chicago: Univ. of Chicago Press, 1995): 282–283.

355. Jones, *The Presidency in a Separated System*, 174.

356. John H. Kessel, *Presidents, the Presidency, and the Political Environment* (Washington, DC: CQ Press, 2001):28.

357. Klinkner, 12–40; and Clifton Brock, *Americans for Democratic Action: Its Role in National Politics* (Washington, DC: Public Affairs Press, 1962): 171–217; and Light, *The President's Agenda*, 49–50.

358. Davis, 49–54; John K.White and Daniel M. Shea, *New Party Politics: From Jefferson and Hamilton to the Information Age* (New York: Bedford/St. Martin's Press, 2000): 77; Frank Sorauf, *Political Parties in the American System* (Boston: Little, Brown, 1964): 126–131; and Parmet, *The Democrats*, 142–219.

359. Leuchtenburg, 114–122.

360. Hardman (ed.), *Rendezvous with Destiny*, 344.

CHAPTER FIVE
JFK, LBJ, AND THE DNC

1. V. O. Key, Jr., *Politics, Parties, and Pressure Groups* (New York: Thomas Y. Crowell, 1950): 422–423; Hugh A. Bone, *Party Committees and National Politics* (Seattle: Univ. of Washington Press, 1958): 9–12, 211–214; and Cornelius P. Cotter and Bernard C. Hennessy, *Politics Without Power: The National Party Committees* (New York: Atherton, 1964): 81–105.

2. Klinkner, 1–4; and Wilder, 93–97.

3. Bone, 219–222; and Cotter and Hennessy, 94–103.

4. David Burner, *The Politics of Provincialism: The Democratic Party in Transition, 1918–1932* (Cambridge: Harvard Univ. Press, 1986): 149–150.

5. Sean J. Savage, *Roosevelt: The Party Leader, 1932–1945* (Lexington: Univ. Press of Kentucky, 1991): 107.

6. Cotter and Hennessey, 101.

7. Klinkner, 41–87.

8. Abraham Holtzman, "The Loyalty Pledge Controversy in the Democratic Party," in Paul Tillett (ed.), *Cases on Party Organization* (New York: McGraw–Hill, 1963): 151–154.

9. Burns, *The Deadlock of Democracy*, 196–203.

10. Porter and Johnson, 387.

11. Numan V. Bartley and Hugh D. Graham, *Southern Politics and the Second Reconstruction* (Baltimore: Johns Hopkins Univ. Press, 1975): 53.

12. Robert J. Steamer, "Southern Disaffection with the National Democratic Party," in Sindler, 160–172.

13. Parmet, *The Democrats*, 20–23.

14. George Roberts, *Paul M. Butler: Hoosier Politician and National Political Leader* (Lanham, MD: Univ. Press of America, 1987): 51–56.

15. Ibid., 55.

16. Paul M. Butler Papers, Box 1, letter, Norman Krandall to Butler, July 29, 1959, ND; and Murphy interview.

17. Ladd and Hadley, 120.

18. Paul M. Butler Papers, Box 1, letter, William Benton to Dean Acheson, Aug. 29, 1957, ND.

19. Reichley, 306–307.

20. Murphy interview; and Klinkner, 14–15.

21. DNC Papers, Box 129, transcript, Nov. 27, 1956 DNC meeting, 206, JFKL.

22. Ibid., 218.

23. Gould, "Never a Deep Partisan," 22; and LBJA Famous Names Files, Box 2, telegram, Sam Rayburn to Paul Butler, Dec. 8, 1956, LBJL.

24. Harry McPherson, *A Political Education* (Boston: Houghton-Mifflin, 1988): 159–160.

25. Broder, *The Party's Over*, 11–13; and LBJA Famous Names Files, Box 2, letter, LBJ to Paul Butler, Dec. 11, 1956, LBJL.

26. Bernstein, *Promises Kept*, 26; and Goodman, 7–16.

27. John M. Bailey Papers, DAC folder, DNC press release, February 27, 1959, LBJL.

28. Klinkner, 22–26; and Ferrell (ed.), *Off the Record*, 342.

29. Murphy interview.

30. Murphy and Doran interviews.

31. Doran interview.

32. Bernard Hennessy, "Dollars for Democrats, 1959," in Tillett, 155–182.

33. OH, Drexel A. Sprecher, Aug. 17, 1972, 16, JFKL.

34. Ibid., 30, 45l; and Roberts, 112–113.

35. HHH Papers, DAC statements, May 5, 1957 and Jan. 28, 1958, MHS.

36. Ibid., DAC statement on civil rights, Feb. 2, 1958, MHS; and DNC Papers, Box 122, minutes of meeting of Democratic State Central Committee of Lousiana, Oct. 8, 1958, 113, JFKL.

37. Drexel A. Sprecher Papers, DAC, "Little Rock—Civil Rights Statement," Sept. 15, 1957, JFKL.

38. OH, Sprecher, 39–44, JFKL.

39. *NYT*, Dec. 7, 1958; and Paul M. Butler Papers, Box 2, telegram, Robert W. Hemphill to Butler, June 25, 1959, ND.

40. Ibid., letter, Butler to JFK, Nov. 3, 1959, ND; and LBJA Famous Names Files, Box 2, clipping, *Philadelphia Inquirer*, July 4, 1960, LBJL.

41. Thomas J. Dodd Papers, letter, Dodd to Butler, June 8, 1959, UCT.

42. Ferrell (ed.), *Off the Record*, 381.

43. Ibid., 382.

44. Murphy interview

45. Ibid., and Roberts, 111.

46. Bernstein, *Promises Kept*, 24–30.

47. Francis Carney, "The Rise of the Democratic Clubs in California," in Tillett, 32–63; and Wilson, *The Amateur Democrat*, 52–58.

48. APSA, *Toward a More Responsible Two Party System*; and Cotter and Hennessy, 213–217.

49. APSA, 17.

50. Sundquist, *Politics and Policy*, 385–529.

51. Ibid., 415.

52. Daniel D. Stid, "Woodrow Wilson and the Problem of Party Government," *Polity*, v. 27, n. 4 (Summer 1994): 553–578; Austin Ranney, *The Doctrine of Responsible Party Government* (Urbana: Univ. of Illinois, 1962): 8–10, and Savage, "JFK and the DNC," 139–148.

53. Sidney M. Milkis, *The President and the Parties* (New York: Oxford Univ. Press, 1993): 50, 179–180.

54. Sam Rayburn Papers, SRH3U55, letter, Don Cain to Ralph Yarborough, Feb. 2, 1960, LBJL.

55. LBJA Famous Names Files, Box 2, letter, Mrs. A. A. Luckenbach to LBJ, Dec. 13, 1956, LBJL.

56. McPherson, 179–180.

57. Evans and Novak, 310–315; and Porter and Johnson, 598.

58. Beck, 233–251.

59. Light, *The President's Agenda*, 49–50; and Sundquist, *Politics and Policy*, 415–416.

60. Milkis, 170–182.

61. Klinkner, 40.

62. Bone, 103–104; and Ralph M. Goldman, 470–472.

63. *PPP*, 1961, 4.

64. Ibid.

65. Stan Opotowsky, *The Kennedy Government* (New York: Popular Library, 1961): 146.

66. O'Brien, 110–111.

67. Savage, *Roosevelt: The Party Leader*, 22–23.

68. Mary McGrory, "The Right-Hand Men—Pierre Salinger, Lawrence O'Brien, and Kenneth P. O'Donnell," in *The Kennedy Circle*, ed. by Lester Tanzer (Washington, DC: Luce, 1961): 80–81.

69. Telephone Conversations, Cassette D, item 10B.4, JFK and Henry Fowler, March 6, 1963, JFKL.

70. POF, memo, JFK to Bailey, Feb. 17, 1961, JFKL.

71. Ibid., DNC press release, June 3, 1961, JFKL.

72. Herbert E. Alexander, "Financing the Parties and Campaigns," in David, 141–142.

73. *CQ, Congressional Quarterly Almanac* (Washington, DC: CQ Press, 1961): 1076.

74. Garcia, 105–145; Poinsett, 98–101; and Henry Lopez, "The President and the Spanish-Speaking Vote," *Frontier* (May 1964): 26–28.

75. Victor S. Navasky, *Kennedy Justice* (New York: Antheneum, 1971): 21, 118–119.

76. POF, Box 138, memo, Charles Roche to John Bailey, Nov. 7, 1963, JFKL.

77. Evans and Novak, 349.

78. Weeks, 21–22; and Soukup et al., 85–89.

79. Patrick Cox, *Ralph W. Yarborough, The People's Senator* (Austin: Univ. of Texas Press, 2001): 172–173.

80. Ralph W. Yarborough Papers, Box 2R 508, letter, Margaret Carter to Henry Hall Wilson, Nov. 15, 1963, UTA.

81. Pycior, 69–70.

82. Eugene Rodriguez, *Henry B. Gonzalez: A Political Profile* (New York: Arno Press, 1976): 114–116.

83. Garcia, 108–145.

84. OH, Clifton Carter, Oct. 15, 1968, 22, LBJL.

85. O'Donnell and Powers, 21.

86. Conkin, 170; Miller, *Lyndon*, 310; and OH, O'Donnell, 38–39, JFKL.

87. Hennessy in Tillett, 155–182.

88. Cotter and Hennessy, 184.

89. Herbert E. Alexander, *Money in Politics* (Washington, DC: Public Affairs Press, 1972): 86–88, 96–98, 100–102.

90. Ibid., 100.

91. *CQ, Congressional Quarterly Almanac* (Washington, DC: CQ Press, 1965): 1551.

92. Ibid., 1571.

93. OH, Lew Wasserman, December 21, 1973, 4–6, LBJL; and Ronald Brownstein, *The Power and the Glitter: The Hollywood-Washington Connection* (New York: Pantheon, 1990): 184–185.

94. G. William Domhoff, *Fat Cats and Democrats* (Englewood Cliffs, NJ: Prentice-Hall, 1972): 42–45; and OH, Arthur Krim, Oct. 8, 1981, 12, LBJL.

95. Brownstein, 190–191.

96. OH, Krim, Oct. 18, 1981, 19, LBJL.

97. Brownstein, 191.

98. Ibid., 192.

99. OH, Krim, Oct. 8, 1981, 21, LBJL.

100. Domhoff, 15–22.

101. Quoted in J. Randy Taraborrelli, *Sinatra: A Complete Life* (New York: Birch Lane Press, 1997): 239.

102. Ibid.

103. OH, Arthur Krim, June 29, 1982, 3–4, LBJL.

104. Brownstein, 200.

105. Broder, *The Party's Over*, 61–62.

106. *CQ, Dollar Politics: The Issue of Campaign Spending* (Washington, DC: CQ Press, 1971): 42.

107. Bobby Baker, 193–194; and Jack Anderson, 46.

108. Beschloss, *Reaching for Glory*, 52–53.

109. WH 6409.01, citations 5413 and 5417, LBJ and Nicholas Katzenbach, Sept. 1, 1964, and LBJ and O'Brien, Sept. 2, 1964, LBJL.

110. Ibid., LBJ and O'Brien, citations 5417.

111. OH, Carter, Oct. 1, 1968, 10, LBJL.

112. Broder, *The Party's Over*, 62–63.

113. Lieberman, 325–326.

114. WH 6402.14, citation 2049, LBJ and Bailey, Feb. 11, 1964, LBJL.

115. WH 6402.13, citation 2006, LBJ and Clifton Carter, Feb. 10, 1064, LBJL.

116. Opotowsky, 148–149.

117. Charles W. Roberts, *LBJ's Inner Circle* (New York: Delacorte, 1965): 91–93.

118. Murphy interview; and Sherrill, 113–115.

119. Author's telephone interview with Bernard Boutin, former OEO official, Jan. 10, 1998.

120. Goodwin, 387–388.

121. Quoted in Patrick Anderson, 377.

122. Murphy interview.

123. OH, Krim, Oct. 1981, 3–4, LBJL.

124. Ibid., 4.

125. *PPP*, 1963–1964, I, 729.

126. White, *The Making of the President 1964*, 378–386.

127. *PPP*, 1963–1964, II, 1154–1155, 1157–1158.

128. Richard L. Schott and Dagmar S. Hamilton, *People, Positions, and Power: The Political Appointments of Lyndon Johnson* (Chicago: Univ. of Chicago Press, 1983): 205.

129. Kearns, 388–399.

130. Broder, *The Party's Over*, 64–77; Beschloss, *Reaching for Glory*, 144; and Shesol, 472–473.

131. (W.) Marvin Watson Files, DNC folder, memo, Cecil Burney to Watson, March 19, 1968, LBJL.

132. OH, Krim, Addendum to June 29, 1982, 5.

133. Herbert E. Alexander, "Financing the 1964 Election," in *Studies in Money in Politics*, v. 2, edited by Alexander (Princeton, NJ: Citizens Research Foundation, 1970): 8.

134. Dallek, *Fallen Giant*, 486, 544–547.

135. Parmet, *The Democrats*, 229–231.

136. LBJ Papers, WHCF, memo, Horace Busby to LBJ, May 23, 1966, LBJL.

137. George Mitchell Papers, Gallup polls, August–Novemeber 1967, BWC.

138. Dan Nimmo, *The Political Persuaders* (Englewood Cliffs, NJ: Prentice-Hall, 1970): 179.

139. Wycoff, 240–241.

140. (W.) Marvin Watson Files, DNC folder, memo, O'Brien to LBJ, Sept. 29, 1967, 31, LBJL.

141. Thomas J. McIntyre Papers, letter, LBJ to McIntyre, Dec. 29, 1967, UNH; and (W.) Marvin Watson Files, letter, George Mitchell to Watson, Jan. 24, 1968, LBJL; and Thomas J. Dodd Papers, clipping, *Washington Star*, Jan. 17, 1968, UCT.

142. Watson Files, DNC folder, memo, O'Brien to LBJ, "White Paper," Oct. 29, 1967, 29, LBJL.

143. OH, John P. Roche, July 16, 1970, tape, II, 77, LBJL.

144. OH, Lawrence F. O'Brien, April 23, 1987, 6, LBJL.

145. Patrick Anderson, 258.

146. Savage, *Truman and the Democratic Party*, 113–116; Clark M. Clifford, Counsel to the President (New York: Random House, 1991): 501–505; and (W.) Marvin Watson Files, Box 19, letter, Arthur Krim to Watson, Nov. 2, 1967, LBJL.

147. Dan T. Carter, *The Politics of Rage* (Baton Rouge: Louisiana State Univ. Press, 1995): 270–285.

148. Beschloss, *Taking Charge*, 310–311.

149. Shesol, 396–399; and David Halberstam, *The Unfinished Odyssey of Robert Kennedy* (New York: Bantam, 1968).

150. LBJ Papers, Confidential Files, Box 77, memo, John Roche to LBJ, Sept. 8, 1967, LBJL.

151. Ibid., memo, Fred Panzer to LBJ, Sept. 13, 1967, LBJL.

152. Ibid.

153. OH, O'Brien, April 23, 1986, 8–9, LBJL; O'Brien, 218–219; and Bruce E. Altschuler, *LBJ and the Polls* (Gainesville: Univ. of Florida Press, 1990): 95–97.

154. Albert Eisele, *Almost to the Presidency* (Blue Earth, MN: Piper, 1972): 262.

155. *NYT*, Dec. 1, 1967.

156. O'Brien, 218.

157. George Rising, *Clean for Gene: Eugene McCarthy's 1968 Presidential Campaign* (New York: Praeger, 1997): 62–65.

158. Gallup, 2104.

159. Altschuler, 89–95.

160. George Mitchell Papers, letter, Herbert Coursen to Mitchell, Nov. 28, 1967, BWC; and LBJ Papers, Confidential Files, Box 77, John Roche to Marvin Watson, Sept. 21, 1967, LBJL.

161. (W.) Marvin Watson Files, Box 1 (1372A), memo, John Criswell to Watson, Dec. 10, 1067, LBJL; and ibid., Box 8 (1372C), letter, George Mitchell to Watson, Jan. 24, 1968, LBJL.

162. Larry Berman, *Lyndon Johnson's War* (New York: Norton, 1989): 123–138.

163. O'Brien, 215–218.

164. DNC Papers, Box 15, clippings, *Des Moines Tribune*, Jan. 24, 1968, and *Salt Lake Tribune*, Jan. 13, 1968, LBJL.

165. James A. Farley Papers, Box 68, speech in Salt Lake City, Jan. 13, 1968, 4, LOC.

166. DNC Papers, Box 15, clippings, *Atlanta Constitution*, Feb. 24, 1968, and *Providence Bulletin*, March 15, 1968, LBJL; and HHH, 354–367.

167. John Criswell Papers, John M. Bailey Name File, DNC pamphlet, Feb. 20, 1968, LBJL.

168. DNC Papers, Box 16, DNC pamphlet, "Campaign '68-No.1," 1, LBJL.

169. Ibid., DNC, pamphlets, "Campaign '68," v. 2, n. 2, Jan. 22, 1968, 3, and "Campaign '68," v. 2, n. 4, Feb. 23, 1968, 1, LBJL.

170. DNC Files, Series 1, 1966–1967 folder, clipping, *Washington Post*, Nov. 24, 1967, LBJL.

171. Ibid., *Washington Star*, Jan. 8, 1968, LBJL.

172. Ibid., Box 100, DC-313 folder, speech, John M. Bailey, Jan. 8, 1968, 6, LBJL.

173. Quoted in Eisele, 292.

174. Eugene McCarthy, "Why I'm Battling LBJ," *Look* (Feb. 6, 1968): 22–24.

175. (W.) Marvin Watson Files, Box 1 (1372A), memo, John Bailey to Watson, Jan. 8, 1968, LBJL.

176. Ibid., 3.

177. Boutin interview.

178. Ibid.

179. Ibid., and O'Brien, 224–225.

180. (W.) Marvin Watson Files, letter, Bernard Boutin to Watson, Dec. 28, 1967, 2, LBJL.

181. Ibid., clipping, *Washington Post*, Feb. 21, 1968, LBJL.

182. Boutin interview.

183. (W.) Marvin Watson Files, memo, John Criswell to LBJ, Feb. 5, 1968, LBJL.

184. Ibid., memo, Spencer Oliver to John Criswell, Feb. 3, 1968, 2, LBJL.

185. Ibid., 4.

186. (W.) Marvin Watson Files, memo, Fred Panzer to LBJ, Jan. 10, 1068, 7, LBJL.

187. Ibid.

188. (W.) Marvin Watson Files, poll and analysis, "A Survey of Opinion among Democratic Primary Voters in New Hampshire," Study #1072, Jan. 1968, 62, LBJL.

189. Ibid.

190. Altschuler, 98.

191. (W.) Marvin Watson Files, memo, John Criswell to Watson, March 9, 1968, LBJL.

192. Ibid., memo, Cecil Burney to Watson, March 7, 1968, LBJL.

193. Rising, 67–68.

194. (W.) Marvin Watson Files, memo, Bernard Boutin to Watson, March 6, 1968, LBJL.

195. Rising, 65–69; Lewis Gould, *1968: The Election That Changed America* (Chicago: Ivan R. Dee, 1993): 34–46; and (W.) Marvin Watson Files, memo, Bernard Boutin to Watson, March 14, 1968, 4, LBJL.

196. (W.) Marvin Watson Files, Quayle poll, "A Survey of Opinion," Study No, 1072, Jan. 1968, 15–16, 61–62, LBJL.

197. *CQ, Guide to U.S. Elections*, 417.

198. (W.) Marvin Watson Files, memo, Bernard Boutin to Watson, March 14, 1968, 4, LBJL.

199. Altschuler, 94–95; and W. Marvin Watson Files, memo, Fred Panzer to LBJ, March 13, 1968, LBJL.

200. Ibid., memo, Ben Wattenberg to LBJ, March 13, 1968, LBJL.

201. Theodore H. White, *The Making of the President 1968* (New York: Atheneum, 1969): 110.

202. James Reston, Jr., *The Lone Star: The Life of John Connally* (New York: Harper and Row, 1989): 338–339.

203. *NYT*, April 1, 1968.

204. HHH, 396.

205. Robert J. Donovan, *Nemesis: Truman and Johnson in the Coils of War in Asia* (New York: St. Martin's Press, 1984): 169.

206. *CQ, Guide to U.S. Elections*, 408.

207. Donovan, *Nemesis*, 143–188; LBJ, *VP*, 31, 530; and Beschloss, *Reaching for Glory*, 179–181.

208. Kearns, 253.

209. *NYT*, March 27, 1968.

210. Ibid.

211. Penn Kimball, *Bobby Kennedy and the New Politics* (Englewood Cliffs, NJ: Prentice-Hall, 1968): 1–31; and Jack Newfield, *Robert Kennedy: A Memoir* (New York: Dutton, 1969): 174–176.

212. Shesol, 8–9.

213. (W.) Marvin Watson Files, Box 2, memos, John Bailey to LBJ, February 28, 1967, and Al Barkan to Watson, January 30, 1968, LBJL.

214. Gould, "Never a Deep Partisan," 22–23.

215. Lieberman, 319.

216. OH, Krim, Addendum to Interview III, March 18, 1984, 1–3, LBJL.

217. Ibid., 9.

218. Ibid., 17.

219. Ibid., 18.

220. Reston, 352–363.

221. John Connally's statement in Robert L. Hardesty (ed.), *The Johnson Years: The Difference He Made* (Austin, TX: Center for American History, 1993): 157–158.

222. Cohen and Taylor, 470.

223. Dallek, *Fallen Giant*, 571–572; and Savage, *Roosevelt: The Party Leader*, 171.

224. Gould, *1968: The Election That Changed America*, 67; Dallek, *Fallen Giant*, 544–547; and Joseph E. Persico, *The Imperial Rockefeller* (New York: Simon and Schuster, 1982): 71–72.

225. John M. Bailey Papers, Box 2, speech by Bailey, January 8, 1968, 5, LBJL.

226. *CQ, The Presidential Nominating Conventions 1968* (Washington, DC: CQ Press, 1968): 132–133.

227. Cohen and Taylor, 470–475; and Adam Clymer, *Edward M. Kennedy: A Memoir* (New York: Morrow, 1999): 122–125.

228. George Mitchell Papers, letters, Doris Cadoux to John Bailey, Aug. 1, 1968, and David Graham to Mitchell, July 11, 1968, BWC.

229. *CQ, Politics in America*, 89.

230. OH, Lawrence F. O'Brien, Dec. 18, 1986, 37, LBJL.

231. *CQ, The Presidential Nominating Conventions 1968*, 127.

232. Ibid., 221.

233. OH, Lawrence F. O'Brien, July 22, 1987, 3, LBJL.

234. OH, Arthur Krim, April 7, 1983, 26, LBJL.

235. O'Brien, 262.

236. Goulden, 366, 368.

237. Ibid., 366.

238. Boyle, 254–255.

239. Goulden, 369.

240. *CQ, CQ Weekly Report* (Oct. 4, 1968): 264.

241. Boyle, 253.

242. Clifford, 594–595.

243. *CQ, Politics in America*, 114.

244. Gallup, 2162, 2168.

245. Domhoff, 14.

246. Ibid., 42–44.

247. Reinsch, 235–237.

248. *CQ, CQ Weekly*, v. 26 (Dec. 13, 1968): 3282–3284.

249. Ibid., 3283.

250. *CQ, Congressional Quarterly Almanac* (Washington, DC: CQ Press, 1965): 1571.

251. Reinsch, 235.

252. *CQ, CQ Weekly*, (Dec. 13, 1968): 3282.

253. Alexander, *Money in Politics*, 66; and *CQ, CQ Weekly* (Dec. 13, 1968): 3283.

254. Quoted in Jamieson, 234.

255. OH, O'Brien, July 22, 1987, 5–6, LBJL.

256. Jamieson, 233–235.

257. Alexander, *Money in Politics*, 82.

258. Gallup, 2168; and O'Brien, 260 261.

259. OH, Lawrence F. O'Brien, July 22, 1987, 9, LBJL.

260. Newfield, *Robert Kennedy*, 60–83.

261. OH, Lawrence F. O'Brien, Aug. 26, 1987, 4, LBJL.

262. HHH, 402–405.

263. Ibid., 362–380.

264. Ibid., 367.

265. LBJ, *VP*, 548.

266. *PPP*, 1968–69, II, 937.

267. Ibid., 1090.

268. HHH, 84–88.

269. APSA, *Toward a More Responsible Two Party System*, 95.

270. *CQ, The Presidential Nominating Conventions of 1968*, 162.

271. Ibid., 179.

272. Ibid., 182.

273. *NYT*, July 11, 1968.

274. WHCF, John Criswell Name File, memo, Criswell to Marvin Watson, Nov. 28, 1966, LBJL.

275. O'Brien, 293.

276. Ibid., 294.

277. Ibid., 294–295.

278. William Crotty, *Party Reform* (New York: Longman, 1983): 131–132.

279. O'Brien, 277.

280. Klinkner, 214.

281. Burns, *The Deadlock of Democracy*, 253–254; and Crotty, 13–33.

282. Frank D. Campion, 260–266; and DNC Files, Box 95, DNC press release, June 2, 1962, LBJL.

283. OH, Lawrence F. O'Brien, Aug. 26, 1987, 20, LBJL.

CHAPTER SIX
THE POLITICS OF CONSENSUS: 1962–1964

1. OH, John M. Bailey, April 10, 1964, 16, JFKL.

2. *PPP*, 1961, 694–695.

3. Ibid., 695.

4. O'Brien, 130, 138.

5. Ibid., 137–138.

6. Lyn Ragsdale, *Vital Statistics on the Presidency: Washington to Clinton* (Washington, DC: CQ Press, 1996): 387.

7. O'Brien, 138.

8. Evans and Novak, 383–384.

9. Ibid., 383.

10. *PPP*, 1962, 573.

11. Philip J. Briggs, "Kennedy and Congress: The Nuclear Test Ban Treaty," in Harper and Krieg, 35–55; and Mary M. Lepper, *Foreign Policy Formulation: A Case Study of the Nuclear Test Ban Treaty* (Columbus, OH: Merrill, 1971): 242–259.

12. Dean Rusk, *As I Saw It* (New York: Penguin Books, 1990): 242–259.

13. White, *Still Seeing Red*, 172; and Kaufman, 148.

14. *PPP*, 1962, 462.

15. Gallup, 1837.

16. Ibid., 1842.

17. Ibid., 1847.

18. Daniel Stevens, "Public Opinion and Public Policy: The Case of Kennedy and Civil Rights," *Presidential Studies Quarterly*, v. 32, n. 1 (March 2002): 11–136.

19. Evans and Novak, 383–384.

20. *PPP*, 1963, 469.

21. Jones, *The Presidency in a Separated System*, 255; and Sundquist, *Politics and Policy*, 263.

22. Bernstein, *Promises Kept*, 110–111.

23. Dan T. Carter, 162–185.

24. Bernstein, *Promises Kept*, 110.

25. Dino Brugioni, *Eye Ball to Eye Ball: The Inside Story of the Cuban Missile Crisis* (New York: Random House, 1991): 101–114.

26. Ragsdale, 197.

27. White, *Still Seeing Red*, 163.

28. Author's telephone interview with former Senator Birch Bayh, Oct. 17, 1997; and *CQ, Guide to U.S. Elections*, 616.

29. Roger Hilsman, *To Move a Nation: The Politics of Foreign Policy in the Administration of John F. Kennedy* (New York: Doubleday, 1967): 177.

30. Ambrose, *Nixon*, 659.

31. Mazo and Hess, 265.

32. Rick Perlstein, *Before the Storm: Barry Goldwater and the Unmaking of the American Consensus* (New York: Hill and Wang, 2001): 120–124.

33. Ambrose, *Nixon*, 657.

34. Totton J. Anderson and Eugene C. Lee, "The 1962 Election in California," *Western Political Quarterly* 16 (June 1963): 396–420.

35. Mazo and Hess, 169–170.

36. Robert Novak, *The Agony of the G.O.P. 1964* (New York: Macmillan, 1965): 84–87; and Stephen Hess and David S. Broder, *The Republican Establishment: The Present and Future of the G.O.P* (New York: Harper and Row, 1967).

37. *CQ, Guide to U.S. Elections*, 492, 611.

38. Mazo and Hess, 293–294; and Graham Molitor Papers, Box 5, IV3A18 Record, memo, Lyn Nofziger, "Analysis of California Election Results," 1962, RAC.

39. Quoted in Reinhard, 165.

40. F. Clifton White, *Suite 3505: The Story of the Draft Goldwater Movement* (New York: Arlington House, 1967): 72–73.

41. MacNeil, *Dirksen*, 187–190.

42. Scheele, 218–219.

43. Ibid., 248–259.

44. Novak, 53–56.

45. Quoted in James A. Michener, *Report of the County Chairman* (New York: Random House, 1961): 301.

46. RNC, *Report of the Subcommittee on Party Organization and Candidate Recruitment* (Washington, DC: RNC, 1962): 1–5.

47. *CQ, Guide to U.S. Elections*, 523.

48. Novak, 88–93.

49. Frank S. Meyer, "The 1962 Elections: The Turning of the Tide," *National Review* 13 (Dec. 4, 1962): 434.

50. Dan T. Carter, 288; and *CQ, Guide to U.S. Elections*, 609.

51. Jonas, 377.

52. Meyer, 434.

53. Paul Gottfried, *The Conservative Movement* (New York: Twayne, 1993).

54. Mary C. Brennan, *Turning Right in the Sixties: The Conservative Capture of the GOP* (Chapel Hill: University of North Carolina Press, 1995): 54–55, 77, 114–115.

55. George H. Nash, *The Conservative Intellectual Tradition in America Since 1945* (New York: Basic Books, 1976): 260–261.

56. Barry M. Goldwater, *The Conscience of a Conservative* (Sheperdsville, KY: Victory Press, 1960): 37.

57. Novak, 179.

58. Gottfried, 35.

59. Novak, 83–84; and Frank Gervasi, *The Real Rockefeller* (New York: Atheneum, 1964): 250.

60. Hess and Broder, 77–78.

61. John A. Stormer, *None Dare Call It Treason* (Florissant, MO: Liberty Bell Press, 1964): 90.

62. Phyllis Schlafly, *A Choice, Not an Echo* (Alton, IL: Pere Marquette Press, 1964): 11.

63. Nash, 76–112; and Brennan, 48–49.

64. Stephen Shadegg, *What Happened to Goldwater?* (New York: Holt, Rinehart, and Winston, 1965): 51; and Reinhard, 174–178.

65. Richard H. Rovere, *The Goldwater Caper* (New York: Harcourt, Brace, and World, 1965): 1.

66. Brennan, 44–62; and Kevin B. Phillips, *The Emerging Republican Majority* (New York: Arlington House, 1969): 461–474.

67. Silvio Conte Papers, Republican Congressional Campaign Committee folder, RCCC newsletter, June 30, 1960, 7, UMA.

68. Rae, *The Decline and Fall of the Liberal Republicans*, 40–61; and Graham Molitor Papers, Box 30, IV3A18 Record, speech by NAR, "The Future of the Republican Party," April 9, 1964, RAC.

69. Gallup, 1715, 1756, 1896.

70. Ibid., 1756, 1896.

71. Ibid., 1756.

72. Silvio Conte Papers, Box 251, speech by Conte, "The John Birch Society," Oct. 21, 1964, 3, UMA.

73. Karl A. Lamb, "Under One Roof: Barry Goldwater's Campaign Staff," in *Republican Politics: The 1964 Campaign and its Aftermath for the Party*, ed. by Bernard Cosman and Robert J. Huckshorn (New York: Praeger, 1968): 13–14.

74. Graham Molitor Papers, Box 5, IV3A18 Record, copy, "Notes on the 1962 Elections," by Daivd S. Broder, 3, RAC.

75. Elmo Roper, "Who Really Won the Elections of '62?" *Saturday Review* 45 (Dec. 15, 1962): 13.

76. Ibid.

77. Ibid.

78. Ibid.

79. POF, Box 28, memo, E. John Bucci and J. V. Toscano to JFK, "Democrats, Coattails, and Kennedy," undated 1962, 10, JFKL.

80. POF, Box 30, memo, Louis Harris to JFK, Nov. 19, 1962, 3, JFKL.

81. Ibid.

82. OH, O'Donnell, 39–40, JFKL.

83. O'Donnell and Powers, 326.

84. Covington and Ellis, 335.

85. O'Brien, 169.

86. Gallup, 1826.

87. Ibid., 1827.

88. Ibid., 1840–1841.

89. Ibid., 1832–1833.

90. Ibid., 1836.

91. Ibid., 1852.

92. "Politics: JFK's Lost Votes," *Newsweek* 62 (July 8, 1963): 21–22; Dan T. Carter, 201; POF, Box 30, memo, Louis Harris to JFK, Nov. 19, 1962, JFKL; and Telephone Conversations, Cassette J, item 28A.2, JFK and Richard Daley, Oct. 28, 1963, JFKL.

93. OH, Richard Scammon, March 3, 1969, 26, LBJL.

94. Quoted in Richard Reeves, 657.

95. Ibid., 656; and Donovan, *The Politics of Poverty*, 106.

96. White, *The Making of the President 1964*, 303.

97. *PPP*, 1963, 868.

98. Ibid., 876.

99. Ibid., 877.

100. Richard Reeves, 658.

101. Eisenhower, *Waging Peace*, 213–274; and Rae, *The Decline and Fall of the Liberal Republicans*, 40–45.

102. Telephone Conversations, Cassette D, item 10B.4, March 6, 1963, JFK and Henry Fowler, JFKL.

103. William Rodgers, *Rockefeller's Follies* (New York: Stein and Day, 1966): 63–65.

104. Novak, 109–110.

105. Rodgers, 52–53.

106. Michael Kramer and Sam Roberts, *"I Never Wanted to Be Vice-President of Anything!": An Investigative Autobiography of Nelson Rockefeller* (New York: Basic Books, 1976): 247–265.

107. Novak, 112–115.

108. White, *The Making of the President 1964*, 80–81.

109. Rodgers, 65.

110. Gallup, 1815, 1826.

111. Novak, 147–150.

112. White, *The Making of the President 1964*, 82–83.

113. Rodgers, 69; and Gervasi, 256–259.

114. Richard Reeves, 655–656.

115. Kramer and Roberts, 277–284.

116. O'Brien, 63.

117. Paul Fay, *The Pleasure of His Company* (New York: Harper and Row, 1964): 259.

118. Sherrill, 81.

119. Clark R. Mollenhoff, *George Romney: Mormon in Politics* (New York: Meredith, 1968): 110.

120. Novak, 88–90; and Hess and Broder, 91–118.

121. Peter Kobrak, "Michigan," in *The Political Life of the American States*, ed. by Alan Rosenthal and Maureen Moakley (New York: Praeger, 1984): 111.

122. Mollenhoff, 202–203.

123. Hess and Broder, 117.

124. Novak, 89.

125. Gallup, 1812, 1815, 1819.

126. Ibid., 1864.

127. White, *The Making of the President 1964*, 83–85; and Rae, *The Decline and Fall of the Liberal Republicans*, 61–64.

128. Rovere, 89; and John H. Kessel, *The Goldwater Coalition: Republican Strategies in 1964* (New York: Bobbs-Merrill, 1968): 93–95.

129. Quoted in Richard Reeves, 656.

130. Lee, *Eisenhower and Landrum-Griffin*, 115.

131. Quoted in Richard Reeves, 655.

132. *PPP*, 1963, 771.

133. Ibid., 828.

134. POF, memos, Louis Harris to JFK, Sept. 3, 1963 and undated 1963, JFKL; I. M. Destler, Leslie H. Gelb, and Anthony Lake, *Our Own Worst Enemy: The Unmaking of American Foreign Policy* (New York: Simon & Schuster, 1984): 17–22; and Daniel M. Ogden and Arthur L. Peterson, *Electing the President: 1964* (San Francisco: Chandler, 1968): 6–7.

135. Brennan, 12.13; Perlstein, 153; and Nash, 272–273.

136. Godfrey Hodgson, *The World Turned Right Side Up: A History of the Conservative Ascendancy in America* (Boston: Houghton Mifflin, 1996): 90–92; and Benjamin R. Epstein and Arnold Forster, *The Radical Right* (New York: Vintage, 1967): 42–43.

137. Perlstein, 5–16.

138. White, *Suite 3505*, 20–21; and *CQ, Guide to U.S. Elections*, 610.

139. Shadegg, 18–30.

140. Perlstein, 61–68.

141. *NYT*, July 24 and 28, 1960.

142. Reinhard, 164–167; Brennan, 53–54; and Nash, 274–275.

143. Shadegg, 44–45; and White, *Suite 3505*, 39–41.

144. Lamb in Cosman and Huckshorn, 13–17.

145. Alexander, *Money and Politics*, 54–55.

146. Perlstein, 214–215.

147. Novak, 176–178.

148. Kramer and Robert, 272–276.

149. *NYT*, July 15, 1963.

150. Ibid.

151. Shadegg, 68–69.

152. White, *Suite 3505*, 199–205.

153. Lamb in Cosman and Huckshorn, 17–18.

154. White, *Suite 3505*, 199–213.

155. Novak, 246.

156. Shadegg, 105.

157. Quoted in White, *Suite 3505*, 119.

158. Gallup, 1854; and Lee Edwards, 196.

159. Carl Oglesby, *Who Killed JFK?* (Berkeley, CA: Odonian Press, 1992): 10.

160. Lee Edwards, *Goldwater: The Man Who Made a Revolution* (Washington, DC: Regnery, 1995): 198.

161. Lasky, *It Didn't Start with Watergate*, 59.

162. Ibid., 61.

163. Lee Edwards, 308–311; and Perlstein, 149–152.

164. Lasky, *It Didn't Start with Watergate*, 61–69; Arthur Larson, *A Republican Looks at His Party* (New York: Harper, 1956): 2–5; and Rae, *The Decline and Fall of the Liberal Republicans*, 60–61.

165. Lasky, *It Didn't Start with Watergate*, 65.

166. Shadegg, 262–263.

167. Ibid., 261.

168. Lasky, *It Didn't Start with Watergate*, 63–66.

169. O'Donnell and Powers, 16.

170. Donovan, *Nemesis*, 39; LBJ, *VP*, 470; and Kearns, 251–253.

171. POF, Box 99, memo from DNC, "Far Right in the Far West," 1963, JFKL.

172. Fred W. Friendly, *The Good Guys, the Bad Guys, and the First Amendment* (New York: Random House, 1976): 34.

173. Ibid., 28–29.

174. Ibid., 33–35.

175. Epstein and Forster, 8–9.

176. Friendly, 38.

177. Ibid., 45.

178. Epstein and Forster, 71–76; Perlstein, 414; and Friendly, 48–53.

179. Beschloss, *Taking Charge*, 189–190.

180. Ibid., 190.

181. POF, Box 99, DNC press release, Nov. 6, 1963, JFKL.

182. Dan T. Carter, 349–350; and John Fischer, "What the Negro Needs Most: A First Class Citizens' Council," in *Politics 1964*, ed. by Francis M. Carney and H. Frank Way, Jr. (Belmont, CA: Wadsworth, 1964): 245–253.

183. Stephan Lesher, *George Wallace: American Populist* (New York: Addison-Wesley, 1994): 260–262.

184. *Boston Globe*, Nov. 5, 1963; and William G. Jones, *The Wallace Story* (Northport, AL: American Southern, 1966): 107–120.

185. Whalen and Whalen, 236–238.

186. Matthew Dallek, *The Right Moment: Ronald Reagan's First Victory and the Decisive Turning Point in American Politics* (New York: Free Press, 2000): 49–50.

187. Ibid., 59–61, 137.

188. George C. Wallace, *Stand Up for America* (New York: Doubleday, 1976): 89; and Jody Carlson, *George C. Wallace and the Politics of Powerlessness* (New Brunswick, NJ: Transaction Books, 1981): 27–44.

189. Dan T. Carter, 203–204.

190. Lesher, 284.

191. Ibid., 272–285; and Jon Margolis, *The Last Innocent Year: America in 1964* (New York: Morrow, 1999): 180–181.

192. *PPP*, 1963–1964, I, 439.

193. Ibid., 432.

194. Lesher, 284.

195. *CQ, Guide to U.S. Elections*, 414.

196. Brennan, 83; *NYT*, April 8, 1964; and Samuel Lubell, "The Changing U.S. Electorate," *Fortune* 70 (July 1964): 132–135.

197. Beschloss, *Taking Charge*, 309.

198. Michael Kogin, "Wallace and the Middle Class," *Public Opinion Quarterly*, 30 (Spring 1966): 107–108.

199. Walter Hixson, *Search for the American Right Wing* (Princeton: Princeton Univ. Press, 1992): 113–174.

200. Beschloss, *Taking Charge*, 309.

201. Ibid., 310.

202. *PPP*, 1963–1964, I, 532.

203. Welsh, *View from the State House*, 188–191.

204. Ibid., 188–191.

205. *CQ, Guide to U.S. Elections*, 360.

206. Welsh, *View from the State House*, 63.

207. Matthew E. Welsh, "The 1964 Primary Election," in *The Hoosier State*, ed. by Ralph D. Gray (Grand Rapids, MI: William B. Eerdmans, 1980): 430.

208. Matthew E. Welsh, "Civil Rights and the Primary Election of 1964," *Indiana Magazine of History*, v. 75 (March 1979): 8–11, 13–20, 22–27.

209. James Thurber, *Party, Patronage, and Recruitment in Indiana Politics* (Terre Haute: Indiana State Univ. Press, 1973): 9–10.

210. Mayhew, *Placing Parties in American Politics*, 94–95; and Frank J. Munger, "Two-Party Politics in the State of Indiana," Ph.D. diss., Harvard University, 1955, 151–182.

211. Welsh in Gray, 437.

212. Welsh, *View from the State House*, 210–211.

213. Ibid., 210.

214. Quoted in Dan T. Carter, 210.

215. Lesher, 289.

216. *CQ, Guide to U.S. Elections*, 415.

217. *NYT*, May 2, 1964.

218. Lesher, 295.

219. Welsh, *View from the State House*, 222.

220. *PPP*, 1963–1964, I, 619.

221. Beschloss, *Taking Charge*, 356.

222. Lesher, 298–300.

223. *CQ, Guide to U.S. Elections*, 415.

224. Dan T. Carter, 215.

225. Margolis, 212.

226. MacNeil, *Dirksen*, 235–237; Hulsey, 196; and Whalen and Whalen, 184–189.

227. White, *Suite 3505*, 429.

228. Lee Edwards, 242; and Lesher, 308.

229. Beschloss, *Taking Charge*, 472.

230. Guthman and Shulman, 76–77.

231. Henggeler, *In His Steps*, 50–91.

232. Lloyd C. Gardner, *Pay Any Price: Lyndon Johnson and the Wars for Vietnam* (Chicago: Ivan R. Dee, 1995): 326–328; and Kearns, 183–184.

233. Guthman and Shulman, 417.

234. Ibid.

235. Heymann, 369.

236. Shesol, 410.

237. Beschloss, *Taking Charge*, 236–237.

238. Heymann, 148–149.

239. Shesol, 183–187.

240. Helen O'Donnell, 62–74.

241. OH, O'Donnell, 12, JFKL.

242. Beschloss, *Taking Charge*, 237–238.

243. Ibid., 238.

244. WH6402.13, citation 2006, phone conversation, LBJ and Clifton Carter, February 10, 1964, LBJL.

245. Lasky, *Robert F. Kennedy: The Myth and the Man*, 195.

246. Beschloss, *Taking Charge*, 240.

247. Gallup, 1868.

248. Schlesinger, *Robert Kennedy and His Times*, 396.

249. WH6403.04, citation 2380, phone conversation, Jack Valenti and Ben Bradlee, March 7, 1964, LBJL.

250. Ibid., citation 2386, phone conversation, LBJ and John McCormack, March 7, 1964, LBJL.

251. Toledano, 294.

252. *New Hampshire Manual for the General Court*, v. 39 (Concord, NH: Department of State, 1965): 428, NHSA.

253. Toledano, 295.

254. *PPP*, 1963–1964, I, 364.

255. Toledano, 295.

256. Shesol, 195–198.

257. Gallup, 1874–1875.

258. Quoted in Margolis, 161.

259. HHH, 288–298; and Allan H. Ryskind, *Hubert* (New York: Arlington House, 1968): 9–21.

260. Beschloss, *Taking Charge*, 419, 515–516, 540.

261. Evans and Novak, 458–487.

262. Gallup, 1883.

263. Guthman and Shulman, 413–414.

264. Evans and Novak, 465.

265. Shesol, 214–221.

266. *PPP*, 1963–1964, II, 919.

267. WH6407.20, citation 4426, O'Donnell and LBJ, July 30, 1964, LBJL.

268. WH6407.20, citation 4436, LBJ and James Rowe, July 30, 1964, LBJL.

269. Ibid.

270. Beschloss, *Taking Charge*, 486–487.

271. Ibid., 487.

272. John F. Martin, 209–212.

273. Harvard Sitkoff, *The Struggle for Black Equality: 1954–1980* (New York: Hill and Wang, 1981): 179–186.

274. DNC Papers, Box 77, brief, Mississippi Freedom Democratic Party (MFDP), 1, LBJL.

275. John F. Martin, 210–211.

276. WH6407.13, citation 4320, phone conversation, LBJ and John Connally, July 23, 1964, LBJL.

277. HHH, 299–300.

278. Stern, 198–200.

279. WH6408.31, citation 5099, LBJ and Walter Reuther, Aug. 21, 1964, LBJL.

280. Clayborne Carson, *In Struggle: SNC and the Black Awakening of the 1960's* (Cambridge: Harvard Univ. Press, 1981): 124.

281. WH6408.33, citations 5121–5122, phone conversation, LBJ, and James Eastland, August 22, 1964, LBJL.

282. John F. Martin, 209–210.

283. Todd Gitlin, *The Sixties: Years of Hope, Days of Rage* (New York: Bantam, 1987): 153.

284. WH6408.35, citations 5173–5174, phone conversation, LBJ and John Bailey, Aug. 25, 1964, LBJL.

285. Ibid.

286. Beschloss, *Taking Charge*, 523–535.

287. Ibid., 524–525.

288. Phone conversations: WH6408.30, citation 5120, LBJ and John Sparkman, Aug. 22, 1964; WH6408.34, citation 5143, Aug. 24, 1964, LBJ and Richard Russell; and WH6408.40, citation 5230, LBJ and Carl Sanders, Aug. 26, 1964, LBJL.

289. John F. Martin, 209–211.

290. Stern, 203–206.

291. Boyle, 193–196.

292. OH, Joseph L. Rauh, Jr., Aug. 8, 1969, 2–18, LBJL.

293. Paul Jacobs and Saul Landau, *The New Radicals* (New York: Vintage, 1966): 22.

294. Joseph L. Rauh, Jr. Papers, Box 86, letter, Aaron Henry and Ed King to John W. McCormack, Aug. 26, 1964, LOC; and Sitkoff, 183–186.

295. Bain and Parris, 315.

296. Margolis, 310–311.

297. Beschloss, *Taking Charge*, 529.

298. William V. Shannon, *The Heir Apparent: Robert Kennedy and the Struggle for Power* (New York: Macmillan, 1967): 21–22.

299. Bain and Parris, 315.

300. DNC, *Official Report of the Proceedings of the Democratic National Convention: 1964* (Washington, DC: DNC, 1968 ed.): 391–437; and *NYT*, Aug. 26, 1964.

301. Evans and Novak, 475.

302. Gitlin, 127–171; Brennan, 75–79; and Sitkoff, 172–178.

303. Reinsch, 193–202.

304. LBJ, *VP*, 101.

305. HHH, 300–303.

306. Beschloss, *Taking Charge*, 538.

307. John O. Pastore Papers, Box 8, clipping, *The Democrat*, Aug. 24, 1964, and letter, James A. Farley to Pastore, Sept. 1, 1964, PC.

308. *PPP*, 1963–1964, II, 1010.

309. Ibid., 1011–1013.

310. Ibid., 1017.

311. *CQ, Politics in America*, 57.

312. Ibid.

313. Democratic platform in Schlesinger and Israel, IV, 3595, 3634.

314. Fred J. Cook, *Barry Goldwater: Extremist of the Right* (New York: Grove Press, 1964).

315. *CQ, Politics in America*, 59.

316. *PPP*, 1963–1964, II, 1059–1061.

317. LBJ, *VP*, 102.

318. Winthrop Griffith, *Humphrey: A Candid Biography* (New York: Morrow, 1965): 289–290.

319. HHH, 309; Beschloss, *Reaching for Glory*, 44–45; and "Businessmen's Vote: It's Going to Be a Tough Decision," *Businessweek* (Sept. 5, 1964): 23–25.

320. Ryskind, 269.

321. Timothy Thurber, *The Politics of Equality: Hubert H. Humphrey and the African American Freedom Struggle* (New York: Columbia Univ. Press, 1999): 162.

322. Quoted in Jamieson, 198.

323. *PPP*, 1963–1964, II, 1052.

324. White, *The Making of the President 1964*, 347–350.

325. Ibid., 348.

326. Lee Edwards, 326.

327. Friendly, 35–37; and Matthew Welsh Papers, copy, *Group Research Report*, v. 2, n. 16 (Aug. 26, 1963), ISA.

328. Lasky, *It Didn't Start with Watergate*, 185–186.

329. Gallup, 1894–1907.

330. *NYT*, Sept. 4, 1964.

331. Perlstein, 483–485.

332. Stephen Shadegg Papers, Box 3H-508, letter and transcript, Dean Burch to Agnes Shaar, Oct. 7, 1964, UTA.

333. White, *Suite 3505*, 414.

334. Quoted in ibid., 438.

335. Brennan, 82–103.

336. Stephen Shadegg Papers, Box 3H-512, speech by William E. Miller, Sept. 15, 1964, 5, UTA.

337. Gallup, 1899.

338. Ibid., 1909–1910.

339. Gallup, 1874.

340. Lubell, *The Future of American Politics*, 1.

341. John B. Martin, "The Election of 1964," in Schlesinger and Israel, IV, 3591.

342. Evans and Novak, 502.

343. Perlstein, 494–495.

344. Ibid.

345. Jamieson, 212.

346. Ibid., 212–213.

347. White, *Suite 3505*, 415.

348. Perlstein, 495–496.

349. White, *Suite 3505*, 415.

350. "Burch Hindsight: TV Badly Used," *Broadcasting* 68 (March 22, 1965): 88.

351. Shadegg, 255.

352. Beschloss, *Taking Charge*, 356–358; and Bobby Baker, 193–199.

353. Beschloss, *Reaching for Glory*, 64.

353. White, *The Making of the President 1964*, 368–369.

355. Beschloss, *Reaching for Glory*, 54–102.

356. White, *The Making of the President 1964*, 371.

357. Reinsch, 205.

358. *PPP*, 1963–1964, II, 1380.

359. Roderick P. Hart, *The Sound of Leadership: Presidential Communication in the Modern Age* (Chicago: Univ. of Chicago Press, 1987): 90–92, 164–165; Wycoff, 11; Nimmo, 129–132; and John Connally Papers, Series 2E, Box 1, letter, John McKee to Clifton Carter, Sept. 23, 1964, LBJL.

360. Evans and Novak, 496; and Patrick Anderson, 334–336.

361. *PPP*, 1963–1964, II, 1138.

362. White, *The Making of the President 1964*, 364.

363. Earl Warren et al., *The Warren Commission Report* (New York: St. Martin's Press, 1964): 1.

364. *PPP*, 1963–1964, II, 1137.

365. Quoted in White, *The Making of the President 1964*, 366.

366. Broder, *The Party's Over*, 46.

367. Peirce, 233–420.

368. Rae, *The Decline and Fall of the Liberal Republicans*, 75–77; Reinhard, 201–203; Silvio Conte Papers, Box 250, speech by Conte, Oct. 21, 1964, UMA; and Edmund S. Muskie Papers, Box 64, folder G, letter, Don Nicoll to Dick Kaplan, Aug. 22, 1964, BTC.

369. Edmund S. Muskie Papers, Box 66, folder 4, letter, James A. Briggs to Muskie, July 8, 1964, BTC.

370. LBJ, *VP*, 103.

371. Ibid.

372. *PPP*, 1963–1964, II, 1152.

373. Ibid., 1158.

374. Ibid., 1249.

375. *CQ, Guide to U.S. Elections*, 361, 500, 616.

376. Harold E. Hughes, *The Honorable Alcoholic: A Senator's Personal Story* (Edina, MN: Jeremy Books, 1979): 152.

377. *PPP*, 1963–1964, II, 1230–1231.

378. Reinhard, 107; Valeo, 107; and MacNeil, *Dirksen*, 325.

379. *CQ, Guide to U.S. Elections*, 361, 501, 1008.

380. Hughes, 182.

381. WH6411.03, citation 6156, phone conversation, LBJ and Harold Hughes, Nov. 4, 1964, LBJL.

382. Ibid.

383. Ibid.

384. Hughes, 210–215.

385. Ibid., 213.

386. LBJ, *VP*, 102–104.

387. Beschloss, *Reaching for Glory*, 41–42.

388. LBJ, *VP*, 103.

389. Broder, *The Party's Over*, 77.

390. *CQ, CQ Weekly Report*, v. 22, n. 42 (Oct. 16, 1964): 2452.

391. Quoted in Gould, "Never a Deep Partisan," 23.

392. WH6411.03, citation 6164, phone conversation, LBJ to Everett Dirksen, Nov. 4, 1964, LBJL.

393. Robert Mann, *A Grand Delusion: America's Descent into Vietnam* (New York: Basic Books, 2001): 390.

394. Leuchtenburg, 148–149; and *CQ, Politics in America*, 60.

395. Stephen J. Wayne, *Road to the White House* (New York: St. Martin's Press, 1980): 56.

396. DNC Records, memos, Matt Reese to John Bailey, Sept. 13, 1963, and Sam Brightman to Bailey, Aug. 10, 1964, LBJL.

397. *NYT*, Nov. 5, 1964.

398. Ibid.

399. *CQ, Guide to U.S. Elections*, 361, 631.

400. *CQ, Politics in America*, 61.

401. Ibid.

402. Black and Black, 199–205; and Rae, *Southern Democrats*, 44.

403. *CQ, Politics in America*, 62.

404. Philip E. Converse, Aage R. Clausen, and Warren E. Miller, "Myth and Reality: The 1964 Election," in Cosman and Huckshorn, 64–65.

405. Gillon, vi–ix.

406. Strout, 274–275.

407. Leuchtenburg, 145.

408. Miller, *Lyndon*, 58; and Donovan, *Nemesis*, 57, 185–187.

409. Conkin, 214.

410. Eric Goldman, 333.

411. Quoted in Evans and Novak, 514–515.

CHAPTER SEVEN
THE POLITICS OF DISSENSUS: 1966–1968

1. Goodwin, 285–309.

2. "Most Disappointing," *Time* (Oct. 30, 1964): 1–2.

3. *CQ, Politics in America*, 61–62.

4. Ibid., 63.

5. Kearns, 238; and Leuchtenburg, 121–160.

6. Hamby, 256–262.

7. Quoted in Miller, *Lyndon*, 497.

8. David Nevin, *Muskie of Maine* (New York: Random House, 1972): 186–187.

9. Kearns, 223.

10. Evans and Novak, 395–396.

11. Bornet, 243.

12. O'Brien, 196.

13. Ibid., 197–198.

14. David Kaiser, *American Tragedy: Kennedy, Johnson, and the Origins of the Vietnam War* (Cambridge: Harvard Univ. Press, 2000): 392–411.

15. *PPP*, 1965, I, 319.

16. Haynes Johnson and Bernard M. Gwertzman, *Fulbright: The Dissenter* (New York: Doubleday, 1968): 203–204.

17. Gallup, 1932–1933.

18. Ibid., 1934.

19. Donovan, *Nemesis*, 107–110.

20. Beschloss, *Reaching for Glory*, 280–281.

21. Ibid., 280.

22. Edwin E. Moise, *Tonkin Gulf and the Escalation of the Vietnam War* (Chapel Hill: Univ. of North Carolina Press, 1996): 226–227.

23. Miller, *Lyndon*, 467.

24. Johnson and Gwertzman, 205–206.

25. *PPP*, 1965, I, 396.

26. Ibid., 472.

27. Johnson and Gwertzman, 212–214; and James Petras, "Dominican Republic: Revolution and Restoration," in *The Great Society Reader*, ed. by Marvin E. Gettleman and David Mermelstein (New York: Random House, 1967): 390–411.

28. Evans and Novak, 553–554.

29. Kearns, 224–225.

30. Wicker, *JFK and LBJ*, 251–252.

31. Richard Whelan, *Drawing the Line: The Korean War, 1950–1953* (Boston: Little, Brown, 1990): 253.

32. Beschloss, *Reaching for Glory*, 281.

33. POF, letter, LBJ to Mike Mansfield, April 12, 1965, LBJL.

34. Beschloss, *Reaching for Glory*, 407–441.

35. Drukman, 174–177.

36. Evans and Novak, 591; and Foley, 58–59.

37. Mann, *A Grand Delusion*, 424–426.

38. Ibid., 8–11; and Kearns, 113–114.

39. Clymer, 79–81; and Nevin, 23–24.

40. White, *Still Seeing Red*, 172–173.

41. Quoted in David C. Bender (ed.), *The Vietnam War: Opposing Viewpoints* (St. Paul, MN: Greenhaven Press, 1984): 26–27.

42. Ibid., 28.

43. Ibid., 31.

44. Ibid., 28.

45. *PPP*, 1966, I, 143–144.

46. Ibid., 145.

47. Ibid., 150–151.

48. Ibid., 157.

49. Johnson and Gwertzman, 235–236; Berman, 89–90; and Altschuler, 44–49.

50. Bernstein, *Guns or Butter*, 368–369; and Kearns, 251–253.

51. Davies, 124–142.

52. Foley, 56–57.

53. Gallup, 56–57.

54. Hugh Sidey, *A Very Personal Presidency: Lyndon Johnson in the White House* (New York: Atheneum, 1968): 194.

55. Beschloss, *Reaching for Glory*, 306; and LBJ, *VP*, 130–137, 370.

56. H. R. McMaster, *Dereliction of Duty* (New York: Harper Collins, 1997): 331–332.

57. David Halberstam, *The Best and the Brightest* (New York: Random House, 1969): 591–593.

58. Beschloss, *Reaching for Glory*, 383–384; and Dallek, *Flawed Giant*, 272.

59. Mann, *A Grand Delusion*, 408.

60. Beschloss, *Reaching for Glory*, 404.

61. Hulsey, 250–251; and Loomis in Baker and Davidson, 252–258.

62. Quoted in MacNeil, *Dirksen*, 291.

63. *New York Times, The Pentagon Papers* (New York: Bantam, 1971): 456–463.

64. *PPP*, 1965, II, 795–796.

65. Ibid., 801–802.

66. Ibid., 795.

67. Leslie H. Gelb, "The Essential Domino: American Politics and Vietnam," *Foreign Affairs* 50 (April 1972): 459–475.

68. Rusk, 499–500.

69. LBJ Papers, Diary Backup File, Box 19, memo, McGeorge Bundy to LBJ, July 14, 1965, LBJL.

70. John E. Mueller, "Trends for Popular Support for the Wars in Korea and Vietnam," *APSR* 65 (June 1971): 358–375.

71. Douglas Pike Collection, George C. Herring, " 'Cold Blood': LBJ's Conduct of Limited War in Vietnam," copy of lecture delivered at U.S. Air Force Academy, 1990, 12–13, TTU.

72. Deborah Shapley, *Promise and Power: The Life and Times of Robert McNamara* (Boston: Little, Brown, 1993): 376–377; Michael Lind, *Vietnam: The Necessary War* (New York: Free Press, 1999): 127–130; and Goodwin, 470–472.

73. George W. Ball, *The Past Has Another Pattern* (New York: Norton, 1982): 280–402.

74. Miller, *Lyndon*, 594.

75. Ibid.

76. McPherson, 444–445.

77. Jacobs and Landau, 3–59; and Jack Newfield, *A Prophetic Minority* (New York: New American Library, 1966): 22–24.

78. Shesol, 9.

79. Bell, 22–25.

80. Ibid., 31.

81. Wicker, *JFK and LBJ*, 181–214; and Reedy, 6–10.

82. Kearns, 138–159.

83. Evans and Novak, 510–513; Sidey, 70–128; and LBJ, *VP*, 102–103.

84. C. Wright Mills, "Letter to the New Left," in Priscilla Long (ed.), *The New Left: A Collection of Essays* (Boston: Porter Sargent, 1969): 16.

85. Ibid., 21.

86. C. Wright Mills, *The Power Elite* (New York: Oxford Univ. Press, 1956): 334–336, 360.

87. Maurice Isserman, *If I Had a Hammer . . . : The Death of the Old Left and the Birth of the New Left* (New York: Basic Books, 1987): 38–46.

88. James Miller, *"Democracy Is in the Streets": From Port Huron to the Siege of Chicago* (New York: Simon and Schuster, 1987): 85–89; and Peter B. Levy, *The New Left and Labor in the 1960s* (Urbana: Univ. of Illinois, 1994): 54.

89. Gregory N. Calvert, *Democracy From the Heart* (Eugene, OR: Communities Press, 1991): 12–18; Rebecca E. Klatch, *A Generation Divided* (Berkeley: Univ. of California Press, 1999): 27–28; and Irwin Unger, *The Movement: A History of the American New Left, 1959–1972* (New York: Harper and Row, 1974): 33–38.

90. Tom Hayden, *Reunion: A Memoir* (New York: Random House, 1988): 28–33.

91. Levy, 15–35; and Calvert, 116–119.

92. Jacobs and Landau, 160–161.

93. Ibid., 161–162.

94. Ibid., 155.

95. Isserman, 188–189.

96. Hayden, 26–27; and W. J. Rorabaugh, *Berkeley at War: The 1960s* (New York: Oxford Univ. Press, 1989): 10–18.

97. Rorabaugh, 15.

98. William H. Chafe, *Never Stop Running: Allard Lowenstein and the Struggle to Save American Liberalism* (New York: Basic Books, 1993): 195–198.

99. Tom Hayden, *Liberal Analysis and Federal Power* (New York: SDS, 1964).

100. Unger, *The Movement*, 76.

101. Ibid., 56; and Hayden, 86–102.

102. Van Gosse, *Where the Boys Are* (New York: Verso, 1993): 61–65.

103. Steven J. Rosenthal, *Vietnam Study Guide and Annotated Bibliography* (San Francisco: SDS, 1965).

104. Ibid., 3.

105. Rorabaugh, 6–15.

106. Ibid., 22–23.

107. Unger, *The Movement*, 93–98.

108. Gosse, 218–222.

109. Kirkpatrick Sale, *SDS* (New York: Random House, 1973): 198.

110. Newfield, *A Prophetic Minority*, 106.

111. William W. Turner, *Hoover's FBI* (New York: Dell, 1971): 185.

112. Hayden, 194.

113. Miller, *"Democracy Is in the Streets,"* 281–282; and Jack Newfield, *Bread and Roses Too: Reporting About America* (New York: Dutton, 1971): 127.

114. Hayden, 357–360.

115. Terry H. Anderson, *The Movement and the Sixties* (New York: Oxford Univ. Press, 1995): 170–171.

116. Marty Jezer, *Abbie Hoffman: American Rebel* (New Brunswick, NJ: Rutgers Univ. Press, 1992): 134–135.

117. Unger, *The Movement*, 142–143.

118. Newfield, *A Prophetic Minority*, 145.

119. Ibid., 72.

120. Staughton Lynd, "Towards a History of the New Left," 8–9; and Frank Joyce, "Racism in the United States: An Introduction," 137–138, in Long.

121. Sara Evans, *Personal Politics* (New York: Vintage, 1980): 51–73.

122. Pycior, 139.

123. Ibid., 153–163.

124. Ibid., 191–192.

125. Garcia, 67.

126. Pycior, 177–178; and Lou Cannon, *Reagan* (New York: G. P. Putnam's Sons, 1982): 117–118.

127. Unger, *The Movement*, 153–156; and Pycior, 203–217.

128. Tony Castro, *Chicano Power* (New York: Dutton, 1974).

129. Ronald Taylor, *Chavez and the Farm Workers* (Boston: Houghton Mifflin, 1975): 4–57.

130. Peter Matthiessen, *Sal Si Puedes: Cesar Chavez and the New American Revolution* (New York: Random House, 1969): 52.

131. Ibid., 111–184.

132. Matthew Dallek, 218.

133. Castro, 28–51; and Walter W. Wilcox, "Farm Policy Issues, 1966–1970," *Social Action*, 32 (Nov. 1965): 6–13.

134. Matthiessen, 363, 367–368.

135. Ibid., 143–145.

136. Ibid., 175–180.

137. Newfield, *Robert Kennedy: A Memoir*, 62–63.

138. Ibid., 81, 214–215.

139. (W.) Marvin Watson Papers, Box 29, memo, John Roche to Watson, March 13, 1968, LBJL.

140. Joseph A. Palermo, *In His Own Right: The Political Odyssey of Senator Robert F. Kennedy* (New York: Columbia Univ. Press, 2001): 226–227.

141. (W.) Marvin Watson Papers, Box 29, memo, John Roche to LBJ, March 14, 1968, LBJL.

142. Cohen and Taylor, 440–445; and O'Neill, 189–200.

143. Thomas P. O'Neill, Jr. Papers, Box 20, newsletter, "Report from Washington," June 1966, 2, BC.

144. Ibid., September, 1966, 1, BC.

145. O'Neill, 199–200.

146. Ibid., 189.

147. Cohen and Taylor, 430–444.

148. Gallup, 1982, 1986.

149. Ibid., 1993.

150. Ibid., 2027.

151. Altschuler, xvii.

152. Berman, 17–19.

153. Murphy interview.

154. DNC Files, clipping, *Harrisburg Patriot*, March 2, 1965, LBJL.

155. Ibid., *Wall Street Journal*, March 30, 1966, LBJL.

156. Ibid.

157. Evans and Novak, 570–582.

158. *PPP*, 1966, I, 3.

159. Gallup, 2037.

160. Altschuler, 63.

161. *PPP*, 1966, II, 1135.

162. Ibid., 1148.

163. LBJ, *VP*, 248.

164. Ibid., 249.

165. Sidey, 150.

166. Quoted in Thomas Powers, *Vietnam: The War at Home* (Boston: G. K. Hall, 1984): 131.

167. Gardner, 318.

168. *The Pentagon Papers*, 520.

169. Sidey, 181–182.

170. *PPP*, 1966, II, 1320.

171. Ibid.

172. Matthew Dallek, 165–172.

173. Brownstein, 226.

174. Cannon, 114–117.

175. Matthew Dallek, 77–79.

176. Cannon, 117–118; and Totton J. Anderson and Eugene C. Lee, "The 1966 Election in California," *Western Political Quarterly*, 20 (1967): 535–554.

177. *CQ, Guide to U.S. Elections*, 519.

178. *CQ, Politics in America*, 67–68.

179. *CQ, Guide to U.S. Elections*, 615.

180. Cohen and Taylor, 412–427.

181. Hess and Broder, 387–388.

182. Drukman, 441.

183. Hess and Broder, 327–328.

184. Powers, 133.

185. George J. Mitchell Papers, 1966 Election File, letter, Mitchell to Fellow Democrat, Nov. 18, 1966, BWC.

186. Ibid., letter, EMK to Mitchell, Nov. 1966, BWC.

187. *CQ, Politics in America*, 67.

188. Ibid., 61–62, 68.

189. Phillips, 437–441; and Thomas Payne, "The 1966 Elections in the West," *Western Political Quarterly* 20 (1967): 517–523.

190. CQ, *Politics in America*, 68.

191. CQ, *Guide to U.S. Elections*, 103.

192. Gary C. Jacobson, *The Politics of Congressional Elections* (New York: Harper Collins, 1992): 27.

193. Stanley and Niemi, 142.

194. Ibid., 127.

195. Jacobson, 26–28.

196. Rae, *The Decline and Fall of the Liberal Republicans*, 86–91.

197. John F. Bibby, "Party Leadership, The Bliss Model, and the Development of the Republican National Committee," in *Politics, Professionalism, and Power: Modern Party Organization and the Legacy of Ray C. Bliss* (Akron, OH: Univ. of Akron, 1994): 19–33.

198. Klinkner, 77–85.

199. *NYT*, Feb. 1, 1968.

200. Hess and Broder, 47–48.

201. Republican Coordinating Committee, *Brief Position Papers and Other Documents* (Washington, DC: RNC, 1966): 6–7.

202. POF, memo, Bill Moyers to LBJ, May 2, 1966, LBJL.

203. DNC Files, Series 1, 1966 Election Folder, clippings, *Washington Star*, Nov. 14, 1966 and *Washington Post*, Nov. 13, 1966, LBJL.

204. *PPP*, 1966, II, 1358.

205. Ibid., 1359.

206. *PPP*, 1967, I, 6–7.

207. Ibid., 8.

208. Ibid., 11.

209. Ibid., 14.

210. CQ, *Politics in America*, 69.

211. Stanley and Niemi, 216.

212. David S. Broder, "Consensus Politics: End of an Experiment," *The Atlantic Monthly* 218 (Oct. 1966): 60–61.

213. Ibid., 63.

214. Ibid., 65.

215. Doris Kearns and Sanford Levinson, "How to Remove LBJ in 1968," *New Republic* 154 (May 13, 1967): 13–14.

216. Ibid., 13.

217. Ibid.

218. Chafe, 265–266; and Ronald Radosh, *Divided They Fell: The Demise of the Democratic Party, 1964–1996* (New York: Free Press, 1996): 27–29.

219. Quoted in Radosh, 40.

220. Ibid., 45.

221. Richard Blumenthal, "New Politics at Chicago," *Nation* (Sept. 25, 1967): 273–276.

222. Radosh, 79.

223. Chafe, 104–107, 254–255.

224. Newfield, *Robert Kennedy: A Memoir*, 177.

225. Chafe, 244–290.

226. Ibid., 246–247.

227. Gillon, 200–202.

228. Lewis Chester et al., *An American Melodrama: The Presidential Campaign of 1968* (New York: Dell, 1969): 265–266.

229. White, *The Making of the President, 1968*, 82–85.

230. Edward Costikyan, *Behind Closed Doors: Politics in the Public Interest* (New York: Harcourt, Brace, and World, 1966): 13–135.

231. Quoted in Chester, 111.

232. Ibid., 71–72.

233. Gillon, 184–185.

234. Eisele, 277–279.

235. Rising, 54.

236. Eisele, 276–277; and *NYT*, Dec. 3, 1967.

237. White, *The Making of the President 1968*, 92–95.

238. Chafe, 280–282.

239. Powers, 287.

240. Rising, 66–68.

241. Allen Young, "McCarthy Is Good Party Man," *Guardian* (Feb. 10, 1968): 5.

242. Chafe, 282–288.

243. Schlesinger, *Robert Kennedy and His Times*, 912–913; and Theodore C. Sorensen, *The Kennedy Legacy* (New York: Macmillan, 1969): 130–133.

244. Heymann, 446–454.

245. Lasky, *Robert Kennedy: The Myth and the Man*, 11–32; Toledano, 362–374; and Nick Thimmesch and William Johnson, *Robert Kennedy at 40* (New York: Norton, 1965): 283–291.

246. Quoted in Shesol, 397.

247. (W.) Marvin Watson Files, Box 25, memo, LBJ to Ben Wattenberg, Dec. 10, 1967, LBJL.

248. *PPP*, 1967, II, 1169.

249. Jules Witcover, *85 Days: The Last Campaign of Robert Kennedy* (New York: Morrow, 1969): 15–44.

250. Clymer, 104–105; and Eisele, 300–301.

251. Quoted in Witcover, *85 Days*, 68.

252. Sorensen, *The Kennedy Legacy*, 138–139.

253. Goodwin, 520–521.

254. Edwin O. Guthman and C. Richard Allen (ed.), *RFK: Collected Speeches* (New York: Viking, 1993): 321.

255. Ibid.

256. Ibid.

257. *NYT*, March 17, 1968.

258. Powers, 291; Lasky, *Robert Kennedy: The Myth and the Man*, 400; and "Politics '68: Kennedy and McCarthy," *Human Events* 28 (March 30, 1968): 5.

259. Quoted in Heymann, 456–457.

260. Ragsdale, 40.

261. Costikyan, 223–224; and Shannon, *The Heir Apparent*, 16–39.

262. Rising, 58.

263. Sam Johnson, *My Brother Lyndon* (New York: Cowles, 1970): 237–238.

264. Schlesinger, *Robert Kennedy and His Times*, 922–923.

265. Gallup, 2112.

266. *NYT*, March 27, 1968.

267. Bruno and Greenfield, 136.

268. Ibid.

269. Guthman and Allen, 333–335.

270. Witcover, *85 Days*, 99–101.

271. Ibid., 116–118; and RFK Papers, PCP, Box 5, memo, unsigned to EMK, Steve Smith et al., March 25, 1968, JFKL.

272. Guthman and Allen, 324.

273. Ibid., 333.

274. Ibid., 338.

275. *PPP*, 1968–1969, I, 410.

276. Ibid., 438.

277. Gallup, 2106, 2113.

278. Ibid., 2112–2113.

279. Altshuler, 98; WHCF, Box 82, Quayle poll on Wisconsin, March, 1968; and (W.) Marvin Watson Files, Box 18, Quayle-NBC poll, March 23–25, 1968 and memo, Jim Wimmer to Watson, March 26, 1968, LBJL.

280. Quoted in O'Brien, 231.

281. *CQ, Guide to U.S. Elections*, 417.

282. Guthman and Allen, 350–351.

283. *PPP*, 1968–1969, I, 470–471.

284. Halberstam, *The Unfinished Odyssey of Robert Kennedy*, 76.

285. Bernard Brock, "1968 Democratic Campaign: A Political Upheaval," *Quarterly Journal of Speech* 55 (Feb. 1969): 26–55; and Jack Newfield, "Kennedy's Search for a New Target," *Life* (April 12, 1968): 35.

286. Guthman and Allen, 357.

287. Ibid., 352–374.

288. Palermo, 179–184.

289. Gould, *1968: The Election That Changed America*, 71–72.

290. Eisele, 331; and *CQ, Guide to U.S. Elections*, 417.

291. Steven V. Roberts, "McCarthy Campaign Enters New Phase," *Commonweal* (April 26, 1968): 165–167; and "Democratic Runners: McCarthy—Man of Conscience," *Economist* 227 (April 27, 1968): 45.

292. Schlesinger, *Robert Kennedy and His Times*, 960–962; and Sorensen, *The Kennedy Legacy*, 142.

293. Roger Branigin Papers, Box 108, folder 15, telegram, Branigin to LBJ, March 28, 1968, FC.

294. Fenton, 174–189.

295. Roger Branigin Papers, Box 108, folder 15, letter, William Carman to Vance Hartke, March 25, 1968, and Birch Bayh to Charles Armington, May 3, 1968, FC.

296. Baldoni interview.

297. Roger Branigin Papers, Box 108, folder 17, letter, John A. Watkins to Branigin, April 4, 1968, FC.

298. Ibid., folder 18, letter, Anonymous "Democrat" to Branigin, April 18, 1968, FC.

299. Ibid., letters, Robert W. Neal, May 1, 1968, Jack Layne, March 31, 1968, and Robert C. Warnick, March 28, 1968, all to Branigin, FC.

300. *NYT*, May 5, 1968; *Time* (April 26, 1968): 22–23; *USNWR* (May 6, 1968): 59–60; and "Election '68: Hoosier Puzzle," *Economist* 227 (April 27, 1968): 41.

301. O'Brien, 60–61, 240–241; and Chester, 173–174.

302. Witcover, *85 Days*, 128–182.

303. Baldoni interview.

304. Palermo, 199–200.

305. Chester, 190–194.

306. Baldoni interview; and Roger Branigin Papers, Box 108, folder 18, letter, J. Byron Hayes to Allen County Democrats, April 15, 1968, and Box 109, folder 1, letter, Marshall H. Hall to Branigin, May 8, 1968, FC.

307. Eisele, 311–314; Chester, 184–185; and Abigail McCarthy, *Private Faces, Public Places* (New York: Doubleday, 1972): 399–404.

308. William vanden Heuvel and Milton Gwirtzman, *On His Own: RFK, 1964–68* (New York: Doubleday, 1970): 347.

309. *CQ, Guide to U.S. Elections*, 417.

310. Chester, 196.

311. Roger Branigin Papers, Box 109, folder 1, letter, Trueman T. Rembusch to Ranigin, May 9, 1968, FC.

312. *CQ, Guide to U.S. Elections*, 417.

313. Newfield, *Robert Kennedy: A Memoir*, 264.

314. Witcover, *85 Days*, 180–181; and RFK Papers, PCP, Box 6, Indiana file, memo, Lawrence F. O'Brien to RFK, April 27, 1968, JFKL.

315. Sorensen, *The Kennedy Legacy*, 148–149.

316. *CQ, Guide to U.S. Elections*, 417–418.

317. Sorensen, *The Kennedy Legacy*, 138–139.

318. Newfield, *Robert Kennedy: A Memoir*, 267.

319. *CQ, Guide to U.S. Elections*, 418.

320. Guthman and Allen, 382; and Witcover, *85 Days*, 197.

321. Witcover, *85 Days*, 198.

322. Gallup, 2123, 2127.

323. Witcover, *85 Days*, 168.

324. Drukman, 435–437.

325. Beschloss, *Reaching for Glory*, 198, 207–210.

326. Drukman, 437–438; *NYT*, May 2, 1966; (W.) Marvin Watson Files, memo, William Connell to Watson, April 19, 1966, LBJL.

327. Guthman and Allen, 387–391.

328. Witcover, *85 Days*, 210.

329. *CQ, Guide to U.S. Elections*, 418.

330. White, *The Making of the President 1968*, 221.

331. Witcover, *85 Days*, 224.

332. Newfield, *Robert Kennedy: A Memoir*, 270–271.

333. vanden Heuvel and Gwirtzman, 369.

334. Pierre Salinger, *P.S.: A Memoir* (New York: St. Martin's Press, 1995): 169–176.

335. Palermo, 218–220.

336. Boyle, 238–244.

337. vanden Heuvel and Gwirtzman, 377.

338. Quoted in Newfield, *Robert Kennedy: A Memoir*, 281.

339. Quoted in Eisele, 320.

340. vanden Heuvel and Gwirtzman, 378.

341. Ibid., 378–379.

342. RFK Papers, PCP, Box 15, press releases, May 1, May 15, June 3, 1968, JFKL.

343. Palermo, 237.

344. Gallup, 2128–2129.

345. Halberstam, *The Unfinished Odyssey*, 162.

346. Ibid., 164.

347. *CQ, Guide to U.S. Elections*, 418; and RFK Papers, PCP, Box 22, press release, May 30, 1968, JFKL.

348. Palermo, 244.

349. Eisele, 320.

350. *CQ, Guide to U.S. Elections*, 418.

351. Witcover, *85 Days*, 183–184; and RFK Papers, PCP, Box 22, memo, David Borden to James Flug, June 4, 1968, JFKL.

352. vanden Heuvel and Gwirtzman, 379, 390–391.

353. Chester, 392; and Chafe, 288–290.

354. Chester, 421–422; and Kimball, 20–22.

355. Halberstam, *The Unfinished Odyssey*, 213–214.

356. vanden Heuvel and Gwirtzman, 380–381.

357. Sorensen, *The Kennedy Legacy*, 279–283.

358. RFK Papers, PCP, Box 2, memos, Bill Silver to William vanden Heuvel, May 2, 1968; Box 9, Fred Berger to Joe Dolan, March 28, 1968, and unsigned, April 27, 1968, JFKL.

359. Palermo, 172.

360. Witcover, *85 Days*, 334–337.

361. Palermo, 253–254; OH, Cesar Chavez, January 28, 1970, 20–21, JFKL; and Newfield, *Robert Kennedy: A Memoir*, 300–304.

362. Burner and West, 220–225.

363. David Wise, "How Bobby Plans to Win It," *Saturday Evening Post* (June 1, 1968): 23–27; and Jerry Bruno Papers, Box 12, scheduling for June 7–17, 1968, JFKL.

364. Chester, 134.

365. Witcover, *85 Days*, 336.

366. Burton Hersh, *The Education of Edward Kennedy* (New York: Morrow, 1972): 289–290.

367. Sullivan, 122–123.

368. Navasky, 361–378; and Cohen and Taylor, 449–450.

369. Jezer, 121–141; and David Farber, *Chicago '68* (Chicago: Univ. of Chicago Press, 1988): 28–55.

370. Strout, 326–328.

371. Clymer, 119–126.

372. Hersh, 282–329.

373. Eisele, 332.

374. *NYT*, June 14, 1968.

375. White, *The Making of the President 1968*, 333.

376. *NYT*, June 24, 1968; and *CQ, Politics in America*, 87.

377. Eisele, 340.

378. Chester, 458–463.

379. Eisele, 342.

380. *NYT*, Aug. 13, 1968.

381. Chafe, 300–301.

382. *NYT*, July 4, 1968.

383. Chester, 463–464.

384. Ibid., 473–474.

385. Ibid., 587–592.

386. *CQ, The Presidential Nominating Conventions of 1968*, 186.

387. *PPP*, 1968–1969, II, 896–903.

388. Ibid., 900.

389. Ibid., 901.

390. Ibid., 905.

391. Quoted in Eisele, 346–347.

392. HHH, 388–389.

393. HHH, 390.

394. Eisele, 347.

395. Ibid., 347–348.

396. *CQ, The Presidential Nominating Conventions of 1968*, 139.

397. Reston, 358–365; and Eisele, 348–351.

398. *CQ, The Presidential Nominating Conventions of 1968*, 89.

399. Parmet, *The Democrats*, 280–281.

400. Joseph L. Rauh, Jr. Papers, Box 29, letter, Aaron Henry to John Bailey, July 17, 1968, LOC.

401. Bain and Parris, 324.

402. Ibid., 324–325.

403. *CQ, The Presidential Nominating Conventions of 1968*, 200.

404. Norman Mailer, *Miami and the Siege of Chicago* (New York: Signet, 1968): 162–164.

405. *CQ, The Presidential Nominating Conventions of 1968*, 213.

406. Ibid., 216.

407. Ibid., 217.

408. Ibid., 214.

409. Quoted in Nevin, 214.

410. *CQ, The Presidential Nominating Conventions of 1968*, 152.

411. Nevin, 212–213.

412. HHH, 390.

413. Ibid., 392.

414. *CQ, Guide to U.S. Elections*, 210.

415. Bain and Parris, 328.

416. HHH, 391.

417. O'Brien, 256.

418. *CQ, The Presidential Nominating Conventions of 1968*, 157, 160.

419. Eisele, 361.

420. *NYT*, Oct. 30, 1968.

421. Quoted in Wicker, *One of Us*, 336.

422. Domhoff, 14–22; and Goodwin, 501–502.

423. Joseph L. Rauh, Jr., Box 11, unsigned ADA press release, Feb. 10, 1968, LOC.

424. Ibid., letter, Robert M. Stein to Rauh, Sept. 30, 1968, LOC.

425. Gillon, 220–223.

426. (W.) Marvin Watson Papers, OF, memo, Larry O'Brien, "A White Paper for the President," Sept. 29, 1967, LBJL.

427. Ibid.; and OH, O'Brien, April 23, 1987, 1–5, LBJL.

428. Thomas J. McIntyre Papers, Administrative Files, undated 1968 campaign pamphlet, "Some Men Talk Change. Others Cause It.," UNH.

429. Edmund S. Muskie Papers, Box CA22, memo, Bill Claire to Larry O'Brien, Sept. 4, 1968, 1, BTC.

430. Ibid.

431. Ibid., Box CA41, DSG memo, "The Republican Platform vs. the Republican Record," Aug. 10, 1968, BTC; and Thomas J. McIntyre Papers, Administrative Files, letter, McIntyre to Paul Marashio, June 14, 1968, UNH.

432. HHH, 397–398, and Bayh and Baldoni interviews.

433. HHH, 398.

434. Gallup, 2162.

435. Goulden, 367–369; and Boyle, 253–256.

436. Carl Solberg, *Hubert Humphrey: A Biography* (New York: Norton, 1984): 388–389.

437. Gallup, 2168.

438. Stanley and Niemi, 106.

439. Jamieson, 233.

440. Edmund S. Muskie Papers, Box CA22, memo, Bill Weeks to Don Nicoll, Oct. 7, 1968, BTC.

441. Wicker, *One of Us*, 363–364.

442. Richard M. Scammon and Ben J. Wattenberg, *The Real Majority: An Extraordinary Examination of the American Electorate* (New York: Coward, McCann, and Geoghegan, Inc., 1971): 205.

443. Edmund S. Muskie Papers, Box CA23, letter, Mrs. Francis Grochowski to Muskie, Sept. 3, 1968; and memo, Larry O'Brien to Don Nicoll, Sept. 5, 1968, BTC.

444. Ibid., Muskie press release, Sept. 5, 1968, BTC.

445. Solberg, 397–398.

446. Thomas J. McIntyre Papers, Administrative Files, 1968 campaign pamphlet, "Some Men Talk about Change. Others Cause It.," UNH.

447. Joe McGinnis, *The Selling of the President 1968* (New York: Trident Press, 1969): 126–141.

448. Reinsch, 237–239.

449. Jamieson, 255–257.

450. Ibid., 242.

451. Scammon and Wattenberg, 169–170; HHH, 400–401; and Edmund S. Muskie Papers, Box CA23, DNC memos, memo, George Carroll to Don Nicoll, Sept. 16, 1968, 2, BTC.

452. OH, Lawrence F. O'Brien, Aug. 26, 1987, 7–9, LBJL.

453. Jules Witcover, *The Year the Dream Died: Revisiting 1968 in America* (New York: Warner Books, 1997): 426–431.

454. Gerald S. Strober and Deborah H. Strober (ed.), *Nixon: An Oral History of His Presidency* (New York: Harper Collins, 1994): 30.

455. Newfield, *Bread and Roses Too*, 158.

456. Halberstam, *The Best and the Brightest*, 662.

457. Broder, *The Party's Over*, 83.

458. Strober and Strober, *Nixon*, 27–30.

459. Miller, *Lyndon*, 640; and LBJ, *VP*, 517–518.

460. *PPP*, 1968–1969, II, 1102.

461. Clifford, 573–594.

462. Ibid., 595.

463. HHH, 405–406.

464. OH, Lawrence F. O'Brien, August 25, 1987, 31–34, LBJL; and Jamieson, 270–272.

465. O'Brien, 269.

466. McPherson, 449; Eisele, 381–383; Miller, *Lyndon*, 524; Gould, *1968: The Election That Changed America*, 143–146; and Shesol, 444–445.

467. Dallek, *Fallen Giant*, 544.

468. Ibid., 580.

469. Strober and Strober, *Nixon*, 27.

470. Eisele, 381.

471. HHH, 400.

472. O'Brien, 252–268.

473. Clifford, 554–558.

474. LBJ, *VP*, 546–547.

475. Bruce A. Murphy, *Fortas: The Rise and Ruin of a Supreme Court Justice* (New York: Morrow, 1988): 517–518.

476. Ibid., 463–526; and "Fortas: LBJ's Mr. Fixit," *Human Events* 28 (July 6, 1968): 3.

477. Domhoff, 14–70; and Brownstein, 202–203.

478. *PPP*, 1968–1969, II, 1111–1112.

479. Ibid., 1112–1113.

480. LBJ, *VP*, 27–41, 549–550; Kearns, 397–398; and Broder, *The Party's Over*, 74–77.

481. Gallup, 2158, 2171.

482. Ibid., 2167.

483. Ragsdale, 133.

484. *NYT*, Oct. 22, 1968.

485. *CQ, Guide to U.S. Elections*, 309, 362.

486. Scammon and Wattenberg, 219–220.

487. *CQ, Guide to U.S. Elections*, 309.

488. Ibid., 362.

489. Stanley and Niemi, 140.

490. Ibid., 128.

491. Ibid., 128; and *CQ, Politics in America*, 83.

492. Joseph A. Pika et al., *The Politics of the Presidency* (Washington, DC: CQ Press, 2002): 58.

493. Ibid.

494. Michael Barone, *Our Country* (New York: Free Press, 1990): 452.

495. Phillips, 231.

496. Ladd and Hadley, 136–177; Black and Black, 199–210, 298–303; and Bartley and Graham, 138–139, 187.

497. *CQ, Guide to U.S. Elections*, 362.

498. Stanley and Niemi, 140.

499. Nie et al., 83.

500. Ladd and Hadley, 160.

501. Phillips, 471.

502. Walter Dean Burnham, *Critical Elections and the Mainsprings of American Politics* (New York: Norton, 1970): 135–174.

503. Broder, *The Party's Over*, 81, 212.

504. Scammon and Wattenberg, 279–305.

505. Stern, 10–20, 133–148.

506. Bernstein, *Promises Kept*, 24–25, 286–288.

507. Theodore J. Lowi, *The Personal President* (Ithaca, NY: Cornell Univ. Press, 1985): 75–76; and Thomas J. Weko, *The Politicizing Presidency: The White House Personnel Office, 1948–1994* (Lawrence: Univ. Press of Kansas, 1995): 24–28.

508. Rae, *The Decline and Fall of the Liberal Republicans*, 47–77; Phillips, 82–93; and Reichley, 316–333.

509. LBJ, *VP*, 470, 529–531; Miller, *Lyndon*, 594; and Kearns, 251–254.

510. Parmet, *The Democrats*, 284–295.

511. APSA, *Toward a More Responsible Two-Party System*, 94.

Selected Bibliography

BOOKS

Aldrich, John H. *Why Parties?: The Origin and Transformation of Political Parties in America.* Chicago: University of Chicago Press, 1995.

Alexander, Herbert E. *Money in Politics.* Washington, DC: Public Affairs Press, 1972.

American Political Science Association. *Toward a More Responsible Two-Party System.* New York: Rinehart and Company, Inc., 1950.

Andersen, Kristi. *The Creation of a Democratic Majority: 1928–1936.* Chicago: University of Chicago Press, 1979.

Bain, Richard C., and Judith H. Parris. *Convention Decisions and Voting Records.* Washington, DC: Brookings Institution, 1973.

Baker, Bobby, with Larry L. King. *Wheeling and Dealing: Confessions of a Capitol Hill Operator.* New York: W.W. Norton, 1978.

Barone, Michael. *Our Country: The Shaping of America from Roosevelt to Reagan.* New York: The Free Press, 1990.

Berman, Larry. *Lyndon Johnson's War.* New York: W.W. Norton, 1989.

Bernstein, Irving. *Promises Kept: John F. Kennedy's New Frontier.* New York: Oxford University Press, 1991.

———. *Guns or Butter: The Presidency of Lyndon Johnson.* New York: Oxford University Press, 1996.

Beschloss, Michael R. (ed.). *Taking Charge: The Johnson White House Tapes, 1963–1964.* New York: Simon and Schuster, 1997.

———. *Reaching for Glory: Lyndon Johnson's Secret White House Tapes, 1964–1965.* New York: Simon and Schuster, 2001.

Bone, Hugh A. *Party Committees and National Politics.* Seattle: University of Washington Press, 1958.

Boyle, Kevin. *The UAW and the Heyday of American Liberalism, 1945–1968.* Ithaca: Cornell University Press, 1995.

Brennan, Mary C. *Turning Right in the Sixties: The Conservative Capture of the GOP.* Chapel Hill: University of North Carolina Press, 1995.

Broder, David S. *The Party's Over: The Failure of American Politics.* New York: Harper and Row Publishers, 1972.

Burns, James MacGregor. *The Deadlock of Democracy: Four-Party Politics in America.* Englewood Cliffs: Prentice-Hall, 1963.

———. *John Kennedy: A Political Profile*. New York: Avon Book Division, 1960.

Califano, Joseph A., Jr. *The Triumph and Tragedy of Lyndon Johnson*. New York: Simon and Schuster, 1991.

Campbell, Angus, Converse, Philip E., Miller, Warren E., and Stokes, Donald E. *The American Voter*. New York: Werbel and Peck, 1964.

Carney, Francis M., and Way, H. Frank, Jr. *Politics 1960*. San Francisco: Wadsworth Publishing, 1960.

———. *Politics 1964*. Belmont: Wadsworth Publishing, 1964.

Caro, Robert A. *The Path to Power: The Years of Lyndon Johnson*. New York: Vintage Books, 1983.

———. *Master of the Senate: The Years of Lyndon Johnson*. New York: Alfred A. Knopf, 2002.

———. *Means of Ascent: The Years of Lyndon Johnson*. New York: Alfred A. Knopf, 1990.

Carter, Dan T. *The Politics of Rage: George Wallace, the Origins of the New Conservatism, and the Transformation of American Politics*. Baton Rouge: Louisiana State University Press, 1995.

Clifford, Clark M. *Counsel to the President: A Memoir*. New York: Random House, 1991.

Clymer, Adam. *Edward M. Kennedy: A Biography*. New York: William Morrow, 1999.

Cohen, Adam, and Elizabeth Taylor. *American Pharaoh: Mayor Richard J. Daley*. Boston: Little, Brown, and Company, 2000.

Congressional Quarterly, Guide to U.S. Elections. Washington, DC: CQ Press, 1985.

Cotter, Cornelius P., and Bernard C. Hennessy. *Politics Without Power: The National Party Committees*. New York: Atherton Press, 1964.

Crotty, William. *Party Reform*. New York: Longman, 1983.

Dallek, Matthew. *The Right Moment: Ronald Reagan's First Victory and the Decisive Turning Point in American Politics*. New York: Free Press, 2000.

Dallek, Robert. *Flawed Giant: Lyndon Johnson and His Times, 1961–1973*. New York: Oxford University Press, 1998.

———. *Lone Star Rising: Lyndon Johnson and His Times, 1908–1960*. New York: Oxford University Press, 1991.

Davis, James W. *The President as Party Leader*. New York: Praeger, 1992.

Donovan, John C. *The Politics of Poverty*. New York: Pegasus, 1967.

Donovan, Robert J. *Nemesis: Truman and Johnson in the Coils of War in Asia*. New York: St. Martin's Press, 1984.

Dugger, Ronnie. *The Politician: The Life and Times of Lyndon Johnson*. New York: W.W. Norton, 1982.

Elliott, Carl, Sr., and Michael D'Orso. *The Cost of Courage: The Journey of an American Congressman*. New York: Doubleday, 1992.

Evans, Rowland, and Robert Novak. *Lyndon B. Johnson: The Exercise of Power*. New York: Signet Books, 1966.

Farrell, John A. *Tip O'Neill and the Democratic Century*. Boston: Little, Brown, 2001.

Foley, Michael. *The New Senate: Liberal Influence on a Conservative Institution, 1959–1972*. New Haven: Yale University Press, 1980.

Freeman, Jo. *A Room at a Time: How Women Entered Party Politics*. Lanham: Rowman and Littlefield, 2000.

Galbraith, John Kenneth. *The Affluent Society*. New York: Mentor Books, 1958.

————. *Letters to Kennedy*. Cambridge: Harvard University Press, 1998.

Gallup, George H. *The Gallup Poll: Public Opinion, 1935–1971*. New York: Random House, 1973.

Garcia, Ignacio M. *Viva Kennedy*. College Station: Texas A and M University Press, 2000.

Gardner, Lloyd C. *Pay Any Price: Lyndon Johnson and the Wars for Vietnam*. Chicago: Ivan R. Dee, 1995.

Giglio, James N. *The Presidency of John F. Kennedy*. Lawrence: University Press of Kansas, 1991.

Gillon, Steven M. *Politics and Vision: The ADA and American Liberalism, 1947–1985*. New York: Oxford University Press, 1987.

Gitlin, Todd. *The Sixties: Years of Hope, Days of Rage*. New York: Bantam Books, 1987.

Goldman, Eric F. *The Tragedy of Lyndon Johnson*. New York: Alfred A. Knopf, 1969.

Goldman, Ralph M. *The National Party Chairmen and Committees*. New York: M. E. Sharpe, 1990.

Gould, Lewis L. *1968: The Election That Changed America*. Chicago: Ivan R. Dee, 1993.

Green, John C. (ed.). *Politics, Professionalism, and Power: Modern Party Organization and the Legacy of Ray C. Bliss*. Lanham: University Press of America, 1994.

Guthman, Edwin O., and Jeffrey Shulman (ed.). *Robert Kennedy: In His Own Words* New York: Bantam Books, 1988.

Halberstam, David. *The Unfinished Odyssey of Robert Kennedy*. New York: Bantam Books, 1968.

Henggeler, Paul R. *In His Steps: Lyndon Johnson and the Kennedy Mystique*. Chicago: Ivan R. Dee, 1991.

Hersh, Seymour M. *The Dark Side of Camelot*. Boston: Little, Brown, 1997.

Hess, Stephen, and David S. Broder. *The Republican Establishment: The Present and Future of the GOP*. New York: Harper and Row, 1967.

Hilsman, Roger. *To Move a Nation: The Politics of Foreign Policy in the Administration of John F. Kennedy* New York, Doubleday, 1967.

Hulsey, Byron C. *Everett Dirksen and His Presidents: How a Senate Giant Shaped American Politics*. Lawrence: University Press of Kansas, 2000.

Humphrey, Hubert H. *The Education of a Public Man: My Life and Politics*. New York: Doubleday, 1976.

Jacobson, Gary C. *The Politics of Congressional Elections*. New York: Harper Collins, 1992.

Jamieson, Kathleen Hall. *Packaging the Presidency: A History and Criticism of Presidential Campaign Advertising*. New York: Oxford University Press, 1984.

Johnson, Lyndon Baines. *The Vantage Point: Perspectives of the Presidency, 1963–1969*. New York: Popular Library, 1971.

Jones, Charles O. *The Presidency in a Separated System*. Washington, DC: Brookings Institution, 1994.

Kaiser, David. *American Tragedy: Kennedy, Johnson, and the Origins of the Vietnam War*. Cambridge: Harvard University Press, 2000.

Kaufman, Robert G. *Henry M. Jackson: A Life in Politics*. Seattle: University of Washington Press, 2000.

Kearns, Doris. *Lyndon Johnson and the American Dream*. New York: Harper and Row, 1976.

Kennedy, John F. *A Nation of Immigrants*. New York: Harper and Row, 1964.

————. *Profiles in Courage*. New York: Harper and Row, 1956.

————. *The Strategy of Peace*. New York: Harper and Row, 1960.

————. *Why England Slept*. New York: Wilfred Funk, Inc. 1940.

Kennedy, Robert F. *The Enemy Within*. New York: Popular Library, 1960.

Kessel, John H. *The Goldwater Coalition: Republican Strategies in 1964*. Indianapolis: Bobbs-Merrill, 1968.

————. *Presidents, the Presidency, and the Political Environment*. Washington, DC: Congressional Quarterly, Inc., 2001.

Key, V. O., Jr. *American State Politics*. New York: Alfred A. Knopf, 1956.

————. *Politics, Parties, and Pressure Groups*. New York: Thomas Y. Crowell, 1950.

————. *The Responsible Electorate: Rationality in Presidential Voting, 1936–1960*. New York: Vintage Books, 1966.

————. *Southern Politics in State and Nation*. Knoxville: University of Tennessee Press, 1985.

Klinkner, Philip A. *The Losing Parties: Out-Party National Committees, 1956–1993*. New Haven: Yale University Press, 1994.

Krock, Arthur. *Memoirs: Sixty Years on the Firing Line*. New York: Funk and Wagnalls, 1968.

Ladd, Everett C., Jr., and Charles D. Hadley. *Transformations of the American Party System*. New York: W.W. Norton, 1975.

Larson, Arthur. *A Republican Looks at His Party*. New York: Harper and Brothers, 1956.

Lasky, Victor. *It Didn't Start with Watergate*. New York: Dial Press, 1977.

————. *J.F.K.: The Man and the Myth*. New York: Macmillan, 1963.

————. *Robert F. Kennedy: The Myth and the Man*. New York: Trident Press, 1968.

Lawrence, David G. *The Collapse of the Democratic Presidential Majority*. Boulder: Westview Press, 1996.

Lazarowitz, Arlene. *Years in Exile: The Liberal Democrats, 1950–1959*. New York: Garland Press, 1988.

Lee, R. Alton. *Eisenhower and Landrum-Griffin: A Study in Labor-Management Politics*. Lexington: University Press of Kentucky, 1990.

Leuchtenburg, William E. *In the Shadow of FDR: from Harry Truman to Ronald Reagan*. Ithaca: Cornell University Press, 1983.

Lind, Michael. *Vietnam: The Necessary War*. New York: Free Press, 1999.

Litt, Edgar. *The Political Cultures of Massachusetts*. Cambridge: MIT Press, 1965.

Lockard, Duane. *New England State Politics*. Princeton: Princeton University Press, 1959.

Lowi, Theodore J. *The Personal President: Power Invested, Promise Unfulfilled*. Ithaca: Cornell University Press, 1985.

Lubell, Samuel. *The Future of American Politics*. New York: Harper and Row, 1965.

MacKaye, William R. *A New Coalition Takes Control: The House Rules Committee Fight of 1961*. New York: McGraw-Hill, 1963.

MacNeil, Neil. *Dirksen*. New York: World Publishing Company, 1970.

————. *Forge of Democracy*. New York: David McKay Company, 1963.

Mann, Robert. *A Grand Delusion: America's Descent into Vietnam*. New York: Basic Books, 2001.

————. *Legacy to Power: Senator Russell Long of Louisiana*. New York: Paragon House, 1992.

————. *The Walls of Jericho: Lyndon Johnson, Hubert Humphrey, Richard Russell, and the Struggle for Civil Rights*. New York: Harcourt, Brace and Company, 1996.

Marmor, Theodore R. *The Politics of Medicare*. New York: Aldine de Gruyter, 2000.

Matusow, Allen J. *The Unraveling of America: A History of Liberalism in the 1960s*. New York: Harper and Row, 1984.

Matthews, Christopher. *Kennedy and Nixon*. New York: Simon and Schuster, 1996.

Mayhew, David R. *Divided We Govern: Party Control, Law Making, and Investigations, 1946–1990*. New Haven: Yale University Press, 1991.

Michener, James A. *Report of the County Chairman*. New York: Bantam Books, 1961.

Milkis, Sidney M. *The President and the Parties: The Transformation of the American Party System Since the New Deal*. New York: Oxford University Press, 1993.

Miller, Merle. *Lyndon: An Oral Biography*. New York: G. P. Putnam's Sons, 1980.

Murphy, Bruce Allen. *Fortas: The Rise and Ruin of a Supreme Court Justice*. New York: William Morrow, 1988.

Nie, Norman H., Sidney Verba, and John R. Petrocik. *The Changing American Voter*. Cambridge: Harvard University Press, 1980.

Nixon, Richard M. *RN: The Memoirs of Richard Nixon*. New York: Simon and Schuster, 1978.

———. *Six Crises*. New York: Doubleday, 1962.

O'Brien, Lawrence F. *No Final Victories*. New York: Ballantine Books, 1974.

O'Donnell, Kenneth P., and David F. Powers. *"Johnny, We Hardly Knew Ye": Memories of John Fitzgerald Kennedy*. New York: Pocket Books, 1973.

O'Neill, Thomas P., Jr. *Man of the House: The Life and Political Memoirs of Speaker Tip O'Neill*. New York: Random House, 1987.

Parmet, Herbert S. *The Democrats: The Years After FDR*. New York: Oxford University Press, 1976.

———. *Jack: The Struggles of John F. Kennedy*. New York: Dial Press, 1980.

———. *JFK: The Presidency of John F. Kennedy*. New York: Dial Press, 1983.

Phillips, Kevin P. *The Emerging Republican Majority*. New York: Arlington House, 1969.

Pomper, Gerald M. *Nominating the President: The Politics of Convention Choice*. Chicago: Northwestern University Press, 1963.

Porter, Kirk H., and Johnson, Donald Bruce (ed.). *National Party Platforms: 1840–1960*. Urbana: University of Illinois Press, 1961.

Powers, Thomas. *Vietnam: The War at Home*. Boston: G.K. Hall, 1984.

Rae, Nicol C. *The Decline and Fall of the Liberal Republicans: from 1952 to the Present*. New York: Oxford University Press, 1989.

———. *Southern Democrats*. New York: Oxford University Press, 1994.

Reedy, George. *Lyndon B. Johnson: A Memoir*. New York: Andrews and McMeel, 1982.

Reeves, Richard. *President Kennedy: Profile of Power*. New York: Simon and Schuster, 1993.

Reeves, Thomas C. *A Question of Character: A Life of John F. Kennedy*. New York: Free Press, 1991.

Reichard, Gary W. *The Reaffirmation of Republicanism: Eisenhower and the Eighty-Third Congress*. Knoxville: University of Tennessee Press, 1975.

Reinhard, David W. *The Republican Right Since 1945*. Lexington: University Press of Kentucky, 1983.

Reinsch, J. Leonard. *Getting Elected: From Radio and Roosevelt to Television and Reagan*. New York: Hippocrene Books, 1991.

Rusk, Dean. *As I Saw It*. New York: Penguin Books, 1990.

Savage, Sean J. *Roosevelt: The Party Leader, 1932–1945*. Lexington: University Press of Kentucky, 1991.

——. *Truman and the Democratic Party*. Lexington: University Press of Kentucky, 1997.

Scammon, Richard M., and Wattenberg, Ben J. *The Real Majority* New York: Coward, McCann, and Geoghegan, Inc., 1970.

Schattschneider, E. E. *Party Government*. New York: Rinehart and Company, 1942.

——. *The Semi-Sovereign People*. New York: Holt, Rinehart and Winston, 1960.

Schlesinger, Arthur M., Jr. *A Thousand Days: John F. Kennedy in the White House*. Boston: Houghton Mifflin, 1965.

——. *Robert Kennedy and His Times*. New York: Ballantine Books, 1978.

Schlesinger, Joseph. *Political Parties and the Winning of Office*. Ann Arbor: University of Michigan Press, 1991.

Sevareid, Eric (ed.). *Candidates 1960*. New York: Basic Books, 1959.

Sherrill, Robert. *The Accidental President*. New York: Pyramid Books, 1967.

Shesol, Jeff. *Mutual Contempt: Lyndon Johnson, Robert Kennedy, and the Feud that Defined a Decade*. New York: W. W. Norton, 1997.

Sorensen, Theodore C. *Kennedy*. New York: Harper and Row, 1965.

Stern, Mark. *Calculating Visions: Kennedy, Johnson, and Civil Rights*. New Brunswick, 1990.

Strober, Gerald S. and Deborah H. Strober (ed.) *"Let Us Begin Anew": An Oral History of the Kennedy Presidency*. New York: HarperCollins, 1993.

Sundquist, James L. *Dynamics of the Party System*. Washington, DC: Brookings Institution, 1983.

——. *Politics and Policy: The Eisenhower, Kennedy, and Johnson Years*. Washington, DC: Brookings Institution, 1968.

Toledano, Ralph. *R.F.K.: The Man Who Would Be President*. New York: Signet Books, 1967.

Unger, Irwin. *The Best of Intentions: The Triumph and Failure of the Great Society Under Kennedy, Johnson, and Nixon*. New York: Doubleday, 1996.

Wattenberg, Martin P. *The Decline of American Political Parties: 1952–1980*. Cambridge: Harvard University Press, 1984.

Whalen, Charles, and Barbara Whalen. *The Longest Debate: A Legislative History of the 1964 Civil Rights Act*. Cabin John: Seven Locks Press, 1985.

Whalen, Richard J. *The Founding Father: The Story of Joseph P. Kennedy*. New York: New American Library, 1964.

Whalen, Thomas J. *Kennedy Versus Lodge: The 1952 Massachusetts Senate Race*. Boston: Northeastern University Press, 2000.

White, F. Clifton. *Suite 3505: The Story of the Draft Goldwater Movement*. New York: Arlington House, 1967.

White, John K. *The Fractured Electorate: Political Parties and Social Change in Southern New England*. Hanover: University Press of New England, 1983.

——, and Daniel M. Shea. *New Party Politics: From Jefferson and Hamilton to the Information Age*. New York: Bedford/St. Martin's Press, 2000.

——. *Still Seeing Red: How the Cold War Shapes the New American Politics*. Boulder: Westview Press, 1997.

White, Theodore H. *The Making of the President 1960.* New York: Atheneum House, 1961.

———. *The Making of the President 1964.* New York: Atheneum Publishers, 1965.

———. *The Making of the President 1968.* New York: Pocket Books, 1969.

Wills, Garry. *The Kennedy Imprisonment.* Boston: Little, Brown and Company, 1981.

Wicker, Tom. *JFK and LBJ: The Influence of Personality upon Politics.* Chicago: Ivan R. Dee, 1991.

Wilson, James Q. *The Amateur Democrat.* Chicago: University of Chicago Press, 1962.

Witcover, Jules. *85 Days: The Last Campaign of Robert Kennedy.* New York: William Morrow, 1969.

ARTICLES

Beck, Kent. "What Was Liberalism in the 1950s?." *Political Science Quarterly* 52 (Summer 1987): 233–258.

Born, Richard. "Reassessing the Decline of Presidential Coattails: U.S. House Elections from 1952–1980." *Journal of Politics* 46 (1984): 60–79.

Bradford, Richard. "John F. Kennedy and the 1960 Presidential Primary in West Virginia." *South Atlantic Quarterly* 75 (Spring 1976): 161–172.

Brauer, Carl M. "Kennedy, Johnson, and War on Poverty." *Journal of American History* 69 (June 1982): 98–119.

Brock, Bernard. "1968 Democratic Campaign: A Political Upheaval." *Quarterly Journal of Speech* 55 (February 1969): 26–55.

Broder, David S. "Consensus Politics: End of an Experiment." *The Atlantic Monthly* 218 (October 1966): 60–65.

Campbell, Angus, and Warren E. Miller. "The Motivating Basis of Straight and Split Ticket Voting." *American Political Science Review* 51 (1957): 293–312.

Campbell, James E. "Explaining Presidential Losses in Midterm Congressional Elections." *Journal of Politics* 47 (1985): 1140–1157.

Converse, Philip E. et al. "Stability and Change in 1960: A Reinstating Election." *American Political Science Review* 55 (June 1961): 269–281.

Cotter, Cornelius P., and John F. Bibby. "Institutional Development of Parties and the Thesis of Party Decline." *Political Science Quarterly* 95 (Spring 1980): 1–27.

Gelb, Leslie H. "The Essential Domino: American Politics and Vietnam." *Foreign Affairs* 50 (April 1972): 459–475.

Hajda, Joseph. "Choosing the 1960 Democratic Candidate: The Case of the Unbossed Delegations." *Kansas Quarterly* 8 (1976): 71–87.

Harris, Joseph P. "The Senatorial Rejection of Leland Olds." *American Political Science Review* 45 (1951): 674–692.

Holloway, Harry. "The Negro and the Vote: The Case of Texas." *Journal of Politics* 23 (August 1961): 522–556.

Huitt, Ralph K. "Democratic Party Leadership in the Senate." *American Political Science Review* 55 (1961): 333–344.

Jonas, Frank H. "Western Politics and the 1958 Elections." *Western Political Science Quarterly* 14 (1959): 241–256.

Kallina, Edmund F., Jr. "State's Attorney and the President: The Inside Story of the 1960 Presidential Election in Illinois." *Journal of American Studies* 11 (1978): 147–160.

Land, Paul G. "John F. Kennedy's Southern Strategy, 1956–1960." *North Carolina Historical Review* 56 (1979): 41–63.

Lawson, Steven and Mark Gelfand. "Consensus and Civil Rights." *Prologue* 8 (Summer 1976): 65–76.

Light, Paul C. "Domestic Policy Making." *Presidential Studies Quarterly* 30 (March 2000): 109–132.

Manley, John F. "The House Committee on Ways and Means: Conflict Management in a Congressional Committee." *American Political Science Review* 59 (December 1965): 927–939.

Matthews, Donald B. "The Folkways of the United States Senate: Conformity to Group Norms and Legislative Effectiveness." *American Political Science Review* 53 (1959): 1064–1089.

Miller, Glenn W. and Ware, Stephen B. "Organized Labor in the Political Process: A Case Study of the Right-to-Work Campaign in Ohio," *Labor History* 4 (1963): 51–67.

Mueller, John E. "Trends for Popular Support for the Wars in Korea and Vietnam." *American Political Science Review* 65 (June 1971): 358–375.

Pomper, Gerald M. "Party Organization and Electoral Success." *Polity* 23 (Winter 1990): 186–206.

Price, Hugh D. "Campaign Finance in Massachusetts in 1952." *Public Policy* 6 (1955): 25–46.

Reichard, Gary W. "Division and Dissent: Democrats and Foreign Policy, 1952–1956." *Political Science Quarterly* 93 (1978): 51–72.

Savage, Sean J. "Franklin D. Roosevelt and the Democratic National Committee." *Social Science Journal* v. 28, n. 4 (Fall 1991): 451–465.

_____. "Hacks and Long Hairs: The Question of a DNC Research Division," *American Review of Politics* 15 (Spring 1994): 57–72.

_____. "JFK and the DNC." *White House Studies* 2 (Summer 2002): 139–153.

_____. "To Purge or Not to Purge: Hamlet Harry and the Dixiecrats," *Presidential Studies Quarterly* v. 27, n. 4 (Fall 1997): 773–791.

Schlesinger, Joseph A. "The New American Political Party." *American Political Science Review* 79 (December 1985): 1152–1169.

Shugart, Matthew S. "The Electoral Cycle and Institutional Sources of Divided Presidential Government." *American Political Science Review* 89 (June 1995): 327–343.

Spragens, William C. "Kennedy Era Speechwriting, Public Relations and Public Opinion." *Presidential Studies Quarterly* 14 (Winter 1984): 78–86.

Stevens, Daniel. "Public Opinion and Public Policy: The Case of Kennedy and Civil Rights." *Presidential Studies Quarterly* 32 (March 2002): 111–136.

Stid, Daniel D. "Woodrow Wilson and the Problem of Party Government." *Polity* 27 (Summer 1994): 553–578.

Sugrue, Thomas. "Crabgrass Roots Politics." *Journal of American History* 82 (September 1995): 551–578.

Photographic Credits

cover   JFK and LBJ, Biltmore Hotel, Los Angeles, 1960. *Courtesy: John F. Kennedy Library*

Plate 1   JFK, Faneuil Hall, Boston, 1946. *Courtesy: Archives of The College of the Holy Cross*

Plate 2   JFK and Jacqueline Kennedy, Assumption College, Worcester, Massachusetts, 1955. *Courtesy: Assumption College Archives*

Plate 3   LBJ with campaign helicopter in 1948. *Courtesy: Jimmie Dodd collection, Center for American History, University of Texas*

Plate 4   DNC chairman Paul M. Butler. *Courtesy: Ideal Baldoni*

Plate 5   Free speech demonstration, Berkeley, 1964. *Courtesy: Bancroft Library, University of California at Berkeley*

Plate 6   Harry S. Truman, JFK, and LBJ, Democratic dinner in Washington D.C., 1961. *Courtesy: Harry S. Truman Library*

Plate 7   JFK, Quonset Point, Rhode Island, 1962. Photo by George W. Locksie, Jr. *Courtesy: Providence College Archives*

Plate 8   LBJ takes oath of office aboard Air Force One, 1963. *Courtesy: Lyndon B. Johnson Library*

Plate 9   LBJ in the White House, 1964. *Courtesy: Lyndon B. Johnson Library*

Plate 10   RFK at a cabinet meeting, 1964. *Courtesy: Lyndon B. Johnson Library*

Plate 11   LBJ, Providence, Rhode Island, 1964. *Courtesy: Providence College Archives*

Plate 12   LBJ and RFK, Brooklyn, New York, 1964. *Courtesy: Library of Congress*

Plate 13   Hubert H. Humphrey at the White House, 1965. *Courtesy: Lyndon B. Johnson Library*

Plate 14   LBJ and Harry S. Truman at the bill signing ceremony for Medicare, 1965. *Courtesy: Harry S. Truman Library*

Plate 15   DNC chairman John M. Bailey in the Oval Office, 1966. *Courtesy: Lyndon B. Johnson Library*

Plate 16   LBJ visiting American troops in South Vietnam, 1966. *Courtesy: Lyndon B. Johnson Library*

Plate 17   LBJ visiting wounded soldiers in South Vietnam, 1966. *Courtesy: Lyndon B. Johnson Library*

Plate 18   Cesar Chavez in 1966. *Courtesy: Library of Congress*

Plate 19   LBJ and John M. Bailey at DNC headquarters, 1967. *Courtesy: Lyndon B. Johnson Library*

Plate 20   Senator Philip Hart and Mayor Jerome Cavanaugh, Detroit, 1967. *Courtesy: Bentley Historical Library, University of Michigan*

Plate 21   Senator Eugene McCarthy, New Haven, Connecticut, 1968. *Courtesy: Minnesota Historical Society*

Plate 22   RFK, Mishawaka, Indiana, 1968. *Courtesy: Mishawaka Public Library*

Plate 23   RFK and Ethel Kennedy, South Bend, Indiana, 1968. *Courtesy: Ideal Baldoni*

Plate 24   Army troops in Chicago, 1968. *Courtesy: Chicago Historical Society*

Plate 25   Army jeeps and barricades, Chicago, 1968. *Courtesy: Chicago Historical Society*

Plate 26   Street demonstration, Chicago, 1968. *Courtesy: Chicago Historical Society*

Plate 27   Police preparing for riots, Chicago, 1968. *Courtesy: Chicago Historical Society*

Plate 28   Antiwar demonstration, Chicago, 1968. *Photo by Earl Seabert. Courtesy: Minnesota Historical Society*

Plate 29   Hubert H. Humphrey and Edmund S. Muskie, 1968. *Courtesy: Ideal Baldoni*

Plate 30   JFK and LBJ, 1960. *Courtesy: "Tip" O'Neill papers, Burns Library, Boston College*

Index